THE HISTORY OF THE EUROPEAN UNION

The European Union celebrated its 60th anniversary in 2017, but celebrations were a crisis of identity. However, as this seminal work shows, the history and ambition of the European Union are considerable. Written by key stakeholders who, between them, acted as architects, adjudicators and arbitrators of the project, it presents the definitive history of the first two generations of the European Union.

This book revisits the birth and consolidation of the great project of a united Europe and the political, institutional, judicial and economical frameworks of the European Union: from the process towards integration, to the advancements and the impasses in building a political union.

The History of the European Union

Constructing Utopia

Edited by
Giuliano Amato
Enzo Moavero-Milanesi
Gianfranco Pasquino
Lucrezia Reichlin

•HART•
OXFORD • LONDON • NEW YORK • NEW DELHI • SYDNEY

HART PUBLISHING

Bloomsbury Publishing Plc

Kemp House, Chawley Park, Cumnor Hill, Oxford, OX2 9PH, UK

1385 Broadway, New York, NY 10018, USA

HART PUBLISHING, the Hart/Stag logo, BLOOMSBURY and the Diana logo are trademarks of Bloomsbury Publishing Plc

First published in Great Britain 2019

Reprinted 2019, 2020

Originally published by Istituto della Enciclopedia Italiana, Rome, 2018

Original title: Europa. Un'utopia in costruzione

A catalogue record for this book is available from the British Library.

Library of Congress Cataloging-in-Publication data

Names: Amato, Giuliano, editor. | Moavero-Milanesi, Enzo, editor. | Pasquino, Gianfranco, 1942- editor.

Title: The history of the European Union : constructing utopia / edited by Giuliano Amato, Enzo Moavero-Milanesi, Gianfranco Pasquino, Lucrezia Reichlin.

Description: Portland, Oregon : Hart, an imprint of Bloomsbury, [2019]

Identifiers: LCCN 2018044041 (print) | LCCN 2018047232 (ebook) | ISBN 9781509917433 (Epub) | ISBN 9781509917419 (hardback : alk. paper)

Subjects: LCSH: Europe—Economic integration—History. | European Union countries—Politics and government. | European Union countries—Economic integration. | European Union—History.

Classification: LCC HC241.2 (ebook) | LCC HC241.2 .H527 2019 (print) | DDC 341.242/209—dc23

LC record available at https://lccn.loc.gov/2018044041

ISBN: HB: 978-1-50991-741-9
ePDF: 978-1-50991-742-6
ePub: 978-1-50991-743-3

Typeset by Compuscript Ltd, Shannon
Printed and bound in Great Britain by TJ International Ltd, Padstow, Cornwall

To find out more about our authors and books visit www.hartpublishing.co.uk. Here you will find extracts, author information, details of forthcoming events and the option to sign up for our newsletters.

TABLE OF CONTENTS

PART VI
POLITICAL CHALLENGES AND DISPUTES WITHIN THE EUROPEAN UNION

PART VII
CONCLUSION

LIST OF CONTRIBUTORS

Giuliano Amato
Judge, Italian Constitutional Court

Giuseppe Galasso
Historian, Professor of Medieval and Modern History. Professor Galasso died in 2018

Giorgio Napolitano
President Emeritus of the Italian Republic

Mario Monti
President of Bocconi University, Senator-for-life of the Italian Republic

Marta Cartabia
Full Professor of Constitutional Law, Vice President of the Italian Constitutional Court

Marise Cremona
Professor Emeritus, European University Institute

Gian Luigi Tosato
Professor Emeritus of International Law and European Community Law, Sapienza University of Rome; Professor of European Community Law, LUISS University, Rome

Jacques Ziller
Full Professor of EU Law, University of Pavia

Sergio M Carbone
Emeritus Professor of Law

Andrea Manzella
President, Center for Parliamentary Studies, LUISS University, Rome

Giuseppe Tesauro
President Emeritus, Constitutional Court of the Italian Republic; Professor Emeritus, University of Naples Federico II

Marco Ventura
Law Professor at the University of Siena

Bruno Nascimbene
Full Professor of European Law University of Milan

Francesco Profumo
President of Compagnia di Sanpaolo

Giovanni Biondi
President, INDIRE – National Institute for Documentation, Innovation and Educational Research

Franco Gallo
Professor Emeritus of Tax Law, LUISS University, Rome; President Emeritus, Constitutional Court of the Italian Republic; Fellow, Accademia Nazionale dei Lincei

Martin Larch
PhD; Head of Secretariat of the European Fiscal Board European Commission

Marco Buti
Directorate General for Economic and Financial Affairs, European Commission

Lucrezia Reichlin
Professor, London Business School

Guntram B Wolff
Director of Bruegel

Justine Feliu
Research assistant in the area of Global and European Macroeconomics-Bruegel

Vera Zamagni
Professor, University of Bologna and SAIS Europe of the Johns Hopkins University

Gianfranco Viesti
Full professor of applied economics, Department of Political Sciences, Università di Bari

Enzo Moavero-Milanesi
Minister of Foreign Affairs and Chairman of the Organization for Security and Co-operation in Europe of the Italian Republic

Pascal Lamy
École des hautes études commerciales de Paris (HEC), Affiliate Professor; Institut des Hautes études internationales et du développement, Genève (IHEID), Distinguished Fellow

Yves Mény
Political Scientist; Adjunct Professor at LUISS University (Rome); Emeritus President, European University Institute

Giorgio Mocavini
PhD in Administrative Law, Sant'Anna School of Advanced Studies, Pisa

Sylvie Goulard
Deputy Governor of the Bank of France

Gianfranco Pasquino
Emeritus Professor of Political Science, University of Bologna; Senior Adjunct Professor, Hopkins SAIS-Europe; Fellow Accademia dei Lincei

Renaud Dehousse
President European University Institute

Joseph HH Weiler
University Professor; Joseph Straus Professor of Law; European Union Jean Monnet Chaired Professor; Co-Director, Jean Monnet Center for International and Regional Economic Law and Justice

Johann Justus Vasel
Professor University of St Gallen, Switzerland

Introduction

The project of political unification of Europe has a history, a present and a future. It is one of the great ideas of the twentieth century, receiving a very important contribution from the Ventotene Manifesto, written in August of 1941 by Altiero Spinelli and Ernesto Rossi with the collaboration of Eugenio Colorni. What might have seemed a utopia at the height of World War II, when the defeat of Nazism was not at all a given, materialised between 1950 and 1957, thanks to the foresight of Konrad Adenauer, Alcide De Gasperi, Robert Schuman and other European statesmen, Paul-Henri Spaak among them. Today it has translated into a construction, at once complex and incomplete. The European Union already represents an ensemble of unthinkable realisations. At the same time it is, still now, a promise rich with possibilities, not devoid of obstacles. In today's world, more or less strongly does the wind of globalisation blow, and the general framework remains variegated and riddled with instability. Authoritarian regimes and personalistic dictatorships have been born and, occasionally, have disappeared. Civil wars have broken out. Authoritarianism and civil wars have as their inevitable consequences oppression and repression, hunger and death, mighty impulses toward the abandonment of those lands and the search for places where life might be lived in peace, with dignity, with opportunity. The European Union is the largest space on the planet in which the rights of the person are protected and promoted; in which the death penalty does not exist; in which democracy is the manner of governmental representation of the Member States and of the Union itself. Precisely because it is a democratic space, the Union is exposed to criticisms. Two elements characterise democracies: the total freedom of criticism (and self-criticism) and the great capacity for self-correction, for learning from mistakes. The Union has progressed, gradually, learning from its mistakes, correcting, improving. The democratic citizens are demanding. They have requested much and they request ever more. They have contributed to the democratisation of the EU institutions, the Parliament, the Commission, the Council. They have exploited to the utmost the potentialities of functionalism, of resource sharing. They seek to influence the procedures and the contents of the decisions of their heads of government in the Council. They have the possibility of being represented in the European Parliament, even if, regrettably, they seldom take advantage of it, preferring, certainly with great variations among the Member States, indifference and abstention. Some have learned that the Court of Justice is capable of defending their rights even against their respective national States. Others know that the instrument of a referendum has become available to them, a referendum requested by a million European citizens from six different States for imposing relevant issues on the order of the day. No one thinks that the democracy of the Union is perfect. Everyone knows that it is perfectible. Many work to perfect it. They are, predominately, the federalists. It is perhaps possible to place the 'United States of Europe' among the utopias, but, certainly, it remains – not only for the committed federalists – an ongoing project.

Not even in the most difficult moments have we believed that, if Europe does not proceed, it must break apart. In truth, the Union has never kept still. It has always taken some step, made some advancement, some progress. It has always, to use words which are often invoked, been able to enlarge, if not to deepen, and, sometimes, to accelerate. Upon celebrating its 60 years of life since that fateful 25 March 1957 of the Treaties of Rome, the Union has contemplated its future possibilities with the five scenarios delineated by the Commission, which have been followed by certain practical proposals for the reinforcement of the decision-making capacities of the Union and for measures in the economic sphere. One does not live on euro alone, but the single currency of 18 of the 28 Member States is a great acquisition of the European Union. It should be defended – as the president of the European Central Bank Mario Draghi forcefully declared in 2012 – 'whatever it takes'. Though not without its drawbacks, the euro is one of the instruments for the maintenance of that prosperity which, over the course of time, has been ensured to all the Member States. Peace and prosperity are the two epochal conquests of the Union: the maintenance of peace together with the commitment to favour democracy and human rights are the two elements underlined in the motivations of the Nobel prize for peace conferred upon the European Union in 2012.

Complex in its construction, dense in its legislative labyrinth and, sometimes, opaque in its functioning, the European Union requires in-depth study to comprehend the mechanisms that oversee the integration of States characterised by historical, administrative, economic and political diversities, diversities which require difficult measures of adjustment and refinement. We do not know if the Union will continue at many speeds, with some Member States daring the others to follow them, proceeding toward a greater integration in a briefer time. We know that not even in federal States do conflicts ever cease. On the contrary, conflicts are often the yeast of changes and of democracy itself. We are certain that the Union is capable of advancing, because all the surveys indicate two great positive phenomena underway today. The percentage of Europeans that recognise their identity as being precisely European, rather than being that of their respective nation or even region of origin, is growing. The people, the European *demos* whose existence is lamented by many, comes to be formed, not only by being exposed to the same laws, but by acquiring awareness of its shared identity, by recognising itself to be a part of, or even the architect of, the supranational construction of the European Union. Moreover, the perception that there exist many more things which bring the Europeans together than which might separate them is growing; above all, the conviction is growing that – contrary to the thoughts and agitations of the so-called souverainists – it will be the European Union which will furnish the best responses with regard to opportunity and justice. While the souverainists hope for a return of the national States which were defined already 50 years ago as obstinate and obsolete by the great scholar of international relations Stanley Hoffmann, those who desire a united Europe strive for effectively supranational solutions.

In the most thoroughly documented way possible, this volume aims to furnish the greatest amount of information available on the roots and the historical path of European integration, on the institutional arrangements of the Union, on the many sectors in which it is active. It intends to offer a wide spectrum of interpretations, from the political, juridical and economic points of view, indicating the problems, assessing Europe's state of health, suggesting certain possible solutions. Much water will pass under the bridges of the

Danube, the Seine, the Tiber, and, the irreducible optimists among us would add, of the Thames, before we arrive, if ever – and, let it be added, as we should like – at a completely federal outcome. However, never do the intermediate stages count so much as on this path; each of them is a bringer of material and symbolic welfare to the European citizens, and also to all those that Europe will know how to welcome. *Hic Bruxelles hic salta.*

Giuliano Amato, Enzo Moavero-Milanesi,
Gianfranco Pasquino, Lucrezia Reichlin

PART I

Common Roots and Shared Values

1

Into the Future of a Common Past

GIUSEPPE GALASSO

I. Roots

It is a well-known fact that the Convention on the future of Europe, held on the basis of the Laeken Declaration of 15 December 2001, completed on 10 July 2003 the work it had begun on 28 February 2002. This labour produced a Treaty establishing a Constitution for Europe, whose draft text was presented in Rome on 18 July of the same year by the European Convention chairman Valéry Giscard d'Estaing. It is also a well-known fact that, after various events, on 29 October 2004, the 25 countries then members of the European Union (EU) signed the Treaty drawn up by the Convention, requiring various ratification procedures for each of the signatory countries. Lastly, it is a well-known fact that this process went on until the 2007 referenda, which saw France and the Netherlands reject the call for ratification, resulting in the de facto final abandonment of the 2004 Treaty.

This failure does not belittle the historical significance of the first attempt to establish an EU Constitution, especially since the Convention that had drafted it was expressly dedicated, as we said, to the 'future of Europe'. It should be added that European public opinion was in a position to follow the Convention's works, because its plenary sessions were open to the public.

Throughout the drafting of the constitutional text to be submitted, one of the points that without a doubt attracted more attention and provided ample material for various kinds of comparisons and discussions was the one concerning the ideal foundations and the historical and cultural values which were to constitute the general and basic principles underpinning the European Constitution. On this subject matter, the text produced by the Convention summarised its aims in the first paragraph of the Preamble. It stated it had drawn inspiration from the cultural, religious and humanist inheritance of Europe, from which have developed the universal values of the inviolable and inalienable rights of the human person, freedom, democracy, equality and the rule of law.

In turn, article 2 of Title I of Part I of the Constitution that had been prepared stated that the EU was founded on the values of respect for human dignity, freedom, democracy, equality, the rule of law and respect for human rights, including the rights of persons belonging to minorities; adding that it understood these values as common to the Member States in a society in which pluralism, non-discrimination, tolerance, justice, solidarity and equality between women and men prevail.

One can hardly say that these formulations were the best that could be hoped for on this subject, but the need for all-round mediation and consensus on a plane where, more than elsewhere, it was necessary to achieve and exhibit a show of unanimity by the contracting parties, may have understandably produced a certain degree of vagueness and wordiness.

Still, it is not surprising that these same issues – so open in themselves to discussion and dissent – have sparked the more notable episodes of controversy or drawn the most puzzling, when not openly hostile, comments from European public opinion. Amid these episodes, for reasons that are all too easy to understand, stands out the unrelenting call of Catholic Church leaders urging Europe's 'Christian roots' to be explicitly, though not exclusively, ranked among the inspiring and founding principles of the Constitution for the EU.

The Catholic world and its culture saw nothing new in this topic, as we all know. In relation to the issues of European integration, we are reminded, for example, of a speech by Alcide De Gasperi at the Paris Parliamentary Conference of 1954, delivered on 21 April. While stating 'that at the origin of this European civilization Christianity is found', he pointed out that he did not intend 'by that to introduce any exclusive confessional criterion into the assessment of our history', but only wanted to speak of the common European heritage, of that unitary morality that exalts the figure and the responsibility of the human person with its ferment of evangelical fraternity [...], with its desire for truth and justice acquired from a millenary experience.

It is easy to see that these are, in substance, the reasons rolled out in successive ecclesiastical and Catholic discourses on the question of European unity from Pope Paul VI up to Pope Francis.

While not included in the failed 2004 Constitution, the debate on Europe's 'Christian roots' has remained very much alive, unsurprisingly perhaps, in Catholic circles; and it is worth mentioning that in a September 2008 conference in Varigotti (Finale Ligure) monsignor Josef Clemens, secretary of the Pontifical Council for the laity, was able to present a detailed account of the Christian roots of Europe through the thoughts of Joseph Ratzinger, who represents a wellspring of ideas and observations on the subject. Pope Francis also touched on the matter, in an interview with *La Croix* on 17 May 2016, although the words he used actually call for even more specific attention. Those roots, he said, are grounded in 'service' and in the 'gift of life', lest we risk falling into 'triumphalism' and 'colonialism'. Yet he then went on to say that 'we must speak of roots in the plural, because there are many'; and added:

> when I hear talk of the Christian roots of Europe, I am sometimes fearful of the tone, which may sound triumphant or vindictive. This is when it turns into colonialism. John Paul II spoke of this in a soothing tone. Europe does indeed have Christian roots. And it is Christianity's duty to irrigate them, but in a spirit of service as in the washing of the feet, as Jesus is said to do in the Gospels.

In what sense did Pope Francis speak of Europe as having 'roots in the plural'? Did he mean that there were others, besides the Christian ones? Or did he want to say that Christianity features such a wealth of motifs and inflections that it does not allow itself to be spoken of except in pluralistic terms, while also taking good care to shun any that might ring triumphant, vindictive or even moralistic? And one is justified in believing that the second answer is right, namely that the plurality contemplated by the pope belongs to the inner essence of Christianity itself.

His predecessor, Pope Benedict, had spoken of Europe's manifold legacies: Greek, Latin, Christian, and the modern age. Benedict XVI thus proved himself to be very much in line with historical literature addressing the concept of Europe and its evolution over the centuries. It is for this very reason – one may well say – that he embodies even more prominently that element at the heart of the contrast over Europe's 'Christian roots' at the time of drafting a Constitution for the EU.

The truth is that on a religious level Christianity cannot be regarded as anything less than a revolution of such force as to impact the course of history and start a new age, based on the final divine Revelation, announced by the prophets and carried out through the redeeming passion of Christ. What comes into being then – Christianity, in fact – is something utterly original and unprecedented, whilst marked by a radical and inseparable unity. Its roots lie embedded in human history from its original moment of fall and damnation, but also exists beyond eternity for the Absolute that transcends all history and time, redeeming man and radically altering the pace of human history.

In this sense, the claim to Europe's 'Christian roots' was quite understandable from a religious point of view, while also poignant, given the depth of meaning that characterises the Christian faith (after all, it may be hardly recalled today, but the claim to those roots did not only come from the Vatican and Catholics, but from other Christian Churches as well). From different points of view, and on different levels than a religious and Christian perspective, the issue does not arise in the same way and in the same terms, nor can it do so. If taken beyond the scope of religious faith, piety, and logic (so to speak), Christianity is wholly steeped in history and, as such, boasts its own historical genesis and its own historical complexity. Viewed under the (albeit dim and humble) light of the historian, Christianity itself stems from many roots, and slowly begins to assert itself until it becomes the dominant force of the age into which it was born, while at the same time transforming itself greatly, in terms of its militancy, but also on a doctrinal and cultural level. The history of Christian churches bears irrefutable witness to this, with its struggles, its heresies and mutual condemnations.

Shifting our discourse to this historiographical level, Christianity arises from the multiple tensions and from the cultural and social yearnings alive within the so-called Greco-Roman empire. In its most essential elements, it came about by harnessing the yearnings and tensions of the land of Jesus, of Hellenistic culture, and of imperial Roman culture. As Joaquín Navarro-Valls told in one of his 2002 speeches, the roots of the European tree grow as deep in the ground of the Golgotha hill as in that of the Acropolis and the Campidoglio. This is true, but it behoves us to remember that the Golgotha hill, mentioned by Navarro-Valls, is not only quite near, but conceptually neighbours the Temple Mount, sacred to the memory of Israel. And from that memory, that Hebrew tradition, and in that context, even geographically, the preaching of Jesus was first born and went forth. Metaphors aside, at the basis of Christianity it is impossible not to identify and not to focus on the world of the Old Testament, to borrow a Christian biblical canon.

Hellenism, Romanitas, Judaism: herewith the three-forked root of Christianity. And it is no mere root. No confession or version of the Christian idea and spirit has ever repudiated or denied the unconditional designation of the Old Testament as an essential and constitutive element of the Revelation; and both the meaning and spirit of the Word in the New Testament have always been understood as stemming from the Old Testament, in its capacity to bring fulfilment and transcendence to the Word.

This genetic and conceptual relationship establishes Judaism as, in many ways, Christianity's primary root. While no less strong, its relationship with the Hellenistic world is far more complex. In this regard, much has revolved around the figure of Paul of Tarsus. In particular, he is credited with a process of Hellenisation of the earliest form of Christianity that is thought to have profoundly changed its spirit to an extent that many far more authoritative theologians and historians believe Paul to have been the true founder of Christianity, which then developed throughout history. Without going as far as that, Paul's mediation between Christian innovation and the Hellenistic world is completely out of the question. More important, however, is the relationship that developed between Christian patristics, both Greek and Latin, and the Hellenic world. Above all, it was Platonism (both in its Middle Platonic and Neoplatonic versions) that provided the thought and theology of Christianity with the categories and ideas of which it felt the need to elaborate conceptually and systematise, that is, to sort and organise within a system, the elements of the Revelation and of the nascent Christian tradition.

Between the second and fifth centuries the Christian world underwent a process of extraordinary importance in the moral and intellectual history of Christianity not only as a religious confession, but also as a centuries-long primary element of the Mediterranean world and, for a much longer time, of the European world. And this process can be appreciated even more when one thinks of that far-from-irrelevant strain of patristic thought, which condemned this Christian appropriation from the pagan world as being an unworkable contamination of truth with falsehood; yet, in its later transition from the professed incompatibility between Christianity and pagan culture to the development of its own thought, it appears to be far from averse to acquiring and utilising doctrines and models derived from ancient philosophy.

In actual fact, it fulfilled a historical need to conceptually strengthen the new wealth of Christian ideas rather than a mere desire or a need for cultural legitimacy. And the fact that the perception of this historical necessity was dealt with by referencing Platonic thought is, once again, an element replete with great historical significance. It meant that what had been constructed in the Hellenic world was truly an 'everlasting purchase'; it had been the acquisition of something – simply said – not strictly limited only to its heyday, but whose intrinsic value rendered it susceptible to a never-ending actuality: after all, this ties in with the hallmarks of that entire civilisation of which even Platonism was an expression.

This is not the only reason why the importance of the meeting between nascent Christian culture and tradition and Greek philosophy (indeed, such a meeting had already occurred in the Jewish tradition) should be emphasised. In fact, the reasoning for this meeting, provided by the Christian writers who carried it through, should be singled out as a distinguishing element here. Even in Greek thought – they said – there were truths to be sought, to be found, and which had to be appropriated. They were truths engendered by that 'seminal' logos, *spermatikòs*, by those presences of the divine in creation, which – as 'seeds of truth' – men may seize upon randomly, sketchily, ecstatically, and inconsistently with their thought. This had occurred especially in the case of some Hellenic thinkers, whose seeds could therefore be picked to the benefit of the conceptual work, of which by now the need was felt.

In the way that the seeds thus picked were understood in relation to the Christian doctrine of the logos, or in the way that Christians would understand and define the logos, the divergences of patristics between the second and the fifth centuries were a great many, also on account of the intrinsic and organic relationship, always reasserted, between logos and Trinity. From the viewpoint that interests us here, the question is not confined to the Christian sphere. The discourse on the logos was an ancient one in Hellenic thought, and was not unknown even to Jewish tradition during the phase of closer ties with Hellenism, if not all-out Hellenisation, undertaken by some of its most important personalities such as Philo of Alexandria with his Hellenistic Judaism. What is worth emphasising here is that, throughout the developments ranging from Stoicism, to Middle-Platonism, to Neo-Platonism, to patristics, the idea of a sapiential tradition is hereby consolidated, bearing the most authentic values of being and living that will go on to spawn a great number of remarkable sequels in European history up to the modern age.

The roots of Christianity are, therefore, complex and multifarious with their three strands: Jewish, Hellenistic, and Roman (three elements that, if examined, would also reveal multifarious roots). Their multiplicity and complexity also render simplistic many traditional notions, according to which Christianity acquired its religious genealogy from Judaism, its methodology and a large part of its conceptualisation from Hellenism, and its legal and institutional sense from Romanitas. It should go without saying that bilateral relations are not the issue here. In each and every one of those derivations it is always the whole pre-Christian body of Christianity that engages with the full gamut of the Christian spirit and of Christian thought. Hence, it is against the backdrop of this all-encompassing relational whole that the individual elements of Christianity hailing from the pre-Christian world must be measured and construed.

Derivations, roots: when all is said and done, the question remains that no derivation or root, however more exceptional or more intense it could be, would detract one iota from the creative originality, the disruptive novelty, the revolutionary inversion of values, or the global otherness of Christianity, in the guise it took between the first and second century, if set against the ancient world of Judaism, Hellenism, and Romanitas. Such was the magnitude of its originality, novelty, inversion, and otherness that, already between the third and fourth centuries Christianity had reached the status of a global and inevitable alternative to the past. In other words, it appeared as the driving force in a world that was experiencing profound changes already in the near future. And soon it would be for all to see what sheer energy that triumphant force carried within itself, with its ability to actively and decisively shape history, while the twilight of the ancient world was becoming more dramatic by the day, bringing about a widespread and ruinous collapse both in the material legacy of its civilisation and in its political-social, cultural, institutional, and legal structures.

II. Borders

The matter of the Christian roots of Europe is thus transformed into the question of the roots of Christianity, viewed as a historical process notwithstanding its religious connotations as Christian Revelation. Basically, these roots take shape – as we have seen – in the threefold nexus of Hellenism, Judaism and Romanitas. This leads one to view this same threefold nexus as the primary root of Europe. And this irrefutable deduction has a two-sided advantage. On the one hand, it affects in no way – as we have said – the conclusive and overwhelming nature of Christianity's originality and novelty; on the other hand, it allows us to trace European roots back to a more befitting time and space – the ancient Mediterranean.

In this sphere Europa/Europe was also known as a mythological name (the former) and as a geographical name (the latter). Its mythological meaning refers to the beautiful maiden, daughter of Oceano and Teti, who was snatched by Zeus in the form of a white bull. As the legend goes, the girl was abducted in Phoenicia, from whence the marauding god carried her away to Crete on his back, and here their union would be consummated. Some authors attach an allegorical meaning to this myth, among the most famous in ancient Greece: the abduction suggests that civilisation is relocated from East to West, just as the beauty of the abducted girl is likened to the superior value of civilisation that is brought from Phoenicia to the Greek island of Crete. While the allegory is suggestive, it is all too clear that it bears more resemblance to an imaginative makeover of an ancient fable by a modern mind.

In fact, the etymology and origin of the name indeed point to a Phoenician root. Their word *ereb* would have described the lands to the west of their Syrian heartland. Hence, Europe would have been the name given to the Western land or lands, and by extension would have applied to the West in general (by the way, even the name Asia, in the opposite sense of East, is thought to be of Phoenician origin or, in any case, borrowed from another Semitic tongue). Later scholars have questioned the Phoenician origin of the word, and did not rule out its Greek origin. For sure, it crops up in Hesiod in the eighth century BC, but again as a mythological name lacking geographical reference. It is hard to say when it acquired its topographical meaning. It makes an appearance again from the fifth century BC onward, in Ionian geographers, and since then it is possible to chart, albeit with some difficulty, the course of its geographical career.

It is quite certain that the name initially described certain regions of Greece: Thrace and central Greece in contrast to the Peloponnese and the Greek islands. The word caught on swiftly, encompassing both westward to the Iberian peninsula, and eastward to the Black Sea, following the routes of Greek expansion across the Mediterranean. And soon enough those same Ionian geographers end up by designating the lands north of the Mediterranean as Europe.

True, the term still retains a certain vagueness. Meanwhile, even though geographical knowledge improved thanks to the accounts of travellers, as well as the campaigns and endeavours of the Roman armies, fleets and imperial administrations up to the Rhine and the Danube, and beyond to Britain, by the end of the age of antiquity, however, actual knowledge of the European continent was altogether patchy and, to a large extent, inaccurate. In the Mediterranean, the European border was quickly identified with the Pillars of Hercules (ie, the Strait of Gibraltar), to the west. To the east it was the river Phasis (today called Rioni) in the Transcaucasian region, and more specifically in western Georgia (the river then ended its course into the coastal marsh called *Paleostom*, where the ancient city of Phasis stood), or alternatively, the Cimmerian Bosporus, that is, the Kerch Strait, between the Crimea and the Caucasian lands, and beyond the Sea of Azov up to the river Tanais, today the mighty Don. Both the western border (a natural and inescapable boundary) and the eastern border remained unchanged for a very long time. In this way, also the continent's southern border was mapped out from east to west.

Beyond the Mediterranean, the outline of the British Isles was known, albeit sketchily; the North Sea was more familiar, but Jutland was mapped little and quite late; and there was no inkling of the Baltic as an enclosed sea. Scania, the southern tip of Scandinavia, was thought to be an island. Only at the end of the fifteenth century did it become clear that Scandinavia is a peninsula bordering on the Barents Sea to the north (explored by ninth and tenth century Norse seamen) and the North and Baltic Seas to the south (thanks to many important trading routes opening up, as well as political developments, already from the tenth and especially from the thirteenth century). Later, in the sixteenth century, other navigators furthered the exploration of the White Sea, going on to reach Novaya Zemlya, but when Arkhangelsk was founded in 1584, trading activity with the most enterprising European countries thrived as much as possible in those extreme North European sea-waters, as had long been the case for the Baltic. Looking west, the outer reaches of the British Isles and Iceland had also become well-known since the eighth century.

By the sixteenth century the western and northern contours of the continent had been charted, and anyone comparing the cartographic depictions of the late age of antiquity (such as the Ptolemy map) with those of Gerardus Mercator (dated 1554) and later, can easily appreciate the giant steps forward made in the understanding of the continent's maritime boundaries. Insofar as the land borders, however, the boundaries were marked – already by ancient geographers, as we have seen – by the Don River as the easternmost reach of Europe. The borderlands east of the Don were unquestionably thought of as Asian territories, so one could say that as late as the seventeenth century, Buda and Krakow were regarded as the last true major European cities of the east. Only in the eighteenth century, under the long reign (1682–1725) of Peter I (the Great) in Russia, were the vast swathes of land up to the Urals fully incorporated geographically (but not only from this point of view) into what was deemed to be a European area; with the definitive backing of the eminent German geographer Carl Ritter in the early nineteenth century, the Urals became known as the cut-off line between Asia and Europe.

On a strictly geographic basis, the choice was not particularly enlightened. The Ural mountain range is known to be of modest elevation on the European side, and does not lend itself well to serve as a border, lacking a clear separation between the great Russian and Siberian plains; while the Caucasus is considered Asian, but even the borders between the Caucasian and Caspian regions are not easy to define.

Also on account of this considerable difficulty in mapping out its eastern borders, as well as for other reasons, to nineteenth-century geographers, Europe ended up looking like a mere peninsular appendix (according to the definition given by Wilhelm von Humboldt) westwards of the much larger (four and a half times) surface of Asia. In 1858 Carl Gustav Reuschle introduced the term *Eurasia* to designate the continuity and, consequently, the unity of the two continental blocks. Considering that the Suez Canal had not yet been constructed, it would have been possible to include Africa in this picture; and, strictly speaking, even the opening of the Suez Canal would not invalidate this observation. It is evident, however, that the limited territorial connection made possible by the isthmus of Suez does not stand up to any real comparison with the continuity and territorial unity between Europe and Asia.

Despite these pieces of evidence, it seems neither advisable nor completely founded to give up on the idea of Europe as an entity in its own right, even geographically speaking. It has been found to occupy, for instance, a central position in the Earth's northern hemisphere, featuring remarkable ease of communication with Africa and with Asia; in the west it borders the Atlantic where this ocean is less wide; and the far reaches of the world, such as

Oceania and Southeast Asia, have become closer after the opening of the Suez Canal. But it is not only on account of its position, which can be defined as central, in the middle of the hemisphere where most of the Earth's land mass is concentrated (and therefore it is called *continental*) that Europe stands out geographically speaking. It is common knowledge that it does not display the striking climatic contrasts that befall other parts of the world; that even for this reason there are no landscapes and natural environments like rain forests or deserts; that there are no high mountain ranges amounting to natural barriers comparable with those of Asia, nor are they flanked by extensive plateaus like those in Asia; that there are not even mountain ranges that frame and enclose an entire horizon, like the Andes in South America; that the complications and the variety of its geographical structure are no less or even greater (considering its much smaller size) than those of other continents; furthermore, there are a number of other elements allowing us to define the European area as more than sufficiently autonomous; and that there is still more to be said if we leave physical geography and move on to anthropic geography.

A remarkable fact is Europe's broad linguistic unity, for example. Already since prehistoric times the continent appears inhabited by populations all speaking Indo-European languages, and this has been preserved until the entire twentieth century. There are only five exceptions: the Lappish and Basque tongues, and those belonging to the Finno-Ugric linguistic group, Hungarian, Estonian and Finnish; Turkish is spoken in the south-eastern corner of Europe in the tiny area around Istanbul (Maltese seems to be wrongly connected to the Semitic group). These are all very modest exceptions, affecting roughly between two and three per cent of the European population.

Another remarkable fact is that, unlike other continents, Europe does not present a compact land mass with few marginal articulations. Instead, it is characterised by numerous islands, by regions clearly defined by natural boundaries that do not render them isolated or remote; by many peninsulas and headlands; by a system of islands developing a short distance from the mainland; by a singularly beautiful coastal articulation.

For these reasons, European geography has often seemed to favour greatly dynamic forms of political pluralism, and strongly pushed for both watchful self-rule and intense relations among the peoples of Europe. In other words, if physical geography beseeches us to look at Europe as a stand-alone unit on a global scale, the repercussions, consistencies or anthropic additions of its physical way of being appear to be greatly enhanced and made extremely evident. In a more specific sense than usual, Europe may be viewed as (no less or more than other parts of the world) an 'anthropogeographic continent', to use German geographer Herbert Louis's terminology, as opposed to the traditional concept of continent in a spatial sense. And its history is such that it ended up by shaping it in a very unique fashion, once again, unlike the rest of the world.

III. Times

A comprehensive knowledge of the definitive scientific basis of European geography was not fully achieved until the late modern age, that is, not before the eighteenth–nineteenth centuries. Besides, a point that has never ceased to be the subject of debate was the question of the historical chronology to be acknowledged as pertaining to Europe, not on a geographical level, but from the point of view of the physical space that ultimately came to be marked out as Europe.

In such terms, the question becomes a great deal simpler, if we are able to identify the time in which it is possible to distinguish more clearly and unequivocally than ever before that historical area that can be reasonably defined as European; and that time is undoubtedly the fall of Rome's empire in the West.

It is common knowledge that such an empire was Mediterranean through and through. For the first and only time in history the lands surrounding the Mediterranean Sea were politically united under Roman sovereignty, from the borders of Mesopotamia to the Rhineland, from Morocco to Romania: a political entity so aware of its Mediterranean character that the great body of water at the heart of it was named *Mare internum*, or *Mare nostrum*. After all, an awareness of the common bond uniting humans drawn to the Mediterranean is much older than the actual domination that Rome exercised over it. It is always worth recalling – and the memory is fully justified – the passage in the *Phaedo*, in which Plato notes that men who dwell between the Pillars of Hercules and the river Phasis (the Georgian river mentioned above) live in a small part of the Earth around the sea, like ants or frogs around a pond.

The notation by Plato (which is set in the framework of a complex reflection on the role of the sea as opposed to the land) is not in itself surprising. In his day, and already for centuries, Mycenaean, Phoenician and Greek navigators had built colonies and set up emporiums along the Mediterranean's shores. Upon encountering and blending into Rome's imperial march, the experience of those navigators and the learning displayed by Greek geographers had given full representation to the uniqueness of the Inland Sea. And the notion of a 'Mediterranean continent' corresponding to Rome's imperial expanse as a veritable geographical setting for the ancient history of the Mediterranean world and its surroundings cannot be dismissed as a mere flight of fancy, attributable to a bunch of imaginative scholars and writers.

In contrast to this continent focused on the Roman *Mare internum*, the European continent sure enough begins to take hold with the collapse of Roman sovereignty, which had established the unity of the Mediterranean sea, thereby ensuring that of the 'Mediterranean continent', while, at the same time, the Continent's boundaries along the Rhine and Danube had been encroached on to the point of vanishing, leading to a lasting association and gradual integration between the lands on this side of the imperial Roman *limes* and those beyond it. Hadrian's Wall in Britain, Augustus' failed expansion across the Rhine, Trajan's limited inroads into Dacian territory beyond the Danube, as well as the constant need to strengthen the imperial *limes* from the Atlantic to the Black Sea and provide for its upkeep are all precedents and conditions that will later pale into insignificance between the fourth and the sixth centuries AD. Rome itself was ousted from its chief role as grand capital of the empire by the 'new Rome', commissioned by Constantine the Great, who gave it his name. Imperial unity, still effective in the last years of Theodosius I, between 392 and 395, ceased with him altogether. The empire definitively split into two parts, Eastern and Western, although its unity continued to be professed in law. In the western part between the fifth and sixth century a series of kingdoms had been founded by the Germanic peoples invading the empire from east and west; in the eastern part the empire continued to exist for many centuries as a Roman empire, but was so transformed in its moral and material basis that later historians called it *Byzantine* (from Byzantium, the city where Constantine established the new Rome); the attempt by emperor Justinian I to reconquer the western part of the empire under his reign (527–565) led to remarkable results, that, however, proved partial and short-lived.

The loss of the empire's western half along with the Germanic conquest of Britain, of the lands from the Rhine to the Alps and the Pyrenees, of the Iberian peninsula and of Italy, undoubtedly mark a profound historical break, which throughout Western Europe clearly sets apart the history of Rome from that which followed. This break is significant enough for us to say clearly that it marks the point in time in which the actual history of Europe per se, as we have always understood it, truly kicks off. At the same time, it behoves us to acknowledge – as with Roman Europe, being equivalent to southern Europe – the geographical limitation of this nascent yet even wider Europe that for a long time will almost entirely be enclosed to the west of the Baltic-Adriatic axis.

Historians later defined the kingdoms set up in the former western half of the Roman empire as Roman-Germanic kingdoms since the invaders (Ostrogoths, Visigoths, Franks, Burgundians, Vandals and others) did not completely destroy Roman institutions and other Roman features in the occupied lands. The same cannot be said for the Anglo-Saxons in Britain and the Lombards in Italy, a fact that profoundly shaped the history of these two countries.

For these and other reasons, many historians have believed there to be a certain continuity between the world before and the one after the Germanic invasions and conquests; and while this is very much a moot point, we can also to some extent agree. Its scope and its historical significance, however, are clearly outweighed by the material collapse of the ancient civilisation that had reached its heyday with the Roman empire. Already from the end of the fourth century and up to its peak in the seventh century, the material and cultural heritage of the Roman world was falling to ruin and being lost with increasing scope and intensity. The former Roman world of the seventh century had become dramatically impoverished: this was evident in the alarming drop in population; in cities being reduced to small, struggling townships; in civil infrastructure (roads, bridges, aqueducts, etc) being in a state of disrepair or heavily damaged, along with all form of communication; in the loss or destruction of the monumental, artistic and cultural heritage (it will suffice to say that the around 85 per cent of Greek and Roman literary or other texts are believed to have been lost); in the almost complete disappearance of the Greek tongue (except in some marginal parts of Italy) from the former Western Roman lands; in the consequent corruption of the proper way of writing and speaking Latin; in the narrow scope for culture and literacy – practically restricted to the clergy and only in its more learned expressions.

On account of all this, one speaks of 'dark ages' throughout post-Roman European history roughly until the fourteenth century. As we shall see, this was an ungracious definition. But the happenings spread over the various centuries that saw the material collapse of the ancient civilisation in the Roman empire's western lands, prolonging its distressing effects, may somehow warrant the use of such a metaphor, in spite of a few episodes, or a short period, of 'lesser darkness' or some hopeful signs of a new dawn (like the all-too-celebrated 'Carolingian renaissance' under Charlemagne). In fact, just as three or four centuries (fourth–seventh century) had passed until the decadence and the material-cultural impoverishment of the late Roman world had reached its highest point, another three or four centuries (eighth–tenth or eleventh) were needed before one could stop speaking of 'dark ages'. At that time Europe experienced a strong upsurge in the sense of a new rebirth of all aspects surrounding civil life, to such an extent that, when the next crisis struck in the middle of the fourteenth century, lasting well into the fifteenth century, neither this downturn, nor all the ones that would later befall Europe were remotely comparable to the catastrophe that had marked the end of the ancient world. This time there was no collapse in the civil backbone of society, indeed, every time the upswings were more impressive and swifter than before, while the material and cultural heritage of the European world would fundamentally and progressively evolve, raising the bar to heights unseen before, in the nineteenth and the twentieth centuries.

There was still no talk, and this for a long time, of Europe and of Europeans. The dominant term used in ancient times for expressing awareness as to one's own civilisation had been the Roman concept of *empire*; and this cultural reference point remained firmly set on the European horizon, as an ideal and as an idea of perfect civilised living. In post-Roman Europe the dominant standard of reference became religious, in accordance with the change of values brought about by Christianity. So one talked of *christianitas, christiana communitas* or *societas, christiana res publica.* It had permeated the very notion of *empire* as evidenced by the expression *sancta romana res publica*, a foretaste of the shift from *empire* to *Roman empire*, as it was known from the first half of the eleventh century, and thence to *Holy empire*, which took hold in the mid-twelfth century, as was the case of the *Holy Roman empire* in the mid-thirteenth, to indicate the 'empire' established under Charlemagne in the year 800.

Only sometime between the thirteenth and fourteenth centuries did this notion of *christianitas* begin to be bound with that of Europe. Later, in the fifteenth century this process of assimilation had become complete. 'Christianus orbis Europam omnem tenet', wrote cardinal Bessarion sometime in the mid-1400s: the Christian world occupies all of Europe; and he could rightly make this claim since, being a native of Constantinople, he construed that *christianus orbis* as also including Byzantine Christianity, which had definitively detached itself from the Roman in 1054. It is no coincidence that, since the fall of Constantinople to the Turks in 1453, the cardinal is said to have proclaimed that they were 'in patria, in domo propria, in sede nostra': in the land, in the actual home, and in the place of us Christians.

The association between *Christianity* and the *Church of Rome* had followed a somewhat parallel route, so that the connection between Christianity and Europe also entailed that the Church of Rome would become identified with Europe; and this idea of Europe representing the Roman Church and, consequently, its pope also took off very quickly. In those days, the Irish monk Columbanus (540 ca.–615), who first moved to France and then to Italy (where he founded Bobbio Abbey) and was an eminent figure in the religious and cultural life of his time, would write to pope Gregory I, describing him as the most beautiful ornament of the Church *totius Europae*; and to pope Boniface IV in 613 as the head *omnium totius Europae ecclesiarum* (*Epistles*, I, 1 and 5). This is all the more significant because in Columbanus' day Western and Eastern Christianity had not yet experienced the first schism, which occurred as a result of image worship in the eighth century.

From the Roman perspective, this Church corresponded geographically to the Europe lying west of the Baltic-Adriatic axis, which (as we have already seen) since the days of Charlemagne had been taking the shape of the western Roman-imperial territories. Hopes of a reunification of the two Churches, Roman Catholic and Eastern Orthodox, in the fifteenth century were never fulfilled in practice. The Christianity associated with Europe was, therefore, Christian-Catholic and pertained to the Church of Rome. In 1458 pope Pius II proclaimed that he would speak of the events that occurred *apud Europaeos aut qui cristiano nomine censentur* ('among Europeans or those who would go by the name of Christians'). Henceforth, the notion of Europe becomes settled (until roughly the eighteenth century) in its close ties and association with the notion of Christianity, but also, increasingly, as a completely autonomous entity in its own right.

Is this to say that in the 'dark ages' and up to the thirteenth or fourteenth century there has been no talk of Europe? Clearly, the answer is no. Let us just cast a quick glance at Dante. He not only recalls Europa's kidnapping by Jove, but mentions the beautiful maiden's abduction in the context of a geographical indication, to indicate Phoenicia, where she was taken, as the Mediterranean's easternmost boundary in opposition to its westernmost, the Pillars of Hercules (*Paradise* XXVII, 83–84). In a geographical sense, the word is found several times in Dante's works: to underscore that the Malaspina's generosity is well known 'throughout all Europe' (*Purgatory* VIII, 121–122); to indicate the place of origin of the Foehn, the dry, warm western wind that in spring gives birth to 'the new leaves, wherewith/Europe is seen to clothe herself afresh' (*Paradise* XII, 47–48); in reference to Byzantium-Constantinople, which stands '[i]n the extreme of Europe', in the furthermost corner of the continent (*Paradise* VI, 5). In one of his *Epistles* (VII, 11) he speaks of a 'three-cornered Europe': that is, of a broadly triangular-shaped Europe enclosed by the Black Sea, the Strait of Gibraltar and an unspecific northernmost point; a Europe over which the empire's authority is by no means limited. In one of his rhymes for the stone-lady (*Io son venuto al punto de la rota*) there is mention of the 'lands of Europe, which never once lose/the seven cold stars' (vv 28–29): as if to mean, the country where the Ursa Major is always shining. In his *De Monarchia* (II, VIII, 7) the strait between the Troas and Thrace, called the Hellespont, is recalled as 'separating Asia from Europe'. Once again, we find a geographical reference, but other references, not just geographical, abound in the *de Monarchia*. In fact, it is said that in the *orbis tripartitus* Europe competed with Asia and Africa to beget the offspring of Aeneas (II, III, 10–13); that also 'maior pars Europam colentium', most of the inhabitants of Europe, as well as the Asians and Africans, do not recognise the power of the Church of Rome as bestowing authority upon the Emperor (III, XIV (XIII), 7); that Italy is the 'most excellent region' (II, III, 16) of Europe. Moreover, in the *De vulgari eloquentia*, Europe is spoken of as a land inhabited by people from the East, and European languages are cited, breaking them down into three groups, namely Greek, also partly spoken in Asia Minor, and the Germanic and Latin languages, the latter further classified into tongues spoken in the Pays d'Oc, Pays d'Oïl, and Pays de Sì (I, viii). Indeed, if it were not such a blatant anachronism, one might almost be tempted to claim that Dante possessed some kind of insight, though very general, into the continent's Indo-European linguistic unity.

If we have somewhat lingered on Dante, it was not only to reel off a number of examples through an important case. We felt the need to quote him because, in this field – as in many others – he most truthfully and authoritatively mirrors post-Roman European culture, wherein the notion of Europe, starting from its geographical meaning, was never forsaken.

The case of the word *European* is different, both as an adjective and as a noun. Latin featured the two forms *europaeus* and *europensis*. The latter can still be found in Isidore Pacensis, an eighth century Iberian cleric who, when describing (*Chronicon*, 59, col 1721) the battle of Poitiers of 732, uses the term *Europenses* twice to indicate the Christian army of the Frankish king Charles Martel, victorious over the Arabs who had crossed the Pyrenees and invaded France. The twofold use of this word may mean that its choice was not entirely random, although its significance and even its usage may be indicative of the author's intent to stress the foreignness of the invaders not only with regard to France, but also to the whole of Europe. Given the complete identification that had quickly established between Europe and Christendom, there is no need to insist on this point: to be *Christian* now meant to be *European*.

A certain delay in the use of the word *European* still persisted, even when using *Europe* instead of *Christianitas* had become commonplace not only as a geographical allocation, but also as the object of specific anthropological histories and notations. 'The mind and the soul of people (*gentium ingenia atque animi*) and the historical memories (*rerum gestarum monumenta*)' – as Valencian scholar Juan Luis Vives wrote in a 1529 pamphlet (*De origine concordiae et discordiae in humano genere*) – 'demonstrate why Asia was able to withstand even the most middling forces of Europe'. After Pius II, and especially since the sixteenth century, there were numerous works dedicated to the history of Europe, even though they lacked the notion of a comprehensive history, 'that would be conceived of and practiced much later' (G Galasso, *Nell'Europa dei secoli d'oro* (2012) 49). Furthermore, the *Sommario dell'istoria d'Italia dal 1511 al 1527* written by the Florentine Francesco Vettori already featured the idea that one cannot write about Italian history without referencing that of other countries with whom Italy's is intertwined: these being Spain and France, the empire and Germany, Switzerland and England, as well as the Ottoman Turks, by now a European power broker that had ultimately lain siege to Vienna. Hence, Vettori too was referring to that 'European Europe' – as it can well be defined – moulded by history and stretching from the Atlantic to, as we said, the Baltic-Adriatic axis. But what was the cause for hesitating to use the word European despite its well-known uses in Latin?

It was not just an Italian phenomenon. In French historical dictionaries we can trace the use of the adjective *europien* to 1563, as a derivation from Latin *europeanus*, hence the modern French *européen* and the English European. In Italian it already features in Giovanni Boccaccio: in his dantesque writings, the adjective *europico* refers to the Greek Mediterranean in opposition to the seas of Africa and Asia, but there are no other instances, and the linguistic form seems crafted upon a learned back-formation by Boccaccio of the noun *Europa*. If the, albeit infrequent, use of the adjectival form may be traced to the mid-sixteenth century, in both France and Italy the noun *Europeans* will have to wait until the eighteenth century (at least 1721, it seems) before making an appearance.

The problem that arises may become less peregrine, if one considers that the political and historical use of the term *Europe* and the use of *European* as a noun/adjective began to circulate and actually gained a foothold at a time that coincided with the period between the Renaissance and the Enlightenment. In other words, it coincides with an age marked by a profound secularisation of the European life and spirit, and in which the world's first, decisive process of Europeanisation was taking place at the same time. It is clear that in this new framework the equivalence between *Christian* and *European*, and between *Christendom* and *Europe* no longer either sufficed or (above all) fulfilled the *Europam colentes*, the inhabitants of Europe, as Dante called them. Even more so, it no longer sufficed or fulfilled that 'European Europe', which had been the indisputable driving force behind European secularisation and expansion.

If this claim holds, it meant that the age of Europe and of Europeans was now in full bloom, reaching its fullest manifestation also with respect to the long season of Christian Europe in which it had quietly matured.

IV. Events

European secularisation and expansion did not entail – it is hardly worth stating – that Christianity and the Christian spirit in Europe had been shelved. These continued to enrich Europe and Europeans with all the stimuli and contributions of their age-old history and their revolutionary ethical philosophy, now spanning 1,500 years; and these values were now the sine qua non of being European. But ever since early post-Roman times, being European had also carried a political theme that would always monopolise the political and ethical-political history of the then emerging 'European Europe': the dual-conflict theme. On the one hand, the unavoidable conflict between gaining (or regaining) a unity akin to the one achieved by Rome in the Mediterranean world, and maintaining and safeguarding a multiplicity of players on the European scene. On the other hand, within the framework of this same multiplicity, an equally hopeless conflict existed between the hegemony exercised by one or more players and a reasonable and well-reasoned (or, rather, contracted and enforced) equilibrium among all major and minor players on the same scene.

The first alternative sustained the imperial notion of Rome along one of the many threads that make Roman legacy one of the most conspicuous chapters in the history of Europe. Unity meant order and peace, and, as peace, it immediately became a firm point of reference also on the part of Christians and on the part of the Church in which Christians recognised themselves. Variety was not in opposition to Unity singularly on account of the unstoppable push of the many Germanic peoples who had settled in the lands of the western Roman empire or had organised themselves in ways far removed from their ancient traditions elsewhere in Europe (and the same goes for those non-Germanic peoples that had made inroads into that formerly Roman sphere). Variety also opposed unity in the form of the autonomist aspirations that gained ground in the former Roman provinces amid local populations who were cut off or far removed from their traditional reference centres or that, under the new conditions, were now in a position to obtain a certain degree of autonomous self-determination. And, once multiplicity was postulated, the facts would determine the outcome of the alternative between equilibrium and hegemony.

For this reason the conflict among Franks, Visigoths and Ostrogoths at the beginning of the sixth century can surely be viewed as 'the first European war'. The Visigoths occupied the Iberian peninsula and parts of France up to the river Loire. The Frankish king Clovis, assisted by the Burgundians, attacked them in a bid to extend his kingdom to the South. If successful, his power and influence would have increased significantly. At Vouillé, in 507, he defeated the Visigoths and pushed them back across the Pyrenees. At that point Clovis and his Burgundian allies were set upon by Theodoric, Ostrogoth king of Italy, who defeated them at Arles in 509. As spoil of war, Theodoric acquired the Provençal coast up to the Rhone, while the Visigoths successfully retook the coastal region from the Rhone to the Pyrenees. The much-feared Frankish hegemony was foiled according to a pattern that would repeatedly play out in later European events.

Such hegemonic tendencies displayed by one of the new Roman-Germanic kingdoms were not thus put to rest. Indeed, they reared their head after the failed attempt by emperor Justinian (527–565) to secure the former Roman western territories of the empire in Italy. Here, the Lombards (as we have said) had not only categorically refused to acknowledge, unlike the other Germanic peoples, any authority of Constantinople over the territories they had invaded, but had also put into effect a twofold partition of the Italian peninsula, whose consequences on the (not merely) political life of the country would last 1,000 years.

The hegemonic design would then be completed by the Franks under Charlemagne. But, meanwhile, other events had developed in the European framework, first of all, starting with the Church of Rome establishing itself as an independent power in the political and civil spheres, and as the undisputed head (through its pope) of canonical hierarchy and of the ecclesiastical world in the theological and religious spheres. The conversion of the Germanic peoples bringing them into obedience, the protection of the populations inhabiting Rome's former empire, the emancipation from imperial protection and from every other form of secular power, the papal primacy in the Church, the work of promoting civil society, culture and heritage conservation through the monasteries, and the setting up of a temporal dominion that constituted a veritable Papal State were among the many aspects underpinning a historical process that can already be considered underway at the time of the papacy of Gregory I (590–604). Hence, a key player – already active for centuries, and immensely influential not only with regard to the history of Europe (that would feel its clout at all times, and often decisively) – had reached full-blown maturity.

The seventh century saw another key player of future world history appear on the Euro-Mediterranean scene: Islam. For the Europe of those times – *in statu nascendi* – it constituted a decisive element towards defining the continent geographically and catalysing its identity. Islam immediately became the *other* against which the Christian world measured itself prejudicially; and this confrontation undoubtedly provided one of the strongest motives for identifying *Christian* with *European*, as we have said before. This same confrontation would take many forms and would drag on from one century to another, running through the whole of European history. The question of its geographical delimitation, however, was settled fairly swiftly, even though, as with the religious confrontation, it would also linger on in various guises, but in very different terms, over the centuries.

Significant episodes in this respect were certainly the repeated assaults carried out by the Arabs against Constantinople between 662 and 679 and in 717–718. In the first case, it was 'Greek fire' – the secret weapon of the Byzantine fleet – that saved the day. The threat was more serious the second time round, but the vigour displayed by emperor Leo III (717–741) succeeded in lifting a siege by massive forces and ensuring the Byzantine reconquest of the western half of Asia Minor. Islamic penetration into the Balkans was put off for a few centuries. With the consolidation of Byzantine power, Europe had nothing more to fear – at least in terms of threats from its south-eastern borders.

In the West, the Arabs had invaded the Iberian peninsula in 711 and quickly extended their rule to the Pyrenees, except for the northwest corner (Asturias, Cantabria and Galicia). Then they crossed the Pyrenees and, as we have already mentioned, drove in the heart of France until Charles Martel, mayor of the palace of the Frankish kings and de facto royal ruler of France, soundly defeated them at Poitiers in 732 (this being the occasion when the aforementioned chronicler Isidore Pacensis spoke of *Europenses*). Traditionally hailed as bringing about the definitive halt to Arab penetration beyond the Pyrenees, the significance of the Frankish victory at Poitiers was later drastically reduced by a part of historiography as a relatively modest victory and military encounter, as it did not truly deal with an invasion, but rather with a series of raiding parties spearheading the vanguard of Arab penetration into France. Indeed, these scholars claimed that the Arabs were present for a long time and kept on making raids and expeditions into French territory. In reality, this attempt to demythicise Charles Martel's endeavour is neither here nor there: Poitiers was the northernmost point reached by the Arabs in Western Europe. The fact that it may have been a raid is historically questionable, and not wholly relevant: in fact many Arab conquests had begun as an incursion. For sure, since Poitiers, there was ever increasing evidence that the Pyrenean border had turned into an unsurpassable boundary for the Arabs themselves, curbing their advance in the West: this is the same fact that the chronicler Isidore had emphasised so much with his use of the term *Europenses*.

In the central Mediterranean, Arab expansion in the ninth century had led to the conquest of Sicily and to temporary occupation and settlements in other Italian islands, in southern Italy and up to Liguria and Provence. But already around the year 1000 a Christian backlash was brewing, resulting in the reconquest of Sicily between 1061 and 1091; triggered the long-lasting experience of the Crusades and the 'Latin kingdoms' in the eastern Mediterranean in 1096; and established the decisive turning point in the Christian *reconquista* of the Iberian peninsula in 1212 with the victory of the kings of Castile, Aragon and Navarre at Las Navas de Tolosa, in Andalusia.

History to come would long confirm the military superiority thus gained, or regained, over the Arab world, with which relations had always been very intense ever since Islam had made its first appearance on the Mediterranean seaboard. Meanwhile, other grandiose events were leaving their mark on Europe.

We have already noted that the alternative between hegemony and equilibrium had immediately come to the fore among the Barbarian peoples invading the Western Roman empire, so that the Goths of Spain and Italy had already clashed with the Franks by the early sixth century. That alternative had been resolved under Charlemagne with the rise of Frankish hegemony and the return of the concept of empire. Charlemagne conquered the kingdom of the Lombards in Italy, subdued Germany from the Rhine to the Elbe and converted the Saxons to Christianity, crossed the Pyrenees and established various fortified towns on their foothills, in Navarre and Catalonia. His dominions now stretched from the rivers Tiber to the Elbe and to the Ebro.

No such thing had been seen in the West since the fall of Rome. And yet, it is hard to believe that the sheer size of Charlemagne's dominions or the extent of his power alone led to his crowning as emperor on Christmas day of the year 800. It has always been mooted whether a new imperial sovereignty in the West was proclaimed at the behest of the Roman Church or of Charlemagne and his court. Yet one can hardly believe that such an initiative could have occurred without some prior agreement between the Church and Charlemagne, as both were pushed to action by their very own motives, which spontaneously converged. Ultimately, even this debate is less important than it appears at a first reading. The main thing was that there would again be talk of an empire in the West, for this meant that a multi-layered awareness of the new era had already begun to take shape.

It was impossible for there to be no talk of Rome, even though no direct reference was made. Still, not all sources agree on this, as some speak of *imperator romanorum*. The *Liber pontificalis*, a particularly relevant authority in this case, speaks of Charlemagne only as 'serene augustus, crowned by God, great and merciful emperor'. Other sources add the words *gubernans Imperium romanum* (governing the Roman empire), a formula preserved by Charlemagne's chancery from 801 until his death in 814. The difference between *emperor of the Romans* or *governing the Roman empire* and the simple title of *sovereign of the Roman empire* or *Roman emperor* speaks volumes about the hesitations and divergences underpinning that proclamation in the year 800. We know that, contrary to custom in Constantinople, pope Leo III did not come forward to bless the sovereign after his proclamation to emperor, but anticipated this move by proclaiming and blessing the new emperor himself in one fell swoop: this marked the starting point to that struggle between the two powers, the pontifical (spiritual) and the political (worldly, civil), for dominance over and submission to one another that would last for centuries.

Charlemagne's imperial title was also questioned by empress Irene from Constantinople, since there could be no imperial titles other than those which furthered Roman tradition, until a deal was struck that put an end to the prickly, and newly arisen, question of two empires. As we have already noted, the eleventh century wording *imperium romanum* for the Carolingian empire does not seem to appear before then (a certificate from 1034 is cited), while the wording *sacrum romanum imperium* was an innovation brought in by the chancery of Frederick I Hohenstaufen around the mid-twelfth century. There is no doubt that – regardless of whichever way or time there was mention of a *Roman empire* – the bedrock of that *renovatio imperii* remained essentially religious. By referring to Charlemagne as 'serene august', religious piety was inextricably bound up with imperial majesty. It is no coincidence that Alcuin of York defined Charlemagne's reign as *regnum Christianitatis*: a perfect definition for this new political-institutional reality.

Was this moment the 'founding of Europe', as tradition has long dictated and is often repeated? If pushed, one can make this claim with far more certainty ex post, in light of Europe's history from that time onward, than from the standpoint of the historical reality of the time. At that time, the overriding tone was certainly the mark of Christianity, as in Alcuin's aforementioned definition; and it was so overriding as to somewhat diminish the importance of the mark of the Roman imperial tradition. And it is not surprising that both the papal curia and Charlemagne's court agreed on this. In Rome, the papacy set itself up to enjoy a more autonomous role than in Constantinople, which persisted in its claims of exercising sovereignty over Rome and in its interference in ecclesiastical affairs, as evidenced by the still recent contrasts over the cult of images. At the same time, the proclamation formula was used by the papacy to bind the new imperial power in the West to a religious basis and to its observance, of which the Church of Rome would have to be considered titular and guarantor. In turn, Charlemagne had surrounded himself with a court that had gradually come to embrace many of the greatest intellectuals of the day: Angilbert, Theodulf, Alcuin, Adalard, Einhard, Peter of Pisa, Paulinus II of Aquileia, Paul Deacon. Actually, the sovereign's cultural policy was broadminded and this is borne out by his superior political personality and the wider horizons to which he aspired. In that court Biblical, Greek and Roman names were used to address one another. But the chosen baptismal name of Charlemagne was David, and this was also a sign of the recurring religious-political connection on the basis of which they acted upon. The sovereign's Davidic title was a clear reference to Jerusalem rather than to Rome. The supremacy attained by the new David had brought about an imperial proclamation that can be likened to an advancement that was hardly oriented to the Roman past. Instead, it looked forward, reckoning on the future of the imperial Christian power built by Charlemagne.

Even less bound up with the imperial promotion of Charlemagne was the Muslim Arabs' outpouring onto the Mediterranean scene. As Henri Pirenne notably argued in his famous 1937 book (*Mahomet et Charlemagne*), that irruption would cause Roman-Germanic Europe to be sundered from its traditional Roman-Mediterranean reference points in both political and economic terms, and so there would be an objective correlation between the expansion of Islam and a general socio-economic setback in Europe, which allowed the Franks to successfully assert their power. In truth, Charlemagne's empire was built in the wake of the aforementioned struggle for hegemony among the Roman-Germanic kingdoms, which had begun long before the prophet Mohammad and Islam erupted so vehemently onto the scene of this story, restricting free movement and stifling the Mediterranean links of those same kingdoms. Above all, the political role taken on by the Germanic potentates on both sides of the old imperial Roman *limes* served as the crucial factor, also novel in itself, that determined the shift in the political axis of the Roman-Germanic world, reaching full maturity under Charlemagne; indeed, it was gradually moving from the Mediterranean to the Rhine valley in the north, where it would always remain even after Islam had long since been beaten back to its original power base, and the Roman-Germanic world had long since turned into modern Europe.

The most important event of the nascent Europe, occurring at the beginning of the second Christian millennium, surely deserves to be identified with the founding of European economy, whose major centres, most advanced manifestations and preeminent expressions were to be found in Italy. Underpinning this phenomenon was a demographic explosion that almost doubled European population in three centuries. More manpower meant that agriculture was developed more intensely, increasing the production, also because, once again, the land was widely settled everywhere. Agriculture could therefore be the driver behind European progress, whose other fundamental and decisive pole was represented by the cities, which reappeared once again – after the far-reaching urban eclipse amid the twilight of the ancient world – to make their mark on European lands not only in formerly Roman provinces, but also in those territories in which city-dwelling was an absolute novelty. The unquestionable role of cities reached new heights when establishing short and long distance trade routes, and commerce proved to be the real driving force behind the great European leap forward in those centuries, also bringing about a major growth in manufacturing, in itself already roused by the increase in population and by the wealth building up in the towns.

This allowed a self-reproducing mechanism to establish itself, which later turned out to be enduring and irreversible, despite the numerous, and often powerful, crises and hesitations throughout the centuries. That mechanism ensured a gigantic 'primitive accumulation' of capital, techniques, networks of relations, equipment, practices, means and systems of communication, upon which all later developments of the European economy were founded. A large market-place also took shape at the time, which tied together the various commercial sectors in Europe's post-Roman age, and extended them organically beyond all the geographical boundaries previously encountered.

In the most intense phase of this development, a 'capital-based realm' was established, so that wealth was increasingly conceived as the availability of capital goods; and it would be methodically and primarily used to create new wealth – unlike what had usually happened until that time and would continue to happen in several large civilised areas outside Europe. What was clearly emerging has been rightly defined as *precapitalism*, in which financial activities took on a prominent role, compared to manufacturing and trade, and were crucially assisted, on the one hand, by special interest relations with the political world that used them to bankroll its own business endeavours and enterprises through hefty loans, and, on the other hand, by a great abundance of new technical resources and new forms of organisation (banks and large trading companies with branches and agencies in many countries, double-entry accounting, bank drafts and bills of exchange: all the trappings of large multinational and multisector business groups for devising multiple ways of allocating and investing capital in many forms that would become commonplace in the distant future).

Both the upheaval and innovations were so great as to raise a number of neither few nor trifling issues in the Christian world that was at the forefront of all this. Difficult questions were raised concerning relations between ethics, religion and economics, even on a largely theoretical scale. That ancient prejudice – first Greek, Roman and then Christian – against mercantile activities that regarded status as ideally warranted by land ownership, was beginning to crumble. In the Christian age mercantile activities were held in even worse esteem. Trade was beset by the extreme difficulty of setting the 'right price'; financial activities were plagued by the overwhelming doubt as to how to differentiate them from undue and unfair speculations; money itself was bedevilled by the materiality of its appearance and for being a vehicle of wealth, the fruit of an *auri sacra fames*, sacred hunger of pernicious gold, as the Latin poet Virgil (*Aeneid* III, 57) used to call it, and even 'dung of the devil', to quote pope Innocent III (following in the footsteps of saint Basil).

These limitations were all quickly tempered, modified, or overcome. The changes were heralded by the return of gold coinage in the West in the mid-thirteenth century, after the practice had been abandoned centuries before, unlike in the Byzantine and Muslim East. And there was certainly no dearth of equally relevant anthropological and cultural repercussions, starting from the one contained in the famous saying that 'time is money'. Above all, one began to take stock of the decisive role of science and technology as fundamental factors underpinning any form of progress or enhancement on a path towards economic growth.

European development from the year 1000 onward truly represented an event of global proportions, both from the cultural point of view (it was at that time that in Europe among other things, universities were born), and from the social point of view, which lay the defining groundwork for future European fortunes. These fortunes would be interspersed, at secular intervals, with epochal crises. Already the fourteenth century witnessed a general crisis – epidemic, demographic, economic, social – of devastating gravity. What happened was nothing on the scale of what had been seen with the collapse of the Western Roman empire. Indeed, the very extent and depth of the crisis testified to the robustness of the European framework built in the previous three or four centuries. It amounted to a restructuring and rescaling of the edifice, not a collapse. Like with the process of development, so too the first seeds of the crisis lay in the countryside. Just over a century was sufficient time to overcome the regression and stagnation phase, during which none of the previous conquests were lost, while the world of culture and science underwent at the same time developments of great importance. Historians have therefore spoken of a new type of crisis, of a 'modern' crisis, that is, a negative crisis, but set within the overall scale of a fundamental process of development under way for three or four centuries, by focusing on cities and commerce. Not for nothing, the fourteenth14th century crisis came to a close with the dawning of one of the most original and relevant ages in European spiritual life, culture and art.

V. Modernity

It was the age of Humanism and the Renaissance. Even before it started, a great innovation had taken place in a particular field, the military, that had always proved to be decisive in historical developments. In fact, the use of firearms had radically altered the notion and practice of war. The infantry resumed its traditional role of 'queen of the battlefield', marking the end of the supremacy of the heavy cavalry, cataphracts, that had dominated the whole post-Roman era, and, at the same time, had been a model of warfare organically linked to the feudal condition. Yet this was not the most important change: especially decisive was the use of gunpowder, invented in China and introduced into European practices during the thirteenth century. Between the fifteenth and sixteenth centuries the new weapons (cannons, muskets, siege mortars, harquebuses) had increasingly gained the upper hand. Their destructiveness from afar was no longer sustainable unless opponents possessed an equal supply of weapons with matching firepower; and the social repercussions of such an innovation were by no means less relevant than its military implications.

An even more far-reaching invention – also 'made in China' – was that of movable type printing. Not widely used in its country of origin, the new technique garnered overwhelming success in Europe, where it was developed by Johannes Gensfleisch Gutenberg, who published his famous *Bible* in 1455. Before the end of the century, already thousands of books had been printed in Europe (called incunabula: books made on a printing press, still in its infancy). What the printing press would mean to Europe and to the world at large, does not even warrant the slightest mention here: suffice it to say that the first true, great medium of mass communication in history was born; and this would impact in particular the circulation of ideas and the conditions of cultural life, as already seen with the advancements brought about by Humanism and the Renaissance.

These too had their hub, their beginning and their highest expressions in Italy. This resulted, first of all, in the awareness that a new day was dawning. It was the Humanists who coined the phrases *media tempestas, media aetas*, meaning the time elapsed since the fall of the Roman empire in the West until their time; and they attributed strongly negative connotations to this 'middle age': for its Latin so far removed from the classical language; for its culture locked in complicated doctrinal schemes and in heavy-going analytical discussions; for its architecture and its art so distant from classical canons.

The return to the heights and harmonies of classicism was not motivated only by artistic rejection and aesthetic preferences, indeed reverting to the ancients (as we said in other cases) often revealed a course of action more geared towards the future than to the past. Behind the classic aesthetic ideal, a whole new consideration of nature was taking shape.

The perfection found in the measures of classicism was such because it was thought to derive from nature and its imitation; and on this basis imitating the ancients and reverting to classicism were seen as a sure-fire way of conquering and affirming one's own new identity. In Humanism, all this basically gravitated around the domain of *artes liberales, humanae litterae*: therefore, literature, art, historiography, philosophy. As such, Humanism was at the heart of the Renaissance. At the heart, that is, of that cluster of elements, not all of which cultural, that between the fifteenth and seventeenth centuries (first in Italy, then elsewhere) betokened a new 'historical spring'; a time that – despite many, and sometimes even important, objections to the contrary – is safely assumed to mark the beginning of the modern age for Europe (modern, from the adverb Latin *modo* = lately, just now, the present, as the Humanists would say to denote their position as opposed to the previous 'dark ages' from which they sought to shy away).

Even Humanism and the Renaissance, as well as the actual Middle Ages, did not constitute a monolithic historical bloc; they were multifaceted worlds with a great deal of ramifications within them, both sectoral and geographical and chronological, akin to a borderland with highly irregular boundaries enclosed between the age that at that time was declared closed (and which stuck with the name *Middle Ages*) and a future in the making where everything was yet to be defined. In keeping with these basic characteristics, there was also the far from systematic heritage made up of ideas and attitudes that constituted its great historical legacy: a new intuition of man inspired by a heroic ideal shaped upon classic cardinal virtues; an ethic founded on human excellence and dignity; a juxtaposition between a superior ethical wisdom (and its resulting anthropological wisdom) and natural science, especially medicine, in its outward perspective as opposed to the true essence of man; the exercise of criticism as a fundamentally ethical and intellectual vocation; civil life as an active, worthy life; new modules of cultural socialisation, such as academies; freedom, peace, utopia, and the new idea of 'raison d'état' as cornerstones of political and social reflection; a historical realism that, in particular ways and measures, gives voice to the large-scale sense of a substantial intellectual and moral secularisation that is undoubtedly evidenced in the broad sense of the Humanistic-Renaissance cultural modules.

Italy was already entering the peak time of this exciting age when, on the morning of 12 October 1492, Christopher Columbus sighted the coastline and the island of the Bahamas archipelago (it is believed, today's Watling) that he named San Salvador: the first strip of American land he set foot on. He then landed in Cuba and Haiti (which he named Hispaniola) before returning to Spain. We know that he intended to discover a western route to the Indies, so as also to gain control of the highly lucrative spice trade; and that, consequently, the native inhabitants of those islands were called *Indios*. We know that it took a few years before people understood that they we were beholding previously unknown lands, standing before a New world as opposed to the old Euro-African-Asian world; and that only in 1507 the German geographer Martin Waldseemüller gave this new world the name of another Italian navigator, Amerigo Vespucci.

If there ever was a momentous event in world history, Columbus's discovery was certainly that. The oft-repeated question as to the supposed discoveries of America before Columbus, and crediting any merit for this, is little more than a laughing matter. Assuming that there had been previous discoveries, for the world they were and remained unknown, as if they had never happened, because nothing about them was ever known. The world never knew of America until Columbus went there in 1492. Even more ridiculous are the allegations that Columbus used secret maps (and even an unknown navigator who was already experienced in the crossing). However, the criterion with which he planned his voyage is of primary importance. For the first time in history, an exploration was organised on the basis of a scientific hypothesis, rather than with the logic of proceeding 'step by step' or looking 'further afield' or 'around the corner'. In fact, the theory rested upon the basis of the supposed roundness or sphericity of the Earth. In a bid to reach the East, it followed that one could also set off and travel westwards: by travelling around the globe, one would surely arrive in the East. It would have certainly been a journey sealed by predictable and tragic failure if the length of the Earth's circumference had been the one calculated by Columbus based on data researched by Arab geographers, a good one-third less than the real size. If the vast expanses between the Spanish coast of departure and the coveted passage to India had not revealed the existence of such a wide-ranging and boundless landmass that provided shelter to Columbus and his sailors when they were now at their wits' ends, no one would have heard of them.

Instead, the Portuguese Vasco da Gama arrived in the Indies by heading eastwards (instead of westwards, like Columbus) and using the traditional method of celestial navigation, and landing in Calcutta in 1498, having rounded the Cape of Good Hope.

Another Portuguese seaman, Ferdinand Magellan, sailing under the Spanish flag, left Spain in September 1519 to look for a passage from the Atlantic to the Pacific along the southern shores of the New world. He found this in the Strait that bears his name in November 1520, and was able to continue his journey into the Pacific, landing in the Philippines in March 1521. There, however, he died. Two of his ships reached the Moluccas, but only one, under the command of Sebastiano del Cano, succeeded in returning to Spain in September of that year.

This was the first circumnavigation of the world. Europeans continued their voyages of exploration of the Earth, discovering other continents (Australia, Antarctica), countless islands, the Northeast Passage (in 1727–28) connecting the Atlantic and Pacific oceans through the Bering Strait (named after the Dane who discovered it) between Russia and America (Alaska), while gradually improving their knowledge of the innermost and far-flung corners of the world, and describing their mountain and water systems, as well as their climate, flora and fauna.

This tremendously challenging undertaking was still underway between the nineteenth and twentieth centuries, and has continued in increasingly sophisticated ways and with more powerful and enhanced technical means than ever before. Geographical discoveries triggered the globalisation of world economic life, which benefited from this quest right from the outset, reaching its peak between the nineteenth and the twenty-first centuries, and extending and intensifying global trade and commerce between various parts of the world to an extent unimaginable when it all began. Economic globalisation has also been accompanied, at an ever-increasing pace since the twentieth century, by a broader Europeanisation of the ways of life, habits and much (if not all) of civil life in non-European countries. European science and technologies were received even more widely, also in those countries that had shown greater reluctance in accepting the European way of thinking and European values.

Meanwhile, a great new rift had appeared in Western European Christendom, after the split of 1054 between Catholics and Orthodox. Beginning in 1517 with a famous initiative by Martin Luther seeking Christian religious reform, the Protestant movement (as it was already designated in 1529) soon took over most of Germany, Denmark, the Scandinavian countries, the Netherlands, much of Switzerland and spread widely throughout other Catholic countries, starting with France. Later, other reformers, and especially John Calvin, further grew the already exceptional scope of the Lutheran initiative, while Henry VIII of England also caused his kingdom to break away from Catholicism, though not strictly for religious reasons.

The reform carried out in this way nullified the ecclesiastical organisation as to the Christian profession of faith. The Church was no longer regarded as the institutional and necessary keeper of the relationship between the faithful and the divine, as it was wholly remitted to the personal and direct experience of the individual worshiper. This was the mainstay of the new religious framework initiated by Luther. It was strictly bound to the doctrine of justification by faith alone, thus flouting the precepts of performing good deeds, the sacramental practices and the demonstrations of piety required by the Catholic Church. It became impossible to speak of the free will of Christians. The damnation resulting from original sin could only be avoided by inscrutable and unchangeable divine decree.

Predestination cancelled the exchange of good works and the administration of the sacraments with salvation. Christians were bound to perform good and pious works on account of their Christian faith, not with a view to achieving salvation. Thus Protestantism revealed its supremely ethical essence. The salvific virtues of performing worthy deeds and the sacraments dovetailed with man's empowerment in his relationship with God that, inescapably, lay in the Christian man's faith and in the complete remission of his destiny to the will of God in no other way attainable to man's Christian feeling and hopes.

The contrast between the Protestant and the Humanist insight into life and the world was, therefore, no less than that between Catholicism and Protestantism, and found its highest expression in the debate on free will between Erasmus and Luther, in which Erasmus supported the notion of Christian free will, against Luther's idea of the bondage of the will. Luther posited that it was a very free bondage, as it was bound with the freedom to have or not to have absolute faith in God and his work, in total remission of man's own individuality and will. Erasmus believed that denying man's will and responsibility in human activity represented an enormous hurdle in terms of the Christian concept of God as infallibly just, but also good and merciful, while in the doctrine preached by Luther God ended up as becoming somehow responsible for both the good and evil committed by men.

Above and beyond the doctrinal contrast, the conflict carried profound implications. For Erasmus, religious life and moral life continued to be one and the same: morality was one of the practical manifestations of religiosity, and was to be taken into account by the latter. For Luther, religiosity was essentially faith; morality was an independent variable of faith, to the point that, in one of his most celebrated passages, he stated that sinners should sin boldly, but their trust in Christ should be bolder still. Luther also appreciated the value of worthy deeds and of the good will they elicited, but limited their meaning to the plane of man's earthly experience of life, which religion transcended in the fullness and autonomy of faith.

Yet, a subtle bond also linked Erasmian, and therefore Italian, Humanism to Humanism on the whole, which Erasmus represented and furthered through the reform movement. The humanist critique had in many cases targeted a Christianity that had disdainfully shut itself off from the world, enveloped in a mysticism that ignored all rationality. The evangelical simplicity of the Christian doctrine had been eulogised, also tending to the idea of a 'natural religion' – constitutive of nature and human experience – that nonetheless traced both nature and humanity back to God. The superior philology of Humanism had also been employed and applied to the texts of the Old and New Testament. And it was no coincidence that many adherents to the Reformation came from the ranks of highly qualified Humanists; and it was even less surprising that such endorsements of the Reformation would trigger over time a series of events that would lead to the modern development of the idea of 'natural religion', of secularism, and of the principle of tolerance.

The Church did not remain inactive before the challenges presented by Protestant success, and fielded a response that demonstrated all its vitality and the wealth of deeply ethical and religious forces. The corrupt, worldly Church, even profane in its own sacramental practice, which had been lambasted by the Reformation, thus became a very active Church, displaying strength and self-confidence in claiming its predominant religious role in the lives of worshipers and in all aspects of social life.

It was not doctrinal innovation or unleashing other forces that would lead to a different way of being Christian. There was a reiteration of the principles of free will and of good deeds in Christian life, of the magisterium of the Church in its capacity as custodian and administrator of the sacraments and as the indisputable guide and teacher of Christian life. All this was, however, accompanied by an extensive drive to bring discipline and higher standards to the clergy and by exercising relentless oversight of the faithful, through the strengthening of the Inquisition and the suppression of thoughts and behaviours deemed to be heretical, and through a strict censorship of cultural life. Papal monarchy in the Church was expanded and bolstered. Its immunity, along with its jurisdictional powers in civil life, were both augmented and forcefully exerted. In the wake of the imperial expansion enjoyed by Catholic powers, primarily Spain, Catholicism found its own way to spread its influence to the New world and elsewhere, even though the ways of achieving this globalisation were not solely those of evangelical preaching.

It would be more than just an historical error to believe that the repressive violence of the Holy Office, the censorial control over life in general and over intellectual activities with the *Index of forbidden books*, along with the restoration and expansion of the pontifical and hierarchical discipline of the clergy and the Christian people amounted to the entire significance of the Counter-Reformation, which would therefore be devoid of any added value. Such a far-reaching and deep-seated undertaking required a degree of faith, a moral and religious commitment, a missionary zeal and a fervour to accomplish works so extraordinary that some Catholic historians have replaced the definition of *Counter-Reformation* with that of *Catholic Reformation*, by way of marking the Catholic Church's comeback from the Council of Trent (1545–63) onward: a Council whose profound and overall reorganisation of Catholic doctrine and discipline lasted four centuries before being revised and variously modified.

Religion was thus allowed to qualify once again, and for a long time hence, among the justifications for ever-frequent wars among the European powers, although, from this perspective, its importance was steadily ebbing, also on account of the continuous developments in all fields of European thought, from political and social doctrines to different philosophical, historical and anthropological disciplines, and to scientific and technical knowledge.

With regard to the latter, in fact, a so-called *scientific revolution* came about in the seventeenth century. A steady yet ongoing build-up of skills, practices, fields of interest, and instruments had been gaining momentum in previous centuries, adding to European intellectual heritage in all fields of knowledge and in all the possible fields of application of new techniques. Impressive indeed is the roster of sixteenth-century intellectual giants (from Leonardo to John Kepler, Nicholas Copernicus, Andrea Cesalpino, Andreas Vesalius, Paracelsus, and Gerolamo Cardano, to name but a few), whose accomplishments have left an indelible mark in the history of the sciences in Europe. One could fairly consider the rightful foundation of modern science to have come to fruition in the times of Galileo Galilei (1564–1642) and Isaac Newton (1642–1727). In short, this foundation consisted in establishing a research method and a conceptual framework such as to allow natural phenomena, in all their expressions and manifestations, to be identified and measured with mathematical and experimental rigour. Reality was to be observed directly, through reasoning and experimentation (the 'sensible experiences' of Galileo) in an effort to capture it in its truest dimensions, render it in exact mathematical (ie, arithmetical and geometrical) data, and replicate it by means of experimentation. Inquiring, experimenting, measuring: only in this way could true science be born, thus marking the end of all 'pseudophilosophy' (Galileo) and the rejection – *hypotheses non fingo* – of any hypothesis not experimentally verified (Newton).

The strength of this method would lie in its reversal of the relationship between science and technique, and in the fact that scientific hypothesis would come before technological research (as we saw with Colombus). This, however, would not erase the part that many an intuition, imagination, random supposition and other like virtuosities have played in furthering technical progress, whether big or small, since the dawn of time; nor quell the variously fruitful interchange between science and philosophy; nor suppress the continually invoked claim to be allowed to act independently of any undue influence (such as that which caused Galileo to be put on trial) outside the rigours of the scientific method.

There had been indeed a shift from the *realm of approximation* to the *universe of precision*, with its uniform approach to nature without differentiating qualitatively between terrestrial and extraterrestrial space. This shift had ushered a new concept of the forces of nature, no longer linked to metaphysical reasons of virtue and quality of bodies, but rather (and solely) to the physical structure of reality. The mere description of the characteristics pertaining to natural phenomena had given way to the study of the constant and fundamental relations between these phenomena (such as Newton's law of universal gravitation). As it was extravagantly claimed, 'Prometheus is unbound', that is to say, the creative genius of man, at one *sapiens* and *faber*, had been set free; and within a few centuries this liberation would bring about a new revolution, this time an 'industrial revolution'. This implied a new way of production that no longer required the exploitation of natural forms of energy, as had happened until that time, but the ability to use machines designed and built by man to produce the forms already known or those that would gradually be discovered. This resulted in a production capacity in the scale of tens to hundreds (and more) times higher than the traditional output. The availability of new forms of power in increasing quantities (from early types, such as steam, to atomic energy) greatly contributed to ensuring the irreversible nature of the progress that is being achieved, up to present-day outer-space exploration, real time communication, the ever-faster and effortless transport of people and things, the miracles of medical and biomedical sciences, right up to the secrets of genetics, the increasingly more effective innovations in pharmacology and prosthetic applications, the immediate and increasingly powerful and perceptible forms of mass communication, and the downgrading of agriculture to a far lesser role in wealth production. All this, in short, amounts to so much progress that our experience of contemporary life makes it almost redundant to notice, with a constant acceleration in the number of inventions and discoveries and astonishing scientific acquisitions.

It is clear that the metaphor of 'Prometheus unbound' was soon supplemented by that of the 'triumph of Minerva'. European thought erected a veritable theoretical temple to human reason, capable of penetrating all the secrets of the world and of achieving continuous and unlimited progress in knowledge as well as in the conditions of man in the world, so that the 'lights of reason' would shine into every nook and cranny of human and natural reality. This paved the way to yet another European cultural revolution of extraordinary importance, the Enlightenment, whose horizon began to cloud over only at the end of the eighteenth century with the appearance of gradually more menacing signs.

VI. Heartland

When these clouds began to loom, the modern age, as we have seen, had struck a positively impressive balance from almost every point of view. Europe had been at that point and for some time already in an undisputed leading position in the world. In the following nineteenth century, and with the industrial revolution, this primacy had expanded and consolidated itself in such a way as to warrant talk of Europe as the Heartland, the centre of the world island, in the sense of this concept as outlined by the American Halford John Mackinder in 1904 (*The geographical pivot of history*). In actual fact, at the heart of his geopolitical theory was the notion that the possession of certain parts of the world would enable any power that controlled or dominated them to hold sway over much larger areas. At a global level, Mackinder's Heartland was the vast Eurasian expanse stretching from the Volga to the Yangtze (Chang Jiang) in China from east to west and from the Himalayas to the Arctic Ocean from south to north. In practice, this geographical position ensured that China or, above all, Russia would achieve world domination. At the time he formulated this concept, however, it was clear that it could apply to Europe, from the Atlantic to the Urals.

Until the early twenty-first century, nothing of the sort could indeed be inferred from the present-day reality, which continued to be characterised by manifest Western superiority. In the world that they had been gradually discovering in the wake of Columbus, Europeans had steadily established their supremacy to such an extent that even up to World War II more than half of the Earth's surface was in thrall to European countries as colonies, or (as in Russia) had even been incorporated to become an integral part of their national territory.

The Europe that had achieved world domination was, in fact, what we called *European Europe*, enclosed between the Atlantic and the Baltic-Adriatic line, which came to include Russia in the eighteenth century. It was a Europe that, while busy conquering the world, at the same time had been fighting on its soil an endless series of wars driven by that alternative between hegemony and balance – already foretold at the beginning of its history with the war between the Franks and Goths mentioned above.

The modern cycle of this dynamic began at the end of the fifteenth century with the so-called Italian wars and continued with varying intensity, but always with high frequency between the sixteenth and the eighteenth centuries, with Spanish dominance until the mid-seventeenth century, followed by French supremacy, and finally, in an effort to strike a balance, yielding under the thrust and stewardship of Britain. Whether their aim was to achieve balance or hegemony, and beyond recurring religious or other ideological motivations, without fail these great wars were waged over power. It soon became clear that power ratios in Europe also implied and included the colonial possessions of European countries in a political game that, far from being merely European, extended to the world stage, in which political globalisation had become as meaningful as its economic counterpart.

The scale of European world domination was by no means merely military and political, technical and scientific. In fact, it relied on a range of great ethical, social and civil values that achieved their full, mature status between the eighteenth and nineteenth centuries. Man as a person – both in the Christian version and in its secular equivalent that had arisen in European thought in the modern age – remained in the foreground, especially with regard to life in the community. Aspects such as the utmost respect for his individuality, the unfettered attainment of his full potential, the framework of his social and natural rights, his freedom of self-expression and self-fulfilment in the most diverse forms and on the most diverse levels, his participation in public life in a manner befitting his nature as a rational and moral being, alongside other connotations of an equivalent nature and meaning were the subject of lengthy conceptual elaboration, which translated into the reality of great political and social movements.

In post-Renaissance Europe, the dominant institutional system consisted of monarchies and republics, characterised by sovereign totalitarianism, social privilege bestowed on the clergy and on aristocracies or oligarchies, the fragmentation of rights, the ensuing legal confusion and judicial unreliability, widespread arbitrariness and wrongdoing at all levels and in every social sector, the absurd distribution of tax burdens, controls and vetoes exercised by all kinds of institutional and corporate bodies, the randomness or the paralysing immobility of the State's territorial or administrative subdivisions, the proliferation of rights and duties under the numerous existing jurisdictions, the coexisting and combined obligation to submit to political and religious orthodoxy, the limitations to personal freedom in its most varied aspects, the overriding weight of executive power above all others in society, as well as its importance with respect to the enduring petty interests and privileges enjoyed by major and minor social groups.

After the French Revolution, this historical condition was defined as *ancien régime*. In actual fact, it was the regime established in Europe in the three centuries, from the fifteenth to the eighteenth, in which a complete first phase of modern statehood had developed. One should not be misled, however, by the confusion and disorder attributed to the political, institutional and social reality engendered by this regime. The fundamental direction underlying the strategy and the actions pursued by the sovereign powers of Europe in those days was very much aimed, overall, at establishing a rationalisation, homogeneity, parification, balance, and equity within the political and social structure. Incidentally, this was the ambitious aim of the French Revolution and, on the whole, it was achieved. A great French historian, Alexis de Tocqueville, in his *L'ancien régime et la Révolution* (1856), said that, in practice, the Revolution had acted as a veritable 'executor of the will' of the *ancien régime*.

VII. Société des esprits

If the Revolution was able to bear such profound significance, it is because ever since its 'dark ages' Europe had, on the whole, persisted in its cultural unity, as well as in a general political-social parallelism, even in the face of the enduring, manifest and relevant differences that have always marked the conditions and the civil life in its countries.

In the centuries of the *ancien régime* this comprehensive and interactive European unity-diversity had actually exacerbated. At the time, Voltaire expressed this, with heightened awareness, in the *Siècle de Louis XIV* (1751):

> Christian Europe, all except Russia, might for a long time have been considered as a sort of great Republic, divided into several States, some monarchical, and others mixt. Of the latter, some were aristocratical, and others popular; but all connected with one another; all professing the same system of religion, tho' divided into several sects; all acknowledging the same principles of public justice and policies, unknown to the other nations of the world (*The age of Louis XIV*, edited by R Griffith, 1st vol (London 1779) 7).

That 'for a long time' certainly referred to the Renaissance, when this European kinship had fully reached maturity, two or three centuries before Voltaire took pen to paper, and before Russia joined the commonwealth of European nations.

And Jean-Jacques Rousseau was no less clear-headed, when he wrote that:

> The powers of Europe constitute a kind of system, united by the same religion, international law and moral standards, by letters, by commerce and by a kind of equilibrium which is the inevitable outcome of all these ties [... given] the continuous mingling of interests that the bonds of blood and affairs of commerce, the arts, colonies have given the sovereigns, and which, without anyone in fact thinking about preserving it, would nevertheless not be as simple to break up as many people think (*Extrait du projet de paix perpétuelle* in *Œuvres complètes*, 3rd vol (1964) 89).

And all the above applied not only to sovereigns and States, but to Europeans as well, on account of 'the unstable mood of the inhabitants, which leads them ceaselessly to travel; the invention of the printing press and the general taste for letters, which has given them a community of studies and of knowledge' (p 89).

As we can see, both in Voltaire and in Rousseau, the element of the community of culture was one of the strongest bonds keeping Europe together. Voltaire spoke with the utmost conviction of 'a Republic of Letters was insensibly established in Europe, in the midst of war, and notwithstanding the number of different religions' (*The age of Louis XIV*, cit, 2nd vol (1780) 311). Since the days of Humanism there had been talk of a *respublica literaria*: the first known occurrence of the term is in a letter by Francesco Barbaro to Poggio Bracciolini dated as early as 1417, and then, from the end of the fifteenth century, it was used increasingly in a constant variety of senses and applications. Still, the concept of the community hinges on intellectuals and scholars, academics and learned folk proficient in *bonnes* or *belles lettres* and in the sciences; on the endless and intense circulation of handwritten letters and the unflagging zeal with which ideas were spread as a result; as well as on the institutions hosting this metaphysical entity, whether universities or academies. The idea that this *république* was a sort of political alternative, more or less ideal, to the absolutism of the powers that be does not seem to hold true. In fact, it was the spontaneous by-product of the breadth and intensity of cultural activity that was increasingly gaining a foothold in modern Europe, as it was facilitated by the spread of the printing press and other favourable conditions in society, including a progressive increase and strengthening of the social class at the forefront of cultural life, along with the exchanges of ideas and intellectual relations. This notion of 'republic of letters' was actually the same as the one held by Voltaire and Rousseau, as we have seen, and that is no coincidence.

Voltaire perceived this emerging 'republic of letters' as a fundamental argument not only for a unified European identity, but also for an internal unity among various European countries: 'Italy and Russia were united by the bonds of science, and the natives of England, Germany, and France went to study at Leyden'; and 'the Arts and Sciences all of them thus received mutual assistance from each other'. The academies had 'helped to form this republic'; and 'the truly learned, of every denomination, have strengthened the bands of this grand Society of Geniuses (*société des esprits*), universally extended, and every where independent' (*The age of Louis XIV*, cit, 2nd vol, 311).

This is why Rousseau felt he could write that Europe is not merely a 'collection of peoples' who have nothing in common but a name, like Asia or Africa, but 'a real society which has its morals, its religion, its customs and even its laws, which none of the peoples who compose it can set aside without soon causing disturbances' (*Oeuvres complètes*, 3rd vol (1964)). A truly perfect synthesis of what Europe had become.

VIII. The West

One only needed to add that, by the time of Voltaire and Rousseau, Europe was no longer that 'European Europe' which we have discussed above, and not only because now Russia had fully become part of it, but above all because European emigration and settlement in the rest of the world had constituted (and would continue to do so) new 'Europes' elsewhere: first off, in Mexico and the rest of Central and South America, then in North America, and finally in Australia and New Zealand throughout the nineteenth century. At first tied to the European countries, from which they depended, these colonies would gradually claim, and obtain, full independence.

The hour of independence first struck in the British colonies, which founded the United States of America after a war that lasted from 1776 to 1783. In Latin America, the independence movements actually took off in 1809. The road to independence for Canada, New Zealand and Australia was more complex, as it dovetailed with the internal developments of political life in Britain. And the many new Europes that had gradually sprung up all over the world eventually were linked to the old Europe, and this combination became labeled 'the West'.

The notion of the West as opposed to the East was an ancient one in the European world, famously going back at least to the Persian wars of ancient Greece, and resurfacing later, even more clearly, in the Roman civil war between Octavian and Marc Anthony. On such occasions, and in contrast with the East, the West was portrayed as the positive pole of human history. It was the world of freedom and dignity of man, first and foremost, in contrast with the Eastern world, seen as a byword for despotism, tyranny, lack of freedom and civil dignity. Ultimately, this was also tantamount to pitting civilisation, on the one hand, against barbarism, on the other, but in a sense that always found its maximum reason for existence in the starkly opposite foundation upon which civil life in these two worlds is supposedly built.

In his day, in the mid-nineteenth century, Carlo Cattaneo explained it perfectly in a passage that, for this and for other reasons, is worthy of being regarded as a classic. He says:

> What do we also mean even today when we call Asia barbaric? It is not that there are no sumptuous cities here, no agriculture and commerce, and more than one kind of flawless industry, and a certain tradition of ancient sciences, and a love of poetry and music, and the pomp of palaces and gardens, and of baths and perfumes and joys and robes and armour and handsome horses and every other form of elegance. But, just like the free Greeks and Romans standing before the Persians and the Syrians, we sense in the midst of all this an aura of barbarism. And this is because, ultimately, those pompous Babylons are cities without municipal order, without law, without dignity; they are inanimate, inorganic beings, incapable of exercising any act bred by reason or free will upon themselves, having yielded to the decrees of fatalism. Their fatalism is not born out of religion, but of politics. Therein lies the chasm between bloated Byzantium and astute Athens, between the contemporaries of Homer, Leonidas and Phidias, and the slothful minions of the Lower Empire (*La città considerata come principio ideale delle istorie italiane*, 1858, in *Scritti storici e geografici*, edited by G Salvemini, E Sestan, 2nd vol (1957) 395–96).

In this passage Cattaneo revisits the original political significance of the Hellenic antithesis between West and East, based on the juxtaposition between *freedom* (for the former) and *serfdom* (for the latter), which did not disdain the culture and material civilisation of the 'pompous Babylons', doomed to the 'fatalism' of serfdom, not on account of religion, but of politics (and, incidentally, this would also be the implied meaning of the long-term confrontation in the Cold War after 1945). It would be trivial, and also inaccurate, to claim that the magnitude of the Europe-Heartland imperial consciousness was simply reflected in its entirety in the passage by Cattaneo. By now, it amounted to the whole consciousness of the West, consisting of European and extra-European Europe alike.

Not surprisingly, even before the French Revolution, one of the new Europes that had thrived elsewhere in the world would send a clear message, through the American Revolution that was hatching between the 1760s and 1770s, concerning the inadequacy of a tradition that bounded the history and sense of European civilisation with an exclusively geographical idea of Europe.

In actual fact, the American message was quintessentially of European stock, with regard to the values and ideals it proclaimed in the Constitution (1787) awarded to the new State. Its system was based on the absence of nobility or class hierarchies; on the substantial equality of rights of citizens as men, that is by right of natural law, and not by privilege or grace granted by others; on popular sovereignty only; on full political and religious freedom; on a strong tendency towards self-government; on the separation between State and Church; on the separation of executive, legislative and judicial powers: in other words, the essence of the theories that European political thought had devised and elaborated on the subject during the seventeenth and much of the eighteenth centuries.

Shortly thereafter, from 1789 onward the French Revolution gave this body of political principles an even more powerful thrust and greater range, through a historical event that failed to bring about a significant regime change and a lasting constitution as in the United States (where the 1787 Constitution was modified only in a few key points, through a series of 25 amendments). Just as the Declaration of the rights of man and of citizens triggered the Revolution in 1789, the first French Constitution of 1792 overhauled so deeply France's social-political order, institutions and legislation that it gained extraordinary political-cultural and idealistic clout, modelling itself as a driving force later in history and the world over.

The French Revolution produced decisive experiences affecting European thought and history. Did equality of rights pertain to the sense of a fundamental juridical principle or imply a further meaning at a substantive level extending to assets and living conditions? Did citizen rights unconditionally curtail the rights of the community, or could the latter, for the sake of the common good, actually override the former and even restrict them without limitations? Did the separation between Church and State and the full secularity of the legal system mean that a community could support itself with no ulterior basis other than that of the claim to and safeguard of human and citizen rights? Were human communities (peoples, countries, nations) conceived as being all equal in their individuality, and would the principles proclaimed in one country be upheld also in all others? To what extent could the distinction between *man* and *citizen* be made, or did this distinction make no sense? And could popular sovereignty be exercised through representatives or did it have to be exercised directly only?

These questions would give rise to the three major issues that would hang over the history of Europe (and, consequently, of the world) throughout the nineteenth and twentieth centuries: the issue of freedom and democracy, the social issue, the national issue. The above questions would also spawn the main trends of European political thought over the following two centuries; the different types of political and social forces at the forefront of the new historical scene; the (not always linear) developments underpinning the various historical phases of these two centuries and their comprehensive, though not consistent, wholeness.

IX. Autumn

A story of ideas and ideals no less intense than the political and social parable that chronicled the mutation of late eighteenth century Europe into that of the early twenty-first century through a series of unprecedented conflicts, tragedies and tribulations. After the 25 years of great unrest and complexities arising from the French Revolution and the ensuing Napoleonic regime, since 1815 a time of relative stability followed, ending with the series of European revolutions of 1848–49. After this, while the national, political, and social ideals dating back to 1789 underwent a gradual, but widespread realisation, already in the second half of the nineteenth century the first symptoms of the dramatic events of the twentieth century had begun to appear: a century (mislabelled as the *short 20th century*) that first saw European world dominance reach its peak, only to then rapidly dissolve within a few decades, from the mid-twentieth century onward, when even its predominance in cultural life and technical-scientific innovation, as well as its military, economic and financial primacy, had shifted across the Atlantic to the United States.

Meanwhile, material progress in Europe had been astonishingly strong, with a considerable rise in living conditions and standards at mass level. However, political stability and security did not achieve much progress, and only after World War II, and the later fall of communist regimes in Eastern Europe, did the situation on the continent appear to reach some form of stability.

The founding of the EU was rightly portrayed as a decisive strengthening factor to this stabilisation, also because it ultimately brought about, in practice, a bipartite separation of the European space, by way of extreme simplification, between the EU area and that of Russia, which had reverted to its great national entity (albeit with various territorial losses) after the long season of Soviet communism.

Despite these new historical conditions, the force of dynamics and dialectics underlying the European spirit failed to find a dimension of peace and tranquillity. In the years of Europe's greatest achievements, a thinker and historian of the stature of Tocqueville predicted 'that the dominant position of the European nations in world affairs would come to an end in a not too distant future' (H Holborn, *The political collapse of Europe* (1951) ix). Tocqueville himself and various other thinkers (Jacob Burckhardt, for example) had begun to raise doubts and fears about the consequences of such a rapid and unfettered growth of industrial society, and how this would affect ethical-political life and freedom. In Italy a most relevant trace of this is found in the 1903–07 writings on contemporary Italian literature (see *La letteratura della nuova Italia*, 4th vol (1915)) by Benedetto Croce. In his *Storia d'Europa nel secolo decimonono* (edited by G Galasso (1991) 426 and ff.) he defined *activism* as a general, and not merely literary tendency to 'do for the sake of doing', no holds barred, in thrall to the myth of speed: *we want to live, Ardi, and do so running* (*Bocca di serchio*, v 121), as that faithful witness of his time, Gabriele D'Annunzio (*Halcyon* (1903)), had written upon addressing his imaginary companion.

Liberalism and democracy were then challenged and refuted as much by the nationalistic as by the socialist and communist ideologies, which largely held the stage in the Europe of the first half of the twentieth century, and proved themselves instrumental in carrying that refutation into totalitarian political regimes. After World War I, *Der Untergang des Abendlandes* (1918–22; Eng transl. *The Decline of the West* (1918 and revised in 1922)) was a huge success. Its author, Oswald Spengler, theorised the end of Europe's lifespan, of its creative and operative force, and of its imperial dominance in the world, as it is subject to the laws of nature, whereby empires and civilisations are born, grow and die, just like any other living organism. Between the two world wars, Edmund Husserl spoke of a crisis of the European sciences and consciousness, and his act of 'linking the sciences, in which he also includes historiography, with European consciousness is a factor of extraordinary insight and great depth', if we consider that 'like history, science is one of the great connotations of European identity' (G Galasso, *Nell'Europa dei secoli d'oro* (2012) 407–08).

X. Post fata

In the aftermath of World War II (which in itself led to a radical setback in the global political significance of the European space, with the exception of Russia, as well as the monstrous experience of the Holocaust, on a moral scale) the European spirit was forced to face a series of relentless challenges (eg, political terrorism, 'holy wars', a torrential flow of cross-continent migrations, radical geopolitical changes in the new worldwide balance) that have been unfamiliar, arduous, and displaying an unprecedented material and moral consistency. In keeping with European tradition, they too were addressed as problems pertaining to man and civilised living. Material growth, economic well-being, and an easier access to wealth were factors that raised once again the age-old question about the antinomy of *being* and *having*, whereof a possible balance, both practical and ethical, was sought. Yet the issue had arisen in a Europe that by now was largely and deeply secularised, laicised, and thoroughly imbued (down to its attitudes, and its health concerns or needs) with the unbelievable advancements of technology and science, increasingly threatened by the temptations and even the apathy brought on by a material affluence that fell short in its scope, and failed to provide satisfying answers to man's problems.

It raised a question that was new, concerning which Western authors from the US would speak of a 'solitary crowd', 'global village' and other metaphors and expressions partly surrounding the concepts of 'mass society', or 'machine civilization', and the like. It was also a problem that had arisen in a Europe at odds with its past and struggling with a whole new kind of relations with the rest of the world. The civil unrest of the late 1960s and beyond was more than eloquent proof of this, also because the whole movement consisted of young people, and the prospect was that of a generational rift that so far has not appeared to have healed. In parallel, Europe was 'in the dock', and the trial was spearheaded by European culture and public opinion and conducted with increasing intensity during the second half of the twentieth century. Its goal was to re-examine and reconstruct Europe's past in such depreciative ways, and with scant meaning and value, as to bereave that past of any chance of playing out its historical heritage and, even more, of representing a worthy ideal for the future. Despite all the above, if we look at the values and ideas progressively wrought by European culture and the European spirit during the triumphant historical career of this small part of the world, an impressive intellectual and moral heritage, they appear not to have yielded under the imperial decline of Europe, with its relegation from Heartland to a geographical area as dependent as others on the changing scenarios of a global political game it no longer controls; they have also demonstrated their state of good health, and that they continue to thrive as a living and vital heritage, as current and active as ever before in the new world geography that has taken shape from the mid-twentieth century onward.

The proud certainties of yesteryear have thus yielded to an implacable restlessness even below the surface of a geographical area that remains among the world's richest and most advanced, and that, through the EU, believes to have rightly found a viable route for a more significant presence, renewed in status and influence.

Is Europe lacking a faith? A Catholic scholar of Humanism closely associated with the controversial thesis of a perennial Humanism, spanning from ancient Greek and Roman culture to Christian patristics and modern Humanism, insisted – with a passion that was not just cultural – on positing the historical reality of a tradition of *wisdom* or *logos* bearing superior ethical and human values, as belonging to European and Christian civilisation and its historical significance. Writing in 1948, he believed that 'the historical cycle that we feel we belong to' was coming to a close; and he saw evidence of this in the end of the logos, that is, of the humanistic tradition, as he understood it, and in the predominance of the values of modern rationalism. 'Today – he concluded – between reason and Logos the great waters roar: faith is an invisible sail, even for those who travel to the sound of its heartbeat. God is far away' (G Toffanin, *La fine del Logos* (1948) VI and 193).

Naturally, it is very difficult to share the views of an eminent scholar so thoroughly wrapped up in his own historical–religious ideas; it is equally hard to share these ideas from other perspectives as well. Still, the point could have been raised that in contemporary Europe, *God* – or, in secular cultural terms, supreme certainties – is distant not only from those who navigate life to the drumbeat of religious faith, but also from those who cultivate other wholly human and worldly values (eg, reason, history, science, etc) made from that same European blueprint, which was embraced so profoundly, and in such abiding virtual exclusivity, by Christianity, in its many denominations.

In short, something far deeper and more meaningful dwells in Europe's present than the dwindling twilight of an imperial past alongside unparalleled cultural and scientific achievements. And perhaps the manner in which Europe will choose to identify and explain this something to itself and to the rest of the world is what shall provide present-day Europe with a raison d'être and a chance to make history that is not unworthy of its past, though measurable on other value scales and orders of magnitude.

This is not to say that Europe must be forced out of itself. As Ernst Troeltsch said, while Odin's spear had inflicted on the European spirit that deep wound, which he associated with historical relativism, it also possessed the virtue of healing the wounds it had caused. One may truly say that, embedded in its own history, Europe:

> carries the seeds and principles of its own new history, measuring itself in the light of world history, against its own dynamics in this history, and reviewing all that can and must be reviewed, but without departing from the vocations most congenial to it (G Galasso, *Nell'Europa dei secoli d'oro* (2012) 411),

without, for the sake of living, losing what makes life worth living (*propter vitam, vivendi perdas causas,* Juvenal, *Satires*, VIII, 84), because that indeed would spell out the end, the true *finis Europae.*

2

The Fundamental Goal of the European Project

GIORGIO NAPOLITANO

I. Before the Treaties of Rome

The Treaties signed in Rome on 25 March 1957 were undoubtedly a milestone in Europe's journey towards unity. They marked the start of a new process of integration, signed by the same six countries that had recognised the Schuman Declaration on 9 May 1950: three of the leading countries in Western Europe – France, Italy and Germany – and three of the smaller countries – Belgium, the Netherlands and Luxembourg (Benelux).

I mentioned 1950, and the crucial step that was taken that year. However, when looking back over history, it cannot be separated from the events and tendencies that preceded it in the years immediately after World War II. A clear line was drawn between then and what Europe had been in the 1930s up until the moment it was so dramatically torn apart – by the attack from Nazism and Fascism – with the war, that became a World War, of 1939–45.

Due to space constraints, this is not the place for me to look back over all 'the Europes' that were imagined in the various historical periods before the contemporary age and the twentieth century (Europes, 2000; Chabod 1974); but there is no doubt that in the 1940s – from the final period of Nazi rule – several ideal scenarios developed in the past were re-examined in detail in various proposals and meetings aiming to draw up a strategy for reconstructing Europe in a new light. In order, these were the Ventotene Manifesto of 1941; the Hague Congress in 1948 and various national parliamentary debates, including those following various federalist motions in the two chambers of the Italian Parliament that was elected in 1948.

From a cultural point of view, at the highest level, there had been signs of a historical watershed in two courses of university lectures on Europe that were held at the same time, albeit not linked in any way. These were the lectures held in the Collège de France in 1944–45 by Lucien Febvre (1878–1956), and those held at the University of Milan in 1943–44 by Federico Chabod (1901–60). At that crucial transition point of history, there had been an awareness in the intellectual world of the need to clear the field of the 'great talking' about Europe and European civilisation, and of the 'enormous confusion' that arose from the predication of the Neue Ordnung, the new European order, by 'the anti-Europe' barbarians. You just have to consider that, at the time of the defeat of Germany in 1945, the concept of Europe was prohibited in France.

With such significant cultural input and the political events I have just mentioned, the ground was prepared for the first constitutive deed – the Schuman Declaration – in a project for cooperation and shared action between European governments.

France had 'always had as her essential aim the service of peace', the starting point for the rest of the Declaration. This aim was applied to the practical reality of relations between France and Germany, the need to pursue reconciliation between these two decisive countries in the heart of Europe, and to uproot the material foundations of nationalistic, competitive policies that led to two disastrous world wars that begun on our continent. This required 'that Franco-German production of coal and steel as a whole be placed under a common High Authority, within the framework of an organisation open to the participation of the other countries of Europe'.

Thus the document presented in Paris on 9 May 1950 by the French Foreign minister Robert Schuman (1886–1963), in its extraordinary capacity for synthesis and anticipation, was in fact the fruit of the creative efforts of the greatest architect of European integration: Jean Monnet (1888–1979). The Declaration affirmed principles that remained cornerstones of the subsequent long march towards European unity. These include the principle of entrusting powers and duties of government transcending the limits of national sovereignty to common European authorities. In the case at hand, focusing action in the immediate term 'on one limited but decisive point', marking what the Declaration defined 'a first step in the federation of Europe'. And the important consequence (even if, after so many decades, still today anything but acknowledged and accepted) is the 'binding' nature of the shared decisions. These were, essentially, the principles and aims solemnly undertaken by the six countries when they signed the Treaty setting up the European Coal and Steel Community (ECSC), establishing the community invention that would be the foundation for the process of European integration and unity.

In this regard, moreover, the text by Schuman (or Monnet and Schuman) included general criteria that this would be an extremely gradual process: 'Europe will not be made all at once, or according to a single plan. It will be built through concrete achievements which first create a de facto solidarity.' There is therefore no doubt about the difference between these words and the more radical, overtly utopian approaches to the prospect of a European Federation.

Despite this, the early 1950s saw the signature of two fundamental treaties – alongside the ECSC, the Treaty establishing the European Defence Community (EDC), signed on 27 May 1952. This latter was extremely important from a political point of view, and not just because it conferred powers in a field that had historically belonged to the jealously guarded absolute sovereignty of the nation States, but because it involved a construction headed by an actual European political community. The reconstruction and testimony provided by Monnet in his Mémoires are extremely interesting. Implanting this powerful strong option of actual political integration onto the choice of a defence community was something that was not born from an intentional political acceleration on the part of the more ardent countries and governments bearing the banner of a federalist vision of the future of Europe. In fact it was the result of dramatic urgency in the development of international relations.

I am referring to the explosion of the war between the two Koreas (1950–53), that sudden transition from a by-now evident cold war to an actual war emergency involving the two major enemy world powers, the Soviet Union and the United States of America. There was in fact widespread alarm in the West at the hegemonic designs and politics of force attributed to Joseph V Stalin. Alarm which, particularly in Europe, showed the need to reinforce the military defence capacity of the Atlantic alliance, acquiring as a military necessity also the support of West Germany, which had by now decisively moved towards the democratic transformation of its laws and the ideal repositioning of its role in the world.

However, the essential point that emerges from Monnet's magnificent account, in this regard, was the unwavering opposition of the great German European Konrad Adenauer (1876–1967) to any reformation of the Wehrmacht, even if part of NATO. He only agreed to approve a contribution from the new Germany to a European defence system headed by a European political authority. This was precisely the choice made by the six founder countries when they decided to adopt a community perspective with the signature of the Treaty on the EDC.

There was a memorable Italian initiative, clearly of a federalist inspiration, that led to the proposal to introduce article 38 into the EDC Treaty. This was drawn up by mutual agreement between Alcide De Gasperi (1881–1954) and Altiero Spinelli (1907–86), and among other things included the creation of a democratically elected EDC Assembly designed in such a way that it would be one of the key elements of a federal or confederal structure.

There is no need to go into detail here about the unfortunate collapse of a political community that was in the process of taking off, under the mortal blow of the rejection of the Treaty establishing the European Defence Community by the French National Assembly on 30 August 1954. This led to urgent, arduous efforts to avoid the collapse of the entire project of European integration and unity. At this point it is clearer how reference to the real historical events of 1951–54 in Europe constitutes an indispensable basis for fully understanding how the Treaties of Rome came about in 1957.

A. From the Messina Conference to the Agreement on the New Treaties: A Major Effort with a Successful Outcome

The major efforts to ensure that the entire European project was not fatally damaged and blocked by the French veto of August 1954 began in June 1955, with the Messina Conference of the six Foreign ministers, presided over by Italy's determined and authoritative minister Gaetano Martino (1900–67). The conference did not reach any clear conclusions, but it took the important decision to appoint an essentially technical intergovernmental committee to work on new treaties. The committee was however headed by a political figure with great vision, Paul-Henri Spaak (1899–1972), a former Belgian prime minister and fervent pro-European. The treaties were then formally signed in March 1957, respectively establishing the European Economic Community (EEC) and the European atomic agency Community (Euratom).

Roberto Ducci (1914–85), a highly professional and intellectual Italian diplomat with a deep-seated belief in Europe, headed the committee responsible for drafting the Treaties, under the leadership of Spaak. Twenty years later he explained how the conflicts and the deadlock of Messina were resolved. This was achieved thanks to the still existing political inspiration which, so recently after the war, had dragged the political leaders of Western Europe towards a project of integration and unity, which was then adopted and launched by the six governments that signed the Schuman Declaration.

And it was also achieved thanks to the effects that, within the international and European context, led to the Franco-British military adventure in Suez, in 1956, and its failure. France and the United Kingdom had found themselves so isolated, exposed and in need of returning within the protective orbit of European cooperation, that they had to stop hair-splitting and work together to resolve the deadlock.

B. The Treaties of Rome: Political Retreat and Economic Growth

The achievements under the leadership of Spaak and the decision to create a European Economic Community were undoubtedly a change of direction. Titles have meanings, and with the new Treaties, the adoption by Europe of the idea of a community that was described as an economic community instead of the planned political community had a precise significance. Was it a step backwards by Europe's leaders after the enthusiastic leap forward that had led them to embrace the more ambitious aims of the EDC treaty? Effectively it was, although it must be clear that this was the objectively inevitable result of the collapse of the more ambitious aims of European integration.

I think it is more dubious to talk (as I myself have done on occasions) about a 'deviation' from the project that first saw light on 9 May 1950. We must not forget that the shared Declaration of the time proclaimed the conviction that bringing about the harmonious shared management of coal and steel production 'would be a true foundation for [...] economic unification' – an aim that was not considered secondary – at least by the two major European countries. In fact the preamble to the Treaty establishing the ECSC was insistent on the prospect of establishing 'common foundations for economic development'. Right from the start the economy was therefore an essential starting point for launching and developing integration starting from the 'limited but decisive point' of industrial integration, initially for coal and steel.

Rather than a 'deviation', the Treaties of Rome represented the decision to focus the process of European integration – initially shared by six countries in Western Europe but potentially open to contributions from a far wider part of the continent – on the simpler terrain of the economy. Despite the fact that the problems and structure of political union were set to one side and left in the background, this consolidated what had already been established in previous years in the sense of building a community, and gave it a strong thrust forwards.

Essentially we can say that the 20 years after the Treaties of Rome saw the creation of a historic construction and a successful institutional, technical and administrative system. This resulted in the development of an extraordinary field of attraction around community Europe – a beacon of liberty and prosperity – for the other countries in the continent and very high levels of prestige worldwide. I believe that it is no exaggeration to describe these 20 years as the triumphant march of the European project – considering also the economic and social results achieved along the way. This march encompassed the adhesion of the United Kingdom to the Community in 1973 and culminated in the entry of three European countries as they gradually freed themselves from long-standing totalitarian systems (Spain and Portugal, which joined in 1986) or more recent military regimes (Greece, which joined in 1981).

Subsequently, as membership of the EEC continued to expand, new development requirements arose in the construction of Europe, based more on the ongoing experience than on predetermined planning. This was the case with regard to financial aspects – first with the creation of the European monetary system (EMS) at the end of the 1970s, and then with its crisis, which led to the need to take the bolder and more consistent step of adopting a common currency. In turn this led to the more general need to move towards political union. In conclusion we can say that the Treaties of Rome undoubtedly marked a political retreat, but also preserved the continuity and future of the community process.

The periods of the Community's life to which I am referring in my brief summary, up to the end of the 1970s, were also times of multiple, recurrent crises and the persistence of unresolved underlying and not even clearly defined problems, inherent in the very concept of the European project that was born from the ruins of World War II.

This long and complex process unfolded against the backdrop of events of global importance, in particular the fall of the Berlin Wall in 1989 and the dissolution not only of the ideological-political-military bloc led by the Soviet Union, but also of the Soviet Union itself. The historic new fact of German Reunification, the result of a difficult confrontation and compromise between the German Democratic leadership in the person of Helmut Kohl and other important European leaders (especially the French president François Mitterrand, 1916–96), was resolved in the major development of the adoption of a single currency. In other words, the birth of the euro and of the European Central Bank (ECB), and the creation of an economic and monetary Union, under the Treaty on European Union (no longer a Community) signed in Maastricht on 7 February 1992.

At this essential stage, in which the issue of political union once more raised its head, the underlying issue that has reappeared at every crucial stage of the process of European integration, and today more than ever, also came to the forefront. I am talking about the problem of sovereignty, national and supranational European sovereignty, and also about the difficulty and reluctance in tackling head on the differences and risks constantly involved in it.

C. The Problem of Sovereignty

This problem also arose at the event that was most fertile in generating motivation and ideas for the future of Europe, that is, the free debate that took place before the Brussels Convention – which was decided at the request of the most frustrated partners, such as the Italian prime minister Giuliano Amato, one of the signatories of the Treaty of Nice (2001) – and at the European Convention on the future of Europe (2002–03), chaired by Valéry Giscard d'Estaing, at which Amato and Jean-Luc Dehaene (1940–2014) were vice-chairs. That workshop to draw up the Treaty and adopt a Constitution for Europe (also known as the European Constitution) was then blocked by the referendums in France and the Netherlands. However, those years of fervid debate generated more than one important driver and the extremely significant parallel outcome that was the Charter of fundamental rights of the European Union, proclaimed in 2000.

The attempt at creating a European Constitution was conditioned by the obsession, especially on the part of Germany (government forces and Länder), with keeping a firm distinction between the competencies of the Union and the sovereign competencies of the nation States. Partners aware of this debate dramatised what they defined as the creeping extension of the Union's remit, in the form of statements and intrusive initiatives by the Commission in Brussels. And while the debate about political union reopened, of which the intention of 'establishing a Constitution for Europe' was undoubtedly part, in the proposal of a more advanced form of integration, the reference to a federal outcome was in any case thoroughly 'rejected'. As Jacques Delors (2004) wrote, 'the word "federal" was still a red flag' (p 363), and not just for the British.

In actual fact the safeguarding of the role of nation States, or even of national identities, was not and had never been at risk, in the intricate process of constructing Europe. It was always clear to those inspiring the process of European integration and unification that this must not threaten the diversity that constitutes Europe's wealth.

The subject had been approached in François Mitterrand's last great speech to the Parliament in Strasbourg on 17 January 1995 (Discorsi sull'Europa (1998) 143–61). He expressed this vision in the most eloquent terms, talking about the 'fruits of centuries of civilisation of which we are the heirs', of 'rich and diverse expressions of our protean genius' (p 152), and describing shared initiatives and programmes that could build a bridge between the European Union and Eastern Europe, which was still suffering from 50 years of isolation, with a view to celebrating their cultural heritage. This was his way of attempting to show that, 'rather than cancelling the cultural identity of nations, Europe was trying to consolidate it' (p 156). He outlined 'the Europe of cultures' as 'the Europe of nations against nationalism' (p 156). Thus he avoided the convenient contraposition between a destiny of uniformity in a united Europe and a defence – against the choices involved in constructing Europe – of national identities closed in on themselves and of the sovereign power of nation States, which could lead to the resurgence of old, new and in any case fatal nationalistic tendencies.

The valorisation of diversity in a united Europe was the principle extensively developed and supported by a highly cultured and politically aware great pro-European Bronisław Geremek (1932–2008), one of the prominent figures of Solidarnosc in Poland.

The Ventotene Manifesto by Spinelli, Ernesto Rossi (1897–1967) and Eugenio Colorni (1909–44) was based on a critical reconstruction of the historical degeneration of the countries of Europe. Despite being inspired by ideologies and movements for national independence that had represented 'a powerful stimulus for progress' (ed (1991) 37), they had become 'divine entities' possessed of absolute sovereignty, which on the outside had resulted in conflictual, aggressive strategies, and on the inside in increasingly centralised bureaucracy and ultimately in totalitarianism.

Looking at what would inevitably follow the predictable and inevitable defeat of Nazi-fascism, the Manifesto already anticipated the risk of the restoration of States based once again on absolute sovereign power. This is what led to the extreme goal of the definitive 'abolition of the division of Europe into national, sovereign States' as the basis for the creation of a federal State. This goal would soon prove to be unrealistic, and was in fact superseded, once Europe was free again. What did remain fundamental in the text of the Ventotene Manifesto was the antithesis to the dogma of the absolute sovereignty of nation States, which referred back to the position taken as early as 1918 by Luigi Einaudi (1874–1961), who in fact became a point of reference for the authors of the Manifesto.

Another thing to emerge was the concrete idea-driver of the transfer to a federal authority of certain powers and areas of sovereignty of the nation States, where these would have had destructive consequences on peace in Europe and ultimately would have led to an overall inability to deal with the reality and problems of the post-war period.

I will come back to the development of Spinelli's thoughts and actions, beyond the early manifestation of his battle for Europe that can be seen in the Ventotene Manifesto. In any case it should be emphasised that the goal of a European federation, as clearly set out in the Schuman Declaration, translated into a political and legal construction in which – to quote Tommaso Padoa-Schioppa (1940–2010) – the Member States were placed 'in a central position within the institutional mechanism', and nations remained (and in certain cases went back to being) 'a fundamental point of reference in the lives of the peoples of Europe' ((2001) 37).

The innovative and openly federalist stance of European political leaders in the years following 1945 was not pure 'ingenuousness'. Men like De Gasperi and Adenauer had been able to clearly comprehend the weight of a major nation State like Germany and a vast empire like the Austro-Hungarian Empire during their formative years and early political experiences. However, they probably overestimated the impact on the nation States of the war unleashed by Nazi-fascism. They saw them as they were seen in the Ventotene Manifesto, which prophesied: 'the fallen governments [will] lie broken'. In actual fact with post-war reconstruction even defeated countries, such as Italy and Germany, recovered more quickly than the federalists could have imagined, through transformation processes that, while undoubtedly containing some elements of restorations, were above all democratic. The patriotic sentiment that the Ventotene Manifesto had identified as a danger to the success of restoration also could and did become fertile ground for a pro-European stance, or, we could say, for European patriotism.

The development of the institutional system of the Community and then the Union thus followed an original compromise between an intergovernmental model and a supranational, federal model, as Padoa-Schioppa again pointed out. In a widespread study some years ago (2002), Biagio de Giovanni described the political construction of Europe as something that was and will be founded on the search for a 'new balance', built on 'a permanent dialogue between the Member States and the Union' (p 41).

However, it has been the desire to shift that balance towards the recovery of decision-making powers by national governments, and towards agreements between governments as an axis for development of the Union that has been a problem on several occasions, showing an underlying lack of clarity about the issue of shared sovereignty at European level. It has also been a problem more recently, during the years of the difficult search for effective responses to the global financial crisis, and specifically, to the crisis in the Eurozone.

D. Ambiguity and Timidity Even Among the Most pro-European Governments

Within the Union the decision to advance the integration process by means of the objectively necessary development of shared sovereignty at a European level should not give rise to objections. However, we are still paying for the consequences of ambiguity and timidity on the part of the national governments that most firmly support European integration and the euro. The leadership and political powers in those countries have not reacted incisively to the spread of not just euro-sceptic but 'euro-denying' positions. Unfounded and instrumental alarmism has been allowed to spread. Even if over the years some the Union's interventions have been inappropriate, even if at times the statements of the Commission on every sort of problem have been needlessly prolific – as Delors himself pointed out – no one could seriously see this as justification for the fear that nation States and their 'residual' sovereignty could disappear. This fear cannot also be due to the real and substantial extension of the area of 'shared sovereignty' through the overcoming of national sovereignty in a monetary sense – with the creation of the euro and the European Central Bank.

The problems involved in considering the future developments of this trend are understandable, as is the need to carefully weigh up the next steps to be taken in other areas involving further transfers of national sovereignty to shared sovereignty at European Union level. However, in order not to give in to positions that tend not to weigh things up or to provide grounds for their position, but to block any progress in that sense, it should be sufficient to remain calmly aware of the profound historical roots of national States and their inherent connection to national identity and sentiment. At the same time we should always be aware that it is objectively impossible to effectively exercise national sovereignty over problems which by now extend way beyond national borders.

In order to master and effectively tackle these problems – no longer solely relating to trade or monetary policy – and in order to manage the common European interest, we need to delegate 'the necessary sovereignty' to shared institutions. As Monnet said so clearly 40 years ago (1976):

> our peoples must learn to live together under freely granted and shared rules and institutions if they want to achieve the dimension they need in order to make progress and to remain masters of their destiny. The sovereign institutions of the past are no longer the framework within which they can resolve the problems of the present (pp 616–17).

The resistance to drawing the necessary conclusions from Monnet's fundamental assumption was both strong and dramatic. The integration process had stalled for some years, and crucial decisions were blocked, despite calls from the five presidents of the European institutions (European Council, European Commission, European Parliament, Eurogroup and ECB). This was a backwards step, which especially called into question the way in which the Union was extended to the Central and Eastern European countries emerging from a subordinate position in the Soviet Union in the early years of the twenty-first century.

Once the Soviet bloc had fallen, there were immediate signs from those countries that they wished to join the ranks of NATO and the European Union. Negotiations with the governments, which became increasingly inevitable during the 1990s, were formally correct, but not within a framework of a preliminary clarification about their definite willingness to delegate parts of their sovereignty to the jointly managed European institutions. It is true that they were countries that had only just recovered their lost independence. They had only recently freed themselves from what was called limited sovereignty, within the Eastern bloc. However, the European institutions should have taken them on in full awareness of the radical difference between their previous status and a voluntary conferment of sovereign powers to a process of shared sovereignty in the democratic context of the European

Union. This was not sufficiently carried out, and the consequences can be clearly seen in the assumption of neonationalist positions by Eastern European governments and countries and their serious challenges to decisions even of the European Council.

As regards the trend in the last ten years for there to be a shift from the community method to an intergovernmental method in the management of the Union, now extended to 28 Member States – with the accession of Croatia in 2013 – a serious and extensive debate is required. It is sufficient to think of the wide-ranging conception of the European Council by Monnet, who was its promoter, that is, as a response to the need for an authority that could overcome the difficulties of the Council of ministers in its various components, burdened by the defence of its national positions, and instead was positioned 'at a crossroads between national sovereignties and common supranational sovereignty' (Monnet (1976) 446). It is then clear how, since the major expansion of the Union, the modus operandi of a redundant Council has effectively been trivialised into a hasty routine.

The extension of an 'intergovernmental drift' undoubtedly calls for a strong institutional rethink. Just as the strategy for reaching the aims of political union must be rethought.

In his speech at the Humboldt Universität in Berlin on 12 May 2000 – the true starting point for the great debate about the future of the Union and of Europe – the German Foreign minister Joschka Fischer raised the question about Monnet's functional approach to the process of European integration. That approach, which according to Fischer was not connected to any final precise plan, had produced results of incalculable historic importance, but had effectively been inadequate when it came to delivering the goals of political integration, on a democratic basis, in Europe.

In the course of the 1990s the expected knock-on effect of developments steadily leading to the process of integration between the markets, the economic and legal systems, and finally the monetary systems, did not take place. There had not been a knock-on effect strong enough to produce a leap forward towards political union. There was once more the need for a more avowed and swift strategy with a federal inspiration. In European politics we are still discussing this need today, even though not everyone recognised it as decisive for the future of the Union.

E. On Ventotene and Altiero Spinelli

In recent years, the Ventotene Manifesto has once again taken a central role in the Italian government's approach to Europe, in an attempt to revisit and appreciate the value of the depth of its inspiration and ideals in our relationship with our partners in the Union.

It is a fact that those (more and more, I hope, in Italy) who wish to enrich their knowledge and understanding of the process of European integration and unity cannot refrain from using the visionary message launched in 1941 by Spinelli, Rossi and Colorni, still imprisoned as antifascists on the island of Ventotene, as a starting point.

However, the role of Spinelli as a constant support to the European cause continued after he was freed for over 40 years, until his death. And his thoughts, as well as his actions, underwent a profound transformation, through many, significant experiences.

This transformation was guided by his firmness of ideals, tireless tenacity, realism and political flexibility that, together, resulted in the extraordinary importance of the original personality of Spinelli in the journey of a united Europe.

The constant development of his positions and attitudes is documented by publications packed with considerations and formulations that went far beyond the vision and platform of Ventotene. In first place is his masterly autobiography *Come ho tentato di diventare saggio* (1984), followed by his diaries, parliamentary speeches and participation in the discussions of the federalist Movement.

In his practical public activity, he did not hold back from taking intransigent positions, making controversial statements and having severe reservations about the decisions and compromises between the governments taking the construction of Europe forward, from one treaty to the next. However, this did not translate into his retirement from realistic involvement in the political and institutional context on each occasion. He ended up working in the most supranational institution of all, the European Commission, becoming an active and competent Member from 1970 to 1976.

Once he had stood as a candidate and been elected to the Italian Parliament (1976) and European Parliament (1979), he became an importance reference point and link for many different political figures and personalities in the Assembly in Strasbourg, working on the structure of that highly successful creative enterprise that was the drafting and approval with a wide majority of the project for a union. This was the most mature point of his far-reaching pro-European ideal and political journey, a long way from the early work that was the Ventotene Manifesto.

That political victory was followed by the defeat – as he considered it – and his considerable disappointment at the fact that the project approved by the European Parliament was not accepted by the heads of State and governments, who refused to abandon the traditional diplomatically intergovernmental process of gradually developing EU legal framework. Spinelli had applied his most radical criticism and caustic wit to the Single European Act that was adopted on that basis in 1987. However, as usual, he followed his convictions and went straight back to work to cultivate the opportunities that even this treaty could, and in fact did, offer.

There are therefore no grounds for identifying Spinelli's role in Europe with the more schematic programme set out in the Manifesto of 1941, as if this had been a statement setting the sense of his Europeanism in stone. And it is gratuitous and misleading to imagine that, over the decades, Europeanism in its sense as an ideal vision and movement has been conditioned on the one hand by a sort of core doctrine of federalist extremism represented by Spinelli, and on the other by an opposing core of exaltation and unmoving defence of sovereign nation States.

Nor does the theory that the undoubted differences between the federalist strategies and methodologies respectively of Monnet and Spinelli constitute a reason to make these two figures antagonists, as has often been suggested when examining developments in the integration process up until the 1980s. Spinelli's words of 1955 clearly show that this is not the case:

> For the last year [Monnet and I] have been pulling a cart like two stubborn donkeys – he in the hope of obtaining a new initiative from governments, and I in the hope of obtaining new impetus from the movements […], but both convinced that due to a sort of mutual liking for each other, which goes beyond any political judgement, we should be helping each other (Spinelli (1989) 260–61).

F. Sixty Years Later: Implementing the Plan for European Integration

On the eve of the 60th anniversary of the Treaties of Rome, ECB president Mario Draghi made a carefully thought-out and passionate speech in Ljubljana (2 February 2017), in which he took a long look back over the past and proposed some essential choices for the future, starting right then. In his reconstruction of the process of European integration, he naturally included the decisive moment when the single currency was adopted and the start of the economic and monetary union, which marked a new fundamental context of shared sovereignty, entrusted to the institutions of the Union. He also included the period after the Maastricht Treaty, which marked that turning point, that is, the years of the crises that rocked and continue to rock the European Union. In other words, the succession of overlapping crises that called into question the Union's policies and direction, its institutional set-up and its very founding ideals: the global financial crisis that bounced back from the United States, which became a crisis of the Eurozone and of sovereign debt, a recession that – it bears repeating – was the most serious since the 1930s, the Greek crisis, and the crisis in the decision-making capacities of the European institutions. This, alongside the crisis in its capacity for growth, produced waves of misgivings among the citizens in our countries, aggravated by the crisis in Europe's internal and external security when faced with attacks by Islamic terrorism and unprecedented waves of asylum seekers and economic migrants.

The analysis of the causes and impact of this series of shocks and critical issues – which raised questions about the survival of the European construct – branched out into a vast number of areas and availed itself of several particularly insightful contributions. One example is *After the Storm*, a collection of essays published in 2015 and promoted by the outgoing president of the European Council, Herman Van Rompuy. This was also based on exchanges of opinion between himself and the authors of the individual essays (including Jürgen Habermas, Amartya Sen, Fritz Scharpf and Pierre Rosanvallon), which mainly focused on key issues such as democracy, solidarity and the EU legal framework. Today it may be surprising that in 2015 'the storm' was already considered to have passed, given that not long afterwards the migratory storm began.

And finally, in sensational confirmation of the impact that the profound crisis of the Union as a whole had had on public opinion and the voters in Member States, the outcome of the United Kingdom EU membership referendum in June 2016 saw a majority of votes in favour of leaving the block, with all the interpretations and the serious and complex implications that this involves.

This was another of the starting points for Draghi's speech. He started by offering an interpretation of the process of integration as a whole, in its response to the aspiration of the peoples of Europe to be able to guarantee their safety against the common threat, that is, a repetition of destructive wars in the same continent and of world wars. Security therefore, in its broadest meaning, pursued at different rates during different phases, but always retaining the vision of deeper integration which was the aim decided on right from the start.

This interpretation provides a crystal clear, perfectly documented assessment of the results achieved and the progress attained thanks to integration. First of all, therefore, vital political benefits such as the 'strengthening of Europe's influence worldwide'. Thanks to integration, a growing part of Western Europe has seen an increase in the growth of its economies and wealth compared with the rest of Europe and with the United States right from the early years; without it Europe would have been condemned to less social and economic progress and greater poverty. Draghi concludes, 'We should be proud of what we have achieved with integration, while not being blind to the challenges that have arisen and the unsatisfactory way we have operated in recent years'. But in his vision, the source of the unsatisfactory responses to the crises of the last few years lies in the unfinished business and ambiguities of the integration process itself, such as those that have left the economic and monetary Union without any form of shared government of the economy and without the indispensable framework of political union, which the unification of the market should, by its very nature, have clearly implied.

The goals of 'completing the economic and monetary Union of Europe' in many senses, including politically and institutionally, were outlined after much collective debate in the report by Jean-Claude Juncker and the other four presidents of the European institutions, most recently in the version of June 2015. However, the first stage of the schedule – from July 2015 to June 2017 – has already passed without anything happening. And this inevitably raises further questions and underlying issues.

What has halted any progress along the path of further developing the integration process, which has been clearly set out in terms that specified the choice of an economic union capable of providing impetus to convergence, employment and the development of a financial union, full banking union, and so on? One obstacle has undoubtedly been the awareness of a clear unwillingness on the part of a large number of the current 27 Member States to proceed in this direction. And therefore the response to Brexit that relies on the continued membership of the Union of all 27 countries and a mere superficial unity has within it the fatal weakness of standing still. Even in the face of devastating emergencies such as the wave of migration and not allowing new shared decisions to tackle it effectively, which the European Council was, and remains committed to doing. Conversely, individual national governments have taken positions and initiatives that are diametrically opposed to the decisions taken by the Council (such as the relocation by quotas of asylum seekers entering the territory of the Union). These have been open challenges to the authority of the common institutions, which have negated the binding character of decisions to which at least informal consent had been given. And underlying all of this, one cannot help noticing the strong tendency (sometimes even expressed in the form of blackmail) not only to reject any further expansion of shared sovereignty, but even to withdraw from all community discipline and to deny founding values of the European project, such as solidarity. A denial that goes hand-in-hand with an unmistakable regurgitation of nationalism in the countries that joined the Union in 2004.

This has led us to the impasse that today – on the 60th anniversary of the Treaties of Rome – is described as unsustainable by the very leaders of the European governments. After a long period of patience, with setbacks and mortifications from some of the governments belonging to the Union, especially those representing the Central and Eastern European countries previously dominated by the ideologies and constraints of the Soviet bloc, the leaders of France, Germany, Italy and Spain have started to react vigorously (in a significant meeting of the four which, as things stand, may or may not have a future). Thus, at the beginning of March 2017, we heard unequivocal words about the need for those who believe in the objective of an integration process that is naturally destined, by its own logic, to become increasingly tighter, to take decisive steps in that direction. Because standing still or moving forward at a snail's pace risks bringing down the whole construction that is Europe. To this end there has been a return to talking about integration that must be explored at different rates.

This is a mandatory commitment. However, it can be interpreted in different ways and is not easy to achieve, especially if it were to be impracticable, with the current rules applying to ratification, to submit the European treaties to review. We can add that we have by now missed out on the historic opportunities for the most comprehensive proposals, which involved differentiation at the time of the major expansion of the Union to ten (2004), 12 (2007) and even almost 30 new Member States. Mitterand's 1991 proposal for a distinction between the wider, more open area of a European Confederation and the core of the smaller Community to be safeguarded and strengthened. Or the proposal, which was vaguer, of Delors for a distinction between a 'Great Europe' united only on some truly vital shared general goals and a Europe moving towards the European Federation imagined at the beginning, in the Schuman Declaration, or (according to the unusual formula of Delors himself) towards a Fédération des Etats-Nations.

Can we now work on enhanced forms of cooperation – sanctioned and regulated by the existing treaties – of which the Schengen Agreement and the agreement on the single currency were ante litteram examples? Can we start from consolidated, or 'structured', forms of cooperation for common defence? Can we imagine a 'network' of enhanced cooperation arrangements ploughing through the land of United Europe at various levels? Can we find the way to guarantee in an equal manner a harmonious structure of effective cooperation and friendship, even if limited, between all the current (and maybe even new) Member States of a variegated 'Great Europe' of tomorrow?

These are questions and issues which we will undoubtedly have to work on. However, it is important to do so with determination and by emerging from behind the veil of reticence and double-dealing that has played too great a part in the story of a united Europe that first saw the light in 1950 and began its productive future in 1957. The perfectly respectable, prudent concept of a gradual approach seen at various times, which prolongs the uncertainty about the aims to be achieved, can no longer hold.

In his speech in Ljubljana in February 2017, Draghi argued that at a time in which the word federal did not appear dangerous and was not censored, the issue of proceeding with all the necessary and practicable stages of integration was, in the shared consciousness of those participating in the European project, a 'question of when, not if'.

Panic about the destruction and disappearance of nation States cannot be used to oppose the stated goal of moving towards a federal union. Presenting the federal union as the outcome of the process of European integration means resolving the age-old, recurring problem of sovereignty, thereby strengthening the supranational dimension of the decisions mooted and implemented in a shared institutional context by the community bodies and the Member States.

These choices, which have become inevitable necessities, were discussed in depth in the run up to the 60th anniversary of the Treaties of Rome. There was widespread discussion in the individual countries and in national and European institutions, as well as in academia and the media. The very virulence of the populist attack on the European project resulted in a shock to public opinion and politicians that sparked off a sort of new pro-European fervour.

The Declaration adopted by the 27 heads of State and government on 25 March 2017 in Rome, which was signed unanimously, as wished, represented a not insignificant success in terms of political image, although it required an effort at conciliatory prudence, leaving open serious unknowns and difficulties for the development of closer integration as a value and key object of the European project in the near future.

In concluding, I do not wish to forget that, historically, a different outcome has been proposed to that key objective, and not through a lesser sense of Europe, but in the form of a more consequential vision in terms of its legal-institutional model, and more politically streamlined overall. I would like to recall at this point, and with great respect despite my difference of opinions, the contribution of an eminent jurist and judge of the European Court, Federico Mancini (1927–99). In an essay he wrote in 1998, which was very rich from a cultural point of view, and summed up his profound intellectual work and his life-long ambitions, he cited the reasons for democracy supporting the choice of 'a State-based Europe' (p 407), as the 'very management of the supranational core [of the Community and therefore of the Union], the single market', was seriously conditioned, as 'democracy will elude Europe until its form of government includes rules and legitimises practices modelled on those of the international community' (p 415). In order to preserve its historic values and its accomplishments, which would otherwise be at risk, according to Mancini, Europe would 'need the tried and tested institutions and procedures that only a State can offer' (p 414). On the one hand, the problem of democracy 'may only be resolved by freeing the Union' from every 'vestige of its original make-up: the essentially international character implanted in its decision-making mechanism' (p 416). And at the same time it would be necessary to overcome 'the inability to conceive of a State except as a nation State, or, in a word, to separate the State from the nation' (p 408).

However, it is the conviction not only of the author – but of an extremely wide-ranging pro-European and federalist political area – that the terrain on which we should continue to build can only be that of the original, unprecedented combination that has been attempted, in the conditions available, of an international agreement signed by the representatives of six Member States (and subsequently, gradually, many others) and a creative constituent act. An original combination, therefore, of a union of Member States and an authentic supranational dynamic.

The final hope is that, in tackling all the problems that still need to be resolved, the original will and political passion can be found once again, practical amends can be made for all the unwillingness, hypocrisy and political opportunism that has freely allowed all kinds of mystification to surround the current status of the process of European unification, and there can be a determined and unequivocal return to an awareness and a pride in being European.

Bibliography

Chabod, F, *Storia dell'idea d'Europa*, eds. E Sestan and A Saitta (Bari, 1974).

de Giovanni, B, *L'ambigua potenza dell'Europa* (Napoli, 2002).

Delors, J, *Mémoires* (Paris, 2004).

Draghi, M, *Security through unity: making integration work for Europe*, 2 February 2017, https://www.ecb.europa.eu/press/key/date/2017/html/sp170202.en.html.

Ducci, R, *Le speranze d'Europa (carte sparse 1943–1985)*, ed. G Lenzi (Soveria Mannelli, 2007).
Febvre, L, *L'Europe. Genèse d'une civilisation* (Paris, 1999).
Hersant, Y and Durand-Bogaert, F (eds), *Europe. De l'antiquité au XXe siècle. Anthologie critique et commentée* (Paris, 2000).
Juncker, J-C (in close cooperation with D Tusk, J Dijsselbloem, M Draghi and M Schulz), *Completing Europe's Economic and Monetary Union* (2015), https://ec.europa.eu/commission/sites/beta-political/files/5-presidents-report_en.pdf.
Mancini, F, 'Per uno Stato europeo' (1998) 377 *il Mulino* 405–18.
Monnet, J, *Mémoires* (Paris, 1976).
Napolitano, G, *Europa politica. Il difficile approdo di un lungo percorso* (Roma, 2003).
Napolitano, G, *Altiero Spinelli e l'Europa* (Bologna, 2007).
Napolitano, G, *Europa, politica e passione* (Milano, 2016).
Padoa-Schioppa, T, *Europa forza gentile* (Bologna, 2001).
Schuman Declaration – 9 May 1950: https://europa.eu/european-union/about-eu/symbols/europe-day/schuman-declaration_en.
Spinelli, A, *Come ho tentato di diventare saggio* (Bologna, 1984).
Spinelli, A, *Diario europeo. 1948–1969*, ed. E Paolini (Bologna 1989).
Spinelli, A and Rossi, E, *Il Manifesto di Ventotene*, Introduction by N Bobbio (Bologna, 1991).
Van Middelaar, L and Van Parijs, P (eds), *After the Storm: How to Save Democracy in Europe* (Tielt, 2015).
All web pages are understood as having last been visited on 22 March 2018.

3

Freedom, Democracy, Rule of Law

GIULIANO AMATO AND NICOLA VEROLA

The search for the founding values of the European Union (EU) is one of the leitmotifs of the integration process. It represents an important interpretation key to understanding the progress made over the last 60 years and, at the same time, one of the most eloquent indicators of the state of health of the European construct in its various historical phases, including the current one.

This chapter sets out to re-evaluate the steps made so far and take stock of the present state of affairs, in the light of the political dynamics of recent years. The first part will be dedicated to retracing the path of the Union's fundamental values, starting from the Treaty of Rome's initial reticence up to the codification achieved with the Treaty of Lisbon, touching upon the Court of Justice rulings, the successive reviews of the Treaties and the affair of the Charter of Fundamental Rights.

The second section will seek to distil the political significance of this lengthy process by explaining the link between the grand developments that have altered the face of the Union over the last 60 years – on the one hand the deepening of competences, and on the other, the enlargement of borders – and the progressive systematisation of fundamental values.

The following three sections will be dedicated to examining the state of health of democracy, fundamental rights and the rule of law in the enlarged Union. We will analyse later, in the sixth part, the mechanisms put in place by the Treaty of Lisbon in defence of fundamental values and, once we have established their limits, we will review the innovative tools that the European institutions are preparing to shield the fundamental value that presently appears to be most at risk of attack: the rule of law.

Lastly, in the final section, we will argue how the defence of fundamental values represents a decisive challenge for the future of the Union. A challenge to be faced with determination and courage if we want to preserve the soul and the raison d'être of the European construct as well as ensure its enduring existence.

I. The Long March of the Fundamental Values of the European Union

A. The Beginnings, from the Case Law of the Court of Justice to the Treaty of Amsterdam

The Treaty of Rome contained no reference to the values that the EU would come to be identified with. Both its provisions and the preamble itself were devoted entirely to the priorities of integration and economic development, with moderate allusions and even more limited concessions to grandstanding and rhetoric. On the other hand, the Economic Community was born as a functional organisation, aimed at promoting economic integration among the Member States, initially, in well-defined fields of action. Only later, with the extension of its competences and the evolution of the institutional framework, would the Community morph into something different and more complex. In doing so, it would progress from the original characterisation of community of interests to that of community of law and, subsequently, from community of law to community of values: a union of States and citizens who share the same rights and duties, and whose common belonging is rooted in a wealth of regulatory beliefs and shared ethical principles.

Fundamental values enter the European legal system thanks to the case law of the Court of Justice (Weiler 1999). With historical judgments in cases such as *Stauder* (12 November 1969), *Internationale Handelsgesellschaft* (17 December 1970) and *J Nold, Kohlen and Baustoffgroßhandlung* (14 May 1974), the Court established that – regardless of the reticence of the Treaties on the matter – European institutions could not fail to ensure an adequate level of protection of human rights, of which the Court itself acted as a guarantor. In the same years it also began to further the vision of European communities as 'communities based on law', the first step towards the affirmation of the of the rule of law as a fundamental value (Schroeder, in *Strengthening the rule of law in Europe*, 2016).

The other European institutions also soon felt the need to overcome that merely functional – and 'value-free' – characterisation of the Union in its initial stages. In 1977 the European Parliament, the Council and the Commission adopted a joint Declaration on fundamental rights, and on 8 April 1978 the European Council, on the eve of the first direct election of the European Parliament, approved a declaration on democracy (annexed to the conclusions) in which it confirmed the will 'to safeguard the principles of representative democracy, of the rule of law, of social justice and of respect for human rights', stating that 'respect for and maintenance of representative democracy and human rights in each Member State are essential elements of membership of the European Communities'. The heads of State and government thus anticipated principles that would be known as 'Copenhagen criteria' for accession, approved by the European Council in 1992, the first of which was (and still is) the: 'stability of institutions guaranteeing democracy, the rule of law, human rights and respect for and protection of minorities'. Earlier still, in a declaration of 14 December 1973, the Council of ministers had included democracy among the founding traits of European identity, introducing an element that, in later years, would monopolise the debate on the accession of Portugal and Spain.

All of these elements – from the judicial rulings to the declarations of the representatives of the governments – would undergo progressive codification throughout the 'twenty-year long constitutional process' spanning the period from the Single European Act to the Treaty of Lisbon.

The first appearance of the founding values in the system of the Treaties dates back to the preamble to the Single Act, in which the signatory States declared themselves:

> determined to work together to promote democracy on the basis of the fundamental rights recognized in the constitutions and laws of the Member States, in the Convention for the Protection of Human Rights and Fundamental Freedoms and the European Social Charter, notably freedom, equality and social justice.

The Treaty of Maastricht, which is the EU Treaty, stated in its preamble:

> Confirming their attachment to the principles of liberty, democracy and respect for human rights and fundamental freedoms and of the rule of law.

The wording was therefore acquiring its final connotations. And it has been noted that this is the first document with constitutional status to mention the rule of law. For sure, it appears here in the European treaties.

That same Treaty would add an important provision to the wording in the preamble; its article F in fact stated:

> 1. The Union shall respect the national identities of its Member States, whose systems of government are founded on the principles of democracy.
>
> 2. The Union shall respect fundamental rights, as guaranteed by the European Convention for the Protection of Human Rights and Fundamental Freedoms signed [...] and as they result from the constitutional traditions common to the Member States, as general principles of Community law.

With this wording, the Treaty codified in practice what the European Court of Justice had already been ruling on since the 1960s.

The Amsterdam Treaty amended article F – which in the meantime had been inserted as article 6 in the ordinary numbering of the Treaty on European Union, TEU – by converting paragraph 1 to paragraph 3 (and narrowing it down to the national identity of Member States, without qualifying this further) and drafting a new paragraph 1 (paragraph 2 remains unchanged), incorporating the democratic principle, in the wording that had been inserted in the preamble of the Treaty of Maastricht a few years earlier:

> The Union is founded on the principles of liberty, democracy, respect for human rights and fundamental freedoms, and the rule of law, principles which are common to the Member States.

In a single article were therefore enshrined as multiple layers some of the fundamental elements of the 'constitutional process' undertaken by the Union since the 1960s: respect for human rights, the contribution of commonly held constitutional traditions, and fundamental values.

B. The Values of the Union in the Constitutional Treaty and in the Treaty of Lisbon

The European constituent legislator would soon be confronted with the systematic need to distinguish the various components of article 6. Thus, the 2002–03 Convention and the subsequent Intergovernmental Conference took the initiative to dedicate an ad hoc article of the Treaty containing a Constitution for Europe to the list of fundamental principles, and specifically renamed 'fundamental values'.

The lexical shift (which also coexisted with the enduring term *principles* in article 21 and in the preamble to the Charter of rights) does not seem to have had a substantial impact from a legal perspective, even if one could long debate the implications of having replaced the term *principles* which carries clear legal connotations with basically a term that transcends the legal framework, such as *values* (Schroeder, in *Strengthening the rule of law in Europe*, (2016) 12 et seq). What is certain is that the choice mirrored a precise constitutional strategy. In the eyes of the European Convention, the Constitutional Treaty could not confine itself to simply stating rules on the organisation of public authorities; indeed, it would also have to contain value-based provisions, such as the ones relating to symbols, whose clear intent is to foster a European collective identity. In its view, the significance and evocative capacity, so to speak, of the word *values* was undoubtedly greater than that of the term principles.

As for the remainder, through the revised article mentioning values, the Convention simply redrafted and polished the wording in paragraph 1 of article 6 of the Treaty of Amsterdam. In doing so, it nonetheless made very important systematic choices. Suffice it to mention that the new article was assigned a privileged position, right after article 1 on the establishment of the Union and before the one detailing the objectives it would strive to pursue. In fact, it became article 2; a choice that would carry both political and legal consequences. The political effects were that, by emphasising the precedence of values over objectives, the Convention sought to highlight the EU's break from its characteristics as an organisation aimed at pursuing limited practical objectives ('purpose-oriented organisation'; Mangiameli, in *The Treaty on European Union* (2013)); the legal effects were that it urged the Court of Justice to model its case-law upon a hierarchy of values (Pinelli, in *Le nuove istituzioni europee* (2010)).

The wording in the European Constitution was adopted, with a few additions, by the Treaty of Lisbon. Consequently, in the consolidated version of the TEU, article 2 now holds that:

> The Union is founded on the values of respect for human dignity, freedom, democracy, equality, the rule of law and respect for human rights, including the rights of persons belonging to minorities. These values are common to the Member States in a society in which pluralism, non-discrimination, tolerance, justice, solidarity and equality between women and men prevail.

Although the transition from the Constitution to the Lisbon Treaty has required a number of other sacrifices (*Le nuove istituzioni europee* (2010)), the legal scope of article 2 has remained unchanged, together with the new status acquired by fundamental values in system of Treaties.

Based on the layout (but not the numbering) of the Constitutional Treaty, the Lisbon Treaty deals with the issue of fundamental rights and freedoms in article 6, albeit in significantly more detail.

This article provides in paragraph 2 that the Union should accede, as such, to the European Convention for the protection of human rights and fundamental freedoms, while taking up in paragraph 3 the well-established formula whereupon:

> Fundamental rights, as guaranteed by the European Convention for the Protection of Human Rights and Fundamental Freedoms and as they result from the constitutional traditions common to the Member States, shall constitute general principles of the Union's law.

Its most innovative provision is paragraph 1, which confers the 'same legal value as the Treaties' to the Charter of Fundamental Rights. As we will see further on, in the section *Fundamental rights in the enlarged Union*, this dry statement represents the crowning accomplishment of a ten-year process which kicked off with the judicial solutions identified by the European Court of Justice, and in the last decade has led to the codification of the fundamental rights of the Union.

The whole gamut of these processes and subsequent revisions of the Treaties can be encapsulated in a confirmatory statement, as well as a punitive measure, in two fundamental provisions of the Treaty. The first is article 49 which holds that 'any European State which respects the values referred to in Article 2 and is committed to promoting them may apply to become a member of the Union'. Hence, sharing the Union's values listed in article 2 is spelled out as a precondition for Union membership, directly impacting the accession negotiations, as we shall discuss in the next section. The second confirmation of the relevance of common values in the EU system is found in article 7 of the Treaty, which provides for specific sanctioning procedures against Member States in which the Union's values may be at risk or infringed even. Said procedures establish the legal force of the list of values in article 2, and not merely its declaratory nature.

II. The Common Values of the Union Caught Between Deepening and Enlargement

A. The Progressive Widening of Competences and the Need to Define Common Framework Values

The sequence we have briefly traced so far is loaded with meaning. The States that breathed life into the European Economic Community are saddled with the failure of the far more federal design at the heart of the European Defence Community, rejected by the French National Assembly; they are also aware that the common purpose upon which they established the Treaty of Rome – the creation of an integrated market – is hampered by far narrower limitations. Their brainchild, for this very reason, would have to be the community of goods and capital rather than of people. And there are plenty of critics who point their finger at the Community, because they see it in these terms and disparage it for this reason. But it is soon clear that the Community is not limited to this aspect, indeed it cannot and will not suffer such a fate.

In his famous declaration of 9 May 1950 announcing the birth of the European coal and steel Community (ECSC), which engendered the European Economic Community, Robert Schuman (1886–1963) had clearly stated that Europe would not be made all at once, but step by step, as solidarity spread among European nations. Well, what could this solidarity be based on? On economic and commercial exchanges alone? Or on the progressive discovery that, setting aside past hostilities, a source of never-ending, mutually destructive wars, there existed a common identity; an idea of Europe that historians like Federico Chabod (1901–60; *Storia dell'idea d'Europa*, edited by E Sestan, A Saitta (1998 2nd ed.)) had already grasped in ancient Greece and followed up to the twentieth century in its subsequent incarnations? And how would it be possible to trust one another, and to adopt principles like that of mutual recognition, as well as common rules, if there were no common fabric of shared principles, above and beyond the commercial ties?

These questions help to explain why the theme of common values (which enable mutual recognition and aim to promote a feeling of common belonging) would soon become interwoven with the theme of the progressive widening of Community competences.

Since the Union's early years, it had already become clear that, despite the postulates of functionalist theory, the sharing of increasingly greater portions of sovereignty would hardly be enough, on its own, to bring about that 'de facto solidarity' necessary for further integration. It was also necessary to presuppose a certain degree of commonality. The cornerstones of the European constitutional system that the Court had begun to define – one only need to think about the direct effect of European provisions on citizens, the primacy of Community law in matters entrusted to its competence, or the mutual recognition of domestic laws – are conceivable only to the point that the values and institutions of Member States are presumed to share a certain degree of consistency. Otherwise, why (for example) should nationals of one Member State automatically deem acceptable production criteria set by nationals of another Member State? And why should national Constitutional Courts accept that rules established at European level prevail over those of the Member States, without national parliaments having a say?

These questions would become unavoidable with the progressive widening of Union competences, extending to sovereign competences (*compétences régaliennes*) such as justice, public security, diplomacy and, increasingly these days, migration control. These fields of action pertaining to public authorities call for greater protection for citizens than simple management of economic activities.

To be sustainable, the deepening of the common market and the progressive widening of the instruments necessary to run it necessitated the definition of a framework of enforceable rights and the constructive listing of a series of common reference values. On these grounds only would it be possible, over time, to foster the growth of a feeling of common belonging.

What the opening sequence at the start of our analysis allows us to capture is the progressive revealing of this common fabric. It is no coincidence that its beginnings go back to 1973 with a Declaration on European identity openly making the connection between European States veer from the field of trade to that of the common embracing of democratic principles. And five years later, in the Declaration on democracy, these principles are fleshed out with a more detailed content (as we have seen), when handling such issues as representative democracy, but also the supremacy of law, social justice and respect for human rights. In the following years the Treaties themselves would transpose the traits of European identity into the codification that would see them enshrined in terms of components (with rule of law replacing supremacy of law, and human dignity, equality and freedom ranking alongside human rights) as well as their origins. These origins will be expressly traced back to those same Member States and to their constitutional traditions, in the wake of the European Court of Justice that, by delving deep into those traditions, unearthed that so-called common heritage in one ruling after another.

What is striking is the progressiveness of this path, which in itself testifies to the aggregating nature of a common fabric, such as to present itself as the core of a constitutional system integrated at European level. And it was interpreted in this light during the years when the integration process was in its heyday (for sure at the time of the Convention on the future of Europe); all this notwithstanding, doubts and misgivings did arise among scholars as to the effective uniformity of intent and significance that the various Member States attached to those identity traits. In fact, they were not born in Europe, but were asserted here as being common to the same Member States. Yet they were common only up to a point, judging by the different histories in which they had matured here and by the implications that still exist to this day. Such narratives had been enriched and diversified as the Union extended its borders and expanded its membership. Which brings us to the second major development undergone by the EU in recent decades: the enlargement process.

B. The Impact of the Enlargement Process on the Values of the Union

The process of enlargement and that of defining fundamental values have been closely linked since their debut. In some respects, the former provided a powerful incentive to the completion of the latter. In other respects, it made it more complex.

With each successive round, enlargement has brought most European countries to join ranks with the six founding States. The Nordic democracies acceded in the 1970s. The States of the Mediterranean and of the Iberian peninsula which had recently cast off the yolk of dictatorship joined in the 1980s. The States of the former Warsaw Pact followed suit with the 'great enlargement' of the early 2000s. With each round, the gradient of heterogeneity within the EU increased. And while one could 'assume' that Member States held shared values in the original Union, this 'unspoken assumption' was no longer sustainable in a Union of 15 and later 28 countries. Once the young and, to some extent, frail democracies first of southern Europe, and then of eastern Europe were added, it became imperative to make certain firm points clear and unequivocal. First of all, to clearly lay down the 'rules of the club' which these countries had now joined, but also to prevent the risk of regressions at a national level. In this effort, the 'ghost of Weimar' proved most effective: the subversion of the German and Italian constitutional order in the 1920s/1930s by utterly legal means. Such a precedent had led most scholars to the conclusion that a text of a constitutional nature could not be limited to setting rules of a procedural nature, but had to go into detail in its description of a nucleus of insuperable values (Wilms 2017).

Hence the reference to the Union's founding values in the most important political documents of the enlargement process, starting with the aforementioned 1978 Declaration on democracy (on the eve of the accession of Spain, Greece and Portugal) and that of Copenhagen in 1992, in the wake of the collapse of the Berlin Wall. Accordingly, we can cite the increasingly clear wording of article 49 of the Treaty which, as we have seen, now explicitly attaches the conditions for applying for Union membership to a State's respect for the basic values listed in article 2.

First and foremost, article 49 sets forth a geographical limitation: only the States pertaining to the European continent may belong to the EU. It is a less obvious criterion than it may seem at first sight, given the difficulty of accurately establishing the borders of Europe, 'une notion géographique sans frontières avec l'Asie et une notion historique aux frontières changeantes' (E Morin, *Penser l'Europe* (1987) 23). Narrowly construed, article 49 lays down that the EU is a regional organisation, and is therefore not likely to extend its borders indefinitely.

Secondly, and more importantly for the purposes of this paper, it adds a value-based criterion to the requirements for applying for membership. To be a member of the Union, it is necessary to share its broad aims and its underlying system of values. This condition cannot be satisfied by passive acceptance, since article 49 does not simply require candidate States to respect the values of the Union; it also requests their commitment in promoting them. This appears fully in keeping with the wording of article 3(5), whereby 'in its relations with the wider world, the Union shall uphold and promote its values and interests' (following an order of priority that is far from random). This dual imperative – respect and promote – means the EU is something more complex than a regional organisation in the classical sense. Its status is raised to that of a community of values, which first of all expects its members to share a number of basic regulatory beliefs and to behave accordingly.

But if enlargement has fuelled the process of assigning an abstract definition to common values, it has also made their practical application more complex. This is because, especially after the 'great enlargement' of the early 2000s, profound differences would emerge as to the interpretation to be given to specific fundamental values: democracy, fundamental rights (which can also encompass, for ease of reading, respect for human dignity and freedom, each mentioned separately in article 2), and the rule of law.

III. Democracy in Europe

A. European Democracies and Democracy in Europe

The first of the European identity traits, democracy, is perhaps the one that has best withstood the impact of enlargement. As we shall see, while slightly different meanings have emerged, so far we have witnessed no competing truths, or radically alternative interpretations, as to its definition. By and large, all current Member States respect the essential standards of representative democracy and they all manifest their will to scrupulously comply with them.

After all, enlargement was brought on by the 'third wave' of democratization in the 1980s and 1990s. And this wave was sustained, immediately after the fall of the Berlin Wall, by the prospect that eastern European countries could join the EU (J Kurlantzick, *Democracy in retreat. The revolt of the middle class and the worldwide decline of representative government* (2013)). The EU's transformational diplomacy at that time proved its worth, ensuring that the countries of the former Soviet bloc would undergo an extraordinarily soft transition towards democracy.

It was by no means a foregone conclusion that the regime change would take place painlessly and (with the partial exception of Romania) without bloodshed; just as one could not assume that the democratic method would take root. And yet, it is a fact that, over the last 20 years, all eastern European countries have witnessed governments of different political persuasions, with dynamics not unlike those recorded in countries with a more long-standing democratic heritage.

The attractive force represented by European values played a fundamental role here. In order to join the 'community of European democracies' it was necessary to embrace at least its fundamental rule: that power is handed down from the people and is fought over by peaceful means through the mechanisms of representative democracy (G Sartori, *Democrazia: cosa è* (1993) 63). This requirement has provided a powerful incentive for the elites in Eastern European countries to exercise a degree of restraint that is truly remarkable, given the scale of their own historical processes.

This is not to say that the overall picture of European democracy is without its fair share of shadows. First of all, it must be borne in mind that the requirement calling for respect of democratic rules, in the sense arising from a systematic reading of article 2, is relatively easy to satisfy. By its nature, it cannot but refer to a 'minimal' concept of democracy, seen as '[…] a set of procedural rules to establish collective decisions, in which the widest possible participation of any interested parties is expected and enabled' (N Bobbio, *Il futuro della democrazia* (1991) XIX). All it takes to meet this requirement is that the representative institutions are appointed through reasonably free and fair elections. Broadening the perspective, however, we know that, in material terms, democracy requires that other conditions are also met, such as media freedom, accountability in public administration, fight against corruption, freedom of association, and independence of the judiciary. Strictly speaking, these conditions fall under the umbrella of other reference values of the European construct, namely, the respect for fundamental rights or the rule of law. Having said that, in the absence of these conditions, even exercising democratic prerogatives effectively becomes a problematic affair. The fact that, in recent years, some of these prerogatives have proved to be not completely immune to the risk of involution (as we shall see) must necessarily cause us to mitigate our, albeit positive, judgement on the state of health of European democracy.

Another shadow is cast owing to the fact that enlargement has revealed the existence of different sensitivities concerning two aspects that are anything but minor when it comes to European democracy: on the one hand, the connection between Community-wide democracy and national democracy and, on the other, the means of exercising the democratic prerogatives.

The first aspect is of considerable importance, since it practically defines how far the integration process can be pushed; and what its *finalité politique* could be. The process can conceivably move in the direction of a fully federal development only insofar as it is willing to adopt, at European level, the methods of democratic investiture typical of national organisations. That is to say, if we acknowledge that European-wide democracy can live side by side, and with equal dignity, with national democracies. On this pivotal element, no real consensus has been reached at European level to this day. An explanation for this can probably be found in the different realities and different historical events that Member States have lived through. The founding countries had collected a fundamentally different set of experiences compared with those countries which were gradually joining the EU: they had given rise to the Communities as a response to the collective trauma of World War II. In the shared consciousness of their ruling classes, this tragedy had been the direct consequence not only of the rabid nationalism of the interwar years, but also of the lack of mechanisms aimed at governing conflicts of interest between States. The old European system based on creating a balance between the major powers had failed miserably. A different solution was sorely needed this time round. And this solution was identified with the creation of supranational mechanisms that would overhaul the notion of competition among European States a turn it into a joint management of common goods. This original commitment has been steadily watered down once the Union's founding members were joined by other countries who were thankfully spared the trauma of World War II or who processed it in a radically different way. This aspect has been boosted with the latest round of membership enlargement.

The collective trauma which eastern European countries were stepping out of in the 1990s was diametrically opposite to the one experienced by the Union's founders. The past they were seeking flight from was 70 years of Soviet domination, trapped within a system that wrapped under the cloak of internationalism what was in fact an imperialistic domination. Once free from this prison, the eastern European States had turned to rediscovering their national roots and emboldened with a strong determination to cling firmly to that sovereignty they had been bereft of for too long. It is no wonder that they approached the integration process on the basis of entirely different assumptions from those that had moved the founding States.

For the newly joined members from the East, subjected to decades of Soviet domination, Europe represented both a bulwark and a safe haven from the ravages of history, not a supranational entity in which their freshly regained sovereignty would be squandered. Consequently, democracy to them meant (then as it does today) allocating a space for national identity and representation through their own national Parliaments that would come before any space allocated for European identity and representation through the European Parliament (I Krastev, 'Europe's democracy paradox' (2012) 7(4) *The American interest* 41–47).

Such increasingly divergent sensitivities have exasperated and turned into a dilemma an otherwise commonplace ambivalence built into every integration process that takes its cue from national identity and thence from national electorates. Democracy in such a context can mean as much representation, hence decision-making weight in the seats of power of EU integration, as well as a refusal to surrender national representation and domestic decision-making centres. This dual interpretation has recently been circulating once again even among the old Community States. In the enlarged Union, one of the fundamental questions forever underlying the integration process has picked up again with rising intensity: is the Union democratic because it is made up of democratic states, or can it/should it be itself democratic? In the first case, it would only be entitled to a kind of secondary democratic legitimacy, flowing from the democratic investiture conferred upon the governments of the Member States. In the second case, though, the Union could even aspire to a primary democratic legitimacy, as European citizens can directly confer their mandate by electing the Strasbourg Assembly.

The constitutional treaty settled the dispute wisely by bestowing a dual source of legitimacy upon the Union: a direct democratic legitimacy, deriving from the investiture by its citizens, and an indirect democratic legitimacy stemming from the will of the Member States. In fact, the opening words of the Constitution – article 1(1) – stated that the Treaty establishing the EU reflected 'the will of the citizens and States of Europe to build a common future'.

The Treaty of Lisbon opted for a similar solution, albeit with less clarity.

Indeed, article 10(1)–(2) of the TEU states that:

1. The functioning of the Union shall be founded on representative democracy.

2. Citizens are directly represented at Union level in the European Parliament. Member States are represented in the European Council by their Heads of State or Government and in the Council by their governments, themselves democratically accountable either to their national Parliaments, or to their citizens.

The composite nature of the EU is thus enshrined, along with its encompassing of both federal and confederal elements (S Fabbrini, *Compound democracies: why the United States and Europe are becoming similar* (2010)).

To speak of a 'draw' between European-wide and national democracy would amount to excessive optimism, however. At European level, there is an abiding sense of deep-seated scepticism about the European Parliament's ability to take on the representation of European citizens in full. This attitude is reflected in the recurring argument that the national governments within the Council do not only represent the Member States (as would be the case if the Council were a genuine 'upper house'), but European citizens as well. And one can detect the same approach in protocols I and II (on the role of national parliaments and on the principle of subsidiarity), which 'insert' national parliaments into European decision-making procedures – almost as if to fill a gap in democratic representation – scoring a point for national democracies.

In maintaining a deep-seated ambiguity on the correlation between national and European-wide democracy, all the Treaty does it to take stock of the uneasiness that for some years has been seeping into the European debate and even legal thought. This is borne out by the inference that the German constitutional court drew from the Federal Republic's Constitution to uphold the unfailing role of the Bundestag on matters concerning European decisions, starting from the premise that the Union's current setup fails to meet the democratic requirements set forth in Germany (K Nikolaïdis, 'Germany as Europe: how the Constitutional Court unwittingly embraced EU demoi-cracy. A comment on Franz Mayer' (2011) 9(3–4) *International journal of constitutional law* 786–92). This kind of mental reservation has recently gained increasingly wider space to manifest itself, if it is true that the more national identities are strengthened when dealing with migratory phenomena, the more the national route to democracy prevails over the European route.

B. The Ambiguous Charm of Populist Democracy

Different sensitivities have emerged, especially in recent years, also on how democracy works. Given their more fragile roots, the eastern European democracies have actually shown to be particularly responsive to the lure of populist movements.

Populism has been rightly said to represent a disease of democracy which, based on the claim of striving to keep its pledges (the power of the people), it nonetheless betrays its substance. Its features include harking back to a mythological and untainted entity such as the 'people', criticism of the elites, 'moralistic' assumptions (all are corrupt), strong identifying national traits and above all a rejection of pluralism. If the true will of the people, through some sort of mystical union, is embodied in the populist movement, those who oppose it run against the will of the people, normally because either they are corrupt or they want to restore the old and discredited elites back to power (J-W Müller, *What is populism?* (2016)).

The rise of these movements is not a prerogative of the new Member States. Similar political groupings have taken hold also in the rest of Europe in recent years and, in some ways, throughout the West (*Populism on the rise. Democracies under challenge?*, edited by A Martinelli, 2016) in the wake of the prolonged economic stagnation and as a reaction against what is perceived as a migration crisis. There is no doubt, however, that the phenomenon has taken root at an earlier time and more forcefully in some eastern European countries. As always, the analysis of complex cases concerning different national situations should be carried out on a case-by-case basis. One can nonetheless put forward a number of explanations as to why populist movements have found fertile ground for growth here more than elsewhere.

The first cause, that is also the most directly intuitive, is that democracy in these countries is less deeply rooted than in western Europe. The democratic 'technique' may be imported with relative ease: it is enough to adopt representative institutions and make sure that popular consultations are carried out. Somewhat more burdensome is the process of incorporating the whole set of institutions that ensure democratic practices run smoothly. We will deal with this topic in greater detail in the section on the rule of law.

It is also likely that eastern Europe's own historical woes go some way towards explaining its relative vulnerability to the populist disease. Even without going too far back in time, to the various nation-building processes throughout the European States, one should bear in mind that, in recent decades, the independence of eastern European countries has undergone a twofold movement of liberation: that of the 'nation against the Soviet-dominated 'block', and that of the 'peoples' against proletarian internationalism. There is no doubt that Poles, Hungarians, Estonians, and Romanians have cast off the Soviet yoke owing to a range of unaddressed political and democratic demands, but also and perhaps above all in their capacity as guardians of an autonomous national identity, which was craving to assert itself.

Naturally, this is not to say that every national liberation struggle is in itself populist. What it does mean, though, is that given certain historical circumstances, it can degenerate into populism. Or, better still, it means that populist forces can take advantage of the people's nationalist fervour and feeling of unity brought on by the struggle for liberation in order to further their own personal agendas.

If we add to this the fact that populist parties in eastern Europe have had an easy job in pointing the finger at old political-administrative elites, in some cases in cahoots with the old regime, or against post-communist elites that were often educated abroad, and in any case 'westernised', therefore arousing the suspicion that they were too far removed from true popular sentiment.

The outcome of this combination of factors is that populist-inspired political forces have so far been particularly successful in the countries of eastern Europe. Emboldened by their claim to represent the 'true people' exclusively, such forces believe that the voters' mandate sanctions their exercise of power with no external interference, and this is why their growing intolerance is directed towards the checks-and-balances mechanisms of liberal democracy as much as towards the external constraints dictated by Union membership. Whereas these political forces observe the external forms of democracy, at the same time, they are in danger of voiding its substance.

IV. Fundamental Rights in the Enlarged Union

A. The Legal Acquis in Support of Fundamental Rights

The second pillar of European identity, respect for fundamental rights, has also managed to absorb the shock of enlargement without particular repercussions. Indeed, in some ways it came out stronger. This particular resilience is due to a combination of factors.

The first one is linked to the fact that a core body of fundamental rights is now universally recognised. From this perspective, especially poignant are the tools developed within the UN, starting with the Universal Declaration of human rights, along with the avenues pursued first by the Commission on human rights, and then by the UN Human Rights Council to promote and encourage respect for human rights and fundamental freedoms by all Member States.

The efforts put in place by the UN system, aided by key players in civil society and the whole gamut of non-governmental organisations (NGOs), have ensured that at least the basic tenets of the human rights doctrine are broadly shared. It has given strong visibility to the most striking cases of rights violations. It has made them the focus of particularly vehement international disapproval. Such sharing, visibility and disapproval have been focused on much more sharply at the European regional level, in particular thanks to the work of the Council of Europe and the European Court of human rights. Respect for fundamental rights is a value that not only defines the identity of the EU, but has risen to the status of a universal value, at least in its fundamentals. Upon joining the EU, the new Member States could hardly bring their own radically alternative views on these matters.

The second factor, strictly bound with the first, stems from the fact that the new Member States were able to become acquainted with – and assimilate, so to speak – the issue of human rights long before joining the Union. The former Warsaw Pact countries have belonged to the United Nations since their inception, and consequently had been involved, albeit with many twists and turns, in crafting the main international legal instruments for the protection of human rights. They had been exposed, if you will, at least insofar as their political elites, to the concepts that were being defined internationally. And it is no coincidence that one of the objectives of the Helsinki Conference, which would give rise to the Organization for security and cooperation in Europe, was precisely to bring about a progressive extension of human rights to the citizens of the Soviet bloc.

To this we should add that, before entering the EU, all the former Warsaw Pact States had followed a ten-year long apprenticeship at the Council of Europe, where they had been able to grasp the contents of the European Convention for the protection of human rights and fundamental freedoms (ECHR) as well as the case law established by the Strasbourg Court.

Thirdly, the solid basis enjoyed by fundamental rights in the enlarged Union is explained by the fact that, by the time of the 'great enlargement', the EU had already consolidated a formidable corpus on this subject. This had grown over the years thanks to the Court's ten-year body of case law, to the legal acquis accumulated in the distinct but adjacent system of the Council of Europe, and to the work undertaken by other European institutions, including (the latest example) the European human rights Agency (established two years after the 'great enlargement'). On account of its clarity and the degree of maturity it has reached, this shared legal acquis leaves little room for radically divergent interpretations.

B. The Role of the Charter of Fundamental Rights

The soundness of this system was certainly assisted by the codification work undertaken by means of the Charter of Fundamental Rights; unsurprisingly, this was devised during the years when the enlargement to the former Warsaw block began to take shape.

The idea had already been put forward by the European Parliament in 1984, with the approval by the Assembly of a draft Treaty establishing the EU (the so-called Spinelli Treaty), but had been shelved for a long time. At Cologne in June 1999 the draft was recovered by the European Council, which mandated a body of delegates of heads of State and government and the president of the European Commission, as well as members of the European Parliament and national Parliaments, to draw up a Charter of Fundamental Rights of the EU.

Understandably lukewarm about the denomination that had been attributed to them, the members of the body, egged on by representatives of the European Parliament, would have rather opted for a more solemn and evocative designation. Drawing on French and American constitutional history, they settled for the term *Convention* (Braibant (2001)). This redenomination would prove to be somewhat successful, as it also inspired the assembly that soon after that would set to work on drafting the Constitutional Treaty.

For the first time, in what has gone down in history as the Herzog Convention, after Roman Herzog (1934–2017), president of the German Constitutional Court (and later president of the Federal Republic) who chaired its meetings, government representatives were able to engage directly with those of the European institutions and national parliaments. This type of hybridisation was to prove extremely fruitful.

The Charter of Fundamental Rights was approved by the Nice European Council in December 2000. For some years it lived in a state of ambiguity – having initially no binding legal force; however, since the outset it has shown its vocation as a guiding force, steering the rulings of the European and national courts, only too pleased to make use of a workable text that codified a subject by its very nature as elusive as fundamental rights.

Ultimately, as we have seen, the Treaty of Lisbon came full circle and integrated the provisions of the Charter by means of an incorporating clause; at the same time the Charter itself was reaffirmed, with some minor changes, in the 2007 proclamation by the three Community institutions (*Carta dei diritti fondamentali dell'Unione Europea* (2017)).

In its preamble the Charter limits itself, in theory at least, to:

> reaffirm […] the rights as they result, in particular, from the constitutional traditions and international obligations common to the Member States […] and the case-law of the Court of Justice of the European Communities and of the European Court of Human Rights.

Its manifest purpose, therefore, is to clarify and illustrate, rather than to innovate. Yet the codification process it embarked on, like all analogous operations, is anything but neutral and its constitutional value is actually extraordinary. In many respects the Charter solemnly establishes the Union's definitive transformation from a community of interests to a community of values. Indeed, it is a community that has finally acquired its own positive set of rights that underpin it.

The Charter also clarifies the link between fundamental rights and the founding values of the Union. Indeed, if article 2 unequivocally includes fundamental rights among the values upon which the European identity is based, their codification within the Charter helps to shed light on the meaning of the individual values mentioned in the aforementioned article. The first Convention had already made the editorial choice to group fundamental rights around six fundamental values or principles, these being dignity, freedom, equality, solidarity, citizenship and justice. Despite the odd mismatch, the Charter reiterates the contents of article 2, to which it is clearly linked. This is not irrelevant, if we consider that individual rights must be interpreted in the light of the reference values they are classified in (Cartabia, in *La Costituzione europea* (2004)).

Finally elevated to the rank of primary norm, the Charter proved itself a valuable source of reference and guidance for the Court of Justice to build a solid and immediately accessible system of guaranteeing fundamental rights. This constitutes an important legal protection for anyone dealing with the EU's institutions, bodies, offices and agencies, as well as with the Member States when implementing European provisions.

And that is not all. While drawing heavily on the case law of the European Court of human rights and constitutional courts, the Luxembourg Court's interpretation of the Charter eventually provided inspiration and stewardship to the other courts, thereby achieving 'an advanced form of circularity' of jurisprudential solutions (*Carta dei diritti fondamentali dell'Unione Europea* (2017) XII). It has been duly noted that the result represents a clear step forward from the point of view of the *ius commune europaeum* (p XII).

With these latest developments, the Union has completed its own internal human rights protection mechanism, which is based on the constitutions of individual Member States, on international obligations and, in particular, on each Member State's accession to the European Convention on human rights established in the framework of the Council of Europe, and on the case law of the EU Court of Justice, which can now rely on a positive list of the fundamental rights of the Union.

The solidity of this mechanism constitutes a mighty bulwark against the risk of regression and involution. Of course, individual violations of fundamental rights are possible, indeed, unfortunately recurrent; conflicting visions on specific issues can still emerge (as is the case, nowadays, regarding what stand to take in dealing with the influx of refugees from Africa and the Middle East). However, it is hard to imagine that these temporary deviations from the common standard may become a systemic problem or stem from radically different interpretations of the obligations to which Member States are bound. If this were to happen, it would mean that all the other 'value-based safeguards' protecting the common European home have already yielded. It would mean that Member States who violate a fundamental value such as respect for human rights have already forsaken democracy or the rule of law or both. And the message would be that the connective tissue of the Union is already in shreds.

V. The Boundary of the Rule of Law

A. A Value Under Consolidation

The third pillar of the common European fabric has proved less tear-proof in the enlarged Union: respect for the rule of law. A number of historical contingent factors, which we will deal with below, have somewhat contributed to its relative vulnerability. However, our analysis will have to start by acknowledging that the very concept of rule of law is less clearly defined, at European level, than the concepts of democracy and respect for fundamental rights.

All the legal traditions represented at EU level agree on the rule of law being a fundamental value, in the absence of which democracy and even the respect for human rights are at risk of being meaningless. Yet there are still diverging views as to what its constituent elements are; largely as a result of the different constitutional routes followed by each Member State. One thing they all have in common is the will to curtail the arbitrariness of political power. In English rule of law, however, the need to curb the discretionary acts of public authorities has always resulted in a strong focus on the practical side of safeguarding individual positions to which liberties and rights are linked. This has always entailed not only that any punitive situation had to be previously established by law, but also that all defendants would be subjected to ordinary court hearings and that general principles protecting individual rights and freedoms arising from the decisions of the judges would enjoy primacy over others. This approach can also lead, in some extended meanings of the concept of the rule of law, to encompass also proportionality in the action of public authorities and safeguarding the legitimate expectations of citizens (Huber, in *Strengthening the rule of law in Europe* (2016)).

The continental equivalents of the rule of law, defined by the terms *Rechtstaat, état de droit, stato di diritto*, pursued a different route, at least until the mid-twentieth century. In their case, the formal aspect of curtailing public authorities was prevalent, and it focused on the central core of the principle of legality. In its continental sense, the rule of law requires above all that lawmakers are bound by the Constitution, and that the executive and legislative powers are bound by the law. Around this central core gravitates a series of corollaries such as the separation of powers, the independence of the judiciary, parliamentary reservation, and judicial review.

Until quite recently, in fact, all that was required of any law on the continent was to legitimise the powers exercised over individuals, and no right of review existed – whether in France, Germany, or Italy. It is true that this was no longer the case (with the partial exception of France) in the decades that witnessed the growth of the European institutions; and it is also true that a substantial and not merely formalistic approach to the rule of law began to appear on the continent as well. Yet it is a fact that different opinions still persist as to the contents of the rule of law – ranging from those who believe its aim is to protect rights and freedoms, and those who consider it only an expression of the need that individuals may be subjected to punitive treatments only insofar as these have been previously pre-established by law.

The existence of different national sensitivities helps to explain the oblique manner in which the rule of law has entered the European legal system. Its first appearance should be traced back to the Court of Justice judgment of 23 April 1986, *Parti écologiste 'Les Verts' v European Parliament*. The political group of the Greens had challenged the decisions of the Bureau of the European Parliament on the allocation of electoral reimbursements. These were certainly measures with legal effects on third parties, but article 173 of the Treaty provides that only measures from the Council or the Commission can be challenged; not those of Parliament. On this matter, the Court held:

> It must first be emphasized in this regard that the European Economic Community is a Community based on the rule of law, inasmuch as neither its Member States nor its institutions can avoid a review of the question whether the measures adopted by them are in conformity with the basic constitutional charter, the Treaty.

And here it mentioned several articles – 173, 177 and 184 – that meant to allow the Court to review without exception any potentially unlawful measures. It is true that these articles only refer to measures of the Council and of the Commission, but when they were drafted the Parliament had only consultative and political powers. It is no coincidence that under the ECSC Treaty, which also gave Parliament deliberative powers, that power to refer for review was not exclude at all. It follows that – concluded the Court – article 173 should be construed so as to include the measures of Parliament itself, when they produce effects on third parties.

This was deemed a 'generous and dynamic' decision (as advocate general Francis Geoffrey Jacobs wrote in a subsequent judgment). But let us tread carefully here. We would be wrong to think that the Court had identified in the rule of law a directly applicable principle and decided only on its basis alone. The Court performed a systematic interpretation that extended article 173 beyond its literal meaning. And to these ends the rule of law served as a general principle that influences the interpretation and therefore the application of a provision – in this case article 173 – and not as a directly applicable provision.

In doing so, the Court heralded a jurisprudence that has remained unchanged. Although repeatedly spurred by the parties, and by the same advocate general, to identify in the rule of law the 'legal norm' infringed in order to exercise the right to review under current article 263 of the Treaty on the Functioning of the European Union, TFEU, it failed to do so. The Court has always identified the breach with the violation of a provision, or even of a principle, attributable to the rule of law, but never coinciding with it. As we shall see shortly, what we usually read is that 'in a community governed by the rule of law' a given right is undeniable, a given act must be subjected to review, but always on the basis of provisions it can be traced back to.

Why exercise so much caution despite the potential for innovation? On account of the presumable awareness that the rule of law is a multifaceted principle and not all its aspects have been accepted by each Member State. It is more prudent – and more consistent with a system in which the rule of law is understood as being common to the Member States – to associate it gradually with principles that are surely shared, and that can be safely regarded as its manifestations. In doing so, those principles are bolstered and the rule of law itself is reinforced.

It so happened that, despite the never-ending doctrinal dispute over the purely formal or even substantial nature of the rule of law, it goes without saying that it also affects substantive criteria and, as Ronald Dworkin (1931–2013) would say, is 'rights based'. In its judgment of

25 July 2002, *Unión de Pequeños Agricultores v Council of the European Union*, C-50/00P (so-called UPA ruling), the Court wrote that:

> The European Community is, however, a community based on the rule of law in which its institutions are subject to judicial review of the compatibility of their acts with the Treaty and with the general principles of law which include fundamental rights.

And in the same perspective, eight years later, we should read judgment of 30 September 2010, *Yassin Abdullah Kadi v European Commission*, T-85/09, wherein it was stated that in the European legal system, based on the rule of law, the freezing of assets belonging to persons suspected of links to terrorist groups is inadmissible, even when this has been mandated by the United Nations Security Council, without the suspect being even heard.

Wedged comfortably and with such flexibility into the European legal system, the rule of law has endured without apparent setbacks its transition from being a *principle* – as defined in article 6 of the Treaty as amended in Amsterdam – to being a *value*, as per the new definition laid down in the Constitutional Treaty and then in the Treaty of Lisbon under article 2. As we have seen in the first section, there are no documented explanations for this transition, although we can hazard a 'political' explanation, in keeping with the constitutional strategy pursued by the European Convention. What is certain, however, is that the term *values* carries greater legal vagueness which, insofar as the rule of law, makes the term better suited to the interpretation given to it by the Court; also, the term responds better to the differences that persist between States and vis-à-vis the Union itself and that sometimes also emerge from the case law. If one thinks of the *Taricco* case, which is still underway thanks to a preliminary ruling ordered by the Italian Constitutional Court, which raises doubts as to whether a decision of the European Court of Justice actually complies with the rule of law. And the question arises from a reading of article 325 – the article dedicated to measures in use to combat tax fraud to the detriment of the Union – that requires direct applicability by the national courts, whereas – in the view of the Italian Constitutional Court – it is a principle that necessitates legislative translation. Here the separation of powers is deemed to be at stake, and there is no doubt – as we shall soon see once examined the Commission's documents – that this principle falls under the umbrella of the rule of law, inasmuch as the independence of the judiciary and other organisational principles.

For sure, having examined the cases referred to both the Court of first instance and to the Court of Justice for review, the principles that these Courts have brought within the scope of that umbrella are far fewer – as mentioned above – than the ones envisaged by the parties: some specific rights enforceable against public authorities – the right to due process, to a reliable and accountable administration, to afflictive measures defined within a given time-frame – and above all access to justice, by always loosely interpreting provisions so that they apply to bodies and acts that may be subject to judicial review, and whose purpose is to protect fundamental rights and equality before the law. It is this latter principle that seems to be most directly affected by the rule of law, in the manner that said principle is upheld by the European Courts; after all, this ties in with what has historically been the first and foremost meaning of the rule of law, thanks to the English courts.

B. The Rule of Law and the Accession Process

In tracing the various national sensitivities on the subject of the rule of law we have left out the group of countries that joined the Union with the latest rounds of enlargement. This is no coincidence. Strictly speaking, these countries were not bearers of their own view on the rule of law simply because the concept was foreign to them.

In the eyes of the Marxist-Leninist ideology that had long subjugated them, the rule of law was an eminently 'bourgeois' notion. A ruse aimed at concealing the State's class origin and the connection made between the class that holds economic power and the State organisation. In practice, a tool wielded by the bourgeoisie to perpetrate its own power and guarantee the conditions for capital accumulation.

After all, the very essence of the rule of law, that is to say the limitation of power, was wholly inconceivable to totalitarian regimes like the ones in eastern Europe. Likewise, they could not fathom its various components and articulations, from the separation of powers to the independence of the judiciary, through to the constitutional union and equality before the law.

It was essential for the Member States and the Commission to bridge this cultural gap and ensure that the candidate countries soaked up the grammar of the rule of law before accessing the Union. So it is hardly surprising that especially swingeing conditions were imposed during the accession negotiations given the context. Under the interpretation that was put forward at that time, the umbrella of the rule of law was extended to its maximum breadth and, not coincidentally, was made to apply not only to safeguarding individual rights, but also to upholding the pillars of the institutional organisation – from the separation of powers, hence judicial independence of judges, to the administrative antidotes against corruption.

This is clearly set forth in the notes with which the Commission summarises the 'Conditions for Union membership' in the relevant chapter on accession negotiations (chapter 23), dedicated to the judiciary and fundamental rights:

> The establishment of an independent and efficient judiciary is of paramount importance. Impartiality, integrity and a high standard of adjudication by the courts are essential for safeguarding the rule of law. This requires a firm commitment to eliminating external influences over the judiciary […]. Legal guarantees for fair trial procedures must be in place. Equally, Member States must fight corruption effectively, as it represents a threat to the stability of democratic institutions and the rule of law […]. Member States must ensure respect for fundamental rights and EU citizens' rights, as guaranteed by the acquis and by the Fundamental Rights Charter (notes by the EU Commission on the Community acquis, https://ec.europa.eu/neighbourhood-enlargement/policy/conditions-membership/chapters-of-the-acquis_en).

The principles set out by the Commission on the conditions for accession to the Union should also apply to States that are already members. However, the manner in which these principles have been applied has been felt rather differently by the two categories. While for Member States compliance with these requirements has been and continues to be taken for granted (this constitutes a major flaw in the system, as we shall see), the verification of compliance with the Union's conditions has been detailed, and at times burdensome, in the case of applicant States. Such meticulousness owes much to the fact that the countries acceding after 2004 were almost exclusively former communist States whose governance systems were inspired by principles far removed from the ones in force in western Europe. It is true to say that the main interest in terms of an institutional common ground for existing Member States, but also for the Commission, lay in the ability of new Member States to effectively control their own borders and, consequently, the migration flows. It is equally true, however, that fulfilling this same aim also called for implementing the requirements in the Commission's notes, namely, administrative systems exempt from corruption as much as possible and independent judicial courts. In this context, the negotiations focusing on chapters such as *Judiciary and fundamental rights* and *Justice, freedom and security* were tough, so much so that things were eventually smoothed by the attitude of the Commission, which interceded by advocating for the applicant countries in their dealings with the Member States (P Ludlow, *The making of the new Europe* (2004)).

Overall, the negotiating mechanism for enlargement set up during the 1990s proved successful, as applicant countries have adopted the wealth of institutions that goes under the name of the rule of law in a very short time; and this is all the more remarkable considering that a long historical development was needed to establish those same institutions in western Europe.

The only aspect that is somewhat doubtful is the degree of assimilation and, so to speak, of internalisation achieved by these institutions, but the question will remain unanswered. What can be said is that – as some maintain – the rationale underpinning the negotiations could have led, on the one hand, to executive powers in applicant countries achieving inordinately high levels of authority, as it falls upon governments to conduct talks with Community negotiators; while bringing about, on the other hand, a Europeanisation (of culture and attitudes) only among the bureaucratic elites at the helm of the negotiations with Brussels, without involving the rest of the population in this process. We would do well to heed this opinion, because it could have a role in explaining the deviances, see below, with which we are grappling today.

C. A Potentially At-risk Value

The relatively frail background of the rule of law helps to explain why this principle, rather than fundamental rights and democracy, is showing the more worrying signs of endangerment today. Those same political organisations that, as we mentioned in the *Democracy in Europe* section, are intent on furthering a 'populist' view of democracy, are in fact displaying growing levels of intolerance towards some of the essential postulates of the rule of law, such as the separation of powers, judicial review, and an independent judiciary. In some cases, they have already stated their intention to tamper with these safeguards; yet the price they are likely to pay for doing so is relatively small. The difference with fundamental rights, that other pillar of the European identity, is quite evident here. Indeed, it is clearly easier to rouse the international community to act against violations affecting people – with their own faces, stories, and ability to arouse empathy – than to rise up in defence of seemingly abstract principles such as the separation of powers or the independence of the judiciary. A government that is bent on undermining the canons of the rule of law without violating, at least at an early stage, the human rights of its citizens would therefore pay a relatively small price in terms of international disapproval. And this is a further explanation of the relative vulnerability of the fundamental value of the rule of law.

One should also consider that violations of the rule of law are in some ways more subtle than the violations of other fundamental values, such as democracy, for example, because they are of an incremental nature. One can clearly identify the moment in which the tenets of democracy, at least in its strictest meaning, are violated. It is when the people's mandate is flouted and elections, even if they formally still take place, cease to be free and fair. On the other hand, the rule of law can be dismantled gradually, imperceptibly even. At the end of the process, democracy will be emptied of substance and the groundwork for serious violations of fundamental rights will be laid. But it will be too late to redress the balance.

But the fundamental reason why the rule of law is in the unenviable position of being the most threatened of all the Union's values is likely to be of a structural nature. In many respects, it can be seen as the foremost bulwark in defence of all the Union's fundamental values. In order to strike at others, whether fundamental rights or democracy, it is first necessary to remove the protections of the rule of law, which centuries of constitutional evolution have put in place precisely to forestall the risk of antidemocratic abuses and involutions. It is only natural then, that this first line of advanced defence should be the first to bear the brunt of the attack from anti-establishment forces.

VI. The Mechanisms in Defence of Fundamental Values in the European Union

A. Monitoring Compliance with Fundamental Values and the Limits of Article 7 of the Treaty

From the review of values such as democracy, fundamental rights and the rule of law we have conducted thus far, it is clear that there are still a few grey areas surrounding the notion of a common European heritage. What does this heritage consist of? Is it the lowest common denominator, from which the European Court of Justice cannot depart, for example, when it admitted to having no other source to draw on other than the common constitutional traditions? Or have the Treaties brought about a novation of the source, thus making it possible to ascribe to democracy and the rule of law an autonomous meaning that is universally applicable? And what legal force does that meaning, whatever it may be, have at its disposal in order to assert itself? Against whom and on behalf of whom?

What emerges is a shifting boundary, resulting as much from the interpretation given by national and European courts to fundamental values, as from the interaction between European institutions and national governments. It is this boundary that must be constantly monitored. To do so, article 7 of the Treaty offers the possibility, depending on the severity of the threat, of resorting to two sanctioning procedures against Member States that fail to uphold the values listed in article 2. In case of a risk of a breach, 'on a reasoned proposal by one third of the Member States, by the European Parliament or by the European Commission', the Council, acting by a majority of four-fifths of its members after obtaining the consent of the European Parliament, may determine that there is a 'clear risk of a serious breach', thus imposing, at this stage, a sanction of a political nature. However, in the most serious cases of overt breach (not in case of a mere risk), it is up to the European Council, acting by unanimity on a proposal by one third of the Member States or by the European Commission and after obtaining the consent of the European Parliament, to determine the existence of a 'serious and persistent breach', and initiate a procedure whereby the offending State may be sanctioned by suspending 'certain of the rights deriving from the application of the Treaties to the Member State in question, including the voting rights [...] in the Council'.

The importance of the procedures envisaged by article 7 is undeniable. In a certain sense, they are presented as the mainstays of the system for they ensure the legal, and not merely declaratory, value of article 2. In legal literature, there is clearly no lack of support for the idea that the Court of Justice could invoke this article directly (von Danwitz, in *Strengthening the rule of law in Europe* (2016)). Yet in practical terms, devoid of the support of article 7, article 2 would likely be far more limited in scope: it would be used as an ideal (and dialectical) reference to brandish during negotiations between Member States and between institutions or, at best, as a hermeneutical criterion that the Courts could resort to when interpreting other provisions of the Treaties. As we shall see, this falls short of what is needed, in the light of the threats the Union is facing.

While the procedures in question actually constitute an element of strength for the Union's value system, it cannot be downplayed that the applicative challenges they present are not negligible. Indeed, they both require ample majorities, a particularly difficult target to meet; this consideration holds especially true for the procedure for serious breaches, for which unanimity in the European Council must be achieved. Also, they both lack gradualness. To openly put a Member State in the dock for serious breaches of article 2 is seen as a particularly traumatic event for the Union, and possibility of suspending its voting rights even more so. It is hardly surprising that, in Community circles, article 7 commonly goes by the eloquent moniker of 'nuclear option'. Also in view of its 'extreme' nature, the risk is that it is triggered too late, when the situation in the Member State in question has deteriorated so much that no outside intervention can hope to change its course. One might surely argue that the purpose of article 7 is to act as a deterrent, and its inclusion in the system of Treaties was precisely with the idea of not having to activate it. But such an interpretation would be guilty of foolhardy optimism. The events of recent years have indeed shown how the growing realisation that article 7 lacks bite has seriously undermined its dissuasive capacity.

In practical terms, we are confronted with a veritable 'bug' in the Treaty system; while it allows, indeed recommends, Member States to pore over the references of candidate States with great attention, in the case of countries within the system, respect for common values can be somewhat taken for granted. This points to some sort of implied assumption whereby no checks and cross-checks need to be performed unless there is, as per the wording of article 7, 'a clear risk of a serious breach by a Member State' or even 'the existence of a serious and persistent breach by a Member State of the values referred to in article 2'.

The shortcomings of article 7 have led Member States and European institutions to question how to bridge the gap between inaction, which is in danger of being mistaken for acquiescence, and resorting to the 'nuclear option'. In recent years, there has been a concerted effort to identify a modus operandi allowing compliance checks to be conducted in a non-traumatic manner, or even by way of routine, so that troublesome situations may be addressed smoothly. Such situations tend to occur today more than in the past, putting a huge strain on that common fabric woven at a time when the integration process was in its waxing phase; one cannot help but wonder whether it still expresses common principles and/or values.

B. The Search for New Tools to Uphold the Rule of Law

The emergency situation has mainly arisen in the field of the rule of law. For the reasons we have seen in *A potentially at-risk value*, the rule of law is the fundamental value that is most exposed to the attacks of anti-establishment forces. But it is not always easy to establish in practice when these attacks turn into serious breaches. By way of example, it is hard to trace the exact boundary between a more or less natural power struggle between State authorities and an actual threat to the rule of law. When does the tug of war between political forces and the judiciary place the latter's independence at risk? And how far can a parliamentary majority rewrite the rules of procedure without encroaching on the prerogatives of the supreme courts?

The experience of these years shows that disputes centring on the respect for the rule of law often lend themselves to different readings; this makes resorting to the already complex procedures of article 7 even less practical. Here more than elsewhere, it was necessary to identify alternative instruments for settling disputes. And the European institutions have done this by essentially following two paths.

The route taken by the European Commission is reminiscent of the infringement procedures, or rather, the so-called EU-Pilot procedures, in which the Community's Executive body initiates a dialogue with the Member States in question prior to triggering infringement proceedings. A number of academics have raised the question as to why the Commission does not resort directly to the instruments bestowed by articles 258 et seq to challenge the Member States for any breaches of article 2 before the Court of Justice (Mastroianni 2017). The answer to this question lies in the difficulty of defining with any accuracy the obligations arising from article 2. As we have seen, this has led the Court to systematically invoke specific provisions of the Treaties to 'shore up' the obligations stemming from article 2. The Commission has done likewise, initiating in recent years a series of infringement proceedings against Hungary for breaches of specific articles of the Treaties (Wilms (2017)). Broadly speaking, this has never happened for the risk of serious breaches of article 2, despite strong pressure to this effect from the European Parliament (*European Parliament resolution of 16 December 2015 on the situation in Hungary*, 2015/2935(RSP)).

In order to remedy the lack of a procedure in the Treaties allowing the EU to engage in consultations with Member States without deploying the 'nuclear option' of article 7, the Commission has resorted to creating an *extra legem* procedure. In spite of objections from some Member States, this course of action undoubtedly falls within its prerogatives. On the one hand, in fact, article 292 TEU confers upon the Community's Executive body a generic power to issue recommendations. On the other hand, the same procedures provided for in article 7 give the Commission, as well as Member States, the 'right of initiative'. Hence, it can surely enter talks with a Member State prior to triggering article 7 to assess whether and how to implement its prerogatives in this area.

The new procedure is set out in the communication from the Commission to the European Parliament and the Council, *A new EU framework to strengthen the rule of law* of 11 March 2014, and is divided into three phases: in the first stage, the EU Executive body makes a first assessment of the situation within a Member State and initiates a structured exchange with its authorities, with the objective of remedying any critical issues. This stage ends with the adoption of a rule of law opinion, of a confidential nature, in which the

Commission informs the State in question of its findings and of the measures it considers necessary to bring the situation under control. The second stage starts by examining the measures adopted by the State following the opinion and may lead to the adoption of a recommendation; in its recommendation the Commission will clearly indicate the reasons for its concerns and formally and officially recommend that the Member State solves the problems identified within a fixed time limit. If also this stage comes to nothing, the Commission decides on what follow-up to give to the proceedings, assessing the possibility, among other things, of activating one of the mechanisms set out in article 7.

C. The Polish Case

The case of Poland has played a pioneering role in the implementation of the new *framework*. On 27 July 2016, the Commission issued a truly analytical recommendation to Poland, which speaks volumes both in terms of the contents attached to the rule of law, and on the unsettling intensity of the deviances that are taking place today within the EU.

The Commission cites – and this is noteworthy in itself – not only the case law of the European Court of Justice, but also that of the European Court of human rights, the documents of the Council of Europe and those of the European Commission for democracy through law, known as the Venice Commission. Drawing from all these sources, the Commission believes that it can draw an open-ended list of the principles falling under the rule of law and capable of fulfilling its essential meaning. And, while similar, the list is more extensive than the one outlined above, that the Commission itself drew up with regard to chapter 23 of accession negotiations. In fact, the principles include:

> legality, which implies a transparent, accountable, democratic and pluralistic process for enacting laws; legal certainty; prohibition of arbitrariness of the executive powers; independent and impartial courts; effective judicial review including respect for fundamental rights; and equality before the law. In addition to upholding those principles and values, State institutions also have the duty of loyal cooperation (Commission recommendation (EU) 2016/1374 of 27 July 2016 regarding the rule of law in Poland).

Against this backdrop, the Commission examined closely the actions taken by the new Parliament in late 2015 and by the government against the Constitutional Court: first of all, the appointment of three judges replacing the three lawfully appointed by the previous Parliament; then the new law changing the Court's decision-making power, by prescribing a two-thirds majority vote, obliging it to handle the cases according to the date of receipt, and introducing disciplinary actions against judges on request of the ministry of Justice and decided by the Parliament in the most serious cases; furthermore, the government's refusal, in March 2016, to publish the Court's ruling that had just declared the law unconstitutional, with the consequence of depriving the ruling itself of legal validity. Finally, the Commission examines recent laws restricting rights and freedoms, with particular attention to the media law, linking its provisions to the obstacles put in the way of their review by the Court. All this leads the Commission to denounce the existence of a 'systemic threat to the rule of law', with particular regard to the separation of powers and the effectiveness of the Constitutional Court's jurisdiction, calling upon the Polish government to take remedial action within three months, addressing the issues detailed in the recommendation. In the three months, no response came from the Polish government.

In the light of its first experience handling the Polish case, it remains to be seen whether the new framework proposed by the Commission would alone suffice to fix the legislative bug in terms of safeguarding the rule of law. A number of reasons seem to suggest that this is not the case. Firstly, one should not downplay the risk that initiating such proceeding prior to triggering article 7 will give rise to a sort of 'game of chicken', with the Member State in question refusing to be placed in the dock and the Commission having to stand its ground so as not to lose face. What happens if the Commission's recommendations remain a dead letter? The Community Executive body would be forced to retreat across the board or, alternatively, to request the initiation of proceedings provided for in article 7. In the first option, its credibility would seriously be undermined. Yet the damage would be equally serious, if not worse, in the second option, if the Commission's course of action were to fail to garner the superqualified majority required by the Treaties. The Union's credentials as a 'community based on law' would suffer a serious blow.

The second reason why Commission's 'framework' alone cannot be relied on, is that the greatest threat to the rule of law today comes from populist political forces who are only too happy to dress their hostility towards the Commission as a struggle between national democracies and Brussels technocracy. Leaving the Commission alone to counteract their illiberal tendencies is tantamount to supplying them with a powerful propaganda tool.

D. The Council's 'Annual Dialogue'

Also for the reasons outlined above, the Council has chosen a different route that in many ways complements that of the Commission. Instead of seeking to formalise an inquisitive procedure against governments suspected of subverting the prescriptions of the rule of law, it has focused on setting up a soft instrument, based on the principles of peer pressure and moral suasion.

Even this seemingly timid step was long met with strong resistance from the Member States, and it took the strong dedication displayed by the Italian presidency of 2014 to reach an agreement. Based on an Italian proposal, on 16 December 2014 the General Affairs Council adopted conclusions establishing an annual political dialogue among all Member States within the Council, to promote and safeguard the rule of law in the framework of the Treaties. In order to secure a deal, the Council went out of its way to stress that the approach of the dialogue would be without prejudice to guarantees (at least from the perspective of the governments concerned), based on the principles of objectivity, non-discrimination and equal treatment of all Member States, and would be conducted 'on a non partisan and evidence-based approach' (*Council conclusions on ensuring respect for the rule of law*, doc. 17014/14, 16 December 2014).

The first two annual rule of law dialogues held under the Luxembourg presidency in 2015 and the Dutch in 2016 served as a testing ground, and focused on a thematic approach, to reduce the risk of sparking protests from some Member States. Thus, the Luxembourg presidency organised a conference on the prevention of anti-Semitism and Islamophobia and promoted a debate on national best practices, while asking the Member States to react to a document on the rule of law in the digital age, while the Dutch presidency used the dialogue to promote a thematic debate on what Member States can do to ensure that fundamental rights are respected when integrating refugees.

Although marked by an overly cautious approach, this course of action has set in motion a mechanism for exchanging ideas on the rule of law without major wrangling, while accustoming Member States to discuss collectively the challenges that they face.

This enabled the Slovak presidency to trigger the future developments clause under the 2014 findings, providing that Member States would 'evaluate, by the end 2016, the experience acquired on the basis of this dialogue'. Also in this phase, Italy played a proactive role, promoting in October 2016 a meeting between some countries of the European Union ('friends of the rule of law' group) on respect for the rule of law in the EU. The countries present (Italy, Austria, Belgium, Denmark, Finland, France, Germany, Greece, Ireland, Luxembourg, the Netherlands, Portugal, and Sweden) signed a joint working paper containing a series of practical proposals on how to strengthen the annual dialogue and, above all, flagging up the possibility of its evolution, potentially converting it into a real periodic review. A procedure of this type would have allowed each Member State's current situation to be reviewed periodically by its partners, akin to what is already happening within the United Nations.

Also thanks to the momentum assured by the 'friends of the rule of law', the General Affairs Council of 16 December 2016 decided on a series of measures aimed at strengthening the annual dialogue, especially in terms of its preparation that will be based on a report by the Commission and the European Agency for fundamental rights. The decision on turning the dialogue into an annual peer review exercise has been put off until a new review, which will occur in 2019. In the presidency's summary, however, it was specified that dialogue should take a twofold form from the next year, comprising, on the one hand, 'a general, interactive discussion about the situation in the Member States' and, on the other hand, a 'thematic discussion' on the challenges faced by the Member States (*Summary on the evaluation of the rule of law dialogue among all member States within the Council*, doc. 14565/16, 17 November 2016).

While the gradualist approach has been maintained, at least Member States have been given the opportunity to engage with each other on how best to address the threats looming over the rule of law at European level. And until 2014, this kind of engagement had no place in the Council.

This constitutes a basic groundwork, upon which much more can be built, in close connection with the other institutions and in a spirit of complementarity with the 'framework' created by the Commission. It is the same approach adopted by the European Parliament when it recently recommended reaching an interinstitutional agreement to set up a unitary monitoring mechanism on democracy, rule of law and fundamental rights (*European Parliament resolution of 25 October 2016 with recommendations to the Commission on the establishment of an EU mechanism on democracy, the rule of law and fundamental rights* (DRF), 2015/2254 (INL)). It is too early to tell whether this initiative will help shore up the action already undertaken by the Commission and speed up the progressive enhancement of the role of the Council. One can safely say, however, that it further confirms the widespread awareness within Community institutions of the need to complete the framework of the instruments at the Union's disposal to ensure respect for fundamental values by all Member States.

VII. The State of Health of Fundamental Values and the Prospects of the European Construct

A. The Risk of a Systemic Crisis Befalling the Integration Process

There are two lessons to be learnt from the latest case (for the time being) centring on the rule of law. The first concerns the very notion of the rule of law – a truly flexible umbrella term that features specific contents routinely highlighted by the criticism it draws. In the case law of the Court of Justice, the dominant theme is the same Court's powers to review legislation; in the negotiations with the candidate countries it has been the creation of an independent judiciary and an impartial public sector, while in the Polish case it is the separation of powers. The rule of law, in its many, distinct facets (which, as the case may be, are defined as its essential components), ultimately coincides with the set of characteristics believed to be typical of a liberal democracy, except those that pertain to the electoral legitimacy of public authorities, which are traced back to that other great founding value of the Union, democracy. When we find it cited alongside other principles/values, clearly held in no less regard by those who drafted the documents we read, we must bear in mind that the rule of law, in its fullest extent, also dwells within the principles that coexist with it; while it appears to be a principle ranked next to others, it is actually a principle that encompasses others. This is what makes the rule of law particularly flexible and legitimises its definition framed by the Commission in the opening passage of the aforementioned *New EU framework to strengthen the rule of law*: the 'backbone of any modern constitutional democracy'; a prerequisite – it goes on to say – for the respect of individual rights.

The definition seems decidedly fitting, and it is even more so in the EU governance system. If it can be said, insofar as individual Member States, that the rule of law is the 'first bulwark' in defence of both fundamental rights and the foundations of pluralist democracy, its function is even further-reaching with regard to the Union. Here the rule of law plays a role akin to that of a lintel: it is the element that holds together a community devoid of coercive powers. In its absence, it is hard to conceive the existence of the other 'constitutional' pillars of the European legal system (we have cited them before: the primacy of European law, direct effect, and mutual recognition), as they are all based on the assumption that legal compliance is a given and that each Member State is endowed with an adequate level of procedures and internal safeguards. Moreover, in its absence, Member States cannot be presumed to maintain that high level of mutual trust which, by itself, can ensure that advanced supplementary choices such as those made over the past 60 years.

And here we run into the second lesson to be learnt from the events we have illustrated so far, and which constitutes the real sore point of our time. Indeed, if some Member States undertake to subvert the precepts of the rule of law at a national level or question its principles at European level – for example, by refusing to comply with the lawfully made decisions of Community institutions – we are not dealing with a mere political issue. We are looking at a systemic, and potentially fatal, crisis in the European construct.

To define the constituent elements of the rule of law and to stress that these concepts are drawn from our common heritage and are therefore shared by the Union and its Member States – in the years when this process was underway (from the Verts case through to the European Convention) – used to be seen as a means of providing the Union with a purely constitutional platform. What seemed to be taking shape was not the Constitution of a national State, but rather the multilevel Constitution illustrated by several authors – from Ingolf Pernice to Andrea Manzella – and essentially made up from the interaction/integration between national Constitutions and the emerging European Constitution. This is why values and rights were now becoming far more important than the free market and the economic rules, which had been the focus of the EU's efforts for the first decades. It was on these foundations that integration was built, European citizenship was enriched with substantive and not blandly procedural content, and the expression 'united in our diversity' acquired a true meaning beyond the rhetorical device.

Today these values are threatened by the risks of involution in some European countries and by the increasingly frequent and vocal protests on the part of anti-establishment political forces.

The Polish and Hungarian cases raise unsettling questions, that we had never had reason to ask ourselves before. Let us not forget that a breach of article 7 had emerged only once before, when, in 1999, the Austrian People's Party formed a governmental alliance with Jörg Heider's Freedom Party (FPÖ). At the time the crisis was quickly defused, but there is no assurance that the same kind of positive and painless outcome is within our grasp today. Also, cracks in the system are not just beginning to show in the two central European countries. The challenge posed by mass migration, that comes on the back of a prolonged economic crisis, is putting enormous strain on all European political systems, abetting the rise of populist movements that are not only anti-establishment (against the European institutions), but often lead the attack on the 'citadel of power' by striking at its very foundations: the values it is built on. Thus, in certain Member States, political forces driven by principles that are clearly antithetical to those that we consider our common principles are in danger of achieving a parliamentary majority. And that is not all, as antithetical principles have begun to make inroads into several national Parliaments, where they are being brandished by smaller political movements, yet strong enough to curb the actions of majority parties, or even push them in their own direction.

B. A Vision of Europe that Europe Cannot Ignore

These developments give rise to distressing questions. If the mutual recognition underlying the common values and principles in article 2 of the Treaty is no more, does the Union still exist? Regardless of the type of institutions it has created, whether governance or sectoral management, from the Central Bank, to the Stability Mechanism, to Frontex, would the base shouldering this whole structure not be doomed to collapse? These are the questions on the agenda at this difficult time we are going through, and the fact that it has come to this raises another question: whether we might have presupposed the existence of a cultural homogeneity that was only assumed and that, once seriously under pressure, has revealed a great many chinks in the armour. That may well be the case. In his lectures on Europe in 1945, Lucien Febvre (1878–1956) warned us that when attempting (once again) to build a united Europe, we had better heed the teachings of history and the profound differences, even hostilities, that it has bequeathed us. Because, history 'once ignored, will exact its revenge' (*L'Europe. Genèse d'une civilisation*, 1999) and the risk is to fail (yet again).

Well, it may be that, trusting in our 'united in diversity' approach, we have overestimated the 'united' and underestimated the 'diversity'. Yet, the process of coalescence of common values we have mentioned here was not make-believe. There was indeed a common heritage which indeed yielded the European precipitate that the EU's institutions sought to extract from it. The Court's rulings, enforcing some of the contents, have been complied with and rarely called into question. The Copenhagen criteria, notwithstanding all the limitations mentioned above, have impacted on the accession negotiations, leading to significant adjustments being made to the institutional frameworks already in force in candidate countries, or still in the pipeline. Finally, the Member States today we call wayward have indeed placed themselves along the watershed, but only after recently amending their Constitutions and adopting equally recent laws. Before then, they sat squarely on the common platform, harbouring their own nationalist attitudes, but not to an extent – or so it seemed – that would set them apart from it.

This is not to say that these ultimate questions are meaningless and that the effects of these chinks are not being felt. These questions make perfect sense, leaving open the potential for a joint effort to address issues that are still outstanding, namely, the need for a dialogue that is first of all of a cultural nature, essential for identifying what we do have in common (and what we cannot go without), while understanding and respecting the reasons of all parties involved, within the constraints set by mutual solidarity.

Having said this, and also because of this, it behoves us to preserve the trust in what we have built, before letting the chinks claim that victory is theirs. To do this, we must start from the realisation that this common platform indeed exists, and we must nurture it more than in the past; on the one hand, upholding its reasons, while, on the other hand, providing non-rhetorical answers to those whose uncertainty and mistrust have led them astray.

C. A Common Heritage to be Rediscovered

If we truly want to dig ourselves out of this hole, perhaps we should start with updating the approach that has so far shaped the discourse on our common European heritage. Perhaps we should stop thinking about the values that define belonging to the European *civitas* as being abstract and timeless, and that only needs to be revealed. And above all we must stop thinking that they can be taken for granted once and for all. The challenge we must accept is to keep on defining them. This means averting the risk of moral relativism, but at the same time acknowledging the intrinsically dynamic nature of common values, which must be constantly reformulated. And this continuous (re)definition process cannot be based upon an authoritative approach, but calls for engaging in constant dialogue among all the Member States of the Union, its institutions, non-governmental organisations, and representatives of civil society.

In light of this, a crucial step has been not only that the Commission has defined its 'early warning' procedure, but also that the Council has decided to provide an institutional framework for the dialogue among the Member States ahead of setting up a mechanism to peer review on one another's adherence to rule of law practices. Over time it could also become a form of monitoring not unlike the one relating to budgets: ultimately, excessive budget deficits are surely not more serious than rule of law failings, so there should be no reason for treating the former with such standardized and greater severity. All the more so, considering that, for the reasons mentioned above, the rule of law crisis can be seen as a far greater threat to the Union's own survival than the economic and financial crisis (Bogdandy, *Ioannidis* (2014)).

It is also true that we are not dealing with numbers here, but with values, national cultures and with our shared culture, along with the interpretations – sometimes necessarily consistent, but also diverging – that follow. It is just as well that dialogue should be the first step, and there are two fundamental reasons for this. First of all, dialogue helps to harmonise the mutual differences that have increased as a result of enlargement: engaging in exchanges and interaction will ensure that peer review parameters are better placed to clarify their own features and, within the bounds of their faultless compatibility, to take stock of otherwise unheeded claims; at this point, these claims will be not only recognised, but the ways in which they shall be addressed shall be brought in line with such compatibility.

Furthermore, we cannot ignore that issues surrounding the rule of law may arise within newly joined Member States, but also affect those with a long-standing European lineage. Certain aspects as to how immigrants are treated, whether asylum seekers or economic refugees, are sometimes at odds with our Constitutions, starting from their detention (albeit for administrative purposes) in the identification and expulsion centres. And again, to what extent national laws governing the building of mosques or the freedom to wear clothing expressing religious identities are compatible with our (allegedly) shared values has already been the subject of a number of European and national Court opinions. But dialogue, and peer review mechanisms, are valuable assets to jointly monitor the common path: in terms of what has been maintained and, for better or for worse, might still change.

The road ahead is long, and we shall find disruptions, rifts, and hurdles along the way. As we have just said, we might even have to acknowledge that the kind of democracy we identify in today is less liberal and more security-minded than the one we had envisaged in our Treaties and documents. Besides, there is no telling that we may even come to realise that, in the end, what unites us – beyond diversity and discrepancy – are still the values and principles that have always fed into the notion of Europe (and which have endured no less taxing times than our own).

Bibliography

Bassanini, F and Tiberi, G (eds), *La Costituzione europea* (Bologna, 2004) (esp G Amato, *Riflessioni conclusive*; M Cartabia, *I diritti fondamentali e la cittadinanza dell'Unione*; F Clementi, *Il Trattato che adotta una Costituzione per l'Europa: dalla Convenzione alla Conferenza intergovernativa*; N Verola, *L'identità dell'Unione*).

Bassanini, F and Tiberi, G (eds), *Le nuove istituzioni europee. Commento al Trattato di Lisbona* (Bologna, 2010) (esp G Amato, *Il Trattato di Lisbona e le prospettive per l'Europa del XXI secolo*; F Frattini, *Il futuro dell'Unione Europea dopo il Trattato di Lisbona*; C Pinelli, *Il Preambolo, i valori, gli obiettivi*; N Verola, *L'identità europea fra eredità e progetto*).

Blanke, H-J and Mangiameli, S (eds), *The Treaty on European Union* (Berlin, 2013) (esp S Fortunato, *Accession to the Union*; C Grabenwarter, K Pabel, *Fundamental rights – The charter and the ECHR*; S Mangiameli, *The homogeneity clause*; S Mangiameli, G Saputelli, *The principles of the federal coercion*).

Braibant, G, *La Charte des droits fondamentaux de l'Union Européenne* (Paris, 2001).

Closa, C, 'The EU needs a better and fairer scrutiny procedure over rule of law compliance' (2015) 1 *Robert Schuman Centre for advanced studies. Policy brief* 1–7.

Closa, C and Kochenov, D (eds), *Reinforcing the rule of law oversight in the European Union* (Cambridge, 2016).

Dehousse, R *Une constitution pour l'Europe?* (Paris, 2002).

Manzella, A, *Sui principi democratici dell'Unione Europea* (Napoli, 2013).

Manzella, A and Lupo, N (eds), *Il Sistema parlamentare euro-nazionale* (Torino, 2014).

Mastroianni, R Pollicino, O and Allegrezza, S et al (eds), *Carta dei diritti fondamentali dell'Unione Europea* (Milano, 2017).

Mény, Y and Surel, Y, *Par le peuple, pour le peuple. Le populisme et les démocraties* (Paris, 2000).

Pernice, I, 'Multilevel constitutionalism and the crisis of democracy in Europe' (2015) 11 *European constitutional law Review* 541–62.

Rodrik, D, 'The future of European democracy' in L van Middelaar and P Van Parijs (eds), *After the storm: how to save democracy in Europe* (Tielt, 2015) 55–65.

'Safeguarding EU values in the Member States – Is something finally happening?' (2005) 52(3) *Common market law Revue* 619–28.

Schroeder, W (ed), *Strengthening the rule of law in Europe* (Oxford, 2016) (esp W Schroeder, *The European Union and the rule of law – State of affairs and ways of strengthening*; A Badó, J Bóka, *Access to justice and judicial independence. Is there a role for the EU?*; PM Huber, *The principle of proportionality*; T von Danwitz, *The rule of law in the recent jurisprudence of the ECJ*; C Closa, D Kochenov, *Reinforcement of the rule of law oversight in the European Union. Key options*; M Claes, M Bonelli, *The rule of law and the constitutionalisation of the European Union*).

von Bogdandy, A and Ioannidis, M, 'Systemic deficiency in the rule of law: what it is, what has been done, what can be done' (2014) 51(1) *Common market law Review* 59–96.

Weiler, JHH, *The Constitution of Europe* (Cambridge, 1999).

Wilms, G, *Protecting fundamental values in the European Union through the rule of law* (Florence, 2017).

Websites

Curti Gialdino, C, *La Commissione Europea dinanzi alla crisi costituzionale polacca: considerazioni sulla tutela dello stato di diritto nell'Unione*, in Federalismi.it, 15 giugno 2016, http://www.federalismi.it/document/editoriale/EDITORIALE_15062016145308.pdf.

Halberstam, D, 'The judicial battle over mutual trust in the EU: recent cracks in the façade', *Verfassungsblog*, 9 June 2016, http://verfassungsblog.de/the-judicial-battle-over-mutual-trust-in-the-eu-recent-cracks-in-the-facade/.

Mastroianni, R, 'Stato di diritto o ragion di stato? La difficile rotta verso un controllo europeo del rispetto dei valori dell'Unione negli Stati membri', *Eurojus.it*, 2017, http://rivista.eurojus.it/stato-di-diritto-o-ragion-di-stato-la-difficile-rotta-verso-un-controllo-europeo-del-rispetto-dei-valori-dellunione-negli-stati-membri-dialogo-con-ugo-villani/.

Pinelli, C, 'Protecting the fundamentals, article 7 of the Treaty on the European Union and beyond', *Foundation for European progressive studies*, 25 September 2012, http://www.feps-europe.eu/assets/9a4619cf-1a01-4f96-8e27-f33b65337a9b/protecting%20the%20fundamentals.pdf.

All web pages are understood as having last been visited on 23 June 2018.

4

Competition and Solidarity in the European Construct

MARIO MONTI

Since its origins in the 1950s, European integration has paid great attention to competition and solidarity, viewing them as two fundamental ingredients for economic and social well being in the Member States, as well as for their economic integration, which in turn was seen as an instrument of growth and as an antidote to the causes of repeated bloodshed.

For a number of years now, however, many have come to view competition and solidarity as antithetical elements. The market economy, liberalisation, the single market and fiscal discipline, all fundamental pillars of European integration, are perceived as the causes of social inequalities and of the disaffection of many citizens with European integration. Competition, the cornerstone of a free market economy, is held responsible for the undeniable difficulties sustained by the weaker social classes. Yet, as we will see below, it is hard to argue persuasively that competition functions against solidarity. Actually, we believe the opposite to be true. It helps to protect the interests of consumers and small businesses and, through its stimulus to growth, to create job opportunities.

In order to acquire the necessary tools to express informed opinions on these extremely current and controversial issues, we need to examine, albeit briefly, the historical and cultural roots that illustrate the major role of competition and solidarity in the European project; followed by the gradual implementation, through successive treaties, of the different components of a social market economy at European level, which include competition and solidarity; and finally, the governance of competition and solidarity, that is, the allocation of the responsibility for implementing the two concepts at the different levels of government, namely, domestic or Community.

Next, we will examine cursorily the main changes that have taken place both in the European integration process and in the global context in which it is taking place; these changes will explain the growing tensions that have arisen between the two, formally harmonious, components of the *competition/solidarity* combination.

Finally, we will examine an issue that may carry very significant consequences for the future of European integration or, at worst, disintegration: what is the state today of solidarity and competition, not with reference to the social and economic players in Europe, but to the Member States themselves? And how can the two concepts evolve in the coming years? We will see that two trends are currently underway. The first is a tendency, and a dangerous one at that unless promptly stemmed, towards greater divergence among Member States in terms of their political cultures, which lies at the root of a growing inadequacy in the European economic governance framework, with serious social repercussions. Today's external environment presents Europe with challenges unseen for many decades. It is possible that these may foster a greater sense of cohesion, soften certain antagonistic attitudes between States, and lead to greater mutual solidarity in the face of common challenges.

I. Historical and Cultural Roots: From the United States, to Divided Germany, to a United Europe

In the second half of the 1940s, when European countries set to work on physically rebuilding their societies and reorganising their institutions after World War II, public policies concerning competition and solidarity were different from one country to the next.

In all countries, to varying degrees and in different ways, intervention mechanisms geared towards the principles of solidarity had already been introduced in previous decades. To heal the wounds that the war had inflicted so heavily on the social and territorial fabric, the number of solidarity-based initiatives multiplied, to the extent of creating in some countries a veritable 'welfare state'.

Not so for competition policy. If social policies in Europe had long been more advanced than in the United States of America, no European country had ever developed an antitrust system, that is, rules designed to ensure that neutral conditions of competition would prevail in the economic system, and the necessary institutions to enforce these rules, which the United States had begun to introduce more than half a century earlier (with the Sherman Act of 1890, the Clayton Act and the Federal Trade Commission Act of 1914) and which had shown their effectiveness, through the enforcement of these rules by the Department of Justice, the Federal Trade Commission, the Attorneys General of the individual Federated States and the Courts.

Two historical-institutional experiences in the United States greatly influenced the shaping of the legal system of West Germany (German Federal Republic), through the post-war American administration in Germany. One was the American antitrust experience or competition policy, to quote the more widely used expression in Europe. The other was the monetary policy pursued in the United States by the Federal Reserve Board. We make a brief mention of this here, although it does not directly affect either competition or solidarity, because there is a notable parallel between the two operations of institutional transplantation from the United States to a divided, post-war Germany.

In the view of the victorious Allied powers, and in particular of the United States, two reasons of an economic nature were among the main causes that led Germany to unleash World War II, a mere 20 years after the World War I: the first was the massive inflation or hyperinflation of the 1920s, which had led to a gross economic inefficiency, deep social tensions and the spread of a general sense of mistrust, all of which favoured the rise to power of Adolf Hitler; the second was the strong concentration of economic and industrial power in a few hands that shared close ties (trust) also with the political powers-that-be, and were mainly active in sectors that would benefit from rearmament (coal, steel, chemical, mechanical industrial groups).

To forestall the possibility of massive inflation occurring again, a central bank independent of government was introduced, modelled on the Federal Reserve Board: the *Deutsche Bundesbank* (German Federal Bank). In an effort to prevent any trusts comprising potentially war-related industries from forming anew, an open policy supporting free market competition, against corporate trusts and cartels, was encouraged; for this purpose the *Bundeskartellamt* (Federal Office on cartels) was set up, mirroring the objectives and intervention procedures adopted by US antitrust regulators, as mentioned above.

In this way, the concerns of the United States and other Western countries, aimed at avoiding the future recurrence of objective conditions that could pave the way to new abuses or deterioration, latched on to an important development in the fields of political philosophy, constitutional doctrine and economic vision begun in the 1930s by the Freiburg school in Germany. Spearheaded by a group of economists (including Walter Eucken, Wilhelm Röpke and Alfred Müller-Armack) not far removed from the economic theories that Luigi Einaudi was developing in Italy, this school of thought was generally liberal, but firmly believed in the incisive role of public authorities since not all forms of competition, if left unattended, lead to a pursuit of common interests, and because market outcomes may sometimes require State intervention so that their consequences in terms of income distribution (and this is akin to 'solidarity') are deemed satisfactory for a democratic society.

The principles of the Freiburg school – applied to West German institutions also on account of autonomous American pressure on Germany after the war – constituted the theoretical basis for Ordoliberalism (*Ordoliberalismus*) and for the social market economy (*Soziale Marktwirtschaft*). The transformation of these schools of thought into effective economic policy measures was above all the work of Ludwig Erhard, the West German minister of the Economy from 1949 to 1963 and chancellor from 1963 to 1966.

Germany's 'economic miracle' in the 1950s and 1960s was largely attributed – on the part of both German and foreign observers – to the consistent and lasting application of the guidelines suggested by the social market economy. Indeed, the same European integration process has, in its various stages, been inspired more by the principles of the social market economy than by Germany's growing economic and political authority among the States participating in this process.

II. The Social Market Economy from Germany to Europe

Insofar as the social and economic aspects are concerned, the various treaties which gave rise to the European Union that we know today can be regarded as the gradual transposition of the essential features of the German model, inspired by the principles of social market economy.

A. Treaty of Paris (1951)

After the Declaration by Robert Schuman, who on 9 May 1950 urged France and Germany, as well as any other country willing to make such a commitment, to pool together the coal and steel industries, which had been converted to manufacturing instruments of war twice in 30 years, the 1951 Treaty of Paris established the European coal and steel Community (ECSC). It included France, Germany, Italy, Belgium, the Netherlands and Luxembourg.

The Treaty set in motion a long and difficult process of building a united Europe, starting from its economic integration, a subject rich in political significance, while not shying away from future ambitions.

In terms of the social market economy, the first element that was 'implanted' in Europe was the market itself, with the creation of a common market, albeit limited to a few, yet fundamental, industry sectors. Alongside this, competition rules were introduced as well. In particular, unfair or discriminatory competitive practices (article 60, para 1) along with all distortive agreements on competition (article 65, para 1), except for specific exemptions (article 65, para 2). Regulations on mergers and acquisitions were established and, though in an embryonic manner, the abuse of a dominant position was prohibited (article 66).

Among its competences, the governing body of the ECSC, known as the High Authority, took on the role of regulator for competition matters: this was the first European supranational authority.

B. Treaties of Rome (1957)

On 25 March 1957, the treaties that established the European Economic Community (EEC) and the European Atomic Energy Community (Euratom) were signed in Rome. Euratom did not have its own competition rules, so the general rules of competition law, introduced by the EEC Treaty (after the specific rules introduced by the ECSC Treaty), applied to the nuclear energy sector as well.

From 1 January 1958, the day that saw the coming into being of the EEC and, consequently, the European Commission, the latter became the European competition authority with general competence (excluding the coal and steel industries that remained under the authority of the ECSC).

The competition rules adopted in the Treaty of Rome have since remained largely unchanged and have been taken up in the more recent Treaty of Lisbon (signed in 2007, and which came into force in 2009). The provisions are reproduced below, with the numbering assigned to the specific relevant articles when transposed into the Treaty on European Union (TEU). The enforcement exercised by the Commission takes place under the supervision of the Court of Justice of the European Union.

Competition rules are set out in Title VII, chapter 1 of the TFEU. Some of them apply to undertakings (section 1), while others address State-granted aid (section 2).

The rules applicable to undertakings are contained in but a few, relatively straightforward articles that are characterised by great adaptability, as the US examples with the Sherman Act and the Clayton Act have shown. The principles are simple and very long-lasting, as they lend themselves to guiding both the behaviour of undertakings and the evaluations of the competition authorities, even in the deeply, rapidly changing manifestations of economic life that, in turn, is influenced by innovation and globalisation.

Article 101 (ex article 81 of the Treaty establishing the European Community, TEC) refers to agreements between undertakings:

> 1. The following shall be prohibited as incompatible with the internal market: all agreements between undertakings, decisions by associations of undertakings and concerted practices which may affect trade between Member States and which have as their object or effect the prevention, restriction or distortion of competition within the internal market, and in particular

those which: a) directly or indirectly fix purchase or selling prices or any other trading conditions; b) limit or control production, markets, technical development, or investment; c) share markets or sources of supply; d) apply dissimilar conditions to equivalent transactions with other trading parties, thereby placing them at a competitive disadvantage; e) make the conclusion of contracts subject to acceptance by the other parties of supplementary obligations which, by their nature or according to commercial usage, have no connection with the subject of such contracts.

2. Any agreements or decisions prohibited pursuant to this Article shall be automatically void.
3. The provisions of paragraph 1 may, however, be declared inapplicable in the case of:
   - any agreement or category of agreements between undertakings,
   - any decision or category of decisions by associations of undertakings, and
   - any concerted practice or category of concerted practices,

which contributes to improving the production or distribution of goods or to promoting technical or economic progress, while allowing consumers a fair share of the resulting benefit, and which does not:

(a) impose on the undertakings concerned restrictions which are not indispensable to the attainment of these objectives;
(b) afford such undertakings the possibility of eliminating competition in respect of a substantial part of the products in question.

Article 102 (ex article 82 TEC) refers to abuse of a dominant position:

Any abuse by one or more undertakings of a dominant position within the internal market or in a substantial part of it shall be prohibited as incompatible with the internal market in so far as it may affect trade between Member States. Such abuse may, in particular, consist in:

(a) directly or indirectly imposing unfair purchase or selling prices or other unfair trading conditions;
(b) limiting production, markets or technical development to the prejudice of consumers;
(c) applying dissimilar conditions to equivalent transactions with other trading parties, thereby placing them at a competitive disadvantage;
(d) making the conclusion of contracts subject to acceptance by the other parties of supplementary obligations which, by their nature or according to commercial usage, have no connection with the subject of such contracts.

Article 103 (ex article 83 TEC) deals with implementation aspects:

1. The appropriate regulations or directives to give effect to the principles set out in Articles 101 and 102 shall be laid down by the Council, on a proposal from the Commission and after consulting the European Parliament.
2. The regulations or directives referred to in paragraph 1 shall be designed in particular:
   (a) to ensure compliance with the prohibitions laid down in Article 101(1) and in Article 102 by making provision for fines and periodic penalty payments;
   (b) to lay down detailed rules for the application of Article 101(3), taking into account the need to ensure effective supervision on the one hand, and to simplify administration to the greatest possible extent on the other;
   (c) to define, if need be, in the various branches of the economy, the scope of the provisions of Articles 101 and 102;
   (d) to define the respective functions of the Commission and of the Court of Justice of the European Union in applying the provisions laid down in this paragraph;
   (e) to determine the relationship between national laws and the provisions contained in this Section or adopted pursuant to this Article.

Article 104 (ex article 84 TEC) lays down transitional rules:

> Until the entry into force of the provisions adopted in pursuance of Article 103, the authorities in Member States shall rule on the admissibility of agreements, decisions and concerted practices and on abuse of a dominant position in the internal market in accordance with the law of their country and with the provisions of Article 101, in particular paragraph 3, and of Article 102.

Article 105 (ex article 85 TEC) defines the powers of the Commission:

> 1. Without prejudice to Article 104, the Commission shall ensure the application of the principles laid down in Articles 101 and 102. On application by a Member State or on its own initiative, and in cooperation with the competent authorities in the Member States, which shall give it their assistance, the Commission shall investigate cases of suspected infringement of these principles. If it finds that there has been an infringement, it shall propose appropriate measures to bring it to an end.
>
> 2. If the infringement is not brought to an end, the Commission shall record such infringement of the principles in a reasoned decision. The Commission may publish its decision and authorise Member States to take the measures, the conditions and details of which it shall determine, needed to remedy the situation.
>
> 3. The Commission may adopt regulations relating to the categories of agreement in respect of which the Council has adopted a regulation or a directive pursuant to Article 103(2)(b).

Article 106 (ex article 86 TEC) deals with public undertakings and services of general economic interest:

> 1. In the case of public undertakings and undertakings to which Member States grant special or exclusive rights, Member States shall neither enact nor maintain in force any measure contrary to the rules contained in the Treaties, in particular to those rules provided for in Article 18 and Articles 101 to 109.
>
> 2. Undertakings entrusted with the operation of services of general economic interest or having the character of a revenue-producing monopoly shall be subject to the rules contained in the Treaties, in particular to the rules on competition, in so far as the application of such rules does not obstruct the performance, in law or in fact, of the particular tasks assigned to them. The development of trade must not be affected to such an extent as would be contrary to the interests of the Union.
>
> 3. The Commission shall ensure the application of the provisions of this Article and shall, where necessary, address appropriate directives or decisions to Member States.

Section 2 is instead dedicated to aid granted by the States. At this point, we enter into a particular area of tasks pertaining to the Commission and the Court of Justice, above it. In fact, only in the European Union are the administrative (Commission) and judicial (Court of Justice) institutions that supervise the compliance with competition rules on the part of undertakings also invested with the task of supervising the Member States, insofar as any aid granted by States. The logic is simple: it would not make sense to strive towards the creation of a single market to improve the efficiency of an economically integrated area, if undertakings were then free to distort the market with behaviours harmful to competition; likewise, it would not make sense to attain a single market in which, while compliant with competition rules in the case of undertakings, States were allowed to grant aid to undertakings or other entities as they please, thus altering the level playing field.

Naturally, extending constraints for the protection of competition to Member States requires the existence of a supranational power, exercised by the Commission and the

Court, conferred upon them in the Treaty by the same Member States, who thus undertake not to breach these rules. This supranational element does not exist in the other jurisdictions with whom the Commission measures itself and cooperates closely. Whether in the United States or Japan, China or Brazil, competition regulators do not have binding powers over their respective parliaments and governments, as is the case with the Commission and the Court in relation to the parliaments and governments of the Member States.

On the subject of State aid provisions, Article 107 (ex article 87 TEC) lays down the following:

> 1. Save as otherwise provided in the Treaties, any aid granted by a Member State or through State resources in any form whatsoever which distorts or threatens to distort competition by favouring certain undertakings or the production of certain goods shall, in so far as it affects trade between Member States, be incompatible with the internal market.
>
> 2. The following shall be compatible with the internal market:
>
> (a) aid having a social character, granted to individual consumers, provided that such aid is granted without discrimination related to the origin of the products concerned;
>
> (b) aid to make good the damage caused by natural disasters or exceptional occurrences;
>
> (c) aid granted to the economy of certain areas of the Federal Republic of Germany affected by the division of Germany, in so far as such aid is required in order to compensate for the economic disadvantages caused by that division. Five years after the entry into force of the Treaty of Lisbon, the Council, acting on a proposal from the Commission, may adopt a decision repealing this point.
>
> 3. The following may be considered to be compatible with the internal market:
>
> (a) aid to promote the economic development of areas where the standard of living is abnormally low or where there is serious underemployment, and of the regions referred to in Article 349, in view of their structural, economic and social situation;
>
> (b) aid to promote the execution of an important project of common European interest or to remedy a serious disturbance in the economy of a Member State;
>
> (c) aid to facilitate the development of certain economic activities or of certain economic areas, where such aid does not adversely affect trading conditions to an extent contrary to the common interest;
>
> (d) aid to promote culture and heritage conservation where such aid does not affect trading conditions and competition in the Union to an extent that is contrary to the common interest;
>
> (e) such other categories of aid as may be specified by decision of the Council on a proposal from the Commission.

Article 108 (ex article 88 TEC) contains rules of substance and procedure:

> 1. The Commission shall, in cooperation with Member States, keep under constant review all systems of aid existing in those States. It shall propose to the latter any appropriate measures required by the progressive development or by the functioning of the internal market.
>
> 2. If, after giving notice to the parties concerned to submit their comments, the Commission finds that aid granted by a State or through State resources is not compatible with the internal market having regard to Article 107, or that such aid is being misused, it shall decide that the State concerned shall abolish or alter such aid within a period of time to be determined by the Commission. If the State concerned does not comply with this decision within the prescribed time, the Commission or any other interested State may, in derogation from the provisions of Articles 258 and 259, refer the matter to the Court of Justice of the European Union direct. On application by a Member State, the Council may, acting unanimously, decide that aid which that

> State is granting or intends to grant shall be considered to be compatible with the internal market, in derogation from the provisions of Article 107 or from the regulations provided for in Article 109, if such a decision is justified by exceptional circumstances. If, as regards the aid in question, the Commission has already initiated the procedure provided for in the first subparagraph of this paragraph, the fact that the State concerned has made its application to the Council shall have the effect of suspending that procedure until the Council has made its attitude known. If, however, the Council has not made its attitude known within three months of the said application being made, the Commission shall give its decision on the case.
>
> 3. The Commission shall be informed, in sufficient time to enable it to submit its comments, of any plans to grant or alter aid. If it considers that any such plan is not compatible with the internal market having regard to Article 107, it shall without delay initiate the procedure provided for in paragraph 2. The Member State concerned shall not put its proposed measures into effect until this procedure has resulted in a final decision.
>
> 4. The Commission may adopt regulations relating to the categories of State aid that the Council has, pursuant to Article 109, determined may be exempted from the procedure provided for by paragraph 3 of this Article.

Again on a procedural level, Article 109 (ex article 89 TEC) provides that:

> the Council, on a proposal from the Commission and after consulting the European Parliament, may make any appropriate regulations for the application of Articles 107 and 108 and may in particular determine the conditions in which Article 108(3) shall apply and the categories of aid exempted from this procedure.

Competition rules have been a cornerstone of European integration and of the Paris (1951) and Rome (1957) Treaties from the outset. It would not have made much sense to speak of Common European Market (as the EEC was called at the time) if competition had been stifled by cartels or restrictive agreements. The same applies to State aid, which, if incompatible with the Treaty, creates unacceptable distortions in the allocation of resources. EU competition policy has successfully implemented, over the years, a strong common approach at European level and a strict enforcement of the rules. When the single market was set up, it was clear that competition policy had a crucial role to play, so much so that it is regarded today as a pillar of the so-called European economic constitution.

Undertakings do not necessarily react to a more competitive environment by improving their efficiency or the quality of their products. They could also try to reduce competitive pressure by engaging in tacit collusion or forming cartels. Alternatively, they could ask for State aid to gain an advantage over their competitors.

Mergers, collusion and State aid are three separate issues, but equally relevant to competition policy.

A greater degree of competition will put pressure on poorly-performing undertakings and on sectors already suffering from structural issues. Furthermore, the wider markets will offer new opportunities to exploit economies of scale. In this context, there tends to be a great deal of company reconstruction operations and an increase in the number of cross-border mergers and acquisitions.

The Commission examines mergers and acquisitions before they can take place. The subject matter is governed by the merger regulation adopted in 1989, reformed by the Council regulation 139/2004.

In the field of mergers, competition authorities have a duty to prevent dominant positions from coming about or being strengthened, while allowing undertakings to innovate and react quickly to the changing market. There should also be an effort to hinder the creation of oligopolies, in which companies, under certain market conditions (significant barriers to entry in the market, presence of the same undertakings in neighbouring markets, weak technological advances, transparent prices, etc) might feel it is convenient to refrain from a vigorous competitive behaviour. This often happens in certain manufacturing sectors. It is no coincidence that many of the mergers that have caused competition problems belong to the manufacturing sector.

Companies in oligopolistic industries may be tempted to engage in tacit collusion or to form cartels. The formation of cartels is one of the most harmful practices for the consumer.

Another reason for concern is that companies that have difficulty in dealing with a more competitive environment might apply for State aid. As a general rule, the Commission views State aid as adding little to lasting economic well-being. On the contrary, experience has shown that they lead to unfair competition between companies, market distortions and inefficient allocation of resources. They also endanger the results of the single market when their effect is to increase barriers to trade.

The only benefits of State aid are, under precise and strict monitoring conditions, those aimed at remedying market imperfections. For example, small businesses are an important and dynamic part of the European economy, as well as a key source of job creation. However, their access to capital markets is limited. Therefore, we can allow various small and medium-sized enterprises (SMEs) to access aid programmes in order to 'level the playing field' by helping them compete. Likewise, regional aid and support for research and development programmes and the environment can, under certain circumstances, be useful to remedy market imbalances and to achieve other policy objectives, such as economic cohesion.

The introduction of the single currency and the process of liberalisation, together with globalisation, have offered and offer great opportunities for the modernisation and strengthening of the European economy. It is evident that many of the advantages that can be drawn from these developments derive in particular from the expected increase in competition in increasingly liberalised and integrated markets. For this reason, competition authorities have a considerable responsibility in positively adapting to these new realities.

If governments or undertakings helped to dampen the functioning of the competitive mechanism, this would not only result in harm to consumers and competitors, but could eventually weaken those businesses and those sectors that initially benefited from this behaviour.

C. Treaty of Maastricht (1992)

By virtue of the combined provisions of the Treaty of Rome and 35 years of its application to a number of Member States that in the meantime had increased from the six founders to 12, the European Community – which under the Maastricht Treaty had adopted the new denomination of European Union – had widely tested two key principles of the social market economy: the market, still undergoing ever-increasing integration and extension, and competition.

Under the Maastricht Treaty, the European construct – after historical transformations such as the fall of the Berlin Wall, which was erected when the EEC was just three years old,

German unification, and the aspiration of former Soviet bloc countries to move closer to the EU until eventually become part of it – set itself highly ambitious objectives, even though they were probably indispensable in order to absorb without excessive strain a Germany enlarged in every sense and to secure the single market against recurring currency crises.

The elements that, having proved to be workable in Germany, Europe wanted to draw from the social market economy were, on this occasion, numerous and demanding: the currency, which would have to be single and solid as the German mark; a European central bank (ECB), as independent as the *Bundesbank* from political power and pressure to dissolve social tensions into higher inflation with the aim of achieving also in the rest of the EU that monetary stability and low interest rates that had characterised Germany; capping the deficit and public debt of the Member States, with penalties for breaches; and banning the European system of central banks (ECB plus national central banks in the single currency zone) from financing the States.

With regard to our *competition/solidarity* combination, what consequences could be expected from such a quantum leap in the integration process?

In terms of competition, it caused the demise of a form of competition against which the Community system created by the Treaty of Rome was powerless: the unfair competition due to competitive devaluations, a scenario which from time to time some States were forced into by currency markets or was brought on by incurred losses of competitiveness. A 'healthy' competition, not distorted, of the type that pushes companies and consumers towards an efficient allocation of resources, would instead benefit from the single currency, which facilitates price comparisons.

And what in terms of solidarity? The question was controversial from the start, and it would have remained so even later, over the years. Many believe that the Treaty of Maastricht has reduced the margins for effective solidarity, as it means national public budgets can be managed less freely, at least insofar as public spending financed by fiscal deficits is concerned. Instead, in the view of others – including the author of this essay – the new treaty does not undermine social solidarity in the slightest. However, there is an important qualitative transformation, and for the better. The Maastricht Treaty restricts the possibility for the government of a State at a given time, to provide social solidarity handouts to its citizens (and voters) at that time, leaving future generations to foot the bill.

There are three ways in which public policies can provide social solidarity. Two of these provide a fake solidarity mechanism and Maastricht restricts them (political prices at odds with the need for competitive markets, deficit social spending that can exceed the set budgetary limits). But Maastricht, by itself, does not restrict the third and only form of true solidarity: public spending, in favour of those who are deemed worthy of solidarity, covered by taxation. We can state that Maastricht, far from being an 'enemy' of social solidarity, is the best instrument for safeguarding future generations.

The Treaty of Maastricht contains far more than the convergence criteria towards the single currency and also far more than a mere recipe for monetary union. It is essentially an 'economic constitution' based on a few essential principles, mentioned above: open and competitive markets; fiscal discipline; independence of central banks; entrusting them with the objective of achieving price stability.

The economic policies of Member States increasingly conform to this economic model. Even countries that fail to comply with the numerical parameters set out by the

Treaty have always chosen to abide by that economic policy model. Without Maastricht, everything would be much more reversible, depending on the fluctuations of national policies.

The concept of social market economy relies on the market mechanism. It is rooted in the experience that this market mechanism is the most efficient way to meet consumers' demand for goods and services, while pushing companies to improve productivity, expand supply, innovate and create jobs. In short, it is acknowledged that market forces are the most efficient generator of prosperity.

Yet, the social market economy does not tolerate laissez-faire capitalism. It acknowledges that a vibrant economy is indispensable for producing the material basis for the existence of human society – along with all other non-economic, human and cultural dimensions. However, it comes with a series of requirements that public bodies are under a duty to safeguard. These State institutions must not leave the economy to its own devices or accept any solution resulting from the way the market operates.

Indeed, what is needed is a clear framework, strictly enforced by public authorities. First off, society's social standards and other objectives must be met. This is reflected, for example, in the individual and collective rights of workers, in the monitoring of working conditions, in the protection of persons with specific needs and so on. Secondly, the efficiency of the markets must not be blocked, curtailed or distorted by improper behaviour on the part of the same players operating in the markets. Hence, a strong regulatory framework on competition and its strict enforcement are of fundamental importance.

If we look at the Treaty, we find the same basic messages typical of a social market economy. Indeed, the Member States have agreed on the creation of a single market in which the forces at work provide the greatest benefit to European consumers. For this reason they have framed strong rules to protect the market against restrictions and distortions, whether they are caused by the same economic operators or introduced by the Member States, in particular through State aid.

The emphasis placed on the benefits for consumers is evidenced by the way in which competition rules are written. In fact, the wording reflects the fundamental idea that the consumer should take full advantage of the generated surplus. Furthermore, the Treaty also reflects the importance of other values pertaining to the 'European model'. And this is particularly evident when it is necessary to strike a careful balance between economic efficiency and social cohesion.

D. Treaty of Lisbon (2007)

With the Treaty of Lisbon, stipulated in 2007 when the Member States were now 27, the European Union also formally takes the definitive step in the choice of its social-economic model: it mentions for the first time in a treaty the 'social market economy'.

In fact, article 3 TEU (consolidated version, former article 2 TEU) states in paragraph 3 that:

> The Union shall establish an internal market. It shall work for the sustainable development of Europe based on balanced economic growth and price stability, a highly competitive social

> market economy, aiming at full employment and social progress, and a high level of protection and improvement of the quality of the environment. It shall promote scientific and technological advance.

Among the various objectives it stated, all of fundamental importance for the Union, two have more structural or constitutive connotations ('an internal market' and 'a social market economy', the latest addition under the Treaty of Lisbon, which had essentially inspired the treaties from Paris onwards), the others are somewhat descriptive of the purposes upon which the various policies emphasising those two structural foundations should be modelled: sustainable development, balanced growth, price stability, strong competitiveness, full employment, social progress, quality of the environment, scientific and technological progress.

For the social market economy it is the culmination of a cultural, political and institutional journey of great significance. Concepts conceived by the school of Freiburg between the two world wars, the experience of American institutions and policies, the singular but full confluence with the US concerns about the future of Germany, are factors that have contributed to give post-war Germany all the features of an innovative experiment: the construction of a social market economy.

The positive results of that experiment have generated an interest for that model in the rest of Europe, culminating in the 'request' to share it at a European-wide level. This transposition has been favoured both by the 'offer' coming from a far from reluctant Germany, and by the bargaining power bestowed upon said country owing to the fact that other Member States, not Germany, were calling for the introduction of the single currency. Indeed, a Germany not keen to share the same currency could easily request that the other countries should effectively adapt their 'economic constitutions' to the model that had enabled its growth and stability. Therefore, both competition and solidarity, essential features of the German social market economy, have seen their respective roles evolve, and generally gain strength, in the European integration process.

III. The Governance of Competition and Solidarity

There is an asymmetry in the Community legal system, shaped by the treaties reviewed above, between the level of governance tasked with the pursuit of solidarity, which is mainly the national level, and the appropriate level for achieving the single market and competition, which is predominantly on a Community basis.

There is obviously a clear logic in this assignment of responsibilities, yet this perceived asymmetry has also led to a negative backlash over time. In the eyes of citizens, most of the 'hard' decisions are taken at EU level (in Brussels) – such are the removals of barriers to the single market that social forces or interest groups would rather maintain, the banning of company mergers, the rejection of certain State aids – while many 'soft' measures are deliberated at national or subnational level, such as unemployment benefits or various allowances.

This has often resulted in an aversion to the EU, in these cases for understandable and well-grounded reasons, which has been compounded by the animosity wrongfully fuelled by national politicians, who in all countries are wont to apportion blame to the EU for whatever people do not like and to take credit for any specific positive outcome, even when these may be the direct consequence of EU interventions.

As regards the allocation of duties in ensuring compliance with competition rules, the EU has introduced a significant change effective from 2004 (the reform and 'modernisation' programme, with regulation 1/2003).

In 1958, when the European Community came into being, no Member State had passed a national law on competition or established a national competition authority, with the exception of Germany. Moreover, in the absence of relevant case law, the surveillance over legislation concerning agreements between undertakings was entirely preventive and had to be necessarily carried out by the Commission. The mechanism was somewhat cumbersome and slow, as well.

Over the years, the number of Member States that had passed a law and established a national competition authority had risen. There was also an abundance of relevant case law, based on the decisions of the Commission and the rulings of the Court of Justice. Finally, the community of expert competition lawyers, who could capably advise companies by submitting competent assessments of possible violations, had grown in size and proficiency. This would entail financial savings and a greater streamlining of operations, without endangering legal certainty for corporations, while promoting a broad decentralisation of the labour market, endowing national competition authorities, as well as national courts, with powers previously reserved to the Commission. It followed that the Commission was able to direct its resources at the most significant cases whether in terms of scope or degree of novelty. With regard to competition, this paved the way to the shaping of a 'governance by network' approach with the Commission at the helm, but ensuring major involvement on the part of the national authorities (that, alongside the Commission, make up the European competition network) and of the national courts.

IV. Integration Subject to the Test of Nationalism and Protectionism

International economic integration has entered a more problematic phase in the last 10 to 15 years, and this is especially true in Europe where greater progress had been achieved since the 1950s. In terms of European policies, this phenomenon has affected more specifically policies aimed at the implementation of the single market and at maintaining conditions of competition therein. In this section we will examine the new challenges facing integration policies, primarily those dedicated to the single market and to competition. In a non-specialist review, as is the case here, we shall discuss economic integration, the single market, and competition with a certain degree of interchangeability.

At present, economic integration in Europe finds itself at a critical juncture, as it faces three challenges.

The first challenge comes from the erosion of the political and social support for market integration in Europe. The single market is seen by many Europeans – citizens as well as political leaders – with suspicion, fear and sometimes open hostility. Two mutually reinforcing trends are at work here: an 'integration fatigue', dampening the appetite for a bigger and stronger Europe and for a single market, and more recently a 'market fatigue', which undermines confidence in the role of the market. The single market today is less popular than ever, while Europe needs it more than ever.

The second challenge comes from uneven policy attention given to the development of the various components of an effective and sustainable single market. Some of the difficulties encountered by the single market in recent years can be traced back not only to the incomplete welding together of the national markets into one European market, but also to the unfinished business on two other fronts: the expansion to new sectors to accompany a fast changing economy and the effort to ensure that the single market is a space of freedom and opportunity that works for all, citizens, consumers and SMEs.

A third challenge comes from a sense of complacency that has gained strength until about the year 2000, as if the single market had been really completed and could thus be put to rest as a political priority. The single market was felt to be 'yesterday's business', in need of regular maintenance but not of active promotion. The shift of attention away from the single market was further strengthened by the need to concentrate the EU's political energy on other challenging building blocks of the European construction: monetary union, enlargement and institutional reforms.

With the entry into force of the Lisbon Treaty in December 2009, all the three major priorities have been achieved, and there is no reason to deflect attention away from the single market. On the contrary, the correct functioning of the monetary union and of enlargement call the single market back on stage.

'It is impossible to fall in love with the single market', Jacques Delors used to say. That the single market is not loved is normal and even reassuring. A market is an instrument, not an end in itself. As the financial crisis has shown, there are risks inherent in the perception of a market as a superior entity, as if it were equipped with the power to guarantee efficiency, even in the absence of adequate rules and strict supervision. Many seem to have forgotten that the market is a good servant, but a bad master. Yet the single market is an essential tool serving the European Union. First, it is a necessary, though not sufficient, condition for the proper functioning of the European economy, just as well-functioning domestic markets are for national economies. Secondly, and even more importantly, a robust single market is key to the overall health of the European Union, precisely because it represents the very foundation of the integration project.

The changes in the context are individually well known, but it is sometimes neglected how profoundly their combined action has changed the way of operating of the single market and what citizens and business expect from it. It will be sufficient to list the key changes, all of which intervened in the 25 years since Delors' White Paper, which in 1985 launched the objective of creating a single (or internal) market for 1992. Some changes took place well beyond Europe: (a) globalisation and the emergence of new economic powers; (b) the technological revolution, due in particular to information and communication technologies; (c) the growing importance of services in the economy; and (d) an increasing awareness of environmental issues and related to climate change.

Besides having to respond to these global changes, Europe's single market has had to cope with a number of deep transformations, which were specific to Europe: (a) the collapse of the Soviet bloc, hence of a threat that had been a key driver of integration; (b) the enlargement of the Union from 10 to 28 Member States (27 once Brexit is completed); (c) much greater economic diversity, also linked to enlargement; (d) the introduction of a single currency; (e) an increase in migrations and in cultural diversity; (f) an open rejection of further (or even present and future) EU integration, through referenda in several Member States; (g) explicit clarification of the limits of acceptability, by one Member State, of further EU integration in the future (ruling of the German Federal Constitutional Court of July 2009); and (h) the Lisbon Treaty: 'The Union [...] shall work for [...] sustainable development [and] a highly competitive social market economy' (article 3 TEU).

Each of these changes, let alone their combined play, has important institutional, economic and political implications on the nature and the functioning of the single market. It will be necessary to keep these implications well in mind, if a new promotion of both is to have the desired effect. The case for the single market needs to be made afresh, in a context that is profoundly different from the one in which the project was launched over 30 years ago. In particular, the globalisation that has developed since then was not created by the European single market. Indeed, a single market, if it is strengthened to resist nationalism and adjourned to be more consistent with other concerns and policy objectives, is the best response to globalisation. In an economic union, the economic, social and environmental welfare of European citizens can be defended better than with economic disintegration and purely national measures.

Nonetheless, a legitimate question may be raised: is it really necessary to have consensus in order to have and to further develop, competition and a strong single market? And if so to what extent? Do not competition and the single market fall within the scope of an area of clear Community competence, with the Commission entrusted with the executive function of enforcing the rules, under the watchful eye of the Court of Justice? At this point a distinction must be made between the enforcement of existing rules and the adoption of new rules or, more broadly, policy initiatives to relaunch and develop the single market.

As regards enforcement, the Commission is indeed entrusted with a set of instruments that it has the right, and the duty, to use as guardian of the treaties, under the sole control of the European Court of Justice and with no need for consensus by anybody else. It is important, however, that enforcement policies, as well as specific enforcement decisions, be conducted and presented in such a way as to generate wide understanding and even consensus. The more vigorous is enforcement, as is needed to ensure a competitive single market, the more it is necessary to explain it persuasively, so as to avoid backlashes against the EU generally and the single market specifically.

As for the adoption of new rules or other policy initiatives to relaunch the single market – including perhaps the granting of further powers or the strengthening of existing enforcement powers – consensus will obviously be required. The degree of consensus necessary will depend on the decision-making rules foreseen by the treaties for the different policy areas. Support by the European Parliament and by the Council will be essential. As far as the Council is concerned, unanimity may be required in some areas, while in others qualified majority will be sufficient. Consensus building – fully engaging the European Parliament, Member States, the Council, stakeholders – will thus be a crucial component of a new strategy aimed at strengthening competition and the single market. The effort to generate consensus will have to show full awareness of the main concerns surrounding the single market today.

The financial crisis that erupted in 2007, the economic and social crisis that has ensued, and more recently the British decision to leave the European Union, has led to an overhaul of the hierarchy of economic and social systems in Europe. The German model, based on the social market economy, has gained wider recognition, while the Anglo-Saxon model has suffered a few setbacks, at least for the time being. This state of affairs may perhaps present Europe with an unexpected opportunity to relaunch integration on a more solid basis, at a time when the economic crisis and the reactions of national governments place the single market in jeopardy, and with it the integration achieved thus far.

The question arises as to whether in Anglo-Saxon countries too much reliance has been put on market mechanisms and too little on regulation, whether the financial sector has not grown too much to the detriment of manufacturing, and whether sufficient attention has been paid to inequalities and welfare systems. There is a tendency to look more favourably to some European countries, such as Germany and, to some extent, France, which have long been followers of social market economy models. Anglo-Saxon countries should not feel ill at ease on account of their partial conversion, however. By the same token, countries with a social market economy should not take pride in this 'reversal of fortunes'. After all, they had been forced to move in the direction of the Anglo-Saxon countries in the previous decade, by introducing economic reforms to increase competitiveness. And they still need to keep on doing so.

This convergence of national economic models towards a middle ground presents Europe with an unexpected political opportunity that would enable it to tackle the growing social challenges while safeguarding integration. In the EU, the two clusters of countries each have their main concerns. The Anglo-Saxon countries and some Northern European countries rightly complain that countries with a social market economy – especially France, but also Germany and others – are often impatient with the existing rules of the single market (including those on the subjects of competition and State aid), let alone accept the actual further development of the single market. Countries with a social market economy complain, also rightly, that the opposition manifested by Anglo-Saxon countries and new Member States to greater coordination of taxation makes it more difficult to achieve social objectives through fiscal policy.

With tax revenues falling as a result of tax competition, this has often affected the ability to fund social programmes. In addition, the more mobile tax bases – capital income, large corporations and highly skilled professionals – tend to move to countries with more favourable tax regimes, thus triggering a trend towards tax minimisation. However, labour income and small businesses, being less mobile, must shoulder a growing tax burden. To avoid frustration in both clusters of countries, as well as the ensuing predictable resentment against Europe in general and the single market in particular, the EU should take this opportunity to promote a fair compromise. First of all, the Commission should confront the Council, the European Parliament and public opinion with a realistic evaluation – in itself rather worrying – of the consequences that growing economic nationalism could have on European integration. The Commission should therefore push for a strategic agreement comprising two elements:

(1) a renewed and binding commitment to the single market, in particular by adopting enhanced mechanisms to ensure compliance with its rules, while taking steps to achieve it, within carefully set deadlines, in those areas in which it is still lacking;
(2) a commitment to introduce even small levels of tax coordination. These should be measures not intended to achieve full tax harmonisation (an unrealistic and unnecessary objective), but to allow Member States to retain their fiscal sovereignty while cooperating on certain parts thereof. If they prefer to defend the principle of fiscal

sovereignty single-handedly instead, the States will witness their sovereignty being steadily eroded due to unfettered tax competition.

This compromise would encourage those countries most inclined to view the single market positively to create an openness in terms of tax coordination (which they may still need, as they have set themselves to make more room for welfare), while securing the future of the single market. For their part, while countries with a social market economy would have to abide by the rules of an effective single market, they would enjoy wider margins to pursue social objectives without having to breach market rules. Both groups would come closer to the model in the Nordic countries, which manage to combine the free market and the social dimension more effectively. Finally, and above all, this agreement would inject new vigour into the European project.

V. Solidarity and Competition between Member States

As we have seen above, the policies of the Member States and the EU influence the conditions of solidarity and competition among social and economic stakeholders. In a way, we can speak of solidarity, as well as of competition, also with regard to relations between Member States. Depending on the circumstances, these relations may be marked by greater or lesser degrees of solidarity and by mutually more cooperative or more competitive attitudes. The phases in which solidarity tends to take priority over competition (or over the *chacun pour soi* approach, as we are dealing with States) are normally those most favourable to further steps towards integration, and vice versa.

The state of relations among Member States, and therefore their willingness and ability to forge exceptional common policies, depends on a number of factors both internal and external to the EU.

Taking a cue from recent experiences, let us examine two cases. The first one, relating to the last 10 years or so, shows that solidarity between States and mutual trust have lost much of their shine, for reasons essentially internal to the EU, in particular with the rise of divergences in national political cultures, also heightened by the crisis. In the second case, a trend seen in the last year, external factors likely to threaten European integration, and perhaps Europe itself, seem to build a momentum towards Member States finding a more coherent and consistent position, in the sense of greater solidarity.

VI. Overcoming Internal Divergences in Favour of Better Common Policies

With the economic, social and political crisis experienced by Europe in the last 10 years and more recently with the intensification of immigration, the sense of cohesion among Member States and their willingness to cooperate closely in pursuit of the broader European interest have been weakened. National priorities have regained status. Mutual distrust has spread among Member States and often through their various public opinions.

Sluggish growth; internal and external security risks; citizens' distrust in national and European institutions; Member States openly opposed to one another; early warning signs of a possible disintegration of the EU. Faced with these difficulties, the approach to economic policies conducted at Community level must necessarily change. Despite the enhancements introduced throughout the years of the financial crisis, the kind of adjustment that is required today cannot be achieved by further tweaking margins, but does not require a 'revolution' either.

Instead, we need to revisit some of the foundations of the current approach, and clearly identify the points that underlie the divergent patterns, increasingly evident, between the visions expressed by the political cultures of our countries.

The 'constructive ambiguity' – increasingly used by ministers and government leaders in the European Councils and at the higher levels of the eurozone to give the impression that deals have been struck – is no longer enough. If a truly shared vision is entirely missing, the compromises made with such difficulty lack credibility, both for the citizens and for the markets. Their different narratives, sometimes irreconcilable, detract from what we are expected to believe to have jointly decided. At the point we have reached, ambiguity can become destructive.

The debates between governments in the Councils are often highly technical. But one seldom wonders what kind of divergent political cultures are created as a result of these contrasts; whether they still make sense in the realities of today; and whether other solutions might be available that could favour both the opposing sides, as well as the European economy, without creating winners and losers, and without resorting to merely cosmetic compromises.

The effort that should be made to understand better the divergences between Member States, and strive to overcome them, mainly concerns three pillars of economic policies, which have come under heavy pressure: the single market, the stability pact, the EU budget. All three themes affect the entire EU-28 (27 after Brexit), although the persisting tensions could lead to particularly serious consequences for the euro area.

A. Single Market: Tensions Between Market Integration and its Rejection on the Grounds of Social and National Policy

The EU strives to be, in the words of the Lisbon Treaty, 'a highly competitive social market economy'. But some countries, for example, the United Kingdom, are more 'market-sensitive', whereas others, like France and in some respects Germany, display a more enhanced 'social' sensitivity. In recent years, in many parts of the world there have been reactions to a globalisation that is much more attentive to the needs of the market than to social concerns or issues linked to national identities. Economic openness is sluggish or giving ground, while protectionism and nationalism are on the rise. This is also the case in Europe, where a fully-fledged single market would be essential for more dynamic growth.

For the single market to be completed, as in the services industry and the digital economy, it is essential to overcome the strong resistance manifested by those who, not unreasonably, view the existence of a market-integrated EU, but divided on social policies, as a factor that increases inequalities. One way to avoid this outcome is to achieve greater coordination of national taxation. Among the opponents of such coordination, the United Kingdom has always played a leading role, being a country that had to face up to the fact that a major part of the pro-Brexit vote had stemmed from the inequalities attributed by many of its citizens to the ills of EU membership. This goes to show that the most ardent supporters of a free market unencumbered by social provisions would eventually lead to the rejection of the single market, and not to its success.

Perhaps, once the United Kingdom (sadly, under many other aspects) will have left the EU, tax coordination will prove to be a little less difficult to attain and the single market will be more widely accepted.

B. Stability Pact: Geographical and Cultural Tensions Lead to Double Jeopardy

Public budgets, once cyclically adjusted, whose deficit is no higher than public investments (in 'real' terms, certified perhaps by the EU) are no threat to the country that adopts them or to the other Member States. Germany is wrong to oppose an economic principle that it had enshrined in its Constitution until a few years ago and that helped her achieve its remarkable post-war economic miracle.

Yet Germany is right, along with other central and northern European countries, to dislike the increasingly frequent use of 'flexibility' in the implementation of the stability pact, even though it has recently appeared to yield to some extent.

Europe needs a strong expansion of investments (whether private, mixed and even public). Under the very same approach to subsidiarity, so dear to the Germans, this expansion cannot be entrusted to a central instrument alone, though very important, such is the Juncker plan. It is therefore crucial that the rules designed to oversee the sound management of national budgets – in the interest of a Europe free from financial tensions but displaying greater growth levels than today, as the EU itself could not survive otherwise – leave the way open to good investments, rather than letting them trickle through the window of 'flexibility'; indeed, this method also lets excessive debt seep through, which is detrimental because not caused by investments, but often by allocations sometimes smack of political expediency.

A solution would be to pass a more credible rule governing investments, while at the same time phasing out the window for flexibility. The only increase in public spending that should encounter favour with both Keynesian French (because it stimulates the demand) and Hayekian Germans (because it expands production capacity, thus amounting to a supply policy in compliance with the ethical principle of keeping future generations in mind) is when making genuine public investments into productive uses. A more respectable rule will also be more respected.

C. EU Budget: Tension Between 'Net Contributors' and 'Net Beneficiaries'

Another source of tension that is poisoning European discourse stems from the woes of a community budget that is obsolete in the structure of expenditure, lacks transparency, and whose financing modalities are undemocratic and regressive.

Along with refugees, migrants, terrorism and the requirements to work for the sake of internal and external security, Member States have recently called on the EU to provide public goods at a European level that countries alone are not able to deliver to their own citizens.

The EU needs to be in a condition to supply these European public goods, with new resources being allocated to these new functions, while a large part of the current expenditure could be saved by scrapping certain programmes or transferring some of their activities to the national level.

This field too will be severely impacted by the UK leaving the EU; indeed there will be a shortfall in the net inflow of resources. However, another aspect that has become increasingly fraught will finally be settled: with the United Kingdom's withdrawal, the 'UK rebate' ('I want my money back', Margaret Thatcher famously stated in 1984) will cease to exist and the same fate will likely befall the rebates that other countries had secured over time to mitigate the effects of the UK's rebate on their budgetary contributions.

VII. Greater Solidarity in the Face of External Threats: How to Exploit them to Secure a Stronger Europe

Sixty years since the EU came into being marks an opportunity to take stock of its standing in the world. In this context, a number of external factors, pertaining to real or potential threats, take on specific importance.

In a nutshell, the EU's weight in the world can be said to be shrinking in quantitative terms, while its qualitative importance has not abated, indeed this has actually increased in some respects.

In terms of world population, the EU's share has been steadily and swiftly declining. Though less speedily, its weight in the global economy is also shrinking.

However, if we look at the values which the EU was founded upon and which it is keen to promote – the founding values of European civilisation and the mode of governance for a community of States – we are confident that their protection and worldwide circulation are still matters of great importance. This is particularly true in a historical phase in which the other fundamental pillar of this values-based community, the United States of America, for the first time appears to have undergone a change of direction.

However, the EU is currently beset by an internal crisis that threatens to bring it down, causing its disintegration. In order to deal with it effectively, the economic and social policies that we have referred to above must be substantially improved, and the policies and attitudes of the Member States vis-à-vis the Union must once again be reconciled with a principle of correctness and a sense of responsibility. In this way it will be possible to stop European integration from breaking up, torn asunder by grassroots nationalist and protectionist movements and, to a (sadly) growing extent, by equally baneful tendencies displayed by political forces and governments with a proven pro-European track record. Caught between two populist forces, the former bottom-up and the latter top-down, the EU would hardly stand a chance of surviving.

If it succeeds in fending off this disruptive onslaught, the EU will have to equip itself quickly to best realise the still largely unused potential that it can derive from a more effective and more functional economic and political integration.

Improving the economic performance of the EU will effectively slow down the decrease in its economic weight in the world. Above all, per capita income will go up and (a particularly urgent move) inequalities would go down, thus helping citizens to reconcile between European integration and social needs, and between the single market and competition on the one hand and solidarity on the other.

Likewise, a more unified and consistent EU engagement in the fields of foreign and defence policy would raise its effective capacity to assert all over the world the values that, as Europeans, are essential for us: the rule of law, democracy based on the separation of powers, protecting the environment and fighting climate change, openness to international trade within rules set and enforced by multilateral bodies and, more generally, a form of multilateral governance of globalisation instead of upholding the law that 'might is right'.

With the election of US president Donald Trump, as unbelievable as it may seem to us, literally each and every one of the principles listed above has been questioned in practice or challenged explicitly from the standpoint of ideology or policy. At the recent World economic forum in Davos (2017), it fell upon president Xi Jinping from the People's Republic of China to advocate the opening up of trade and that globalisation should be rightfully governed by multilateral organisations such as the G20 and the World Trade Organization.

But what assurances can the world have, what assurances can Europe itself have, if such a conspicuous rift has opened up between the great powers? The government of the United States, a country with a deep-rooted democratic tradition, despite some of its new president's attitudes and initiatives, is now calling for forms of protectionism. Yet on the other hand, the defence of free trade is taken up by a country which Europe values highly on many levels, but not on its record of 'democracy' or respect for human rights. It is more evident than ever that the EU must fill a void, stepping up in tenacious defence of both democracy and an open international economy, based on the consistency and credibility it has demonstrated for decades. But to be taken seriously, and to play a decisive role in shaping the future mainframe of the economy and international policy, the EU must wield such a strength that draws upon an economy capable of adapting to the new division of labour on a global scale, but without alienating its citizens, and speaks with one strong voice in the world. The two prerequisites, instead of stepping up, would tarnish and fall into irrelevance if the centrifugal thrusts represented by the strict national interests of individual European countries were to win the day.

Moreover, signs of greater cohesion among Member States seemed to be on the rise throughout 2017. It was evidenced in the response to the intermittent deluge of criticism and controversy that characterised president Trump's initial dealings with the EU and its Member States. It is evidenced in the positions, which have so far been much more convergent than expected, that the 27 Member States have taken as regards the negotiations with the United Kingdom on exit terms and conditions.

VIII. Solidarity and Competition in Italy

And what about Italy? How can we briefly describe our country's standing in the current European framework?

Let us start with the institutional aspect. Italy, as it is known, is one of the six founding States of the European Economic Community and of the European atomic energy Community and, earlier still, of the European coal and steel Community.

Today Italy ranks among the 28 EU Member States (soon to be 27 after the United Kingdom's withdrawal from the Union). For a long time we have been members of two areas of strengthened integration, which several States do not belong to either as a result of their own choices or because they have so far failed to meet the predefined requirements: Europe's Schengen border-free area allowing for the free movement of people, and the eurozone, made up of countries that share the same currency, the euro. Italy joined the eurozone from the beginning, after a flurry of activity in the mid-90s to contain public spending; as for the Schengen area, Italy joined a few years after the first members; in those years, one would say today, Italy belonged to the 'second speed' Europe in terms of free circulation.

From a political point of view, Italy's stance has historically been one of the most favourable to integration. It is a less well-known fact that Italy has played a key role in addressing the EU Council at various times, crucial for the integration progress. For example, fundamental decisions were taken when Italy was holding the rotating Council presidency; these include the introduction of a directly elected European Parliament in 1979; the Single Act that would lead to the single market (Milan European Council, 1985); and the groundwork for the birth of the single currency (Rome European Council, 1990).

From an economic point of view, it is broadly recognised that membership of the EU has been a fundamental factor in Italy's growth and modernisation. Opinions are more divided, however, when it comes to weighing up the effects that adopting the euro have had on Italy's real economy. Still, it is a fact that the single currency has shielded our country from extreme currency fluctuations and financial turbulence in the wake of international crises, and has contributed significantly to contain interest rates, with positive effects on the cost of refinancing the public deficit.

Measured against other eurozone countries, Italy stands out for its weak growth rate, largely due to the delays in making the necessary structural reforms that should have swiftly followed the adoption of the euro.

The process of redressing the balances of Italy's public finances has moved along more rapidly, but is still unfinished business. The ratio of government debt to gross domestic product is still among the highest in Europe, although the rate of return of the government deficit has been more satisfactory. Indeed, the excessive deficit procedure against Italy was closed in the spring of 2013, a unique case among the countries of Southern Europe, including France. Likewise, Italy was the only country in Southern Europe to have withstood the severe financial crisis of 2011–12 without having to appeal for aid from the EU and the International Monetary Fund. In other countries these institutions had to step in and seize control of the economy through the so-called troika (European Commission, European Central Bank and International Monetary Fund) which in fact replaced national governments and Parliaments.

Among the major eurozone economies, the general assessment is that, in spite of some delays, Italy has made more progress than France in terms of both structural reforms and above all, budgetary discipline. This has put Italy in a position to assert itself more adequately, compared to France, when engaging with the European institutions and with Germany on the guidelines defined at EU level. At the same time, along with France, Italy is helping to put pressure on the EU and Germany to ensure that the rules of budgetary discipline are formulated and implemented while safeguarding more the needs of economic growth. In particular, by applying a more favourable treatment for public investments (as long as they are real investments and actually made in tangible assets) within the rules on public budgets.

With its strengths and weaknesses – whether historical, political, economic, or financial – briefly described above, Italy is poised to play decisive games for its own future, for the EU, and for the EU's role in the world. The three levels must now be seen as closely bound together. Ultimately, over the coming years Italy's economic, political, and identity-giving role on the world stage will depend on the progress it achieved at home, on the respect it will elicit and on the influence it will wield in the EU, as well as on the importance that the EU will succeed in having in the world – also thanks to Italy's contribution.

If Italy's participation in the EU and the euro area is to be effective and fruitful, our country will also continue to benefit from the positive influence it has successfully drawn from European law and its regulations on competition and solidarity.

Italy passed its own law on competition and set up the relevant Authority relatively late in 1990, but framed it in very consistent terms with Community law. As a result of the work of the European Commission and the Italian Competition and Market Authority, which have often acted in conjunction, the promotion of competition rules has penetrated many sectors of the Italian economy that had been shielded from it for a long time. But much remains to be done, considering this field is of such paramount significance for the revival of growth, competitiveness and employment.

By the same token, thanks to its membership of the EU Italy has been subject to a positive wave of modernisation in the methods and instruments through which solidarity is provided. Fake forms of solidarity – where often one hand (inflation) would snatch the monetary benefits paid by the other hand to the needy – were excluded from partaking of the euro, with a single monetary policy aimed at containing inflation. Also, the single market and competition have greatly reduced the direct interference of public authorities in the markets (think of political prices), as these hampered growth and employment, while leading to inefficiencies in the allocation of resources. There are still important areas for directing public policies to solidarity objectives, but European regulations and criteria represent a filter that has cut off the supply of sham solidarity measures, already paid for by living but unaware taxpayers, through hidden tariffs, or by unborn contributors, our future generations.

Bibliography

Amato, G and Ziller, J, *The European Constitution: cases and materials in EU and Member States' law* (Cheltenham, 2007).

'A symposium on Monti's legacy' (2005) 1(1) *Competition policy international*, https://www.competitionpolicyinternational.com/cpi-11/.

Baker, JB and Salop, SC, 'Antitrust, politica della concorrenza e disuguaglianza' (2016) 1 *Mercato, concorrenza e regole* 7–34.

European Parliament, *Tax competition in the European Union*, 1998, http://www.europarl.europa.eu/workingpapers/econ/pdf/105_en.pdf.

Goulard, S, and Monti, M, *La democrazia in Europa: guardare lontano* (Milano, 2012).

Monti, M, *Competition in a social market economy* (Freiburg, 2000), http://ec.europa.eu/competition/speeches/text/sp2000_022_en.pdf.

Monti, M, *Una nuova strategia per il mercato unico al servizio dell'economia e della società europea*, Report to the President of the European Commission, José Manuel Barroso, May 2010, https://www.ecc-netitalia.it/files/Una%20nuova%20strategia%20per%20il%20Mercato%20Unico_Mario%20Monti%20-%20Maggio%202010.pdf.

Napolitano, G, *Europa, politica e passione* (Milano, 2016).

Pitruzzella, G, *Relazione annuale dell'Antitrust*, 16 May 2017, http://www.agcm.it/stampa/news/8753-relazione-annuale-dell-antitrust-presentazione-del-presidente-giovanni-pitruzzella-16-maggio-2017.html.

Van Miert, K, *Le marché et le pouvoir : souvenirs d'un commissaire européen* (Bruxelles, 2000).

Please see also:

International Competition Network, *History*, http://www.internationalcompetitionnetwork.org/about/history.aspx.

European Competition Network, http://ec.europa.eu/competition/consumers/cooperation_en.html.

All web pages are understood as having last been visited on 14 May 2018.

The author wishes to thank Elisabetta Olivi for her contribution to the discussion of this topic and for pre-editing the text.

5

The Charter of Fundamental Rights of the European Union

MARTA CARTABIA

I. The Origins, Processes, and Reasons that Led to a Charter of Fundamental Rights

It took 50 years for the European Union (EU) to adopt a Charter of fundamental rights. The Treaty of Rome, which established the European Economic Community in 1957, omitted the protection of individual rights entirely. This omission could not have gone unnoticed at that point in history, which was particularly sensitive to the rights of persons. The Charter of Fundamental Rights of the European Union, proclaimed at Nice in 2000, attained legally binding status in 2007, with the approval of the Treaty of Lisbon. Today it ranks among the most important sources of EU law.

1957–2007: 50 years later, the founding Treaty was finally endowed with a proper bill of rights. This dynamic stands out as highly unusual, if not totally unique, in the history of constitutionalism. Generally speaking, in modern times, declarations of rights are an integral part of the founding documents of any new legal system. When not included in the Constitution itself, a bill of rights is, nevertheless, generally issued at the same time as the Constitution. This was the case with the American Constitution, the first ten amendments to which, including the delineation of individual rights, were approved in 1789 and took effect starting in 1791, a short time after the Constitution itself was ratified. In fact, since the French and American Revolutions in the eighteenth century, individual rights have been an essential component of every constitution. As article 16 of the Declaration of the rights of man and of citizens famously proclaimed: 'Any society in which no provision is made for guaranteeing rights or for the separation of powers, has no Constitution.'

The EU does not fit into the typical pattern for two distinct reasons. First, its founding treaties do not even mention individual rights. The reasons for this omission have been investigated and analysed extensively and need not be repeated here. Secondly, and more worthy of further consideration, is the fact that the gap was filled only 50 years later, when the original treaties were finally amended to include a complete, detailed, and modern rights charter.

So, the question is not so much, 'Why a Charter of rights for the European Union?' but rather, 'Why then? Why 50 years later? Why the long delay?' After all, despite the original omission, effective protection of fundamental rights had been a well-established part of the European system since the 1970s, thanks to the case law of the Court of Justice.

The story is well known. In a series of cases brought before the Court in the 1950s and 1960s, all claims that would have required European recognition of rights recognised under domestic law were rejected. National courts, particularly the German and Italian constitutional courts, became understandably concerned that Union institutions would be able to dodge any scrutiny based on fundamental rights. The principles of supremacy and direct effect, if respected to the utmost degree, threatened to render national constitutional guarantees inapplicable to Union rules. By the same token, since the European Communities had not signed the European Convention of Human Rights (ECHR), the residual protection provided therein would also be inapplicable.

In response to pressure from the national courts, the Court of Justice began to change its position, starting with the 1969 *Stauder* case. There the Court began to hold that fundamental human rights were 'enshrined in the general principles of Community law and protected by the Court' (judgment 12.11.1969, *Erich Stauder v City of Ulm-Sozialamt*, case 29/69), as unwritten general principles, binding on all of the European institutions. Later on, treaty revisions gradually strengthened fundamental rights protection in the EU. Among these revisions, which predated the extensive changes made by the Charter and the Treaty of Lisbon, it is worth mentioning the steps taken to protect fundamental rights in what was then article F(2) of the Maastricht Treaty and the addition of a procedure for punishing Member States for serious and persistent violations of fundamental rights and freedoms to the Treaty of Amsterdam (then article 7 of the Treaty on European Union, TEU).

In order to identify fundamental rights, the Court of justice has long relied on a variety of different sources. In particular, it gave a great deal of weight to the common constitutional traditions of the Member States (judgment 17.12.1970, *Internationale Handelsgesellschaft mbH v Einfuhr- und Vorratsstelle für Getreide und Futtermittel*, case 11/70) and to international treaties for the protection of fundamental rights to which Member States were signatories (judgment 14.5.1974, *J Nold, Kohlen-und Baustoffgroßhandlung v Commission of the European Communities*, case 4/73), especially the European Convention of human rights and the case law of the European Court of human rights (judgments 15.5.1986, *Marguerite Johnston v Chief constable of the Royal Ulster constabulary*, case 222/84; 18.6.1991, *ERT AE v Pliroforissis and Kouvelas*, C-260/89; 22.10.2002, *Roquette Frères SA v Directeur général de la concurrence, de la consommation et de la répression des fraudes*, C-94/00). The European Convention has long been a key, special 'source of inspiration' for the Court, even without being formally binding. The Court of justice has always emphasised the autonomy of EU general human rights principles vis-à-vis both the national legal cultures and constitutional traditions and the European Convention. So much so that when the Court was asked to give an opinion about the accession of the EU as such to the European Convention, it answered in the negative (opinion 2/94).

The final result of this evolution was the settled establishment of judge-made protection of human rights in the EU, although the European Court's case law in this vein has been frequently called into question by legal scholars, who have accused it of chiefly intending to bolster the arguments for European integration (J Coppel and A O'Neill, 'The European Court of Justice: taking rights seriously?' (1992) 29 *Common market law review* 669–92; JHH Weiler and NJS Lockhart, 'Taking rights seriously: The European Court and its fundamental rights jurisprudence – part I' (1995) 32 *Common market law review* 51–94).

What need was there, after the gap had been filled by the Court, to adopt a written charter of fundamental rights? Who stood to benefit from such an initiative? To address this issue properly, it is worth recalling that the Charter of Fundamental Rights was not intended to replace the other sources of fundamental rights, but rather to complement them. In fact, the current version of article 6 of the TEU lists at least three formal sources for EU human rights. The first is the Charter itself. The second is the ECHR, which will become formally binding on the EU if the EU accedes to it, as envisaged in article 6.2 of the TEU. The third are the 'general principles' of EU law, the body of legal principles, including human rights, which have been articulated and developed by the Court of justice over the years, drawing from the national constitutional traditions, the ECHR, and other international treaties signed by the Member States. Today, the constitutional framework of the EU boasts an impressive array of human rights provisions. Even at the time of its drafting, the Charter could have been considered redundant (JHH Weiler, 'Editorial: does the European Union truly need a Charter of rights?' (2000) 6 *European law journal* 96).

It is unclear whether individuals actually benefit from this superabundance of instruments for the protection of rights. The Charter was primarily intended to restate existing rights, rather than add to the list. Several critics have pointed out that if the Charter was meant simply to reiterate the guarantees that the European Court had already laid down over the years, it would be useless and ineffective, if not outright damaging for the individual. More documents, more charters and more courts do not necessarily result in more guarantees for the individual. On the contrary, the multiplication of norms, structures, and procedures can result in overlaps, conflicts, and lack of clarity, all to the detriment of the individual. The combination of different sources – national, supranational, and conventional – is all but easy to understand. The difficulty of identifying the most appropriate of the various remedies, and confusion about their different roles, may lead complainants to knock at the wrong door, or may even deter people whose fundamental rights have been breached from seeking the legal remedy to which they are entitled.

Here it is important to note that, after the Charter entered into force, the European Commission launched a publicity campaign to raise public awareness of the rights it contains and the appropriate legal remedies connected with them (European Commission, COM(2010)573). The reasons for drafting the Charter of Fundamental Rights at the turn of the twenty-first century were not, in short, based exclusively on concern for the individual person. In order to complete the picture and understand the many reasons behind the Charter, it may be useful to recall the spirit and the atmosphere of the European Union at the end of the last century. Two major elements deserve to be emphasised. First, the legal culture at the time was dominated by the doctrines of neo-constitutionalism, which focused on rights and courts. At the time, constitutional thought tended to emphasise individual rights over the law and constitutional adjudication over parliamentary legislation. From the institutional point of view, courts were at the centre and Parliaments were at the margins. In keeping with this, judicial review was the preferred place for providing safeguards for the individual, rather than legislation and acts of Parliament. Secondly, the process of European integration needed a push toward closer political union. To that end, the European institutions were considering a genuinely constitutional move, which eventually resulted in the proposal of a Treaty establishing a Constitution for the European Union, approved in October 2004 (but later abandoned after the negative results of referendums in France and the Netherlands). In this context, the Charter of Fundamental Rights was intended as a precursor for a future Constitution of the Union.

This historical context helps shed light on the two-part nature of the Charter. On the one hand, it stressed the central position of the individual in the European legal order – the Europe of its citizens. On the other, it provided the perfect channel for broader reform headed toward constitutionalism in the European Union. The Charter had an intrinsic value as an amplifier for 'rights talk', and, at the same time, it had the beneficial side effect of laying the pedagogical groundwork for an all-encompassing constitutional turn in the Union.

As Miguel Poiares Maduro observed in 2003, the drafting of the Charter may be interpreted both as a simple consolidation of the *aquis communautaire* in the area of fundamental rights, and as the bill of rights of a political community – the first, essential constitutional document of the true 'social contract' of a new political community. The two-part objective of the Charter is clearly visible in the wording of the *Conclusions of the European Council Presidency*, Cologne, 3–4 June, 1999, annex IV:

> Protection of fundamental rights is a founding principle of the Union and an indispensable prerequisite for her legitimacy. The obligation of the Union to respect fundamental rights has been confirmed and defined by the jurisprudence of the European Court of Justice. There appears to be a need, at the present stage of the Union's development, to establish a Charter of fundamental rights in order to make their overriding importance and relevance more visible to the Union's citizens.

In short, the Charter was not adopted to fill a gap in the protection of individual rights. As the European Council recognised, the Union had been committed to individual rights for decades already. Drafting the Charter was an exercise in visibility, intended both to display what the European Union had already accomplished in the area of human rights and to restate its commitment, as a tool for bolstering the legitimacy of a tighter union between European peoples. Putting human rights at the core of the supranational order had potential to raise up a strong, visible, and incontestable political ideal, something the Union was longing for.

Many commentators have emphasised that guaranteeing a higher degree of legitimacy was quite explicitly the chief aim of drafting the Charter, and that the drafting process was designed accordingly (de Búrca (2001)). The drafting was carried out outside the framework of the European treaties, and, therefore, a new convention was established that could be configured as an experimental, open, and deliberative forum for constitutional discussion. This was unlike the traditional State-dominated conferences, where diplomats could engage in tough bargaining behind closed doors. The convention was a high-profile body, made up of representatives of the heads of State and the governments and of the president of the Commission, as well as members of the European Parliament and national Parliaments. The proceedings that followed were open to participation by social and interest groups and brought about a *grand débat* on the Constitution for Europe. This experiment fuelled a great deal of optimism that Europe would move toward constitutionalism. Then, however, matters took a different turn, and the treaty that would have instituted a European Constitution was not ratified. But the Charter had already come to be, and it endures today. For years, despite having been solemnly proclaimed at Nice in December 2000 and attached to the Treaty on the European Union through the Lisbon revision in 2007, it remained a non-binding document. So, the Charter both pioneered the European constitutional experiment in the early twenty-first century and survived its failure, effectively becoming an additional instrument for the protection of individual rights.

In the pages that follow, I will assess the impact of the Charter on the protection of fundamental rights in Europe, highlighting its most important outcomes and pointing to the most problematic areas that remain to be resolved. We will consider the effect that the Charter has had on the European institutions, particularly on the European Court of Justice, and the changes it has provoked in the systems of the Member States, above all in the national constitutional courts. We will not spend time here on questions of the compatibility between the adoption of the Charter and the Union's adherence to the European Convention on human rights under article 6.2 of the TEU. After the intense negotiations that followed the commencement of the Treaty of Lisbon, the adherence process seems to have come to an abrupt stop in the wake of the negative opinion expressed by the Court of justice (opinion 2/13). The uncertainty of its prospects suggests that it would be unwise to linger on the topic of the protection of rights in a constitutional Europe, even though this would have the great distinction of subjecting Union institutions to an 'external' adjudicator, whose decisions would also be binding upon all the Member States.

II. The Charter and EU Institutions

The adoption of the Charter did not transform the European Union into a human rights organisation (von Bogdandy (2000)), nor did it entirely convert the European Court of justice into a human rights tribunal (de Búrca (2013)). The Charter did not alter the objectives, focus, or activities of the Union's legal order or institutions. Its field of competence was, and still is, defined by the conferral principle, since the legal basis for the actions of European institutions is established by the treaties. Fundamental rights act as *limits on*, rather than *justifications of* new forms of intervention or expanded activity by European institutions.

In a way, this has always been the case. The protection of fundamental rights enshrined in the general principles of law as spelled out by the European Court of justice has always pertained to European institutions, and it was meant to implement the constitutional spirit of 'limited government' in the European constitutional framework, as well. The general principles of EU law derived from the common constitutional traditions of the Member States, among which the ECJ also includes fundamental rights, theoretically applied to European institutions as well as to the Member States when measures were implemented at the European level. In reality, however, before the Charter entered into force, the case law of the European Court of justice on fundamental rights was directed chiefly at the Member States when acting within the scope of EU legislation, and the Court displayed a high degree of deference as far as the European institutions were concerned.

Things changed after the Treaty of Lisbon. The European Court in recent years has heard a growing number of challenges to EU legislation that plead violations of human rights as a ground (Peers (2011), pp 283 and 291). The Court has begun to take these claims seriously and, in a number of cases, the Court has actually struck down EU legislation or administrative acts.

To be sure, the field of application of EU fundamental rights has not undergone any change since the Charter entered into force. As laid out in greater detail below, article 51 reaffirms some important and well-established principles that were already present in ECJ case law, which has consistently held that fundamental rights are a benchmark of validity for both European measures and national ones, provided that the latter fall within the field of application of European law. However, whereas the European Court has always been generous and courageous in interpreting the scope of its powers in relation to State actions, on the contrary, only after the Charter was given the same value as the treaties did measures adopted by European institutions began to be regularly submitted to judicial review and occasionally struck down by the European Court.

After the Charter entered into force, it became mandatory that 'the Union must be exemplary' with respect to fundamental rights, 'not only for people living in the Union but also for the development of the Union itself', in order to 'build mutual trust between the Member States and, more generally, public confidence in the Unions policies' (European Commission, COM(2010)573). In the past, the European Union had been accused of telling others (Member States, third countries and new entrants) what to do in the field of human rights, without acting in accordance with its own preaching. 'Don't do what I do, do what I tell you to do', as Joseph Weiler and Sybilla Fries put it ((1999), p 147). In the twenty-first century the Union can no longer afford to make such mistakes. And, since it desires to be exemplary, it cannot create causes for complaint; every legislative and administrative act must be above reproach when it comes to respect for fundamental rights. To this end, the Commission has produced a method for monitoring EU legislation, and submitting all proposals to multiple checks, from the initial drafting phase to the finalisation of the text (European Commission, COM(2010)573).

As mentioned above, since the ratification of the Treaty of Lisbon, the European Court of justice has begun to hand down decisions invalidating European measures for violating rights protected by the Charter. For example, in the *Schecke* case of November 2010 (judgment 9.11.2010, *Volker und Markus Schecke GbR and Hartmut Eifert v Land Hessen*, joined cases C-92/09 and C-93/09), some regulatory provisions were found to contradict article 7 of the Charter, which protects the right to private and family life, and article 8, which deals with the protection of personal data.

The protection of privacy and personal data subsequently prompted the Court of justice to strike down all of directive 2006/24/EC, which dealt with the storage of data generated or processed in connection with the provision of publicly available electronic communication services or of public communication networks (judgment 8.4.2014, *Digital rights Ireland Ltd v Minister for communications, marine and natural resources and others and Kärntner Landesregierung and others*, joined cases C-293/12 and C-594/12). The case was brought before the Court by way of references for preliminary rulings by the Irish Supreme Court and the Austrian Constitutional Court. They complained that the directive permitted interference in private life (as guaranteed by articles 7 and 8 of the Charter) in order to make available a wide range of personal data about internet traffic and the locations of natural and legal persons, for the purpose of the prevention, investigation, detection, and prosecution of serious crimes. Although the Court held that the purposes of the directive – the fight against organised crime and terrorism – genuinely satisfied an objective of general interest, it nevertheless determined that, under a proportionality test, this objective did not justify a broad data retention measure like the one established by directive 2006/24/EC.

A balanced approach to security issues had already given rise to the long Kadi saga (judgments 21.9.2005, *Yassin Abdullah Kadi v Council of the European Union and Commission of the European communities*, T-315/01; 21.9.2005, *Ahmed Ali Yusuf and Al Barakaat international foundation v Council of the European Union and Commission of the European Communities*, T-306-01; and 3.9.2008, *Kadi and Al Barakaat v Council of the European Union and Commission of the European communities*, joined cases C-402/05 P and C-415/05 P). It ended with the Court of justice striking down Union measures implementing the anti-terrorism resolutions of the United Nations (UN) Security Council, which allowed for the freezing of resources. The Court held that the measures limited the fundamental rights protected by the Charter (and by the ECtHR – the European Court of Human Rights), specifically with reference to the right to an effective legal remedy and to property rights. The various facets of the *Kadi* case have been the focus of extensive analysis (for one, see G de Búrca, 'The European Court of justice and the international legal order after Kadi' (2010) 51(1) *Harvard International Law Journal* 1–49).

Similarly, in the more recent *Schrems* case (judgment 6.10.2015, *Maximillian Schrems v Data protection commissioner*, C-362/14), the Court of justice declared the Commission's safe harbour decision invalid (decision 2000/520/EC), since it authorised the practically unlimited transfer of personal data to the US intelligence authority, without an effective legal remedy ensuring protection against such interference. The Court held that this compromised the essence of the fundamental right to respect for private life.

These and many other examples demonstrate that the EU Charter's entry into force had immediate impacts, strengthening the position of the Court of justice in relation to other European institutions, particularly when it is called upon to act like a Union constitutional adjudicator, rather than an adjudicator of European integration. In particular, in the *Digital rights* case mentioned above, two national Supreme Courts made recourse to references for a preliminary ruling asking the Court to verify the validity of a decision, rather than to interpret European provisions, as more typically happens. Therefore, if before the Lisbon Treaty entered into force the rights protection assured by the Union primarily affected the Member States, with this decision, the Court of justice showed that it could be used to determine the validity of Union regulations, and struck down one of them in its entirety. This case, then, is truly emblematic of the benefits of lively interaction between courts in the European constitutional context, as will be discussed in further detail below.

The strengthening of the European Court's constitutional role manifests itself in a variety of ways. For one thing, the Court now faces the political institutions of the Union as an independent actor, and is less and less reluctant to invalidate their acts, be they legislative or administrative in nature. Moreover, the Court speaks with a distinctive dialect that is easily recognised in the human rights discourse that has universally pervaded the field of law in recent years. The Court, stressing the constitutional autonomy of the European Union, is developing a new brand of protection of individual rights. On the one hand, the jurisprudence of the European Court is fully a part of western legal culture, fuelled by the values shared by all the liberal democracies and inspired by the 'constitutional tradition common to the member states'. On the other hand, the European Court articulates the content and limits of individual rights in a distinctive tone. The Court's originality derives not so much from the names and the number of rights written in the Charter, but rather from its interpretation of them. In fact, the list of rights included in the Charter repeats, by and large, the rights enumerated in the national constitutions of the European countries and in the most relevant international instruments.

It is true that the array of rights included in the Charter is more complete and has been updated compared with those found in older documents. This is because it was drafted at a time that allowed it to reflect various changes that have had an impact on contemporary society, including scientific and technological advances. Yet, it is the interpretative approach that leads to original outcomes, that is, the legal reasoning and balancing processes conducted by the Court of justice. For example, we can see in the cases mentioned above that the European Court is particularly concerned about the right to privacy and data protection, the essence of which is to be preserved even in an age of terrorist attacks and other serious security threats. In other systems, transparency, freedom of information, or security concerns override other relevant interests and rights. In the jurisprudence of the European Court, security concerns are relevant, high-ranking interests, capable of justifying some restrictions to individual fundamental rights, but they are not absolute priorities capable of justifying any constriction whatsoever.

III. The Charter and the Member States

This shift in gears for the Court of justice – its more marked autonomy and more dynamic activism in expanding its protection of fundamental rights after they were established by the Charter – was foreseen to some extent by the Member States. Some of them sensed that the act of writing down the rights protected within the European Union would not be without costs, which would most certainly include a stronger Court of justice. The Court's increased authority would, in turn, compress the space for preserving the diverse national traditions, which are marked by a pronounced pluralism in the field of human rights.

Preserving their own identities and constitutional traditions in the field of fundamental rights has become a high-priority concern for some Member States. They have expressed it both in their requests to accurately and precisely define the scope and boundaries of the Charter and of the fundamental rights it contains, as well as through firm demands that their national constitutional identities be respected. This identity component (*Guastaferro* (2012); *Faraguna* (2015); *Fabrini, Pollicino* (2017)) has been linked to the contents of particular rights – which are open to different interpretations depending upon the context – as well as to the essential nucleus of competences to be kept under Member State control. Respect for these competences, preservation of constitutional identities, and defining the field of application of the Charter of rights are all interconnected questions.

These factors, taken together, have caused a number of tensions, traces of which appear in some of the general provisions of the Charter, in the protocols attached to the Treaty of Lisbon, and in the case law of the European Court, but which are also detectable in decisions by the national constitutional courts. More precisely, they show up in the on-going, lively legal dialogue that has characterised the relationship between the national jurisdictions and the Court of justice over the last decade.

The reality is that the mere drafting of the Charter of rights has had contradictory effects. There is no doubt that it helped trigger the Court of justice's move toward active leadership, by encouraging its interventions to guarantee rights. But, to some degree, the codification of rights has also had a paralysing effect, and sparked a combative dynamic. This is particularly true with regard to those national actors most inclined to fear that issues based on fundamental rights may be used as powerful tools for eroding their national sovereignty.

On the legal plane, the winds of *souverainism* have even reached some national constitutional courts.

A. The Treaty of Lisbon Protocols

While the Treaty of Lisbon was being negotiated, the representatives of the UK and Poland staunchly opposed the drafting of the Charter and sought, at the very least, to limit its potential impact. Their efforts succeeded in guaranteeing a sort of special regime for their own nations. On Great Britain's initiative, Protocol No. 30 to the Treaty of Lisbon was approved to define the application of the EU Charter of fundamental rights to Poland and the UK. It states:

> Article 1
>
> 1. The Charter does not extend the ability of the Court of Justice of the European Union, or any court or tribunal of Poland or of the United Kingdom, to find that the laws, regulations or administrative provisions, practices or action of Poland or of the United Kingdom are inconsistent with the fundamental rights, freedoms and principles that it reaffirms.
>
> 2. In particular, and for the avoidance of doubt, nothing in Title IV of the Charter creates justiciable rights applicable to Poland or the United Kingdom except in so far as Poland or the United Kingdom has provided for such rights in its national law.
>
> Article 2
>
> To the extent that a provision of the Charter refers to national laws and practices, it shall only apply to Poland or the United Kingdom to the extent that the rights or principles that it contains are recognised in the law or practices of Poland or of the United Kingdom.

This protocol drew public, political, and legal attention because it was interpreted as a form of opting out of the Charter or, in any case, as indicating that the Court of justice and the national courts were backing down from the prerogative to review the legitimacy of State-level legislation under the Charter. Nevertheless, the protocol on the whole, despite some murkiness owing to the different goals of the two signatory States (Arnull, in *The EU Charter of fundamental rights* (2014) 1610; as well as JC Piris, *The Lisbon Treaty: a legal and political analysis* (2010) 14), merely restates principles already present within the rights of the Union, without making any significant new additions. What is probably most revealing is the protocol's explicit reference to title IV of the Charter, which signals a clear lack of trust on the part of the two countries for the EU attitude toward social rights, albeit for opposite reasons, as declaration No. 62 annexed to the Lisbon Treaty makes clear.

Poland and the UK were not alone in their misgivings about the Charter. The Czech Republic also wanted to emphasise its views in a declaration annexed to the Lisbon Treaty (No. 53, Declaration by the Czech Republic on the Charter of Fundamental Rights of the European Union). This resulted in sensitive negotiations that triggered a process that is still on-going, which intends to (among other things) extend the scope of protocol No. 30 to that Member State. And, after Ireland came back with a negative vote in its first referendum concerning ratification of the Treaty of Lisbon, the European Council had to approve clarifications about the rights relating to life, family, education, security and defence, worker rights, and social policy in order to pave the way for later Irish ratification. Leonard FM Besselink provides a good overview of the Member States' attitudes toward the Charter in the 2012 study he conducted for the *Fédération internationale pour le droit européen*.

The Member States' reservations, which they expressed in a variety of ways, largely involve two principal areas. First and foremost is the issue of the level of protection of social rights by the Union. The European national systems – despite sharing the social democracy model – have always taken different positions on the topic of social rights. The Court of justice, in its attempts to find a point of agreement, has often made decisions that one Member State or another has taken exception to, as was the case with the well-known and extensively debated decisions handed down in December 2007 (judgment 11.12.2007, *International transport workers' federation and Finnish seamen's union v Viking line ABP and OÜ Viking line Eesti*, C-438/05, and 18.12.2007, *Laval un partneri Ltd v Svenska Byggnadsarbetareförbundet, Svenska Byggnadsarbetareförbundets avdelning 1, Byggettan and Svenska Elektrikerförbundet*, C-341/05).

This is such a burning issue that difficulties in harmonising the levels of social rights protection are responsible for the distinction that has been drawn between *rights* and *principles*, found in articles 51.1 and 52.5 of the Charter. The distinction was intended to temper the direct applicability of certain rights, including primarily social rights. Not by chance, the Explanations relating to the Charter of fundamental rights (2007/C 303/02) list articles 23, 25, 26, 33, 34, and 37 among the principles to be *observed* (as opposed to rights to be *respected*). All of them deal, directly or indirectly, with social issues:

> The provisions of this Charter which contain principles may be implemented by legislative and executive acts taken by institutions, bodies, offices and agencies of the Union, and by acts of Member States when they are implementing Union law, in the exercise of their respective powers. They shall be judicially cognisable only in the interpretation of such acts and in the ruling on their legality (article 52.5).

Distinctions of this kind are not altogether unfamiliar for Italian scholars. In Italy an attempt was made to weaken the innovations effected by the 1948 Italian Constitution by creating a sophisticated distinction between *precept rules* and *programmatic rules*. The latter were meant to be the chief concern of the legislator, which alone was supposed to be endowed with the necessary powers to implement them. By the same token, they were removed from the control of the judiciary, including the Constitutional Court, so that courts would be unable to ensure that they were effectively applied without intermediation by parliamentary law. Nonetheless, the Constitutional Court, from its very first judgment No. 1 of 1956, held that this distinction was illegitimate and that all constitutional rules were equally directly applicable for purposes of the constitutional review of laws.

Alongside social rights, some Member States are also concerned about the different interpretations of rights that touch on 'ethically sensitive' subjects. This concern can be seen explicitly in declaration No. 61 of the Republic of Poland on the Charter of fundamental rights of the European Union. These rapidly evolving areas are particularly revealing of the cultural differences and the constitutional pluralism that mark the European continent. Abortion, assisted suicide, assisted reproduction, euthanasia, family, and marriage are some of the topics that are approached from different cultural perspectives in the various Member States. It seems that the competences of the European institutions should not touch directly upon these areas, which appear to fall under the competences reserved for the Member States. Nevertheless, the various national and supranational actors often overlap, and cases concerning abortion, marriage and same-sex unions, transsexual rights, and experimentation on human embryos have long been brought before the Court of justice

(Cartabia (2007)). This has led to misgivings on the part of some States, which are sensitive to issues concerning the preservation of their constitutional identities and the values enshrined in their national constitutions.

The reactions of the Member States at the time the treaties legally recognising the EU Charter of Fundamental Rights were ratified suggest that we cannot take for granted the existence of a *ius commune Europaeum* in this field. The drafting of the charter of rights provides a shared baseline, not a finish line. In light of the dynamic visible in the individual concrete cases, the new sets of problems emerging in the life of society, and new advancements in science and technology, the balancing between opposing values must always be newly recalibrated. This means that the polyphonic voices of Europe must be able to be heard, sometimes even in counterpoint (M Poiares Maduro, *Contrapunctual law: Europe's constitutional pluralism in action*, in *Sovereignty in transition*, (ed) N Walker (2003) 502–37) in order to express renewed harmony.

B. The Boundaries of the Charter

One of the greatest concerns at the time the Charter was drafted was to prevent it from becoming a vehicle for surreptitiously expanding the competences of the Union and simultaneously eroding those of the Member States. Fears of a creeping expansion of Union powers dominated both the discussions on the drafting of the Charter and the steps that followed, up to the commencement of the Lisbon Treaty. One sign of the high level of Member States' concern about this point is the number of provisions that deal with the topic of the delimitation of competences, even if only to reiterate essential principles.

Article 6.1 of the TEU, immediately following the recognition that the Charter's value is equal to that of the treaties, states that: '[t]he provisions of the Charter shall not extend in any way the competences of the Union as defined in the Treaties'. Article 51(2) of the Charter, following the stipulation in section (1) that the Union and the Member States 'shall therefore respect the rights, observe the principles and promote the application thereof in accordance with their respective powers', goes on to reemphasise that '[t]he Charter does not [...] establish any new power or task for the [Community or the] Union, or modify powers and tasks as defined in the Treaties'. Again, declaration No. 1 annexed to the final act of the intergovernmental conference which adopted the Treaty of Lisbon, which concerns the Charter of Fundamental Rights of the European Union, returns to the same topic to state that '[t]he Charter does not extend the field of application of Union law beyond the powers of the Union or establish any new power or task for the Union, or modify powers and tasks as defined by the Treaties'. And another declaration, No. 18, was also dedicated to the issue of competences, restating principles that had always shaped the Union and that had already been laid out in the treaty provisions mentioned here above.

The Member States' chief concern was to categorically rule out the possibility that the rights recognised by the Charter could be interpreted as an autonomous legal basis for justifying new actions on the part of European institutions, through the adoption of regulatory or administrative acts or policies that did not otherwise fall under the powers attributed to the Union. The centralising effect on powers that has taken place in other federal contexts – particularly in the United States of America after the adoption of a common Bill of Rights – was taken as a historical caveat, the import of which was not to be underestimated.

The highest risk area for potential invasion by competence creep is the delimitation of the EU Charter's scope of applicability. The relevant section is found in the first part of article 51.1 of the Charter of fundamental rights, which states: '[t]he provisions of this Charter are addressed to the institutions, bodies, offices and agencies of the Union with due regard for the principle of subsidiarity and to the Member States only when they are implementing Union law'. The existing provision was the result of a turbulent drafting process, as evidenced by the many linguistic revisions it underwent in the various drafts. Some of these versions identified the boundaries of the Charter's application to the Member States in reference to the 'field of application of Union law'. Others restricted it to cases in which the States 'implement community regulations' (Ziller (2017), pp 1050 et seq). These seemingly similar linguistic constructions pose the interpretative question of whether the expressions 'field of application of Union law' and 'implementation of Union law' are equivalent.

After the commencement of the Charter, the Court of justice seemed initially inclined to embrace an expansive interpretation of article 51. Extensive debate surrounded the case of *Åklagaren v Hans Åkerberg Fransson* (26.2.2013, C-617/10) and its application of the *ne bis in idem* principle (enshrined in the Charter at article 50) to Swedish law, which allowed the same person to be submitted to multiple proceedings to impose criminal and administrative sanctions for a single act of tax evasion related to the value added tax (VAT). In that case, the Court of justice held that there was a sufficiently clear link between the applicable national rules and community law to justify the projection of the rights protected by the Charter within Swedish law. The judgment stressed that the criminal proceedings brought against the accused were 'connected in part to breaches of his obligations to declare VAT', and that that form of tax was connected in various ways with Union law. Among these connections was the fact that the financial resources of the Union itself include funds levied via the application of a uniform rate to the harmonised VAT assessment. Accordingly, the Court held that the case fell within the field of application of the Charter, on the basis of article 51, over the specific objections of the Commission and the governments of numerous Member States who intervened in the case, and despite the opposing opinion submitted by advocate general Pedro Cruz Villalón. The Court first recalled – with a reference to its earlier case law – that the fundamental rights guaranteed in the legal order of the European Union are 'applicable in all situations governed by European Union law, but not outside such situations', and reiterated that, if a law does not fall within the scope of EU law, the Court has no jurisdiction. Then, the Court went on to conclude that the case was bound up with Union law and that, therefore, it did have jurisdiction to answer the questions referred to it and to provide all the interpretive guidance necessary for an evaluation of the national law's compatibility with the *ne bis in idem* principle enshrined in article 50 of the Charter. This was because, the Court held, 'situations cannot exist which are covered in that way by European Union law without those fundamental rights being applicable. The applicability of European Union law entails applicability of the fundamental rights guaranteed by the Charter'.

This decision drew fire from many sides, from scholars as well as from some national constitutional courts, for the tenuousness of the link it found between national and Union law, concerning which, as mentioned above, the Court seems to articulate a 'vaguely tautological' test (F Fontanelli, 'The implementation of European Union law by Member States under article 51(1) of the Charter of fundamental rights' (2014) *Columbia journal of European law* 193–247).

Not by chance, beginning in early 2014, the Court of justice has repeatedly come back with judgments on this topic, which is so sensitive for its relations with the national constitutions and national judiciaries. These later judgments attempt to comply with a more restrictive approach and to carefully spell out the factors or characteristics that demonstrate a strong enough link with EU law to bring national legislation under the provisions of the Charter and, therefore, under the jurisdiction of the Court of justice.

For example, one of the most notable and discussed cases was that of *Cruciano Siragusa v Regione Sicilia – Soprintendenza Beni Culturali e Ambientali di Palermo* (6.3.2014, C-206/13), which dealt with illegal construction, environmental protection and landscape conservation. In that case the Court held that the rights enshrined in the Charter did not apply, holding that the mere overlapping subject matter, covered by both the EU and national laws, was not enough. Rather, implementing EU law 'requires a certain degree of connection above and beyond the matters covered being closely related or one of those matters having an indirect impact on the other' (para. 24). Again, in the case of *Emiliano Torralbo Marcos v Korota SA, Fondo de garantía salarial* (27.3.2014, C-265/13), the Court of justice declined to answer a preliminary question, observing that the Spanish law governing the payment of judicial fees did not amount to an implementation of Union law, nor was it influenced by Union law.

Conversely, some weeks later, in the case of *Robert Pfleger and others* (30.4.2014, C-390/12), the Court reiterated, in line with case law that had been well established long before the commencement of the Lisbon Treaty, that Member States who invoke 'overriding reasons in the public interest' to justify measures restricting free circulation are obliged to respect fundamental rights, as guaranteed in the legal system of the Union. In that case, which involved Austrian laws regulating games of chance, the Court acknowledged the existence of a certain margin of appreciation for States, but held that the TFEU (*Treaty on the Functioning of the European Union*) had been violated as well as, *ipse facto*, articles 15 and 17 of the Charter, concerning the freedom to choose an occupation, the right to work, and property rights.

At around the same time, the Court decided *Pelckmans Turnhout NV v Walter Van Gastel Balen NV and others* (8.5.2014, C-483/12), a case about open hours and obligatory weekly closing periods for businesses, which was referred by the Belgian Constitutional Court with a question about the compatibility of the national law with the duty of non-discrimination enshrined in articles 20 and 21 of the Charter. The Court held that it did not have jurisdiction and that the case did not fall within the field of application of the Charter, reasoning that any effects of the national laws regulating business hours and provision of services 'are too uncertain and indirect for the obligation laid down to be regarded as being capable of hindering that freedom'.

A short time later, in *Víctor Manuel Julian Hernández and others v Reino de España and others* (10.7.2014, C-198/13), the Court held that the Charter did not apply to a case that involved Spanish labour legislation that ensured certain worker guarantees not provided for by European law, but established exclusively under national law, albeit in a field certainly not outside Union powers.

The examples could go on and on, as Koen Lenaerts and José Antonio Gutiérrez-Fons have demonstrated in their thorough analysis (in *The EU Charter of fundamental rights* (2014)), but for present purposes the list can stop here. It suffices simply to point out the high number of cases taken by the Court of justice over a short space of time. Immediately after the Lisbon Treaty's entry into force, many national judges submitted requests for preliminary rulings by the Court of justice intended to clarify the precise scope of article 51. But despite the large number of decisions on this issue handed down by the European Court, in a rapid succession of different situations, the matter does not seem to be definitively settled.

An interesting interpretation of these approaches is offered in a study conducted by Eleanor Spaventa (2016) for the European Parliament. The investigative analysis she carried out leads to the conclusion that article 51 of the Charter has been subject to 'diversified' application by the Court of justice. In areas marked by a strong Union interest – particularly an economic one or an interest connected with the sectors of the internal market – the Court of justice tends to apply the Charter to Member States generously, as it did in the *Fransson* case cited above (case C-617/10) and in *Ivo Taricco and others* (8.9.2015, C-105/14), which directly concerned Italy and to which we will return shortly. It is equally clear that, in cases totally unrelated to Union competences, the Court is extremely careful not to make undue intrusions into the national legal orders (as in, for example, the *Siragusa*, *Torralbo*, and *Hernández* cases mentioned above). The problem areas are those in which the Union plays a coordinating role with regard to regulatory schemes that fall under the powers of the Member States to establish. These include, in particular, European arrest warrants and matters of immigration, citizenship, and asylum. In these areas, the Court has maintained a very cautious approach, holding that the rights protected by the Charter apply only 'in exceptional cases'. This restrictive interpretation of article 51 should be corrected, because it is precisely in these areas, in which the Union's task is to coordinate national laws without harmonising them, that the need for a common standard of protection for fundamental rights is most acute, in order to favour the growth of mutual trust between Member States.

If we consider the issue from the point of view of the national legal systems, greater consistency and, therefore, greater clarity in interpreting the Charter's field of application is an increasingly urgent matter, including for the sake of effective respect for national identities. This element, which is inherent to the basic political and constitutional structures of the Member States, is explicitly recognised by the Lisbon Treaty in article 4.2 TEU. It is interesting to observe that many of the divergences between the ECJ and the national Constitutional (or Supreme) Courts in the area of fundamental rights concern the Charter's field of application and end up bringing in the issue of respect for national constitutional identity. This area is the subject of intense dialogue – or heated debate, if you like – in the European constitutional sphere, driving all the various players to try to strike a new balance.

C. The European Court and the National Courts: Dialogue and Conflict the Case of Italy

The national Courts, especially the Supreme and Constitutional Courts, have not been passive in the face of the incorporation of the Charter of rights into the European legal system on an equal footing to the treaties. Many of them have sensed the sea change and have been active on the European constitutional stage, soliciting interpretations from the Court of justice on a variety of different grounds.

In addition to the many questions submitted to the Court of justice concerning the Charter's field of application, like those mentioned above, it is interesting to note that the commencement of the Treaty of Lisbon coincided with the increased use of references for preliminary rulings under article 267 of the TFEU by national Supreme and Constitutional Courts. Traditionally reluctant to use a procedural tool that involves the European Court of justice in the definition of legal issues from national-level proceedings, in recent years many national Supreme and Constitutional Courts have jumped in, opening themselves up to frank and constructive conversation – and sometimes open debate – with the European Court. Although, until very recently, references for preliminary rulings were used only in exceptional cases, and almost exclusively by certain Courts (particularly the Constitutional Courts of Belgium and Austria), after the commencement of the Treaty of Lisbon, many national constitutional jurisdictions took the path laid down by the trailblazers of European constitutional dialogue.

These overlapping events – the Charter's rise to legally binding status and the heightening of constitutional conversation among the high courts – cannot be explained as a mere coincidence of timing. The questions referred to Luxembourg by the national Constitutional Courts have often focused on issues connected with the scope of the fundamental rights protected by the Charter. This was the case, for example, in *Stefano Melloni v Ministerio Fiscal* (16.2.2013, C-399/11), which involved a request by the Spanish Constitutional Tribunal concerning the level of protection of due process rights for purposes of applying the rules concerning European arrest warrants. Another such case was the Digital rights case mentioned above, in which the Court of justice accepted a question about the validity of a European directive, jointly brought by the Constitutional Court of Austria and the Irish Supreme Court, for violating the right to privacy and to the protection of personal data. More recently, in the *Taricco* case mentioned above, the Italian Constitutional Court requested a preliminary ruling on a question relating to the guarantees of legality and legal certainty of criminal offenses. It is not implausible to conclude that, with the Charter of rights' entry into force, the national Constitutional Courts sensed the need to recover a meaningful and central role for themselves in the dynamic of European integration, on a purely constitutional level like that of the protection of fundamental rights, after a long period of marginalisation and self-exclusion from it (Cartabia, Celotto (2002)).

In the case of Italy, in particular, it is useful to note that, ever since it was solemnly proclaimed in late 2000, the Charter of Fundamental Rights has been met with warm appreciation on the part of both ordinary judges and the Constitutional Court, even if it serves more often as a rhetorical tool than as a proper parameter of judgment. A great number of recent cases drawn from constitutional case law reveal this tendency to formally refer to the Charter, without, however, effectively grounding the judgment on the cited parameter. The Constitutional Court has done this in the context of the best interest of minors (article 24.2 of the Charter, judgment Nos. 27 of 2017, 239 of 2014, and 31 of 2012); the proportionality of penalties (article 49.3 of the Charter, judgment No. 236 of 2016); the right to work vacations (article 31.2 of the Charter, judgment No. 95 of 2016); the independence of collective bargaining (article 28 of the Charter, judgment No. 178 of 2015); and the right of a decent existence for people who lack resources (article 34 of the Charter, judgment no. 168 of 2014). Similarly, the following principles have also been considered by the Court: the *lex mitior* principle (judgment No. 236 of 2011), the dignity of the person (judgment No. 82 of 2011), public hearings (judgment No. 93 of 2010), informed consent to medical treatment (judgment No. 48 of 2008), and administrative due process (judgment No. 182 of 2008). In post-2000 cases on the facts, on legitimacy, and on constitutionality, there is a very common tendency to use this kind of purely rhetorical reference to the European Union Charter of rights – references intended to stress that the recognition of some rights and principles extends beyond the national borders. This is intended to buttress arguments that are actually drawn from an analysis of national parameters.

However, when it comes to cases where the rights protected by the Charter, as interpreted by the European Court of justice, are laden with meanings that are significantly new and different from the ones already guaranteed under traditional Italian constitutionalism, the Constitutional Court has been more careful to channel the Charter's field of effectiveness within its proper limits and to stipulate with some rigor the precise reach of the rights protected at the EU level. In particular, the Court has done this with regard to issues relating to criminal law and criminal procedure. In such cases, the Constitutional Court has frequently held that the rights and principles guaranteed by the Charter 'are relevant solely in relation to situations to which Community law (now Union law) is applicable' (judgment Nos. 303 of 2011 and 210 of 2013). The Court was even more explicit in a case involving issues of national criminal procedure law, the facts of which touched on the principle of publicity as it related to hearings for the imposition of preventive measures on dangerous individuals. The Constitutional Court referred to article 51 of the Charter, holding that that provision 'means that the Charter cannot constitute an instrument for protecting fundamental rights beyond the competences of the European Union, as has moreover been repeatedly asserted by the Court of justice'. Here the Court showed that it is well aware that a prerequisite for applying the Charter is that the case under examination falls under European law (judgment No. 80 of 2011).

In this kind of case, we can sense an awareness that the pluralism found in the various legal traditions can be so diverse as to give rise to real conflicts. And the Constitutional Courts, in such instances, feel particularly bound to their role as interpreters and guardians of national constitutional values.

At times, this particular 'vocation' and, we might say, this faithfulness to national tradition, expresses itself in the form of attributing relevance exclusively to the principles of the national constitution, deliberately sidelining the corresponding principles protected under the legal system of the European Union (one example, among many, is judgment No. 213 of 2016 of the Italian Constitutional Court). At others, the Charter is considered alongside constitutional and supranational parameters, all taken as a whole and without an analysis that considers its provisions individually (some examples of this, drawn again from the Italian Court, include judgment Nos. 235 of 2014, 7 of 2013, and 245 of 2011). These cases do not delineate the specific contribution made by the Charter, but neither do they draw a distinction in the levels of protection, which are kept artfully separate.

In conclusion, we cannot rule out that in some eminently improbable, but still possible, situations (as the Italian Court said long ago, in judgment No. 183 of 1973), the different view of the European Union could go so far as to come into conflict with the values protected by the Italian Constitution. This would trigger the divisive role of the so-called counter-limits, which express the need to protect the supreme and imperative principles of the constitutional system. These fundamental pillars are considered so crucial for the constitutional structure that they must be sheltered from interference of any kind, internal, supranational, or international (judgment No. 1146 of 1988). Even if this were to occur, it would not change the fact that there is a possibility to react in proactive, constructive, and dialogue-centred ways, or rather take the opposite approach and react in a defensive or combative manner. The Italian Constitutional Court, in its request for a preliminary ruling in order No. 24 of 2017 – a response to the European Court of justice's decision in the *Taricco* case – chose to take the former route. Stressing the indispensable value of the principles of legality and legal certainty of criminal law (guaranteed by article 25 of the Italian Constitution as well as by other legal traditions, particularly continental ones) the Constitutional Court decided to present the requirements of internal constitutional law within the European forum. In this way, it avoided, at least as a first step, initiating a conflict between the two systems. With that decision, the Italian Court demonstrated that the national constitutional traditions have not been surpassed or eclipsed by the entry into force of the European Union Charter of rights. It remains possible for them to be the lifeblood of constitutional law in Europe today, providing precious interpretive support for broadly shared values as part of a common experience, in which the rights of the person constitute, in an exemplary way, an element of 'unity in diversity'.

Bibliography

Besselink, LFM, 'The protection of fundamental rights post-Lisbon. The interaction between the Charter of fundamental rights of the European Union, the European convention on human rights (ECHR) and national constitutions' in *Reports of the XXV FIDE Congress Tallinn 2012*, vol. 1, *The protection of fundamental rights post-Lisbon* (Tallinn, 2012) 1–139.

Bifulco, R, Cartabia, M and Celotto, A, *L'Europa dei diritti. Commento alla Carta dei diritti fondamentali dell'Unione Europea* (Bologna, 2001).

Cartabia, M 'L'ora dei diritti fondamentali nell'Unione Europea', in M Cartabia (ed), *I diritti in azione* (Bologna, 2007) 13–66.

Cartabia, M and Celotto, A, 'La giustizia costituzionale in Italia dopo la Carta di Nizza' (2002) 6 *Giurisprudenza costituzionale* 4477–507.

de Búrca, G, 'The drafting of the EU Charter of fundamental rights' (2001) 26 *European law review* 126–38.

de Búrca, G, 'After the EU Charter of fundamental rights: the Court of justice as a human rights adjudicator?' (2013) 20 *Maastricht journal of European and comparative law* 168–84.

Fabbrini, F, *Fundamental rights in Europe* (Oxford, 2014).

Fabbrini, F and Pollicino, O, 'Constitutional identity in Italy: European integration as the fulfillment of the Constitution' (2017) 6 *EUI Law department working papers*, http://cadmus.eui.eu/handle/1814/45605.

Faraguna, P, *Ai confini della Costituzione. Principi supremi e identità costituzionale* (Milano, 2015).

Gianniti, P, (ed), *I diritti fondamentali nell'Unione Europea. La Carta di Nizza dopo il Trattato di Lisbona* (Bologna-Roma, 2013).

Guastaferro, B, 'Beyond the exceptionalism of constitutional conflicts. The ordinary functions of the identity clause' (2012) 31 *Yearbook of European law* 263–318.

Peers, S, 'The rebirth of the EU's Charter of fundamental rights' (2011) 13 *Cambridge yearbook of European legal studies* 283–309.

Peers, S, Hervey, T, Kenner, J, and Ward, A, (eds), *The EU Charter of Fundamental Rights* (Oxford-Portland (Oreg), 2014), (in particular K Lenaerts, JA Gutiérrez-Fons, *The place of the Charter in the EU constitutional edifice*, 1559–93; A Arnull, *Protocol (No. 30) on the application of the Charter of fundamental rights of the European Union to Poland and to the United Kingdom*, 1595–1612).

Poiares Maduro, M 'The double constitutional life of the Charter of fundamental rights of the European Union', in T Hervey and J Kenner (eds), *Economic and social rights under the EC Charter of fundamental rights. A legal perspective* (Oxford, 2003) 270–99.

Spaventa, E, 'The interpretation of article 51 of the EU Charter of fundamental rights: the dilemma of stricter or broader application of the Charter to national measures', Study for the PETI Commission, 2016, http://www.europarl.europa.eu/RegData/etudes/STUD/2016/556930/IPOL_STU(2016)556930_EN.pdf.

Trucco, L, *Carta dei diritti fondamentali e costituzionalizzazione dell'Unione Europea* (Torino, 2013).

von Bogdandy, A, 'The European Union as a human rights organization? Human rights and the core of the European Union' (2000) 37 *Common market law review* 1307–38.

Weiler, JHH and Fries, SC, 'A human rights policy for the European community and Union. The question of competences', in P Alston (ed), *The EU and human rights* (Oxford, 1999) 147–66.

Ziller, J, 'Art. 51. Ambito di applicazione' in R Mastroianni, O Pollicino, S Allegrezza, F Pappalardo and O Razzolini (eds), *Carta dei diritti fondamentali dell'Unione europea* (Milano, 2017) 1042–58.

All web pages are understood as having last been visited on 24 April 2018.

Thanks are due to Dr Alessandro Baro for his help in drafting this chapter.

PART II

The European Union and its Institutional System: Basic Principles, Competences and Responsibilities

6

The Treaties that Created Europe

MARISE CREMONA

I. The Treaty Family

In the familiar face of an adult woman, an old friend might see not only an older version of the woman's younger self, but also traces of the child she once was. In the treaties currently governing the European Union (EU), which seem in some ways scarcely recognisable as altered versions of the EEC Treaty which came into force in 1957, we do nevertheless see elements of the original Treaty of Rome. So much has changed: the titles of the treaties, the name of the organisation that they establish, the arrangement of the provisions, the accumulation of protocols and declarations, and even their stated aims. And yet many core provisions – the bones of the European construction – are remarkably little changed. These include, for example, the provisions governing the four freedoms (the free movement of people, services, goods and capital), competition and agricultural policies, and the jurisdiction of the European Court of Justice (ECJ). It is interesting to note that it is precisely these provisions – which have been more or less taken for granted and to some extent eclipsed in commentators' and scholars' attention by more recent and apparently more exciting innovations such as monetary union, security and defence, and migration policy – that have emerged as 'red lines' in the negotiations on the exit of the United Kingdom from the European Union. They are perceived as vital to the integrity of the European Union and are not to be compromised.

This chapter will examine the treaties that have contributed to the construction of what is now the European Union, starting from the establishment of the European Coal and Steel Community (ECSC) in 1951. It will focus on the most important treaties, the aim being to trace their inter-relationships so as to get a better picture of the genealogy of the current treaty framework, its inherited characteristics as well as more recent innovations. Behind the metaphor with which we began, the more prosaic truth is that despite the almost uninterrupted process of reform over the last 15 years the structures of the European Union display a high degree of continuity and are strongly path-dependent. What are the characteristics that emerge from this combination of change and continuity?

In the first place there is the creation of a system of interconnected treaties. The project of the European Community, and now of the European Union, has never been founded on a single treaty, despite the initial pre-eminence of the Treaty of Rome. It has always been based on a series of related treaties, although the ways in which they connect have altered. This is perhaps one of the distinctive features of the construction of Europe, and maybe it is no coincidence that attempts to merge all the treaties into one – albeit never comprehensively – have always failed.

In the second place there is the dual nature of these treaties. This duality has emerged over time, from the Van Gend en Loos judgment (5.2.1963, *NV Algemene Transport- en Expeditie Onderneming van Gend & Loos v Netherlands inland revenue Administration*, case 26/62) to opinion 2/13 (18.12.2014) of the European Court of Justice. They are indisputably instruments of international law, and the Member States as contracting parties are ultimately the 'masters of the Treaties' ('die Herren der Verträge': de Witte 2012). However, they are also more than this: according to the European Court of Justice they constitute the 'constitutional charter of a Community based on the rule of law', albeit concluded 'in the form of an international agreement' (opinion 1/91, 14.12.1991, paragraph 21). The treaties are not simply expressions of a reciprocal contractual relationship, nor even of a collective set of commitments and goals. They establish an autonomous legal order capable of governing relationships between the actors in the system, of determining its relations with other legal norms – national and international laws in particular – and of entering into new international commitments (Weiler (1991)). The precise nature of the European Union Constitution and its relation to the constitutions of its Member States is not the subject of this chapter. Nevertheless the characteristics of the EU treaties which evidence their dual character as treaty and – in a certain sense – Constitution have influenced their structure and evolution.

In the third place, there is the relation between framework and detail. A distinguishing feature of the original Treaty of Rome was said to be its character as a *traité-cadre*, and early commentators highlighted the way the EEC Treaty established relatively broad principles, the detailed implementation of which required completion by the legislative institutions and the Court of Justice. The independence of these legislative and judicial institutions constituted one of the key features of the EEC, identified by Pierre Pescatore in his *Le droit de l'intégration* in 1972. And the teleological method of interpretation of the European Court of Justice derived (or at least derived support) from the framework nature of the founding treaties.

At the same time, the treaties contain a high level of detail. They do not merely establish legislative structures; they prescribe substantive commitments and precise obligations, including rights defined with sufficient precision as to be directly enforceable by individuals. In this sense the treaties can also be described as *traité-loi*. As the scope of Community and then Union law has increased, so have the substantive provisions of the treaties, but this expansion of the treaties is not simply the result of the advance of Union law into new fields; existing competences are spelled out in more detail, decision-making rules are ever more complex and successive treaty revisions have attempted to codify developments in law and practice so that treaty provisions become longer and more convoluted. Behind this tendency are reiterated attempts to balance the flexibility and dynamism needed to respond to new challenges with concerns over 'competence creep' and the desire to ensure that the Member States can indeed retain control over the EU's expanding powers.

In the fourth place there is the variety of competence structures contained in the treaties and differentiation in the participation of the Member States. Here there has been significant change over time. While the original Treaty of Rome granted competences but said nothing about their nature, the Treaty on the Functioning of the European Union (TFEU), the successor to the EEC and EC Treaties, now identifies explicitly at least five types of competence.

And whereas the treaties of 1951 and 1957 established rules which applied equally to all the Member States, from the Maastricht Treaty (Treaty on European Union, TEU, 1992) onwards, the treaties began to introduce different types of differentiated integration.

These characteristics emphasise the degree to which the EU treaties have moved away from traditional instruments of international law while at the same time maintaining the central importance of the Member States.

In this chapter we will examine three phases in the development of the treaties. While these overlap to some extent, they will enable us to bring into focus these different characteristics at different points in time. We will not look so much at the substantive content of the treaties (otherwise this would become a history of European integration), but rather at their architecture and interrelationships. Bruno de Witte (2009) has explained the term 'treaty architecture' as the way that the treaties and their protocols 'are arranged in relation to each other' and their internal structure; it refers, he said, 'to the way the Treaties look before one examines their actual content' (p 9).

The first phase is the one in which the treaty system was initially established, and which saw the emergence of the distinctive characteristics of the legal order of the 'European Communities', legally distinct yet closely integrated. The second phase was marked by growing complexity and at the same time by growing fragmentation and differentiation. It was characterised by attempts to incorporate new forms of integration into the framework and by the creation of a new organisation alongside the European Communities: the European Union, with its own treaty, specific competences and legal nature. A third phase was marked by a failed attempt to manifest in treaty form the constitutional character of the treaties and by an (only partially successful) attempt to simplify the treaty structure. These experiments and the current treaty framework, which derives from the 2007 Treaty of Lisbon, are testament to the resilience and adaptability of the treaties.

To do justice to the treaties which have helped to create Europe, we should also take account of their 'extended family': the accession agreements; the treaties between Member States that, while not among the founding treaties of the EU, nevertheless form part of the broader legal environment (such as the Treaty of stability, coordination and governance in the Economic and Monetary Union, also known as the European Fiscal Compact); and some of the Union's external agreements, such as the agreement on the European Economic Area (EEA), which play an important part in the construction of the wider Europe. It will not be possible to cover these in such a short chapter; this is not a sign of their lack of importance, but rather of a lack of space.

II. Establishing the Framework

The three original founding treaties date from 1951 (Treaty of Paris, establishing the ECSC) and 1957 (the two Treaties of Rome, establishing the EEC and the EAEC, European Atomic Energy Community, also known as Euratom). A fourth founding treaty was signed in Maastricht in 1992, creating the European Union. The ECSC, which came into force in 1952, was designed to last 50 years and it was allowed to expire in 2002, its functions subsumed into the European Community.

How were these first three treaties of the 1950s (the ECSC, EEC and Euratom) structured?

First we notice that while the ECSC Treaty was relatively short (100 articles), the treaties founding the EEC and Euratom were much longer (248 and 225 articles respectively). These were supplemented by protocols on the Statute of the Court of Justice and on privileges and immunities and, in the case of the ECSC, by a Convention on transitional arrangements. In comparison, the current Treaty on the European Union has 55 articles and the TFEU has 358, albeit supplemented by 37 protocols. The complexity of the current treaties is thus not simply a function of their greater length.

The structure of the ECSC Treaty was simple: it opened with provisions establishing the aims and basic principles of the 'common market, common objectives and common institutions' (article 1), followed by provisions on the institutions, and substantive provisions on the management of the coal and steel industries. The Preamble clearly stated that the treaty's ultimate goals were political and far-reaching (the contracting parties were 'resolved to substitute for historic rivalries a fusion of their essential interests; to establish, by creating an economic community, the foundation of a broad and independent community among peoples long divided by bloody conflicts; and to lay the bases of institutions capable of giving direction to their future common destiny'), but the treaty itself is prosaic and sectorially focused. In its institutional provisions, it laid the foundation for the new forms of institutional structure which came to be defined as supranational, dividing power between the four institutions: the Council of Ministers, the High Authority (precursor to the Commission), a Common Assembly and the Court of Justice (Pescatore (1972), Eng transl (1974) 13). The ECSC had its own legal personality and the ability to conduct external relations (article 6).

The EEC and Euratom Treaties, concluded in 1957 and coming into force in 1958, built upon the ECSC Treaty both institutionally and substantively. The scope of the EEC Treaty was of course broader, including in principle all types of goods and services. The sectoral ECSC and Euratom Treaties were more concerned with market management than the EEC Treaty, an approach echoed by the EEC Treaty's provisions governing the Common Agricultural Policy (CAP). However, the fundamental idea of establishing a common market based on principles of free movement, non-discrimination and safeguarding competition provided a common framework.

With the birth of the two Treaties of Rome we can see the emergence of the family of European treaties. It would have been possible to draft a single new treaty incorporating the powers of the ECSC, Euratom and the EEC (de Witte (2009) 9), but this did not happen. Instead, there were three separate treaties, each establishing a Community with its own legal personality, competences, and the ability to act internationally: three separate but connected European Communities. Apart from sharing some goals, what made these treaties a family? Essentially three features: first, an identity of Member States; secondly the institutional framework and thirdly the express provisions linking the treaties.

The three Communities had the same original six Member States, and it is noticeable that from the start the accession of new members was envisaged – it was to be an open club – but it was accepted politically, albeit not legally required, that any accession would be to all three Communities. This was not an inevitable requirement, especially since the Communities were separate legal entities governed by separate treaties, although the shared institutions would have made a differentiated membership difficult. But more important, the identity of membership emphasised the linked character of the Communities, which even from 1957 were referred to collectively as the 'European Communities,' and their founding treaties. The unity of membership established from the start also had implications in later years, as other ways of accommodating different views on the direction of further integration needed to be found.

The three Communities were always designed to be linked institutionally, and in a relatively short time these links became even closer. From the start they shared two institutions, the Assembly and the Court of Justice, in accordance with a Convention on certain institutions common to the European Communities, drawn up at the same time as the two Treaties of Rome. Then in 1965 the Merger Treaty (*traité de fusion*) did not merge the Communities, but did provide for a single Council and a single Commission. Despite the fact that these were shared institutions, their powers derived from three separate treaties, and it was therefore still necessary to determine the legal basis for acting under the powers of one or another (or a combination) of the three treaties. From this point of view, the mandate of a single Court of Justice with the ability to adjudicate on the allocation of competence between the treaties was important.

The treaties also contained provisions on their inter-relations. According to article 232 of the EEC Treaty its provisions 'shall not affect' those of the ECSC, 'in particular in regard to the rights and obligations of Member States, the powers of the institutions of the said Community and the rules laid down by the said Treaty for the functioning of the common market for coal and steel'; a similar provision referred to the Euratom Treaty. Although this might appear to be a *lex specialis* clause designed to protect the sectoral treaties, it was not interpreted by the Court as completely excluding issues concerning coal and steel or Euratom from the scope of the EEC Treaty.

Instead, the Court ascertained whether the specific matter under discussion had a legal basis in the ECSC or Euratom Treaties; if not, then the EEC Treaty could and should apply. In opinion 1/94 on the conclusion of the WTO (World Trade Organization) agreements, for example, the Court held that 'since the Euratom Treaty contains no provisions relating to external trade, there is nothing to prevent agreements concluded pursuant to article 113 of the EC Treaty from extending to international trade in Euratom products' (opinion 1/94, 15.11.1994, para. 24). The issue of international trade in coal and steel was more debatable, since a provision in the ECSC Treaty did refer to commercial policy, reserving this to the Member States (article 71, ECSC). Nonetheless the Court maintained that this provision 'can only have reserved competence to the Member States as regards agreements relating specifically to ECSC products' (opinion 1/94, 15.11.1994, para. 27). Agreements on trade in goods in general, including coal and steel – as was the case of the GATT (General Agreement on Tariffs and Trade) and WTO agreements – came under the general commercial policy powers of the European Community. Thus although there was no formal hierarchy between the treaties, and the ECSC and Euratom treaties had their own distinct spheres of action, we can see the EEC Treaty becoming the central treaty, providing an overarching coherence to the group.

The Single European Act (SEA) of 1986 contains a modest 34 articles but was a significant addition to the European Communities family of treaties. In the first place, it brought about the first substantial revision of the EEC Treaty since its birth, earlier amendments having mainly concerned its sphere of application (management of the consequences of decolonisation, the accession of new Member States and the withdrawal of Greenland).

The SEA falls into two parts; one (Title II) consisting of amendments to the three existing treaties and the other (Title III) of provisions on European Political Cooperation (EPC), adding a fourth member of the family. The initial articles (Title I) form a chapeau, declaring the unified aims of this now four-part framework and institutionalising the role of the European Council.

In its revision of the EEC Treaty, the SEA established the goal of the internal market as an area without internal frontiers with its own legislative competence characterised by qualified majority voting, and included explicit grants of competence in fields such as the environment, social policy and economic and social cohesion, which had until now required the use of the 'flexibility clause' (article 235, EEC Treaty). It also conferred greater powers on the European Parliament, with the introduction of the new cooperation procedure. These revisions made it clear that substantive treaty amendment was feasible, and the SEA effectively inaugurated a 20-year period of successive treaty reform, with the Treaties of Maastricht (1992), Amsterdam (1997) and Nice (2001); the failed Constitutional Treaty of 2004 and the Treaty of Lisbon of 2007. The failure of the Constitutional Treaty and the arduous process of gestation and ratification of the Treaty of Lisbon (Piris (2010) 25–63) has halted (at least temporarily) this period of continual change, as well as leading to calls for revision of the treaty amendment procedures and a renewed recourse to alternative mechanisms, including inter-Member State agreements operating alongside the European Union treaties.

In addition to these amendments, Title III of the SEA formalised and institutionalised the practice of coordinating the foreign policy of Member States which had developed under the name of European Political Cooperation since the 1970s. This addition of a fourth dimension to the three European Economic Communities was significant in several ways which bear on our subject. For the first time, the European integration project had a distinct foreign policy mandate. Each of the three Community treaties had created an organisation with the capacity and the competence to enter into international commitments. In its judgment on the European Agreement on Road Transport (31.3.1971, *Commission of the European Communities v Council of the European Communities*, case 22/70), the Court held that external competence may be derived from provisions of the EEC Treaty that do not explicitly refer to external action, opening up the possibility of more extensive external relations in spheres including transport, fisheries, social policy and the environment. However, these powers were economically rather than the politically conceived and were not fundamentally concerned with the establishment of an international identity for the Community. The SEA struck a new note in its Preamble, which is reflected in the present treaties:

> Aware of the responsibility incumbent upon Europe to aim at speaking ever increasingly with one voice and to act with consistency and solidarity in order more effectively to protect its common interests and independence, in particular to display the principles of democracy and compliance with the law and with human rights to which [the Signatory States] are attached, so that together they may make their own contribution to the preservation of international peace and security in accordance with the undertaking entered into by them within the framework of the United Nations Charter.

We have here the foundation for the EU's external mission, further crystallised in the Maastricht Treaty and currently set out in articles 3(5) and 21 of the TEU, which now forms such an important part of the EU's identity.

Secondly, the SEA was an attempt to bring into the European treaties a new policy field that had developed outside them, a process which would be repeated a few years later in the field of borders and migration with the integration of the Schengen acquis into the Treaty on European Union. The title 'Single European Act' signals the intention to create a unified regime, and the SEA refers to the European Communities as being 'founded' on the three constituent Community treaties, declaring that they share with the EPC the objective 'to contribute together to making concrete progress towards European unity' (article 1, SEA). However, the provisions concerning EPC were not integrated into the EEC Treaty and – and this is the third important aspect – retained their intergovernmental nature. One of the most striking indications of this was the use of the expression 'High Contracting Parties' instead of Member States in Title III of the SEA, but it is also evidenced by the absence of any jurisdiction for the Court of Justice (article 31, SEA) and the more limited role of the Commission, which is 'fully associated with the proceedings of Political Co-operation' (article 30(3)b, SEA), but without its normal Community prerogative of initiative. The EPC provisions in the SEA alluded to the relationship between the two types of regime cohabiting under the same roof, stipulating that the EPC was to be 'consistent' with the external policies of the EC, entrusting the responsibility for this to the presidency and to the Commission (article 30(5), SEA), but without providing any 'practical interaction rules' (Lak (1989) 290). For the first time, the European treaties accepted a new policy field that did not share the normal 'Community method' of decision making, and the tension between these different institutional methodologies, criticised at the time (Pescatore (1987)) and which reached its height in the Maastricht Treaty's pillar-based structure, can still be traced today in the Lisbon Treaty regime.

The last point draws attention to an important aspect of this period of building the treaty framework: the recognition that the treaties that established the European Communities were undoubtedly international treaties, but they were also something more. This development was the result of interaction between the Court of Justice and its primary and secondary interlocutors, in particular the Commission, national courts, Member State governments, and scholars. As ECJ Judge Federico Mancini said in 1989, 'if you had to summarise the orientation characterising the case law produced in Luxembourg from 1957 onwards, you could say that it coincided with the drawing up of a Constitution for Europe' (p 595).

The 'essential characteristics' of the legal order established by the treaties that two years later would lead the Court of Justice to refer to the EEC Treaty as a 'constitutional charter' include the Court-made doctrines of primacy and direct effect (opinion 1/91, 14.12.1991, para. 21). Other characteristics can certainly be added, ranging from the doctrine of pre-emption (Mancini (1989). 603) to the development of the Court's fundamental rights case law. The separation within the SEA of the amendments to the Community treaties from the provisions on the EPC was a sign that the Member States had recognised both the legal character of the *acquis communautaire* and the Court's powerful influence in shaping that character. Another sign could be said to be the start, in the context of the European Communities, of the practice of appending declarations to the new treaty designed in some cases to preempt judicial interpretation. The SEA contains 11 general declarations and nine declarations from individual Member States. Subsequently the practice, like that of using protocols, has burgeoned: the treaties in force contain 50 general declarations and 15 declarations from one or more Member States.

III. Architectural Complexities

The SEA may be said to have started the process of increasing complexity which then became, in the Maastricht Treaty, almost an organising principle of treaty reform. The Treaty of Maastricht came into force in 1993, at a time when major geopolitical change was reshaping Europe, and it represents an attempt to respond to those changes and to launch a new phase in European integration. At the same time, the underlying nature of the European project's constitutive instruments as treaties imposed the need to find ways of accommodating the Member States' differences alongside their desire to be part of the common enterprise. For the first time, ratification of the new Treaty by all Member States was not a straightforward process. Thus one feature of the Treaty of Maastricht was acceptance, for the first time, of differentiation: that not all Member States would necessarily participate in each new initiative. The major new policy additions were each characterised by opt-outs or derogations: the Economic and Monetary Union (EMU), the Common Foreign and Security Policy (CFSP) and cooperation in Justice and Home Affairs (JHA). This was one form of fragmentation.

The Treaty of Maastricht sought to bring together within a single framework the European Communities, the new Common Foreign and Security Policy (which represented a considerable step forward in the institutional development of EPC) and existing cooperation on migration, borders and criminal justice that had taken place outside the Community treaties, and would become known as cooperation in Justice and Home Affairs. Like the SEA, the Treaty of Maastricht combined amendments to the Community treaties with a body of provisions establishing new fields of action, each with their own institutional and decision-making structures, thus introducing a second form of fragmentation. However, unlike the SEA it created a new entity to provide an overarching framework housing the different 'pillars' of integration: the European Union.

The treaty structure of the European Union at its inception illustrates concretely the different forces at play. On the one hand, the desire to bring together the different elements of the European integration project into a single structure, so as to limit the risk of further fragmentation. On the other hand, the desire to protect the *acquis communautaire* contained in the three Community treaties from the risk of being diluted by the less integrated forms of cooperation represented by the CFSP and JHA. The precise legal nature of the European Union was left undefined and was subject to different interpretations: it was not even clear whether it had a separate legal existence (Curtin (2001) 351). It was presented in the Treaty as 'a new stage in the process of creating an ever closer union among the peoples of Europe', which was 'founded' on the European Communities (article A, TEU). It was given a set of objectives (article B, TEU) which, alongside 'maintaining in full' and 'building on»' the Community acquis, emphasised the policies newly introduced into the Community treaties (EMU and citizenship) and the TEU (CFSP and JHA). At the same time, the European Communities maintained their separate existence side-by-side (or as part of) the new European Union, and were not subservient to it: the new policies are described as 'supplementing' those of the European Communities and, most importantly, they were not to 'affect' the Community treaties (article M, TEU). Thus, the Treaty on European Union became one of the family of European treaties, but it was an additional layer placed on top of a composite construction. The foundation was the European Communities, and reading the Community treaties one would hardly have been aware that the European Union existed (there were some clues, such as the creation, in the EC Treaty, of citizenship of the Union).

Much has been written about the Treaty of Maastricht and its simultaneous move towards Union and fragmentation, the pillar-based structure that led to the epithet 'a Europe of bits and pieces' (Curtin (1993)). As de Witte explains, in time both political practice and scholarly understanding accepted that the European Union was a 'stable legal reality', and that it was legally and institutionally linked to the European Communities (de Witte (2009) 14). The key to the link was in the Maastricht Treaty's provision in article C of the TEU for a 'single institutional framework'. This had two dimensions: first, alignment of the institutional provisions in the EC, ECSC and Euratom treaties and, secondly, the sharing of institutions between the Communities and the EU policies of CFSP and JHA. As the institutions became more used to working within a single framework, albeit according to different procedural rules and producing acts with differing legal effects, the experience of coexistence made possible the move towards greater convergence in the Constitutional Treaty and the Treaty of Lisbon.

Some steps towards this convergence were taken with the 1999 Treaty of Amsterdam, which, while retaining the pillar structure, started the process of bringing into 'normal' Community structures some aspects of the JHA, at the same time reforming again Community decision-making processes and increasing the power of the European Parliament through co-decision. Both of these moves, as well as some cleaning up of the Community Treaties and the inclusion in the Amsterdam Treaty's Final Act of consolidated and re-numbered versions of the EC Treaty and the Treaty on European Union, are evidence that the Union and its Member States were attempting to provide a stable foundation for European integration. We can also see the constitutional 'pull' of the Community method. It is notable however that, despite discussions on merging the four treaties into one, and a number of experiments in that direction, the existing treaty framework was not altered. Nor was the eventual attempt to do so in the 2004 Constitutional Treaty ultimately successful.

The 2000 Treaty of Nice did not essentially make any immediate contribution to the EU's treaty architecture. It was designed to adjust the institutional and decision-making structures in the run-up to the major enlargement that was to take place in 2004. But the resulting text, with its baroque compromises, complex protocols and the difficult process of achieving this less-than-optimal outcome gave momentum to the call for simplification and laid the foundation for the 2001 Laeken Declaration, which launched the process leading to the drafting of the Constitutional Treaty.

In considering the increasing complexity of the treaty framework, we have so far highlighted the introduction of the Treaty on European Union with its additional pillars and its separate but integrated relationship to the Community treaties (3.9.2008, *Yassin Abdullah Kadi and Al Barakaat International Foundation v Council of the European Union and Commission of the European Communities*, joined cases C-402/05 P and C-415/05 P, paragraph 202), as well as differentiated integration in the form of policy opt-outs. Three further aspects of this complexity should briefly be mentioned.

The first is the introduction in the Treaty of Amsterdam of a new form of flexibility: enhanced cooperation. To some extent this can be seen as part of the Community's enlargement plan: the desire to avoid blockages in the decision-making process by enabling some Member States to move ahead within Community structures. As with policy opt-outs, enhanced cooperation tackles the problem of the convoy moving at the speed of the slowest component, preserving the concept of unity but accepting the reality of differentiation.

For some time this remained only a potential cause of greater complexity, since it was little used (indeed it seemed designed to discourage its use). However, more recently it seems to have found more favour, and has been used to create the European Unitary Patent as well as for legislation on private international law on divorce, for the creation of a European Public Prosecutor, and a financial transaction tax. Together with the various opt-out regimes, especially those that make it possible to opt into individual pieces of legislation, these initiatives make it increasingly difficult to identify exactly which elements of Community law apply to which Member States. As nicely put by de Witte (2002) 1257), as a result of the Amsterdam Treaty the '*maquis communautaire*' became even denser than before.

Another type of complexity reflects the tendency towards ever-greater specificity in defining Union policies. In some cases (such as environmental policy) this results from explicitly defining new policy frameworks that had emerged from existing competences; in other cases new policies are included (such as those on employment introduced by the Treaty of Amsterdam) or existing embryonic provisions are expanded. For example: the SEA contained a single article on EPC, this rose to 11 articles on the CFSP in the Treaty of Maastricht, and in the current TEU we find 23. The Treaty of Maastricht contained nine articles on JHA, essentially establishing fields and modalities of cooperation; the current TFEU contains a title on the Area of Freedom, Security and Justice containing five chapters and 22 articles. The amendment by the Treaty of Nice of the definition of the common commercial policy in article 133 of the EC, rendered parts of it almost incomprehensible even to specialists, and if it had not been radically restructured by the Treaty of Lisbon it would no doubt have led to extensive litigation (see opinion 1/08, 30.11.2009). The treaty provisions on decision-making have also expanded and grown more complex. At the time of the Laeken declaration there were 15 different types of legal act, some – as Jean-Claude Piris (2010) has pointed out – with different names but similar legal effects, others with similar names but different legal effects: 'This phenomenon did not contribute to enhancing the readability and understanding of the Treaties' (p 93).

The third type of complexity concerns the introduction of a new source of Union law and its relationship with existing sources: the Charter of Fundamental Rights, adopted in December 2000 and given binding force by the Treaty of Lisbon. There is considerable overlap between the rights set out in the Charter, certain rights contained in the EU treaties, and the fundamental rights guaranteed by the European Convention on Human Rights and derived from the constitutional traditions common to the Member States, which are recognised and applied by the Court as 'general principles of Union law' (article 6(3), TEU). These relations are still being worked out, although it appears that in practice the Court of Justice will tend to refer in the first instance to the Charter. From the perspective of this chapter we should note that the Charter would have formed part of the Constitutional Treaty, and despite the fact that formally speaking it is not a protocol annexed to the treaties in force, it has been taken out of its 'legal limbo' (de Witte (2002) 1279) and given 'the same legal value as the Treaties' (article 6(1), TEU), thus becoming part of EU primary law.

However perhaps the greatest problem has simply been the difficulty caused by an accretion of legal texts. In 2004 there were three basic treaties (the EC Treaty, TEU and Euratom) with a total of 36 protocols, nine amending or supplementary treaties, and six accession treaties (without counting the protocols, this makes a total of 18 treaties), all with provisions in force (Piris (2006) 57). As Stephen Weatherill stated, 'The problem lies in the accumulation of texts, breeding ever-deepening intransparency. Change which is not intelligible is likely to cause alienation' ((2000) 18). It was this sense of the need to make the Community and Union treaties more accessible and thereby, it was thought, enhance their legitimacy that was behind the political support for a 'simplification' project and ultimately the Constitutional Treaty (de Witte (2002)).

IV. The Resilience of the Treaties: The Treaties as Palimpsests

In a counterpoint to the movements towards greater complexity and fragmentation that we have been tracing, we can see moves towards trying to achieve simplification and greater unity. Interestingly, these have tended to represent not a desire to return to simpler, less challenging forms of integration but an impulse towards 'more Europe' and greater integration, to fulfil the promise of European unity already mentioned in the preamble to the ECSC Treaty of 1951. This was, as expressed by de Witte, an approach to treaty architecture 'which was constitutionally inspired rather than pragmatic, and in which reforms of treaty structures were intended to pave the way for (rather than follow and codify) a substantive deepening of the integration process' (de Witte (2002) 1263).

The story of the Constitutional Treaty has been told many times and will not be repeated here (Piris (2006); Amato, Bribosia, de Witte (2007); de Witte (2009) 16–20; Piris (2010) 15–25). Within the scope of this paper we may note the following points.

The process that started with the Laeken Declaration of 2001, despite the fact that this was the first time that the heads of State and of government used the word constitution, was not the first attempt to unify the treaties. We might mention in particular the Spinelli project of 1984, a project of the European Parliament (de Witte (2009) 11–12), and a project on a 'basic treaty' undertaken in 2000 by the European University Institute on behalf of the Commission (de Witte (2002) 1270–72).

In effect the Constitution Convention process, unusual though it was in terms of Community and Union treaty revision, was the culmination of a long conversation between different institutional and non-institutional actors.

There were two distinct dynamics in this conversation. The first saw unification of the treaties primarily in terms of simplification, bringing together the existing texts into one treaty framework, clearly identifying the acquis and eliminating the confusion attendant on the simultaneous existence of three or four organisations, each with their own legal personality (the ESCS expired in 2002 and the Union's legal personality was at the time not fully accepted). Simplification could also include reformulating the more obsolete and less transparent provisions of the treaties, although this was not a merely technical task given that the lack of clarity was often the result of hard-fought battles and compromises (de Witte (2002) 1278, recalling that 'monument of intransparency' represented by the new rules in the Treaty of Nice on qualified majority voting in the Council). The second position argued in favour of a reorganisation of the treaties, together with the possibility of some clarification or revision, for example by integrating the CFSP and/or JHA pillars into Community decision-making procedures. This reorganisation would also allow for a distinction between a shorter and simpler 'basic treaty', containing the fundamental constitutional provisions, and a second treaty (or set of protocols) containing the details of the different policy fields.

In addition to greater clarity, it was argued, this division would also allow a differentiation in treaty revision processes, entrenching the 'basic treaty' and allowing a simplified procedure for revision of the more technical policy provisions. Given the difficulties experienced with treaty revision in the post-Maastricht period, this was an appealing prospect.

The Constitutional Treaty project adopted aspects of both these approaches. It was a single treaty, but contained various parts, the first of which was designed as a sort of 'basic treaty' or fundamental constitutional framework. The articulation between the different parts was not always smooth, and indeed determining the criteria for allocating the provisions was not straightforward, given (for example) that in the Community treaties the delimitation of competence was normally dealt with in policy-specific provisions (de Witte (2002).1274). The adoption of a single treaty implied the merger of the Communities and the Union into a single entity, and it was not surprising (despite the regrets of some) that the chosen successor was the Union and not the Community. It also implied the incorporation of the Charter of Fundamental Rights, which was simply added as a separate part of the treaty. The Constitutional Treaty was certainly a simplification, in the sense of a single treaty, a degree of rationalisation and a clearer statement of the Union's primary objectives. However, the resulting text was very long and complex and the links between the constituent parts were not always clear.

There was also the question of the extent to which the new treaty should incorporate a codification of the Court's case law. Since the most fundamental constitutional doctrines of Community law have been developed through case law, to reject this outright would have resulted in a thin and somewhat misleading expression of the new constitution for the Union. On the other hand it is always difficult to attempt to codify complex case law, and it risks 'freezing' the law at a certain point in time, hindering further development. The Constitutional Treaty was fairly circumspect on this point. The primacy of Union law was included, and in a few instances a codification was attempted, not always successfully (eg, in relation to exclusive external competence), but there was no wholesale attempt to incorporate case law on, for example, the direct effect of treaty provisions or directives, or Member State liability under the Francovich doctrine (19.11.1991, *Francovich v Italian Republic and Bonifaci and others v Italian Republic*, joined cases C-6/90 and C-9/90).

As some have pointed out, it was not at all obvious that the simplification and reorganisation project would become a process of constitutional-building. The Laeken Declaration, by raising this possibility, paved the way for an intense debate on whether or not it was appropriate – and indeed possible – to draw up a constitution for Europe. While significant from a political point of view, the constitutional terminology adopted in the title did not change the legal nature of the text as an international treaty, as evidenced in the provision on ratification and entry into force (de Witte (2012) 32). So, too, the 'de-constitutionalisation' that took place with the transformation of the Constitution into the Treaty of Lisbon did not involve any changes to the legal status of the texts themselves.

The Treaty of Lisbon was designed to achieve a certain amount of simplification and reorganisation, retaining many of the revisions agreed in 2004 and incorporated into the Constitutional Treaty, but abandoning the idea of a single text. It is drafted as a treaty amending the TEU and the EC Treaty (the latter renamed as the Treaty on the Functioning of the European Union, TFEU), and retaining the basic structure and differentiation between the EU and EC Treaties, while making significant amendments to both.

The decision to act through an amending treaty and to retain the separated treaty architecture was obviously predominantly driven by the need to demonstrate both that the Treaty of Lisbon was something different from the Constitutional Treaty (and that the public voice evidenced in the negative referendums on the Constitution had been heard), and that the new Treaty did not in fact make major constitutional changes to the status quo – and that therefore new referendums did not need to be held (Cremona (2012)).

As stated in the mandate of the Intergovernmental Conference agreed by the European Council in June 2007, which formed the basis for the Treaty of Lisbon negotiations, 'the constitutional concept, which consisted in repealing all existing Treaties and replacing them by a single text called "Constitution", is abandoned. [...] The TEU and the Treaty on the Functioning of the Union will not have a constitutional character' (European Council, doc. 11177/1/07, REV 1, Brussels, 20.7.2007). The solution adopted in the Treaty of Lisbon was more than a simple cosmetic exercise (it was not simply the Constitutional Treaty in disguise), but at the same time it produced results significantly different from the former treaty structure (Cremona (2012)), most notably in connecting the two treaties firmly together as the common foundation for the European Union, which 'shall replace and succeed' the EC (article 1, TEU; article 1, TFEU).

The two treaties are of equal legal value and the Union is now founded on both treaties rather on the European Communities. The reference in the former TEU to retaining and developing the *acquis communautaire* has also gone. In fact all references to the *acquis communautaire* as such have disappeared (although ironically some other uses of the term 'acquis' remain, signalling continuity: article 20(4) TEU, for example, refers to the accession acquis in the context of enhanced cooperation, and article 87(3) TFEU refers to the Schengen acquis). If EC priority has disappeared, the TEU, despite its more general and institutional provisions, is not given a more fundamental status than the TFEU, although we should note that the simplified revision procedure only applies to (parts of) the TFEU so in some sense the TEU provisions are more entrenched.

The two treaties are bound more closely together than the EU and EC Treaties. In a clever piece of drafting, 'the Treaties' is used as a term not only in article 1 TEU and article 1 TFEU but throughout. Thus, for example, in article 17(1) TEU we read that the Commission 'shall ensure the application of the Treaties, and of measures adopted by the institutions pursuant to them' and article 19(1) TEU provides that the Court of Justice 'shall ensure that in the interpretation and application of the Treaties the law is observed'. On the other hand, such reference to 'the Treaties' is not entirely systematic, and tends to replace earlier references to 'this Treaty' in the equivalent provisions in the EC Treaty. The two treaties are linked in other ways. Some issues are dealt with across both treaties with consequent cross-referencing between them. Thus the concept of European citizenship is introduced in article 9 TEU among the provisions on democratic principles, the details being found in articles 20–24 TFEU; and according to article 52 TEU the territorial scope of the treaties is defined in article 355 TFEU. The division and allocation of matters between the two amended treaties is not as logical as that between Part I and Part III of the Constitutional Treaty. For example, the general provision on types of competence is found in the TFEU (article 2), while the fundamental competence-related principles of conferral, subsidiarity and proportionality are found in the TEU (article 5). The provisions establishing the institutions are contained in the TEU, but those concerning the decision-making processes, types of legal acts and jurisdiction of the Court are in the TFEU. In fact neither of the treaties could stand alone. The TEU would possess objectives and institutions but no powers or policies (apart from the CFSP). The TFEU would establish the power to act, but nothing on the principles governing its exercise, the establishment of the institutions or even the creation of the Union.

Furthermore, the TEU contains a series of 'common provisions' applicable to both treaties. A single set of values, principles and objectives applies to both treaties and to all policies. A single set of legal acts applies across both treaties and all policy areas (although legislative acts are excluded from the CFSP). The provision on consistency in the TFEU (article 7) refers to all the policies and activities of the Union and to all its objectives, as defined in the TEU. The only substantial area of activity that is divided between the two treaties – external action – contains a set of general principles and objectives (article 21, TEU) that are explicitly stated to apply both to the CFSP in the TEU (article 23, TEU), and to the provisions on external action in the TFEU (article 205, TFEU). It is perhaps less clear to what extent the 'provisions having general application' in the TFEU (articles 7–17, TFEU), such as environmental protection, and equality, should be applied to action taken on the basis of the TEU (in particular the CFSP). Given the express partial derogation in the provision on the protection of personal data (article 16(2), TFEU), it seems reasonable to assume that the other provisions of general application apply across both treaties.

Legally speaking, this highly integrated structure implies that we have moved from the 'separate but integrated' legal orders of the pre-Lisbon treaties to a single legal order governing a single entity with a single legal personality. One consequence of this, already clear in the case law of the Court of Justice, is that although the CFSP is still subject to 'specific rules and procedures' (article 24(1), TEU), the general rules of the treaties apply unless explicitly excluded or modified. Since 2009 we have seen a gradual 'normalisation' of the CFSP, to the effect that while it clearly occupies its own legal and policy space and there is no evidence that the Court is seeking to establish a preference for the use of non-CFSP competences (14.6.2016, *European Parliament v Council of the European Union*, C-263/14), the CFSP is nevertheless part of the same legal order as the rest of the EU, subject to the same general objectives and principles – including respect for fundamental rights and the rule of law.

The architecture of the treaties post-Lisbon is thus radically different from the preceding treaty system. For the first time we have two treaties designed to work together, even if the articulation between them is clumsy in places, and even though the basic two-treaty structure is the result more of historical path-dependency and political exigency than of structural planning. And here we can see a paradox of a kind: despite the significant changes just discussed, the context in which the Treaty of Lisbon was drafted has resulted in texts that retain distinct traces and signs, in their structure and in their substantive content, of their earlier forebears. Despite the many criticisms levied against the treaties over the years for their lack of consistency, for being at once too detailed and full of gaps, they have proved both resilient and adaptable to change. The Lisbon Treaty revision has to some extent removed redundant layers and accretions that had built up over the years, cleaning and simplifying the treaty architecture. But the treaties are a sort of palimpsest: they are texts which have been used and re-used and on which traces of earlier texts still remain.

V. Coda: The Euratom Treaty

When discussing the post-Lisbon treaty structure the Euratom Treaty is often left out. Here we will briefly mention its structural relationship to the Union, without however being able to take a broader perspective on the future of Euratom within (or outside) the Union (Södersten (2018)). Before the Treaty of Lisbon, Euratom was one of the Communities on which the Union was founded: the Euratom acquis was protected by article 47 TEU alongside the EC acquis and article 305(2) EC provided that the EC Treaty should not derogate from the Euratom Treaty. Today the position seems rather different. Most striking is that the Union is founded on the TEU and on the TFEU and there is no mention of Euratom anywhere in the text of these two founding treaties, indeed nothing to indicate that Euratom is part of the Union. The protocol on the amendment of the Euratom Treaty was annexed to the Treaty of Lisbon and therefore does not appear among the protocols annexed to the TEU and the TFEU in the consolidated versions published in the EU's Official Journal. Within the treaties, all the provisions linking Euratom to the Union and its founding treaties have been placed in the Euratom Treaty itself. This has the advantage that amendments to the Euratom Treaty, and therefore to its position within the Union, can be made without the need to amend the TEU and the TFEU, but its effect is to make Euratom almost invisible. Almost, but not completely, as some of the protocols to the TEU and the TFEU are also annexed to the Euratom Treaty, and protocol No. 36 on transitional provisions includes the Euratom Treaty among the treaties defined for the purposes of the protocol.

Somewhat paradoxically, given the silence in the TEU and the TFEU on the place of Euratom within the Union, the amendments to the Euratom Treaty introduced by protocol No. 2 annexed to the Treaty of Lisbon integrate Euratom more closely into Union structures, by repealing the pre-existing institutional and decision-making provisions and replacing them with the relevant provisions of the TEU and the TFEU. This was achieved by a simple reference in article 106a(1) of the Euratom Treaty to the relevant articles in the TEU and the TFEU. The provisions thus incorporated into the Euratom Treaty include those concerning the institutions (excluding the European Central Bank), the provisions on accession and withdrawal, the revision of the treaties (only the ordinary revision procedure), the jurisdiction of the Court of Justice, the types of legal act and decision-making procedures, including article 15 TFEU on transparency, and financial and budgetary provisions.

On the other hand, the general provisions on the Union's values and objectives, on the principles of sincere cooperation, the conferral of competences, proportionality and subsidiarity are not directly incorporated into the Euratom Treaty, nor is article 6 TEU on fundamental rights. Might these 'common provisions' also apply by inference to Euratom, on the grounds that they apply generally to the Union in all its activities and Euratom is part of the Union? An indication is provided by the inclusion, among the articles which are applicable to Euratom, of article 7 TEU, which concerns sanctions against a Member State that is found to be in serious breach of Union values. The inclusion of this provision is presumably intended to ensure that the suspension envisaged by article 7 of 'certain of the rights deriving from the application of the Treaties to the Member State in question' can also include rights derived from the Euratom Treaty. But if the sanction extends to suspension of Euratom rights, then consistency requires that the values thus protected should also be applicable to Euratom-based action.

A further indication of the relationship between the TEU, TFEU and the Euratom Treaty is provided by article 106a(3) of the Euratom Treaty, according to which 'the provisions of the Treaty on European Union and of the Treaty on the Functioning of the European Union shall not derogate from the provisions of this Treaty', and which replaces article 305(2) EC and article 47 TEU. Its inclusion in the Euratom Treaty rather than in the TEU or the TFEU emphasises that the relationship between the Euratom Treaty and the Union's two founding treaties is governed by the former. This combination – the incorporation of the institutional, law-making and budgetary provisions, and the non-derogation clause – together suggest that the Euratom Treaty should be characterised as a special sectoral regime operating within the Union framework (12.2.2015, *European Parliament v Council of the European Union*, C-48/14). However, apart from the fact that these conclusions are drawn by inference rather than made explicit in the treaties, the oddity persists that Euratom remains a separate organisation with its own legal personality (article 184, Euratom Treaty) in parallel with the EU, somewhat undermining the simplification achieved by the Treaty of Lisbon. Undoubtedly these anomalies and the somewhat ambiguous position of the Euratom are the result of uncertainty as to its future. The legal solutions adopted in structuring the treaties are designed to make changes to that position relatively easier to implement than if revision to the EU treaties were required.

Bibliography

Amato, G, Bribosia, H and de Witte, B, *Genèse et destinée de la constitution européenne* (Bruxelles, 2007).

Cremona, M, 'The two (or three) treaty solution. The new treaty structure of the EU' in A Biondi, P Eeckhout and S Ripley (eds), *European Union law after the Treaty of Lisbon* (Oxford, 2012) 40–61.

Curtin, D, 'The constitutional structure of the Union. A Europe of bits and pieces' (1993) 30 *Common market law review* 17–69.

Curtin, D, 'Emerging institutional parameters and organised difference in the European Union' in B de Witte and E Vos (eds), *The many faces of differentiation in EU law* (Antwerp, 2001) 347–77.

de Witte, B, 'The pillar structure and the nature of the European Union: Greek temple or French gothic cathedral?' in T Heukels, N Blokker and M Brus (eds), *The European Union after Amsterdam* (The Hague, 1998) 51–68.

de Witte, B, 'Simplification and reorganization of the European treaties' (2002) 39 *Common market law review* 1255–87.

de Witte, B, 'The question of the treaty architecture: 1957–2007' in A Ott and E Vos (eds), *Fifty years of European integration – foundations and perspectives* (The Hague, 2009) 9–20.

de Witte, B, 'The European Union as an international legal experiment' in G de Búrca and JHH Weiler (eds), *The worlds of European constitutionalism* (Cambridge, 2012) 19–56.

Lak, MWJ, 'Interaction between European political cooperation and the European community (external) – existing rules and challenges' (1989) 26 *Common market law review* 281–99.

Mancini, F, 'The making of a Constitution for Europe' (1989) 26 *Common market law review* 595–614.

Pescatore, P, *Le droit de l'intégration: émergence d'un phénomène nouveau dans les relations internationales selon l'expérience des Communautés Européennes* (Leiden, 1972) (Eng transl) *The law of integration: emergence of a new phenomenon in international relations, based on the experience of the European Communities* (Leiden, 1974).

Pescatore, P, 'Some critical remarks on the "Single European act"' (1987) 24 *Common market law review* 9–18.

Piris (Justus Lipsius), J-C, 'The 1996 Intergovernmental conference' (1995) 20 *European law review* 235–67.

Piris, J-C, *The constitution for Europe: a legal analysis* (Cambridge, 2006).

Piris, J-C, *The Lisbon Treaty. A legal and political analysis* (Cambridge, 2010).

Schütze, R, *European Constitutional law* (Cambridge, 2015).

Södersten, A, *Euratom at the crossroads* (Cheltenham, 2018).

Weatherill, S, 'Flexibility or fragmentation: trends in European integration' in J Usher (ed), *The state of the European Union* (Harlow, 2000) 1–18.

Weiler, JHH, 'The transformation of Europe' (1991) 100 *Yale law journal* 2403–83.

7

The Institutional Framework of the European Union

GIAN LUIGI TOSATO

I. Introductory Remarks

In times of crisis such as those we live in (terrorism, mass immigration, economic stagnation, unemployment, banking crises, Brexit, anti-European political movements), there is strong need for a serious debate about Europe. Lacking in leadership, values and relevance, Europe seems almost resigned to suffer an irreversible decline. There is also no shortage of doomsayers, who see a recurrence of the circumstances that led to the two world wars of the last century. Hence the need to raise questions on the issue of European integration, and ask ourselves where we are, how we got here, and which prospects lie ahead of us. Such questions are particularly relevant to all those who believe that the current adversities can only be warded off through a greater union of European citizens, and not by dangerously retreating into one's own national domain.

This chapter is divided into three parts, complemented by a few final considerations. The first part aims to clarify the scope and legal framework of the paper. It commences by defining what is meant by the Union's 'institutional framework' – identifying its components and clarifying the parameters of our enquiry. A classification will then be drawn up of the institutions under review, according to their origin and evolution, their composition and nature, as well as the tasks and objectives assigned to them. Finally, questions of a systematic nature will be raised, in a bid to ascertain the extent to which this institutional framework fits into a unified reconstruction or whether it requires further specifications and differentiations.

The second part analyses the role of political institutions within the European Union. It takes a close look at their involvement in the exercise of the normative (constituent and legislative) and executive (governmental and administrative) functions. Our analysis will be based on the Treaty of Lisbon, but we will also look at developments leading up to it, as well as to its subsequent evolutions, especially those that stemmed from the Euro crisis.

In the third part we will proceed to make a series of evaluations of the institutional framework previously described. The objective of our exercise will be to assess to what extent this framework complies with the fundamental principles of EU law, such as the rule of law, the democratic legitimacy and the balance of powers. Based on the outcome of these assessments, we will seek to establish which form of government the EU Constitution is modelled on, especially in respect of the coexistence of, and interaction between, intergovernmental and supranational elements.

The EU's institutional framework can be defined in either broad or narrow terms. The narrow concept includes only those bodies that article 13 of the Treaty on European Union (TEU) expressly identifies as EU institutions: the European Parliament (EP), the European Council (EC), the Council, the Commission, the European Court of Justice (ECJ), the European Central Bank (ECB), and the Court of Auditors. The wider conception includes other bodies, some of which are directly provided for in the Treaties, others are the fruit of EU secondary legislation. This wider conception is recognised in a number of provisions of the Treaties (among others, articles 9 and 17, TEU, articles 15 and 16 of the Treaty on the Functioning of the European Union, TFEU) and the Charter of fundamental rights (article 41). In these provisions reference is made not only to the 'institutions', but also to other 'bodies' and 'entities' of the Union.

Among these other bodies and entities, the Treaties directly contemplate the president of the European Council and the president of the Commission, whose prerogatives are, to a certain extent, independent of their respective institutions (article 15(6) and article 17(6), TEU respectively); the High Representative for Common Foreign and Security Policy (CFSP), who holds the dual role of chairman of the Council for Foreign Affairs and vice president of the Commission (article 18, TEU); the Committee of Permanent Representatives of the Governments of the Member States (COREPER), a Council's auxiliary body (articles 16(7), TEU and 240(1) TFEU); the European System of Central Banks (ESCB), constituted by the ECB and the central banks of Member States (article 282, TFEU and protocol No. 4 of the Lisbon Treaty); national parliaments, called upon to contribute directly to the proper functioning of the Union (article 12, TEU). The Treaties also contemplate two advisory bodies, the Economic and Social Committee and the Committee of the Regions (article 300, TFEU) as well as a financial institution, the European Investment Bank (EIB; articles 308 and 309, TFEU).

The broad conception of the institutional framework also covers the so-called European agencies. Some are directly envisaged by the Treaties, such as Eurojust (article 85, TFEU), Europol (article 88, TFEU) and the European Defence Agency (article 1 of protocol No. 10 of the Treaty of Lisbon). Others (nowadays quite numerous, almost 40 in fact) were created through EU legislation. Agencies perform a variety of functions (regulatory, executive or merely consultative and research-oriented) in areas that require special technical expertise (energy, electronic communications, environmental protection, pharmaceutics, food safety, banks, etc).

This chapter will, primarily, focus on the narrow conception of institutional framework, namely, on the institutions *stricto sensu* of the Union, as they play a central role on the European scene. Yet we will also take stock of the broader conception, that is, of those other bodies and entities covered by EU law, to pinpoint interactions between the latter and the EU institutions.

II. The EU Institutions: Their Origin, Structure and Functions

EU institutions can be differentiated according to their origin and structure, and to the tasks assigned to them. As we shall see, however, these are not necessarily strict and clear-cut distinctions.

From the perspective of their inclusion in the EU structure, one can speak of 'old' and 'new' institutions. The first group includes the EP, the Council, the Commission and the ECJ, which have accompanied the European integration process since its inception with the European Coal and Steel Community (ECSC) in the early 1950s. Conversely, the EC, the ECB and the Court of Auditors may be regarded as 'new' institutions, as they have only been formally acknowledged as institutions under the Treaty of Lisbon. However, upon closer scrutiny, there is something 'new' even in the 'old' institutions and something 'old' also in the 'new' ones.

Formerly European Community institutions, the 'old' institutions became EU institutions only when the European Community was incorporated into the Union. Furthermore, they underwent a series of significant innovations over time. Consider for example the members of the European Parliament (MEP), who since 1978 have been elected by direct universal suffrage (they previously used to be elected among the national parliamentarians), or the legislative powers acquired by the EP over time (it was originally entrusted with a mere advisory role). As for the 'new' institutions, the EC has been the subject of a long evolution: it dates back to the summit meetings of the 1960s, saw its role (outside the European Community) first formalised in 1974, and was progressively included into the EU since the Single European Act was passed in 1986.

A distinction is traditionally made between intergovernmental institutions (EC and Council) and supranational institutions (EP, Commission, ECB, ECJ and Court of Auditors), based on their different structure.

Intergovernmental institutions typically comprise members of national governments (heads of State or government in the case of the EC). They represent the Member States and are express bearers of their interests. By contrast, a shared element with supranational institutions is that their members are persons individually appointed, without any subordination towards their own States. MEPs represent the citizens of the EU not the Member States; similarly, the other supranational institutions are entrusted with the mission of pursuing the interests of the EU rather than those of the Member States.

The aforementioned difference between intergovernmental and supranational institutions is not rigid. Supranational institutions also possess intergovernmental traits and the opposite is true of intergovernmental institutions.

With the exception of MEPs elected directly by European citizens, members of other supranational institutions are elected or nominated by the Member States (the ECJ and Court of Auditors) or by the EC (the president of the Commission and the ECB Governing Council) or in accord with the Council (the members of the Commission). Thus, these institutions present an intergovernmental feature in the phase of their formation. By contrast, the president of the EC is individually elected, carries out his duties freely and does not act as a collective representative of Member States. The High Representative for CFSP, who chairs an intergovernmental body (the Foreign Affairs Council), is also elected on an individual basis; and its independence is strengthened by being also a member of the Commission (a vice president).

EU institutions may also be differentiated pursuant to the classic distinction between legislative, executive and judicial functions. The EP and the Council are legislative, the EC and the Commission executive, the ECJ and the Court of Auditors judicial institutions. In addition, there is another distinction, which is partly overlapping with the preceding one, between political institutions and supervisory institutions. The former include the legislative and executive institutions, as they contribute to establish the direction of EU policy; judicial institutions belong to the latter, as they are called upon to ensure compliance with the law.

Even the above distinctions, however, require to be specified, both because there is no rigid division of functions amongst the EU institutions and also because the exercise of 'political' power (and therefore the choice of ends and means of EU activities) takes on different forms and varying degrees.

Let us consider the legislative function for example: the decision-making power belongs to the EP and the Council, but that of initiative is normally reserved to the Commission (articles 289(1) and 294, TFEU). In addition, the legislative process involves national Parliaments called upon to express compliance with the principle of subsidiarity (Lisbon protocol No. 2); furthermore, regulatory powers are increasingly exercised by specialised agencies.

Similar considerations apply to the executive and to the judicial function, albeit with their respective peculiarities. The EU executive branch is made up of the EC and the Commission, but executive duties are also assigned to the Council. Also, specialised agencies contribute largely to the Commission's activities. With regard to the judicial function, the ECJ (in its various ramifications: article 19(1) TEU) naturally plays a central role. Yet compliance with EU law is also ensured by the Commission, being the traditional guardian of the Treaties (article 17(1), TEU), as well as by the national courts, which have rightly been defined as ordinary courts of European law (ECJ, judgment of 10.07.1990, *Tetra Pak Rausing SA v Commission*, case T-51/89, paragraph 42).

The ECB deserves a special mention. It exercises executive functions in monetary matters, but may also be included among the political institutions. In fact, although the goals of its actions are laid down in the Treaties, it is for the ECB to decide upon the instruments to achieve them (M Selmayr, 'How political are the institutions of economic and monetary union? The cases of the European Central Bank and the European Commission' (2015) *ECB Legal Conference* 261–275, www.ecb.europa.eu/pub/pdf/other/frommonetaryuniontobankingunion201512.en.pdf).

We will come back in greater detail to various issues outlined above. It is important to recall here that EU law has its own peculiarities, which are not always attributable to models borrowed from other legal systems.

III. A Unified or Fragmented System?

This issue came starkly to the fore with the creation of the three pillars of Maastricht (1992), two regulated by the Treaty on European Union (CFSP and JHA, *Justice and Home Affairs*) and one by the Community Treaty (the economic pillar). The institutions were also divided between the two treaties: the European Council was included in the Treaty on European Union, while the traditional Community institutions were enshrined in the Community Treaty. Hence the problem to bring unity to such a fragmented institutional framework.

The situation is now changed. With the Treaty of Lisbon (signed on 13 December 2007, and which came into force on 1 December 2009) we have two Treaties (the TEU and the

TFEU), but there is only one entity (the EU), which has incorporated the three previous pillars and the entire institutional system. Nevertheless, some differences persist among the CFSP, the area of freedom, security, and justice (formerly the JHA), and the economic sector.

There have always been differences throughout the integration process. One only need think of the European Monetary System (EMS), the Schengen and Prüm agreements, the Social Charter, the Charter of rights: not all Member States were involved in such initiatives. However, in the area of economic integration, a broader division is now emerging between the EU and the Eurozone; between the Europe of the single market, involving all EU Member States (still 28 before Brexit) and the Europe of the Euro, which includes only the Member States that have adopted this currency (19 at present). A series of monetary, financial and economic policy regulations apply only to the Eurozone. Moreover, the Eurozone features an institutional framework that is partly borrowed and partly runs parallel to that of the EU.

While the Eurozone makes use of certain of the established EU institutions (Commission, EP and ECJ), it also relies on two new entities: the Euro Summit, which brings together the heads of State and government from the euro countries, and the Eurogroup, which is made up of the finance ministers from the same countries (Lisbon protocol No. 14, Fiscal Compact, article 12). It is patent how the two intergovernmental institutions of the EU (European Council and Council of Europe) are replicated inside the Eurozone.

The insertion of the EC and the Council into the Eurozone has proved to be a relatively simple affair. It was enough to withdraw from these institutions the government representatives of non-Euro States. Similarly, the decision-making bodies of the ECB (Governing Council, Executive Committee) do not pose particular problems, as they are made up of Eurozone citizens only. Less straightforward appears the use of supranational institutions within the Eurozone, since they represent all Member States and feature a unitary structure. Resorting to them, may cause decisions related to the euro to be influenced by the interests of non-euro countries.

In truth, there is no reason for such concern in the case of ECJ judges, individually selected for each of the Member States and appointed by common accord of the governments of the Member States. The treaties require that they are chosen among legal experts whose independence and probity is beyond doubt. The same can be said for the Commission, whose members comprise one citizen for each Member State (at least for now, until the downsizing provided for in article 17(5) TEU). Commissioners are chosen individually and are bound to act autonomously and independently.

The most sensitive issue concerns the EP. Its members represent the citizens of the Union as a whole, but are elected through national procedures and sometimes vote according to national party lines. This breeds a certain reluctance to accept that MEPs from non-Euro States have the right to decide on euro-related issues. As a radical solution to the problem, the Eurozone could be provided with its own distinct parliamentary assembly. More simply, and without prejudice to the EP's singleness, the right to vote on euro-related matters could be reserved exclusively to MEPs from Euro States. As an alternative, such matters could be delegated to a special EP Committee consisting solely of said MEPs.

IV. Allocation of Powers among Political Institutions

Having provided a general overview of the institutional framework, we will proceed to a more analytical investigation into the role of the political institutions of the EU. The choice to restrict our enquiry to such institutions is dictated by the limited scope of this chapter. We shall therefore deal with the allocation of normative and executive powers among these institutions, distinguishing between constitutional and legislative powers within the normative function, and between governmental and administrative powers within the executive function.

A. Constitutional Power

The survey of this theme could come to a swift conclusion, given that the constitutional powers belong to Member States and not to the EU institutions. These are tasked with producing secondary rules, as a manifestation of legislative power, but not primary rules, which are an expression of constitutional powers. Primary rules define the constitutional setup of the Union and are embodied in the founding treaties. Indeed, as the German Constitutional Court (*Bundesverfassungsgericht*, BVG) pointed out, Member States are and remain 'masters' of the treaties (BVG, judgment of 30.06.2009, *Lissabon-Urteil*, paragraph 150). On one specific occasion, a bid was made to overthrow this scheme: the Altiero Spinelli's project of February 1984. As it was, Member States were swift to reaffirm their exclusive constitutional power and the project was abandoned. Even the so called constitutional treaty of 2003, rejected by the French and Dutch referenda, was formally a treaty rather than a Constitution (GL Tosato, 'Il nuovo Trattato costituzionale per l'Europa: Trattato o Costituzione?' (2003) [2004] 130–131 *Queste Istituzioni* 31–40).

Nonetheless, the EU's institutions can take part in the revision procedures of the Treaties. The revision initiative can come from the EP and the Commission, as well as from national governments. Also, there is no way of moving on to the more international stages of the procedure (intergovernmental conference, ratifications) without the prior approval of the EC (articles 48(4) and (5), TEU). The EC's decision takes on particular significance in the two instances of simplified revision: in one it avoids the intergovernmental conference, in the other it also eschews ratification, replaced by the power granted to a national Parliament to make its opposition known (articles 48(6) and (7), TEU). In this second case (the so-called *passerelle* clause moving from unanimity voting to majority voting in the Council, and from special legislative procedures to the ordinary legislative procedures), the EP also has a say as it may block the EC's decision.

It is true that the EC always decides unanimously, that is, with the consent of all national governments. But one has to distinguish between two different types of acts: on the one side, a decision (even a unanimous one) adopted by the EC, which is an act issued by an EU institution and directly attributable to it; on the other side, an agreement among States, which is based on international law and which is attributable to the States that have ratified it. In the first case, the act falls within the scope of EU law, in the second outside the EU legal framework.

A similar problem applies to resolutions made by heads of State and government, which may deemed to be agreements between States or acts of the EC. In some cases they are expressly stated to be resolutions taken at a meeting of the EC, but outside its scope (eg, the Decision of the heads of State or government, meeting within the European Council, concerning a new settlement for the United Kingdom within the European Union, 18–19 February 2016). In these cases we undoubtedly have agreements made by Member States in simplified form, as permitted under international law. But if no such clarification is present, those resolutions may be attributed to the EC; so the question arises as to whether they constitute an exercise of executive or constitutional powers. The first solution appears preferable if the act is only meant to implement existing EU competences; the second option is, instead, more appropriate if the act entails the furthering of existing competences. Some EC or Eurozone summits resolutions aimed at countering the euro crisis raise the above questions.

B. Legislative Power

Legislative power is firmly tied to the well-known trio (Commission, EP, Council) that exercises this power in accordance with the traditional Community method: the Commission puts forward draft legislation, the EP and the Council decide on its adoption.

The exercise of this power has undergone significant changes over time, mainly affecting the EP. Initially endowed with a purely advisory role, the EP has gradually acquired greater influence, generally through its own initiatives subsequently reflected into the Treaties. This is witnessed by the Single European Act (1986), the Treaties of Maastricht (1992), Amsterdam (1997), Nice (2001) and lastly Lisbon (2007). This latter Treaty has finally acknowledged that the EU's ordinary legislative procedure is characterised by a codecision process, in which the EP and the Council have equal status.

A few grey areas still remain, however. In a number of cases, not necessarily of minor importance, the ordinary procedure is replaced by special procedures, in which decision-making powers are held by the Council exclusively, while the EP retains a mere advisory role or (more rarely) an approval function (article 289(2), TFEU). This weakens the role of the EP, whose opinions are mandatory, yet not binding; and even with regard to the special procedures where the EP's approval is required, the EP can only block the enactment of laws, but not actively participate in their drafting.

The above limitation applies in particular to budgetary matters. The Treaty states solemnly that the annual budget of the Union is jointly established by the EP and the Council (article 310, TFEU). Nevertheless, the EP enjoys powers of codecision (or something to that effect) only insofar as the Union's expenditure is concerned (article 314, TEU). On the subject of revenue, the Council makes the decisions and the EP is only consulted; and not even the Council enjoys full, unrestricted powers, since its decisions may only come into force subject to their approval by Member States. In any case, the EP lacks the power of taxation, which constitutes one of the traditional prerogatives of representative assemblies.

The evolution of legislative procedures has also affected the Commission, which has seen its role weakened in some respects and strengthened in others.

The former is evident in respect of the Commission's power of initiative. This power remains one cardinal prerogative of the Commission, as its proposals can only be modified by the Council unanimously; moreover, the Commission may amend or even withdraw its proposals until they are finally adopted by the Council (ECJ, judgment of 14.04.2015, *Council v Commission*, C-409/13). Still, the Commission's initiative may be instigated (and influenced in its content) by the EP, by the Council and even by the EC. Accordingly, the Commission's autonomy hinges largely on the authority of its president and of its cabinet as a whole: its proposals may have a decisive weight or, quite the opposite, appear as the mere implementation of political impulses coming from other institutions.

By contrast, the Commission's role appears to have gained strength in a different context. Alongside the legislative acts (to which the above remarks apply), the Treaty of Lisbon officially acknowledges the existence of delegated and implementing acts: a legislative act may delegate to the Commission the power to adopt them (articles 290 and 291, TFEU). Undoubtedly, this is a secondary legislative function, subject to strict substantive and procedural limits. Nevertheless, it can take on increasing importance, as evidenced by the powers conferred to the Commission in financial and banking matters.

C. Governmental Power

This power, understood as the power to set the political direction of the Union, can be deemed to belong to all the EU's political institutions: indeed, not just to the EC and the Commission, but also to the EP, the Council and the ECB. All these institutions are called upon to make political choices with regard to the objectives and tools of the actions to be taken. It is nevertheless true that the highest-level policy options, those aimed at establishing the fundamental direction of the integration process, fall upon the EC and the Commission, which by no coincidence are known as the Union's Executive.

The EC is entrusted with the task of providing the Union with 'the necessary impetus for its development' and with defining 'the general political directions and priorities thereof' (article 15(1), TEU). The Commission shall promote 'the general interest of the Union' and take 'appropriate initiatives to that end' (article 17(1), TEU). These two formulations are not perfectly symmetrical, yet they outline a dual form of government for the Union, that calls for an assessment of the manner in which the role of the EC interacts with that of the Commission.

According to current opinion, in the past the Commission represented the driving force behind European integration, while the EC was a forum for long-term strategies. However, the situation changed after Maastricht, and especially following the financial crisis: under this opinion, the leading executive role has now been acquired by the EC. Evidence of this evolution is found in the frequency of the EC's meetings (they used to be no more than three a year, now they are almost monthly) and the subject matter of its resolutions (they are no longer limited to strategic guidelines, but contain detailed indications of the measures to be taken). It is thus maintained that the role of the Commission has been significantly scaled down; it Cooks now confined to the mere implementing of decisions taken by the EC.

While one may express broad agreement with this narrative, it nonetheless deserves to be clarified in some respects.

First, Maastricht does not seem to represent such a dividing line in the relations between the two executive bodies. The relations between them have always fluctuated, and even before Maastricht the impetus for major developments in European integration came from the EC (not yet incorporated into the Union). Think of such cases as the 'empty chair crisis' (caused in June 1965 by French president Charles de Gaulle's decision to boycott the meetings of the Council of ministers of the EEC), which was overcome with the signing of the so-called Luxembourg Compromise (1966); the direct election of European parliamentarians (1976), previously elected among national MPs; the creation of the European Monetary System (EMS, 1979), in a bid to put an end to uncontrolled currency fluctuations. All these developments were triggered by the EC or at least saw its active involvement. The same may be said for the promotion of new policies (environment, employment, consumer protection), which were subsequently incorporated into the Treaties. Clearly, the EC played a significant executive role well before Maastricht.

Secondly, the new post-Maastricht trend has not affected the Commission's competences. It is true that Member States, while conferring to the European Union competences in areas previously considered national prerogative (CFSP, Justice, Economic and Social Policies), have managed to retain control over these areas also at a European level. In fact, the decision-making powers have been concentrated in the hands of intergovernmental institutions (EC and Council). But the role of the Commission in managing the internal market has remained unaltered. Furthermore, the Commission has been progressively involved in new areas, such as the provision of financial assistance to Member States, the supervision over national budgets, the banking crisis resolution procedures.

Thirdly, the strengthening of EC has become more marked during the euro crisis years. Anti-crisis measures have required a delicate balancing between conflicting principles of EU law: solidarity on the one hand (article 3(3), TEU) and full and exclusive responsibility of each Member State for its own liabilities (the *no bailout* clause, article 125, TFEU). Such a balancing mechanism is likely to exceed the limits of executive powers, and fall into the scope of constitutional powers instead. Indeed, in a situation that could put the euro area financial stability at risk, decisions have been taken which could entail financial transfers among Member States. Whatever the precise nature of these decisions, there is no doubt that only the EC could be legitimised to adopt them.

It is thus correct to say that after Maastricht, and above all throughout the recent crisis, the predominant role of the EC has come to the fore. But this has not undermined the Commission's traditional prerogatives relating to the internal market, since it affects competences in new areas attributed to the EU. And even in these new areas, the Commission has been gaining increasing powers in the oversight and implementation of applicable rules. Moreover, in some cases, as with the Banking Communication (30 July 2013) and that on the flexibility criteria in the implementation of budgetary rules (13 January 2015), the Commission has proven its determination to make policy choices autonomously from the EC.

Ultimately, the Union continues to feature a dual executive system, rooted in the EC and the Commission. The pendulum has oscillated over time between these two poles; as of late, it has swung towards the EC for the reasons stated above. But the trend has already shifted to a more balanced position, which should consolidate itself once the more acute phase of the crisis has passed. In any case, we are faced with two institutions that are not hierarchically subordinated to one another, and must jointly act in the exercise of the executive power. Their relations are subject to the general duty of sincere cooperation, which the Treaty imposes on all the institutions of the Union (article 13(2), TEU).

D. Administrative Power

A discussion on administrative power, understood as the power to apply general rules to specific cases, involves the following questions: (a) what is the extent of the competence attributed to the Union; (b) which institutions are involved in its exercise and (c) how the EU's institutions interact with the administrative apparatus of Member States.

(a) The existence of administrative powers wielded by the Union is not the rule but the exception. The Union essentially functions as a legislator, while the States implement the legally binding laws that it passes: this is clearly stated in article 291(1) TFEU. In principle, therefore, the Union is based on a system of decentralised administration. However, the cases of centralised administration have grown over time. Certain cases are the subject of specific provisions in the Treaties: they are the provisions of Community origin in the field of agriculture, transport and competition, as well as those introduced with the Maastricht Treaty on CFSP and budgetary discipline. Other and more numerous cases have been added through the Union's legislation.

Indeed, after establishing the rule mentioned above (in paragraph 1), article 291 TFEU provides for a derogation in general terms (in paragraph 2). In order to ensure a uniform application, a legislative act of the Union may authorise the Union to adopt 'mplementing acts': a term that includes both normative and administrative acts. A further legal basis for extending the Union's administrative powers is provided by article 114 TFEU, which deals with the harmonisation of national laws. Thanks to an evolutionary interpretation, this provision allows the Union not only to adopt uniform rules but also to centralise their application at a European level (ECJ, judgment of 06.12.2005, *United Kingdom of Great Britain and Northern Ireland v European Parliament and Council of the European Union*, C-66/04, paragraph 64).

In conclusion, there seems to be a wide possibility of replacing the system of decentralised administration through Member States with the centralised administration by the Union.

(b) The administrative powers of the Union are shared among the Commission, the Council, the ECB and the specialised agencies. In principle, the Commission has enforcement responsibility in the field of the single market and competition, the Council on CFSP and economic policies, the ECB on monetary matters, the specialised agencies in the specific areas entrusted to them.

The Commission's administrative powers have been extended in the context of the euro crisis. The constituent acts of the so-called rescue funds – the European Financial Stability Facility (EFSF) and the European Stability Mechanism (ESM) – assign a central role to the Commission (along with the ECB and the International Monetary Fund, IMF). It is up to the Commission to propose the granting of funds, oversee their proper use, sign the memorandum of understanding with the beneficiary State and subsequently verify its implementation. Furthermore, as a result of subsequent revisions of the Stability and Growth Pact (most recently, the so-called Six Pack and Two Pack legislation), the Commission's control over national economic policies has been extended, particularly for those States whose budgetary situations are deviant.

The above developments have also strengthened the Commission's role vis-à-vis the Council. Through the mechanism of reverse-majority voting, the Commission's proposals on excessive deficit and macroeconomic imbalances procedures almost amount to decision-making. In fact, they are construed as adopted unless the Council rejects them by a qualified majority; and this is somewhat unlikely to occur given the commitment by Euro-States to support the Commission's proposals (Fiscal Compact, article 7).

Lastly, let us briefly turn to the ECB and the specialised agencies. We have already mentioned the functions attributed to the ECB along with the Commission and the IMF (the so-called troika) on the management of rescue funds. In addition, the ECB's administrative power has grown considerably with the centralisation at the European level of supervisory tasks over credit institutions. In this way, the ECB's powers have extended from the monetary to the banking sector. As to the specialised agencies, they perform a complementary, sometimes even substitutive, role with regard to the Commission's activities. The nature of the powers that may be conferred to these agencies raises a number of delicate questions, which will be discussed later.

(c) The two methods of administrative implementation of EU law, the centralised and the decentralised method, are often integrated within the so-called networks of authorities. These ensure coordination between European and national institutions according to different legal models.

A first model is represented by the ESCB, which brings together the ECB and national central banks in the exercise of an exclusive competence of the Union (monetary policy). Within the ESCB, the ECB exercises a hierarchical preeminence over the national central banks, which are called to ensure the proper implementation of the ECB's decisions. A second model is exemplified by the network of antitrust authorities, which operates in a regime of shared competences between the Union and the Member States. Here there is no hierarchical subordination of the national authorities vis-à-vis the Commission; nonetheless, the latter enjoys a dominant position, primarily through the power to take over a case pending before a national authority and deal with it directly. The network created in the banking sector can be directly related to this model. A third model is outlined by entities such as the Agency for the Cooperation of Energy Regulators (ACER) and the Body of European Regulators of Electronic Communications (BEREC), which coordinate the activities of national regulators in two areas pertaining to the administrative competence of the States (energy and electronic communications). In this case, the Commission operates from the outside through non-binding legal instruments.

The trend towards bringing the centre of gravity of administrative functions from national into EU authorities raises the question as to what extent this is compatible with the principle of subsidiarity (article 5(3), TEU). The more there is a shift towards a centralised administration at a European level, or even towards decentralisation at State level but with national authorities subject to the Commissions powers of direction and substitution, the more the issue of subsidiarity appears problematic.

V. Evaluations

A. From the Perspective of the Principle of Legality

After analysing the EU's institutional framework, it is appropriate at this point to check to what extent the institutional framework of the EU complies with fundamental principles of European law.

Our enquiry starts with the principle of legality, that is expressly acknowledged in article 2 TEU as one of the values upon which the Union is founded. Even before being enshrined in the Treaties, this principle was duly upheld by the ECJ that described the European framework as a 'community of law' (judgment of 23.04.1986, *Parti écologiste 'Les Verts' v European Parliament*, case 294/83, paragraph 23). Indeed, the principle of legality (*rule of law*) has shaped the process of European integration since its inception.

The principle in question requires that the institutions of the Union act within the limits of their powers and in conformity with the procedural and substantive conditions set out in the Treaties (article 13(2), TEU). It also implies the presence of a judicial body (in our case the ECJ) in charge of ensuring that such conditions and limits are respected (article 19, TEU).

The ECJ has significantly extended the principle of legality by subjecting to its control all the acts having legal effects passed by any institution, body or entity of the Union. In ascertaining the effects of an act, the Court does not dwell on its formal legal status and denomination; it rather undertakes a substantive analysis which may even take into account the manner in which an act is perceived by the parties concerned (judgment of 31.03.1971, *Commission v Council*, case 22/70, paragraphs 38–43). In so doing, the Court has looked beyond the categories of acts to which the Treaties explicitly attribute a legally binding effect (regulations, directives, decisions). It has recognised that rights and obligations can be produced also by a host of non-typical acts (communications, guidelines, letters, etc), and consequently has subjected them to its jurisdiction (see Villani (2017) 359 ff.).

Reviewing the legality of an act requires first to verify the competence of the issuing body (article 263(2), TFEU). This implies a twofold investigation: first, it is necessary to establish whether the act might overstep the boundaries of the Union's powers as a whole; secondly, whether it might encroach on the competence of another entity. The considerations below relate to the first instance; the second aspect will be discussed when dealing with the principle of institutional balance.

The Union's competences are only those conferred upon it by the Treaties: all the others continue to belong to the Member States (articles 4(1) and 5(2), TEU). It is the well-known principle of conferral which, by its very nature, has a twofold impact. The exercise of a competence not attributed to the Union does not affect European law alone; it also affects national law, where it determines an infringement of Member States' prerogatives. Thus, Member States share an interest in verifying compliance with the principle of conferral, and in blocking the enforceability of potentially ultra vires acts adopted by the Union.

This issue is at the centre of the dispute between the ECJ and the BVG in relation to the ECB's Outright Monetary Transactions Program (ECJ, judgment of 16.06.2015, C-62/14; BVG, rulings 07.02.2014 and 21.06.2016, *Gauweiler* case). The ECJ claims it has exclusive jurisdiction over the legality of the Union's acts, including the control over the principle of conferral (cf P Craig, 'The ECJ and ultra vires action: a conceptual analysis' (2011) 48 *Common market law review* 395–437). On the other hand, the German Court acknowledges the priority, not supremacy, of the European Court. In other words, the BVG is prepared to concede that the matter should be addressed by a preliminary ruling of the ECJ, but it also reserves the right not to follow the ECJ's decision in case of acts deemed substantially ultra vires and therefore seriously prejudicial to the national competences.

It is plain to see that each of the two courts (ECJ and BVG) has supremacy within its own jurisdiction, but neither of them can claim unconditional supremacy over the other.

Potential conflicts cannot be resolved hierarchically; they may only be overcome by means of that principle of sincere cooperation to which all European and national institutions are legally bound (article 4(3), TEU).

B. From the Perspective of the Principle of Institutional Balance

EU law does not strictly comply with the classic principle of the separation of powers. An executive body (the Commission) is involved in the exercise of the legislative function, having the exclusive power of initiating legislation. Moreover, the executive function is shared among a number of institutions (Commission, EC, Council). At EU level, the principle of the separation of powers is superseded by that of institutional balance, which pursues a similar goal: to avoid a concentration of powers and create a system of checks and balances.

The institutional balance within the Union has obviously changed over time. Broadly speaking, this evolution has primarily affected the EP and the EC, the former as the bearer of the interests of European citizens, the latter as the bearer of the interests of Member States. The EP has been steadily strengthening its role until it came to acquire legislative and budgetary decision-making powers. The EC occupies a central place in the Union's government.

The principle of the balance of powers requires, first of all, that no institution may overstep the boundaries of its competences to the detriment of those of other institutions. This is what is laid down in article 13(2) TEU, which states that each institution is required to act within the limits of the powers conferred upon it. As the ECJ has stated, the Treaties have established:

> a system for distributing powers among the different Community institutions, assigning to each institution its own role in the institutional structure of the Community and the accomplishment of the tasks entrusted to the Community. Observance of the institutional balance means that each of the institutions must exercise its powers with due regard for the powers of the other institutions (judgment of 22.05.1990, *European Parliament v Council of the European Communities*, case C-70/88, paragraphs 21–22).

Furthermore, the principle under consideration requires that the institutional balance established by the Treaties shall not be altered through the delegation of powers. Each institution is called to exercise its own competences directly: these may be divested and delegated to others, only provided that precise limits are respected. The delegation of legislative power from the EP and the Council to the Commission can only cover non-essential elements of the matters to be regulated (article 290, TFEU). The same kind of limitation applies in the case of delegations to Union agencies. In accordance with the *Meroni* doctrine (judgment of 13.06.1958, *Impresa Meroni & Co v High Authority of the ECSC*, case 10/56), only partially mitigated in a recent case (judgment of 22.01.2014, *United Kingdom v EP and Council*, C-270/12), the delegation to these agencies of 'a discretionary power implying a wide margin of discretion' is precluded. Only the delegation of 'clearly defined executive powers' may be permitted; and only provided that the exercise of such powers can 'be subject to strict review in the light of objective criteria determined by the delegating authority'.

The principle of institutional balance also implies a positive duty of cooperation. This duty does not only concern the relations between the Union and the Member States, it equally applies to EU institutions in their relations with one another. It binds them not only to refrain from infringing the competences of another institution, but also to facilitate their proper performance. Thus, with regard to the Commission's power of initiating legislation, the Commission may always withdraw its proposal until it has been definitively adopted. But the ECJ has stated that such a withdrawal must be motivated by 'convincing elements', for the Commission cannot block the exercise of the legislative powers attributed to the EP and the Council (judgment of 14.04.2015, *Council v Commission*, C-409/13).

The principle of institutional balance must be respected also by Member States. In the *Pringle* case, the ECJ held that this principle does not bar the EU institutions to be involved in entities (such as the ESM) created by States outside the Union (judgment of 27.11.2012, *Thomas Pringle v Government of Ireland and others*, C-370/12). The Court stated, however, that the tasks attributed to the Commission and of the ECB in the ESM could be considered lawful under the Treaty only provided that their responsibilities within the Union would not be distorted. The principle of institutional balance must be safeguarded in these cases as well.

C. From the Perspective of the Democratic Principle

Criticism of democratic deficit has always accompanied the process of European integration. Initially, it was levelled at the marginalisation of national Parliaments that failed to be offset by the powers attributed to the EP. Later, it was directed against the powers of the Commission, an executive body consisting of technocrats lacking democratic legitimacy. More recently, this criticism has challenged the leading role of the EC and the determining powers assumed within it by the stronger Member States. Lastly, the target has shifted to the ECB, accused of widening its scope of action in a regime of virtual unaccountability. These examples are enough to convey the degree of sensitivity surrounding the issue.

The democratic principle, which under article 2 TEU is one of the values the Union is founded upon, is subsequently specified by article 10 TEU in terms of representative democracy. The European people as a whole, namely the citizens of the Union, are represented by the EP; Member States are represented by the EC and the Council, being institutions composed of national governments. In turn, national governments represent their own citizens, namely the various peoples that make up the Union. Accordingly, the democratic principle rests upon two channels of representation, one referring to the European people as a whole and the other to the distinct peoples of the Member States.

It is therefore essential to verify how these two channels concur in the performance of the Union's legislative and executive activities.

The legislative function seems to be suitably well monitored from a democratic point of view by the powers of codecision generally attributed to the EP along with the Council. Even in the absence of codecision powers, the EP has not failed to make its voice heard. In the case of the regulation conferring to the ECB the supervision over the banking sector, the EP consultation under article 127(6) TFEU has de facto become an approval, thus transforming the status of this legislative procedure from special to ordinary. The EP has weighed in with authority also in the case of extra-EU agreements, such as those setting up the ESM and the Single Resolution Fund. It did so, firstly, challenging the need to get out of the legal system of the Union; and secondly, having a say anyway in the rules adopted.

A supplementary democratic protection in normative matters is provided by national Parliaments in three ways: by exerting control over the stances taken by their own governments inside the Council; by issuing opinions on the EU's legislative proposals on the subject of subsidiarity (Lisbon protocol No. 2); by submitting all agreements concluded by Member States outside the Union to the mandatory parliamentary approval.

The 'democratic' question is somewhat more delicate and complex with regard to the executive function.

Let us start with the Commission. Its president is selected jointly by the EC and the EP, while its members are appointed by agreement between the Council and the EP. The setting up of the Commission requires, therefore, that the two channels of representation are involved. The channel representing the European citizens is gaining relevance as a result of the so-called *Spitzenkandidat* system (which links the choice of the president of the Commission to the outcome of the European elections). Once duly set up, the Commission is subject to the traditional political scrutiny of the EP, which can dismiss the whole cabinet in a vote of censure.

No such power is granted to the Council over the Commission, but this affects the representation of the citizens of the Member States only to a limited extent. Indeed, the Council is in a position to watch over the Commission's legislative proposals, requesting their submission or amending their content. The reverse-majority voting system undoubtedly strengthens the role of the Commission in the excessive deficit and macroeconomic imbalances procedures; but the Council always has the last word, as it can outright reject the Commission's proposals.

The question of the EC's democratic legitimacy appears more problematic. In principle, it should be guaranteed by the national Parliaments, to whom the EC members are politically accountable. This does not ensure full legitimacy, however. Every national Parliament oversees the conduct of its own government within the EC, but this power of oversight does not extend to the collective actions of the EC in its role of EU institution. As for the EP, the political control powers conferred upon it by the Treaties only apply to the Commission. The democratic legitimacy of the EC appears, therefore, incomplete with regard to the citizens of the Member States and substantially absent in respect of the people of Europe as a whole.

There are three avenues available to the EP to try to overcome this democratic shortcoming: the first is to address directly the EC, the second to pass through national Parliaments, the third to act through the Commission.

With regard to the first approach, the EP can exert some influence on the EC through its president's opening speech at the commencement of the EC meetings. It may also do so in connection with the reporting to the EP made by the president of the EC at the end of such meetings. In addition to these tools expressly provided by the Treaties, the EP can intensify the relations established with the EC president by way of practice (exchanges of letters, meetings, written questions); perhaps, it could consolidate these developments by means of an interinstitutional agreement. The second approach, that of the collaboration between EP and national Parliaments, finds an explicit basis in protocol No. 1 of the Treaty of Lisbon, as supplemented by article 13 of the Fiscal Compact. An interparliamentary conference dedicated to the issues of economic and financial governance has already been established.

A third approach remains open: the president of the Commission is a standing and voting member of the EC. For sure, his role inside a forum of heads of State or government is a minor one, but he can make his voice heard, especially as his appointment has now gained greater political standing. Thanks to its powers of control over the Commission, the EP may influence the conduct of the Commission's president within the EC.

The issues of democratic legitimacy are being perceived as increasingly compelling in the Eurozone, both for the greater importance that the latter has gained in times of crisis, and in view of its foreseeable future developments. As mentioned before, the EC and the Council of the Union are replicated inside the Eurozone by two bodies consisting of similar intergovernmental makeup, the Euro Summit and the Eurogroup. Here, a particular difficulty for the EP stems from its composition that reflects the EU in its entirety. The fact that MEPs from non-Euro States may have a say in euro-related matters, has generated much controversy. The possible ways of overcoming this difficulty have been previously discussed.

VI. A Composite Institutional System

The above considerations on the institutional balance and the democratic legitimacy underline the need for a cooperative interaction between supranational and intergovernmental elements of the EU institutional framework.

The principle of institutional balance does not merely require that decision-making powers be divided among multiple decision-making centres so as to guarantee a system of checks and balances. The principle also mandates that the interests of the two constituent entities of the EU (Member States and European citizens) be duly represented and balanced.

The EU's intergovernmental institutions primarily bear the responsibility for national interests. Their decisions must necessarily take into account the various needs and demands of Member States. It is therefore not conceivable that the protection of the general interests of the European citizens may be entrusted to the EC and the Council alone. In the event of conflicts, the interests of Member States are likely to prevail over those of European citizens, especially if the conflict involves the stronger States. It is no coincidence that the voting system within these institutions guarantees to all (in the case of the EC) or at least to the major States (in the case of the Council) a power of veto that may bar the adoption of specific resolutions.

Conversely, supranational institutions are naturally geared towards looking at the demands of the European people. They are called to pursue the general interests of the Union, including those of the Member States. But it is inevitable that institutions such as the EP and the Commission are motivated to favour the interests of European integration over national interests. Their composition, and majority voting system, are pushing them in this direction.

It is thus confirmed that a fundamental value of the Union, such as the institutional balance, cannot do without the cooperation of supranational and intergovernmental institutions. No doubt that, at different times, the balance of powers can shift towards one pole or the other. In times of crisis or major conflicts between Member States, it is natural for intergovernmental institutions to play a central role. Problems of this nature call into question the responsibilities of Member States, as holders of the EU's constituent powers.

Yet even in these circumstances, the contribution of supranational institutions remain essential, as evidenced by the degree to which the Commission and the EP have been involved in dealing with the recent euro crisis.

Similar remarks apply to the democratic legitimacy issue.

Representative democracy, upon which the Union is founded pursuant to article 10 TEU, is based on the two channels of representation set out therein, being that of the citizens of the Member States and that of the citizens of the Union as a whole. The former are democratically represented by their national Parliaments, the latter by the EP. The joint and cooperative action of the two channels is needed in order to ensure the democratic legitimacy of the Union.

The idea that the said channels could function separately would presuppose the presence of two separate constitutional systems within the Union: one intergovernmental (foreign policy and economic policies) and the other supranational (single market). The two systems would refer to two equally distinct executive bodies: the first to an intergovernmental institution (the EC), which draws its democratic legitimacy from national Parliaments, and the second to a supranational institution (the Commission), legitimised through the EP. However, given the close interactions among all the constituent parts of the Union, the theory of two separate systems does not appear convincing.

One needs therefore to go back to the necessary complementarity of the two bases of democratic legitimacy. The isolated control exercised by the EP over the Commission and by national Parliaments over the EC cannot suffice. This set up is clearly incomplete: in the first case, the EC escapes the scrutiny of the EP, in the second the Commission that of national Parliaments. Again, in the first instance, the EC lacks the legitimacy afforded by the citizens of the Union, in the second the Commission lacks the legitimacy conferred by the citizens of the Member States. Hence the need for national Parliaments and the EP to cooperate in exercising the power of control conferred upon each of them. A more intensive inter-parliamentary cooperation would certainly help to achieve this result.

Under the two tenets of institutional balance and democratic legitimacy, the composite nature of the Union's institutional system is thus substantiated. The joint action of supranational and intergovernmental institutions is a fundamental requirement. Their relative weight may shift over time, but a strong and consolidated preeminence of intergovernmental institutions would be incompatible with the constitutional setup of the European project.

VII. Final Considerations

The Union's institutional framework has been criticised for complying with standards of formal legality, which are matched by a poorly balanced, scarcely democratic and inefficient system. This is no groundless criticism, but it should be viewed in the context of the European integration process.

The project of building a united Europe is based on the consent of the participating States: past attempts to unify it by force have yielded disastrous results. The process of consensus building is laborious, requires constant compromises, entails deviations from the main route, slow and belated decision-making, stalemates and an inconsistent systematic design. These are the inevitable consequences of the mandatory search for consensus.

Nevertheless, the integration process has shown its vitality especially in times of crisis. On a number of occasions it found itself in serious jeopardy: the de Gaulle claims (1960s), the unfettered currency fluctuation (1970s), the rejection of the Constitutional Treaty (2004), the recent economic and financial crisis (2008 onwards). In all these circumstances, Europe has proven its capability to face the difficulties, indeed its determination to move forward the European integration process.

However, improvements are urgently required. Europe needs to be perceived as a provider of economic growth and social protection; and that it is willing to make its voice heard on the wider international scene. Only by doing so, will it be possible to counter the spread of national-populist movements and the consequent risks of disintegration of the European project.

There is no dearth of workable legal instruments, even without resorting to a radical revision of the Union's founding treaties (an unrealistic prospect at least in the short term). Significant developments in the fields of the EU's institutional structure, its governance and policies can be achieved on the basis of the existing framework (interinstitutional agreements, enhanced cooperation, special measures for the Eurozone) or with small-scale revisions of the Treaties (articles 48(6) and (7), TEU) or even through extra-EU arrangements. Legal instruments are not in short supply, but the political will to trigger them is sorely needed.

Bibliography

Amato, G and Gualtieri, R (eds), *Prove di Europa unita. Le istituzioni europee di fronte alla crisi* (Bagno a Ripoli, 2013).

Daniele, L, *Diritto dell'Unione Europea* (Milano, 2014).

Daniele, L, Simone, P and Cisotta, R (eds), *Democracy in the EMU in the aftermath of the crisis* (Torino-Berlin, 2017).

Fabbrini, S, *Which European Union? Europe after the euro crisis* (Cambridge, 2015).

Fabbrini, F, Hirsch Ballin, E and Somsen, H (eds), *What form of government for the European Union and the Eurozone?* (Oxford, 2015).

Gaja, G and Adinolfi, A, *Introduzione al diritto dell'Unione Europea* (Roma-Bari, 2014).

Habermas, J, *The crisis of the European Union* (Cambridge, 2012).

Jacqué, J-P, 'The principle of institutional balance' (2004) 41(2) *Common market law review* 383–91.

Lenaerts, K and Van Nuffel, P, *European Union law* (London, 2011).

Puetter, U, *The European Council and the Council. New intergovernmentalism and institutional change* (Oxford, 2014).

Schütze, R, *European Union Law* (Cambridge, 2015).

Tesauro, G, *Diritto dell'Unione Europea* (Padova, 2012).

Tizzano, A (ed), *Verso i 60 anni dai Trattati di Roma. Stato e prospettive dell'Unione Europea* (Torino, 2016) (specifically LS Rossi, *Equilibri istituzionali e metodi di integrazione dell'Unione: quale ruolo per la "nuova" Commissione europea?* 65–89).

Tosato, GL, 'L'integrazione europea ai tempi della crisi dell'euro' (2012) 3 *Rivista di diritto internazionale* 681–703.

Tosato, GL, 'How to pursue a more efficient and legitimate European economic governance' (2016) 3 *IAI Working Papers*.

Vai, L, Tortola, PD and Pirozzi, N (eds), *Governing Europe. How to make the EU more efficient and democratic* (Bern, 2017).

van Gerven, V, *The European Union. A polity of States and peoples* (Oxford, 2005).

Villani, U, *Istituzioni di diritto dell'Unione Europea* (Bari, 2017).

8

The Acquis: European Union Law and So Many Laws

JACQUES ZILLER

I. European Union Law, a Target for Eurosceptics

Following the example of the criticisms levied from the mid-1980s by the British prime minister Margaret Thatcher, it has become fashionable to criticise European 'bureaucracy' and the 'democratic deficit' of the European Union (EU) and, in particular, to rail against the European Commission for the invasive character attributed to EU law.

As far as the so-called democratic deficit is concerned, it may be useful to remember that the expression was initially coined in 1997 by Richard Corbett, an assistant of Altiero Spinelli and president of the Young European federalists, therefore by definition not a Eurosceptic. For him it was a case of highlighting the absence of power in legislative matters of the European Parliament with regard to EC Treaties, before the reforms introduced by the Maastricht Treaty (1992). The concept was then taken up and developed by the British political scientist and politician David Marquand – who has held important advisory roles for the European Commission, and is therefore also not an Eurosceptic – to describe the European Community before the Maastricht Treaty. The fortune of the expression 'democratic deficit' probably lies with the fact that it is used for totally different purpose, both by supporters of greater European integration of a more political nature, and by the so-called Eurosceptics. The former group want to expand the powers of the European Parliament and the other forms of democratic participation in the functions of the Union, while the latter use the argument of the democratic deficit to ask for the powers transferred to the Union to be returned to the Member States.

To return to the accusations regarding the invasive nature of EU regulations, which are supposed not to be in line with the proximity principle according to which decisions must be taken as closely to citizens as possible, examples considered bizarre or pointless are often given, such as, for example, the regulations governing the technical specifications for windscreen wipers, which were even referred to in a TV advertisement during the 2009 European Parliament election campaign. Criticisms of this nature are based on fundamental ignorance about the goals and benefits of bringing together the legislative, regulatory and administrative provisions of Member States within the internal market.

The criticisms mainly feed on a perception that is in actual fact unfounded, and concerns a supposed absence of control over what is considered European bureaucracy – the word bureaucracy often lumping together Commission officers, European commissioners themselves and even the Members of the European Parliament. Leaving aside the lack of good faith of many of its proponents, such criticisms also reveal a total ignorance of the checks and balances exercised within the European Commission, by the Council on the Commission, by the Court of justice (ECJ) and by Member State Parliaments and governments on compliance with principles concerning the distribution and exercise of competence.

More recently, there have also been criticisms of supporters of stronger European integration, according to which the Union should only deal with important things such as internal and external security, economic growth and employment, rather than producing detailed regulations governing certain characteristics of agricultural or industrial products, or the equivalence of professional qualifications.

This type of criticism may have the purpose of reducing the breadth of the support, coordination and complementary competences. Exercising these powers takes up a not insubstantial part of the Union's budget funds. However, it does not produce large quantities of Union regulations, because such competences 'shall not entail harmonisation of Member States' laws or regulations', as specified by article 2.5 of the Treaty on the functioning of the European Union (TFEU). In fact some criticisms of this type may also be the fruit of ignorance about the role of legislation in ensuring the maintenance of the internal market and development of an area of freedom, security and justice, the two pillars of integration within the EU.

The abundance of legislation directly or indirectly produced by the institutions of the European Union should not, however, be considered a fault in itself. It is important to understand why and how such abundance is linked to the very concept of European integration, as it has been developed since the Treaty of Paris establishing the European coal and steel Community (ECSC), which came into force on 23 July 1952, 65 years ago.

It is also important to understand that the existence of such legislation constitutes a guarantee of rights and freedoms, and not a series of bureaucratic constraints with no reasonable basis. That said, it is undeniable that there are some areas of EU law that are pointlessly detailed, and not always restricted to what is necessary to achieve the aim of the law in question. In order to combat this phenomenon, ECJ case law has gradually developed to include the application of the principle of proportionality, generated first and foremost by referrals, for example, initiated by individual citizens and enterprises. This development has been followed by actions by the Commission – generated both by initiatives of its presidents (including Jacques Delors, Romano Prodi and José Manuel Barroso), and at the request of governments of individual Member States – regarding the application of the same principle, together with the principle of subsidiarity. These actions have been summarised since the beginning of this century by the words 'better regulation'.

As the title of this essay suggests, Union law comprises many different types of laws and many different disciplines regulated by law. On the one hand there is the body of law produced by the EU institutions since the entry into force of the Community Treaties, known as the EU acquis and, on the other, legislation produced by the institutions of the EU Member States to implement the acquis. Unlike the situation in many Member States, since the Maastricht Treaty there have been specific principles, procedures and mechanisms for ensuring in the best possible way that the legislation and regulations produced by the Union institutions are of impeccable technical quality and comply with the principles of proportionality and subsidiarity, in other words, better regulation.

II. The Concept of the European Union 'Acquis'

The terms Community ''acquis, Union 'acquis', Schengen 'acquis' are part of the lexis of those that have been involved in the policies and institutions of the EU since the 1970s. The French word 'acquis' is used in all the Union languages, including English, Italian, German and Spanish, because there is no single word in those languages that exactly corresponds to the noun 'acquis' – literally 'what has been acquired'.

The word 'acquis' refers, on the one hand, to the body of positive EU law existing at the time of speaking or of writing. Beyond this summary of a technical nature, the word 'acquis' also contains an implicit reference to the fact that there is no going back from the degree of European integration thus achieved.

Ever since the negotiations that led to the first expansion of the European Communities, in 1973, to include Denmark, Ireland and the United Kingdom, the principle according to which the so-called Community acquis must not be amended in the event of expansion has been agreed by the governments of the Member States and the candidate countries. In fact it was a matter of emphasising, in particular with regard to the British government, that the accession of new Member States should not change the purpose of an 'ever closer union'. It is important to remember that in the 1950s the British governments had been invited to join Belgium, France, Germany, Italy, Luxembourg and the Netherlands in the establishment first of a coal and steel community, then in a common market and an atomic energy community for civil purposes, but that they had decided not to join the enterprise of the six because they were against the supranational aspects of the institutional and legal system conceived with the Community Treaties and had not, therefore, been able to participate in the formulation of the rules and principles applicable to the Community's scope of action.

According to the definition proposed by the European Commission in its 1992 publication, *The challenges of European enlargement*, the 'acquis' includes:

> the content, principles and political objectives of the Treaties; the legislation adopted in implementation of the Treaties, and the jurisprudence of the Court of justice; the declarations and resolutions adopted within the [Union's] framework; the [Community's] international agreements and the agreements between Member States connected with the [Community's] activities.

The position of principle of the Member States and the institutions of the Union regarding maintenance of the acquis means that the only adaptations to the Treaties contained in a treaty of accession are those concerning the composition of the Union institutions, bodies and organisations, up until 2014 the number of votes for calculating a qualified majority of the Council and the European Council, the official languages of the treaties and the geographical scope of application of the treaties.

However, with regard to the essence of the Union's goals and policies, a treaty of accession may include adaptation periods – all such treaties have included this provision. They however do not contain permanent exemptions for a new Member State, unlike the case of revision treaties, such as the Treaties of Maastricht, Amsterdam, Nice and Lisbon, which were accompanied by protocols governing specific positions with regard to some policies on the part of Denmark, Ireland and above all the United Kingdom. The concept of acquis has therefore been used to avoid 'cherry-picking' or the choice of only participating in some policies by a candidate for accession, since it goes against the very idea, already expressed in the preamble to the founding treaties of the European Community, of an ever closer union between the people of Europe. Instead, with the Treaties of Maastricht, Amsterdam, Nice and Lisbon compromises have been reached between existing Member States of the Union, which were thought to accept the general purpose, and the institutional and judicial system of the Union.

Before calling the referendum of 23 June 2016 on what has become known as Brexit, British prime minister David Cameron often stated that the United Kingdom would never have been part of an ever closer union, but only of the single market and some related policies. These statements were in full contradiction of the fact that Edward Heath's government, which had led the negotiations for the United Kingdom's Membership, and Parliament, which had adopted the European Communities Act of 1972, had accepted the principle of the acquis. In fact, until Cameron's government, no British government had asked to be exempted from the acquis: the governments of Harold Wilson, Margaret Thatcher, John Major and Tony Blair had only asked, on the one hand, for a revision of the contribution to the budget of the Union and, on the other, not to participate in new policy developments that the other Member States wished to endorse.

The word 'acquis' even crops up in the last sentence of article 87 of the TFEU and the protocol (No. 19) on the Schengen acquis integrated within the scope of the EU. In fact, the agreement signed on 14 June 1985 in Schengen, Luxembourg, by the representatives of Belgium, France, Germany, Luxembourg and the Netherlands – which involved the gradual suppression of systematic controls at the borders of these States, and cooperation in the matters of visas, immigration and policing made necessary by this abolition – was then integrated by a series of more precise provisions, with the implementation Convention signed by the same Member States on 19 June 1990, and a series of more specific agreements based on the Convention. These were specific agreements between just half of the Member States, agreed in order to test the avant-garde idea of closer integration. Given the success of the cooperation – shown by the subsequent adhesion of a further eight Member States, as well as Iceland and Norway – the incorporation of the body of rules contained in the Schengen Convention, as well as the agreements for implementing the Convention, were put on the agenda of the negotiations that led to the Treaty of Amsterdam in 1997.

While not wishing to impede this step towards European integration, the British government under the leadership of Tony Blair asked to continue not taking part in the suppression of controls, but to be able to take part in some useful regulations, including the fight against crime and terrorism. There followed discussions about the communitarisation of the Schengen acquis in order to indicate the fact that, with the Treaty of Amsterdam, the institutions of the Union – above all the European Parliament, Commission and ECJ – had acquired the competence to integrate and amend previous regulations, turning them from intergovernmental agreements into EU law.

From the mid-1980s onwards, there has increasingly been talk of the acquis, sometimes pejoratively, to refer to the growing quantity of laws symbolised by the impressive number of pages of the Official journal of the Union in which binding laws – decisions, directives and regulations – are published, as well as recommendations, communications, etc. that, while not being legally binding, are usually considered part of European law.

Journalists, politicians and even academics – economists, political scientists and legal experts – often state that 80% of the legislation applicable in Member States comes from Europe. In actual fact there is no way of actually calculating this percentage – if only because it is not possible to know whether the benchmark to use is the number of directives, regulations and decisions of the Union applicable in the Member States, or alternatively the number of internal laws and regulations adopted to implement the policies, or the number of articles, sub-sections or paragraphs, or even words contained in the laws. All attempts to do so, including efforts by sociologists, have failed thus far. In fact, the reference to 80% of the laws was made by the then president of the European Commission Jacques Delors, who used it as a tool for communicating with entrepreneurs in the Member States to explain how, through the implementation of the White Paper of 1985 on the completion of the internal market by 31 December 1992, the legal framework applicable to their businesses would be simplified. In 80% of cases (a rough estimate) a single common European law would in fact apply to their businesses instead of twelve different regulations, given that on 1 January 1986 there were 12 Member States.

III. Law as Method for Implementing Common Policies

The law is only one of the tools for implementing public policies in a modern State. Laws and regulations serve not only to lay down common rules for life within a society, but also to determine the framework for State intervention in order to protect widespread interests – such as protection of the environment or the landscape – as well as for the creation and maintenance of infrastructures and for the creation and maintenance of social protection systems, and so on. However, the majority of these legal regulations would be without effect without the human and financial resources necessary for implementing the policies.

The model of European integration chosen thus far has never been that of a State, but rather that of cooperation between States, where most of the human and financial resources belong to the Member States and the local independent bodies that comprise them. As a result, the role of common rules is far more important for the development and functioning of European integration and cooperation between EU Member States than the role of the budget and the employees of the EU in implementing common policies. Nonetheless it should be emphasised that the Union's legal system is also based on a decentralised model, and therefore includes not only the law produced directly by the institutions of the Union – known as EU-derived law – but also that produced independently by the Member States.

The law therefore has a particularly important role for the EU. This is not only because, as article 2 of the Treaty on European Union (TEU) reminds us:

> The Union is founded on the values of respect for human dignity, freedom, democracy, equality, the *rule of law and respect for human rights*, including the rights of persons belonging to minorities (Author's italics),

but also, precisely, because the law is the instrument that has enabled the development and maintenance of the common market (now internal market) and the area of freedom, security and justice of the EU.

The rules necessary for a life in common among citizens, enterprises and associations in an area shared by all the Member States of the Union are therefore defined and integrated in an important set of rules of what is called EU-derived law, that is, in directives, regulations and decisions of the Union. Given the decentralised nature of the EU legal system, as well as EU-derived law there are numerous laws and regulations promulgated by Member States for the implementation of common policies. To these EU and Member State laws and regulations we also have to add a series of international agreements between the Union and third countries or international organisations that are indispensable for regulating activities that are not internally restricted to the Union. First and foremost, the battle against pollution and measures to tackle climate change, the protection of animal and plant species (environmental policy), as well as the trading of goods and services between the Union and third countries (known as the common commercial policy).

Articles 289, 290 and 291 of the TFEU clearly highlight the fact that the Union regulations take the form of legislative acts – to use the term used in EU law to indicate the laws – adopted by both branches of the Union's legislative power, the Parliament and the Council. These acts may contain provisions giving the Commission the power to adopt implementing regulations, which complement the basic acts with details (normally of a technical nature) necessary for them to be fully operational. The result is that the quantity of regulations produced by the institutions of the Union cannot be measured simply by analysing the underlying legislative activity. The result is also that those not involved in the process often struggle to understand that the Commission, which participates in legislative activity because it puts the proposals necessary for the discussion and adoption of Union 'legislation' to the Parliament and the Council, is not a legislator in the true sense when it adopts delegated or executive acts. The confusion is understandable, given that on the one hand there are *legislative* directives, regulations and decisions, and on the other *delegated* or *implementing* directives, regulations and decisions. In actual fact it is less complicated than it may seem. Just as the governments of the Member States exercise regulatory power by adopting delegated decrees implementing the laws, the Commission also has regulatory power, when explicitly required by the underlying legislative act.

To understand the necessity for common regulations, regardless of the opinion one may have of the content and form of each specific directive, each regulation or each decision of the Union, it is important to bear in mind the roles of the judges and the public administration in implementing common policies. In the case of ordinary international treaties, countries agree coordinated actions, leaving to each party not only the choice of how to implement the agreements, but also the time, the form and above all the specific content of the laws and regulations necessary to implement the treaties – with the risk of significant disparity in the rights guaranteed under the treaties to people, enterprises, associations, etc. Whereas the EU bases itself on the idea that the different institutions in the Member States are bound by their common law. Consequently the administrations of the Member States, as well as their courts and tribunals, have the duty of guaranteeing their citizens and legal persons that the rights – and obligations – imposed by EU law are effectively applied.

This concept is particularly clear in the preliminary ruling mechanism by which Member State judges apply to the ECJ, as it guarantees the standardised application and interpretation of EU law in all Member States. This explains the need for precise, clear and unequivocal laws (these are the conditions set out by the ECJ for EU law's to be directly applicable since its judgment of 5 February 1963, *van Gend en Loos*, case 26/62). 'Directly applicable' means that individuals may ask a judge in the Member State in which they operate under EU law as well as public authorities to apply the relevant Union laws to resolve a dispute, issue an authorisation or pay a grant without the need for further intervention by the legislator or government of the country in question.

There are also international treaties containing extremely precise and detailed rules, especially international trade agreements such as the *General agreement on tariffs and trade*, which comprises more than 500 articles. However, unlike EU law, these agreements do not normally set up a comprehensive system, ensuring not only that the agreement is implemented in all the signatory countries, but also that its application and interpretation do not differ between one country and another.

IV. A Paradox: More European Legislation Means Less Regulation in Europe

In order to understand the need or otherwise for common European regulation, we need to understand the logic of the area being regulated, before deciding on the substance of the regulation.

The choices made by the governments of the six founder Member States of the European Communities in the 1950s have ensured that the common market is still a core concept of EU law. The choices were dictated not so much by theoretical concepts as by the international scenario at the time, and the fact that the political forces of all six countries were not unanimous when it came to the purpose or the form of European integration. Despite the fact that the competence of today's EU has been greatly extended when compared to the European Communities of the 1950s, the majority – by a long shot – of the regulations, directives and decisions that have an impact on the lives of individuals within the Union can be directly or indirectly linked to the operation of the internal market. Since the 1990s a body of laws more specifically related to the operation of the area of free circulation of people outside of trade has gradually developed.

A market is traditionally defined, in a few words, as an area where there is an exchange of goods and services, that is, products of human activity, as well as of labour and capital, that is, production factors. Whether or not this is a comprehensive and accurate definition from the point of view of the science of economics is not relevant for the topic we are dealing with in this chapter, because it is simply the definition of the market based on the relative provisions drawn up by the authors of the Treaties of Paris and Rome. The concept was implicit in the Treaties of 1951 and 1957, and was explicitly formulated from the Single European Act of 1986 with the text now included in article 26 of the TFEU, according to which:

> The internal market shall comprise an area without internal frontiers in which the free movement of goods, persons, services and capital is ensured in accordance with the provisions of the Treaties.

The provisions of the Treaties, which in this have remained unchanged since the Treaty of Rome of 1957, are particularly brief. In fact, unlike the usual international trade agreements, which first of all contain lists of products with the various duties that can be charged on products imported or exported, as well as the various quantities that can be imported, the Treaty of Rome simply contains general principles applicable to the free circulation of goods. Member States are barred from applying duties and charges 'having equivalent effect' (article 30, TFEU) and quantitative restrictions on imports are prohibited (article 34, TFEU) as they are on exports (article 35, TFEU), along with 'measures having equivalent effect'. A quantitative restriction is a numerical restriction – expressed in units, weight, volume, etc – on the quantity of goods of a certain type that can be imported or exported into and from a country. The above principles have the purpose of creating and maintaining a single market rather than a series of markets more or less open to trade.

That said, the common or internal market is not the same thing as that of a single State, but comprised six States in 1958, the year the Treaty of Rome came into force, and 28 States in 2017. Moreover, these are sovereign States. Article 36 of the TFEU draws the conclusions:

> The provisions of articles 34 and 35 shall not preclude prohibitions or restrictions on imports, exports or goods in transit *justified on grounds of public morality, public policy or public security; the protection of health and life of humans, animals or plants; the protection of national treasures possessing artistic, historic or archaeological value; or the protection of industrial and commercial property* (Author's italics).

In other words, the Member States remain free to regulate the manner in which goods are placed on the market in order to safeguard the public interest, whether these are produced in the country itself or imported from other Member States.

These principles show that putting the same goods on the market may be regulated by laws and decrees in each of the Member States, even if the differences in national regulations make it more difficult, if not impossible, to sell goods in an EU Member State other than the one in which the goods were produced. There are two limitations on the freedom to regulate of Member States. In the first place, if the regulation has the same effects as those of quantitative restrictions, they may only regulate for the purposes described in article 36. In the second place, as provided for by the rest of article 36 TFEU, 'Such prohibitions or restrictions shall not, however, constitute a means of arbitrary discrimination or a disguised restriction on trade between Member States'. In other words, regulations may not be used for protectionist purposes.

At this point it is necessary to mention the theory developed by the Nobel prize-winning economist, Dutchman Jan Tinbergen, in 1969, regarding the common market. According to Tinbergen, in the construction of the common market, it is important to distinguish between the initial logic of negative integration, that is, the abolition of all the obstacles that can get in the way of developing a transnational market (duties, prohibitions, quantitative restrictions and regulations of equivalent effect) and the construction of a common regulatory framework in order to avoid distortions to free circulation, and corrections to the common market. Only by accompanying negative integration with positive integration measures can we achieve a regulated common market that is not simply a lawless jungle where the strongest win.

Examination of the provisions of the TFEU clearly shows that its authors wished to make both types of integration possible. Alongside articles 34, 35 and 36, which establish principles of negative integration, are articles 101–107, which give the Union the competence to regulate competition in order to prevent undertakings behaving in such a way that is damaging to consumers, in the short or the medium term. These are first of all prohibitions on anti-competitive agreements between undertakings (article 101, TFEU) and abuse of dominant positions by one or more undertakings (article 102, TFEU). In addition, articles 114 and 115 give the Union legislators jurisdiction for the 'approximation of the provisions laid down by law, regulation or administrative action in Member States' which have as their object the establishment and functioning of the internal market. And it is these articles – article 115, the content of which has remained unchanged since the Treaty of Rome, and article 114, the content of which was introduced with the Single European Act of 1986 – that are the major source of European regulations, especially those most criticised by the Eurosceptics, and by the proponents of European integration focused solely on 'what is important'.

The example of the windscreen wipers mentioned in the introduction enables us to understand the paradox that we are dealing with in this section. Regulation (EC) No 661/2009 of the European Parliament and of the Council of 13 July 2009 concerning type-approval requirements for the general safety of motor vehicles, their trailers and systems, components and separate technical units intended thereof – a legislative act – was made operational by an implementing act for the said Regulation, Commission Regulation (EU) No 1008/2010 of 9 November 2010 concerning type-approval requirements for windscreen wiper and washer systems of certain motor vehicles, published in the EU Official journal (No. L 292 of 10 November 2010, together, among others, with Commission Regulation (EU) No 1009/2010 of 9 November 2010 concerning type-approval requirements for wheel guards of certain motor vehicles). The actual content of the Commission regulation is quite short: three pages, with a total of seven articles; but the regulation also contains an Annex I – Administrative documents for EC type-approval of motor vehicles with regard to their windscreen wiper and washer systems, an Annex II – Administrative documents for EC type-approval of windscreen washer systems as separate technical units and an Annex III – Requirements for windscreen wiper and washer system with four appendices. The total Regulation takes up 19 pages of the Official journal.

It is easy to cite this text to criticise the European Union and to claim that Europe should spend time resolving more important problems than those of windscreen wipers. However, it is important to ask what would happen if such a European law did not exist. In this case there could be 28 laws or decrees – one for each Member State of the Union – regulating the technical specifications of windscreen wipers, as well as the type of documents and procedures applicable when putting such products on the market. A small manufacturer of windscreen wipers operating in Italy with the capability of manufacturing excellent quality, low-cost windscreen wipers could be required to produce 28 different types, and would also have to request a certificate of conformity for each country in the EU. For a small to medium-size undertaking this could represent a significant cost that would effectively prevent access to the markets of other EU countries and therefore have the same effect as an import ban. In a case such as that of windscreen wipers it is not simply possible to apply the technique of mutual recognition, according to which goods complying with the regulations in the country in which they are produced, or imported from a third country not belonging to the European Union, must automatically be accepted in all the other Member States. It is in fact legitimate for a Member State to set technical specifications for windscreen wipers, given that their operation is essential for road safety. In fact it corresponds to 'grounds […] of public security; the protection of health and life of humans', as we read in article 36 TFEU.

In order to enable our windscreen wiper manufacturer to sell them in a market of almost half a billion people, it is therefore necessary for the technical standards and certification procedures to be the same for the whole market. This happens precisely through regulation: European windscreen wiper regulation in actual fact makes it possible to considerably reduce the body of regulations and procedures that apply to the activity of undertakings.

In the sectors and for goods for which there are no EU-wide common regulations, there just needs to be regulation in a single Member State, and no specific rules for such goods in the others, to create an obstacle to free circulation. The victim of such a situation (manufacturer, consumer or intermediary) could appeal to the courts in the country where the regulation exists to cancel its effects, which would be expensive in terms of both time and costs. In addition to the costs of appealing to the courts of the country in which the problem exists, there are the costs of the national courts sending an application for a preliminary ruling to the ECJ. This is because in order to guarantee that the same parameters are applied throughout the internal market, only the ECJ can ultimately decide whether the effect of a regulation is equivalent to that of a prohibition or quantitative restriction, and whether it can be justified for reasons of public interest.

With the appropriate nuances due to the difference in subject, the above reasoning also applies to the option for an undertaking or a self-employed person to provide services throughout the market, or for a citizen to go to another country to benefit from a service – such as specific medical treatment – without paying more than in their country of residence. The same goes for the option for an EU citizen to seek employment and to work in a Member State other than their own, and for the option of making investments in another Member State.

The principles and legislative mechanisms developed to ensure that the internal market works effectively with the four freedoms of movement (of goods, services, workers and capital) are also used to ensure the free movement of EU citizens not only for business purposes. The result is that numerous European regulations are necessary in order to bring about both the area of freedom, security and justice and the internal market. The result is also that, overall, the European regulations reduce the total number of regulations within the EU.

V. Better Regulation

The fact that the legislation and regulations produced by the European institutions are fully justified in order to ensure the construction and operation of the area of freedom, security and justice and of the internal market common to the whole of the EU does not necessarily mean that they are truly limited to what is strictly necessary, or that the drafting standards of directives, regulations and decisions are high enough to ensure their comprehension by all stakeholders. Since the mid-1980s this issue has led the EU institutions, headed by the Commission, to seek concepts, ideas and methods to improve the quality of regulation and reduce the bureaucratic costs resulting from it.

These efforts date back to the programme presented by the European Commission under the leadership of Jacques Delors in the form of the Commission's 1985 *White Paper on the completion of the internal market* (European Commission, COM(85) 310 final), approved by the European Council in Milan in June the same year, which led to the agreement of the Single European Act in 1986. The White Paper addressed the matter that there were still numerous obstacles to the free circulation of people, goods, services and capital more than ten years after the deadline established by the Treaty of Rome, which had provided for a transition period of a maximum of 12 years (therefore from 1958 to 1970), after which no such obstacles would be permitted. These were the result, among other things, of regulation existing in the various Community Member States, which their governments often justified as being necessary in order to safeguard the public interest, in accordance with article 36 of the Treaty of Rome (which corresponds to the current article 36 TFEU). As a solution, the Commission proposed a list of 300 measures to be adopted by the Community in the form of directives or regulations to replace thousands of national laws and decrees, where it was not possible simply to use the mechanism of mutual recognition to enable freedom of movement. The goal presented by the Commission and approved by the European Council was to adopt such measures by 31 December 1992. The Commission proposed, wherever possible, to have recourse to a qualified majority vote of the Council, which was indispensable in order to reduce the time needed to adopt common rules (on average six or seven years until the entry into force of the Single European Act on 1 July 1987).

The White Paper not only proposed the adoption of three hundred measures in just four years; it also proposed a new approach to the approximation of Member State legislation in order to reduce the workload and time required by the European institutions, and to guarantee the involvement of the interested parties, especially of undertakings, in drafting the rules. According to this 'new approach', the approximation of legislation should no longer have the purpose of standardising the law applicable to a sector, but only the protection of health and life of humans, animals or plants and the protection of industrial and commercial property. The proposals for directives and regulations by the Commission were only intended to set out the principles essential for such protection, while the technical details were delegated to bodies responsible for technical 'standardisation' such as the European Committee for standardization (CEN), the purpose of which is to harmonise and produce technical regulations in Europe in conjunction with national and supranational regulatory bodies such as the International Organisation for standardization (ISO), or industry bodies such as the European Committee for electrotechnical standardization (Cenelec) in the case of electrical engineering.

When visiting the various Member States to present the project for implementing the internal market, Delors also met with Members of the governments of the German Länder (in Germany, the federal provinces are called countries). They pointed out that, in some cases, the regulations that were supposed to be replaced by European regulations were concurrently within the competence of both the Federation and the Länder, and that in order to decide whether a regulation should be adopted at a federal or a regional level the principle of subsidiarity was used. After this Delors increasingly referred to this principle, and at the intergovernmental conference of 1991 at which the Treaty of Maastricht was adopted, the Commission proposed that subsidiarity should be introduced into the Treaty of Rome as a general principle. The principle of subsidiarity became not only the war-horse of the Länder, but also of the governments of some other Member States, first and foremost the UK.

After the negative outcome of the referendum of 2 June 1992 that prevented Denmark from ratifying the Treaty of Maastricht, the Major government, which was taking its turn to hold the EC presidency, organised a summit in Edinburgh in December. Together with the search for a solution that would enable the Danish government to propose a new text for referendum without changing the Treaty of Maastricht, the European Council's agenda had as a focal point the implementation of the principle of subsidiarity written into the EC Treaty as article 3B, in identical wording to that of the current article 5.3 of the TEU.

The conclusions of the Edinburgh summit therefore contained the first components of a method that would, via a series of formalised consultations, guarantee consideration of the principle of subsidiarity by the Commission in the drafting of its proposals for decisions submitted to the European legislator. Among other things, the Commission committed to presenting an annual report to the European Council and Parliament on the application of the principle of subsidiarity. This method was subsequently formalised with a protocol (No. 7) on the application of the principles of subsidiarity and proportionality, adopted with the Treaty of Amsterdam that was signed on 2 October 1997. The protocol – now replaced by the protocol (No. 2) of the same name, adopted with the Treaty of Lisbon – provided in article 9 for the submission each year to the European Council, the European Parliament and the Council of a report by the Commission on the application of article 5 to be forwarded also to the Economic and Social Committee and the Committee of the Regions.

From 1999, the annual report was entitled Better Regulation. According to the first paragraph of the 1999 report, 'better regulation' means not only correctly applying the principles of subsidiarity and proportionality, but also making legislation simpler, more readable and more accessible. This also led to greater efficacy and greater acceptability of community actions.

The initial title of the English version of the report, *Better Law-making*, was replaced by the title Better Regulation, in line with Commission's 2001 *White Paper on European Governance* (communication from the Commission of 25 July 2001, [COM(2001) 428 Final – Official journal C 287 of 12 October 2001]). Since this White Paper, drawn up at the initiative of the president Romano Prodi, the Commission has developed an agenda, that is, a series of points to be implemented, for better regulation. Under the presidency of Barroso from 2004 to 2014, the Commission continued along these lines, developing tools, procedures and working mechanisms. Since Jean-Claude Juncker took over the presidency in 2014 the Commission has even appointed the first vice-president of the 'better regulation' programme, Frans Timmermans, also the custodian of the Charter of fundamental rights and the Rule of law in all the Commission's activities. The Commission has since presented a large 'better regulation' package, which resulted first and foremost in the 'Interinstitutional Agreement between the European Parliament, the Council of the European Union and the European Commission on Better Law-making, of 13 April 2016' (*Official journal of the European Union*, L 123/1, 12 May 2016).

The main tools of the interinstitutional agreement of 2016 are the multiannual programming of legislation, the systematic use of impact assessments, public and stakeholder consultation and feedback, ex-post evaluation of existing legislation and a 'regulatory fitness and performance programme (REFIT)'. The agreement also contains a series of provisions regarding transparency and coordination of the legislative process, the application and implementation of Union legislation and simplification. The impact assessments should map out alternative solutions and, where possible, potential short and long-term costs and benefits, assessing the economic, environmental and social impacts in an integrated and balanced way and using both qualitative and quantitative analyses. [...] should also address, whenever possible, the 'cost of non-Europe' and the impact on competitiveness and the administrative burdens of the different options, having particular regard to SMEs ('Think Small First'), digital aspects and territorial impact.

The interinstitutional agreement also includes a page dedicated to the acts and implementing measures which, as we have seen, constitute the largest part of Union legislation. The agreement provides that whenever broader expertise is needed in the early preparation of draft implementing acts, the Commission will make use of expert groups, consult targeted stakeholders and carry out public consultations, as appropriate, which may not seem much, given the importance of such acts. The point is that delegated acts and implementing measures are adopted solely by the Commission, based on the measures incorporated into legislative acts. The next step is to take a look at the *Commission Staff working document: better regulation guidelines* (European Commission, [COM(2015) 215 final]), a document of 91 pages, to get an idea of the procedures and tools (better regulation 'toolbox') that the Commission uses to ensure better regulation, bearing in mind that some have been developed and used for almost two decades, while others are new.

In conclusion, it seems appropriate to quote from the 2015 Communication from the Commission to the European Parliament, the Council, the European Economic and Social Committee and the Committee of the regions, *Better regulation for better results – An EU Agenda* (SWD(2015) 110 Final):

> Better regulation is not about 'more' or 'less' EU legislation; nor is it about deregulating or deprioritising certain policy areas or compromising the values that we hold dear: social and environmental protection, and fundamental rights including health – to name just a few examples. Better regulation is about making sure we actually deliver on the ambitious policy goals we have set ourselves.

Bibliography

Arena, A, Bestagno, F and Rossolillo, G, *Mercato unico e libertà di circolazione nell'Unione Europea* (Torino, 2016).

Dente, B, *Le decisioni di policy. Come si prendono, come si studiano* (Bologna, 2011).

Grilli, A, *Le origini del diritto dell'Unione Europea* (Bologna, 2009).

Nugent, N, *The government and politics of the European Union* (London, 2017).

Pescatore, P, *Le droit de l'intégration* (Bruxelles, 2005).

Piris, J-C, *The Lisbon Treaty: a legal and political analysis* (Cambridge, 2010).

Tinbergen, J, *International economic integration* (Amsterdam, 1965).

Wallace, H, Pollack, MA, and Young, AR (eds), *Policy-making in the European Union (New European Union)* (Oxford-New York, 2010).

9

The Principle of the Primacy of EU Law Over the National Legal Systems of Member States

SERGIO M CARBONE

I. The Effectiveness of Community Law: The Peculiar Coordination Between the EU and Member States

A legal system that determines the rules of behaviour of natural persons and companies is largely dependent on their effective enforcement by and against their addressees. The ensuing regulations therefore need to become incorporated and functional in an organisation endowed with adequate characteristics and tools capable of ensuring their implementation and effective enforcement. It follows that only such implementation and enforcement of the rules guarantee the vitality of the law and the stability of the system to which it belongs, allowing it to stand the test of time.

In this respect and within this framework, the majority of the rules belonging to the legal system of the European Union (EU) are addressed and enforceable immediately and directly towards individuals and companies as recipients of the precepts set forth, in a bid to attain the aim related to its effectiveness in the sense mentioned earlier. Since its very beginning, then, Community law has been characterised in a particular way precisely because the European Economic Community (EEC) did not limit itself to contemplate obligations and ensuing rights for States. It has also been made clear that Community law constitutes a new kind of legislation in which 'the States have limited their sovereign rights, albeit within limited fields'; in this sense, the subjects of this legal order 'comprise not only Member States but also their nationals' (Court of Justice (ECJ), 5.2.1963, *NV Algemene Transport- en Expeditie Onderneming van Gend & Loos v Netherlands inland revenue Administration*, case 26/62).

It is thus acknowledged that 'independently of the legislation of Member States', Community law operates directly, also when it comes to negative obligations to perform, with regard to its final recipients, by giving them rights and obligations as long as we are dealing with regulations whose content is 'clear and unconditional'.

Moreover, even if European integration and Community law possess the aforementioned characteristics, they do not bring about the overcoming of the nation State and cannot be likened to the functional organisational model of the federal State. In fact,

Member States are the ones equipped with an organisational apparatus capable of passing concrete operational measures in order to impact on natural and legal persons as well as their own domestic bodies or entities.

Under the characteristics specified here, Community law is incorporated into a frame scarcely attributable to traditional institutions. It is in fact a regulatory and organisational system based on a cooperation scheme between national legislation and Community law, in which the States are no longer entirely sovereign, and the system attributed to the EU is not yet entirely equipped with fully sovereign powers. This, to the extent that the EU may not exercise exclusive control over the powers assigned to it, as they depend on the founding Treaties, and their actual implementation is still left to the Member States in their capacity as subjects of international law. Yet, despite such a delicate balance, the effectiveness of Community law and its actual implementation, with its prevalence over national laws, have never been questioned thanks to the aforementioned positive balance, cooperative relationship and loyal cooperation between the European Union/Community and Member States. A relationship of this kind has, for quite some time now, made it possible to claim that 'the EEC Treaty even though it has been concluded by an international agreement, constitutes the constitutional charter of a community of law' (ECJ, 14.12.1991, opinion 1/91).

Therefore, a key cornerstone of such a construct is the explicit nature of the so-called primacy of Community law over the domestic law of Member States. Such a key principle has actually guaranteed the concrete application of its immediate and direct efficacy upon individuals and companies, in relation to which rights and obligations are directly applicable in all Member States and enforceable by (and against) both national and EU institutions. Obviously, the operation of the respective competencies has to be coordinated on the basis of a collaborative relationship based on loyal cooperation and solidarity between the States and the EU, from which both the above-mentioned primacy of Community law and the constitutional characterisation of the successive Treaties leading up to the present-day EU depend.

II. The Affirmation of the Primacy of Community Law: Early Case Law

The meaning and unambiguous affirmation of the above-mentioned primacy have been progressively clarified during the 60 years of the EU's existence. After all, since the very beginning the Community legal system has never harboured any doubts about the existence of this primacy, regardless of the fact that it was never specifically mentioned in any of the Treaties established over the course of the constitutional evolution that has led to the current formulation of the Treaty of Lisbon (signed on 13 December 2007, in force since 1 December 2009), later supplemented by subsequent protocols and amendments to some of its provisions, also following the accession of Croatia.

The only express reference to this principle in Community law is found in declaration no.17 annexed to the final act of the Intergovernmental Conference which adopted the Treaty of Lisbon, where it is recalled that:

> in accordance with well settled case law of the Court of Justice of the European Union, the Treaties and the law adopted by the Union on the basis of the Treaties have primacy over the law of Member States, under the conditions laid down by the said case law.

And to confirm such primacy and its nature as a fundamental principle of Community law, let us quote below the content of the Council's Legal Service opinion of 22 June 2007, transposed in the document 11197/07/JUR260, which states that non-inclusion of the primacy principle in the Treaty of Lisbon 'shall in no way change the existence of the principle and the existing case-law of the Court of justice', placing particular emphasis on recalling certain expressions to this effect contained in one of the first rulings of the Court of justice.

The matter at hand was decided in the ruling of 15.7.1964 in *Flaminio Costa v ENEL*, case 6/64. On this occasion, it was actually held that Community law:

> stemming from the treaty, an independent source of law, could not, because of its special and original nature, be overridden by domestic legal provisions, however framed, without being deprived of its character as community law and without the legal basis of the community itself being called into question.

In this way the principle upheld was that the scope of the Treaties establishing the European Community entails a transfer of sovereignty from the Member States, whose effect forestalls their exercising of sovereign powers through acts that run contrary to the provisions of Community law. Therefore, any acts (legal or administrative) adopted violating this preclusion must be 'disapplied' in the exact same way in all the Member States. Any other solution would undermine the harmony and uniformity of enforcement of Community law.

And it is in this very perspective that the principle of Community law primacy was expressly restated in the *Simmenthal II* case (ECJ, judgment of 9.3.1978, *Amministrazione delle finanze dello Stato v Simmenthal SpA*, case 106/77) with the purpose of affirming that Community law (whether stemming from the Treaty or from measures of its institutions), whenever directly applicable, shall 'render automatically inapplicable any conflicting provision of current national law, but […] also preclude the valid adoption of new national legislative measures […] incompatible' with Community legislation.

Such an effect, so clearly expressed and directly attributable to the correct application of the direct effects of the Community principles and their prevalence over national legislative acts, has (even more so) found full affirmation with regard to administrative acts. Hence, the Court of justice did not hesitate to state that, given the aforementioned case law precedent, it would be contradictory to hold that, unlike the courts, a public authority would not be required to cast aside domestic regulations found to be incompatible with Community law (ECJ, 22.6.1989, *Fratelli Costanzo SpA v Comune di Milano*, case 103/88).

III. The Progressive Evolution and Extension of the Effects of Community Law Primacy

As well as being upheld with increasing emphasis over the following decades, the scope of the principle of Community law primacy has been clarified by attaching it to a number of effects that go beyond those mentioned above.

To begin with, it was clarified that, by applying domestic law to individuals and companies, judges and public authorities must take into account and comply with the provisions of directives addressed to Member States only; and this holds true regardless whether such legislation may contain clear and precise provisions directly applicable to individuals and companies, or whether domestic laws may precede or follow a directive against which they may be interpreted in a manner that is more or less consistent with its contents. In fact, any domestic court judge called upon to interpret an internal provision is required to do so 'in the light of the wording and the purpose of the directive in order to achieve the result pursued by the latter' (ECJ, 13.11.1990, *Marleasing SA v La Comercial Internacional de Alimentación SA*, case 106/89).

Using even more forthright language in favour of the prevalence to be generally assigned to Community law, also when interpreting domestic legislation, it has been stated that national courts 'are bound to take recommendations into consideration [...] in particular where they cast light on the interpretation of national measures [...] or Community provisions' (ECJ, 13.12.1989, *Salvatore Grimaldi v Fonds des maladies professionnelles*, case 322/88). The obvious clarification was that, by so doing, well-established national court decisions, as well as specific explanatory guidelines adopted with administrative measures, may be lawfully overcome.

Again by virtue of the principle of Community primacy, the effects relating to the principle of res judicata as per Article 2909 of the Italian civil code were also overhauled, when they precluded the application of EU provisions both with regard to the Member States' duty to recover any aid given in violation of Community law (ECJ, 18.7.2007, *Ministero dell'Industria, del Commercio e dell'Artigianato v Lucchini SpA*, C-119/05) and in order to ensure effective application of Community tax rules (ECJ, 3.9.2009, *Amministrazione dell'Economia e delle Finanze and Agenzia delle entrate v Fallimento Olimpiclub Srl*, C-2/08). On the grounds of these same principles, both national provisions and rulings by national courts have been struck down whenever confronted with Community provisions whose mandatory nature determines their illegitimacy, since Community bodies are themselves competent for assessing such matters as illegitimacy.

It got to the point that in a landmark, and still hotly-debated, judgment of the Court of justice (17.12.1970, *Internationale Handelsgesellschaft mbH v Einfuhr- und Vorratsstelle für Getreide und Futtermittel*, case 11/70) it was held that:

> the validity of a community measure or its effect within a Member State cannot be affected by allegations that it runs counter to either fundamental rights as formulated by the constitution of that State or the principles of a national constitutional structure.

IV. The First Reactions of Italian Law Restricting the Primacy of Community Law

The views expressed on the principle of Community law primacy, and particularly on its effects, were far from shared by a number of influential constitutional justice authorities, especially in the first decades of the EEC. These included, above all, the German, French and Italian Constitutional Courts.

With particular reference to the position held within the Italian legal system, the scope and effects of Community law primacy, in the meaning outlined in the above paragraphs, had to come to terms with a whole range of positions and objections which tended to greatly undermine its useful effect.

First of all, in the first decision handed down by the Italian Constitutional Court on this matter, in the same case (*Flaminio Costa v ENEL*) ruled on by the Court of justice a few months later (see the above paragraph), and contrary to the outcome reached in that occasion, the impact of Community legislation on domestic law was substantially equated to that of international agreements. According to this approach, the Community legal system did not become part of the Italian legal system by virtue of its own strength. Article 11 of the Italian Constitution, invoked by the Constitutional Court to enable the limitation of sovereignty provided for in the Community Treaties, was however not deemed suitable also for crediting an ordinary law (relating to the implementing act of the Community Treaty) with a degree of efficacy that transcends its own scope; in any case, article 11 would not be capable of acknowledging a degree of efficacy also greater than that of ordinary laws in its own regulations and those laid down in the sources derived from it.

It follows that, with regard to this law, 'the body of laws subsequent to the latter one must hold fast, in accordance with the principles of the succession of laws over time'. If this presence were to bring about a violation of the Treaty, only 'the responsibility of the State at the international level' would matter (Constitutional Court, judgment 1.3.1964, No. 14) with no direct effects on the domestic legal system. This position is deeply rooted, on the one hand, in a dualistic view of relations between international law and domestic law, and, on the other, in an evaluation of the Community legal system that ranks it much like any other international treaty on Italy's participation in an international organisation.

Faced with these conflicting premises, if compared to those made by the Court of justice around the same time, there was an evident need for a decisive shift in direction that would enable a move towards the positions established within the Community. It is not surprising, then, that in immediately subsequent years, the general consensus was to take this route starting from a statement already expressed during the aforementioned *Costa v ENEL* ruling on the suitability of an ordinary law to introduce legislation from Community institutions into Italian law, by way of derogation from the principle of exclusive competence only awarded to those bodies envisaged by the Constitution.

It has been noted that article 11 of the Constitution does authorise ordinary laws to execute also written agreements such as the Community treaties, which also entailed significant limitations of sovereignty. Moreover, the effects obtained by the clear separation between domestic and Community legal systems were specified, to the point that Community law was awarded its own independent character, distinct from international law. Therefore, on the strength of its being 'a wholly different legal system from the domestic one', it was impossible to apply the ban on appointing special judges (article 102 of the Constitution) as well as the principle of judicial protection under the conditions and guarantees afforded by article 113 of the Constitution (Constitutional Court, judgment of 27.12.1965, No. 98, *Acciaierie San Michele SpA (in liquidation) v High Authority of the ECSC*).

In other words, it was exactly the separation of the two legal systems, which gravitated inside two different operational orbits, which prevented the respective regulations from coming into conflict. At the same time, one could not fail to observe that the effectiveness of Community law and its actual application were to a large extent dependent on the laws of the Member States and, at least in this respect, could encounter limitations to their domestic enforcement. In fact, each of these legal systems was 'only responsible for assessing whether, in its own domain, there can be acknowledgement of laws enacted by bodies that are not its own'.

In this way, steps were taken to establish a relationship between the two legal systems (Community and Member States) which, although formally autonomous and distinct, could coexist and make use of mutual collaboration to ensure full efficacy of their respective regulations.

V. The Rapprochement Between Constitutional and Community Case Law

The Constitutional Court made a further decisive move towards the positions of the Court of justice when it ruled on the *Frontini* case (27.12.1973, No. 183), in which all the issues raised in previous decisions were strengthened in a pro-European sense, encouraged in this approach also by the parallel and convergent experiences of the Dutch, Luxembourgish, Belgian and German Courts. It follows that article 11 of the Constitution represents a sure foundation of the EEC Treaty's legitimacy and guarantees its smooth running, being a determining factor in the pursuit of the aims set forth therein. And at the same time, it is expressly recognised that in doing so:

> Italy and the other promoting States have conferred and recognized certain sovereign powers directly to the EEC, constituting it as an institution characterized by an autonomous and independent system.

And it is precisely as a result of this statement that, in the opinion of the Court, Community legislative acts 'must not [even] be subjected to State provisions of a reproductive, integrative or executive nature that may in any case delay or affect their coming into force'; indeed, they must be granted 'full mandatory efficacy and direct application' that can under no circumstances be subject to compliance or dependent on the possible lack of financial resources to cover any related expenses, as article 81 of the Constitution requires for any law introducing a new or increased financial burden. In this way, the full efficacy and direct application of Community law were expressly extended also to cases in which the single piece of Community legislation provided for personal or capital performance imposed despite the legislative basis provided for to this effect by article 23 of the Constitution.

These statements foretold the total and absolute alignment of constitutional case law with Community law, relating to the primacy awarded to Community law over any domestic law at odds with the decision adopted within the scope of its competences. Such a position was not exempt from criticism that, on the one hand, highlighted its predominantly 'political' character and, on the other, gives full weight to the need to verify – under penalty of a weakening of those counter-limitations set forth in the aforementioned *Acciaierie San Michele* ruling (Constitutional Court, 27.12.1965, No. 98) – the balancing of the limitation to State sovereignty, and evaluating these counter-limitations on an individual basis, in relation to the interests and values safeguarded by the State principles vis-à-vis those laid out in the Community legislation. Such case-by-case balancing would have created uncertainty in relation to the high-priority need for an unequivocal assertion guaranteeing the effectiveness of Community law and its prevalence – to be achieved without 'meddling' from the domestic legal systems of the Member States; this would also rule out, inter alia, the possibility that Community legislation (and in particular regulations) could be directly affected by a constitutionality verification procedure or a referendum.

VI. The Coincidence of the Effects of Community Law Primacy

Having outlined the new course of constitutional law, the convergence of its effects with the outcomes or, at least, with the practical consequences of Community case law deciding on matters of Community law primacy could not be far behind. Yet, with judgment No. 132 of 13.10.1975, relating to ICIC (*Industrie Chimiche Italia Centrale*), the Constitutional Court did not hesitate to state that laws subsequent to (even if temporarily reproducing) Community regulations should have been struck down as constitutionally illegitimate and not directly disapplied by ordinary judges.

While this approach was openly disputed by the overwhelming majority of the doctrine (yet upheld by authoritative constitutionalists) and by the Constitutional Court's aforementioned statements, in actual fact it was not entirely incompatible with the outcomes aimed at guaranteeing the prevalence of Community legislation over domestic law. Moreover, it proved to be extremely cumbersome, as it required procedures that necessarily delayed the application of Community law, following criteria and methods at odds with the common approach in other Community countries, including Germany; indeed, although Germany exercised a centralised control over matters of constitutionality, it had developed a shared system of verifying the compatibility of national legislative acts with Community law, and entrusted it to ordinary judges.

As a result of these needs being fulfilled, and following the leading Community law case represented by the *Simmenthal II* case, cited in the paragraphs above, even the Constitutional Court, with decision No. 170 of 8.6.1984 relating to the *Granital* case (the so-called La Pergola judgment, from the name of its rapporteur), aligns itself with this last position. By reaffirming the characteristics of an independent and distinct legal system inherent to Community law as opposed to the domestic one, it appears that, within its field of applicability, Community law must be recognised as such without being subject to influencing and meddling from national laws that should, therefore, have been disapplied in favour of their Community counterparts precisely because they operate in a different material scope. In this way the prevalence of Community law was also guaranteed by ruling out any possibility of conflict with State legislation, by virtue of the mere identification of the respective areas of application, a procedure that had to be necessarily entrusted to an ordinary judge, as better specified in judgment of 7.2.2000, No. 41. To such an extent, that within the scope reserved to it, there was no hesitation in claiming (even at the time of judgment No. 117 of 1994) that Community law may also derogate from provisions of a constitutional status.

Yet, this very last point necessarily entailed less of a separation, and more of 'a progressive integration of the national and community legal systems' and, consequently, 'significant changes to the domestic legal system', according to the unequivocal pronouncements made in the aforementioned Constitutional Court case, No. 41/2000. So, the opening premises centring on the dualist and separatist relations between Community and domestic law gave way to (de facto) monistic conclusions supporting integration between the relevant systems based on criteria whereby the primacy of Community law over domestic law was also upheld by the Constitutional Court, after the troubled path mentioned above, and whose effects were substantially consistent with those of the Court of justice.

A matter that remains unresolved is the identification of the exact scope of the so-called counter-limitations within the national legal system when faced with undue or illegitimate interference from Community law with respect to the fundamental principles of the Italian constitutional order. The degree of effectiveness of these control systems and their actual implementation are still vague, even though the Constitutional Court's jurisdiction is acknowledged, and they may be invoked only when Community provisions address the whole system in such ways and with effects as to constitute 'a breach of the fundamental principles of our constitutional law or not respectful of the inalienable rights of human beings' (Constitutional Court, judgment of 21.4.1989, No. 232). On the other hand, these counter-limitations are also intended to operate in conjunction with internal regulations aimed at 'preventing and prejudicing ongoing compliance with the Treaty and its core principles' (Constitutional Court, order of 28.12.2006, No. 454).

The primacy of Community law and the consequent disapplication by ordinary judges, and by all the State bodies in their varying range of organisational components, of any domestic legislation at odds with it, is no longer questioned in any shape or form, and neither in all its applications. All the more so since endorsing this solution also brought tangible benefits from the amendments to article 117 of the Constitution following the enactment of constitutional law No. 3/2001, which expressly confirmed the previous jurisprudential interpretation on the relationship between Community law and domestic law; this being no longer solely entrusted to the wording of article 11 of the Constitution. And this to the extent that, even recently, the primacy of Community law has been expressly reiterated once and for all:

> also with respect to constitutional rules, identifying as its only boundary when running contrary to the fundamental principles of the State's constitutional setup or to the inalienable rights of the individual (Constitutional Court, judgment of 24.6.2010, No. 227),

and these are precisely what we understand as so-called counter-limitations.

VII. The Expression of the Primacy and Direct Effects of Community Law

The most significant evolution in the extent to which the principle of Community law primacy was applied, was especially notable with regard to its effects also extending to rules contained in directives or relating to general EU law principles that have been progressively awarded ever greater 'direct effects' also vis-à-vis individuals and companies.

In actual fact, as the foregoing paragraphs have shown, the principle of non-application of national laws by reason of their incompatibility with Community law was adopted, in its first years, specifically in the case of clear, precise and complete Community rules only. These rules were the product of legislative acts characterised by their immediacy and adopted with respect to all addressees, including individuals and enterprises. In other words, these treaty provisions or regulations owe as much to their statutory form as to their express content, and reject any right to appeal or any contrasting effect from national legislation over which they must prevail. There is no doubt that, since the initial period of the Community law applicability, this effect should also be granted to those rules whose scope in the given sense should arise from their interpretation as a result of an infringement procedure (Constitutional Court, judgment of 11.7.1989, No. 389) with the consequence that the related effects were extended universally.

The aforementioned expansive force of Community law prevalence over domestic law with the consequent disapplication of the latter yielded far less obvious and blatant results when ordinary judges were tasked with immediately identifying and actuating this effect, also with regard to the provisions contained in directives. Although characterised by a broad scope, these provisions are directed at Member States only and, while they are not mandatory in all their components, they are binding upon States to achieve a specific goal within a specifically defined time frame.

Consequently, in order to meet the goal envisaged by the directive it must be transposed and supplemented by the necessary provisions to render it concretely operational and applicable within each national legal system, which is responsible for adopting to this effect 'forms and means' appropriate to its specific characteristics. Indeed, it is precisely 'through the medium of the implementing measures adopted by the Member State' that the effects of the directive 'extend to individuals' (ECJ, 19.1.1982, *Ursula Becker v Finanzamt Münster-Innenstadt*, case 8/81).

After all, even in the 1980s and 1990s it had already been swiftly pointed out that the said transposition of the directive does not require specific legislative or administrative activity, provided that there are already:

> general principles of constitutional or administrative law [...] [which] guarantee that the national authorities will in fact apply the directive fully and that, where the directive is intended to create rights for individuals, the legal position arising from those principles is sufficiently precise and clear and the persons concerned are made fully aware of their rights (ECJ, 23.5.1985, *Commission of the European Communities v Federal Republic of Germany*, case 29/84).

In this way directives and their effects have been likened to those of regulations not only when their content is clear, precise, complete and unconditional, but also when existing legal principles in the Member States allow their necessary integration even in the absence of any further specific regulatory intervention. At the same time, the disapplication of national legislative and administrative provisions is sanctioned when these are at odds with the provisions of a directive, at least in cases where it possesses all the features necessary for its implementation by the national courts. In this way, it appears that 'legislative or administrative provisions that fail to comply with a mandatory and sufficiently precise obligation imposed by the directive cannot be enforced by a national authority against an individual' (ECJ, 7.7.1981, *Rewe-Handelsgesellschaft Nord mbH et Rewe-Markt Steffen v Hauptzollamt Kiel*, case 158/80).

A. The Primacy Effects of Directives Lacking Directly Applicable Provisions to Individuals and Businesses

Within the scope of the so-called 'horizontal' effects attributable to directives, following the rationale outlined above, the courts did not hesitate to disapply even well-established, specific national legislation and existing case law whenever found not to comply with EU law. In fact, it has been held that legislation other than regulations, such as directives, may have the same scope and direct effect over individuals and businesses so as not to undermine their useful effect:

> in particular, where the Community authorities have, by directive, imposed on Member States the obligation to pursue a particular course of conduct, the useful effect of such an act would be weakened if individuals were prevented from relying on it before their national courts and if the latter were prevented from taking it into consideration as an element of Community law (ECJ, 1.2.1977, *Verbond van Nederlandse Ondernemingen v Inspecteur der Invoerrechten en Accijnzen*. Case 51-76).

It follows that a Community citizen who has complied with the obligations laid down in a directive may (and must) successfully seek the disapplication of national rules which are incompatible with the above obligations, even if they have not yet been incorporated into domestic law, at least when these are 'unconditional and sufficiently precise' obligations (ECJ, 5.4.1979, *Criminal proceedings against Tullio Ratti*, case 148/78).

In such a case, individuals and companies may also invoke directives with the aforementioned contents before the national courts in order to 'seek an order against the administrative authorities', precisely because public administration bodies are also required 'to apply the provisions of the directive [by disapplying] provisions of national law which conflict with them' (ECJ, 22.6.1989, *Fratelli Costanzo SpA v Comune di Milano*, case 103/88).

As said before, the same does not apply when the directive is invoked by the State against individuals and companies. In fact, on the occasion of the famous case *Berlusconi and others* (ECJ, 3.5.2005, *Silvio Berlusconi, Sergio Adelchi, Marcello Dell'Utri and others*, joined cases C-387/02 and C-403/02), it was rightly held that a directive cannot be invoked as such by the authorities of a Member State against individuals because:

> a directive cannot, of itself and independently of a national law adopted by a Member State for its implementation, have the effect of determining or aggravating the liability in criminal law of the persons [accused].

As already shown, the foregoing does not exclude that in any case Member States law must be construed up to the limits imposed by interpretation criteria, in accordance with the requirements of the directives irrespective of whether said rules precede or follow the deadline set for the full implementation and integration of the directive itself (ECJ, 5.10.2004, *Bernhard Pfeiffer and others v Deutsches Rotes Kreuz, Kreisverband Waldshut eV*, joined cases C-397/01–C-403/01). Clearly, the interpretative effort cannot be stretched to the point of allowing a *contra legem* interpretation; in this case, as mentioned before, the domestic rule may be set aside, but only if the contents of the directive are unconditional and sufficiently precise.

Even in the event that a Community directive should lack the appropriate characteristics for it to be directly effective, with the consequent setting aside of the conflicting national provisions, it shall not in any case be deprived of effects. In this case, the necessary verifications must take place through an incidental procedure before the Constitutional Court, in which these directives operate as an 'intermediate law' for the purposes of adjudicating on the constitutionality of the conflicting domestic rules 'for alleged breach of art. 11 and art. 117(1) of the Constitution' (Constitutional Court, judgment of 24.6.2010, No. 227).

VIII. The Evolution of Principles for the Protection of Human Rights

The evolution traced with regard to the direct effects acknowledged by 'clear, precise and unconditional' directives, with their consequent primacy over conflicting domestic rules that ordinary national courts must directly disapply, has brought about the extension of identical effects in favour of 'general principles' enforceable in Community law. On the one hand, we are dealing with principles laid down in the norms of the Treaty on European Union (TEU) and the Treaty on the functioning of the European Union (TFEU) which have the characteristics of self-executing provisions and, on the other, with the unwritten principles found in current EU legislation also flowing from the subject matter of derived norms and principles common to the legal systems of the Member States or found in international legislative instruments to which the EU adheres, especially if referred to in the very own provisions of the Treaty of Lisbon.

It comes as no surprise, then, that the Court of justice has not hesitated to make use of the regulatory provisions of the European Convention for the protection of human rights (ECHR) in this regard, owing to the ever wider recognition of the leading role that it has assumed internationally in the protection of human rights, and to the many references to the Convention in the Treaty of Lisbon and in the EU's Charter of fundamental rights. In fact, it has been known for a long time that, even though the EU has still not adhered to this Convention, its provisions, including the case law resulting from its implementation, are deemed to be effective also within the EU and they enjoy the same primacy over conflicting national legislation as Community law. This is enough to ensure that national legislation may be disapplied regardless of the existence of a specific international obligation assumed in the matter by the EU vis-à-vis the contracting States of the ECHR.

In support of the above, article 6 TEU has recently been invoked, and in particular its paragraph 3, on the basis of which:

> fundamental rights, as guaranteed by the European Convention for the protection of human rights and fundamental freedoms and as they result from the constitutional traditions common to the Member States, shall constitute general principles of the Union's law

recognised in its own sphere of application and not only as a 'source of inspiration for the discovery of general principles of EU law', as held at the time of the *Nold* judgment (ECJ, 14.5.1974, *J. Nold, Kohlen-und Baustoffgroßhandlung v Commission of the European Communities*, case 4/73).

But that is not all. In actual fact, the ECHR assumes a definitive binding status within the EU legislative system, enjoying relative primacy over national legislation also with regard to the protocols relating to it, at least to the extent in which they are in force within those States that have ratified them. The protection granted by the ECHR must be allowed to extend its scope, in accordance with the provisions of the aforementioned protocols and at the discretion of the Member States, provided that this does not run against EU legislation, and in particular without prejudice to the unity and effectiveness of EU law, as the Court of justice recently clarified in the *Hernández* case (10.7.2014, *Víctor Manuel Julian Hernández e a. contro Reino de España*, C-198/13).

Nor can it be construed to the contrary that the effects of the ECHR described above could only be justified under the Treaty of Maastricht as expressly established by reason of a specific legal obligation to comply with the Convention; indeed, there is no such express obligation under the Treaty of Lisbon, since the current wording of article 6.3 TEU was adopted instead. As has been recently observed, one certainly cannot construe this amended formulation of the Treaty of Lisbon as a will to scale back the obligations and effects ascribed to the regulatory content of the ECHR in the aforementioned sense, and the will to undertake an objective regression in the protection of personal rights compared with the past.

Based on the foregoing arguments, it is possible to integrate the direct effects of some of the principles found in Community law through the use of ECHR provisions as well as the Strasbourg Court's relevant case law. In this way the contents and the extension of the corresponding personal rights are specified, making them more tangibly operational and enforceable throughout the EU's legal system.

IX. The Effects of the Charter of Fundamental Rights and of the ECHR

Similar integration effects also take place in cases where the recognition of the above-mentioned principles is possible through their codification, as undertaken by the Charter of fundamental rights of the European Union.

Indeed, article 51 of the Charter must be construed by acknowledging that the scope of such a regulatory tool, despite its formulation, cannot be construed as being directed at the States only, and specifically as being capable of limiting or affecting the direct applicability of general principles whose criteria are likely to establish and shape individual rights within EU law. Even though they are rightly formulated in such a way as to produce direct effects also in relations between individuals, the principles contained in the Charter and in the ECHR must in any case be credited with the interpretative efforts aimed at strengthening and clarifying the extent of Community rules and principles. This facilitates the recognition of their direct effects in favour of individuals and companies within the operational scope of EU law, with the ensuing precedence over (and disapplication of) national legislation in contrast with these effects.

It is precisely in this sense that the evolution of Community law is justified and legitimised also with regard to recent developments in the *Mangold* case (ECJ, 22.11.2005, *Werner Mangold v Rüdiger Helm*, C-144/04) up to the *Kücükdeveci* case (ECJ, 19.1.2010, *Seda Kücükdeveci v Swedex GmbH & Co. KG*, C- 555/07), in which the above-mentioned principles were expressly upheld with specific reference to direct horizontal effects and to primacy applied to the principle of non-discrimination on the grounds of age.

On the strength of the aforesaid case law, rather than enshrining the direct effects of directive 2000/78/EC that codified this principle, this directive has simply been referenced as a source of knowledge and the wellspring of a general principle already existing in Community law. It was found that the specific circumstances relating to the practical implementation of the contents, the underlying principles gaining ground in the EU, along with the common traditions of Member States all warrant this presence and the aforementioned declaratory function of the directive in question.

Crucially, in a bid to bolster this declaratory effect, article 21 of the EU Charter of Fundamental Rights, article 13 of the EC Treaty in force at the time, along with the provisions of article 14 of the ECHR, were invoked; the reason for this being that all these articles are designed to strike down any form of discrimination even on the grounds of age. On the other hand, the fact that this prohibition should abide in Community law as a mainstay of its constitutional principles had already been asserted on various occasions.

Recognising the existence, the direct applicability and the consequent primacy of the aforesaid principles, ascertainable also through the declaratory value that may have been accomplished by specific directives, does not rule out the possibility that limitations to their scope may be enforced and/or specific restrictions may be placed on the rights exercised, when calls are made to set aside national legislation that curtails the directive's scope and effects. First of all, particularly relevant in this regard are the conditions and limitations that can be relied on pursuant to article 6.1, paragraph 3 TEU, article 52 of the EU Charter of Fundamental Rights, along with the ECHR provisions. In the latter regard, the limitations that can lawfully be applied must not go beyond those permitted under the ECHR, in keeping with the effort to coordinate these provisions with those of the aforementioned EU Charter of Fundamental Rights under article 52 thereof. The purpose here was to ensure the necessary consistency between the Charter and the ECHR 'without thereby adversely affecting the autonomy of Union law and of that of the Court of justice of the European Union'.

In any case, the limitations to rights and freedoms must be in the public interest or warranted by the need to safeguard the rights and freedoms of others, even if the necessary evaluation would be made taking into account the criteria of each national jurisdiction along with any specifications that the various States may have adopted. These limitations and their corresponding methods of application, however, must not be disproportionate to the aims pursued which warranted their use. In fact, the margins of discretion that States possess in this regard should not produce the result of frustrating the actual uniform effectiveness and primacy of Community principles.

This leads to a system that affords adequate protection of the rights guaranteed by Community law principles so as to ensure their full effectiveness and direct effects on individuals and companies with the consequent setting aside, if justified, of any conflicting national legislation, or of any detrimental effects of such legislation considered excessive in establishing the limitations to the exercise of rights protected by EU law.

Specifically, as recently highlighted by the Court of justice (in the *Rasmussen* case, judgment of 19.4.2016, *Dansk Industri (DI) v Succession Karsten Eigil Rasmussen*, C-441/14), the enforcement of principles and rights recognised by Community law constitutes a duty which must be imposed on all the authorities of the Member States, including jurisdictional ones ensuring 'the full effectiveness' and 'disapplying if need be any provision of national legislation contrary to that principle'.

Naturally, the evaluation of the legitimacy and application of the limitations set by national legislation for the exercise of the principles and rights accorded under Community law will be all the smoother given that they are expressly recognised as such when their scope is identified in specific EU legislative acts. Moreover, the corresponding effects must be evaluated regardless of the abstract potential of the specific act to generate both direct effects on individuals and horizontal effects in the case of relations between individuals; we should rather be evaluating their scope as a source capable of identifying the presence of certain community principles in its capacity as a source of cognisance as to the existence of those very same principles.

Bibliography

Adinolfi, A, 'Rapporti fra norme comunitarie e norme interne integrate da sentenze additive della Corte costituzionale: un orientamento (… 'sperimentale') del Consiglio di Stato' (2006) 89(1) *Rivista di diritto internazionale* 139–44.

Amalfitano, C and Condinanzi, M, *Unione Europea: fonti, adattamento e rapporti tra ordinamenti* (Torino, 2015).

Baratta, R, 'La cosa giudicata non limita il principio della primauté ... peraltro espunto dal progetto di riforma dell'Unione Europea' (2007) 12 *Giustizia civile* 2659–62.

Carbone, SM, 'Corte costituzionale, pregiudiziale comunitaria e uniforme applicazione del diritto comunitario' 2007 12(3) *Il diritto dell'Unione Europea* 707–17.

Condorelli, L, 'Il caso Simmenthal e il primato del diritto comunitario: due corti a confronto' (1978) 1 *Giurisprudenza costituzionale* 669–76.

Gambino, S, 'Identità costituzionali nazionali e primauté eurounitaria' (2012) 3 *Quaderni costituzionali* 533–61.

Itzcovich, G, *Teorie e ideologie del diritto comunitario* (Torino, 2006).

Ivaldi, P, 'Diritto dell'Unione Europea e processo costituzionale' (2013) 1 *Il diritto dell'Unione Europea* 191–224.

Mastroianni, R, 'L'ordinamento giuridico nazionale nei rapporti con le regole comunitarie e dell'Unione Europea. La posizione della Corte costituzionale italiana' (2009) 48(3) *Diritto comunitario e degli scambi internazionali* 437–65.

Orlandi, M, *L'evoluzione del primato del diritto dell'Unione Europea* (Torino, 2012).

Parodi, G, *Le fonti del diritto. Linee evolutive* (Milano, 2012).

Ronzitti, N (ed), *L'articolo 11 della Costituzione. Baluardo della vocazione internazionale dell'Italia* (Napoli, 2013).

Sorrentino, F, *Le fonti del diritto italiano* (Padova 2009, 2015).

Tizzano, A, 'Ancora sui rapporti tra Corti europee: principi comunitari e cd controlimiti costituzionali' (2007) 3 *Il diritto dell'Unione Europea* 734–44.

Vecchio, F, *Primazia del diritto europeo e salvaguardia delle identità costituzionali* (Torino, 2012).

'Actes de colloque La primauté du droit de l'Union Européenne: intégration et valorisation du principe. 50 ans après l'arrêt de la CJCE, Costa c/ Enel' (2014) *Europe* annex to No. 7.

10

Legislation and Legislative Procedures Between the Parliament, the Council and the Commission

ANDREA MANZELLA

I. Toward the 'Better Regulation'

In 2016, the European Parliament, the Council and the Commission – the institutional triangle within which the Union's legislative activity takes place – signed a final agreement on 'better regulation' ('Interinstitutional agreement on better law-making reached by the European Parliament, the Council and the European Commission', *Official Journal* L 123, 12 May 2016). In this agreement every European citizen can easily read what is effectively a manifesto for good law-making, and can compare the more effective supranational approach with the way in which governments and national Parliaments usually proceed. Indeed the order of the new European legislation is based on three pillars: planning, quality of law-making and assessment of its impact and continuing validity.

The long-term planning coincides with the appointment of a new Commission. This government plan is initiated by the Commission, but is based on dialogue, and therefore on conclusions shared by all three institutions. After this, the Commission's annual work programme is drafted for each year of the parliamentary term and contains the main legislative proposals for the following year. These include proposals for repeals, recasting of legislation, simplifications and withdrawals of draft legislative acts that have not yet been approved.

This interinstitutional 'manifesto' therefore indicates that in order to ensure that a legislative programme remains up to date it is essential also to include non-legislation as well as legislation for the purpose of simplification. The quality of law-making depends above all on the efficacy of the consultations that need to accompany the law-making process from beginning to end: discussion with the social parties, in the form of consultations with the public and with stakeholders, and discussion among the institutions, which must reflect in a 'sincere and transparent' manner the balance of powers between the Parliament, the Council and the Commission depending of the stage of procedures. This balance is defined in the treaties and internal rules of procedure of the three institutions and finds in the Community method the paradigm through which the institutional triangle operates. However, the quality of law-making also and above all depends on the 'joint responsibility' of the three institutions in producing a body of law that guarantees legal certainty and is therefore as 'simple and as clear as possible' and 'avoids overregulation and administrative burdens for citizens, administrations and businesses, especially small and medium-sized enterprises ("SMEs")'. The 'manifesto agreement' goes on to say that legislation must be designed 'with a view to facilitating its transposition and practical application and to strengthening the competitiveness and sustainability of the Union economy'.

Therefore, at the Union's highest institutional level there is awareness that legislation is also an economic factor that can have a positive or negative effect on business, making it simpler or burdening it with pointless costs. This 'economy of legislation' is clearly referred to in three essential caveats for good law-makers: 'to legislate only where and to the extent necessary'; 'the analysis of the potential "European added value" of any action should be fully considered'; assessing the 'cost of non-Europe' in the absence of the proposed action. This leads to a prior impact assessment based on these parameters, identifying the impact of the various alternative solutions, 'having particular regard to [...] digital aspects and territorial impact'.

Finally in the conception of European legislation, there is full awareness of the possible transience of law-making in relation to changes in society and international events. This underlies the conceptual pillar of reviewing the legislation in force and the related public policies, a pillar which in fact could recommend the preventive use of 'review clauses' in legislation, or of 'sunset clauses' to limit the application to a fixed period of time. In any case at the planning stage the Commission informs the Parliament and the Council of the evaluation of existing legislation 'based on efficiency, effectiveness, relevance, coherence and value added': all conditions that must be verified with 'public and stakeholder consultation' and with 'measurable indicators as a basis on which to collect evidence of the effects of legislation on the ground'. The Commission will 'in particular encourage the direct participation of SMEs and other end-users in the consultations. This will include public internet-based consultations'. This is therefore the end-point – provisional, like every degree of maturation in the process of European integration – of the Union's law-making 'conscience'. A point that could be a good standard to upgrade the body of law in many countries.

Of course there is always (and always will be) a significant gap between the good intentions, so clearly set out, and the reality of Union matters. However, there is a complicated story behind this gap that in part justifies it (certainly much more than the hundred-year old histories of the nation-States). There is a close link between the history of European law-making and an analysis of the Union's current legislative procedures, in the sense that each of the procedural stages internally mirrors the tensions and equilibriums that marked that history.

The long path towards parliamentary legislation, which in key areas coincides with the 'great history' of integration, is in fact the search for a difficult balance between the institutions. The original role of these institutions was to execute the objectives 'entrusted to the Community' (article 4 of the Treaty establishing the European Community, TEC), to which they had to add the far more ambitious goals for the Union, to 'promote its values' and to 'serve its interests, those of its citizens and those of the Member States' (article 13 of the Treaty on European Union, TEU). However, this balance would be best defined as constitutional, because it coincides with the gradual formation of a democratic type of order, in which the element of representation of European citizens eats into and ultimately conditions the decision-making power of the national governments in the Council. Conversely, the Commission, with its independent powers of arbitration, oscillates from its position wedged between the two political powers, in one phase acting as an active protagonist and in the other as an executive secretariat.

The Court of Justice, which for sixty years has been assigned the task to 'ensure that in the interpretation [...] of the Treaties the law is observed' (article 164, TEC, article 19, TEU) in an unaltered formula, rationalises and supports the constitutionalisation of the law and its balance with the case law establishing the primacy of Community law, and its direct effect on the law of the Member States and on the correct joint presence of the institutions in the decision-making processes (with special focus on the representative principle). In turn, the law-making process sees the same institutional players involved in a complex balancing act between the political and economic interests they represent, and the interaction with national parliaments and the people ultimately affected by the laws.

II. The Growing Powers of the European Parliament as a Legislator

The history of European law-making was, for almost 20 years, that of legislation not requiring parliamentary decisions. The Council of Minister of the Member States and the Commission – with members 'of indisputable independence' appointed by joint agreement with the governments (article 157, TEC) – adopted regulations, directives, and decisions in the strict sense (article 189, TEC). Of course, the parliamentary Assembly established with the founding treaty (article 137, TEC) had a say: but only via a consultation procedure. Its opinions therefore accompanied the growth of the original Economic Community through its most delicate phases and policies the custom union (article 14(7), TEC), the common agricultural policy (article 43(2), TEC), freedom of establishment (article 54(1), TEC), the freedom to provide services (article 59(1), TEC), the common transport policy (article 71(1), TEC) and the rules on competition (article 87(1), TEC).

Moreover, the consultation of the Assembly had a not insignificant procedural impact. The Commission was able to alter its initial proposal – 'particularly in cases where the Assembly had been consulted on the proposal concerned' – until such time as the Council had acted (article 149, TEC). This means that the opinions of the Assembly made up of delegations from national parliaments could play a driving role in amending the Commission's proposal. And by means of subsequent interinstitutional agreements, the Commission undertook to provide express justifications for rejecting parliamentary amendments and even to withdraw legislative proposals that had been rejected by the Parliament.

Another parliamentary source, on a secondary level, and tied to the result to be achieved, was only envisaged when the statutory format of the directive referred as for the 'form' and 'means' of action to the competence of the domestic institutions (article 189, TEC). Such a referral is, therefore, implicit: it is subject to the requirement by the national constitutional systems of a parliamentary intervention.

In fact, from 1957 to 1979, the members of the Assembly, appointed by the national parliaments, used their dual mandate to bring the European positions back to their national parliaments. This was then reflected in the mandate given to the governments for discussions in Europe. At that time a synergy had developed between the European Parliament and the national Parliaments that was gradually lost over time.

However, in the original unyielding a-parliamentary set-up of the European Communities there was a fault line. And the European parliamentarism took advantage of this opening to build its legislative powers. The fault line was the ancient power of the purse, the budget approval, which had not been possible to pinch from the first parliamentary Assembly, 'composed of delegates whom the Parliaments [of the Member States] shall be called upon to appoint from among their members' (article 138, TEC).

This budgetary power was very limited: 'The Assembly shall be entitled to propose to the Council amendments to the draft budget', but in the end it was the Council that 'shall finally adopt the budget by means of a qualified majority vote' (article 203, TEC).

Only with the 1975 Treaty of Brussels were increased financial powers assigned to what from 1962 was able to call itself the European Parliament. These affected both the budget of the previous financial year (the 'budget discharge' decision) and, and above all, the power to reject the budget for the following year, with the consequent obligation for the Commission to start the whole procedure again from scratch.

A joint declaration by the Parliament, the Council and the Commission in March 1975 marked the intention of the three institutions to find an agreement for legislative acts having 'significant financial implications'. This agreement also showed the first opportunity for legislative debate between the Parliament and Council without filtering by the Commission. In fact, it contained a select committee conciliation procedure that was a precursor to what, many years later, would become standard conciliation procedure incorporated into the ordinary law-making process. However, it should be remembered that there were a few exemplary cases in which the Council interpreted the formula of 'significant financial implications' in a flexible manner and with a certain *favor parlamenti.*

Nonetheless, it took 12 years for European law-making to become parliamentary-oriented legislation, with the cooperation procedure set out in the Single European Act (1986). Almost directly as a result of this, the Council took on a role comparable to that of a second chamber, second also in chronological terms because law-making initiatives on the part of the Commission were examined in the first instance by the Parliament. The legislative debate took place between the Assembly and the Commission. The Council intervened on the text once it was normally amended by Parliament, and formed a common position on it by a qualified majority. The text of the Council's common position was then put before Parliament for a second reading, either for final approval or for new amendments. The *navette* then went back to the Council, which could definitively adopt the text or approve it with its amendments, but in this case it had to do so unanimously. This considerable complication of the procedure within the Council had constitutionally significant consequences. In the first place, an alliance between the Parliament and the Commission in the ordinary process of drafting a text; the Commission's monopoly on law-making initiatives therefore remained such, but when the proposal reached the Council it had been subject to parliamentary debate that could have led to amendments. In the second place, the Parliament could exercise its power to reject a legislative proposal due to irreconcilable differences with the Commission (which might result in the withdrawal of the text), or the Council could fail to reach unanimity on its position within a three-month period. In the majority of cases, these procedural complications led the Council to incorporate the parliamentary amendments adopted at the first reading. In its structure and practical consequences (involving Parliament in the essential harmonisation legislation for the creation of the common market), the cooperation procedure thus marked the beginning of Parliament effectively having power over the legislative process.

The Maastricht Treaty (1992) is generally famous for its economic and financial convergence criteria that Member States have to comply with in order to join the economic and monetary union (and to remain members, as it has gradually been discovered). However, for the purposes of European integration, in a democratic-parliamentary constitutional system, the introduction of two key provisions was far more important. These were the European citizenship and the codecision legislative procedure. Both provisions are closely dependent on a democratic turning point. The rights relating to citizenship, in fact, include active and passive voting rights in the European Parliament elections, whichever the Member State of residence and on equal terms with the citizens of that State. The codecision procedure (at the time limited to 15 subject-matters) meant the European Parliament and Council became colegislators practically on equal footing.

Compared with the previous cooperation procedure, which continued to exist for other subject-areas, the new procedure meant that the Parliament-Council's *navette* did not just end with the common position adopted by the Council on the text shaped by the interaction between the Commission and the Parliament. In fact, under the codecision procedure, if the Council does not accept such a text, this leads to a third phase: the establishment of a conciliation committee comprising representatives of the Parliament and the Council in order to find a compromise test, with the mediation of the Commission. This text would then have to be adopted by a qualified majority of the Council (except for subjects where unanimity is required) and a simple majority of the European Parliament.

With the codecision procedure structured in such a way – and in particular with the conciliation phase it incorporated – European legislation became parliamentary legislation. There is now a direct dialogue between the two Chambers, downgrading the Commission's role to an albeit essential one of independent arbitrator. A path was taken in reaction to the constant pressure from public opinion and case law against the democratic deficit that made it irreversible.

The 1997 Treaty of Amsterdam extended the codecision procedure to the majority of subject matters under the Union competence. Finally, the 2009 Treaty of Lisbon further extended these subject matters, making the codecision procedure the 'ordinary legislative procedure' as it is defined in the official text of the Treaty. Its core is the joint adoption of a regulation, directive or decision by the Parliament and the Council on a proposal of the Commission (article 289, TFEU). In fact, the Treaty of Lisbon seems to go further. By precluding the European Council of the heads of State and government (the new institution introduced by article 15, TEU) from exercising legislative functions, it reserved this power for the pair Parliament-Council. However, the economic crisis has unfortunately shown that this legislative domination was fictional, given that the major legislative directions and inputs in this context (and something more than just 'directions') were formed in the European Council. Indeed the practice has shown a sort of abusive exercise of legislative powers by the European Council. By politically endorsing the multiannual financial framework, the European Council has implicitly supported the adoption of around 60 regulations, thereby updating the European legislation every seven years. It is a sort of mass adoption of the main legislation with a financial impact. Despite this, the Treaty of Lisbon established a normal procedure that effectively marked the level of democratic commitment of European law-making.

It has therefore taken 52 years (the period of time between the Treaty of Rome and the Treaty of Lisbon) for an international agreement, by definition intergovernmental, to develop a system in which the democratic element slowly but surely prevailed. This involved the shift from second-level parliamentary elections to direct elections, and increased the quality of the European Parliament's powers from mere consultation to those of checking the budget of the 'common enterprise' and again to those of colegislator, responsible for the implementation through legislation of the founding objectives of the European integration.

In this process of parliamentary empowerment, and more so than ever before, we may glimpse how a utopia has become reality, albeit an unfinished one, as is the case with every democratic process.

III. The Ordinary Legislative Procedure

Every stage of the Union's legislative procedures seems to embody on a microscopic scale the tensions and the difficult balance between the institutions that have featured the development of European legislation, which is so closely linked to the great history of integration. However, in recent years there has been an increasingly clear attempt also to respond to the widespread accusations of a democratic deficit coming from the political community. As if the Union institutions, having appeased a similar internal confrontation, felt the need to show a common front to external threats of legal and political delegitimisation.

The accusations of a lack of democracy that initially came from the federalist movements ('the best enemy of good') then became the arch defence of a sort of parliamentary exclusivism on the part of national assemblies through the case law of constitutional courts, and finally degenerated into actual cracks in the whole construction of the Union. In the critical phase, which is still ongoing, the call on national Parliaments to act as interlocutors in the decision-making process was if anything far too late. And this despite the fact that the problem (and the remedy) had become gradually clear for some time. The creation of the Conference of parliamentary committees for Union affairs (COSAC, 1989), the declarations annexed to the Maastricht Treaty (declaration 14 even talks about interparliamentary cooperation as an assize in between the European Parliament and national Parliaments) and the protocol on the role of national parliaments in the European Union annexed to the Treaty of Amsterdam are all stages that led to the formulation of the Lisbon Treaty, according to which '[n]ational Parliaments contribute actively to the good functioning of the Union' (article 12, TEU). What is more, the establishment of two Interparliamentary Conferences (on common security and defence in 2012 and on governance of the Eurozone in 2013) seemed to pave the way towards a mutual exchange of legitimation between the European Parliament and national Parliaments in order to determine an effective parliamentary influence on what were eminently intergovernmental policies (therefore removed from the competence of both the European Parliament and national Parliaments). In fact, since Lisbon it has been possible to talk about an actual 'Euro-national Parliamentary System', considering the panoply of all the other powers attributed to national Parliaments by the Treaty (article 12) and the interaction between them and the European Parliament.

However this trend is slow in producing effective results due to the short-sighted resistance in legislative bodies, both on the 'unionist' and the national side. The two Interparliamentary Conferences we have mentioned should have acted as a precursor to more extensive interparliamentary cooperation 'by means of Conferences' established by subject-matter, whereas they were in fact encapsulated within the programme of an anodyne 'European week' (as if they were ordinary conferences of experts and not of parliamentary bodies). These reciprocal misunderstandings meant that the role of national Parliaments in the Union has remained essentially restricted to a purely defensive and – what is more – totally fragmented role, thus overlooking the weight that a proactive and, above all, collective role might carry in terms of democratic persuasion (in the procedures of Interparliamentary Conferences comprising representatives of the relevant parliamentary committees). There is therefore a lack of a systematic connection that could have avoided the – debatable – views of the German constitutional case law on a lack of democratic powers. The democratic nature of the legislative process of the European Union must therefore be evaluated first and foremost within the stages that make up what is the ordinary legislative process: the codecision procedure.

(a) Article 17 of the TEU states that '[u]nion legislative acts may only be adopted on the basis of a Commission proposal', but during the drafting of a proposal one can detect an entire pre-legislative cycle. First of all, the Commission has to specify the legal basis, that is, the provision of the Treaty attributing competence to the Union to take action in order to regulate a given subject-matter. The Commission's initiative then has to take two routes: the prior assessment of the quality of the legislative proposal and of its consistency with the Union's annual and multiannual programmes. As mentioned, this quality control results in four distinctive judgements of the initiative, based on: its 'necessity' with regard to the existing legislative framework; its 'European value added'; the cost of 'non-Europe' (ie, in the absence of said initiative); and calculation of the administrative burdens resulting from the introduction of the new provisions. These requirements and the ex-ante impact assessments must be examined in consultation with the addressees of the proposal, as illustrated by the various forms of communications (white papers and green papers).

The monopoly on legislative initiatives therefore lies with the Commission, but the substance of the initiative is shared, due to the conventional bond with the other two institutions that will be involved in the process. It is in that framework that national parliaments step in. They receive the consultation documents drafted by the Commission as soon as they are published. Most important they are transmitted the draft legislative acts presented to the Parliament and the Council (once the legislative initiative has taken on its final form). There is then a 'white' period lasting eight weeks. The initiative is suspended in order to allow national assemblies to send their reasoned opinions as to whether the draft complies with the principle of subsidiarity (and proportionality, according to the institutional practice, see article 5, TEU). This is the moment when the role of national parliaments, albeit in a defensive sense, emerges in the European legislative procedure with institutionally relevant effects (in accordance with protocol No. 2 annexed to the Treaty of Lisbon).

The second route the Commission's initiative has to take is to check its consistency with the Union's annual and multiannual programmes, which take the form of an inter-institutional agreement (article 17(1), TEU). The importance of the consistency with the programming activity has become more significant since the latest developments of the Union. The parliamentarisation of the investiture of the Commission's president – after the European elections have been 'unified' by the presentation of supranational *Spitzenkandidaten* by the various European political 'families' (2014) – has led to a 'Coalition Commission'. This definition, taken from current parliamentary terminology, also incorporates the change in the legal – and not just political – significance of the programming activity set out under the Treaty. In fact such activity identifies the core of the coalition agreement triggered by the parliamentary election of the president of the Commission. This means that 'the general interest of the Union' that justifies the Commission's monopoly on legislative initiatives no longer springs forth like a technocratic Minerva from the solitary head of Jove-the Commission. Instead it is the general interest that gives life to parliamentary agreement, which, based on a programme, has led to the election of the president of the Commission and to the approval of the individual commissioners and of the Commission as a whole. This influence on the democratic credentials of the European legislative process is even more important if we consider that when we talk about a legislative initiative, we are not just dealing with the initial act of a legislative procedure, but also with the powers that the Commission has throughout the process, including in particular the power of withdrawal until the act is formally adopted. In a public announcement the president of the Commission has linked the power of withdrawal not so much to a procedural technique aiming at simplifying the legislation but rather at a principle of political discontinuity at the start of the parliamentary term. This explicit claim of a break (between parliamentary terms and, hence, between different Commissions) seems to confirm the almost executive nature of the Commission's initiative – of proposal or withdrawal – with respect to the political programme of its investiture. Basically it is a new approach that considerably consolidates the majority of the European Parliament, currently under pressure from a euro-hostile opposition, around the Commission's president and his programme. And this strengthening of the parliamentary majority should be mirrored in legislative procedure.

Leaving aside the primary source of legislative initiatives – that appears to be found in the gradual introduction of the parliamentary appointment of the Commission – thus far two other 'initiative's initiatives' have had little influence. The Commission's reason for presenting 'appropriate proposals' may in fact also come from a majority of members of Parliament (article 225, TFEU) or from one million European citizens (article 11, TEU).

This recent participatory innovation introduced by the Treaty of Lisbon has certainly not made a significant impact compared to the expectation. However, it is interesting to note that in official European Parliament's documents, this 'citizens' initiative' is seen as a form of future competition with the parliamentary 'initiative's initiative'. In the first place there is in fact a clear difference in the democratic commitment. On the one hand there is the burdensome collection of signatures from one million citizens, with 'minimum thresholds' reached in at least seven Member States. On the other, it is certainly easier to achieve a majority of members of the European Parliament via the aggregating mechanism of the parliamentary groups. In the second place, the European citizens' initiative has, at least in theory, greater political resonance than parliamentary initiative, both in itself – as an opportunity for a transnational political debate – and for the possibility of being heard in the European Parliament and for the legally 'due' reaction of the Commission.

Of course we are still talking about an 'initiative's initiative' because the monopoly on legislative proposals attributed to the Commission by the Treaties is not up for discussion. But the concern of the European Parliament for its own initiative also tells us that in the democracy of the public the announcement effect has taken on exaggerated implications. And not just in a virtual sense, but in actual terms: whether in political conduct, in the search for consensus and ultimately in the processes of democratic legitimation.

Just as in a kaleidoscope, the interests of social parties and the positions of European institutions and of Member States' governments and parliaments come together during the stage of the legislative initiative. The initiative is therefore always taken by the Commission, but it is not a 'naked' product, it is 'clothed' in these multiple contributions.

(b) The Commission presents the proposal simultaneously to the European Parliament and the Council (article 294(2), TFEU). However, the proposal may come as a 'non-novelty' for the Parliament. The committee responsible may in fact have already decided to appoint a 'rapporteur to follow the preparatory phase of a proposal [...] listed in the Commission Work Programme' (rule 47(3), Rules of procedure of the European Parliament, REP). As for the Council, this institution undoubtedly follows the formation of the proposal through the Committee of permanent representatives of the Member States' governments (Coreper).

The two legislative Chambers therefore begin their examination of the proposal in parallel, but the Council's position is normally adopted after the vote in Parliament at this initial stage. This parliamentary stage is marked by four preliminary checks aiming at evaluating the draft legislative act's full compliance with the 'fundamentals' of the Union system.

The first check concerns the full compliance with the rights, freedoms and principles contained in the Charter of Fundamental Rights of the European Union (article 6, TEU). The Charter is still called the 'Nice' charter because in December 2000 it was the subject of a premature proclamation by the presidents of the European Parliament, the Council and the Commission: a good seven years before the Treaty of Lisbon, which has given to the Charter binding force and the same value as the Treaties, came into force. Created by a parliamentary convention, it has always remained in the foreground, and is therefore a natural parliamentary code of conduct, defended by a procedural cornerstone (current rule 38, REP) and by the mechanism of a committee with cross-sectional competence responsible for the parliamentary interpretation of the Charter. It is perhaps not a long shot to see in parliament's protective fencing-off of the Charter a certain 'patriotism of rights' that is in line with the tumultuous opinion of 18 December 2014 in which the Court of Justice declared that the draft agreement on the Union's accession to the ECHR (European Convention for the Protection of Human Rights) was 'not compatible with EU law'. What this means is that a specific rationale has been endorsed in the European legal order by the European Parliament and the Court of Justice whereby the choice underlying the European case law on rights is also shared and deeply rooted in the political mindset at supranational level. Therefore, underlying the Court's opinion on the draft accession agreement to the ECHR is the concern for avoiding a potential crisis of rejection triggered by the activism of a judge, the European Court of human rights, not closely tied to the rules 'of the European Union house'.

The second check deals with the legal basis of the draft legislative act, which the Court of Justice defines as an essential element for greater understanding of its scope and its validity (see 1 October 2009, *Commission v Council*, case C-370/07). The Parliament's rules of procedure assign this assessment to its committee on legal affairs, with a significant reference to article 5, TEU. In the first place, therefore, there is the question of the principle of conferral (rule 39, REP). This is what defines the fundamental position of the Union in its relationship with the Member States and the scope of its competence.

The third check involves the control of compliance with the principles of subsidiarity and proportionality. Again the recommendations of the committee responsible for compliance with the principle of subsidiarity prevail over the committee responsible for the subject-matter (rule 42, REP).

A specific procedure is initiated when the European Parliament receives 'reasoned opinions on the non-compliance of a proposal' from a national Parliament (in accordance with protocol No. 2 annexed to the Treaty of Lisbon). If, in fact, such opinions are supported by a majority of the national Parliaments, the committee responsible may even recommend that the plenary session rejects the proposal, by a majority of the votes cast. This is the point when national Parliaments can have the maximum procedural impact on the European legislative process (rule 42(6), REP).

The fourth preliminary check involves the financial compatibility, based on the regulation establishing the multiannual financial framework (article 310(4), TFEU). Here, in addition to the committee responsible for the subject-matter, a specific role is played by the committee responsible for budgetary issues. Besides its ordinary advisory role on matters of financial coverage, this committee can also report its conclusions to the Parliament on its own initiative before the vote on the proposal takes place (rule 41, REP).

Once gone through the four checks, the proposal is ready for its first reading. However, this cannot take place until the committee responsible for the subject-matter has appointed a rapporteur who has drawn up a comprehensive report (rule 49, RPE). This report can provide the basis for a phase of negotiations with the Commission and the Council (outside of the first reading in a formal sense). This may in fact be the first of the 'trilogues' to be held: informal contacts (behind closed doors) between the institutions responsible for European legislation. The distant example of 1975 has in fact had a mole-like burrowing effect and in its perfected form has become standard practice for the search, as efficient as possible, for consensus between the institutions, each of which has its own legitimate range of interests.

These trilogues appear in the rules governing the European Parliament and in the Interinstitutional Agreements, but not in the constitutional system of the Union. However, as has been written, they are an 'inherent and in any case inescapable part of it', guaranteeing its effectiveness. This is at the cost of the principle of transparency in the law-making process, despite the fact that the Treaty of Lisbon took care to ensure that there is a public session also for the Council 'when it deliberates and votes on a draft legislative act' (article 16(8), TEU). The need to balance between promptness and effective results of the European legislative process (which are also a factor of its legitimation), on the one hand, and transparency of all the reasoning behind it, on the other, was thus resolved in favour of the former two needs.

From this point of view, the ordinary European legislative procedure appears to have a dual structure: the formal stages regulated by the treaties and the informal stage with its sequence of trilogues. A river the course of which is mapped out everywhere accompanied by a subterranean groundwater conduit. At the final confluence the conclusion could well be that the latter contributed the most water. Careful observers focus their criticism on the trilogues on the composition of the parliamentary negotiating team, often reduced to the bare minimum (although, alongside the rapporteur and committee chair the influence of shadow rapporteurs linked to the various political groups has been growing) and on the lack of clarity in their negotiating mandate. These factors seem to exaggerate the negotiating space in which the various trilogues take place, to the considerable detriment of a real knowledge of the preparatory work.

However, we are not dealing with a drift away from the law towards the *arcana imperii* of *interna corporis* (in which the Court of Justice just said that it does not wish to be involved: judgment 14.4.2015, *Council of the European Union v European Commission*, case C-409/13). The scope and legal basis of the legislative initiative remain intact in the hands of the Commission at least until the Council has completed its first reading. Up until then the Commission may in fact amend (article 293(2), TFEU) or even withdraw its proposal, should it consider that the agreement between the colegislators at first reading could distort the objectives of its initiative. The Court of Justice's decision in this regard also provided its interpretation of the constitutional balance, to be calculated in the objective positioning of the institutions with respect to the general interest of the Union, rather than in the dynamic shifts in importance of powers and counter-powers during negotiations (14.4.2015, C-409/13). It is also important to consider that the Commission possesses a lethal weapon to protect its proposal. Indeed, if the Commission does not agree with the amendments, the Council is obliged to seek unanimity within its ranks, an increasingly difficult task (except in the case of voting on a 'joint text' of the Conciliation Committee, as will be seen: article 294.10, TFEU).

(c) The effectiveness of the previous negotiations is what determines the larger number of legislative acts approved at the first reading (in the 2009–14 parliamentary term, 448 out of 526 legislative acts were approved at first reading, ie, 85%). When negotiations lead to a provisional agreement, the committee responsible for the subject-matter approves it by way of a single vote by majority and tables it for consideration before the plenary of Parliament (rule 69f, REP). If the Parliament approves it, it is the turn of the Council to decide on the basis of its first reading. If the Council approves it, the act is definitively adopted in the formulation corresponding to the position of the European Parliament (article 294(4), TFEU). However a new trilogue can start, especially if a parliamentary text that has significantly altered the previous provisional agreement is sent to the Council. The parliamentary negotiating team will have the original position of the Parliament as its mandate (rule 69d, REP). If there is an agreement on the parliamentary text after the negotiations, then the cycle is completed.

(d) If this is not the case, it is the turn of the Council to adopt a position at first reading. When the text is sent to Parliament, a parliamentary second reading phase begins. Both institutions – with the Commission as intermediary – will have the option of opening a further trilogue (rule 69e, REP). Again a new provisional agreement will be possible, which the committee responsible will therefore table for consideration by Parliament at second reading. At this point Parliament is presented with three alternatives: to approve the position adopted by the Council at first reading or to express tacit consent to it (in such cases the act is adopted in the formulation that corresponds to the position of the Council); to reject the Council's position by an absolute majority (in this case the cycle ends with rejection of the act); or to propose amendments to the Council's position (chiefly based on the provisional agreement that emerged from the trilogue). In this last case the *navette* therefore goes back to the Council, which may approve all of the amendments in order to definitively adopt the act, closing the legislative cycle.

(e) 'Where the Council informs Parliament that it is unable to approve all of Parliament's amendments to the Council's position', a new negotiating phase begins, which this time is formal, and calls upon the Conciliation Committee (rule 70, REP). Within six weeks, the Conciliation Committee (with the representatives of the three institutions, the political composition of the parliamentary delegation shall mirror the proportion of political groups in Parliament: rule 71, REP) may agree on a joint text. This will be added to Parliament's agenda for approval by a single vote, without the possibility of presenting amendments. This is the third reading. If the Conciliation Committee is unable to approve a joint text within six weeks all the work of the three institutions will have been in vain. The act will not be adopted. Parliament will be informed by a declaration, *palabras y plumas el viento las lleva*.

However, leaving aside the possible negative outcome of normal legislative work, a sword of Damocles hangs over the ordinary legislative procedure until its completion. The extension of this procedure to new sensitive subject-matters by the Treaty of Lisbon in fact introduced the possibility, as a counter-weight, for each Member State to suspend it. Therefore when the ordinary legislative procedure applies to sensitive issues (eg, social security and criminal matters: articles 48, 82 and 83, TFEU), each Member State may appeal to the European Council. In this way, the body that is precluded, by definition, from exercising legislative powers (article 15(1), TEU) may paradoxically operate an emergency brake which has a significant effect on ordinary legislative procedures. This is suspended, and the European Council may send the text back to the Council which takes the procedure forward on the basis of the observations made or may definitively end the procedure and even ask the Commission for a new proposal.

The introduction of this political guarantee into the decision-making process has reassured everyone and has convinced the most suspicious EU Member States to apply the ordinary legislative procedure to some policies, waiving unanimity in such cases. The clauses with an emergency brake effectively apply to three areas of high political sensitivity: measures of coordination of social security systems for migrant workers (article 48, TFEU); judicial cooperation in criminal matters (article 82, TFEU) and the establishment of common rules for some crimes (article 83, TFEU).

This, therefore, is the European ordinary legislative process: a *navette* that is far more complex than that of traditional parliamentary systems. It includes a complicated web of transparent and less-transparent phases in which the initial draft legislative act acquires depth and new emphasis; simple and qualified majority voting, informal consent and formal unanimity. The ultimate aim is to find a balance not between legal powers but between institutions that often have very different political and economic interests. The whole process is like a biography of the efforts to build the EU, in protean forms and with the difficulties of Sisyphus, over a period of 60 years.

IV. The Consultation Procedure

The story of European law-making therefore has an end-point in the ordinary legislative procedure. Its formal architecture may appear tiring, but the interinstitutional negotiations have the virtue of speeding up the process. However the story is also one of persistence. It almost seems as if the famous *acquis communautaire*, an irreversibility clause against any attempts at de-integration, also casts its shadow over the preservation of procedures that only an established practice of non-application could cancel out.

The original procedure of consultation, which applied to the appointed parliamentary Assembly, survives in the life of the European Parliament as a special legislative procedure (article 289(2), TFEU). The structure is always the same: after the Commission presents its proposal, the Council may adopt the act, but only after the European Parliament has expressed its opinion. This opinion is mandatory, or the legislative act would be invalid, but it is not binding for the Council. The Court defined it as 'the means which allows the parliament to play an actual part in the legislative process of the Community' (29.10.1980, case 138/79). But it also added that if Parliament did not express an opinion within a reasonable period of time – thus failing to comply with the fundamental principle of sincere interinstitutional cooperation (article 13(2), TEU) – the Council may adopt the act without further delay (30.3.1995, *European Parliament v Council of the European Union*, case C-65/93). In the event that the Council wishes to substantially modify the proposal, it must again consult the Parliament.

Despite its residuality and speciality, the consultation procedure in which Parliament is without a veto and subordinated to the Council characterises some very politically and socially sensitive issues. It is not inaccurate to see in the following list of matters subject to consultation the protection of a (thus far) unassailable domination of Member States rather than the persistence of an ancient procedure.

This evaluation is further backed by the fact that in the treaties the consultation procedure is almost always accompanied by the requirement of unanimity for adoption by the Council. This is the case for subjects such as social security and social protection (article 21(3), TFEU); citizenship, passive eligibility and municipal elections (article 22(1), TFEU); family law with cross-border implications (article 81(3), TFEU); police cooperation (article 87(3), TFEU); cross-border judicial and police operations (article 89, TFEU); fiscal measures applicable to energy (article 194(3), TFEU); methods of association of third countries (article 203, TFEU) and the Union's own resources (article 311, TFEU).

Having been excluded from the adoption of the final decision, the Parliament has therefore attempted to give a specific emphasis to its opinions. Before the committee responsible for a subject-matter proceeds to vote, it may ask the Commission to state its position on all the amendments that the committee intends to table (rule 78b, REP).

Moreover, the parliamentary influence continues to apply after approval of the opinion by the Assembly. The chair and rapporteur of the committee responsible are appointed to monitor the progress of the draft 'in order to ensure that any undertakings given by the Council or the Commission to Parliament concerning its position are properly observed' (rule 78d, REP). Should the Council alter or intend to alter the initial draft, the President of the Parliament shall, at the request of the committee responsible, call on the Council to consult the Parliament again (rule 78e, REP). However, the committee responsible could even resort to the extreme remedy of calling on the Commission to withdraw its proposal (rule 78d(3), REP).

As can be seen, these are a series of caveats to ensure that, albeit at the consultation stage, the parliamentary participation in the legislative process is truly effective, as the Court of Justice has urged.

V. The Issue of Delegation

As in all modern parliamentary systems, the procedure by which the legislature delegates its powers to other institutions marks a critical moment in the harmony of the system. Monitoring the terms of the delegation instrument, and in particular compliance with the criteria and guiding principles to which the delegated power is subject, is a key problem when analysing any legislation. In the EU legal system, the problem of delegation is more complex for two reasons. In the first place, due to the absolute lack of homogeneity between the two legislative Chambers: the one representing citizens and the other the Member States. In the second place, because the system does not allow the delegation of legislative powers. The very term delegation has a singular and, one could say, incorrect meaning here. In fact, the treaty gives the Commission the non-legislative power to supplement or amend a legislative act (article 290, TFEU). The mechanism is very hard to interpret from a legal point of view even though it has been considerably successful at a practical level, since the ambiguous definition has facilitated flexibility and effectiveness in its use.

The delegation of power is in fact formally ruled out for the essential elements characterising the issue, while delegation is permitted for supplements or amendments – by means of 'non-legislative acts of general application' – to non-essential elements of the basic legislative act. The only legally possible interpretation – with which practice appears to comply – is that by means of this mechanism there is an unspoken 'delegislation' regarding the necessary elements for supplementing the act of delegation: in other words, a delegation of power that is almost legislative in nature. However, EU law is far more precise and compliant with the commonly accepted principles of legislative delegation when establishing the requirements for the basic act. This in fact must explicitly specify the objectives, content, scope and duration of the delegation of power as well as the conditions to which it is subject, conditions that may vary according to the type and political importance of the subject.

In fact it appears that the delegation in the EU is still based on the spirit of negotiation that, due to the singular nature of the Union's supranational legal system, pervades the whole story and the procedures leading to the adoption of EU legislation.

The flexibility attributed to the parliamentary committee responsible in the difficult distinction between essential and non-essential elements of a legislative act in fact seems to a certain extent to be offset by a careful regulation of compliance by the Council and, in particular, by the European Parliament. The procedure that is set in motion when the Commission refers a delegated act to the Parliament is extremely trenchant. The committee responsible for the subject-matter can, in a proposed resolution, raise objections to the delegated act and may contain a request to the Commission to present a new delegated act taking into account the recommendations formulated by Parliament. In extreme cases of divergence, it may adopt a proposed resolution that revokes all or part of the delegation of powers, although this revocation must be approved by a parliamentary vote with an absolute majority. However, to set the seal on the supplement or amendment carried out and the agreement reached, a *nihil obstat* recommendation may be adopted if there is no objection even without a parliamentary vote (rule 105, REP).

In this extreme procedural circuit – of a non-legislative act that supplements or amends the non-essential elements of a legislative act and, *nemine contradicente*, is considered to be approved without a parliamentary vote – it almost seems as if EU legislation has rediscovered something of its distant origins. However this point is reached after the procedure for the delegation has seen a sequence of consultations of social parties, discussions and negotiations that have given it the substantive democratic nature that is constantly sought after in the Union's law-making process.

If anything (and this regards all of the Union's legislative procedures), the question could be whether it is truly impossible to combine effectiveness and transparency. In other words, whether making procedures leaner could be compatible – and in fact be justified – with greater transparency. In the sense that broad knowledge – disseminated by computers, which by now are the prevalent media – of the politically key points of the procedure and real interests involved in them could lead to 'democratic lobbying' for the general interests of the Union. In other words a stimulus for (not only) better but faster regulation in pursuit of the objectives of the Union.

VI. Conclusion

When casting a final eye over the topic as a whole it is impossible not to notice that the process of parliamentarisation of Union legislation (despite the invasive presence of the European Council as 'legislator', and despite the treaties) has involved two fundamental and, in a certain sense, irreversible stages. On the one hand, the generalised application of the ordinary legislative procedure has facilitated a change of culture within the institutions, especially within the Council, showing that the role of the European Parliament cannot be considered an incidental part of the procedure, but can provide an added value thanks to its internal capacity for mediation. On the other hand, the loyalty element in the election of the president of the Commission has strengthened the relations between the Commission and the Parliament.

Parliament has taken on an increasingly full role in the entire legislative process, from definition of the legislative priorities to the preparatory stage, and from the purely legislative stage to the assessment of policies and legislation. Parliament's influence has become particularly important in defining the legislative priorities. And an important consequence of this has been the semi-institutionalisation of majority meetings of the President of the Commission with the leaders of political groups. The European method of law-making increasingly resembles the 'homespun' method of national parliamentary systems.

Bibliography

Adam, R and Tizzano, A, *Manuale di diritto dell'Unione Europea* (Torino, 2014).

Cannizzaro, E, *Il diritto dell'integrazione europea* (Torino, 2014).

Corbett, R, Jacobs, F and Shackleton, M, *The European Parliament* (London, 2016).

De Feo, A, *History of budgetary powers and politics in the EU. The role of the European Parliament (Part II: The nonelected Parliament 1957–1978)* (Bruxelles, 2015).

Fasone, C, 'European economic governance and parliamentary representation. What place for the European Parliament?' (2014) 2 *European law journal* 164–85.

Ibrido, R and Vosa, G, '"Forma" e "forme" negli assetti di organizzazione costituzionale dell'Unione Europea' in *Il Filangieri 2014* (Napoli, 2015) 182 et seq.

Lupo, N, 'L'iniziativa legislativa nella forma di governo dell'Unione Europea e il ruolo dei parlamenti nazionali' in *Il Filangieri 2014* (Napoli, 2015) 17 et seq.

Manzella, A, 'The European Parliament and the national parliaments as a system' in S Mangiameli (ed), *The consequences of the crisis on European integration and on the member States* (Milano, 2017) 47–82.
Manzella, A and Lupo, N (eds), *Il sistema parlamentare euro-nazionale* (Torino, 2014).
Piccirilli, G, 'Atti legislativi dell'Unione Europea' in *Digesto delle discipline pubblicistiche* vol 6 (Torino, 2015).
Rugge, G, 'Il ruolo dei "triloghi" nel processo legislativo dell'UE' (2015) 4 *Il diritto dell'Unione Europea* 809 et seq.

11

Safeguarding Rights in EU Law Between the Commission and the Court of Justice

GIUSEPPE TESAURO

I. The Defining Elements of the European Union's Legal System and the Role of the Judge

The close relationship between the characteristics and evolution of a legal system and the way in which the system of judicial control is configured and operates, along with its role in the interpretation and application of the law, is a recurring element in modern democracies, inspired by a healthy debate between the rights and obligations of its protagonists and by the appropriate redress mechanisms. Especially in the case of judges at the top of the system, their response to social needs, issued through their rulings, may be the product of one or more legal cultures, however it can leave a specific impression in the evolution of a legal system, finding a reason to consolidate itself, developing through the case law, and ultimately working its way into the key passages that mark the evolution of that system.

These elements can also be found in the legal system of the European Union (EU), in the key passages that have marked the progress of case law spanning more than half a century. And therein lies something even more specific and different.

The system of judicial review that has been maintained until today in its essential terms as well as in its finer points, except for some additions, lies at the heart of the EU, not only of its legal system. It simultaneously embodies the EU's strength and its pledges, being the instrument of that Community of law which represents the exemplary way of being (and is the pride and joy) of the European Community design set out in the 1957 Treaty of Rome and upheld in the Lisbon Treaty (signed on 13 December 2007, and entered into force on 1 December 2009), in the Treaty on European Union (TEU) and in the Treaty on the Functioning of the European Union (TFEU); all these designations are now and have replaced the original ones (I will take the liberty of making the occasional use of the old term Community, especially in its adjectival form, rather than embrace new-fangled phrases).

One should immediately point out that the EU's legal system is founded on the principle of conferral of competences and powers, whereby the Union acts within the limits of the powers that States have conferred upon it in the Treaties to pursue the goals that they have set out; this construct has been emphasised on several occasions and with unusual zeal in the TEU and in the TFEU, as if it had not always been an undisputed, fundamental principle inherent in the system. This principle affects the allocation of powers both between Member States and the Union, and between the EU's institutions, and for this reason a special constitutional relevance is bestowed upon the competence of the Court of Justice for all matters concerning the interpretation and application of Community law. This competence is exclusive to the Court, as is the competence to settle disputes between Member States, which cannot be submitted to any other method of settlement (article 344, TFEU, formerly article 219, European Economic Community, EEC Treaty).

The legal scrutiny over the Union's acts falls under the specific competence of the EU judge only, who are under a duty to verify and control their legitimacy, also with regard to the claim that an institution has exceeded the limits of its jurisdiction, extending to the Court itself. It is true to say that verifying the timely compliance of the principle of separation of powers between the Union and its institutions, on the one hand, and between the Union and the Member States, on the other, becomes especially important, also from the standpoint of general legal theory, to the extent that many have expressly made a connection between this issue and the question of the erosion of State sovereignty in favour of the Union. On the other hand, the very fact that the framework of powers has been secured by the principle of conferral has led to the necessary consequence that, under the Treaty, Member States have attributed to the Court of Justice the jurisdiction to interpret and verify the legitimacy of Community acts. And the Court has clung tightly to its competence in these matters, routinely denying it to national courts unless on a temporary and precautionary basis, and only by way of exception (see judgments of the Court of 22.10.1987, *Foto-Frost v Hauptzollamt Lübeck-Ost*, case 314/85; 21.02.1991, *Zuckerfabrik Süderdithmarschen v Hauptzollamt Itzehoe and Zuckerfabrik Soest GmbH v Hauptzollamt Paderborn*, 143/88 and 92/89; 21.03.2000, *Association Greenpeace France and others v Ministère de l'Agriculture et de la Pêche and others*, C-6/99).

Normally, the interpretation of Treaties, even those establishing international bodies, is up to the contracting States, and any differences are dealt with through the methods put in place for this purpose by international law, with the possible risk of at least some temporary instability in the institutional framework. Yet the contracting States of the Community Treaties undertook to confer upon a Community institution, on an exclusive basis, the task of interpreting the Treaties, with the specific aim of achieving Community-wide consistency and uniformity of application. And it is a truly relevant and significant competence, as it is added to the regulatory powers delegated exclusively or concurrently to EU law-making bodies. The specific nature of the Community – in particular the main goal of furthering integration among Member States by creating an area of free movement of goods and factors of production, with an impact on the legal position not only of the Member States but also of individuals – did not allow a system of regulation that received an interpretation and, along with it, a divergent application in the Member Countries, beyond a natural and only temporary diversity. This has resulted in Community judges being granted the last word as regards the interpretation of EU law and the verification of the lawfulness of its acts. A different solution would have undoubtedly undermined the integration plan, by allowing differences and thereby even profound discrimination between Member States – and consequently between individuals; the outcome of this would have been a truly judicially-determined Tower of Babel that we can certainly do without.

The issue of jurisdiction has always been the subject of a latent debate – especially among scholars of constitutional law and of domestic law in general – often founded upon a hasty and therefore superficial reading as to the true meaning of the separation of competences under the Treaties, both directly and through the conferral of specific material competences. Significant steps have been made in this field, in particular in the case law of the German Constitutional Court. In a first judgment concerning the ratification of the Treaty of Maastricht (1992), commonly referred to as the *Maastricht Urteil* (judgment), the Karlsruhe judges asserted the right of the national court to review the legitimacy of the exercise of powers by Community institutions and agencies with respect to the delegation of powers conferred upon the Union by the German Parliament, to see whether their acts remain within the limits established by the Treaty (*Bundesverfassungsgericht* (BVerfG), 12.10.1993, case 2134/92, '*Europäische Grundrechte Zeitung*' (1993) 429 and ff). It follows that any Community act which, in the view of a national court, failed to remain within the limits of the rights conferred on the Union might well be held to be unlawful by that same national court, and therefore inapplicable in that Member State. The Constitutional Court's argument was grounded on seemingly cast-iron logic: as Member States remain firmly in control as the 'masters of the Treaties' (*Herren der Verträge*), the limits within which they have sacrificed a part of their sovereignty can never be exceeded. I truly believe one cannot argue with this quite undisputed postulate. However, the German constitutional court ignored one element: that Member States not only conferred upon the Union regulatory powers in certain areas (principle of conferral of powers), but also designed a system of judicial review of the legality of their exercise, under the exclusive jurisdiction of the Court of Justice. As a consequence, no scrutiny, either logically or legally conceivable, is permitted outside that system of judicial review, also contemplated by the Treaty, that falls within the surrendering of sovereignty and sharing of competences which Member States chose to carry out freely, consciously and therefore democratically. In other words: no one can doubt that Member States are masters of the Treaties, for they can amend Treaty provisions or even exercise the right of withdrawal from the Union in the ways provided; however, this certainly does not mean that, whether on a case-by-case basis or in the light of the circumstances at the time, Member States can unilaterally take back ownership of a competence that they collectively agreed from the outset to confer to the Community system of judicial review (MacCormick (1999)).

The error that can be glimpsed in the 1993 ruling of the German Constitutional Court, moreover, does not solely hinge on its failure to identify the precise and express conferral upon the Court of Justice of the powers to review the legitimacy of Community acts. It should be added, in fact, that if each national court had retained the power to verify the legitimacy of Community acts within the limits of the rights conferred on them by the Treaty, we would not have a single system of law. One can hardly imagine the kaleidoscope of interpretations that would ensue. Likewise, if Member States, by way of lawful execution of their supremacy over the Treaties, were to amend them in the sense of the *Maastricht Urteil* cited above, one would have to ascertain whether and to what extent it would make sense to speak of a legal system of the Union and of a Community of law. On top of that, it is rather telling that the States have never even contemplated amending, besides its number and place in the Treaty, the content of the provision (now article 19, TEU), which has always attributed to the Court of Justice the right to have the last word on the interpretation and application of EU law.

A similar position taken by the German constitutional court can be found in its ruling on the ratification of the Lisbon Treaty (BVerfG, 30.06.2009, 2 BvE 2/08, '*Neue Juristische Wochenschrift*' (2009) 2267; Ziller (2009)). In dealing with the question of constitutional legitimacy of the law, in relation to the significant changes it introduced, the Constitutional Court rejected all doubts as to its constitutional compatibility, underlining that the Lisbon Treaty confirmed the principle of conferral of powers, while noting that the ensuing development that takes place, which cannot be determined in every detail, must be allowed nonetheless (paragraph 237). Also, as regards the separation of powers allowed by the national Parliament, it held that 'if legal protection cannot be obtained at Union level', the German Constitutional Court will carefully review whether the acts are the expression of the powers conferred (paragraph 240). In this way, the judge overseeing the laws has at least acknowledged at 'Union level' its duty to ensure 'legal protection'. Indeed, while it is significant that the position of the German Constitutional Court has never seen practical application yet, the power-duty of the Court of Justice to review the validity of Community acts under the Treaty has not been called into question either (see also the BVerfG *Honeywell* ruling, 30.08.2010, case 1 BvR 1631/08, which is linked to the European Court of Justice ruling on the *Mangold* case on the subject of age discrimination).

Besides, the principle of conferral of powers also features a different aspect, in particular with regard to compliance with the scope defined within the bounds of the rights established by the Treaties, as stated in article 19 of the TEU ('The Court of Justice of the European Union shall, in accordance with the Treaties, rule [...]'). European case law has repeatedly pointed to this limitation of the jurisdiction of EU institutions, including that of the Court, which in this respect has often declared its lack of jurisdiction and therefore rejected the referral on the grounds of inadmissibility (judgment 05.10.2010, *J McB v L E*, C-400/10 PPU, paragraph 51). This is the case when the legal instrument the Court is called upon to interpret cannot be considered an act of a Community institution (judgment 06.10.1987, *Marcel Demouche v Fonds de garantie automobile*, case 152/83, paragraph 19); or that EU law is not applicable to the case at hand, since it deals with a wholly domestic scenario, that is to say, when the subject-matter of the dispute is not connected in any way with any of the situations contemplated by Community law (judgment 29.05.1997, *Friedrich Kremzow v Republik Österreich*, C-299/95, paragraphss 15 to 16; order of the Court of 06.10.2005, *Attila Vajnai*, C-328/04, paragraph 13). At the same time, while it has emphasised that its powers must be exercised in compliance with the relevant rules of international law (judgment of 21.12.2011, *Air Transport Association of America and others v Secretary of State for energy and climate change*, C-366/10, paragraph 123), the Court also clarified that when it is called upon to interpret provisions of international law, its interpretation can only apply to a set of competences attributed to the Union by the Treaties, declaring its manifest lack of jurisdiction to interpret and hold applicable the relevant provisions of international law in a specific *ratione materiae* and *ratione temporis* outside the framework of Community law (judgment of 12.07.2012, *Gennaro Currà and others v Bundesrepublik Deutschland*, C-466/11, on the issue raised by the victims of massacres committed by German armed forces in Italy during World War II; and judgment of 27.11.1973, *Magdalena Vandeweghe and others v Berufsgenossenschaft für die chemische Industrie*, case 130/73, paragraph 2).

II. The Features of Judicial Review and the Central Role of the Preliminary Ruling System

The EU's legal system is broadly based on certain fundamental elements. The first one is rooted in the extensiveness of the judicial review mechanism, which impacts the consistency of the legal system seen as a whole, and consequently the legitimacy of the acts of Community institutions alongside the laws, acts and practices of the Member States. The result is achieved on two distinct, but functionally connected, procedural levels. The first procedure is that of direct review by the Court, and may be triggered by EU institutions, Member States or individuals, resulting in a ruling of the ECJ. The second is the preliminary ruling procedure based on cooperation between the national court and the EU's judiciary, which results in an indirect review by the Court of Justice, and the final judgment on the case resting upon the national courts. Among the direct referrals to the Court, the most relevant for our purposes are actions seeking annulment and for infringement. The action for annulment consists in appealing against an act adopted by the EU institutions on the grounds that it is flawed and has a detrimental effect, so that it is held to be null and void. On the other hand, the infringement procedure seeks to put an end to a Member State's breach of EU law and, therefore, to ensure that the State in question changes its behaviour accordingly, making it consistent with the relevant provisions, even prior to (and rather than) formally pursuing the actual infringement. The indirect judicial review system (preliminary ruling referral) has gained decisive importance on matters concerning the competences of the Court of Justice, as it is exercised whenever a question arises before a national court on the interpretation of a provision of EU law or the validity of legal instruments of European institutions, and, being a question of law, it must be answered for the case to be settled. Indeed, a sizeable portion of legal issues directly or indirectly governed by EU law are of practical relevance at a domestic level; either because the national authority enforces the EU provision directly, or because national regulations implementing EU law have been introduced that govern the relations between the parties. In the pathological structure of legal relations, EU law is mainly applied by the national courts which, thanks to the preliminary ruling mechanism, have the power, or obligation – if the court is of last instance – to request the Court of Justice to give a preliminary ruling on the interpretation or validity of a provision of EU law, when such a ruling is instrumental in settling the dispute before it.

The second fundamental element of the EU is the tried and tested method of interpreting provisions which, compared to the traditional canons of legal hermeneutics, may be defined as 'teleological', but is more simply expressed through interpretative choices that are functional to the development of the integration process – this being a fundamental objective of the Treaty. It is a dynamic principle, which aims to provide timely support to the equally dynamic evolution of society. It is not a new principle, and has been repeatedly cited in international case law and formally enshrined in article 31(1) of the 1969 Vienna Convention on the law of treaties (judgment of 29.11.1956, *Fédération charbonnière de Belgique v High Authority*, case 8/55). In addition to this, we have the fundamental provision of article 4 TEU which, in recalling the obligation of the Member States to uphold the objectives of the Treaty and the obligation to facilitate Community institutions in the fulfilment of their tasks, has proven to be of key importance in understanding the entire Treaty, including the Preamble (Quadri (1965); Porchia (2008)).

The third element consists in the consideration given to individuals, and conveyed into a system for the protection of rights, including fundamental rights, that can stand up to any comparison. In the original design and wording of the Treaty, individuals did not appear exactly at the forefront of the legislators' minds; in practice, the EU judiciary have resorted to utilising individuals to enhance the system and strengthen even its seemingly less important ramifications.

The mechanism that has been found to be the most effective and that has best marked the key milestones in the evolution of the EU legal system is undoubtedly the preliminary ruling system, inspired by the model for reviewing the constitutionality of laws also used in Austria, Italy and Germany. Judicial review based on the preliminary ruling system has marked the achievement of the integration objectives set out in the Treaties more than any other initiative, legislation or policy, promoted by the institutions or by the Member States themselves. Indeed, the preliminary ruling system was instrumental in decisively strengthening the bond and, thereby, the consistency between the legal systems of Member States and that of the Community; its success is evidenced by the creation of that border-free area, which is the ultimate goal of the overall design, and makes it possible to rebut the utterly misleading stereotype about the exclusively economic dimension of the European integration process that ignores the true essence of the EU. When exercising its preliminary ruling competences, the Court of Justice seized the opportunity to give its interpretation on EU law not in abstract terms, but on the basis of its impact on the national legal system of the referring court, so that the domestic judge's decision may actually affect the individual's subjective legal position uniformly throughout all Member States.

An equally important role was played by the sundry legal cultures and their influence on how the case law developed through the preliminary ruling system. The impact of national legal systems, alongside the legal effects of several international conventions, has been characterised by more various and, ultimately, more relevant aspects than those resulting from other cooperation initiatives held between States. Mutual contributions are in fact inherent in the system. Showing consideration for the law of the Member States and, more broadly, for 'other' regulations aside from EU law constitutes a necessary and integral part of an EU judge's way of being and acting. It is not so much a matter of occasionally recalling this or that provision from another legal system; nor is it a matter of applying a foreign provision to which reference is made, as is customary with international private law provisions; and it is much less a comparative method, which is referred to all too often and usually inappropriately by devotees of domestic and comparative law. It is rather a dialogue between legal systems and between judges from different legal systems, and this, with its continuous exchange of experiences and values, constitutes the real asset of judicial review in its struggle for consistency throughout the EU's legal system as a whole. National judges and EU judges have worked in an integrated way. And a solid proof of this synergy, almost a form of complicity, are those passages in EU case law whose impact upon the Community framework, not just its legal system, has been far more significant, revealing its fundamental characteristics and highlighting its implications under every possible profile (Tesauro (1993)). With regard to the integration process, the leading role of the Court of Justice and, where appropriate, of the General Court has steadily emerged. This role warrants attention above all in relation to two general basic themes: one is the nature of the Union's legal system, particularly as regards its relationship with national legal systems and the scope of the judicial review system; the other is the principle of the effectiveness of the protection of rights arising under the Community legal system as a whole.

III. The Relationship with the Legal Systems of the Member States

Called upon to ensure legal compliance in the interpretation and application of the Treaty, the Union judiciary appeared originally designed to act as a guardian of compliance with respect to the mutual obligations that the contracting States had signed, in other words as a judge overseeing the rights and duties of the Member States. After all, the mainstays of the rules of the common market of goods, people, services and capital, were founded on as many obligations of the Member States. However, precisely when it came to assessing one of the main obligations of the States aimed at creating the common market, that of refraining from introducing new customs duties and charges having equivalent effect and even eliminating them progressively – the cornerstone of the common market – the Court of Justice laid the foundations for the construction of a peculiar model of legal system and of Community of law.

The case was *Van Gend en Loos*, initiated by a Dutch customs authority judge in 1962, who sought a preliminary ruling on the interpretation of article 12 of the Treaty (today, article 30, TFEU), on the prohibition of the introduction of new customs duties and charges having an equivalent effect on intra-Community trade in goods; the question was raised as to whether the rule had 'direct application within the territory of a Member State, in other words, whether nationals of such a State can, on the basis of the article in question, lay claim to individual rights which the courts must protect' (judgment of 05.02.1963, *Van Gend & Loos v Netherlands Inland Revenue Administration*, case 26/62, paragraph 1). Despite the strong opposition of some governments intervening in the proceeding, the Court addressed the issue, grasping its significance in terms of the nature of the Community legal system, of its relations with national legal systems and of the role of individuals – as well as, in a preliminary view, of its own role. And in doing this, it issued an array of findings and statements, albeit in the simple and essential dimension of the time, on the meaning of the fundamental article of the Treaty which entrusts the Community judge with guaranteeing legal compliance in the interpretation and application of the Treaty. Indeed, the Court held that, by setting up a common market whose operations directly affect the Community's nationals, the Treaty of Rome did not merely establish mutual obligations between the contracting States just like any other international agreement. The Member States had intended to create:

> a new legal order of international law for the benefit of which the States have limited their sovereign rights, albeit within limited fields, and the subjects of which comprise not only Member States but also their nationals.

Community law therefore not only imposes obligations on individuals, but grants them subjective rights, not only expressly but also 'by reason of obligations which the Treaty imposes in a clearly defined way upon individuals as well as upon the Member States and upon the institutions of the Community'.

Among the many important statements contained in this famous ruling by the Court, that everyone has alluded to on every occasion, I wish to point out a particular aspect. If the Treaty of Rome establishes a series of rights and obligations for the Member States, Community judges were indeed intended to play a key part in this, but their role was that of judge of the rights and obligations of States: this is the way in all forms of organised cooperation governing international relations. In the *Van Gend en Loos* case, however, the

Court highlights the importance of the role of individuals in the system; this is especially true in terms of their role as front-line keepers of the European Union's principle of legality; however, in their capacity as holders of subjective legal positions strictly dependent on Community provisions, they are also entitled to trigger the judicial review mechanism on the consistency of the legal system as a whole. The Community judge glimpses its own different role, while at the same time revealing it from a specular point; it is that of judge of the duties and rights of individuals. This is no small achievement and not without consequences on the evolution of the Court's case law and on its role in the Community integration process.

The subsequent evolution, through the most striking developments in the case law, all but confirms the Court's abiding care and attention in consolidating the legal system also (or perhaps, especially) by enhancing the subjective legal position of individuals: and this on the basis of an interpretation of the Treaty unconstrained by any traditional model of organised cooperation between sovereign States. It is not long before the Court of Justice adds other relevant pieces to the construction of the framework, while striving for consistency with the national legal systems. This time, the dialogue is not only with an ordinary judge who refers a matter for a preliminary ruling, but also – remotely – with the Italian Constitutional Court.

In the case of *Costa v ENEL*, a conciliator from Milan brought before the Court of Justice and the Italian Constitutional Court the matter as to whether the law nationalising Italy's electric power industry (in the early 1960s) was compatible with the Treaty, which would have forbidden it, and for this reason, with article 11 of the Italian Constitution, which permits limitations to sovereignty, and therefore would not uphold a subsequently enacted conflicting national law.

The Constitutional Court decides first (ruling No. 14/1964), stating, as many recall, that article 11 of the Constitution indeed allows limitations of sovereignty by reason of Italy's participation in certain international bodies under ordinary law, but assigns no particular value to it compared to other laws, being that the principle of the primacy of later laws is firmly upheld. Ultimately, breaches of the Treaty may result in the State's liability on an international level, but this does not reduce the full effectiveness of the subsequent contrasting law: as we can see it is a plain example of regulatory dualism.

A few months later, the Court of Justice hands down its ruling with a diametrically opposite effect (judgment of 15.07.1964, *Flaminio Costa v ENEL*, case 6/64). Under the Treaty, the Court held, the States handed over certain powers to the Community, without limits of duration, along with autonomous bodies, legal personality, external representation, and therefore have created a binding system for States and their citizens. If the effectiveness of Community law were to vary from State to State according to successive laws, the obligations contracted would not be absolute, but conditional on the whim of the next day, so that one would struggle to see the reasoning behind the express provision of exemptions and the procedure to allow them. The transfer of powers to the Community implies that a subsequent legal measure incompatible with Community law is completely ineffective.

Shortly afterwards, in the *Acciaierie San Michele* case, a decision of the High Authority of the European coal and steel Community (ECSC, today Commission) was challenged both with a direct action for annulment before the Court of Justice, and before the Court of Turin. The Italian court, in turn, raised a question before the Constitutional Court as to the legitimacy of the provisions of the Treaty which, amongst other things, granted to the

Court of Justice exclusive jurisdiction over the High Authority's legal acts. The undertaking therefore petitioned the Court of Justice to stay proceedings pending the Constitutional Court's ruling, invoking the absolute authority of the Italian judge's upcoming ruling and the obligation to stay the proceedings as these would fall upon all the courts with jurisdiction over Italian citizens, including the Court of Justice.

This time the Community judge replied first (order of the Court of 22.06.1965, *Acciaierie San Michele SpA (in liquidation) v High Authority of the ECSC*, case 9/65). And very simply he noted that from the instruments of ratification that have determined the strength of the Treaties, it is clear that the Member States have adhered to the Treaty all equally, definitively and without any reservations, other than those ritually set out in the Protocols, and that therefore any claims by citizens of Member States questioning such adherence would be contrary to EC law; also, any decision to suspend judgment would be tantamount to reducing the Community to a cipher by regarding the instrument of ratification either as only partially accepting the Treaty, or as the means of according to it different legal consequences in the Member States, essentially allowing a diversity of treatment among the citizens of the Community; ultimately, 'any application the purpose of which is to establish discrimination of this nature which no law of ratification could introduce into a Treaty prohibiting such discrimination' shall be 'dismissed as contrary to Community policy'.

The Constitutional Court then ruled on the question of constitutional legitimacy in December 1965, taking a first step backwards in terms of the previous *Costa v Enel* case (ruling No. 98/1965). It held that the judicial review system entrusted to the Court of Justice over Community acts was inadmissible with respect to the national legal system; and, in any case, that judicial protection in the Community legal system is afforded by a body that is made up and operates in accordance with rules in keeping with the relevant fundamental aspects of the Italian legal system.

The *Simmenthal* case (judgment of 09.03.1978, *Amministrazione delle Finanze dello Stato v Simmenthal SpA*, case 106/77) provided the opportunity for the Court of Justice to take up once again the issue of relations with national legal systems, but also to underline the need to give immediate and uniform application to Community rules.

In the case at hand, in a reference for a preliminary ruling, an Italian court referred to the European Court the question as to whether the obligation to activate the prior constitutionality judgment in order to set aside national legal measures contrary to Community law was not in itself incompatible with Community law, and, specifically, with the need to give immediate and uniform application throughout all Member States to Community provisions, also to protect the subjective legal rights created for individuals. The Luxembourg Court criticised the Italian constitutional case law that prevented the ordinary judge from applying the provision of Community law in contrast with a national measure, without first referring the matter to the Constitutional Court and awaiting its decision; and this to the detriment of the immediate application of the Community provision and hence to its effectiveness and efficacy. The Court of Justice held that direct applicability should be understood as meaning that provisions of Community law must have full, complete and uniform effect, for the States and for individuals, in all the Member States; this also applies to all national courts, whose task is to protect the rights conferred on individuals by Community law. On the basis of the principle of primacy of Community law, the Court went on to say, the provisions of the Treaty and the acts of the institutions, if directly applicable, have the effect of preventing the valid enactment of new national legislative acts incompatible with those Community provisions and acts, to the extent that any national court must apply Community law in full and protect the rights it confers upon individuals, by refraining from applying any conflicting provisions of domestic law, enacted either before or after the Community provisions. The conclusion was therefore that any provision or practice (in this case the national constitutional case law) that denies the power to immediately apply the Community rule instead of conflicting national legislation is incompatible with Community law, and this without the need to wait for the national legislature or other constitutional authority to strike down such national provisions. Needless to say, the Court of Justice's judgment in the *Simmenthal* case then led the Italian Constitutional Court to amend its case law and to recognise the ordinary judge's competence not to apply any national law in contrast with a Community provision with direct effect, except for violations of the fundamental principles of the State's constitutional system or of the inviolable rights of the person (judgment 170/1984).

Hence, these are the conceptual bases upon which the Community judicature has defined the nature of the Community and the scope of its rules with regard to the legal systems of the Member States. Using the classic criteria of legal hermeneutics, in particular that of the purpose of rules and their practical effect, the Court has made an essential contribution to the integration plan since the early years. It is clear, however, that the result – the primacy of Community law – is not a last-minute discovery, if it is true that a fundamental and ancient principle of international law, enshrined in the case law and in the Vienna Convention on the law of Treaties, prevents States from invoking national legislation against those commitments they have freely underwritten by signing an international treaty.

The principle of the primacy of EU law over national legislation has been repeatedly upheld and consolidated in several passages of the case law of the Court of Justice and of the General Court (among the many judgments, see those of 28.06.2001, *Gervais Larsy v Institut national d'assurances sociales pour travailleurs indépendants (Inasti)*, C-118/00, paragraphs 51–52; of 09.09.2003, *Consorzio industrie fiammiferi (CIF) v Autorità garante della concorrenza e del mercato*, C-198/01, paragraph 48; on the primacy of EU law also over constitutional provisions, judgment of 17.12.1970, *Internationale Handelsgesellschaft mbH v Einfuhr- und Vorratsstelle für Getreide und Futtermittel*, case C-11/70; judgment of 11.01.2000, *Tanja Kreil v Bundesrepublik Deutschland*, C-285/98; judgment of 16.12.2008, *Michaniki AE v Ethniko Symvoulio Radiotileorasis e Ypourgos Epikrateias*, C-213/07), to the point that it has become an undisputed general principle of the system. This is evidenced by the fact that in a declaration (No. 17) concerning primacy annexed to the Final Act of the Intergovernmental Conference which adopted the Treaty of Lisbon, it was deemed sufficient to reference the Court's well settled case law on the matter, as well as an opinion of the Council Legal Service, designed to bolster its meaning and scope.

Particular mention should also be made of a case that has aroused great interest in the literature, while at the same time drawing much criticism, since the decision of the Court of Justice has mainly been construed as an attack on the fundamental principle of res judicata and hence of legal certainty: the *Lucchini* case (judgment of 18.07.2007, *Ministero dell'Industria, del Commercio e dell'Artigianato v Lucchini SpA*, C-119/05). The extraordinary nature of the case is truly noteworthy, since it is not easy to find such a display of 'ignorance or negligence' – to quote the attorney general of the case – with regard to the unquestioned articulation of competences between the Commission and national courts on the subject of State aid; the former having exclusive competence to assess the compatibility of the aid measures with the common market, and the latter only being competent to establish that the obligation to notify the Commission has been complied with and, limited to this purpose, that the measure is consistent with the notion of aid. It has long been common ground that national courts have no competence to assess the legitimacy of State aid, and even less to question the incompatibility established by a Commission decision, which is subject to the exclusive scrutiny of the Community judicature; national courts lack all the more jurisdiction when, as in the present case, the decision is final as it has not been challenged before the natural judge, which is that of the EU. It follows that while the conditions for a preliminary ruling were not satisfied, the court could enforce the application of that Community decision in lieu of any contrasting legislation or administrative act. The fact is that the Italian courts had not even addressed the relevant aspects of Community law on this subject. The Italian State Council had rightly raised the matter in terms of primacy, having referred the question thus:

> In the light of the principle of the primacy of immediately applicable Community law [...] is it legally possible and compulsory [...] to recover aid [...] even though a final civil judgment has been delivered confirming the unconditional obligation to pay the aid in question (paragraph 40).

The Court of Justice replied to the (almost rhetoric) question framed in the request for a preliminary ruling referred by the State Council that the Commission's exclusive competence over matters of State aid is a binding principle in the national legal systems, 'as a result of the principle of the primacy of Community law' (paragraphs 52 and 62). Therefore, the Court concludes, Community law precludes the application of a provision of national law, such as article 2909 of the Italian Civil Code, in so far as the application of that provision prevents the recovery of State aid granted in breach of Community law in a decision of the Commission which has become final.

As we can see, the judgment settles the matter as to whether the principle of the primacy of directly applicable Community law over any conflicting national legislation – whereby the national judge and administration are required to apply the former in lieu of the latter – may be set aside, in short circumvented, by means of a final ruling in contrast with that same provision of Community law. And the Court of Justice, which both before and after the *Lucchini* case had expressly stated the duty to uphold the fundamental principle of *res judicata*, could not help but issue a negative response – at least in a case of such gross 'carelessness' shown by national judges; and this because neither the principle of primacy, being one of the qualifying principles of the Community legal system, nor the definitive nature of an unchallenged decision by the Commission, also confirmed by the Court of Justice, could be called into question in any way.

IV. Effectiveness of the EU's Legal System

On this basis, the Court's attention turned to the issue of the effectiveness of the Union's provisions and the protection of the rights that those provisions confer upon individuals. And if the issue of harmonisation with national legal systems has been the subject of a continuous dialogue especially among the constitutional judges of Member States, the main topic of discourse among ordinary judges has been the effectiveness of the Community legal system, centring on the preliminary ruling mechanism, and confirming its key role throughout the whole process of European integration, not just in terms of legal system. Another exemplary evidence of this consideration also on behalf of Member States, and rendered in article 19 TEU (section 1, sub-section 2), is the reference to the obligation ('Member States shall') to provide remedies sufficient to ensure effective legal protection 'in the fields covered by Union law'.

After all, the Court had already openly shown this kind of attention in its judgment on the *Van Gend en Loos* case, manifesting a veritable culture of integration, of which many of the decisions of the following decades, up to the present day, are clear offshoots. Ultimately, on that occasion the Court grappled with the question of what substantial importance, in a legal system such as that of the Community (but actually in any legal system), should be attached to the verification of the timely fulfilment of a State's obligation that affects an individual's legal position, if that same individual lacked a corresponding right to that obligation being duly and effectively fulfilled. The answer could only be positive, yet it raised a further question: what is the practical worth of a right granted to individuals by a rule, in the present case a Community provision, if they could not assert the right themselves directly before a judge? And in this regard the Court held that the remedy for breaches of obligations by Member States could not be limited to the infringement procedure, an instrument born out of international law, and whose activation relies on the discretionary powers of the Commission. Instead, individuals would have to be able to assert before the national court their right (not to pay new duties) which arose from the obligation of the State (not to introduce new duties) to which the infringement relates.

This was a fundamental choice for the Court. And it was a choice that marked the next leg of the journey, with the enhancement of all the tools of judicial protection available, with a view to steadily growing the legal system. In the *Van Gend en Loos* case, once the Luxembourg Court has established that the rule is capable of yielding direct effects not only as a result of the wording but also on the basis of its end goal, it recognises that the rights conferred on individuals by Community law may amount to 'consideration' of precise obligations imposed on the Member States or the institutions; this is to say that a clear and unconditional prohibition on the part of the State is matched by a corresponding right of the individual to its compliance, but also that the individual has the right to assert its legal position directly before the national court based on Union provisions. By the same token, the Court assigns direct effect to those provisions contained in directives that do not merely state a result to be achieved but, much like a regulation, also set out the means and ways to achieve that result: in short, they are clear, precise and liable to being immediately applicable, and therefore not conditional on any formal provision enacted by a national authority. I am referring to that case law which, having recognised the direct effect also pertaining to provisions of directives under certain conditions and limited to their so-called vertical effects, sets out to penalise the slowness and deliberate sloppiness displayed by Member States when transposing directives (judgment of 04.12.1974, *Yvonne van Duyn v Home Office*, 41/74, paragraph 12; judgment of 05.04.1979, *Tullio Ratti*, 148/78, paragraph 22; judgment of 02.12.1997, *Fantask A/S and others v Industriministeriet (Erhvervministeriet)*, C-188/95, paragraph 54; judgment of 14.07.1994, *Paola Faccini Dori v Recreb Srl*, C-91/92, paragraphs 21–23).

First of all, the Court has focused on clarifying, defining, and sometimes reconstructing the material content of Community rights and obligations, as well as qualifying their impact on the legal position of the end-users; afterwards, it proved itself increasingly sensitive to the profiles that directly impact the means and the level of protection of rights. It was less preoccupied, and not only, with its own competences and with the level of protection it ensured, but also with the guarantees afforded by the national courts, pushing itself to verify their adequacy and consistency with the requirements of the Community legal system. This has led to the growing tendency to 'communitise' the degree of 'effective protection', that is to say, to verify each and every time the compatibility of the levels of protection under the national legal systems with Community law; in so doing, the general limit to the national court's procedural autonomy is identified with the principle – clearly derived from the principle of effectiveness – whereby national procedural rules must not be so framed as to make it virtually impossible, or excessively burdensome, to exercise the rights afforded by Community law. The pursuit of an objective such as system harmonisation is to a large extent dependent on the cultural tradition upholding the effectiveness of the protection of rights, declined according to the paradigms of the Community's whole legal culture, and shaped in equal measure by common law and continental legal systems.

And this composite culture has begotten the case law whose aim is to set up a system of judicial review and protection of rights as comprehensive and effective as possible; and it is no coincidence that such case law benefits more from the preliminary ruling mechanism than from all the other remedies provided by the law.

The *Simmenthal* ruling is certainly among the most relevant passages in the case law of the Court of Justice, aside from the question of harmonisation between Community law and national legislation, and especially as regards the particular attention it pays to the need for effectiveness in Community law. And this was confirmed more than once over the following years.

Among the most relevant practical applications of this particular attention, it is worth recalling some explanatory passages in the case law. On the subject of interim relief in the *Factortame* case, the Court reaffirmed the national court's duty to guarantee the effectiveness and therefore the immediacy of judicial protection through measures capable of protecting a right conferred by Community law, if necessary beforehand, and pending its final validation by the Court's ruling (judgment of 19.06.1990, *The Queen v Secretary of State for Transport, ex parte: Factortame Ltd and others*, case 213/89), even at the cost of setting aside the application of a rule. Also on another occasion, the Court of Justice found that, in order to ensure the full effectiveness of the judgment to be given on the existence of the rights claimed under Community law, a national court has the power-duty to ensure as a precautionary measure the effectiveness of the future ruling, even in the presence (*Simmenthal*) of national legislative provisions which might prevent this (judgment of 13.03.2007, *Unibet (London) Ltd and Unibet (International) Ltd v Justitiekanslern*, C-432/05, paragraph 67).

And the Court has repeatedly upheld the same principle, so that once again any national legislative provision or practice – which might impair the effectiveness of Community law by stripping the national court, competent for enforcing such law, of the power to set aside national legislative provisions that might prevent, even temporarily, Community rules from having full force and effect – are incompatible 'with requirements that are the very essence of Community law' (*ex multis*, the aforementioned *Gervais Larsy* case). No less important are the passages of the case law which confirmed the completeness of the legal system. Let us consider those decisions that have upheld the need for effective judicial protection of the rights of individuals, unsurprisingly related to the principle of loyal cooperation laid down in article 4(3) TEU (formerly article 10 of the Treaty), to affirm the State's financial liability for breach of Community law, first of all in the event of violations by the legislator, in particular for the incorrect or failed implementation of a directive (judgment of 19.11.1991, *Andrea Francovich* and *Danila Bonifaci and others v Italian Republic*, joined cases C-6/90 and C-9/90), or for violation of a provision of the Treaty despite having direct effect (judgment of 05.03.1996, *Brasserie du pêcheur SA v Federal Republic of Germany* and *The Queen v Secretary of State for transport, ex parte: Factortame Ltd and others*, joined cases C-46/93 and C-48/93). A further step, nonetheless consistent with the objective of ensuring effective protection of the rights of individuals, was the assertion of the responsibility of the State for infringements attributable to a national court (judgment of 30.09.2003, *Gerhard Köbler v Republik Österreich*, C-224/01; judgment of 13.06.2006, *Traghetti del Mediterraneo SpA v Repubblica italiana*, C-173/03), which is largely entrusted with the responsibility for the correct application of Community law and can therefore make a decisive contribution to the effectiveness of the overall system under review. In fact, the Court did not fail to note that:

> In the light of the essential role played by the judiciary in the protection of the rights derived by individuals from Community rules, the full effectiveness of those rules would be called in question […] if individuals were precluded from being able, under certain conditions, to obtain reparation when their rights are affected by an infringement of Community law attributable to a decision of a court of a Member State adjudicating at last instance (judgment in *Gerhard Köbler* case, paragraph 33),

to the point of declaring any national legislation, in this case Italian law, which establishes that the State is not liable as a result of the judge's irresponsibility, incompatible with Community law (judgment of 09.12.2003, *Commission of the European Communities v Italian Republic*, C-129/00).

In the *Kühne & Heitz* case, the Court succeeded in combining the obligations deriving from the *primauté* of EU law with the principle of legal certainty linked to the authority of a final decision (judgment of 13.01.2004, *Kühne & Heitz NV v Produktschap voor Pluimvee en Eieren*, C-453/00). The Community justices stated that a rule of Community law interpreted by the Court on the basis of a preliminary ruling must be applied by a national administrative body even to legal relationships which arose or were formed before the Court gave its ruling on the question on interpretation. It follows that, given that legal certainty is one of a number of general principles recognised by Community law and that Community law does not require administrative bodies to reopen an administrative decision, such an obligation does exist under certain circumstances and in particular when: national law has the power to reopen that decision at the request of one of the parties; that decision becomes final only as a result of a judgment of a national court ruling at final instance based on an interpretation of Community law which, in the light of a subsequent judgment of the Court, was incorrect; that the interested party complains to the administrative body requesting the revocation of the administrative act immediately after becoming aware of the ruling of the Court of Justice on the *Kühne & Heitz* case.

Specific mention is reserved here to the recognition of a general principle such is the right to full and effective judicial review, which played a fundamental role in the case law and, consequently, in the development of the Union's legal framework (judgments of 15.05.1986, *Marguerite Johnston v Chief Constable of the Royal Ulster Constabulary*, case 222/84; 25.07.2002, *Mouvement contre la racisme, antisémitisme et la xénophobie ASBL (MRAX) v Belgian State*, C-459/99, paragraph 100, in particular on the subject of residence permits and expulsions; 29.10.2009, *Virginie Pontin v T-Comalux SA*, C-63/08; the aforementioned Unibet judgment, paragraph 36; 18.03.2010, *Rosalba Alassini v Telecom Italia SpA, Filomena Califano v Wind SpA, Lucia Anna Giorgia Iacono v Telecom Italia SpA* and *Multiservice Srl v Telecom Italia SpA*, joined cases C-317/08, C-318/08, C-319/08, C-320/08). The case law has developed the principle of the effectiveness of judicial review especially in the light of the need for uniformity as to the level of protection in the Union. This has brought forth, on the one hand, the criterion that the protection of rights conferred by Union rules must be at least equal to that afforded by rights granted under national rules (principle of equivalence); on the other hand, as mentioned above, it has introduced the principle whereby the national system of remedies must be such as not to make virtually impossible or excessively burdensome the exercise of rights conferred upon individuals by Union rules (principle of effectiveness, judgments of 09.11.1983, *Administration of the State v SpA San Giorgio*, case 199/82, paragraph 14; 20.09.2001, *Courage Ltd v Bernard Crehan and Bernard Crehan v Courage Ltd and others*, C-453/99, paragraph 29; 02.10.2003, *Weber's Wine World Handels-GmbH and others v Abgabenberufungskommission Wien*, C-147/01, paragraph 103). The consequences have been a gradual communitisation of the level of adequacy as regards judicial protection along with the introduction into national systems of new or otherwise more favourable remedies to the individual (by way of example, precautionary measures protecting a party's interests *ante causam* in relation to tenders: judgment of 15.05.2003, *Commission of the European Communities v Kingdom of Spain*, C-214/00, paragraph 98; order of the court of 29.04.2004, *Dac SpA v Azienda ospedaliera Spedali Civili di Brescia*, C-202/03). This is confirmed in detail in article 19 TEU (paragraph 1, section 2), which explicitly places an obligation on Member States to provide remedies sufficient to ensure effective legal protection in the fields covered by Union law.

V. The Protection of Fundamental Rights

The sensitivity of the Court of Justice towards the rights of individuals, aimed at guaranteeing them a decent existence, has insisted on the central role of individuals as such, regardless of the status assigned and recognised to them in each instance. In this perspective, the Court has paid great attention to the protection of fundamental rights, which constitutes a crucial part of the subjective legal position of individuals. The reticence of the 1957 Treaty of Rome on such an important subject, with the exception of the prohibition of discrimination on the basis of nationality and the freedoms linked to the economic activities of individuals, was soon offset by a very rich body of case law, already starting from the 1970s. Also driven by encouraging developments from the Italian Constitutional Court (ruling 27.12.1965, No. 98) and the German Constitutional Court, the Court of Justice stated that fundamental rights, as they result from the constitutional traditions of Member States and the ECHR (*European Convention of Human Rights*), are part of the general legal principles whose compliance it ensures (judgments of

12.11.1969, *Erich Stauder v City of Ulm – Sozialamt*, case 29/69; 17.12.1970, *Internationale Handelsgesellschaft mbH v Einfuhr- und Vorratsstelle für Getreide und Futtermittel*, case 11/70; 14.05.1974, *J. Nold, Kohlen- und Baustoffgroßhandlung v Commission of the European Communities*, case 4/73; 28.10.1975, *Roland Rutili v Ministre de l'Intérieur*, case 36/75; 02.05.2006, *Eurofood IFSC Ltd*, C-341/04; 25.01.2007, *Salzgitter Mannesmann v Commission*, C-411/04 P; on a similar statement by the Court, judgment of 28.01.1992, *Speybrouck v Parliament*, T-45/90; on the 'special significance' to be attributed to the 1950 Rome Convention, see, in particular, judgments of 18.06.1991, *Elliniki Radiophonia Tiléorassi AE and Panellinia Omospondia Syllogon Prossopikou v Dimotiki Etairia Pliroforissis and Sotirios Kouvelas and Nicolaos Avdellas and others*, 260/89, paragraph 41; 14.10.2004, *Omega Spielhallen- und Automatenaufstellungs-GmbH v Oberbürgermeisterin der Bundesstadt Bonn*, C-36/02, paragraph 33; 27.06.2006, *European Parliament v Council of the European Union*, C-540/03, paragraph 35; as well as opinion 2/94 of 28.03.1996, paragraph 33). In addition to the Union's acts, the jurisdiction of the Court of Justice over the protection of fundamental rights has extended to national acts implementing EU law and exceptions to fundamental freedoms justified by the Member States with the need to protect fundamental rights (see the aforementioned judgment *Elliniki Radiophonia Tiléorassi*, paragraphs 41–44; on the necessary reconciliation between the need to protect fundamental rights and guarantee the freedoms of movement under the Treaty, see judgment of 12.06.2003, *Eugen Schmidberger, Internationale Transporte und Planzüge v Republik Österreich*, C-112/00, paragraph 71). Therefore, only national rules that do not establish a sufficient connection with Community law fall outside the scope of the Court's supervision (judgment of 29.05.1997, *Friedrich Kremzow v Republik Österreich*, C-299/95).

The Court has seized the opportunity to invoke the key fundamental rights, from the right to property (judgment of 03.12.2009, *Faraj Hassan v Council of the European Union and European Commission* and *Chafiq Ayadi v Council of the European Union*, joined cases C- 399/06 P and C-403/06 P) to the non-retroactivity of criminal law, from observance of the rights of the defence and the right to a hearing judgment (21.09.1989, *Hoechst AG v Commission of the European Communities*, joined cases 46/87 and 227/88, paragraphss 55–57) to the right to a fair trial within a reasonable time, from the respect of private life (09.11.2010, *Volker and Markus Schecke GbR* and *Hartmut Eifert v Land Hessen*, joined cases C-92/09 and C-93/09) and human dignity (above-mentioned ruling in Omega case) to freedom of expression and pluralism in information.

Article 6(3) TEU has also formally consolidated the Court's case law, expressly categorising fundamental rights as general principles of EU law and clearly recalled the Court's case law on the matter, transposing on a regulatory level its dual reference to constitutional traditions common to the Member States and to the ECHR. The Charter of fundamental rights of the European Union (or Charter of Nice), which the Lisbon or reform Treaty formally elevated to the same status as the Treaties, laid down a set of fundamental rights, based on the values of dignity, freedom, equality, solidarity, European citizenship and justice, already recognised by the Treaties, by the ECHR, by the Constitutions of the Member States and, above all, by the Court of Justice. After all, the purpose of the Charter was not to bring innovation, but to assert and formalise the affirmation of a series of values, within the limits and according to the framework of competences already set forth in the case law of the Court of Justice. The commitment to boost the visibility of the protection of fundamental rights was also spelled out in article 51 of the Charter, which clearly states that the Charter does not 'establish any new power or task for the Union, or modify powers and tasks as defined in the Treaties'.

Having said that, with the issue of the EU's accession to the ECHR settled by the Court's adverse opinion (opinion 2/13 of the Court of Justice of 18.12.2014), it is clear that today the overall mechanism for the protection of fundamental rights in the EU finds its main benchmark in the EU Charter of fundamental rights. In the new wording of article 6 TEU, in fact, the Charter is the primary source, while the reference to the general principles and common constitutional traditions of the Member States appears to be a complementary source. This is evidenced by the first rulings following the entry into force of the Treaty that clearly show the Court's intention to give priority to the Charter (the aforementioned Schecke and *Eifert v Land Hessen* case; judgment of 05.10.2010, *J. McB v L. E.*, C-400/10 PPU; judgment of 01.03.2011, *Association Belge des Consommateurs Test-Achats ASBL and others v Conseil des ministres*, C-236/09). As for the Charter's relationship vis-à-vis the common constitutional traditions (article 53), the Court tends to narrow the scope of the reference to the Charter, in the name of the principle of the primacy of EU law, inasmuch as it would allow a Member State to set aside EU legal rules which are fully in compliance with the Charter (judgment of 26.02.2013, *Stefano Melloni v Ministerio Fiscal*, C-399/11, paragraphss 57 et seq.).

It is worth noting that, in view of the EU's accession to the ECHR and with the formalisation of the primary law status of European Charter of Fundamental Rights among Community sources of law, the Lisbon reform in a way failed to bring about the 'communitisation' of the ECHR; therefore the relationship between the ECHR and the internal legal systems are still, albeit to varying degrees, firmly rooted in the choices of the individual Member States, also in terms of the consequences to be drawn by a national court in case of conflict between the rights guaranteed by that convention and a provision of national law (judgment of 24.04.2012, *Servet Kamberaj v Istituto per l'edilizia sociale della Provincia autonoma di Bolzano (IPES) and others*, C-571/10, paragraphs 62–53; judgment of 26.02.2013, *Åklagaren v Hans Åkerberg Fransson*, C-617/10). Furthermore, the Luxembourg court has clearly stated that the ECHR does not constitute a legal instrument which has been formally incorporated into European Union law (see aforementioned judgment in *Åklagaren v Hans Åkerberg Fransson*).

Moreover, it must be equally ruled out that, simply because the Charter has been formally incorporated into EU law, it may extend the field of application of European Union law beyond the powers of the Union (among others, judgment of 15.11.2011, *Murat Dereci and others v Bundesministerium für Inneres*, C-256/11, pargrapha 71, cited in the *Gennaro Currà* case, paragraph 25), as some judgments handed down by ordinary judges had wrongly held, notwithstanding article 51 of the same Charter, and of a general principle of legal theory (Criminal Court of Cassation case No. 5770/2010; State Council ruling of 02.03.2010, case No. 1220; Lazio TAR (regional administrative tribunal) ruling of 25.05.2010, No. 11984, Civil Court of Cassation, Section III, ruling of 22.03.2011, No. 6548, Lazio TAR ruling of 24.10.2012, No. 8748; see in the correct sense, Constitutional Court ruling of 11.03.2011, No. 80, preventive measures, paragraphs 5.3–5.6 on the points of law under review).

VI. The Commission's Role in Upholding Rights Before the EU Judge

The pages of EU law written by the Court of Justice would (probably) have a markedly different flavour without the European Commission's contribution to the protection of fundamental rights and freedoms laid down in the Union's constitutional texts.

The history of the EU, in fact, bears witness to a relationship of identification between the two institutions in pursuing the aims set out in the Treaties and in relation to the respective functions and powers established therein. Moreover, by express provision of the Treaties, the Commission promote the general interest of the Union and takes appropriate initiatives to that end; it ensures the application of the Treaties and of Union law under the control of the Court of Justice (article 17, TEU).

As a result of this, a number of cases which have left their mark on the Union's legal order and EU case law have been brought before the Court by the Commission as infringement proceedings against Member States pursuant to article 258 TFEU. In fact, the infringement procedure is closely associated with the role bestowed upon the Commission as guardian of the Treaties and of the Union's acts; in the EU system, the normal assumption is that the European executive body is tasked with triggering this procedure against a Member State that has failed to fulfil an obligation under the Treaties. It should also be noted that the arguments put forward by the Commission in these proceedings are – very often – accepted in the Court rulings and this ever since the EU system's earliest days.

As we cannot retrace here the 60 years of work undertaken by the two institutions at hand, let us briefly recall the objectives they have fulfilled in terms of social policy, approximation of laws, free provision of services and movement of workers, freedom of establishment and/or citizenship. Indeed, in numerous cases of proceedings against Member States for failing to fulfil their obligations, national provisions creating unequal treatment between workers who have not exercised their right to free movement and migrant workers, to the detriment of the latter, have been held to be incompatible with the Treaties. In this way, the principle, now known, has been affirmed to the effect that, even if these provisions are applied indistinctively, they deters workers from leaving their Member State of origin in order to work in another Member State, or in an EU institution, and therefore constitute an impediment to the free movement of workers contrary to article 45 TFEU (judgment of 21.01.2016, *European Commission v Republic of Cyprus*, C-515/14, and the case law cited there).

As regards the freedom of establishment, again thanks to the Commission, the Court has been able to clarify that Member States may require that citizens of other Member States possess the necessary linguistic knowledge in relation to the nature of the job offered (article 3(1), regulation No. 492/2011/EU). However, the linguistic requirement must be implemented in a proportionate and non-discriminatory manner (judgment of 05.02.2015, *European Commission v Kingdom of Belgium*, C-317/14; judgment of 06.06.2000, *Roman Angonese v Cassa di Risparmio di Bolzano SpA*, C-281/98; see also judgment of 23.02.2016, *European Commission v Hungary*, C-179/14; judgment of 16.04.2015, *European Commission v Federal Republic of Germany*, C-591/13; judgment of 11.12.2014, *European Commission v Kingdom of Spain*, C-576/13).

Following an action brought by the Commission, EU case law goes so far as to openly uphold the right of the migrant worker's child to rely on EU legislation granting maintenance and education (regulation No. 1612/68) to obtain funding for studies subject to the same conditions as are applicable to the children of national workers, and no additional residence requirement may be imposed on them (judgment of 26.02.1992, *MJE Bernini v Minister van Onderwijs en Wetenschappen*, C-3/90; judgment of 08.06.1999, *CPM Meeusen v Hoofddirectie van de Informatie Beheer Groep*, C-337/97).

More broadly, it is the opinion of the EU Court that the principle of equal treatment laid down in article 45 TFEU prohibits not only direct discrimination based on nationality, but also all indirect forms which lead to the same result. And the residence requirement may constitute indirect discrimination. It is clear that, even if the requirement applied in the same way to nationals and other EU citizens alike, it would naturally be easier for national workers to meet and would therefore be liable to disadvantage migrant workers in particular. Furthermore, it is the opinion of the Commission, upheld by the Court, that such a requirement is even more discriminatory for frontier workers and their children, who, by definition, reside in a Member State other than the Member State of employment (on this subject, the nationality requirement for access to the notarial profession imposed by national legislation is discriminatory and contrary to article 49 TFEU: judgment of 10.09.2015, *European Commission v Republic of Latvia*, C-151/14).

It follows that, along these lines, a principle was affirmed that is by now indisputable for the EU order, namely that it is for the national authorities which plead an exception from the fundamental principle of freedom of movement for persons to show in each individual case that their rules are necessary and proportionate for the purposes of attaining the aim pursued. In other words, as a result of the common objective envisaged by the Commission and the Court of Justice, the irrefutable principle of freedom of movement for workers within the European Union constitutes a fundamental right and that any national obstacle can be justified only: if it relates to an objective that is compatible with the Treaty; by overriding reasons relating to the public interest; if it is appropriate to achieve the legitimate objective pursued; if it does not go beyond what is necessary to achieve that objective (judgment of 14.06.2012, *European Commission v Kingdom of the Netherlands*, C-542/09).

It should be recalled that the Commission's role has been of fundamental importance also in relation to social policies to protect workers with disabilities who require different treatment. In fact, following an action brought by the Commission, the Court of Justice stated that it is the responsibility of the Member States to impose on all employers the obligation to take effective and practical measures, where needed in a particular case, for all persons with disabilities, establishing a general framework for equal treatment in employment and occupation and allowing such persons to access employment, to work, to be eligible for promotion or to receive training (judgment of 04.07.2013, *European Commission v Italian Republic*, C-312/11; judgment of 11.04.2013, *HK Danmark v Dansk almennyttigt Boligselskab* and *C Dansk Arbejdsgiverforening*, joined cases C-335/11 and C-337/11).

The same approach is also highlighted in the extensive case law on the implementation of the principle of equal treatment for men and women with regard to access to employment, vocational training and promotion, and working conditions (*ex multis*, judgment of 13.11.2008, *Commission of the European Communities v Italian Republic*, C-46/07; judgment of 23.02.2006, *Commission of the European Communities v Republic of Austria*, C-133/05; judgment of 08.11.1983, *Commission of the European Communities v Kingdom United Kingdom of Great Britain and Northern Ireland*, case 165/82; judgment of 06.07.1982, *Commission of the European Communities v United Kingdom*, case 61/81; judgment of 30.01.1985, *Commission of the European Communities v Kingdom of Denmark*, case 143/83).

Furthermore, the important milestones achieved in terms of citizenship are also a direct result of this line of action. On several occasions, the Commission's oversight has enabled the Court to affirm that article 20(1) TFEU confers the status of citizen of the Union on every person holding the nationality of a Member State (judgment of 20.09.2001, *Rudy Grzelczyk v Centre public d'aide sociale d'Ottignies-Louvain-la-Neuve*, C-184/99; judgment of 11.07.2002, *Marie-Nathalie D'Hoop v Office national de l'emploi*, C-224/98). Also, thanks to the correct interpretation of the Treaties by the institutions in question, every citizen of the Union may rely on article 18 TFEU, expressly prohibiting any discrimination on the grounds of nationality, within the scope of application of the Treaties, where such situations shall include exercising the fundamental freedom to move and reside in the territory of the Member States granted by article 21 TFEU (judgment of 12.05.1998, *María Martínez Sala v Freistaat Bayern*, C-85/96; judgment of 15.03.2005, *Dany Bidar v London Borough of Ealing and Secretary of State for education and skills*, C-209/03; judgment of 18.11.2008, *Jacqueline Förster v Hoofddirectie van de Informatie Beheer Groep*, C-158/07; judgment of 13.04.2010, *Nicolas Bressol and others, Céline Chaverot and others v Gouvernement de la Communauté française*, C-73/08). Likewise, students from Member States who pursue their studies in other EU countries, providing they are nationals of a Member State, may enjoy the right as citizens of the Union to move and reside freely within the territory of the Member State without direct or indirect discrimination on the grounds of their nationality (*ex multis*, judgment of 04.10.2012, *European Commission v Republic of Austria*, C-75/11; article 18 TFEU; directive 2004/38/EC).

And again, to quote a further example of the institutional synergy to the advantage of EU policies, as a result of the Commission's action, the Court disallows the difference in treatment between natural persons transferring all the assets related to an activity carried out on an individual basis to a company with its head office and effective management in the national territory and those who carry out such a transfer to a company with its head office or its effective management in the territory of another Member State of the European Union (judgment of 21.12.2016, *European Commission v Portuguese Republic*, C-503/14). Similarly, at the Commission's request, the Court held that the obligations laid down in articles 56 and 63 TFEU bar EU States from introducing and maintaining a tax reduction in respect of contributions paid to a savings pension in so far as that reduction is applicable only to payments to institutions or funds established in the Member State (judgment of 23.01.2014, *European Commission v Kingdom of Belgium*, C-296/12).

Ultimately, there is no doubt that the EU's fundamental principles and freedoms, in the familiar wording known to us today, made their first steps in the Commission, conceived in the various opinions framed at the end of the pre-litigation stage of infringement proceedings. And it goes without saying that the Court of Justice guarded them until they reached full maturity and legal affirmation, also thanks to its uniform interpretation of the Treaties and of EU secondary legislation.

Bibliography

Adam, R and Tizzano, A, *Manuale di diritto dell'Unione Europea* (Torino, 2014).

Beaudouin, C, *La démocratie à l'épreuve de l'intégration européenne* (Paris, 2014).

Ciccone, R, *Il rinvio pregiudiziale e le basi del sistema giuridico comunitario* (Napoli, 2011).

Condinanzi, M, Lang, A and Nascimbene, B, *Cittadinanza dell'Unione e libera circolazione delle persone* (Milano, 2006).

Craig, P 'Pringle and use of EU institutions outside the EU legal framework: foundations, procedure and substance' (2013) 9(2) *European constitutional law review* 263–84.

Damato, A, 'Politica economica e principi democratici: osser vazioni sul ruolo della Commissione' in A Damato and P De Pasquale (eds), *Politica economica e monetaria dell'Unione Europea. Procedura legislativa e ruolo delle istituzioni* (Napoli, 2016) 55–72.

Ferraro, F, *La responsabilità risarcitoria degli Stati membri per violazione del diritto comunitario* (Milano, 2008).

MacCormick, N, *Questioning sovereignty* (Oxford-New York, 1999).

Pesce, C, 'Corte di giustizia dell'Unione Europea, principio democratico e trattati in materia economica' in A Damato and P De Pasquale (eds), *Politica economica e monetaria dell'Unione Europea. Procedura legislative e ruolo delle istituzioni* (Napoli, 2016) 151–68.

Porchia, O, *Principi dell'ordinamento europeo. La cooperazione pluridirezionale* (Bologna, 2008).

Porchia, O, 'Il ruolo della Corte di giustizia dell'Unione Europea nella governance economica europea' (2013) *Il diritto dell'Unione Europea* 593 et seq.

Quadri, R, 'Commento all'art. 5', in R Quadri, R Monaco, A Trabucchi (eds), *Trattato istitutivo della Comunità economica europea. Commentario* 1st vol (Milano, 1965) 54.

Tesauro, G, 'The effectiveness of judicial protection and cooperation between the Court of justice and the National Courts' (1993) *Yearbook of European law* 3 et seq.

Tesauro, G *Diritto dell'Unione Europea* (Padova, 2012).

Tizzano, A, 'Le competenze dell'Unione e il principio di sussidiarietà' (1997) *Il diritto dell'Unione Europea* 229 et seq.

Tizzano, A, 'Alle origini della cittadinanza europea' (2010) *Il diritto dell'Unione Europea* 1031 et seq.

Villani, U, 'Osservazioni sulla tutela dei principi di libertà, democrazia, rispetto dei diritti dell'uomo e stato di diritto nell'Unione Europea' (2007) *Studi sull'integrazione europea* 27 et seq.

Villani, U, *Istituzioni di diritto dell'Unione Europea* (Bari, 2016).

Ziller, J, 'Solange III' (2009) 5 *Rivista italiana di diritto pubblico comunitario* 973–95.

PART III

The European Union and the People: Rights and Opportunities

12

Non-discrimination and Protection of Diversity and Minorities

MARCO VENTURA

Emerging from the founding fathers' dream of a peaceful and developing Europe, the project of the European construction is based on unity in diversity. At the heart of the project was the faith in the possibility to build unity through recognition and protection of diversity. Hence the fight against discrimination on grounds of sex, race, ethnicity, skin colour, social origin, genetic characteristics, language, religion or personal beliefs, political opinion or of any other nature, membership in a national minority, birth, disability, age, sexual orientation. Non-discrimination and protection of diversity and minorities has thus become the leading principle for both an historical process of convergence within Europe, and the building of an unprecedented transnational legal mechanism.

I. Non-discrimination in the Process of the Construction of the European Union

The process through which the European Community and the European Union (EU) have progressively recognised and protected diversity and minorities has reflected the history of Europe over the last 60 years, and has made a fundamental contribution to this history. Such process has been accompanied by socio-cultural transformations of European diversity in the context of the political and legal dimensions of European integration.

To trace the principal stages of the enunciation of principles and their legislative implementation, it is necessary to begin from the three defining factors of the period between 1957 and 2017.

The first factor is constituted by the history of the different countries – political and legal – from which the common constitutional traditions relating to the protection of human rights as identified by the jurisprudence of the European Court of Justice, and elevated to a general principle of EU law in article F of the 1992 Maastricht Treaty (now article 6(3) of the Treaty on European Union, TEU), as well as the duty to respect the national constitutional identities of Member States as provided for in article 4, according to the subsequent wording of the Treaty of Lisbon (2007), have emerged.

The second factor is represented by the contribution of international supra-European law. As subjects of the international community, parts of the United Nations system and of other international extra-European systems, starting from NATO, but also as actors of bilateral or multilateral relations, the Member States of the Union have experienced international policies and instruments on diversity, on minorities and on non-discrimination, which have determined their orientation in the internal debate of the EU.

The third factor, finally, comes from the development of human rights in European integration in a broad sense, in particular through the Council of Europe, the European Convention on Human Rights (ECHR) and the CoE Framework Convention for the Protection of National Minorities' of 1995, on the one hand, and the Organization for Security and Cooperation in Europe (OSCE), on the other. In the construction of non-discrimination in Union law, the Strasbourg institutions, and the Court, have had particular significance. The principle expressed in article 14 of the Convention, always to be applied in conjunction with other articles of the Convention, has had a deep impact. Article 14 ECHR provides that:

> the enjoyment of the rights and freedoms set forth in this Convention shall be secured without discrimination on any ground such as sex, race, colour, language, religion, political or other opinion, national or social origin, association with a national minority, property, birth or other status.

In its conditions, development and results, the contribution of the European Union system to the protection against discrimination and to the safeguarding of diversity and minorities is inseparable from these three factors (national, international and European in a broad sense). It is from the crucible of these various experiences, with their fragility and contradictions, and in the peculiar adventure of the Community and the European Union, that an approach of the EU to diversity and minorities and the correlated anti-discriminatory law were born.

A. From the Origins to the Respect for Diversity and to Anti-discriminatory Safeguards after the Treaty of Maastricht and Amsterdam

Since the 1957 Treaty of Rome, non-discrimination, diversity and minorities have been understood in a peculiar sense from the point of view both of structure and substance. As far as structure goes, Community safeguards had to be organised in a way consistent with the competences first of the Community, and then of the Union. Such competences were instrumental in the creation of an area of free movement of persons, services, goods and capital. In the 1957 Treaty which instituted the European Economic Community (EEC), the principle of non-discrimination was laid down in a general way as regards nationality, through the commitment to the 'abolition of any discrimination based on nationality between workers of the Member States as regards employment, remuneration and other conditions of work and employment' (article 48, now article 45(2) TFEU) and specifically through the ban against speculating on the lower costs of female labour so to distort competition; article 119 (now article 157 TFEU) in this respect, prescribes '[e]qual pay without discrimination based on sex'.

In the subsequent decades, the substance and the structure of the safeguards slowly changed as a consequence of the expansion of competences, the recognition of fundamental rights (first of all through the work of the Court of Luxembourg), the enlargement to new countries and, above all, the project of political unity in the 1980s, which then became the three-pillar architecture with the Maastricht Treaty and the 1997 Treaty of Amsterdam.

While the recognition of the 'national identity' of the Member States appears with article F of the Maastricht Treaty, thus balancing a closer integration, the consolidated version of the Treaty establishing the European Community (TEC) – designation taken up by the Treaty of Rome after the TEU – following the 1997 Treaty of Amsterdam then confirms the ban on discrimination based on nationality (articles 11, 12, 39, TEC) and sex (article 141, TEC), but broadens the scope of the term *discrimination* in four directions:

(1) Further grounds of non-discrimination. The Treaty expressly forbids the discrimination between citizens of the States and in the trade between States in the area of enhanced cooperation (article 11, TEC) and 'discrimination based on sex, racial or ethnic origin, religion or belief, disability, age or sexual orientation' (article 13, TEC). While discrimination based on nationality and sex was already covered in the Treaty of Rome, the extension to new grounds of discrimination is a significant step forward, one which transposes the fundamental rights doctrine of the Court of Justice and makes the Union converge to the system of the European Convention on Human Rights.
(2) The fight against discrimination. The commitment to the fight against various forms of discrimination is added to the ban on discriminatory measures. In that respect, article 13 TEC provides that the Council, upon approval by the European Parliament, 'may take appropriate action to combat discrimination based on sex, racial or ethnic origin, religion or belief, disability, age or sexual orientation'.
(3) Explicit and articulated application of non-discrimination based on nationality to the common market. The Treaty expressly forbids discrimination based on the country of origin or of destination in a general way 'in the exchange between the Member Countries' (article 11, TEC) and specifically in supply and markets (article 31, TEC), in the common organisation of the agricultural markets (article 34, TEC), in the free movement of capital and payments (article 58, TEC), transport (article 75, TEC), and in State aid (article 87, TEC).
(4) Typology of discrimination. While it does not define them, the Treaty employs the categories of arbitrary discrimination (articles 30 and 58, TEC) and of direct and indirect discrimination (article 184, TEC).

While anti-discrimination safeguards were enlarged and deepened in 1997, after the Maastricht Treaty the reference to the cultural, linguistic and national differences was explicitly subsumed in the law of the European Union treaties. The commitment to respect the 'cultural and linguistic diversity' of the Member States (article 149, TEC) and 'to respect and to promote the diversity' of the Union (article 151, TEC) corresponds to the recognition of 'cultural and linguistic diversity of the Union' (article 149, TEC). The development of the Member States' cultures, article 151 TEC further specifies, has to take place with regard to their 'national and regional diversity'. Moreover, if culture is the place of diversity, it is also the place of community and union, in accordance with the 'common cultural heritage' (article 151, TEC).

B. Broad Recognition of Diversity, Minorities and Non-discrimination in the Principles of the Nice Charter

In the Charter of Fundamental Rights of the European Union (or Nice Charter) of 2000, a non legally binding document until the Treaty of Lisbon of 2007, the original development project through free movement is consolidated around the 'common values' of 'human dignity, freedom, equality and solidarity', the principles of democracy and of the rule of law and the construction of an 'area of freedom, security and justice' through the citizenship of the Union. In this framework, in accordance with the model drafted in the Maastricht Treaty, the recognition of diversity coincides with a legally stronger and politically more conscious integration project. In the preamble of the Charter, the 'preservation' and the 'development' of the 'common values' are thus to be understood as 'respecting the diversity of the cultures and traditions of the peoples of Europe' and of the 'national identities of the Member States'.

In comparison with the Treaty, the Charter extends both the catalogue of the protected diversities and the anti-discrimination safeguards themselves. Alongside the cultural and linguistic diversity and the national identity already recognised after the Maastricht and Amsterdam Treaties, in fact, the diversity of the 'traditions of the peoples of Europe' (preamble) and 'religious [...] diversity' (article 22) are now identified as equally important.

The 'value' of equality enshrined in the preamble is made legally binding through the ban on discrimination in the Charter. While including the grounds of article 13 TEC – sex, race or ethnic origin, religion or personal beliefs, handicaps, age or sexual tendencies – the non-discrimination principle of the Charter is significantly broader. In particular, at article 21, 'ethnic origin' becomes 'ethnic or social origin', and four new grounds are introduced: 'genetic features', 'political or any other opinion', 'property' and 'birth'. The generic protection of 'linguistic diversity' is specified through a ban on discrimination based on 'language'. Discrimination based on nationality becomes discrimination on the basis of citizenship through the ban in article 21 of 'any discrimination on grounds of nationality', 'within the scope of application of the Treaties' and 'without prejudice to the special provisions of those Treaties'. A reference to minorities appears for the first time in the primary legislation of the Union with the ban, also in article 21, of discrimination based on 'membership of a national minority'.

C. The Implementation of the Principles in the Anti-discrimination Directives

The signing of the Nice Charter, despite its original non-legally binding nature, and the adoption of the motto 'unity in diversity' made 2000 a turning point for non-discrimination and equality in the European Union. Even more, 2000 was momentous for the adoption of two directives on employment discrimination: directive 2000/78/EC, which establishes a general framework for equal treatment in the field of employment and working conditions, and directive 2000/43/EC on racial discrimination.

These directives have both an historical and a legal significance. On the one hand, they represent a qualitative leap in the implementation of principles: indeed, they make explicit the instrumental function of the anti-discrimination safeguards as regards the attainment of a high level of employment and social protection, the improvement of living standards and quality of life, economic and social cohesion, solidarity and the free movement of persons; they define violations and prescribe remedies; they bind Union and national institutions and encourage the promotion of anti-discrimination policies. On the other hand, the directives circumscribe the safeguards, limiting their field of application and creating a system of uneven protection between areas and grounds of discrimination, which puts pressure on the Union's policies and the Court of Justice.

The consolidation and the extension of safeguards against indirect discrimination are fundamental to the directive on employment; such safeguards were already introduced with the 1976 directive on equal treatment between men and women (76/207/EEC) and developed by the Court of Justice. Article 2(2) of the 2000 directive on employment, defines the difference between direct and indirect discrimination in this way:

> (a) direct discrimination shall be taken to occur where one person is treated less favourably than another is, has been or would be treated in a comparable situation, on any of the grounds referred to in Article 1;
>
> (b) indirect discrimination shall be taken to occur where an apparently neutral provision, criterion or practice would put persons having a particular religion or belief, a particular disability, a particular age, or a particular sexual orientation at a particular disadvantage compared with other persons.

The legislative framework was subsequently enriched with directives that implemented the principles of equal opportunity and equal treatment between women and men, in matters of employment and work: directive 2004/113/EC and especially directive 2006/54/EC.

On the one hand, the Commission emerged as a key actor through anti-discrimination policies and the actions in support of the Union's diversity – in particular in support of fundamental rights, against xenophobia, and for the inclusion of the Roma communities – as well as through the diversity charters for companies and the partnership with institutions such as the Fundamental Rights Agency. On the other hand, the Court of Justice authored seminal decisions in the theorisation and implementation of non-discrimination. This happened in 2005 with the *Mangold* case (judgment of 22.11.2005, *Werner Mangold v Rudiger Helm*, C-144/04) on discrimination based on age, in which the Court identified the general principle of equal treatment as having direct horizontal effect; in 2008 with the *Tadao Maruko* case (judgment of 01.04.2008, *Tadao Maruko v Versorgungsanstalt der deutschen Bühnen*, C-267/06), on discrimination based on sexual orientation; in 2010 with the *Kücükdeveci* case (judgment of 19.01.2010, *Seda Kücükdeveci v Swedex GmbH & Co KG*, C-555/07), again on the issue of discrimination based on age, in which the Court reinforced the *Mangold* ruling; and in 2014 with the *Association de médiation sociale* case (judgment of 12.01.2014, *Association de médiation sociale v Union locale des syndicats CGT and others*, C-176/12), in which the Court further clarified under what conditions a general principle of EU law can be directly applied in a dispute between private parties.

D. Respect for All Minorities and the Principle of Non-discrimination in the Treaty of Lisbon

With the Treaty of Lisbon and the transformation of the charter of fundamental rights in a legally binding instrument, the twofold protection against discrimination on the one hand, and in favour of diversity and minorities on the other, was consolidated and expanded further.

In the consolidated version of the Treaty on European Union after Lisbon, indeed, a general recognition of minorities appears for the first time in primary EU law. Repeating the preamble of the Nice Charter, article 2 proclaims respect for human rights as a founding 'value' of the Union, including 'the rights of persons belonging to minorities'. Even if this reference does not confer to the Union any specific competence regarding minorities, it paves the way for further developments, particularly in the recognition of the status of minorities and the right of minorities to self-determination and autonomy.

In continuity with the previous primary legislation, article 4(2) TEU mandates respect by the Union for 'the equality of Member States before the Treaties', and develops article F of the Maastricht Treaty so as to prescribe respect for 'their national identities, inherent in their fundamental structures, political and constitutional, inclusive of regional and local self-government'.

Recognition of diversity is also embedded in article 3(3) TEU committing the Union to 'respect its rich cultural and linguistic diversity', in the sphere of the safeguarding and development of 'Europe's cultural heritage'. In this matter, the consolidated version of the Treaty on the Functioning of the European Union (TFEU) reiterates the principles and rules of the founding Treaty of the Union as amended by the Amsterdam Treaty. On the subject of education, both cultural and linguistic diversity are recognised (article 165 TFEU), and also national and regional diversity, from which the common cultural heritage emerges (article 167 TFEU). On the subject of culture, article 167 confirms the commitment of the Union to 'respect and to promote the diversity of its cultures'.

The Treaty of Lisbon is even more significant on non-discrimination. Article 2 TEU reiterates the reference of the Nice Charter to the 'values' of equality and non-discrimination. The status of the general principle of non-discrimination is no doubt boosted by this provision. This principle is presented as deriving from the values 'common to the Member States' and 'respect for human dignity, freedom, democracy, equality, the rule of law and respect for human rights', as well as a part of a set of defining features of European society, which must be 'a society in which pluralism, non-discrimination, tolerance, justice, solidarity and equality between women and men prevail'. Article 3(3) TEU further defines discrimination. Discrimination is associated, on the one hand, with 'social exclusion', and on the other, with the promotion of specific values, in particular 'social justice and protection, equality between women and men, solidarity between generations and protection of the rights of the child'.

The most significant novelty is, however, article 10 TFEU, in which the goal of combating 'discrimination based on sex, racial or ethnic origin, religion or belief, disability, age or sexual orientation' is adopted by the Union as a general precondition '[i]n defining and implementing its policies and activities'. Hence the title *Non-discrimination and citizenship of the Union* of the second part of the founding Treaty – which is a synthesis of chapter III of the Nice Charter dedicated to equality and part II of the TEC dedicated to citizenship. Combining citizenship and non-discrimination, the second part of the TFEU includes article 18 on discrimination based on nationality, a reiteration of article 12 of the TEC, and article 19 on the measures which may be adopted by the European Council and Parliament 'to combat discrimination based on sex, racial or ethnic origin, religion or belief, disability, age or sexual orientation', a reiteration of article 13 of the TEC, with some adjustments in terminology ('disability' instead of 'handicap' and 'sexual orientation' instead of 'sexual tendencies').

The TFEU innovates also with regard to the Union's action in the field of humanitarian aid, a field which was absent from the previous treaties: along with impartiality and neutrality, non-discrimination is defined as a guiding 'principle' for actions in this area (article 214 TFEU).

The TFEU repeats references of the TEC to discrimination based on sex (article 157 TFEU reiterates article 141 TEC) as well as those regarding free movement in the single market.

At the end of the first decade of the twenty-first century, Union law presented a broad spectrum of principles and instruments guiding and shaping the interaction between grassroots organisations, civil society, national and regional governments, articulations of the European Union, and bodies external to the Union. Such interaction is crucial for the development of the various dimensions of non-discrimination and the very protection of diversity and minorities in Europe.

II. The Dimensions of Non-discrimination

The Lisbon Treaty establishes a European Union system in which diversity and minorities are recognised and in which anti-discrimination has been developed into a sophisticated system of protection.

Faced with such an opportunity, civil society and institutions have the responsibility first of applying the available instruments, and secondly of planning and executing the next steps, for example through the introduction of a horizontal directive.

In using the system and planning and executing the next steps, actors are confronted with four fundamental dimensions, substantive and structural equality and citizenship; the diversity of nations, regions and peoples, as well as cultural and linguistic diversity; and the diversity and minorities safeguarded by anti-discrimination law.

A. The Single Market

The single market and freedoms of movement constitute the first dimension of non-discrimination and the protection of diversity and minorities.

A reason is that the single market belongs to the very structure of the Union, even after the extension of the Union's competences to the economic union and to the Union citizenship, and after the addition of the two pillars of foreign policy and common security, and of police and judicial cooperation. The single market was for decades, and still is, a primary reference framework of EU law.

A second reason is that the single market delimits and characterises the scope of protection, as illustrated above in the case of employment directives. This makes the Union system more limited, but also deeper and more effective, if compared to the protection systems of the ECHR and the OSCE. The single-market dimension affects the protected grounds, for instance gender, in the case of discrimination of women in the labour market, or religion, in the case of collision between religious freedom and business freedom.

B. Equality and Citizenship

The second dimension of equality and citizenship can be identified through the combination of chapter III of the Nice Charter, dedicated to equality, and part II of the TFEU, dedicated to the Non-discrimination and citizenship of the Union. Here diversity and minorities are part of a project of multiple citizenship, complementary to national citizenship, founded on the conviction that plurality is a value according to the principle of 'pluralism' enshrined in article 2 TEU.

Within the dimension of equality and citizenship, non-discrimination is elevated next to citizenship in the systematics of the TFEU and plays the triple role of the principle through which equality is developed, the clasp between equality and diversity in the construction of a citizenship of equal and diverse individuals and, finally, the bridge between the single market, for equal and diverse economic actors, and the common citizenship, for equal and diverse citizens.

C. Diversity of Nations, of Religions and of Peoples and Cultural and Linguistic Diversity

The third dimension regards the 'diversity of the cultures and traditions of the peoples of Europe' and the 'national identities' of the Member States, as envisaged in the preamble of the Nice Charter and in article 4 TEU, and the 'national and regional diversity' of the Union in article 167 TFEU.

This dimension coincides with the macro-diversity of the Union – diversity of States, nations, regions and peoples – formulated in terms of local traditions and national identity. The recognition and protection of macro-diversity respond to the political necessity of reassuring people with regard to the effects of the project of progressive integration and harmonisation. In this respect the terms 'traditions' and 'identity' take on a particular salience: while setting a limit to plans for change, they also define a value to be protected and promoted.

If Member States have been protected against national discrimination since the first steps of the EEC, with article 4 TEU the Union now guarantees 'the equality of the Member States before the Treaties'. At the same time, national identity, never before defined in its limits, extends itself so far as to guarantee Member States in 'their fundamental structures, political and constitutional, inclusive of regional and local self-government'.

This third dimension furthermore concerns 'the cultural and linguistic diversity' established by article 22 of the Charter of Fundamental Rights, as also mentioned in article 165 TFEU on education.

Cultural diversity is also mentioned by the Nice Charter preamble, which prescribes respect for 'the diversity of the cultures and traditions of the peoples of Europe', and article 167 TFEU, again on education, in which the Union commits 'to respect and to promote the diversity of its cultures'. A diversity of culture, a unitary entity differentiated internally, therefore coexists with a diversity of cultures, which, as one can deduce from the whole of the Charter's preamble, interprets cultures as collective entities comparable to peoples and nations.

Linguistic diversity is further protected by the inclusion of language among the forbidden grounds for discrimination in the Charter of Fundamental Rights and the TEU.

D. Diversity and Minorities Safeguarded by Anti-discrimination Law

The fourth dimension comprises those characteristics which are specifically protected from discrimination. For these characteristics the Nice Charter does not employ the word 'diversity', except in the case of culture, language and religion, and yet each of them is undoubtedly an expression of a form of diversity. The risk of discrimination identified on the historical and social level, to which specific legal safeguards correspond, is in fact by definition connected to the diversity borne by individuals or groups, which is itself the reason for the unfavourable treatment inflicted on them. From the catalogue contained in article 21 of the Nice Charter, the broadest statement of discrimination grounds in Union's primary law, it is possible to derive the commitment of the Union to recognise and protect diversity of sex, race, skin colour or ethnic or social origin, genetic characteristics, language, religion or personal beliefs, political or any other opinion, belonging to a national minority, property, birth, disability, age or sexual orientation.

Analogously, a minority qualifying for protection is implicitly defined as any group of individuals united by one of these characteristics, and of a numeric presence such as to distinguish it, by virtue of this characteristic, from a majority. Apart from the case, which is made explicit in the Nice Charter, of national minorities, linguistic minorities in particular come to mind. They are not recognised expressly in primary EU law, yet they are expressly protected in national and international law. Even if primary law does not explicitly recognise minorities other than national minorities, the broad and general recognition of minorities in the Lisbon Treaty reinforces the tie between the characteristic protected against discrimination and the protection of possible minorities united by the characteristic in question. In some cases, such as that of linguistic or religious minorities, there is a clearly established connection between grounds for discrimination, dynamic forms of social and political recognition and the relevant legal protection of minorities. In other cases, such as that of the equality of gender and the rights connected to sexual orientation, the identification for example of a LGBTQI (*Lesbian, Gay, Bisexual, Transgender, Queer, Intersex*) minority is certainly founded on a socio-political reality, but still legally problematic.

Supposing one can proceed from characteristics protected against discrimination to implicitly recognised and protected forms of diversity and minorities, this occurs with different degrees of intensity of protection, on the basis of the characteristic in question and of the corresponding source in Union's law. According to this methodology, the following categories can be identified:

(a) diversity protected through the mechanism of article 19 TFEU, that is, through measures which might be taken by the Council to 'combat discrimination based on sex, racial or ethnic origin, religion or belief, disability, age or sexual orientation';
(b) diversity protected under secondary legislation, in particular regarding the super-protected factors of sex and race, thanks to directive 2000/43/EC, which forbids racial discrimination, and directives 2004/113/EC and 2006/54/EC, which forbid discrimination based on sex and regarding employment, while directive 2000/78/EC forbids discrimination based on 'religion or belief, disability, age or sexual orientation';
(c) diversity protected through the fundamental rights of freedom, as in chapter II of the Charter of Fundamental Rights. In various ways, this diversity reflects individual or collective articulations of the freedom of private and family life (articles 7 and 9), of thought, conscience and religion (articles 10 and 14(3)), of expression of opinion (article 11), of assembly and association (article 12), of the arts and sciences (article 13), the right to education (article 14) and property (article 17);
(d) diversity of sex/gender, the only one for which the Nice Charter employs the expression 'equality', thus reinforcing the protection established by the dimension of non-discrimination with a principle of equality and the legitimisation of affirmative measures in favour of the disadvantaged sex. In particular, according to article 23, '[t]he principle of equality shall not prevent the maintenance or adoption of measures providing for specific advantages in favour of the under-represented sex'. Alongside protection of the diversity of sex/gender is now to be found, at least in the jurisprudence of the Strasbourg and Luxembourg courts, what article 3 of directive 2006/54/EC defines as discrimination 'arising from the gender reassignment of a person';
(e) diversity of age, with particular reference to children and the elderly. In this case, beyond the general ban on discrimination based on age, articles 24 and 25 of the Nice Charter articulate the contents of the rights to protection of the two categories. According to article 24, children 'shall have the right to such protection and care as is necessary for their well-being' and '[t]hey may express their views freely', which is to be taken into consideration 'on matters which concern them in accordance with their age and maturity'. In all actions relating to children, whether taken by public authorities or private institutions, 'the child's best interests must be a primary consideration'. In this respect, '[e]very child shall have the right to maintain on a regular basis a personal relationship and direct contact with both his or her parents, unless that is contrary to his or her interests'. Regarding the elderly, article 25 establishes recognition and respect on the part of the Union for the 'rights of the elderly to lead a life of dignity and independence and to participate in social and cultural life';
(f) diversity of disability. Here too the Charter does not limit itself to non-discrimination based on disability, but positively adopts the principle of 'integration', stating in article 26 that '[t]he Union recognises and respects the right of persons with disabilities to benefit from measures designed to ensure their independence, social and occupational integration and participation in the life of the community';

(g) the dimension of diversity of religion or beliefs. This diversity is recognised and protected in six different ways: (1) the preamble of the TEU recognises the inspiration deriving from the 'religious and humanist inheritance of Europe', therefore considering religion as a pluralistic, diverse element; (2) article 22 of the Charter of Fundamental Rights recognises expressly 'religious diversity' along with cultural and linguistic diversity; (3) anti-discriminatory legislation protects implicitly religious diversity in the Nice Charter (article 21 forbids discrimination based on 'religion or belief') and in article 19 TFEU; (4) religious diversity is protected, again implicitly, in secondary legislation, in particular in the 2000 directive on employment discrimination, and (5) by norms on human rights, as in chapter II of the Charter of Fundamental Rights, and specifically in articles 10 and 14(3) on freedom of thought, conscience and religion and of manifestation of religion or belief, and the connected prerogatives of the parents in the education of their children; and finally (6) religious diversity is implicitly protected, in its institutional dimension, by article 17 TFEU, in particular in paragraph 3 whereby the Union recognises 'the identity and the specific contribution' of 'churches and religious associations or communities' and 'philosophical and non-confessional organisations'.

From the seven dimensions of diversity derives a complex picture, whose entirety can be observed and interpreted only if multiple viewpoints are adopted. The overall picture of diversity depends on the following aspects: (a) the boundaries and the contents of each type of diversity; (b) the interaction between one diversity and the other and in particular their collaboration (when several kinds of diversity lend themselves to being combined by the actors so as to strengthen one another) and competition (when on the other hand the actors employ one kind of diversity against another); (c) their position in the hierarchy of legal sources; (d) the degree of their legal protection; (e) their development in secondary legislation and in the Union's policies; and (f) the relationship of each type of diversity with the principle of non-discrimination and with anti-discriminatory protection.

Besides being diachronic, as is indicated in the first part of this essay, and systemic, as is indicated in its second part, the development of anti-discrimination protection and protection of diversity and minorities is also geopolitical. In that sense, the globalisation of the last decades, and the historical phase beginning in the new millennium with the attack on the Twin Towers (2001) and the wars in Afghanistan (beginning in 2001 and still ongoing) and in Iraq (2003–11), the economic-financial collapse and the migration crisis have exposed the European project to a double tension, both from within and from without. The emergence of new diversities and new minorities underlie this tension, and challenge the project of unity in diversity and anti-discriminatory protection.

Religious diversity is a crucial test for European integration in general and in particular for anti-discrimination policies and the protection of diversity and minorities, as demonstrated by the European Court of Justice rulings in cases pertaining to the definition of religious persecution (judgment of 05.09.2012, *Bundesrepublik Deutschland v Y and Z*, joint cases C-71/11 and C-99/11), on conscientious objection in order to acquire the right of asylum (ruling of 26.02.2015, *Andre Lawrence Shepherd v Bundesrepublik Deutschland*, C-472/13) and on discrimination for the prohibition to wear an Islamic veil at the workplace (judgment of 14.03.2017, *Achbita and Bougnaoui*, C-157/15).

III. The Religious Dimension of Non-discrimination

Two factors explain why religious diversity occupies a special place in the architecture of non-discrimination within the European Union: first, the general importance of religion in the private life of individuals and groups and in the public life of European societies; secondly, the specific importance of religious diversity in European history in general and the history of European integration in particular.

On the first level, religion is a decisive factor in the life of individuals. It matters for those who believe and follow the precepts of their own faith in its rites and in every aspect of their lives. Religion consequently has a significance also for those who, though not believing, find themselves inevitably in contact with believers and experience the effects of the beliefs and practices of those believers. In particular, religion conditions the approach of individuals and groups to the diversity which is safeguarded by the European Union. Indeed, the religious factor has an impact in terms of traditions and identity, culture, politics, individual and collective psychology and, most immediately, through the role that religious institutions, communities and authorities play in legitimating or fighting discrimination.

On the second level, the weight of religious diversity in European history and in particular in European integration needs to be taken into account.

Religious diversity manifests in European history first through three large categories of diversity:

(a) diversity among Abrahamic religions of the Mediterranean basin: Judaism, Christianity and Islam;
(b) the internal diversity within each religion: for example in Christianity, between Protestants, Catholics and Orthodox Christians, in Judaism between Reformed and Orthodox Judaism, in Islam between the Shia and the Sunni; and
(c) the internal diversity of every Christian Church: for instance in Protestantism between the Evangelical Lutherans and Calvinists, in Orthodox Christianity between the various Patriarchates, and in the Church of Rome between Polish and Spanish Catholics.

Another category needs to be added to the three large categories of internal diversity in the religious world: namely, that between believers and non-believers, which took on particular cultural, socio-political and even legal significance with the process of secularisation, by virtue of which the religious space in the public sphere has been limited, religious practice and faith have declined, and religion itself has been called into question. Diversity within the religious world and diversity between religion and non-religion feature in European history with enormous individual and collective variations, with mixed and mobile identities and practices, which have rendered the landscape particularly complex and diverse.

European religious diversity has characterised the political formations and the legal profile of the national States. The peace of Westphalia (1648) established the union between throne and altar through State confessionalism – the 'establishment of religion', in the terminology arising from the experience of the Church of England's secession from Rome and the connected supremacy of the king over the national Church (1534).

Elsewhere in Europe, under the Ottoman Empire, a new management of religious diversity was being attempted. While in confessional Christian Europe the emergent citizenship was made to coincide with membership to the State Church, in the Ottoman Empire a system of personal statutes determined by the religious confession of reference ruled, with significant advantages for Muslims.

The European path is therefore characterised by the evolution of the relations between religious majorities and minorities internally, wherever the history of religious freedom coincided with the progressive enfranchisement of individuals and groups who did not conform to the dominant population and faith, and externally, wherever the European States intervened in defence of Christian minorities – in particular in the Ottoman Empire – or clashed in the colonies with unknown forms of religious diversity, as happened in India with Hindu-Muslim syncretism or in the Far East with Confucianism and Taoism.

At the beginning of the twentieth century, the religious persecutions of modern Europe seemed distant, but religious diversity and protection of religious minorities remained dramatically relevant in the conflicts of the old continent. Complicity of some Christians and Christian communities with Nazism and Fascism, and the signing of the agreement between the Holy See and Benito Mussolini (1929) and Adolf Hitler (1933), did not prevent the persecution of many Christians and coincided with the extermination of the Jews and the Jehovah's Witnesses. Communist Russia imposed State atheism through bloodshed. In the colonies, meanwhile, religious diversity inflamed the fight for national independence: in 1948 the British partition in India and Palestine opened a long phase of religiously-motivated conflicts and massacres.

A. Religious Diversity in the Project of the Single Market

After World War II, religious diversity was crucial to the project of European integration. The Universal Declaration of Human Rights of 1948 and the European Convention of 1950 proclaimed religious freedom. The bipolar division of the world between the free capitalist market and the planned economy, between liberal democracy and Marxism-Leninism, dramatised the diversity between believers and non-believers. On the other side of the curtain, State atheism translated into large-scale religious oppression and persecution. The American model, on the other hand, reconciled non-confessional religious freedom (the establishment of religion is prohibited by the US Constitution) and capitalist liberal democracy. Seemingly the religious factor contributed to European integration only insofar as freedom of religion and increasing acceptance of religious diversity were central to the human rights narrative. The religious element seemed to be absent from the Treaty of Rome and from integration through the single market. In reality, the contribution of religion to the single market was fundamental, in the form of theoretical resources (Christian thought on free trade and on the autonomy of civil society), economic resources (Christian and Jewish entrepreneurs), employment and political resources (labour unions and Christian parties), not to speak of the direct commitment of Churches and faith communities to the market place, private property and capitalism.

As far as the free market was then progressively realised, the law of the European Union has established an area of free movement of services, capital, goods and persons for faith communities as well, which is to say, an open space for religious competition.

Religious actors are now invited to a playground very similar to the American free market of faiths. Minority religions and especially new religious movements such as the Church of Scientology, which are still struggling with the fundamental inequality of national laws on religions, find an involuntary ally in the European Union. Mainstream Churches, on the other hand, feel exposed: the protection still guaranteed to them by national laws is indeed threatened by the anti-protectionist expansion of Union law. Midway through the 1990s, while the Treaty of Amsterdam was being negotiated, the religious actors who most stood to lose from the impact of the Union on religious national protectionisms expressed their concern regarding a Union system which was more hospitable toward religious diversity and more egalitarian in its internal law, thus favouring new religious movements. With declaration No. 11, annexed to the Treaty of Amsterdam, in which the Union purports not to prejudice the status of the Churches and religious communities as regulated in national law, a process was initiated which would culminate ten years later, with the Lisbon Treaty in the first two paragraphs of article 17 TFEU, according to which:

1. The Union respects and does not prejudice the status under national law of churches and religious associations or communities in the Member States.
2. The Union equally respects the status under national law of philosophical and non-confessional organisations.

Commonly interpreted as a rule excluding the competence of the European Union on the status of religious communities, thus reassuring the majority Churches anxious about losing their advantageous domestic legal status, article 17 has in reality a very limited sphere of influence. On the one hand, the reality of religion can hardly be squeezed into what might correspond to a clearly defined field of competence; on the other hand religious actors constantly invade the territories of Union competence, from employment to culture, from asylum right to social enterprise. A European law on religion is by now a reality: the jurisprudence of the European Court of Human Rights is certainly an essential part of it, but the law of the European Union also contributes to it significantly, starting with its anti-discrimination laws.

B. Religious Non-discrimination in Employment

European Union law has a profoundly ambivalent relation with religious diversity. On the one hand it protects it, and even incentivises it, in the name of that freedom of choice on which the market is founded; on the other hand it recognises its specificity and its fragility and it protects it from the market. The fullest manifestation of this ambivalence – of a religious diversity protected simultaneously through and against the market – is the anti-discrimination law's approach to religion, in particular through the directive on employment discrimination.

On the one hand, the directive includes religion among the characteristics protected from discrimination: the widest religious diversity is thus safeguarded according to the egalitarian and liberal-competitive logic of the single market. On the other hand, however, the directive concerns itself with public or private employers, 'the ethos of which is based on religion or belief' and exempts them under certain conditions, from respecting the principle of non-discrimination.

Thus in this connection article 4(2) of directive 2000/78/EC reads:

> in the case of occupational activities within churches and other public or private organisations the ethos of which is based on religion or belief, a difference of treatment based on a person's religion or belief shall not constitute discrimination where, by reason of the nature of these activities or of the context in which they are carried out, a person's religion or belief constitute a genuine, legitimate and justified occupational requirement, having regard to the organisation's ethos. This difference of treatment shall be implemented taking account of Member States' constitutional provisions and principles, as well as the general principles of Community law, and should not justify discrimination on another ground.

The directive therefore carries in itself two polarities which stand in tension to one another: it defends religious diversity through non-discrimination and defends religious diversity (of the employer) from non-discrimination.

The directive on employment has profoundly influenced national laws on religious freedom, above all in the United Kingdom through the Human Rights Act. The directive has also been central to decisions of the European Court of Justice (as in the aforementioned *Achbita* and *Bougnaoui* cases of 2017) and of the European Court of Human Rights (as in the decisions of 23.09.2010, *Schüth v Germany*, No. 1620/03, and *Obst v Germany*, No. 425/03; of 09.07.2013, *Sindicatul Pâstorul cel Bun v Romania*, No. 2330/09, and of 12.06.2014, *Fernández Martínez v Spain*, No. 56030/07).

C. The Dialogue of the European Union with Religious and Philosophical Organisations

While the expansive force of anti-discrimination law and of the Union's policies, and the uncontrollable trajectories of religious diversity reveal the impossibility of any political project aimed at shielding European law on religion from the law of the European Union, religious organisations multiply efforts to interact with EU decision-makers and bodies. Article 17 TFEU itself, whose first two paragraphs would establish the Union's commitment to 'not prejudice' the status of religion, enshrines in its third paragraph the principle of cooperation between the Union and religious actors: 'Recognising their identity and their specific contribution, the Union shall maintain an open, transparent and regular dialogue with these churches and organisations.'

Through the cooperative principle of article 17, a fundamental peculiarity of the European Union's approach to religious diversity is set out, and also of European integration in its entirety: that is to say, equality toward the end of protecting religion and non-religious belief.

Since the decision in the *Kokkinakis* case (judgment of 25.05.1993), the European Court of Human Rights has clarified that the textual reference of article 9 ECHR to the 'freedom to manifest one's religion or beliefs' represents 'in its religious dimension, one of the most vital elements that go to make up the identity of believers and their conception of life, but it is also a precious asset for atheists, agnostics, sceptics and the unconcerned.' Subsequent developments consolidated the concept of the unity of freedom of thought, conscience and religion, synthesised in the expression 'freedom of religion or belief' and its acronym FoRB coined by the Norwegian Centre for human rights. Freedom of religion or belief is now the key concept, and expression, for the various European institutions and the Union itself, which adopted it in the 2013 *EU guidelines on the promotion and protection of freedom of religion or belief*, drafted by the European External Action Service.

Article 17 TFEU recognised at the same time the 'Churches' and the 'religious associations or communities' and the 'philosophical and non-confessional organisations'. How equal this recognition really is, remains to be seen. The Holy See, for example, reads the article as excluding equivalence between the first organisations and the second. For its part, the *Ombudsman* of the European Union has found discriminatory the decision by the EU Commission to disregard the consultation request formulated by a philosophical and non-confessional organisation under the terms of article 17, third paragraph.

The English formula 'religion or belief' of article 9 of the ECHR and article 10 of the Charter of Fundamental Rights of the Union is the same used in the other sources of Union law, including article 19 TFEU and article 21 of the Charter of Fundamental Rights in the area of non-discrimination. The category 'religion or belief' therefore includes diversity within religious beliefs (encompassing old and new, large and small, majority and minority religions) and diversity between religious beliefs and non-religious beliefs.

The religious diversity of the European Union is thus a true diversity 'of religion and belief' in the sense that it does not limit itself to religions, but extends to every creed and conviction, including those of the atheists, agnostics, sceptics and unconcerned. This is a diversity recognised and protected, not only through anti-discrimination protection, but also through internal and external policies and, in particular, through the dialogue with religious and non-confessional organisations.

D. New Diversities and New Minorities

Diversity of religion or belief has changed profoundly during the construction of the European Union. New majorities and minorities have taken their place alongside the traditional ones in the European landscape. It is possible to identify the following categories: (1) majorities within the individual countries, and across them, which identify themselves with national and cultural traditions and identity, therefore attracting not only members of the relevant religion or church, but also non-believers. A majority of this kind was mobilised, for example, to defend the display of the crucifix in Italian public schools after the first 2009 ruling against it of the European Court of Human Rights in the *Lautsi* case, and obtained in 2011 a contrary appeal decision (judgment of 18.03.2011, *Lautsi and others v Italy*, application No. 30814/06); (2) mainly immigrant minorities who defend their own rules, as for example, the prescription to wear the veil, for reasons which are at the same time cultural and religious; (3) majorities variously composed of believers and non-believers, who support reforms opposed by many religious communities, such as the introduction of same-sex marriage; (4) minorities, also composed of believers and non-believers, who fight for the reform of consolidated aspects of the European law of religion, such as public funding of Churches; (5) ex-majorities that consider themselves to be 'new minorities', such as those Christians resorting to conscientious objection in order to display religious symbols or refuse complicity with homosexual couples (as in the *Eweida and others v Great Britain* case in 2013 (judgment of 27.05.2013, Application No. 36516/10, 48420/10, 51671/10, 59842/10).

New majorities and new minorities are interchangeable. They can deconstruct and reconstruct themselves, and in this way they reflect a European diversity in constant flux.

The general principle of the respect for diversity and minorities, and the non-discrimination law of the Union itself, lend themselves to the most various uses, instrumental to mutually contradictory claims and strategies.

Policies and the law change as European diversities change. The quest for recognition and protection coming from traditional diversities – such as those of religion, sex, race and nationality – is changing, and new diversities emerge, such as those related to sexual orientation and gender identity on the one hand and cultural identity on the other. The response of the European Union to these diversities, both new and old, will depend in a substantial way on its policies on information and communication technologies in a society deeply influenced by artificial intelligence. In 2012, within the EU Commission, the Directorate General for communications networks, content, and technology (DG Connect) has been created. In collaboration with the various institutions of the Union, DG Connect elaborates policies (from financing to research and cooperation with ICT and media companies) and legal measures for the protection of diversity in social media, the fight against fake news and incitement to hatred, the promotion of quality journalism, and awareness regarding the function of algorithms and the ethics of information technology. The challenge for non-discrimination, diversity and the minorities in Europe is now situated in the intersection between the physical world and the virtual space, between human and artificial intelligences, between human beings and machines.

Bibliography

Beaman, L, *Deep equality in an era of religious diversity* (Oxford, 2017).

Bell, M, *Anti-discrimination law and the European Union* (Oxford, 2002).

Cavilli, C, *La non discriminazione nell'Unione Europea* (Bologna, 2008).

Chege, V, *Multidimensional discrimination in EU law: sex, race and ethnicity* (Baden-Baden, 2011).

Coglievina, S, *Diritto antidiscriminatorio e religione. Uguaglianza, diversità e libertà religiosa in Italia, Francia e Regno Unito* (Tricase, 2013).

Ellis, E, *EU anti-discrimination law* (Oxford 1999, 2015).

Fuchs, D and Klingemann, H-D (eds), *Cultural diversity, European identity and the legitimacy of the EU* (Cheltenham-Northampton, 2011).

Hill, M (ed) *Religion and discrimination law in the European Union*, Proceedings of the 23rd Congress of the European consortium for Church and State research (University of Oxford 2011, 2012).

McCrea, R, *Religion and the public order of the European Union* (Oxford, 2010).

Stiglitz, J, *The price of inequality* (London, 2012).

Tizzano, A (ed) *Verso i 60 anni dai Trattati di Roma: Stato e prospettive dell'Unione Europea* (Turin, 2016).

Tridimas, T, *The general principles of EC law* (Oxford, 2006).

Ventura, M, *La laicità dell'Unione Europea. Diritti, mercato, religione* (Torino, 2001).

Ventura, M, *Libertà religiosa e divieto di discriminazione nel diritto dell'Unione Europea* 2010 (3–4) *Il diritto ecclesiastico* 487–96.

Ventura, M, 'L'articolo 17 TFUE come fondamento del diritto e della politica ecclesiastica dell'Unione Europea' (2014) 2 *Quaderni di diritto e politica ecclesiastica* 293–304.

13

The European Union: An Area for Freedom, Security and Justice

BRUNO NASCIMBENE

The creation of 'an area of freedom, security and justice' (AFSJ) appears among the main objectives pursued by the European Union (EU). Indeed, under article 3(2) of the Treaty on European Union (TEU, in force since 1 December 2009, as amended by the Lisbon Treaty), '[t]he Union shall offer its citizens an area of freedom, security and justice without internal frontiers, in which the free movement of persons is ensured in conjunction with appropriate measures with respect to external border controls, asylum, immigration and the prevention and combating of crime'.

The Union shall not only 'offer' this area of freedom, security and justice, but shall 'constitute' it, as laid down in article 67 of the Treaty on the Functioning of the European Union (TFEU, in force since 1 December 2009, following the changes introduced by the Lisbon Treaty to the Treaty establishing the European Community, TEC).

Under the Treaty of Maastricht – in force since 1 November 1993, it established the European Union and modified the Treaty establishing the European Economic Community (TEEC, the so-called Treaty of Rome, in force since 1 January 1958) – and under the Treaty of Amsterdam – in force since 1 May 1999 – the area is determined, at first on a limited basis – with the Treaty of Maastricht providing (article B) that one of the objectives of the Union is 'to develop close cooperation on the justice and home affairs' – and then in a broader (in relation to justice and home affairs) and more contemporary form. The subsequent Treaty of Amsterdam (article 2) provides, in fact, that one of the Union's objectives is to 'maintain and develop the Union as an area of freedom, security and justice, in which the free movement of persons is assured in conjunction with appropriate measures with respect to external border controls, asylum, immigration and the prevention and combating of crime'. The 'communitisation' of the area, following the abolition – as pointed out below – of the 'three-pillar' structure that made up the European 'construct', takes place in its entirety, only with the entry into force of the Lisbon Treaty.

The reason for the tardy creation of area lies in the fact that, in the beginning, the main objective of the three European Communities was to constitute an 'economic Europe', and the integration process was indeed limited to economic aspects. Subsequently, integration also became political and social, with the consequence that the creation of an area of freedom, security and justice became an indispensable part of it.

There is no definition of an 'area of freedom, security and justice' to be found in the Treaties and in the secondary acts. It is therefore necessary to deduce it from other sources.

While it first began as a judicial area, we shall see that over time different profiles were added, such as immigration, asylum, cooperation in criminal matters and among law enforcement agencies. Freedom, security and justice can be considered cornerstones of the European integration model, contributing to the construction of a common area in which citizens move freely and receive effective protection.

I. A Historical Reconstruction

At the start of the integration process, the only traces relating to the subject were to be found in article 220 of the TEEC: it stated that the Member States would enter into negotiations with a view to securing the protection of persons, the mutual recognition of companies and simplification of the formalities governing the reciprocal recognition and enforcement of judgments of courts and of arbitration awards.

The slow (and belated) creation of an area of freedom, security and justice begins, as we said, with the Treaty of Maastricht, which created a Union founded on three 'pillars': the European Communities, the common and foreign security policy (CFSP) and cooperation on justice and home affairs (JHA). The subject matter thus fell into the third pillar, inserting a new title VI into the TEU (*Provisions relating to cooperation in the areas of justice and home affairs*, articles K-K9).

With the Treaty of Amsterdam, a few third-pillar matters – such as asylum, visa, immigration, and other policies related to free movement and judicial cooperation in civil matters – were shifted to the first pillar (articles 61–69, TEU, title VI). However, its communitisation was only partial, as it excluded police and judicial cooperation in criminal matters that remained in the third pillar, characterised by intergovernmental cooperation (articles 29–42 TEU, title VI).

As we have mentioned, the Lisbon Treaty completed the process of communitisation, by abolishing the three pillars and unifying the regulations in this area in part III, title V of the TFEU (*Area of freedom, security and justice*, articles 67–89). The whole subject has thus been subject to the common rules of the Treaties, except for some peculiarities in relation to the other Union's internal policies.

II. Objectives and Characteristics

The objectives to be pursued with the creation of the AFSJ are: (a) ensure the absence of internal border controls for persons; (b) frame a common policy on asylum, immigration and external border control; (c) ensure a high level of security; and (d) facilitate access to justice (article 67, TFEU).

The area must be constituted in compliance with fundamental rights and the different legal systems and traditions of the Member States, pursuant to article 67 TFEU. This provision contains an implicit reference to article 6 TEU, to the Charter of Fundamental Rights of the European Union (also known as the Charter of Nice, signed on 7 December 2000 in the French city by the European Parliament, the Council and the Commission; modified by the same institutions on 12 December 2007 in Strasbourg), to the rights protected by the European Convention for the Protection of Human Rights and Fundamental Freedoms (better known as the European Convention on Human Rights, ECHR, signed on 4 November 1950 in Rome) and those derived from the constitutional traditions common to EU countries.

The protection of fundamental rights and national interests must be balanced. The Union proposes to operate in an area where States have always tried to preserve their sovereignty: it is precisely for this reason that the Union must take due account of national needs and prerogatives. A general reference to respect the 'national identities, inherent in their fundamental structures, political and constitutional' of the Member States, is contained in article 4(2) TEU, and a specific reference, in relation to establishing the area, to the 'different legal systems and traditions' of the Member States, is made in article 67(1) TFEU.

The possibility of activating the so-called emergency brake mechanism (articles 82(3) and 83(3) TFEU) is a clear manifestation of this principle. Indeed, when a Member State considers that a draft directive would affect fundamental aspects of its criminal justice system, it may request that the ordinary legislative procedure in the context of judicial cooperation in criminal matters (approximation of criminal law, both procedural and substantive) be suspended. The same purpose can be attached to the exercise of the responsibilities incumbent upon Member States with regard to the maintenance of law and order and the safeguarding of internal security (article 72, TFEU), as they are entitled to introduce exceptions to rules of EU law. Under this provision, Member States are authorised to adopt acts even where the Union has exercised its competence, thereby derogating from Union law.

The nature of the competence over this 'area' is shared (article 4, letter j, TFEU). The Union's proposals and legislative initiatives must comply with the principles of subsidiarity and proportionality, the respect of which national Parliaments are specifically called upon to monitor (article 69, TFEU, which refers to protocol No. 2 on the application of the principles of subsidiarity and proportionality). Member States, on the other hand, may intervene to the extent that the EU has not exercised its competence or decided to cease exercising it. As a rule, legislative texts are adopted according to the ordinary legislative procedure (ex article 294, TFEU), with a clear strengthening of the European Parliament compared to the past, when its role was only marginal. Though less relevant today, there is still 'competition' between the integration method and that of intergovernmental cooperation, providing for the exclusive competence of the States or unanimity (legal immigration, article 79(5), TFEU; geographical demarcation of borders, article 77(4); matters pertaining to the free movement of persons, such as passports, identity cards, residence permits or similar documents, article 77(3)), or enhanced cooperation in the context of judicial cooperation in civil matters concerning family law with cross-border implications (article 81(3)), of judicial cooperation in criminal matters and police cooperation (articles 82(3), 83(3), 86(1), 87(3)).

Some Member States participate differently in the AFSJ (the so-called differentiated application). In particular, Denmark does not take part in the adoption of measures under title V of the TFEU, with the exception of measures determining the third countries whose nationals must be in possession of a visa when crossing the external borders of the Member States, and those representing a development of the so-called Schengen acquis, which will be discussed shortly (protocol No. 22).

The United Kingdom and Ireland, on the other hand, participate only in the adoption and application of specific measures, as a result of an opting-in decision, a clause which allows the State to participate on a case-by-case basis in the adoption of a measure or application of a measure already adopted (protocol No. 21).

III. The AFSJ Sectors

The area of freedom, security and justice consists of four different sectors: the area of freedom (policies relating to border controls, asylum and immigration), judicial cooperation in civil matters, judicial cooperation in criminal matters, police cooperation.

As well as an 'internal' dimension, the area also features an 'external' dimension, since the Union may conclude agreements and arrangements or implement forms of cooperation with third-party States and international organisations, in parallel with the creation of an internal policy. On the subject of immigration, see article 79(3) TFEU on the conclusion of readmission agreements (and the Commission communication COM[2011] 743 of 18 November 2011, *The global approach to migration and mobility*); on combating terrorism and organised crime (and on the transfer of passenger name record (PNR) data), see the approach taken by the Court of Justice (judgment of 30.05.2006, *Parliament v Council and Commission*, C-317/04 and C-318/04, ECLI:EU:C:2006:346), as well as the approach taken by the Court on judicial cooperation in civil matters and the competence to conclude agreements (opinion 1/03, 7 February 2006, *Competence of the Community to conclude the new Lugano Convention on jurisdiction and the recognition and enforcement of judgments in civil and commercial matters*, ECLI:EU:C.2006:81).

IV. The Area of Freedom

Recent events – such as the so-called crisis in the Mediterranean – have placed the issues of asylum, immigration and external border controls at the centre of public and political attention. The absence of a common policy, or its shortcomings, on the subject matters indicated has been the subject of extensive scrutiny, drawing also criticism and disapproval.

The area of freedom is governed by a common principle: that of solidarity and fair sharing of responsibility among States. For the purpose of applying this principle, the Union has the power to adopt 'appropriate measures' (article 80, TFEU).

The rationale stems from the fact that Member States, in particular because of their geographical position, are subject to different pressure from immigration and, consequently, have different burdens to meet.

The European Parliament has recently highlighted the need to adopt a holistic approach to border management based on the principle of solidarity, which strengthens the common asylum policy, in order to reduce the migratory pressure on the States hosting the largest number of refugees and asylum seekers (resolution of 29 April 2015, 2015/2660[RSP]). However, it is far from simple to establish the extent of equitable burden-sharing and how to promote these actions among the Member States.

The so-called Schengen agreements underpin the evolution of the regulatory system. They are also defined as Schengen acquis, and are made up of a series of acts relating to the gradual phasing out of checks at common borders between various EU countries, and include: the actual Schengen Agreement (officially the Agreement between the governments of the States of the Benelux Economic Union, the Federal Republic of Germany and the French Republic on the gradual abolition of checks at their common borders) signed in Schengen, Luxembourg, on 14 June 1985; the Schengen Convention (officially the Convention implementing the Schengen Agreement), signed in Schengen on 19 June 1990; the various international application and implementation acts.

Although they essentially address the issue of border controls, as mentioned, these agreements have influenced the creation of the area of freedom, security and justice (and still do). The legal framework resulting from the cooperation falls within the EU system under a special protocol (No. 19), since not all Member States had signed these agreements. Integration was achieved through 'enhanced cooperation' among Member States in the institutional and legal framework of the Union (on the definition of enhanced cooperation, see article 20, TEU, and on the implementation of judicial cooperation in civil matters see the concerns on the specific point, infra). The positions of the United Kingdom, Ireland and Denmark with respect to the Schengen acquis, on the other hand, are governed by specific protocols (Nos. 21 and 22).

The area of freedom (articles 77–80, TFEU) is divided into three common policies concerning: (a) border control; (b) asylum; (c) immigration.

As regards border control, the Union is developing a policy aimed at establishing a common management of external borders and at eliminating internal border controls (article 77, TFEU).

An area without internal border controls requires adequate and standardised checks at external borders, in order to safeguard the free movement of people internally, and prevent threats to public order, security and public health in the Member States. The central pillar governing this aspect is represented by the so-called Schengen Borders Code (EU regulation 2016/399, 9 March 2016): it establishes the requirements and conditions that foreigners must satisfy for entry and short stay.

Currently, the so-called Schengen area (consisting of European countries that, according to the Schengen acquis, have abolished checks on people at their common borders) is made up of 26 countries (of which 22 are Member States of the Union). External borders are defined on a residual basis, such as those between a Schengen State and a non-Schengen State. Therefore, the borders with non-Schengen Member States (such as Bulgaria, Croatia, Cyprus, Ireland, Romania and the United Kingdom) are considered external. On the other hand, internal borders are those with States which are not part of the EU, but which participate in this area (Iceland, Liechtenstein, Norway and Switzerland).

Given that to identify geographically a country's borders (in accordance with international law) falls under the exclusive competence of the Member States (under article 77(4), TFEU, as we have said), the Schengen Borders Code provides that the entry of nationals of third-party countries into the Schengen area is subject to the fulfilment of five cumulative and comprehensive conditions: (a) to have a valid travel document; (b) to hold a valid visa (if required, pursuant to EC Regulation 539/2001, 15 March 2001); (c) to justify the purpose and conditions of the intended stay and have sufficient means of subsistence; (d) not being the subject of a Schengen Information System alert (article 24 of EC Regulation 1987/2006,

20 December 2006); (e) not be considered a threat to public policy, internal security, public health or the international relations of any of the Member States.

In 2005 Frontex (the European Agency for the Management of Operational Cooperation at the External Borders, EC Regulation 2007/2004, 26 October 2004) was set up for coordinating border control efforts in a more incisive way, providing support especially to those Member States facing the greatest pressure from immigration. Frontex was transformed into a fully-fledged European Border and Coast Guard Agency (EU Regulation 2016/1624, 14 September 2016), in coordination with the border and coast guards of Schengen Area Member States. Endowed with a revised, more extended mandate, and with more incisive powers than Frontex (having considerably more financial resources, personnel and equipment available), the new Agency aims to bridge those operational gaps that had been singled out for criticism over the years, especially by those countries (like Italy) most affected by migration and asylum flows.

Inherent to border controls are powers such as the exercise of inspection and enforcement, with the risk of affecting people's fundamental rights. In this regard, the Schengen Borders Code provides that checks must be carried out with due respect for human dignity, the principle of proportionality and the prohibition of discrimination, as well as international protection obligations and the principle of non-refoulement. It is up to the national legal systems to ensure adequate and effective means of redress in any case of violation of these rights. The Schengen Borders Code also provides for 'a Community Code on the rules governing the movement of persons across borders' (on the protection of fundamental rights see, among others: the Court of Justice judgment of 17.01.2013, C-23/12, *Mohamad Zakaria*, ECLI:EU:2013:C:24, esp. paragraph 40; the European Court of human rights ruling of 23.02.2012, *Hirsi Jamaa and others v Italy*, appeal 27765/09). Indeed, checks at internal borders are prohibited regardless of a person's citizenship. They can only be reintroduced in the event of a serious threat to public policy or internal security.

Despite the 'last resort' nature of these checks, since 2015 they have been temporarily reinstated by many European countries – with reasons that can be traced back to public policy and national security – mainly due to the exceptional inflow of migrants as well as concerns over terrorist attacks. The situation seemed critical enough as to imperil the capacity of some States to fulfil their commitments undertaken in all areas of the Schengen acquis. This led the European Commission to draw up a 'roadmap' to restore the normal functioning of the Schengen system (COM[2016] 120 final, 4 March 2016) in full. Also, the situation is even more complex on account of the internal border controls that six States (Austria, Denmark, France, Germany, Norway and Sweden) are currently keeping in place (on the functioning of the derogation system, see article 29 of the Schengen Borders Code).

On the subject of asylum, the Union shall develop a common policy on asylum, subsidiary protection and temporary protection with a view to offering appropriate status to any third-country national requiring international protection and ensuring compliance with the principle of non-refoulement (article 78, TFEU). In a free-movement area without internal borders, a common asylum policy must necessarily be adopted. The flows of asylum seekers are not constant, and EU Member States have a shared responsibility to receive and accommodate them in a dignified manner, guaranteeing fair treatment and ensuring that their case will be examined according to standard rules. The 1951 Geneva Convention on the status of refugees (expressly referred to in article 78, TFEU) represents the cornerstone of the international legal framework on asylum, as defined in 2011 by the EU's so-called qualifications directive (directive 2011/95/EU, 13 December 2011), and by the Court of Justice in some of its rulings (see, eg, judgment of 02.03.2010, *Aydin Salahadin Abdulla and others v Bundesrepublik Deutschland*, joined cases C-175/08, C-176/08, C-178/08 and C-179/08, ECLI:EU:C:2010:105; judgment of 19.12.2012, *Mostafa Abed El Karem El Kott and others v Bevándorlási és Állampolgársági Hivatal*, C-364/11, ECLI:EU:C:2012:826).

The Union has implemented the principles enshrined in the Convention, but offers a broader and more favourable framework for those seeking protection. This protection includes not only asylum, but also subsidiary and temporary protection. Thanks to the communitisation of the subject, a set of rules has been established that constitutes the Common European Asylum System (CEAS) that, along with the aforementioned qualification directive, includes: the so-called procedures directive (2013/32/EU, 26 June 2013); the so-called reception directive (2013/33/EU, 26 June 2013); the so-called displaced persons directive (2001/55/EC, 20 July 2001); the so-called Dublin III regulation (EU 604/2013, 26 June 2013); the so-called Eurodac regulation (EU 603/2013, 26 June 2013).

Foreign nationals subject to the risk of serious human rights violations in their own countries can therefore access three different forms of international protection, with different conditions and different levels of guarantees offered. The first form is that of refugee status, which is recognised to third-country nationals or stateless persons at risk of persecution in the country of their nationality or of habitual residence. The second form is that of subsidiary protection, granted to those at risk of suffering serious and unjustified harm in their country of origin. The third form is that of temporary protection, granted to displaced persons in the event of a massive inflow owing to their evacuation. It consists of a provisional and collective guarantee without individual determination whether members of the group of persons affected might be refugees under the Geneva Refugee Convention (article 78(2), letter a, b, c, TFEU).

A fundamental right relating to asylum is the right to non-refoulement, or the practice of not forcing refugees or asylum seekers to return to a country in which they are liable to be subjected to persecution. This principle is applicable to any form of transfer (forced or informal) and non-admission at the border, and exceptions apply when there are reasonable grounds for regarding the person as a danger to the security of the host country (on this principle see article 19(2) of the cited Charter of Fundamental Rights and a few Court of Justice rulings, including: judgment of 18.12.2014, *Center public d'action social d'Ottignies-Louvain-La Neuve v Moussa Abdida*, C-562/13, ECLI:EU:C:2014:2453, and judgment of 24.06.2015, *HT v Land Baden-Württemberg*, C-373/13, ECLI:EU:C:2015:413).

With regard to immigration, the Union undertakes to enforce a common policy aimed at ensuring the efficient management of migratory flows, the fair treatment of legally resident third-country nationals, the prevention and combating of illegal immigration and trafficking in human beings (article 79, TFEU). There are two types of actions in pursuit of this common policy: one in case of legal immigration; the other addresses illegal immigration. With regard to legal migrants, the Union is competent for adopting measures relating to the common visa policy and other short and long-term residence permits, to the conditions of entry and residence, and to the rights of legally resident third-country nationals. On the other hand, determining the volume of admission of third-country nationals for work purposes remains a matter responsibility for Member States to decide (the so-called reservation of sovereign rights: article 79(5), as mentioned above).

Regulations on legal immigration are still patchy, as they cover only a few, specific sectors, including: family reunion; the stay of long-term resident foreign nationals; the conditions of entry and residence of certain categories of workers, students, trainees, researchers, au pair workers; the set of rights guaranteed to employed persons (directives: 2003/86/EC, 22 September 2003; 2003/109/EC, 25 November 2003; 2016/801/EU, 11 May 2016; 2009/50/EC, 25 May 2009 ; 2014/36/EU, 26 February 2014; 2014/66/EU, 15 May 2014; 2011/98/EU, 13 December 2011).

Likewise, the Union has the power to adopt measures addressing illegal immigration and irregular stay, including expulsion and repatriation. The EU's main legislative instrument is the so-called returns directive (2008/115/EU, 16 December 2008), which has achieved minimal harmonisation in this area. It defines the common rules concerning the conditions, standards and procedures for returning illegally staying third-country nationals. In transposing the directive, a wide margin of discretion is left to the States that nonetheless must uphold fundamental rights, especially with regard to the principle of non-refoulement that must be effectively implemented so as not to frustrate its useful effect (on the interpretation and application of the directive, see the principles affirmed, among others, in the following Court of Justice judgments: 28.04.2011, *Hassen El Dridi*, C-61/11, ECLI:EU:C:2011:268; 06.12.2011, *Alexandre Achughbabian v Préfet du Val-de-Marne*, C-329/11, ECLI:EU:C:2011:807; 05.06.2014, *Bashir Mohamed Ali Mahdi*, C-146/14, ECLI:EU:C:2014:1320; 01.10.2015, *Skerdjan Celaj*, C-290/14, ECLI:EU:C:2015:640).

Furthermore, the Union has the power to conclude readmission agreements, consisting of international agreements with third-party countries that have committed themselves to readmit their nationals who entered a Member State irregularly. This type of agreement is viewed as a useful tool for combating illegal immigration, in a bid to break the business model of human traffickers and remove the financial incentive to enter the Union through illegal channels.

The cooperation between the Union and Turkey, about which ethical questions have been raised, is controversial by reason of a statement (issued by the European Council and the Turkish Government on 18 March 2016) in which it was agreed that all irregular migrants, new irregular migrants, and asylum seekers whose applications had been declared inadmissible, crossing from Turkey into the Greek islands as from 20 March 2016 would be returned to Turkey (the repatriations, as of 1 June 2016, are implemented on the basis of the so-called EU-Turkey Readmission Agreement, Council decision [EU] 2016/551 of 23 March 2016). The statement lacks the typical format of international agreements and has not been concluded according to the procedures specifically provided for in the Treaties (article 218, TFEU, which provides that the European Parliament be immediately and fully informed). The Court of the European Union has declared that it lacks jurisdiction to rule over the legitimacy of this act, skirting the issue of the repatriation of asylum seekers based on the highly contentious assumption that qualifies Turkey as a 'country of first asylum and safe third country', making it guarantor of the protection of fundamental rights (Court orders, 28 February 2017, *NF, NG and NM v European Council*, T-192/16, T-193/16 and T-257/16, ECLI:EU:T:2017:128,129,130).

With regard to combating crime and illegal immigration, including judicial cooperation in criminal matters (which will be discussed below), there is a clear need for a 'transversal' reading of the rules applying to irregular immigration and to judicial cooperation in criminal matters (on the fight against trafficking in human beings see articles 79(4), letter d, and 83(1), TFEU). As for the problems posed by the massive influx of asylum seekers and the shortcomings of the so-called Dublin system (addressing the right to asylum, it was established by the Dublin Convention – signed in that city on 15 June 1990 – and entered into force on 1 September 1997) – given the risk that asylum seekers may be transferred to a Member State that is responsible for examining an asylum application but is unable to ensure treatment in accordance with article 4 of the Charter of Fundamental Rights and article 3 of the European Convention on Human Rights (prohibition of inhuman or degrading treatment) – the Court of Justice has taken, albeit indirectly, the view that the system is in need of reform (among the various judgments, see that of 21.12.2011, *NS v Secretary of State for the Home Department and ME and others v Refugee applications commissioner and minister for Justice, Equality and Law Reform*, joined cases C-411/10 and C-493/10, ECLI:EU:2011:865, recalling the approach taken by the European Court of Human Rights).

A. Judicial Cooperation in Civil Matters

The main objectives of judicial cooperation in civil matters are legal certainty and effective access to justice. Indeed, the diversity and complexity of the legal systems of the EU's Member States should not be a barrier to this, in the sense that citizens must not be hindered in exercising their rights. For this reason it is indispensable to have criteria for the easy identification of the competent court and for determining applicable law, as well as procedures for its rapid and effective recognition and/or enforcement.

The area under review is the one in which Member States first felt the need to establish a cooperation, initially between one another and, later, within the European Union: as we have seen, article 220 TEEC provided that Member States would 'so far as is necessary, enter into negotiations with each other with a view to securing for the benefit of their nationals [...] the simplification of formalities governing the reciprocal recognition and enforcement of judgments of courts or tribunals and of arbitration awards'. This provision laid the groundwork for the Brussels Convention of 27 September 1968 (on jurisdiction and the enforcement of judgments in civil and commercial matters), followed by the so-called Brussels I and then Brussels II regulations (more on that below).

Article 81 TFEU outlines the framework built around these rules, stipulating that the Union shall develop judicial cooperation in civil matters having cross-border implications, based on the principle of mutual recognition of judgments.

The object of the cooperation is the civil sphere: while the Treaty gives no clear definition thereof, the Court of Justice makes a contribution (in the negative sense) stating that a situation can be regarded as falling outside the scope of civil matters when a public authority is involved and it 'is acting in the exercise of its public powers' (see the judgment of 11.04.2013, *Land Berlin v Ellen Mirjam Sapir and others*, C-645/11, ECLI:EU:C:2013:228). The competence in question can be exercised only when the matter has cross-border implications, that is, only when the situation is connected to several States.

Just as with other sectors of the 'area', at the root of the whole system lies the principle of mutual trust between Member States; indeed, one of the ways of implementing this principle is through the mutual recognition of judicial and extrajudicial decisions. The latter case consists in allowing decisions issued in one Member State to have effects in other Member States, with the final aim of equating 'foreign' decisions to 'national' decisions.

With a view to developing this cooperation, the Union may adopt measures for the approximation of national provisions and regulations of the States. Normally, the adoption of legislative acts takes place according to the ordinary procedure, except in matters of family law with cross-border implications (where the unanimity of the Council is required, after consulting the European Parliament). In this matter (article 81(3), TFEU) the instrument of enhanced cooperation was relied on mainly because of the impossibility of achieving unanimity (see EU regulations: 1259/2010, 20 December 2010 in the area of the law applicable to divorce and legal separation; 2016/1103, 24 June 2016 in the area of jurisdiction, applicable law and the recognition and enforcement of decisions in matters of matrimonial property regimes; 2016/1104, 24 June 2016 in the area of jurisdiction, applicable law and the recognition and enforcement of decisions in matters of the property consequences of registered partnerships).

The European Union is competent to adopt harmonisation measures on matters that, firstly, fall under the scope of international private and procedural law: concerning jurisdiction, recognition and enforcement of judgments and extrajudicial decisions issued in another Member State, and on choice-of-law rules (acts concerning jurisdiction and the recognition and enforcement of judgments include: regulation [EC] 2201/2003, 27 November 2003, in matrimonial matters and the matters of parental responsibility; regulation [EU] 1215/2012, 12 December 2012, on jurisdiction and the recognition and enforcement of judgments in civil and commercial matters, the so-called Brussels II, which repealed [EC] 44/2001, 22 December 2000, so-called Brussels I, which succeeded the earlier Brussels Convention of 1968, as mentioned above; legislation on choice-of-law rules and issues relating to applicable law includes: regulation [EC] 593/2008, 17 June 2008, on the law applicable to contractual obligations, the so-called Rome I, and regulation [EC] 864/2007, 11 July 2007, the so-called Rome II).

In exercising its competence, the Union has mostly relied on the legislative instrument of the regulation, as it is more suited to bringing about a real unification of the rules, replacing those provisions contained in national laws. The legislative intervention focused mostly on sectoral policy areas, so that a comprehensive and overreaching body of rules on the subject was not drawn up after all: on the subject of family law, see the aforementioned legal instruments; on the subject of maintenance obligations (jurisdiction, applicable law, recognition and enforcement of decisions and cooperation in such matters), see regulation [EC] 4/2009, 18 December 2008; in matters of succession (jurisdiction, applicable law, recognition and enforcement of decisions, acceptance and enforcement of authentic instruments, and on the creation of a European Certificate of succession), regulation [EU] 650/2012, 4 July 2012; on insolvency proceedings, regulation [EC] 2015/848, 20 May 2015. A second aspect of the cooperation relates to activities aimed at cross-border cooperation between national courts, such as the taking of evidence and the service of documents in civil or commercial matters (regulations: EC 1206/2001, 28 May 2001; EC 1393/2007, 13 November 2007).

The Union is also competent for taking the necessary measures to ensure that citizens have simple and effective access to civil justice for the settlement of cross-border disputes (article 81, TFEU, article 47, Charter of Fundamental Rights; directive 2002/8/EC, 27 January 2003, and regulation EC 1896/2006, 12 December 2006, which deal with, respectively, the definition of minimum common rules relating to legal aid and the creation of a European order for payment procedure; also recalling directive 2008/52/EC, 21 May 2008, on certain aspects of mediation in civil and commercial matters).

B. Judicial Cooperation in Criminal Matters

The progressive removal of controls at the EU's internal borders has considerably facilitated the free movement of European citizens; however, it has unfortunately made it easier to carry out transnational criminal activities, which have become an increasingly international phenomenon. Thus, it has become necessary to establish a common European criminal justice area, characterised by mutual support between national authorities.

From the very beginning, this kind of cooperation has been met with a series of limitations, first of all owing to the difficulty for most of the Member States to accept external competence in this matter, as they considered national sovereignty and criminal justice to be closely linked. In this respect, it is sufficient to recall the aforementioned procedure of the 'emergency brake' (articles 82(3) and 83(3), TFEU), as well as the limitation to the jurisdiction of the Court of Justice to review the validity or proportionality of operations carried out by the police or other national law enforcement agencies of a Member State, both on the exercise of the responsibilities incumbent upon Member States with regard to the maintenance of law and order and on the safeguarding of internal security (article 276, TFEU; limitation applying in both criminal and police matters).

First of all, it is necessary to define what is meant by criminal matters: as for civil matters, the Treaty does not provide a clear definition. To date, there is no clear notion of what constitutes a criminal offence at Union level: 'criminal matters' shall therefore refer to those cases in which criminal proceedings take place in a Member State, and these are subject to compliance with the appropriate procedural safeguards, regardless of their formal qualification (Court of Justice, 14 November 2013, *Marián Balàž*, C-60/12, ECLI:EU:2013:733).

Cooperation in criminal matters in the Union shall be based on three aspects: (a) the mutual recognition of judgments and judicial decisions (article 82, TFEU); (b) the approximation of the laws and regulations of the Member States (articles 82 and 83, TFEU); (c) crime prevention (article 84, TFEU).

As for the first aspect, it is the basis for judicial cooperation in criminal matters. The prerequisite is the mutual trust among Member States that the legal systems of other Member States are sufficiently consistent in upholding common values such as democracy and human rights. The recognition of judicial decisions pose a number of problems, mainly concerning the lack of appropriate procedural guarantees and the absence of a common framework on matters relating to jurisdiction.

The Union has committed itself to adopting a series of measures aimed at filling these gaps, and specifically: laying down rules and procedures for ensuring recognition throughout the Union of all forms of judgments and judicial decisions, preventing and settling conflicts of jurisdiction between Member States, supporting the training of the judiciary and judicial staff, as well as facilitating cooperation between judicial or equivalent authorities of the Member States. The principle of *ne bis in idem*, or the prohibition of double jeopardy, under which an individual who has already been convicted by a final judgment in one Member State cannot be prosecuted in another Member State for the same acts, has been established in the case law of the Court of Justice as absolutely relevant under the mutual recognition framework (among others, see the judgments of 11.02.2003, *Hüseyin Gözütok* and *Klaus Brügge*, joined cases C-187/01 and C-385/01, ECLI:EU:C:2003:87, and the judgment of 29.06.2016, *Piotr Kossowski*, C-486/14, EU:C:2016:483; for a clear affirmation of the principle, see article 50 of the Charter of Fundamental Rights).

The second aspect of this cooperation revolves around the approximation of criminal law, both in terms of substantive and procedural rules. Regarding the substantive aspect, establishing minimum rules with regard to the definition of criminal offences and sanctions in particularly serious crimes with cross-border dimension, aims to combat the so-called eurocrimes, such as terrorism, sexual exploitation, human trafficking and corruption. The approximation of procedural rules, on the other hand, aims to facilitate mutual recognition of judgments and judicial decisions and police and judicial cooperation in criminal matters (eg, mutual admissibility of evidence, rights of parties to the proceedings).

The third aspect consists of the competence to carry out supporting action in crime prevention. Especially noteworthy, in this regard, is the setting up of a European Crime Prevention Network (EUCPN, decision 2009/902/EU, 30 November 2009), and, for the purpose of developing cooperation, the work of Eurojust (an EU agency established by Council decision 2002/187/JHA, 28 February 2002). A European Public Prosecutor's Office, provided by article 86 TFEU, has not yet been set up (even though 16 Member States have triggered initiatives for strengthened cooperation).

A number of legislative instruments have been adopted concerning the different profiles mentioned here. These include, insofar as the application of the principle of mutual recognition of decisions, various framework decisions on the European arrest warrant and the surrender procedures between Member States; on the application of the principle of mutual recognition to financial penalties; to confiscation orders; to judgments in criminal matters imposing custodial sentences or measures involving deprivation of liberty; to judgments and probation decisions with a view to the supervision of probation measures and alternative sanctions; to supervision measures as an alternative to provisional detention (2002/584/JHA, 13 June 2002; 2005/214/JHA, 24 February 2005; 2006/783/JHA, 6 October 2006; 2008/909/JHA, 27 November 2008; 2008/947/JHA, 27 November 2008; 2009/829/JHA, 23 October 2009); also, a couple of directives: on the European protection order; on the European criminal investigation order (2011/99/EU, 13 December 2011; 2014/41/EU, 3 April 2014). As regards minimum provisions or standards, especially in procedural matters, there are several relevant directives on the right to interpretation and translation in criminal proceedings; on the right to information in criminal proceedings; on the right of access to a lawyer in criminal proceedings and in European arrest warrant proceedings; and on the right to have a third party informed upon deprivation of liberty and to communicate with third persons and with consular authorities while deprived of liberty; on the strengthening of certain aspects of the presumption of innocence and of the right to be present at the trial in criminal proceedings; on establishing minimum standards on the rights, support and protection of victims of crime; on procedural safeguards for children who are suspects or accused persons in criminal proceedings; on the right to legal aid (2010/64/EU, 20 October 2010; 2012/13/EU, 22 May 2012; 2013/48/EU, 22 October 2013; 2016/343/EU, 9 March 2016; 2012/29/EU, 25 October 2012; 2016/800/EU, 11 May 2016; 2016/1919/EU, 26 October 2016). As for the so-called eurocrimes, several framework decisions have been adopted, concerning: rules on terrorist offences; minimum provisions on the constituent elements of criminal acts and penalties in the field of illicit drug trafficking; combating certain forms and expressions of racism and xenophobia by means of criminal law (2002/475/JHA, 13 June 2002, replaced by directive 2017/541/EU, 15 March 2017; 2004/757/JHA, 25 October 2004; 2008/913/JHA, 28 November 2008) and directives on preventing and combating trafficking in human beings and protecting its victims; on the protection of the euro and other currencies against counterfeiting by criminal law (2011/36/EU, 5 April 2011; 2014/62/EU, 15 May 2014).

Significant progress has been achieved in this field, despite its characteristic reliance on intergovernmental cooperation, which – as stated above – has always influenced the overall development of the sector.

C. Police Cooperation

Police cooperation (articles 87–89 TFEU), essentially aimed at combating serious crime and terrorist activity, is an important element with a view to creating a genuine area of freedom, security and justice. Strictly linked to criminal cooperation, it (article 87 TFEU) involves 'all the Member States' competent authorities, including police, customs and other specialised law enforcement services in relation to the prevention, detection and investigation of criminal offences'.

A primary role is played by the European Union's law enforcement agency (Europol, article 88, TFEU) qualified (EU regulation 2016/794, 11 May 2016) as the European Union Agency for law enforcement cooperation, tasked with supporting and strengthening action by the Member States' police authorities and other law enforcement services and their mutual cooperation. Cooperation with Eurojust is strict, especially with regard to serious cross-border crime, terrorism and forms of crime which affect a common interest covered by a Union policy.

Measures concerning operational cooperation between the competent authorities of the Member States may be the subject of enhanced cooperation, in case of the absence of unanimity in the Council (article 87(3), TFEU). An important limitation is that any operational action by Europol must be carried out in liaison and in agreement with the authorities of the Member State or States whose territory is concerned, since the application of coercive measures shall be the exclusive responsibility of the competent national authorities (article 88(3), TFEU). A special legislative procedure is laid down (article 89, TFEU) as regards the conditions and limitations under which the competent authorities of the Member States may operate in the territory of another Member State in liaison and in agreement with the authorities of that State.

Cooperation between Europol and Eurojust and the joint strategy to ensure the best possible protection for citizens, with particular regard to the more recent phenomena of terrorism and the increase of crimes committed on the net (improving practical collaboration and information exchange between police and judicial authorities), seem to have become increasingly closer in practice. A number of important acts are worth recalling here, such as Council framework decisions on joint investigation teams; on the protection of personal data processed in the field of judicial and police cooperation in criminal matters (2002/465/JHA, 13 June 2002 and 2008/977/JHA, 27 November 2008).

V. Conclusions: Progress and Perspectives

There is no doubt that significant progress has been made in establishing an area of freedom, security and justice; however this process still requires further actions and interventions. The actions undertaken so far should be seen as only the beginning of a path still to be perfected. An essential tool for this purpose is mutual trust: a principle that must indeed be declined in all its forms. The approximation of legislation is essential for increasing trust between States and enabling mutual recognition. In short, a 'virtuous circle' consisting of approximation, trust and recognition must be put in place and perfected. Even if rules are far from equivalent across all Member States, trust can still allow their recognition, because attention must be paid to the aim pursued.

As for immigration, it is noted that the European Union has been affected by an unprecedented inward flow, brought on by economic need or by the desire to escape poverty, war or persecution. Measures to address the crisis should be directed towards eliminating its root causes and increasing aid for people in need of humanitarian assistance, both within and outside the Union, in a spirit of solidarity (a programme of to-do actions, implementing the European Agenda on migration, COM[2015]240 of 13 May 2015, is set out in the plan put forward by the Commission on 2 March 2017, IP/17/350, with a renewed EU action plan on return and a set of recommendations to Member States on how to make return procedures more effective).

A spirit of close cooperation and integration is also crucial for judicial cooperation in civil, criminal and police matters. On this last issue, particularly sensitive on account of terrorist activity, we can recall the reinforced actions envisaged by the European Agenda on security (2015-2020, COM[2015]185 of 28 April 2015), which stress the relevance of mutual trust between States, a prerequisite for cooperation and, as we have said, an essential element of the area as a whole.

The Union has set itself the goal of achieving ambitious goals, such as the actions needed to create a genuine area of freedom, security and justice which includes all the sectors mentioned above. States should become more aware of the indispensability of creating this space, and demonstrate greater willingness to place limitations on their sovereignty by implementing common interventions, thereby making it possible to achieve over time an effective area of freedom, security and justice, without borders.

Robert Schuman, former French minister for Foreign Affairs, in his Paris speech on 9 May 1950 (the so-called Schuman Declaration) showing both foresight and realism, stated that 'Europe will not be made all at once, or according to a single plan. It will be built through concrete achievements which first create a de facto solidarity'.

Bibliography

Schuman Declaration – 9 May 1950, https://europa.eu/european-union/about-eu/symbols/europe-day/schuman-declaration_en.

Adinolfi, A, 'La libertà di circolazione delle persone e la politica dell'immigrazione' in G Strozzi (ed) *Diritto dell'Unione Europea. Parte speciale* (Torino 2015) 63–166.

Amalfitano, C, 'Spazio giudiziario europeo e libera circolazione delle decisioni penali' (2009) 1 *Studi sull'integrazione europea* 73–120.

Caggiano, G, 'L'evoluzione dello Spazio di libertà, sicurezza e giustizia nella prospettiva di un'Unione basata sul diritto' (2007) 2 *Studi sull'integrazione europea* 335–88.

Caggiano, G (ed), *I percorsi giuridici per l'integrazione: migranti e titolari di protezione internazionale tra diritto dell'Unione e ordinamento italiano* (Torino, 2014).

Carbone, SM and Tuo, C, *Il nuovo spazio giudiziario europeo in materia civile e commerciale* (Torino, 2016).

Daniele, L, *Diritto del mercato unico europeo e dello spazio di libertà, sicurezza e giustizia* (Milano, 2016).

Di Pascale, A, 'Le politiche dell'immigrazione e asilo dell'Unione Europea: alcune riflessioni sui primi quindici anni', in M Carta (ed) *Quale futuro per l'Europa tra crisi, rilancio e utopia*, in Proceedings of the Study Conference (Rome 2014, Soveria Mannelli 2015) 241 et seq.

Draetta, U, Parisi, N and Rinoldi, D (eds), *Lo spazio di libertà, sicurezza e giustizia dell'Unione europea: principi fondamentali e tutela dei diritti* (Napoli, 2007).

Favilli, C, *Spazio di sicurezza, libertà e giustizia*, 2014, in the Law online section at www.treccani.it.

Fletcher, M, Herlin-Karnell, E and Matera, C (eds), *The European Union as an area of freedom, security and justice* (London-New York, 2016).

Hailbronner, K and Thym, D, *EU immigration and asylum law. A commentary* (München, 2016).

Labayle, H, 'L'espace de liberté, sécurité et justice dans la Constitution pour l'Europe' (2005) 2 *Revue trimestrielle de droit européen* 437–72.

Labayle, H, 'La nouvelle architecture de l'espace de liberté, de sécurité et de justice' in C Kaddous and M Dony (eds), *D'Amsterdam à Lisbonne. Dix ans d'espace de liberté, de sécurité et de justice* (Bâle-Bruxelles, 2010) 3–27.

Nascimbene, B, 'Il 'diritto degli stranieri'. Le norme nazionali nel quadro delle norme di diritto internazionale e comunitario', foreword to B Nascimbene (ed), *Diritto degli stranieri* (Padova, 2004) XXXI–LIV.

Nascimbene, B, 'Il diritto di asilo. Gli standard di tutela dell'Unione Europea e il confronto con gli standard internazionali' in LS Rossi (ed) *La protezione dei diritti fondamentali. Carta dei diritti UE e standard internazionali*, Atti del XV Convegno SIDI [Italian international law society], Bologna 10–11 giugno 2010 (Napoli 2011) 25–48.

Nascimbene, B, 'Lo spazio di libertà, sicurezza e giustizia a due anni dall'entrata in vigore del Trattato di Lisbona' (2011) 4 *Diritto, immigrazione e cittadinanza* 13–26.

Peers, S, *EU Justice and home Affairs Law*, 1st and 2nd vols (Oxford, 2016).

Salerno, F, 'La cooperazione giudiziaria in materia civile' in G Strozzi (ed), *Diritto dell'Unione Europea. Parte speciale* (Torino 2015) 483–531.

I wish to thank Dr Francesca Gelmini, PhD in EU law, for her revision of this paper and its bibliography.

14

Education and Training in Europe: Students and the Erasmus Programme

FRANCESCO PROFUMO AND GIOVANNI BIONDI

On 15 June 1987, by proposal of the European Commission, the Council of the European Economic Community (today the EU Council), with decision No. 327, adopted the European region action scheme for the mobility of university students (Erasmus).

If on the one hand this measure marks the starting point of one of the most significant experiences of the Union, at the same time it should be recalled how this was also one of the results of a 30-year-long political and institutional path, along which the idea of promoting a common area for training and education in Europe was consolidated bit by bit, beginning with the premises posited already in 1957 in the Treaty establishing the European Economic Community. In particular in articles 118 and 128, which declare respectively:

> Without prejudice to the other provisions of this Treaty and in conformity with its general objectives, it shall be the aim of the Commission to promote close collaboration between Member States in the social field, particularly in matters relating to
>
> - employment,
> - labour legislation and working conditions,
> - occupational and continuation training,
>
> The Council shall, on a proposal of the Commission and after the Economic and Social Committee has been consulted, establish general principles for the implementation of a common policy of occupational training capable of contributing to the harmonious development both of national economies and of the Common Market.

In the following decades, these conditions, which were initially limited to professional training, were grafted with important decisions endorsed by the Member States; and these have determined the realisation of one of the surest paths in the sometimes complicated process of constructing a united Europe. Erasmus immediately played a fundamental role in this area, both for the number of European (and non-European) citizens involved, and for the concreteness and the efficacy of the results obtained, regarding which more will be said later.

It is indeed difficult to grasp the full scope of the programme without considering the international, political, and institutional framework within which it was developed after 1987, above all in light of the growing centrality recognised to the university, which over the course of some three decades has assumed an ever more central role.

Precisely on the occasion of the anniversary celebrations for the founding of two of the oldest European universities – the ninth centenary of the University of Bologna and the eighth of the Sorbonne – in 1988 and in 1989 the *Magna charta universitatum* and the *Sorbonne Declaration* were respectively undersigned, in the first case by 388 rectors and deans of European and non-European universities, and in the second by the ministers of Education of France, Germany, Great Britain and Italy. These last formalised their commitment on that occasion 'to encouraging a common frame of reference, aimed at improving external recognition and facilitating student mobility as well as employability' (*Sorbonne Declaration*), effectively launching a complex programme of structural and convergent redefinition of the European universities, defined in its entirety as the Bologna Process.

On 19 June 1999 a new declaration was undersigned in Bologna, this time by the ministers of Education of 29 countries, aimed at the commitment 'to create a European space for higher education' (Associazione Treellle, *Università italiana, università europea?*, Quaderno No. 3, September 2003, p 57), a commitment concretely carried forward through a series of ministerial meetings which have since then been convened every two years to monitor the results obtained. The ultimate goal was to arrive, by 2010, at the creation of a European space for higher education (*European Higher Education Area*, EHEA) – a target reached inasmuch as the EHEA was officially formalised during the ministerial conference of 2010, convened for that year in Budapest and Vienna.

It is not possible to give an account here of the individual measures that have built, step by step over 30 years, the juridical and institutional skeleton of the project of international collaboration in the field of training and education, but it is important here to underline how every institutional decision in this long period was accompanied by a growing political and social sensibility that has transversely involved countries and supranational institutions, widening the original intent of 1957 – connected mainly to professional common development – to a broad range of issues (such as the right to education in the Union and beyond its borders) and to a broader audience of beneficiaries (no longer only universities, but also upper secondary schools, no longer only students, but also – and in increasing numbers – teachers). The Erasmus programme, as has been mentioned, represents one of the most fruitful experiences of this long and complex path, not only in what concerns the realisation of the specific institutional objectives, but also, and above all, for the contribution it has made to the yet more complex process of building European citizenship.

In the 1996 *Report to UNESCO of the International Commission on education for the twenty-first century* (a commission chaired by Jacques Delors), the passage which analyses the function of the common vocational training projects, Erasmus included, offers an effective summary of the virtuous circle initiated by international mobility:

> The purpose of these programmes is to allow the participating countries to collectively garner benefit from the advantages that they separately possess at each educational level, compensating in this way for the national shortcomings. This cooperation consents young people, students in particular, to take advantage, from the available study courses in the various Member States of the Union, contributing thereby to a better mutual comprehension between peoples (Delors (1997) 178).

I. From Erasmus to Erasmus+

In relation to its initial organisation, the structure of Erasmus has undergone numerous evolutions, two of which have brought about deep structural and organisational changes. The decision of 15 November 2006 of the European Parliament and of the Council instituted the Lifelong learning programme (LLP), which grouped together all the initiatives of European cooperation in the field of education and training, by integrating the previous Leonardo initiative (established in 1994 and dedicated to vocational training) and Socrates initiative (of 1994, for school education and higher learning) into a single programme. Erasmus thus became one of the LLP subprogrammes to manage the activities of exchange, cooperation and mobility from 2007 to 2013.

EU regulation No. 1288/2013 of the European Parliament and of the Council established the passage to Erasmus+, the new Union programme for education, training, youth and sport, which was launched on 1 January 2014 and will last until 2020.

Figure 1 The Erasmus+ Program is designed to support the efforts of the Countries participating in the program with a view to lifelong learning, by bringing into relation the support of formal, non-formal and informal learning in the areas of education, training, and youth

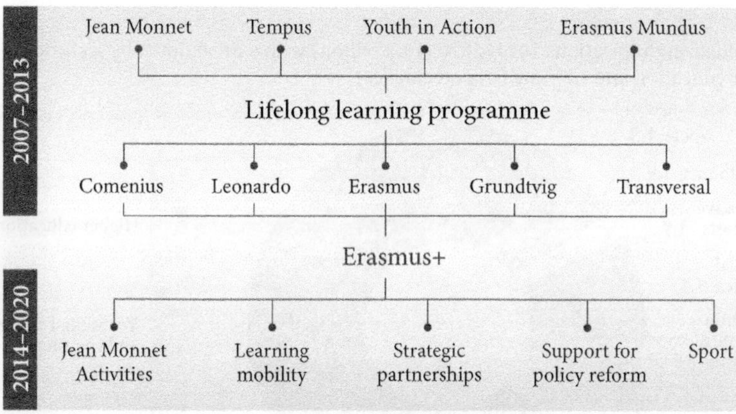

Structured around certain key actions (Jean Monnet activities; individual mobility for learning; strategic collaboration on the subject of innovation and exchange of best practices; support for policy reform and, for the first time, sporting activity), Erasmus+ has introduced some significant innovations since its first phase. First among these is an important enlargement of the subjects involved, from university students alone to all students aged between 13 and 30; thus the inclusion of support for sporting activities and, from the financial point of view, a significant increase in the budget provided for the previous programme.

Among the objectives of the new programme is to set up measures which are aimed at stemming the increasing youth unemployment rate in Europe, as is made explicit in point 16 of the aforementioned EU regulation No. 1288/2013:

> The crucial role played by vocational education and training (VET) in helping to achieve a number of targets set out in the Europe 2020 strategy is widely acknowledged and defined in the renewed

> Copenhagen process (2011-2020), taking into account, in particular, its potential in addressing Europe's high level of unemployment, especially youth unemployment and long-term unemployment, promoting a culture of lifelong learning, countering social exclusion and promoting active citizenship. Quality traineeships and apprenticeships, including those in micro-enterprises and small and medium-sized enterprises, are needed in order to bridge the gap between the knowledge acquired through education and training and the skills and competences required in the world of work, as well as to enhance the employability of young people.

When Erasmus+ was launched in Europe in 2014, the youth unemployment rate in some countries exceeded 50 per cent, and the total of unemployed young people was about six million. In the face of these statistics, it became apparent that more than two million jobs were vacant, while employers complained of the difficulties in finding qualified employees that could answer to the real requirements of the market. The programme aims therefore at reducing this discrepancy through opportunities in study, training or job experiences and volunteering abroad.

For this purpose, and with a view to lifelong learning, Erasmus+ integrated school education (Comenius programme), the higher education (Erasmus), the subprogramme of international higher education (Erasmus Mundus), education and the vocational training (Leonardo Da Vinci) and adult learning for adults (Grundtvig), along with, as mentioned, a new sector dedicated to the sports activities.

Figure 2 Budget appropriations 2014–2020 (14.7 billion) with a breakdown by sector of the funds allocated for education and training (in percentages)

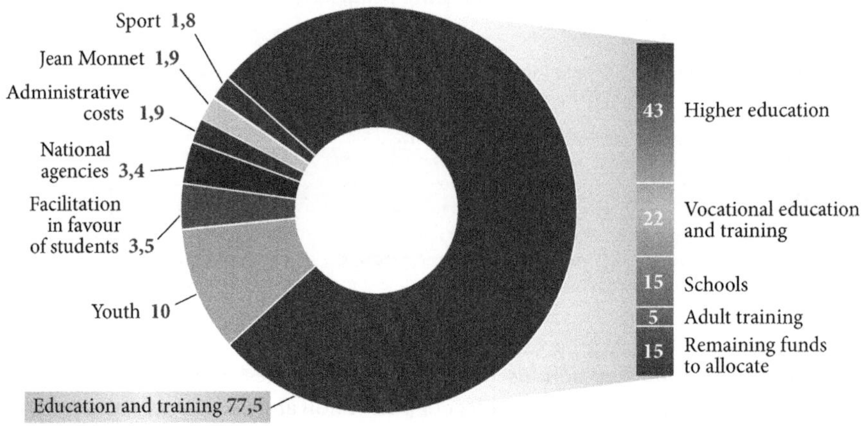

Source: European Commission, Erasmus+ in detail (https://ec.europa.eu/programmes/erasmus-plus/sites/erasmusplus/files/erasmus-plus-in-detail_en.pdf).

For each of these areas there will be support for the reinforcement of teaching and learning methods, of new programmes and vocational training for teaching staff and youth workers, as well as of a closer cooperation between the educational world and the job world. The budget of 14,7 billion euro planned for the 2014–20 period includes estimates concerning inflation, and shows an increase of 40 per cent as compared to precedent appropriations. Additional finances are also allocated for mobility in the field of higher education and for the formation of capacities through the involvement of third countries (see figure 2).

II. Erasmus and Italy: The Protagonists and the Numbers

From 1987 to 2016, almost four million university students were involved in the Erasmus programme, a record number to which Italy contributed about 10 per cent. After Spain, Germany and France, Italy is indeed the fourth country for the number of students who leave for other European destinations.

Beyond this numerical contribution, Italy also furnished Erasmus with a fundamental conceptual and project contribution: indeed, the basic idea and the launch of the programme must be largely recognised as the work of two Italians, the educator Sofia Corradi and the jurist Domenico Lenarduzzi. In 1969, in her role as consultant to the Conference of Italian rectors, Corradi drew up – following a personal history of qualifications obtained abroad and not recognised at home – some notes, that for the first time suggested the possibility of university students playing a part in their own study plan in foreign universities: a few lines that would become the basis for all the following developments in the area of student mobility. This commitment, which the educator pursued with constancy, earned her in 2016 the conferral of the prestigious European Carlo V Award for her career and, as is stated in the motivation, especially for:

> her great commitment and contribution to the process of European integration by means of the design and implementation of the ERASMUS initiative of the European Union, as well as her work and endeavour on behalf of academic mobility, focussing on young European students as a guarantee of tomorrow and the future of Europe.

Lenarduzzi, once Director-General of the European Commission's Educational policy and today honorary director, at a time when education was not part of the areas of collaboration between the States, had the intuition and then the tenacity to launch what was at that time a pilot project, but which subsequently would enter as a leading programme into the construction of the European Union. Even the choice of the acronym Erasmus was his idea.

As regards the data relative to its reception, Italy is in the fifth place, shortly after Spain, Germany, Great Britain and France.

The number of European students that choose Italy for study or to carry out internships exceeds 20,000 individuals. In Italy (2016–17) 244 institutes of higher learning participated, including universities, art schools and secondary schools for language mediators, to which higher colleges of technology have been added in recent years.

The average age of the more than 20,000 Italian Erasmus students is 23 years old so far as study experiences go, and 25 years old for internships. Women constitute 59 per cent of the total number of students to depart for study and 63 per cent of the interns; the former principally head towards Spain, France, Germany and Portugal, and the interns for Spain, Great Britain, Germany and France.

In 1987, out of 3,244 European students to depart from 11 countries, 220 were Italian (see table 1). From Great Britain 925 departed, 895 from France and 649 from Germany. 33 countries presently take part in the programme, and the number of Erasmus students will probably arrive at some four million in 2017, 30 years after the programme's launch.

Table 1 Mobility trends in Europe and in Italy from 1987 to 2015

Academic Year	Number students European Union	Number students Italy
1987–88	3,244	220
1988–89	9,914	1,365
1989–90	19,456	2,295
1990–91	27,906	3,355
1991–92	36,314	4,202
1992–93	51,694	5,308
1993–94	62,362	6,808
1994–95	73,407	7,217
1995–96	84,642	8,969
1996–97	79,874	8,907
1997–98	85,999	9,271
1998–99	97,601	10,875
1999–00	107,666	12,421
2000–01	111,092	13,236
2001–02	115,432	13,940
2002–03	123,600	15,216
2003–04	135,586	16,810
2004–05	144,037	16,419
2005–06	154,421	16,341
2006–07	159,308	17,179
2007–08	182,697	18,364
2008–09	198,523	19,414
2009–10	213,266	21,039
2010–11	231,408	22,031
2011–12	252,827	23,377
2012–13	268,143	25,224
2013–14	272,497	26,335
2014–15	292,086	31,087
2015–16(1)	291,121	33,977

Source: www.indire.ita.

(1) Estimate relative to *Call* 2015.

III. The International Mobility of Erasmus+

The Erasmus+ mobility action, which involves non-European countries through the International credit mobility (ICM), was launched in 2015 and provides for periods of study between three and 12 months for student mobility, and a variable duration of five days to two months for teaching activities and training for teachers and technical administrative employees. This action requires a commitment on the part of institutes of higher education to manage both exit mobility and entry mobility in the partner countries. In a spirit of boosting the attraction of European systems of higher education, the programme strongly pushes reception, both in the area of student mobility and in the field of initiatives dedicated to academic staff.

In the 2016–17 period, the budget provided to Italy in the sphere of international mobility was increased by 13 per cent, in part on account of the enlargement of the programme to partner countries in the African, Caribbean, and Pacific areas (ACP). 52 projects were financed, as against the 89 presented by the Italian candidate institutes of higher education, and the budget assigned to Italy by the European Commission was around 13 million euro. These funds will finance 3,102 people, including students and teachers who will be in a condition of mobility (+25 per cent as compared to 2015), and will go to defray the costs of:

(a) 1,986 instances of entry mobility from non-European countries, including students, teachers and academic staff, principally from the Russian Federation (195), Albania (191), Serbia (159), Georgia (121) and Israel (109);
(b) 1,116 instances of exit mobility, who from Italy take as their destination countries in the rest of the world, primarily the Russian Federation (140), followed by Georgia (84), Serbia (80), Israel (75) and Albania (61).

Among the Italian universities that most attract students from around the world, the University of La Sapienza in Rome is in the first place, followed by the University of Milan, the Alma Mater of Bologna, the University of Padua, and the Polytechnic University of Turin. With regard to the mobility toward non-European countries, the first five Italian institutes by number of students departing are the Alma Mater of Bologna, the Ca' Foscari of Venice, the Tuscia University, the Polytechnic of Milan and Parma University.

IV. Erasmus Mobility for the School

Erasmus is especially famous for the opportunities it offers to the university world, but over the years the European programmes for education and training (as has been mentioned above, Socrates I and II from 1995 to 2006, LLP 2007–13, Erasmus+ 2014–20) have sustained mobility activities and cooperation in projects also in the field of school education.

Specifically, in 1995 the teachers of school institutes were able to carry out in-service training activities, with scholarships that allowed them to attend courses in Europe. From 1995 to 2013 16,773 Italian teachers departed to carry out mobility of this kind.

Similarly, from 2014 to 2016 in the programme Erasmus+, this kind of mobility allowed 5,339 individuals, including teachers and employees of the school, to carry out in-service training activities: training courses, job shadowing activities, and periods of teaching within European schools. From 1995 to 2013, the Comenius assistantship measure for future teachers was also activated, which has given the opportunity to about 2,160 young people to experience teaching activities in European schools.

As regards the projects of cooperation between schools, from 2000 to 2017 about 5,200 projects were realised (school partnerships, strategic partnerships), which allowed Italian school institutes to work in cooperation with European schools and to realise activities of mobility for teachers and students for a total of more than 143,000 persons.

Table 2 Erasmus+: origin and destination of students (2014–2015)

	Origin
France	39,985
Germany	39,719
Spain	36,842
Italy	31,051
Poland	16,735
United Kingdom	14,801
Turkey	14,665
Netherlands	12,397
Belgium	8,632
Czech Republic	8,226
Portugal	8,034
Austria	6,609
Romania	6,406
Finland	5,598
Sweden	4,635
Greece	4,516
Hungary	4,421
Lithuania	4,417
Denmark	4,251
Slovakia	3,819
Ireland	3,029
Bulgaria	2,179
Slovenia	1,987
Latvia	1,837
Norway	1,723
Croatia	1,679

Estonia	1,278
Cyprus	581
Luxembourg	538
Iceland	340
Malta	331
Republic of Macedonia	77
Liechtenstein	45
Total	291,385

	Destination
Spain	42,537
Germany	32,871
United Kingdom	30,183
France	29,558
Italy	21,564
Poland	13,101
Portugal	11,459
Netherlands	11,445
Belgium	10,666
Sweden	9,754
Czech Republic	8,330
Turkey	7,925
Finland	7,910
Ireland	7,216
Austria	7,052
Norway	5,610
Denmark	5,518
Hungary	5,403
Greece	3,653
Lithuania	2,615
Romania	2,573
Malta	2,295
Slovenia	2,248
Slovakia	1,791
Estonia	1,579
Croatia	1,541

Latvia	1,447
Bulgaria	1,095
Cyprus	928
Iceland	712
Luxembourg	694
Liechtenstein	55
Republic of Macedonia	55
Total	291,385

Source: European Commission, Erasmus+, 2017 (http://www.erasmusplus.it/i-paesidi-destinazione-degli-studenti-erasmus/).

V. The Erasmus Stories

As 2017 is the 30th anniversary of Erasmus, it might be interesting to recount the programme through the stories and 'the voice' of those who were its protagonists, because today's Europe, though presently in difficulty, belongs above all to those who have contributed to constructing the community of the 'Erasmus alumni', and this cannot be erased even by the most steadfast anti-Europeans.

Among the pioneers, which is to say the students who carried out the Erasmus experience in the first years of the programme, we find illustrious personages like the High Representative of the Union for foreign affairs and security policy, Federica Mogherini, the writer Roberto Saviano, the economist Andrea Sironi, or popular figures in the entertainment world like the actor Luca Argentero. Apart from these cases of very notable personages, it is evidently in the commoner stories that the programme has succeeded in expressing the best of its potential and capitalising on the formative and professional results for which it was created.

To cite but a single example, the Ice cream team, winner of NASA's 2016 international space apps challenge in the Galactic impact category, is a group constituted by seven young people, average age 29, who are characterised by competencies acquired and enriched by passion, creativity, constancy, resourcefulness, but also by Erasmus journeys in international mobility.

A. From the Lifelong Learning Programme (LLP) to Erasmus+

On the Move for Learning! LLP Stories was published in 2013 by the national agency for Erasmus+, the *Istituto nazionale di documentazione, innovazione e ricerca educativa* (*Indire*), is a collection of stories: stories of Comenius, Erasmus, Grundtvig and Leonardo da Vinci, stories of a Europe lived in the first person thanks to the opportunities offered by the Lifelong learning programme to participate in a linguistic exchange, in a training course, in a study visit or an internship, to pass a long period of time in a country different from one's own for study or professional training. The young are the principal protagonists of this mobility experience: from the alumni of upper secondary schools, who thanks to the individual mobility granted to Comenius students spend a part of the scholastic year in a school of another European country, hosted in families for at least three months, to newly graduated youths who choose to experience an assistantship with the objective of travelling the road to a teaching career, to Erasmus students, in mobility for study or placement. However, LLP mobility involves all learning phases, with no age barriers. Indeed, the first story recounts how even fourth-graders were able to participate, thanks to the Comenius project and to the courage of their teachers, in a project meeting in London. Then there are the teachers, the educators, the trainers who, in the Comenius and Grundtvig mobility for in-service training, found motivation and incentive to adopt more modern didactic approaches and a new way of relating to students and learners. Among the stories of Grundtvig, there are even those of the role of European mobility for work with people affected by forms of disability and the mobility dedicated to the elderly in the area of the projects for senior volunteering. Thanks to the collaboration with the LLP national agency for Leonardo da Vinci, with its headquarters at the *Istituto per lo sviluppo della formazione professionale dei lavoratori* (ISFOL), it was possible to include a chapter dedicated to Leonardo mobility: the interviews carried out by the employees of ISFOL with the recent young graduates in mobility for professional training, as well as the stories of the students of secondary schools that had the opportunity to carry out an internship of initial training in another European country, have enabled us to draw a more comprehensive picture of the meaning of LLP mobility. A lowest common denominator characterises all these experiences: the desire to put oneself out there, to know, to discover, to face new challenges, to enrich themselves and to grow, from the human and professional points of view, and to live in full participation with the complexity and the beauty of being a European citizen. The work on learning mobility done in 2012 by the LLP national agencies, Comenius, Erasmus, Grundtvig and Study Visits, through a primary investigation on the impact of mobility actions within the Lifelong learning programme, has given rise to the publication of a very accurate and exhaustive document, 'La mobilità europea per l'istruzione e la formazione – Indagine sull'impatto di LLP dal 2007 al 2012', *I quaderni del Lifelong learning programme* (2012) 20.

VI. Conclusion

From the beginning of the Erasmus programme in 1987 up till today, the total number of European university students involved approaches four million, to which number one must add the school students. This experience, one of a kind in the world, has been watched with interest by all the countries outside Europe. The project has succeeded in evolving over time to respond to new needs, at a moment in which the European Union is in a state of severe employment crisis. Its 'state of health' is well summarised by the conclusions of the 2015 report (European Commission 2015), that have done the math on the activities of the first year of Erasmus+; the report underlines how, out of 725,000 interviewees, 96 per cent of the participants in the programme declare themselves satisfied by the experience, 96 per cent say they have improved their skills, and 80 per cent feel better prepared to find a job. Not only that, but Erasmus+ has proved itself to be a flexible instrument, useful for effectively confronting the complex political situation in terms of social inclusion, and probably addressing in this way the highest and most difficult challenge of the European Union.

Bibliography

Bettin Lattes, G and Bontempi, M, *L'identità europea tra vissuto e istituzioni* (Firenze, 2008).

Cappè, F (ed) *Generazione Erasmus: l'Italia dalle nuove idee* (Milano, 2013).

Chessa, S, *Formazione universitaria e mobilità studentesca in Europa. Una lettura sociologica* (Milano, 2010).

De Rita, G and Trombetti Budriesi, AL (eds), *La mobilità internazionale degli studenti universitari. Valutazione delle politiche ed esperienze innovative* (Bologna, 2006).

Delors, J, *Nell'educazione un tesoro. Rapporto all'UNESCO della Commissione internazionale sull'educazione per il XXI secolo* (Roma, 1997).

European Commission, *Annual report 2015*, 2015, https://ec.europa.eu/programmes/erasmus-plus/sites/erasmusplus/files/erasmus-plus-annual-report-2015.pdf.

The reference site for the Erasmus programme in English is https://www.erasmusplus.org.uk/.

All web pages are understood as having last been visited on 27 June 2018.

15

Tax Harmonisation

FRANCO GALLO

I. Social and Fiscal Policies at the Early Stages of the European Union's Journey

In the original framework of the Treaties, fiscal policies, like social policies, were not the subject of a specific competence of the European institutions. This was due to the prevalence of the German approach, strongly influenced by the Ordoliberal School (Joerges 2005), according to which the harmonisation of national social systems with national fiscal systems should have been the automatic consequence of the process of market integration. Article 117(2) of the original Treaty establishing the European Economic Community (TEC) is clear on this matter, when addressing the promotion of improved living and working conditions of workers, stating that:

> They [Member States] believe that such a development will ensue not only from the functioning of the common market, which will favour the harmonisation of social systems, but also from the procedures provided for in this Treaty and from the approximation of provisions laid down by law, regulation or administrative action.

The outcome was the defeat of the alternative French position and, in particular, of its prime minister, Guy Mollet (1905–75), who had fought hard to ensure that the harmonisation of national social policies – including the funding of social security systems – would fall under the prerogatives of the new European Economic Community as a precondition for the successful integration of the markets of the Member States.

The affirmation of this view – first in the Ohlin and Spaak reports (1956) and then, as we have seen, in the Treaties themselves – responded to an original, dual ranking of needs: on the one hand, that of committing the new-born European institutions to the construction of the common market as a priority; on the other hand, to ensure full respect for the sovereignty of the Member States in the sphere of social and redistributive policies, all strictly reserved for national democratic processes. In this light, the reduced powers assigned to the Community in the field of social and fiscal policy were framed into a logic of 'mere compensation for the socially undesirable effects of economic integration' (Mechi (2003) 79).

Even the period spanning the main harmonisation directives of 1975, 1977 and 1980 on the subject of corporate crisis management – a phase that cannot be underestimated also because it represents a first departure from the ordoliberal approach – must be framed in a functionalist (D'Antona (1996)) and 'non cohesive' perspective, aimed at creating common social rules geared only towards the principle of non-distortion of competition. Anyhow, this phase petered out in a relatively short time (Treu (2004)), thus showing up the fragile prospects of harmonisation of social and fiscal norms if left to the unanimous approval of the nation States – an objective notoriously difficult to achieve.

Let us examine how this rugged, uneven course has shaped, in particular, fiscal policies, distinguishing the area of indirect taxation from that of direct taxation.

As for the first type, the express provision in the Treaties of rules aimed at the harmonisation of taxation strictly related to goods and their circulation has certainly yielded positive results. Suffice it to recall the adoption, through the European Union VAT directive, of a single European model of value added tax, and of that on the manufacture of products (excise duties) and even the plan for a single customs duty, applied in Member States without having to go through Parliament, and therefore, only as an automatic consequence of the transfer of sovereignty established with the signing of the Treaties of Rome pursuant to article 11 of the Italian Constitution.

As for the subject of direct taxation, the lack of express provisions demanding harmonisation was justified by the original belief that these taxes constituted an instrument of social policy and income redistribution that fell within the exclusive competence of the Member States.

This did not prevent EU institutions from progressively becoming aware, at least theoretically, that as the Community construction progressed, there was also a need to adjust national taxation levels, even direct taxes, to a common model. The studies promoted by the Commission on this subject are of particular note as they looked favourably on the harmonisation of income taxes (Neumark Report of 1962 and Segrè Report of 1966), as are, above all, the proposals for directives aimed at favouring the processes of concentrations between undertakings, especially the 16 January 1969 proposals on the tax regimes applicable, respectively, to corporate reorganisations and profit distributions between parent companies and subsidiaries of different Member States.

In the intentions of the Commission, these proposals should have constituted the initial stage of a broader programme for the harmonisation of direct taxes (see the Commission communication to the Council of 26 June 1967, *Programma d'armonizzazione delle imposte dirette*, 'Bollettino delle Comunità europee', 1967, suppl. No. 8, 6–21).

But this ambitious project has ground to a halt over the unanimity requirement, which, by attributing preemptive powers to each State, has brought the harmonisation process to a virtual standstill.

II. From Tax Harmonisation to Coordination

From the second half of the 1980s and, in an increasingly subtle way, during the 1990s up to the year 2000, the European Union (EU) was forced to fall back on the mere coordination of social and fiscal policies, with a view to pursuing a few selected common objectives. With this in mind, indeed it has taken such policies upon itself, but rather than going down the (blind) alley of striving to adapt national systems to a common model, it has confined itself to a 'government of diversity' (Torchia (2006)) of these systems, relying on non-legislative sources – the so-called soft law – to overcome the obstacle of unanimity. In the field of social policies, the Single European Act of 1986 saw the casting aside of the strategy pursuing harmonisation through directives in favour of intervention models aimed at convergence rather than regulatory standardisation. As for fiscal policies, while it is true that Commission communication outlining fiscal coordination dates back to 1997, it is also true that the decision to abandon the project of overall income tax harmonisation (throughout approach) in favour of a strategy focused on single aspects of corporate taxation with cross-border relevance (piecemeal approach) should be traced back to the end of the 1980s, with the enactment of directives on the taxation of cross-border dividends and on cross-border corporate reorganisations.

It so happened that the positive strategy launched in Lisbon in 2000, aimed at foreshadowing the EU's new 'social route' firmly attached to the catalogue of rights included in the Charter of Nice, has ultimately been entrusted to these weak forms of governance. The open method of coordination (OMC) adopted, in fact, has merely resulted in certain objectives being set at Community level, with Member States reporting on progress to the European institutions, but with no binding legal obligations strictly speaking (Bano (2003), Massa (2006)), leading towards unification or, at the very least, cooperation or harmonisation. In particular, with regard to direct taxation, the instructions contained in the recommendations, guidelines, multilateral agreements, interpretative notes, communications and resolutions have played a considerable role in monitoring, stimulating and guiding the fiscal policy of the Member States, but still at a mere coordination level. One need only consider, on the subject of taxation of dividends, the COM (2003) 810, Communication from the Commission to the Council of 19 December 2003, *Dividend taxation of individuals in the internal market*; on the subject of the system for cross-border loss relief, the COM (2006) 824, Communication from the Commission to the Council of 19 December 2006, *Tax treatment of losses in cross-border situations*; and, finally, on the subject of exit taxation, COM (2006) 825, Communication from the Commission to the Council of 19 December 2006, *Exit taxation and the need for coordination of Member States' tax policies*.

It must be said that the ups-and-downs of the road to a successful integration of social and fiscal policies have in some way contrasted with a certain activism displayed by the European Court of Justice (ECJ). Indeed, by leveraging the principle of non-discrimination on the grounds of nationality and its associated fundamental freedoms, the ECJ has repeatedly challenged national rules governing the employment, tax and benefit systems on a number of points.

This was achieved through a mechanism dubbed by academics as induced transformation of national social and taxation rules; a mechanism that, generally, has operated by removing domestic provisions contrary to Community law, but sometimes, and not infrequently – whenever the principles set forth by the Court of Justice fit into a single alternative model – it also operated by 'adding' to national law provisions it deemed consistent with the Treaties. It suffices to consider the highly significant example surrounding the method of alleviation of double taxation of company profits, where we witnessed a switch, driven by EU case law, from the imputation to the exemption method.

But even these strong actions by the Court of Justice failed to bear fruit, since they must in any case operate at the same plane as, not in substitution of, those undertaken by the other Community institutions.

At present, the fiscal policy landscape, much like that of social policy, appears strongly contested and, in any case, disappointing in terms of concrete results. Actually, I would even go as far as to say that, compared to social policy, it is even less encouraging.

All the Commission's initiatives aimed at creating common, even optional, tax regimes in the field of direct taxation have failed miserably, smashing against the insurmountable wall of the unanimous consent rule. Consider, for example, the proposal for a directive of 16 March 2011, COM (2011) 58, on a common consolidated tax base for multinational companies (known by the acronym of CCCTB, *Common Consolidated Corporate Tax Base*), or Home State Tax pilot scheme for smaller companies (Commission communication of 23 December 2005, COM (2005) 702); these all being issues on which serious discussions among Member States have never even begun. And again, let us consider the proposal for a directive on the Financial Transaction Tax (FTT), which – regardless of its theoretical acceptability or actual practicability – struggles to make significant headway despite the enhanced cooperation of the 11 Member States in a context that, by definition, should include only like-minded States.

A few positive signs come from the coordination action undertaken by the Commission in the struggle against tax avoidance, where it is easier to reach a consensus among the main European States, especially against the backdrop of an economic crisis, such as the current one, which lays bare the weaknesses of many a State budget. Hence, welcome in this context are both directive 2016/1164/EC, adopted on 12 July 2016, laying down rules against tax-avoidance practices that directly affect the functioning of the internal market, to be transposed by Member States by the end of 2018; and the agreement reached by the Ecofin Council on 21 February 2017 for extending anti-tax-avoidance rules to cases involving non-EU countries, to be implemented by Member States by the end of 2019.

The truth is that the hurdles along the route to tax harmonisation have been very high, and cannot be overcome by tackling the unanimity rule alone. In the current historical phase, the tax competition ban between States – which should be an essential instrument for harmonisation and dismantling tax dumping practices between the States themselves – has been only limited to certain tax competition scenarios that are deemed harmful and unfair as they are liable to affect the location of production activities within the States. The reference is to the code of conduct for business taxation, adopted as a mere resolution by the Ecofin Council on 1 December 1997. This code was aimed at countering distortions to both financial and industrial investments in the cadre of what commissioner Mario Monti envisaged as the beginning of a new phase of Community action inspired by a 'global approach' to taxation. However, it gave a very limited definition of harmful tax competition, only targeting the introduction of new fiscal measures aimed to non-residents, which could have a significant impact on the location of business activities within the EU, and therefore constituting, as such, harmful tax competition. Consequently, the many significant differences in business taxation that are resolved in general schemes of low corporate taxation, applicable indiscriminately to residents and non-residents, have remained outside the tax competition ban. At present, the criteria for tax base determination and tax rates present a highly diverse and fragmented picture throughout the various EU countries, which could create distortions and discriminations and, consequently, trigger opportunistic behaviour both on the part of the Member States, providing low rates to encourage foreign businesses to set up shop, and of individual taxpayers, keen to exploit the most favourable tax regimes.

As we have seen, the few active coordination and convergence policies have been achieved thanks to the case law, as well as soft-law legal instruments and, in any case, relying on the strength of actions whose direct source lies mainly in general Community principles. Only some of these principles need mentioning here: the approximation of national law to the extent necessary for the functioning of the common market (article 3, letter h TEC); the competence of the Council to decide unanimously on directives aimed at the approximation of national laws of the Member States as directly affect the establishment or functioning of the common market (articles 94 and 95, TEC); the removal of those disparities deriving from internal provisions that distort competition (article 96, TEC); finally, the abolition of double taxation within the Community (article 293, TEC).

In the wake of these principles, a number of directives or conventions have been adopted, having a variety of aims; these include removing the tax obstacles to cooperation, abolishing double taxation of dividends, interests and royalties in dealings between parent companies and subsidiaries, taxing extraordinary infracommunity transactions, and abolishing double taxation resulting from profit adjustments between associated companies. Also in pursuit of these principles, the Court of Justice has recognised that national tax rules, as a tax competition tool, may, under certain conditions, be disregarded by the courts in all cases where they are found to infringe the fundamental freedoms guaranteed by the Treaty and the general principle of non-discrimination; and to distort competition and specifically result in State aid.

All this – as we have said before – has occurred episodically owing to the lack of express provisions requiring the harmonisation or coordination of direct taxes. And there could be no other way. As we have seen, the justification for this regulatory omission lies in the original belief that direct taxes constitute an instrument of social policy and redistribution of income that falls under the exclusive responsibility of individual Member States. Limiting the tax competition ban to the aforementioned cases of harmful competition was, therefore, consistent with the school of thought prevailing at the time the Treaty of Rome and the same code of conduct were drafted. By adopting this approach, the Community held a legitimate interest in removing distortionary factors in the field of direct taxation (and corporate tax in particular), but only given privileged tax regimes or specific harmful preferential practices established for non-residents only, and implemented precisely to lure mobile tax bases and business activities. The political corollary attached to this principle was that a general tax reduction applied by individual States did not merely fall within the tax practices to be rooted out through harmonisation processes at EU level; indeed, it could even be construed as a worthy aspect linked to a healthy tax competition between States, which converted into an equally beneficial and binding stimulus to reduce public spending (Timmermans, Klaver, Vording (1999)). It follows that assigning preemptive powers to each individual State was born out of this approach, causing a stalemate in the harmonisation process.

One cannot share this opinion, however, if we examine it – and that is how it should be – from the perspective of greater European integration. In an economically integrated and single currency area, the significant abiding differences in corporate taxation actually amount to an equally significant burden on the competitiveness of European industry, owing to its failure to take full advantage of the potentials of integration. It is especially hard to grasp how these differences, just because they are so widespread, can be deemed consistent with the smooth running of the markets and, also, not liable to cause serious distortions in the localisation of business activities and a rise in administrative costs. Even if the 1997 code of conduct were strictly enforced, it would be difficult to stop altogether cases of negative competition based on general low-tax schemes – such as the ones practiced, for instance, by Ireland and some Eastern European countries – applicable to residents and non-residents without distinction. One way of putting an end to this, would be to further develop (in an almost objective and economic way) the notion of harmful tax competition – rejected by the code of conduct on the basis of questionable value judgments and individual regulatory assumptions – to gradually reach a definition that also reviews tax competition effected through national systems as a whole.

In the EU's current state of integration, this problem is impossibly hard to address and to solve in coordination with 28 States – actually, with 27, once the United Kingdom's withdrawal from the EU has been finalised. Still, it would be a start to admit that there is a problem, that its solution is strictly dependent on greater EU integration, and that now is the time to lay the foundations for solving it, refusing to settle for biased 'political' definitions of harmful competition.

III. Harmonisation, Tax Coordination and the Principle of Non-discrimination

It should be noted that, with regard to the general framework of the Treaties, whereas harmonisation and fiscal coordination do coexist, they do not extend, in any case, to the principle of non-discrimination in taxation; the principle states that – with reference to fundamental freedoms provided for by the Treaties – foreign nationals and foreign products shall not be subjected to any taxation which is other or more burdensome than the taxation to which nationals of that other State in the same circumstances are or may be subjected. Even if the desired approximation of national tax laws were achieved, it does not automatically follow that this principle would be set aside, just as its timely application by the Court of Justice would not be an alternative to the process of harmonisation and coordination. These two statements must be justified more accurately.

The first statement is a negative answer to the question, which scholars have long been grappling with: whether tax discrimination and the resulting distortion effects in cross-border relations may be overcome by merely striving for a sufficient degree of harmonisation of the various tax systems, without having to rely on applying the principle of non-discrimination. The negative answer to this question comes easy and is based on the simple finding that while harmonisation or coordination help to root out the distortions hindering the common market, they are not alternatives to the principle of non-discrimination, which has a different and wider scope of application. Even if we were in the presence of tax systems displaying an advanced state of harmonisation, it could well be that situations of 'arbitrary discrimination' of a protectionist nature or of 'disguised restriction' still abide or derive from that same process of approximation; and these can only be removed by the Court of Luxembourg's prompt enforcement of the principle of non-discrimination.

My argument here is that the opportunities to induce tax savings can arise from those same existing Community legislative instruments of harmonisation. The more cunning taxpayer could obtain a fiscal advantage that would not be due otherwise, by relying on measures introduced by the Community legislation to foster the integration process among the States. Therefore, yet a further need arises in relation to tax integration instruments: to ensure that they are not misused by perpetrating directive/treaty shopping.

The second proposition answers the following closely-related question: whether, symmetrically, applying the principle of non-discrimination is enough on its own to solve the problem of differentiated harmful treatment, so that fiscal harmonisation is no longer necessary.

The answer here is negative as well, and is grounded in the observation that the discrimination ban, although a basic cornerstone in Community law, is not a perfect remedy capable of remedying any injurious fiscal situation with regard to cross-border relations. In the way it has been framed in the Treaties, this principle is actually limited, in the sense that it addresses those forms of discrimination that result in possibly higher taxation, in one Member State, being applied to goods and to nationals belonging to other Member States, and not – as would be ideal in a post-integration scenario – in lower taxation being applied to those goods and nationals (the so-called reverse discrimination), which can also create a distortion with regard to the goods and nationals belonging to the tax-collecting country. In a now old, but still standing, judgment of 13 March 1979, case C-86/78 (*Grandes distilleries Peureux v Directeur des Services fiscaux de La Haute-Saone et du territoire de Belfort*), the EU Court of Justice held the French law on spirits monopolies not to be in conflict with the prohibition of article 95 (now article 110 of the Treaty on the Functioning of the European Union, TFEU) when it provides an imposition on national products of internal taxation in excess of that on imported products.

The principle of non-discrimination counters the protectionist tendencies of the Member States only, and does not strike at measures that these countries may adopt to attract goods and, above all, investments from other Member States. With the exception of the ban on customs duties and charges having equivalent effect – a strict and absolute prohibition which has led the Court of Justice to challenge, in this context, also forms of 'reverse' discrimination (see judgments of 16.07.1992, *Administration des douanes et droits indirects v Léopold Legros and others*, C-163/90; 09.08.1994, *René Lancry SA and others v Direction générale des douanes and others*, joined cases C-363/93, C-407/93, C-408/93, C-409/93, C-410/93 and C-411/93, 14.09.1995, *Maria Simitzi v Dimos Kos*, joined cases C-485/93 and C-486/93; 09.09.2004, *Carbonati Apuani Srl v Municipality of Carrara*, C-72/03) – the same Court ruled that:

> disparities of this kind do not come within the scope of Art. 95 (now Art. 110 TFEU), but result from special features of national laws which have not been harmonized in spheres for which the Member States are responsible (see the ruling in the case C-86/78, paragraph 33 and, consistently, the judgment of 24.10.1996, C-217/94, *Eismann Alto Adige Srl v Ufficio IVA di Bolzano*, paragraph 21).

Despite a number of advocates general petitioning the Court for a reversal on that point (above all, see the conclusions of 6 May 2004 of advocate general Miguel Poiares Maduro, in the aforementioned case C-72/03, and the conclusions of 28 June 2007 of advocate general Eleanor Sharpston, in the case *Government of the French Community and the Walloon Government v Flemish Government*, C-212/06), the Court of Justice has always reiterated, from a Community perspective, the irrelevance of purely internal situations within the domain of individual Member States (in the context of the freedom of establishment and the free movement of services, see judgment of 01.04.2008 of the aforementioned case C-212/06, paragraphs 38–39, order of the Court of 19.06.2008, *Marc André Kurt v Bürgermeister der Stadt Wels*, C-104/08, the judgment of 01.07.2010, *Emanuela Sbarigia v USL RM/A and others*, C-393/08, paragraph 23 and following, and the decision of 22.12.2010, *Omalet NV v Rijksdienst voor Social Zekerheid*, C-245/09, paragraphs 12–16).

Ultimately, in the view of the Court of Luxembourg, the principle of non-discrimination does not extend to 'inverse' or 'reverse' tax discrimination applied to non-residents to encourage foreign investment: unlike the principle of domestic equality, it is indifferent to purely internal situations, as there is no obligation to achieve an equal tax treatment between national and foreign products or nationals, but only an obligation not to discriminate against the latter category in a more unfavourable manner than nationals (the so-called internal parity) or than other foreign products (the so-called external parity).

Such tax competition situations may only be mitigated by resorting to forms of tax harmonisation and coordination, which would coexist with the principle of non-discrimination and are left exclusively to the initiative of the Community institutions.

If the form of tax competition that leads States to give more and more tax breaks to foreign investments and to undermine the basis of coexistence through harmful distortions is to be avoided, there is no choice but to embrace the harmonisation programme – which, I repeat, the Treaties do allow, but do not enforce on direct taxation – or the less ambitious one, that of the mere approximation of national provisions which have a direct impact on the establishment and functioning of the internal market.

IV. OECD Proposals and the Stance of the G20

The issues developed above have been taken on board by the OECD (*Organization for Economic Cooperation and Development*), which, especially in recent years, has put forward several proposals in order to contain at least negative factors like tax planning.

An important proposal concerns the permanent establishment and, above all, digital enterprises. It is aimed at creating a new connecting factor based on 'a significant digital presence' of OTT (*Over-The-Top*) companies in the economy of the territory of a Member State other than the one of residence. Crucially, in a bid to identify the taxable presence, it has outlined a series of parameters, unlike the traditional ones, which range from the type of business actually undertaken by the company in the territory to the way contracts are concluded and the payment methods through which prices are paid by the contracting parties. For its part, the EU Commission has so far ducked the issue by adopting various recommendations and a communication dedicated to tackling 'aggressive tax planning' and proceeding to identify third-party countries that do not comply with the minimum standards of good tax governance. But it has continued to hang on to the unsatisfactory distinction between harmful tax competition (ie, discriminatory against non-residents) and virtuous or fair or beneficial tax competition (Gallo (2015)).

These actions by Commission and the indications of the OECD are certainly tokens of goodwill, but have so far been of little use in dampening the negative effects of tax competition on the subject of taxation of the digital economy.

Another OECD initiative that seems to have been more successful is the so-called BEPS (*Base Erosion and Profit Shifting*) action plan. This plan was drawn up on behalf of the G20 and served as a guideline to the European Commission for the drafting of a directive

(2016/0011/CNS) containing the so-called anti-avoidance package with particular regard to the following points:

- strengthening the fight against aggressive tax planning in terms of the sham nature of abusive transactions;
- contesting tax rulings that afford undue advantages on transfer pricing (the reference is to the operations of Apple in Ireland, of Fiat Corporation in Luxembourg, of Starbucks in the Netherlands);
- combating tax evasion on intellectual property perpetrated through intangibles;
- extending the rules on CFCs (*Controlled Foreign Corporations*);
- controlling the debt ratio of transactions between multinationals;
- implementing Patent box rules in relation to the nexus between business activity and fiscal incentive;
- reviewing hybrid mismatch arrangements, namely, narrowing the so-called tax arbitrage to prevent tax payers taking advantage of the differences between the different tax systems.

The desired effect is that these proposals will not remain unfulfilled, like many others, and that they may be translated into appropriate, generally applicable instruments of fiscal harmonisation.

The only time when this negative trend was bucked, involving the OECD itself and the EU Commission, occurred only as a result of factors unrelated to the European context and did not affect corporate taxation anyway. The reference is to the rules designed to put some kind of stop on tax competition, aggressive planning and tax evasion, at international level. These rules are contained in Tax Information Exchange Agreements on the automatic exchange of information on foreign accounts held in the financial systems of each signatory country. The agreement was signed on 10 October 2014 in Berlin by 58 countries and, as of 2017, its implementation has begun. It was enough for the United States and other important States to show resolve in demanding to automatically obtain any relevant information concerning their residents for security reasons and to combat tax evasion that made it virtually impossible for countries considered tax havens to avoid compliance with the agreement. Countries such as Luxembourg, as well as the Cayman Islands, Singapore and San Marino were forced to sign. Moreover, this was the driving force behind similar agreements recently signed between Italy and Switzerland, Liechtenstein and the Principality of Monaco.

V. Conclusions

It follows from the foregoing that we cannot fail to acknowledge the objective difficulty of attaining a substantial approximation of the tax laws of the Member States on the subject of direct taxation in the short and medium term – and notwithstanding the EU's current setup as a mere alliance of States. In fact, given the current situation of 'integration without a goal', it seems unlikely that we will achieve homogeneous and, in any case, harmonised tax systems without a defined political organisation to be held accountable for the process.

It might seem a trivial and perhaps utopian statement, but there can be no doubt that, from a longer-term perspective, the only way to overcome the difficulties surrounding approximation is by linking fiscal integration to the abolition of the principle of unanimity. And this will only happen if greater political integration is achieved according to the model and based on the experience of the federal union of States, with the consequent attribution of 'substantial' powers to the European government and Parliament. In this case, it is not to say that the whole range of tax burden differences existing in individual countries should be removed for the sake of ensuring uniformity within their tax systems; or that, at any rate, harmonisation is the sole instrument capable of achieving approximation, instead of opting for merely coordinating or setting common minimum levels of tax, or establishing one or more federal European taxes. The best solution will hinge on the level of institution building achieved by the EU, as much as on the capability of the future tax systems of Community and of the individual Member States to comply with them.

In this drawn-out transitional phase from a pre-federal State (or federation in progress, if you like) to an out-and-out federal State, the process of positive and negative integration among national laws will have to move forward at different speeds; nonetheless, all will have to comply with the fundamental principles of subsidiarity and proportionality, while abiding by the two general rules of Community law primacy over the laws of the individual States (when subsidiarity does not apply, that is) and the direct applicability of this principle with regard to the public administration of each Member State and to its nationals. Against this backdrop, the future European tax model will mark the end of the line for the gradual process of approximation, and cannot be separated from the type of federal structure that the EU will decide to adopt. And it may also extend to setting up a European federal direct tax, in addition to current VAT and excise, to finance federal spending, perhaps even partially. After all, this lies at the heart of the proposal for a council directive No. 683 of 25 October 2016 on a common consolidated corporate tax base for groups of European companies beyond a certain size (which is accompanied by the proposal for a directive No. 685 of the same day on a common corporate tax base for the same type of companies) whose aim is to set up a European corporate tax to be paid in the Member State where the parent company of the group is resident for tax purposes. This tax should include other corresponding taxation already determined by the Commission itself, such as environmental taxes and the financial transaction tax (Gallo (2015)).

But precisely because this would be a federal-style tax system, national taxes – that would have to coexist with the new tax – need not be strictly harmonised with each other; and, more importantly, neither would regional and local taxes, especially if the latter will be increasingly based on the principle of equitable and mutual benefit or of consideration. This kind of taxes can continue to be freely determined, with different margins of autonomy, by each Member State, national region and local authority can, with different margins of autonomy, continue to freely determine this kind of taxes, which can also function as a tool to enable reasonable tax competition (especially in terms of tax rates) according to the traditional patterns of fiscal federalism. They may be subject to coordination by the European Union and the European Parliament when their regulatory differences become relevant in terms of common macroeconomic policies, and clash with the basic principles of the federal European Union. While not actually shaking up the fiscal systems of the individual States, this should however at least lead to a need to revise the Treaties or, better still, to incorporate into the future European Constitution a provision granting the Union certain powers of coordination. Such powers would be justified not with the sole purpose of putting an end to harmful distortion practices regarding non-residents – as it is now – but as an essential tool for decentralisation and multilevel cooperation.

If the goal of speeding up the integration process is to be met, one must first recover the spirit of Maastricht and restore full identity to the EU in terms of public finance and social policies. The emphasis placed upon the social market economy over the last 20 years is no longer enough. The value scale underlying the Community system would have to be overhauled, as it is still grounded in the economic principle (typical of free trade systems) of external and internal tax neutrality. In such a scale, at least for the time being, national and Community systems are presumed to be non-comparable, and taxation – including both indirect, and necessarily harmonised, taxes and direct taxes – is mainly viewed through the (shall we say) negative lens of the unity of the internal market and of the four fundamental freedoms of the European tradition. A different idea of taxation should be put forward instead, namely, as a revenue-raising device essential for developing and safeguarding livelihoods according to the principle of fair distribution (Gallo (2015)).

To be clear on this, a single economic governance means granting the EU also regulatory powers of taxation legitimised by the vote of the European Parliament that allow the EU to pursue its own allocation, stabilisation and redistribution policies. The democratic principle of no taxation without representation should also work the other way round: no representation without taxation (Padoa Schioppa (2002)). In short, there can be no centralisation of monetary and social policies without at the same time having the availability of own revenues, along with those that constitute the tax system of individual Member States and local authorities. A European tax system is an essential step to ensure that the Union replaces the social State as a joint provider of security for its citizens.

In particular, revenue from federal taxes should be earmarked for financing both specific interventions and a European development plan – aiming to cover standardised social protection spending – that would one day create a first embryo of a federal budget – by possibly adding revenue from the distribution of 'common taxes' (German style) co-decided by the European Parliament and national assemblies.

As regards the perimeter within which it is possible to start this process, the starting point is certainly the euro area, where there has already been an ever-growing interdependence insofar as the management of the economy and of the currency, and where it is possible to foresee further developments in a federal direction. From this point of view, many parties have rightfully put forward the proposal of setting up a ministry of Finance of the euro area that would have the responsibility of activating the economic and fiscal federation; it would also be responsible for the handling of the banking union, as well as of crisis management tools like the European Stability Mechanism (ESM).

It is clear that the pooling, at European level, of certain policies (eg, defence and military expenditure) currently within the competences of the Member States should, in any case, lead to the positive effect of tightening national budgets. The transfer of costs from national States to the federal State and the creation of a European tax system should, in particular, lead to a parallel tax burden decrease at State government level and, consequently, to the 'trimming' of national tax systems.

Once stripped of harmful tax competition practices, the tax system of a future federal union should be based on the same principles that govern the systems of individual States and whose source, even now, is to be found as much in their respective national Constitutions, as in the Charter of Nice and in the current Treaties as well. These principles are consensus, equality, taxpaying capacity, solidarity and subsidiarity. We shall focus on the first two not because they have to be considered more important, but because, in the moments of transition from one axiological value system to another, they are the ones that can most affect the process of political democratisation of the EU.

With regard to the principle of consent – which in domestic law corresponds to the principle of statutory provision in the field of set performances – it should be construed in the fuller sense that tax levies must be democratically decided by the representative bodies of the communities upon whom the amounts levied are imposed; where the reference to consent obviously means that the levy, regardless of the formal instrument adopted, must have its legitimacy in the will of the people and, in any case, of the subjects authorised to impose financial charges. This means that, just as State taxes must be approved by the national Parliaments, federal taxes must be approved by the European Parliament, whereas common charges must be co-decided by both Parliaments.

As for the principle of tax equality, it should be identified with distributive justice and reasonableness, that is, with the same notion of equality as contemplated in the individual national Constitutions. It should be assumed as a general and imperative rule, whereby an individual's best and most advantageous position must correspond to that individual's greater contribution to the public expenditures. In current Community legislation, however, while equality has properly risen to the status of fundamental value thanks to the binding nature it acquired through the Charter of fundamental rights, for fiscal purposes it still amounts essentially to a discrimination ban; it therefore lacks the intensity of protection that it enjoys under national constitutional law, and that it should enjoy by law under a future federal Union (Gallo (2012). This is because by virtue of the principle of preservation of national tax systems that may be inferred from the Treaties, EU law still views taxation more as a possible factor distorting competition – and therefore to be constrained, harmonised, coordinated and controlled from a neutralist point of view – than a revenue-raising device essential for developing and safeguarding livelihoods according to the principle of fair distribution.

In future, social justice and fiscal justice at European level should play out in this federalist view; consequently, social justice should display its function as a qualitative and, above all, quantitative benchmark for assessing the performance of the fiscal policies aimed at upholding it. After all, as Europeans we would not find it hard to facilitate this conjunction and to establish this correlation, since it would be a matter of formalising values already in place within national legal systems, and since Europe is so proud of its liberal and social solidarity traditions. Still, whatever the political orientation of their governments, all States have taken these traditions to heart as an absolute and explicit manifesto commitment. Universal health coverage, free education from kindergarten to university, welfare for the less fortunate, unemployment benefit and other services have represented a concrete sign of this commitment, to the point of becoming a source of identity and pride, especially if compared with the experience of the United States and the ruthlessness of its welfare system, only partly mitigated by the controversial health reform carried out by president Barack Obama, but then reduced by president Donald Trump in 2017. What we have briefly outlined here is a goal whose path to realisation is fraught with obstacles and difficult to achieve. But it is also a goal with no alternatives if a true European political union is to be built. However, when and how this will actually come about is a matter that belongs to our still uncertain and inscrutable future.

Bibliography

Bano, F, 'Diritto del lavoro e nuove tecniche di regolazione: il soft law' (2003) 1 *Lavoro e diritto* 49–76.

Boria, P, *Diritto tributario europeo* (Milano, 2005) 4-9, 34, 66.

D'Antona, M, 'Sistema giuridico comunitario' in A Baylos Grau, B Caruso, M D'Antona and S Sciarra (eds), *Dizionario di diritto del lavoro comunitario* (Bologna, 1996) 3–46 (esp 22).

Del Federico, L, *Tutela del contribuente ed integrazione giuridica europea* (Milano 2010) 13–47.

Gallo, F, *Ordinamento comunitario e principi fondamentali tributari* (Napoli, 2006).

Gallo, F, *Le ragioni del fisco: etica e giustizia nella tassazione* (Bologna 2007, 2011).

Gallo, F, 'Il ruolo dell'imposizione dal Trattato dell'Unione alla Costituzione europea' (2009) 5 *Rassegna tributaria* 1486–92.

Gallo, F, *L'uguaglianza tributaria* (Napoli, 2012).

Gallo, F, *Giustizia sociale e giustizia fiscale nell'Unione Europea fra integrazione e unificazione* (Napoli, 2015).

Guerra, MC and Zanardi, A (eds), *La finanza pubblica italiana – Rapporto 2007* (Bologna, 2007) (esp S Giannini, C Maggiuli, *La Corte di giustizia europea, l'autonomia degli Stati e il processo di integrazione delle imposte dirette nel mercato unico* (211 et seq); L Greco, R Vuillermo, *Aiuti di Stato e federalismo fiscale* (255 et seq)).

Jacobsson, K, *Soft regulation and subtle transformation of States. The case of EU employment policy* (Stockholm, 2002) 26.

Joerges, C, 'What is left of the European economic Constitution? A melancholic eulogy' (2005) 30 *European law review* 461–89.

Massa, M, 'Modelli e strumenti del governo delle politiche sociali a livello nazionale e comunitario' in P Bianchi (ed), *La garanzia dei diritti sociali nel dialogo tra legislatori e Corte costituzionale* (Pisa, 2006) 11–48 (esp 30).

Mechi, L, 'La costruzione dei diritti sociali nell'Europa a sei (1950–1972)' (2003) 14 *Memoria e ricerca* 69–82 (esp 79).

Melis, G, *Coordinamento fiscale dell'Unione Europea*, in *Enciclopedia del diritto* (Annali, I, Milano, 2007) 394–419.

Padoa Schioppa, A, *Improving effectiveness of the institutions, in Institutional reforms in the European Union: memorandum for the convention* (Roma, 2002) 105–30.

Sacchetto, C, 'Il diritto comunitario e l'ordinamento tributario italiano' (2001) 1 *Diritto e pratica tributaria internazionale* 3–47.

Snyder, F, 'Soft law e prassi istituzionale nella comunità europea' (1993) 1 *Sociologia del diritto* 79–109 (esp 80).

Timmermans, AJM, Klaver, J and Vording, H, *No tax harmonisation. Why a single tax system is harmful to small EU members* (The Hague, 1999).

Torchia, L, *Il governo delle differenze. Il principio di equivalenza nell'ordinamento europeo* (Bologna, 2006).

Treu, T, 'Le regole sociali europee: quali innovazioni?' (2004) 1 *Europa e diritto privato* 33–52 (esp 34).
Trichet, JC, 'Governance economica europea. Verso una federazione economica e fiscale per eccezione' (2013) 2 *Il Mulino* 273–80.
Tryfonidou, A, *Reverse discrimination in EC law* (Kluwer, 2009).
Tryfonidou, A, 'Resolving the reverse discrimination paradox in the area of customs duties: the Lancry saga' (2011) 22(3) *European business law review* 311–36.
Weiler, JHH, *The constitution of Europe: do the new clothes have an emperor? And other essays on European integration* (Cambridge, 1999).

Websites

Gallo, F, *Regime fiscale dell'economia digitale, audizione presso la VI Commissione finanze della Camera dei deputati nell'ambito dell'indagine conoscitiva sulla fiscalità nell'economia digitale*, 24 February 2015, http://www.salviniescalar.it/wps/portal/salviniescalar/le-risorse/pubblicazioni.
Majocchi, A, *La priorità: il Fondo europeo per lo sviluppo e l'occupazione*, 9 December 2013, http://nuovo.csfederalismo.it/it/pubblicazioni/commenti/801-la-priorita-il-fondo-europeo-per-lo-sviluppo-e-l-occupazione.
Tamborini, R, *Perché è il momento di una tassa sulle transa- zioni finanziarie*, 'nelMerito', 19 November 2010, http://www.nelmerito.com/index.php?option=com_con-tent&task=view&id=1205&Itemid=71.
All web pages are understood as having last been visited on 28 May 2018.

PART IV

The EU Economic and Monetary Union and Actions for its Sustainable Development

16

The Economic Governance of the Euro Area

MARCO BUTI AND MARTIN LARCH

On 7 February 1992, a small town in the Dutch region of Limburg was catapulted into the collective conscience of Europe and its citizens. On that most likely cold and humid winter day the Foreign and Finance ministers of then 12 Member States of the European Economic Community (EEC) signed the Treaty on European Union (TEU) better known as the Maastricht Treaty. This Treaty included the roadmap to the single European currency, the euro, which was eventually introduced some seven years later in January 1999.

The launch of the euro went beyond the conversion of national currencies into a single currency. It came with the understanding that macroeconomic stability in a context of growing economic integration required a common and effective governance framework transcending national borders. In fact, the Maastricht Treaty was not the beginning of monetary and economic integration in Europe. It was a particularly important step in an ongoing process adding a single currency to the single market.

Although the product of a tedious political process the economic governance framework of the Maastricht Treaty was firmly grounded in the then dominant macroeconomic paradigm. Based on experience accumulated since the mid-1980s, overall macroeconomic stability was assumed to hinge on two key macroeconomic conditions: low and stable inflation and sound fiscal policy. Accordingly, the Maastricht architecture rested on two pillars: an independent monetary authority mandated to achieve price stability, and common rules for national fiscal policies aimed at safeguarding the long-term sustainability of public finances. As long as the respective mandates and rules were abided by, the euro area was expected to stay clear of major dislocations.

As the single European currency is approaching its 20th birthday, we look back over periods of both successes and tensions. In the first 10 years, the euro area managed to safeguard overall macroeconomic stability ostensibly confirming the intellectual underpinnings of the Maastricht architecture (*The euro: the first decade* (2010)). With hindsight, the success was transient and did not run deep. The large dislocations of the post-2007 crises unearthed important shortcomings in the governance framework and the prevailing macroeconomic paradigm. Most importantly, the cross-country spill-overs ensuing from economic integration, especially in the financial system, turned out to be much more important and harmful than expected and could not be absorbed within the existing set of common rules and institutions.

At some point, when macro-financial tensions ran particularly high, concerns were raised about the euro area's capacity to defend the single currency project. In many cases, offering an effective response to the crisis would have required Treaty changes and taken too much time. Far-reaching and timely responses could only be brokered at the Member States level outside the formal governance framework via intergovernmental agreements. However, the Eurogroup, the forum of euro area Finance ministers, which effectively exercises political control over euroarea matters, was often divided.

Despite the perceived or real difficulties in finding effective solutions to burning issues during the last crisis, today's governance framework, although still not perfect, has evolved considerably compared to the architecture originally laid down in the Maastricht Treaty. It has been strengthened, amended and complemented in important ways. Like most governance frameworks that evolve over time in response to new challenges, it is not a seamless or homogenous set of rules and institutions. It encompasses elements of different institutional nature yet inspired by one common goal: to effectively bridge the gap between the scope of national governments and the cross-country nature of economic activity in the broader context of European integration.

I. History and Economic Rationale

A. The Road towards Economic and Monetary Union

Economic integration and its governance have been at the core of the post-World War II European project from inception. The declared objective of the Treaty establishing the European Economic Community (TEEC) known as the Treaty of Rome, signed on 25 March 1957 and came into force on 1 January 1958, was a common market characterised by the free movement of goods, services, capital and people. The European Commission was endowed with important tasks aimed at eliminating tariffs as well as quantitative trade restrictions and restrictions on capital movement, ensuring the right of establishment of firms across all Member States and enforcing common rules on competition. It is actually quite striking to see how much of today's Economic and Monetary Union (EMU) is rooted in the provisions of the Treaty of Rome. In particular, the foundations (and sometimes even more) of what later would effectively become the European single market, were already laid down in this Treaty.

By contrast, the framework for macroeconomic policymaking was comparatively light. The Treaty of Rome merely asked Member States to regard fiscal and monetary policies (the Treaty of Rome actually speaks of conjunctural policy) as a matter of common concern and to coordinate them within the Council of ministers (henceforth Council). The Commission, the executive body of the EEC, had the right to put forward policy proposals, yet any decision required unanimity in the Council. Since most Member States had their own currency, the Treaty of Rome also included provisions on how to manage nominal exchange rates. Member States were expected to coordinate their exchange rate policies so as not to jeopardise the underlying balance of payments (the balance of a country's transactions with the rest of the world).

Overall, while the Treaty of Rome did recognise the obvious need to coordinate macroeconomic policies in a common market, governance provisions merely amounted to soft coordination with no real power neither on the part of the European Commission nor the Council. This limitation was due to the reluctance of sovereign countries to surrender sovereignty as well as to prevailing economic conditions and international arrangements. At the end of the 1950s all EEC Member States were accumulating surpluses giving them a sense of comfort. In addition, the gold exchange standard (a monetary system under which the main reserve currency, the US dollar, kept its connection with gold while other countries had the possibility to exchange their dollars stock to a fixed exchange rate), although temporarily suspended in the aftermath of the great depression, was de facto reintroduced with the Bretton Woods agreements of 1944. Under these arrangements, participating countries, including EEC countries, pegged their nominal exchange rate to the US dollar and central banks could exchange dollar holdings into gold at an official rate determined by the US Treasury. Consequently, a separate monetary arrangement for the EEC was considered to be unnecessary.

The assessment changed around the time the international convertibility of the US dollar to gold was eventually ended (under the Nixon administration in August 1971). Faced with increasing currency fluctuations of their own, the EEC launched a series of successive initiatives aimed at strengthening economic and monetary governance. Already in 1969, the Council mandated the Luxembourg prime minister and Finance minister Pierre Werner to lead a reflection process aimed to identify options for a gradual creation of an EMU. The report of the group (*Rapport au Conseil et à la Commission concernant la réalisation par étapes de l'union économique et monétaire dans la Communauté*) outlined a three-stage process covering 10 years, including the possibility of a single currency.

In 1971, the EEC agreed in principle to the roadmap and launched the first stage with the introduction of the so-called European currency snake in March 1972. Its objective was to contain the degree of currency fluctuations by pegging all the EEC currencies to one another. However, a wave of currency crisis on the back of the first oil shock in 1973 hampered the effectiveness of the snake. In an attempt to fight the impact of economic recession, some EEC Member States abandoned the idea of coordination and decided to unilaterally devalue their currency and to abandon the snake altogether. By 1976 only Germany and countries tracking the Deutschmark (Belgium, Luxembourg, the Netherlands and Denmark) still adhered to the snake.

A new attempt was launched in 1979 when, following an initiative by the President of the French Republic, Valery Giscard d'Estaing, and the German Chancellor Helmut Schmidt, the European Monetary System (EMS) entered into force. At the core of the EMS was the European Exchange Rate Mechanism (ERM) which included four important elements: (a) the European Currency Unit (ECU) as a weighted average of the participating currencies; (b) a parity grid of bilateral rates where fluctuations of the nominal exchange rate had to be contained within a predefined margin; (c) multilateral credit facilities to extend loans to countries facing temporary difficulties; (d) changes of parities subject to a joint agreement.

The system proved to be more stable than the European currency snake. It formally remained in place until the end of the 1990s, when the single currency was introduced, and is actually still in place as ERM II for Member States intending to adopt the euro. At the same time, its survival hinged on periodical adjustments dictated by diverging economic conditions across Member States. Because of its strong productivity growth and virtuous macroeconomic policymaking Germany became the de facto anchor of the ERM.

Other countries had to keep up with the German benchmark or risk breaching the agreed band of currency fluctuations. This situation sparked misgivings in several countries, especially after the Bundesbank tightened monetary policy in response to the economic boom ensuing German reunification. A critical moment was reached in the second half of 1992, when Italy and the UK withdrew from the system (the UK had only joined in 1990) and several other countries started having major difficulties keeping their exchange rates within the established bands. To safeguard the ERM, wider bands of +/– 15 per cent were introduced in August 1993. Italy joined ERM again in 1996.

Grievances vis-à-vis Germany as the ERM anchor were also a driving force behind new initiatives towards a more collegial form of monetary integration. It had become clear that, in order to be sustainable – both economically and politically – economic and monetary integration required a governance framework that went beyond the soft coordination or the onus to follow best performers. Moreover, the Single European Act of 1986 had provided new impetus to the completion of the single market, which had been stalling compared to the original ambitions of the Treaty of Rome. In that context, policymakers took ultimately the view that it would be difficult to reap the full benefits of a single market with unstable exchange rates.

In April 1989, Jacques Delors, then president of the European Commission, presented an eponymous report, mandated by the heads of States and government of the EEC a year earlier (*Report on economic and monetary union in the European Community*). The report set out the roadmap to the EMU subsequently transposed into the governance framework of the Maastricht Treaty: delegation of monetary policy to a new centralised and independent institution coupled with a stronger coordination of national fiscal and structural policies on the basis of common rules. Trying to manage the interplay between different macroeconomic tools at the central level made sense from an economic point of view. Some saw it also as an opportunity to emphasise coordination as opposed to convergence by competition.

The Maastricht architecture remained broadly unchanged until 2008 when the post-2007 crises imposed new reflections and reforms. First, the coordination of fiscal and structural policy was enhanced assigning more competences to the European Commission. Secondly, crisis management mechanisms were put in place to offer financial assistance to ailing Member States. Thirdly, the banking union was launched to account for the growing importance of financial systems.

B. The Economics of the European Single Currency

Attempts to coordinate exchange rate developments in Europe predate those undertaken since the onset of post-World War II European integration. They include the Latin European Monetary Union in 1865–78 or the Scandinavian Monetary Union in 1873–1914. What they all have in common, in spite of many idiosyncrasies, is the fundamental tension between providing a stable framework for economic integration on the one hand and protecting local interests on the other, whenever previously agreed parities turn out to be too costly for the domestic economy. In a system of flexible exchange rates frequent and large movements in the relative value of currencies will hurt trade and give rise to financial market instability. In a system of fixed exchange rates, diverging price developments impose painful adjustments to preserve competitiveness.

When the Treaty of Rome was signed, the EEC Member States were embedded in the Bretton Woods system of fixed but adjustable exchange rates. According to the prevailing economic orthodoxy, fixed exchange rates were the foundation of macroeconomic stability in a system of free trade and capital mobility. Cross-country differences in competitiveness were expected to be primarily corrected via wage and price adjustment, unless the International Monetary Fund (IMF), the enforcer of the Bretton Woods agreements, agreed to realignment as part of an adjustment programme involving policy conditions.

The European currency snake was a loose agreement among participating Member States. It did not encompass instruments apt to commit participating Member States to monetary policies that would support the agreed exchange rate parities and bands. In the face of a turbulent external economic environment – such as the first oil shock in 1973 – different EEC Member States followed different macroeconomic policies to stabilise their economies. Some like Germany, the Netherlands and Belgium, showed more determination to fight inflation, others like France and Italy followed a different course. Against this background, fixed exchange rates were simply not sustainable, even in the absence of free capital mobility, since inflation causes external imbalances as a consequence of the real appreciation of national currencies.

The EMS of 1979 meant to strengthen the system of mutual monetary support. The central bank of a country under pressure would receive loans from the central banks of countries with appreciating currencies. Such loans would effectively allow Member States to defend the parity beyond their individual holdings of foreign reserves. For instance, if the currency of a country came under pressure it would have to support the fixed exchange rate by trading foreign reserves for its own currency. However, since foreign reserves are typically limited it was just a matter of time before a parity had to be given up. In such a case, monetary autonomy was not an option, unless the central banks of appreciating currencies (who by definition were accumulating foreign reserves) would help out. In addition, realignments, if they were to happen, had to be agreed jointly and unanimously, subject to negotiations and conditions.

While the system of mutual support and joint exchange rate management under the EMS turned out to be longer-lived than the snake, it underscored a fundamental trade-off: either national macro policies, especially monetary policy, are geared towards an agreed fixed exchange rate or recurring realignments are accepted to address persisting differences in the rate of inflation. Until the early 1990s, the EMS followed the latter path, namely to accept cross-country differences in economic conditions which from time to time would lead to a readjustment of the exchange rate parity.

New challenges to the European economic integration and its governance have arisen with the full liberalisation of capital flows introduced by the Single European Act. Since 1986 restriction on capital movements between residents of Member States had been gradually removed and in 1990 full capital mobility was achieved. In the early 1960s Marcus Fleming (1962) and Robert Mundell (1963) formalised the key implications of capital movements for macroeconomic policies in open economies. Applying the standard Keynesian framework to a small open economy, their seminal work had shown that with cross-border capital mobility fixed exchange rates implies the loss of monetary autonomy. The underlying mechanism is quite simple. If capital is allowed to move freely across jurisdictions, it will tend to move towards countries where its return, measured by the domestic interest rate, is higher than the international interest rate. Conversely, it will tend to leave those countries where the internal return would be lower. Hence, a fixed exchange rate can only be sustained if monetary policy commits to keeping the domestic interest rate aligned with the international rate and abandons the goal of stabilising the domestic economy.

The more general insight of Mundell and Fleming is characterised as the 'impossible trinity': it is impossible to have all three of the following at the same time: (a) a fixed exchange rate; (b) free capital mobility; (c) independent monetary policy. In an extension of the 'impossible trinity', Tommaso Padoa-Schioppa (1992), one of the fathers of the euro, added free trade of goods and services as a fourth element to underscore that the free exchange of goods and services as envisaged in the Treaty of Rome could not be taken for granted.

The Delors report and subsequently the Maastricht Treaty moved economic governance into a new direction. They proposed – and eventually formalised – a framework which, in light of the constraints imposed by increasing cross-border capital mobility under the 'impossible trinity', decided to accept the benefits of stable exchange rates by giving up the monetary autonomy at the national level. The speculative attacks on European currencies in 1992–93 which eventually forced the UK and Italy to leave the ERM, laid bare the limits of mutual support under the EMS. In a context of increasingly integrated and deeper capital markets the commitment of unlimited mutual support simply lost its credibility. At the same time, repeated currency realignments and competitive devaluations had hampered the smooth functioning of the single market for goods and services giving rise to tensions between Member States.

The Maastricht governance framework took the ultimate step to rule out currency fluctuations by virtue of a single currency backed by a centralised monetary authority. In parallel, the Maastricht Treaty introduced common rules for the conduct of national fiscal policies, that later (1997) became part of the Stability and Growth Pact (SGP). The constraints imposed by the SGP were motivated by the interactions between monetary and fiscal policymaking, that is by the understanding that in a monetary union independent national fiscal authorities do not fully internalise the effects of fiscal indiscipline on inflation and, ultimately, on the monetary commitment of the centralised monetary authority. Hence, the SGP is meant to protect the centralised monetary authority (Uhlig (2003)).

Under the SGP rules, Member States are expected to achieve sustainable budgetary positions around which automatic stabilisers are allowed to work freely so as to smooth out country-specific shocks, while the European Central Bank (ECB) takes care of common economic shocks (*Economic Policy in EMU* (1998)). The rule-based character of the SGP embodies the widespread understanding documented in the literature that, under normal conditions, fiscal discretion, as opposed to rules, leads to suboptimal results and to the accumulation of national debt in view of the many political aspects or specific interest groups that come into play in the political arena (Taylor (2000); Alesina, Perotti (1994)).

The preferred degree of integration of fiscal policymaking envisaged in the Delors report went actually beyond what was subsequently codified in the Maastricht Treaty. Nevertheless, the authors of the report were fully aware that there was no political consensus for further economic integration. In particular, the report rightly anticipated the difficulty for the euro area to find the right policy mix in a monetary union without a substantial centralised budget. Although this evaluation did not envisage the specific situation that the euro has been facing since 2012, it has been vindicated in a more general sense. In spite of unprecedented monetary easing by the ECB since 2012, including through unconventional policy measures, inflation has remained below its target. At the same time, national fiscal policies cannot or do not provide additional demand support under the SGP rules. As a result, and in the absence of a centralised fiscal capacity, such as a larger EU budget, monetary policy is overburdened and is not able to achieve the right policy mix.

The Delors report also thematised another economic-policy issue, the importance of which would forcefully come to the fore with the post-2007 crises. As Member States give up the exchange rate as adjustment instrument and domestic fiscal policies are constrained by common rules, the burden shifts towards structural policies as means to avert or correct diverging economic developments. In particular, labour and product markets would have to become sufficiently flexible to absorb country-specific shocks. The optimal currency area (OCA) theory identifies several criteria determining whether countries qualify for a currency union, in particular wage and price flexibility, labour mobility, economic openness, fiscal as well as financial integration (Mundell (1961)). When the euro project was designed, there were doubts as to whether the OCA criteria were sufficiently met by the Member States. At the same time, many pundits expected these criteria to be endogenous: not satisfied ex ante, they would be met ex post as participation in the euro would result in increasing trade integration and force policymakers into structural reforms (Obstfeld (1997)). However, this expectation was not met in practice. In spite of the convergence of Gross Domestic Product (GDP) per capita and nominal variables, a structural divergence took hold: Germany and some other core countries became more intensive in tradeables, whilst in peripheral countries non-tradeables increased in relative terms. This structural divergence was at the roots of the large current account imbalances within the euro area. During the economic upturn preceding the post-2007 crises, productivity developments diverged significantly across countries confronting governments with formidable adjustment needs once the crisis hit.

A crucial issue the Delors report, and subsequently the Maastricht Treaty, did not anticipate was the potentially destabilising role of financial markets as subsequently evidenced by the prominent financial dimension of the post-2007 crises. This blind spot was neither accidental nor a sign of negligence. The two-pillar architecture – centralised monetary policy coupled with common rules for national fiscal policy – was strictly designed around the then prevailing consensus in mainstream macroeconomics on how to ensure overall macroeconomic stability: keeping inflation low and stable and conducting public finances so as to achieve the 'divine coincidence' of output at around potential and inflation in line with the central bank's definition of price stability. Financial supervision and regulation were not considered to be a macroeconomic policy tool. As long as they were properly deployed to ensure the soundness of individual banks no macroeconomic implications were expected (*Rethinking macroeconomic policy* (2010)).

Trust in the effectiveness of sound monetary and fiscal policy was not a matter of faith. It was motivated by the much reduced volatility of economic growth and inflation in most advanced economies since the mid-1980s, dubbed great moderation, which coincided with improved macroeconomic policymaking. While other factors such as luck or better inventory management are also indicated as contributing factors, progress in macroeconomic policymaking was considered to be crucial (Bernanke (2004)).

The great moderation paradigm had to be revised on the back of the post-2007 crises with important implications for euro area governance. When the ripples of the US financial crisis reached Europe it became clear that prevailing arrangements were not sufficient to safeguard overall macro-financial stability. To start with the fragmentation of financial regulation and supervision along national borders proved to be a major obstacle in finding solutions to issues with important cross-border implications. As a result, the governance framework of the euro area was extended towards the creation of a banking union including the common supervision and regulation of banks. In analogy to the 'impossible trinity' of Mundell, Dirk Schoenmaker (2013) highlighted the 'financial trilemma' involving financial stability, cross-border banking and national financial policies. He pointed out that any of the two of the three objectives can be achieved together, but not all three.

The financial crisis also brought to the fore the crucial question of what to do in case systemically important actors or sectors (typically banks or governments) risk insolvency. The answer enshrined in the Maastricht Treaty was, and formally still is, the so-called no-bail-out clause whereby Member States must not be liable for, or assume the commitments or debts of, any other. However, when actually confronted with the risk of a sovereign default, at the height of the euro crisis in 2010–11, policymakers concluded that a strict implementation of the no-bail-out clause came at the risk of a euro area break-up. They faced the fundamental trade-off underlying both Mundell's 'impossible trinity' and Schoenmaker's 'financial trilemma': unless countries want to forgo economic integration or stability, national sovereignty has to give way to common solutions. In 2010, the ministers of the euro area countries decided to create a common facility to raise debt to finance assistance programmes for ailing governments. Four years later the European Union also decided to put in place a single resolution fund for banks.

II. Rules and Institutions of the Euro Area Economic Governance Framework

By now, the governance framework of the euro area covers, with different degrees of centralisation, all main areas considered to be crucial for macroeconomic stability: monetary, fiscal, financial and structural. We will present them in turn in dedicated subsections. Upfront, a few general considerations are in order.

The governance framework of the euro area encompasses three different approaches: (a) the Community method with the established division of executive and legislative powers as per the Treaty; (b) the delegation of specific tasks to independent institutions or bodies; and (c) the intergovernmental approach.

Under the Community method, the Council is the ultimate decision maker when it comes to the implementation of EU laws. It acts on proposals of the European Commission, the 'guardian of the Treaty'. Within the Council, the Eurogroup (composed of the finance ministers of euroarea countries) plays an important role in relation to matters pertaining to the euro area. The Eurogroup was established in 1998 as an informal coordination and consultation forum and was subsequently formalised under the Lisbon Treaty in 2007. The Eurogroup meets in private before the regular meetings of the Economic and Financial Affairs Council (ECOFIN, composed of economic and financial ministers of all EU Members States). Since 2004 it has a non-rotating president elected for two and a half years. Only the Eurogroup States vote on issues relating to the euro in the ECOFIN. Although the Eurogroup remains an informal body its influence has grown considerably over time. Especially during the post-2007 crises, it turned into a pivotal forum for finding answers to pressing policy issues which could not be addressed in a timely fashion via the Community method.

While the delegation of specific policy tasks can be considered to be a special case of the Community method, the intergovernmental approach is fundamentally different. It relies on multilateral agreements under international law. Intergovernmental solutions come with up and downsides. The clear downside is that their implementation escapes the division of power and the accountability arrangements of the Community method. As an upside, intergovernmental solutions take generally less time, especially if they touch upon issues that would require a change of EU primary law under the Community method.

<table>
<tr><th colspan="8">Economic and monetary union (EMU)</th></tr>
<tr><th colspan="2">Single market</th><th colspan="3">Single currency</th><th colspan="3">Banking Union</th></tr>
<tr><th colspan="2">Treaty of Rome 1957
Single European Act 1986</th><th colspan="3">Maastricht Treaty 1992</th><th colspan="3">EU heads of State and government agree to create Banking Union: single market provisions of Treaty</th></tr>
<tr><td rowspan="6">Free movement of goods, services, workers and capital
Implementation via
• competition law
• public procurement
• company law
• intellectual, industrial and commercial property
• financial supervision and regulation (see banking union)</td><td rowspan="6">Communitary policy</td><td>Monetary policy</td><td>ECB independent institution</td><td rowspan="3">Communitary policy</td><td>Single supervisory mechanism</td><td>ECB independent institution</td><td rowspan="3">Community method + intergovernmental approach</td></tr>
<tr><td>Fiscal policy</td><td rowspan="2">Member States subject to common rules</td><td>Single resolution mechanism</td><td>SRB independent institution</td></tr>
<tr><td>Structural policies</td><td colspan="2">Single rulebook</td></tr>
<tr><td colspan="6">Crisis management [(1)]</td></tr>
<tr><td colspan="6">Greek loan facility (GLF), European financial stability mechanism (EFSM); European financial stability facility (EFSF); European stability mechanism (ESM)</td></tr>
<tr><td colspan="6">Intergovernmental (with exception of EFSM)</td></tr>
</table>

(1) Details on EU instruments to handle crisis are available at http://ec.europa.eu/info/business-economy-euro/economic-and-fiscal-policy-coordination/eu-financial-assistance.

Source: European Commission.

A. Monetary Policy

Monetary policymaking in the euro area is carried out within a fully centralised framework, which, in essence, has not changed since inception. It has been delegated to the Eurosystem, which consists of the ECB and the national central banks of the euro area. It is governed by the decision-making bodies of the ECB, the Governing Council and the Executive Board. The Governing Council includes the six members of the Executive Board plus the governors of the national central banks of the euro area countries. The Governing Council formulates the monetary policy for the euro area, while the Executive Board is responsible for its implementation by giving instructions to the national central banks.

One of the most defining features of the ECB is its independence. The Maastricht Treaty explicitly stresses that:

> neither the ECB, nor a national central bank, nor any member of their decision-making bodies shall seek or take instructions from Community institutions or bodies, from any government of a Member State or from any other body (article 107).

In tandem, article 107 of the Maastricht Treaty also commits any institutions and bodies as well as Member States to respect the ECB's independence. The very strong emphasis on independence mirrors a broad-based consensus among the economic profession on how to ensure effective monetary policy. This consensus translated into a wave of independence laws precisely in the late 1980s when the Delors report was drawn up. The Reserve bank of New Zealand was granted independence in law in 1989. The Bank of England, the Riksbank in Sweden and the Bank of Japan became legally independent in the 1990s.

The members of the Executive Board are expected to be recognised experts in monetary policy making and banking. Expertise and professional experience, as opposed to political affiliation, are essential to bolster the credibility of an independent institution. In a similar vein, to protect the members of the Executive Board from pressure to use monetary policy in an opportunistic manner for short-term political goals, they are appointed for an eight-year non-renewable term.

Importantly, and in line with most other central banks in advanced economies, the independence of the ECB pertains to the use of instruments, while the goals of monetary policy are determined by the Treaty and are an expression of the will of the legislators. The ECB's primary objective is to maintain price stability. Subordinated to this primary goal, the ECB can also support the more general objective of a harmonious and balanced economic development. According to some observers, mainly from the United States, the independence of the ECB goes beyond the use of instruments, since the operative definition of price stability is not included in the Treaty, but is chosen by the ECB itself.

The counterpart to independence is accountability. The ECB is primarily accountable to the European Parliament by submitting and presenting an annual report on its tasks and activities. Over the years, the ECB has established further channels of accountability that go beyond the Treaty requirements. Every three months the ECB's president appears before the Committee on economic and monetary affairs of the European Parliament. The ECB's accountability is further strengthened via increased transparency, for instance through extensive press conferences after rate-setting meetings (including the publication of minutes, so-called accounts, of the rate-setting meetings) or other means of communication with the general public.

B. Fiscal Policy

Fiscal policy remains a prerogative of Member States but is to be exercised within the remit of the SGP, a set of rules laid down in primary and secondary EU legislation (*The Stability and Growth Pact* (2001)). Although the SGP applies to all EU Member States, some provisions, such as enhanced budgetary monitoring, fines and sanctions, do not apply to non-euro area members. In all parts of the SGP, legally binding decisions are taken by the Council with qualified majority on a recommendation from the European Commission.

The country under discussion does not participate in the vote. In most cases, non-euro area member countries do not participate in the voting on euro area countries.

Since its inception in 1997, the SGP has been amended three times, in 2005, 2011 and in 2013. The amendments responded to lessons learnt from the implementation of the SGP. As a result of the successive amendments there has been an increase in both the flexibility and also the complexity of the SGP. The increase in flexibility was a reaction to the widely-held view that the original rules were too rigid, most importantly that the rules did not account for economic circumstances. The most prominent 'envoy' of this view was Romano Prodi who, on 17 October 2002 (in an interview to Arnaud Leparmentier and Laurent Zecchini of the French newspaper *Le Monde*, 'La France sera en minorité si elle n'est pas le levain de l'Europe') characterised the SGP as 'stupid' due to it being too rigid. Growing complexity is partly due to political constraints, where the need for impartiality and equality of treatment between Member States has led to a consensus that this is best achieved through increasingly detailed rules rather than the exercise of judgement.

The SGP consists of two parts: the preventive and the corrective part. The corrective part, known as the excessive deficit procedure (EDP), applies to Member States that breach Treaty requirements to keep the general government deficit below 3 per cent of GDP and the general government gross debt at below 60 per cent of GDP or diminishing sufficiently towards that level at a satisfactory pace. It encompasses a detailed list of procedural steps aimed at correcting an excessive government deficit or debt. The opening of an EDP entails Council recommendations for corrective action with which the Member State must comply or face an escalation in the procedure. For euro-area Member States each new step of the EDP entails the possibility of sanctions which range from the lodging of a non-interest bearing deposit at the opening of the EDP to an annual fine in the case of persistent non-compliance.

The preventive part requires Member States to achieve and/or maintain a medium-term budgetary objective (MTO) which pursues a triple aim: (a) ensuring a safety margin against the risk of breaching the 3 per cent of GDP deficit threshold of the Treaty; (b) ensuring rapid progress towards long-term sustainability of public finances taking into account the budgetary impact of aging population; (c) taking (a) and (b) into account, allowing room for budgetary manoeuvre over the cycle. The MTO is country specific. As long as the MTO is not achieved Member States are expected to implement an annual budgetary adjustment towards it. A higher adjustment is expected when economic conditions are favourable, with a lower adjustment being possible when conditions are more difficult.

Motivated by the lessons of the post-2007 crises, amendments were introduced to both parts of the SGP in 2011. The recognition that fiscal policy decisions during economic good times are crucial in enabling stabilisation during times of recession led to a strengthening of the preventive arm. In parallel, the transformation of the crisis into a sovereign debt crisis put debt on an equal footing with the deficit in the corrective arm. The sanctions applicable to euro-area Member States under the corrective arm were intensified and a degree of automaticity was added to the voting procedure, while sanctions were also introduced to the preventive arm for the first time. The degree of automaticity consists in applying reversed qualified majority voting: sanctions are considered approved unless there is a qualified majority in the Council against them. Last but not least, Member States were asked to strengthen domestic budgetary frameworks and to make them compatible with EU rules.

In March 2012, all EU members, except Czech Republic, the United Kingdom and Croatia, signed the Treaty on stability, coordination and governance (TSCG), an intergovernmental agreement aimed to underline the responsibility of national fiscal policy in the EMU. In title III of the TSCG, with the Fiscal compact, Member States are asked to introduce into the national legislation an automatic correction mechanism to address deviations from the MTO.

Additional rules for euro area countries entered into force in 2013. Two are worth highlighting here. First, participating Member States are required to submit annually their draft budgetary plans to the European Commission and the Eurogroup by 15 October. Based on an overall assessment, the European Commission adopts and publishes an autonomous opinion. If the draft budget is found to be in serious conflict with EU fiscal rules the Member State concerned is asked to submit a revised draft. Secondly, participating Member States were asked to establish fiscal advisory councils, who, by virtue of an independent assessment of fiscal policymaking, would enhance the accountability of national governments vis-à-vis voters.

C. Structural Policies

Initially, structural policymaking was the area with the thinnest and least codified governance framework. It essentially relied on soft coordination as defined in article 103 of the Maastricht Treaty. The main instruments of coordination are Council recommendations originally known as broad economic policy guidelines (BEPGs) and more recently renamed country-specific recommendations (CSRs). The CSRs encompass policy advice that ultimately aim at ensuring a proper functioning of the EMU; in more concrete terms the objective is to make sure Member States remain on a balanced path of economic development and avoid persisting and significant divergences compared to each other.

Since monetary policy is centralised and discretionary fiscal policy is constrained by common rules, structural policies are de facto the only instrument under the full control of national governments to safeguard competitiveness within the single currency area. At the same time, there were very limited means of enforcement in case a Member State runs policies that are not consistent with the CSRs. The only option foreseen by the Maastricht Treaty was a recommendation by the Council, a kind of warning to the Member State concerned. Beyond such a warning no further steps were foreseen; in 2009, with the Lisbon Treaty the Commission was given the faculty to issue the recommendation directly. Prior to the post-2007 crises, the warning was used only once and not very successfully when, on a recommendation from the Commission, in 2001 the Council found fault with Ireland's pro-cyclical fiscal policy during a period of strong growth. The Irish government essentially ignored the recommendation.

In a bid to boost the reform momentum beyond soft coordination a number of initiatives were launched in the wake of the post-2007 crises. In March 2011, following a Franco-German plan, the Euro Plus Pact was adopted, an intergovernmental agreement, in which participating Member States (all EU members except Czech Republic, Hungary, Sweden and the UK) committed to undertake structural reforms and to track progress through regular reviews and the identification of best practice. The actual impact of the Euro Plus Pact has been very limited. While formally still in force the Pact has been dormant for years.

The community framework for structural policies was strengthened in 2011 with the so-called Six pack, a set of five EU regulations and one directive. Among other things, the Six pack put in place the macroeconomic imbalances procedure (MIP), which is grounded in one crucial insight: there are macroeconomic elements beyond inflation and public finances that are crucial for the overall stability of an economy. Spain and Ireland, countries that were in full compliance with the provisions of the pre-crisis governance framework, experienced a deep recession and eventually had to ask for financial assistance, because their construction and housing sectors had gone through a major boom-bust cycle. House price developments or other important macro variables, although regularly and consistently monitored by the European Commission, could not trigger any formal surveillance step.

The MIP relies on a detailed analysis of an array of macroeconomic indicators including the current account balance, indicators of competitiveness, the stock and increase in private and public sector debt, and house prices. In case several indicators exceed a predefined threshold, the country in question will undergo an in-depth review to determine whether it is experiencing economic imbalances or excessive imbalances. The difference between economic imbalances and excessive imbalances is crucial for the procedural follow-up. Countries experiencing imbalances will receive CSRs which remain in the realm of soft coordination. In contrast, countries experiencing excessive imbalances are required to submit and implement a corrective action plan. Failure to do so can trigger a crescendo of sanctions starting with an interest-bearing deposit, followed by an annual fine. Like in the case of an EDP, the decision to impose sanctions is taken by reversed qualified majority, that is, they are deemed adopted unless the Council rejects the Commission recommendations within a given period.

D. Financial Regulation and Supervision

Apart from confirming the mainstays of the single market, including the free movement of capital, the Maastricht Treaty did not foresee any EU governance framework for the banking sector. The supervision of banks remained completely decentralised. The banking sector was not expected to endanger the smooth functioning of the EMU, as long as national supervisors kept a close eye on individual banks.

As indicated above, the post-2007 crises led to a radical rethink of the prevailing macroeconomic paradigm and led to an extension of the euro area governance framework. In June 2012, the heads of government and States of the EU agreed to create a banking union that would encompass a centralised supervision of banks, a common resolution framework and common rules for the protection of savers.

The main objective of the banking union is to break the vicious circle between banks and sovereigns which during the 2010–11 euro crisis was threatening the macrofinancial stability of some Member States with tangible risks for the euro area as a whole. The objective is pursued along two avenues: risk reduction and risk sharing. Centralised supervision on the basis of common rules helps make bank failures much less likely, while, should banks end up in difficulties, a centralised resolution mechanism defines a common framework for an orderly wind down including the question of who pays how much. Central supervision and resolution are mandatory for euro area countries and are open for non-participating Member States.

The governance model chosen for the centralised supervision and resolution of banks largely follows the model of monetary policy. Supervision and resolution are delegated to independent institutions run by experts on the basis of a mandate formulated and adopted by the EU legislators. Bank regulation stays within the Community approach with the Council and the Parliament as legislators acting on proposals by the Commission.

The EU regulation on the Single Supervisory Mechanism (SSM), which entered into force in November 2013, assigns the supervision of significant euro-area banks to the ECB in cooperation with the national supervisory authorities. The decision-making body of the SSM is the ECB Governing Council. However, decisions are prepared by the Supervisory Board of the SSM, which is composed of a chair (appointed for a non-renewable term of five years) and a vice-chair chosen among the members of the ECB Executive Board, four ECB representatives and the representatives of the national supervisors. The ECB Governing Council adopts draft decision prepared by the Supervisory Board under the 'non-objection' procedure: the decision is deemed adopted if the Council does not object within a given period.

Assigning monetary policymaking and financial supervision to the same institution has raised questions about potential conflicts of interest. The ECB may face a trade-off between monetary and financial stability when banks under the supervision of the SSM face liquidity constraints: financial stability may require lower interest rates, monetary stability higher rates. However, the case is not clear-cut and there are also arguments against a separation of the two tasks (Goodhart, Schoenmaker (1993)).

The common framework for the resolution of banks is implemented through the Single Resolution Mechanism (SRM) underpinned by an eponymous EU regulation. The SRM entered into force in August 2014 and is directly responsible for the resolution of banks supervised by the SSM. The governing body of the SRM is the Single Resolution Board (SRB) organised as an independent EU agency; it has its own legal personality and is separated from other EU institutions.

Upon notification from the ECB that a bank is failing or about to fail, the SRB prepares a resolution plan which will typically include recourse to the Single Resolution Fund (SRF). The SRF is sourced by contributions from banks in the participating Member States. The fund is being gradually built up with a target level of at least 1 per cent of the amount of the covered deposits of all credit institutions within the banking union to be reached by the end of 2023. Within the SRM, the SRF will be used as a last resort and only after own funds of the institutions under resolution have been bailed-in. To overcome a possible shortfall of funds during the SRF build-up an intergovernmental agreement has been reached in December 2015 whereby participating Member States will provide credit lines to the SRB.

First steps were also taken to create a single deposit insurance scheme. At the end of 2015 the Commission put forward a concrete legislative proposal as a further step towards a full banking union. However, the proposal was not received favourably by some Member States and has not made any progress.

Since financial markets are integrated at a global level, common regulation and supervision in the EU banking union cannot abstract from the international context. Significant differences in the regulatory and supervisory environment could give rise to harmful arbitrage or even undermine financial stability. Taking into account the economic environment may also be relevant for monetary and possibly even fiscal governance in the euro area. However, due to the high degree of mobility of capital and the sheer amount of global cross-border transactions, financial regulation and supervision are a particular case. That is why an important part of the EU legislation underlying the banking union is consistent with prior agreements reached in the relevant international forum, the Basel Committee on banking supervision.

III. The Political Economy of the Euro Area Governance Framework

With the notable exception of monetary policymaking and, very recently, the SSM and SRM, which are run by independent agencies, the implementation of the euro-area economic governance framework has been challenging since inception. In part, difficulties are explained by the need to progressively adapt the framework to new and evolving insights about how the single currency area works. To an important degree, however, the implementation of the framework was simply not in line with the letter and spirit of the underlying legislation, or available instruments have simply not been applied. In most areas, a clear gap has emerged between the stated objectives of the governance framework and actual outcomes, where the wedge is being driven by the political economy of the decision-making process.

The Council, the EU institution which ultimately holds the decision-making power, is not a homogenous entity that exclusively pursues the interest of the EU or the euro area as a whole. Rather, it encompasses different and often diverging interests that may evolve over time. The ministers participating in the Council meetings are accountable to their national constituencies or more specifically, to the national constituencies supporting the national government. Moreover, ministers in the Council, as politicians in general, are not self-effacing decision makers pursuing the common good: they are motivated by a specific ideology and the prospect of re-election. From this point of view, the Council does not differ from national institutions. They both encompass representatives of different national or subnational interests driven by opportunistic motives.

A prominent example is the pro-cyclical nature of fiscal policymaking, especially in economic good times. As indicated in section II.B, under the SGP Member States are expected to keep their budget balance at a sustainable level and to let automatic stabilisers iron out country-specific shocks. A complex system of rules and procedures is available to ensure compliance.

Yet, the actual track record of the SGP in ensuring counter-cyclical fiscal policies and sustainable public finances has been mixed at best. There is ample evidence indicating that while the SGP may on average have reduced the size of government deficits, Member States still tend not to take advantage of economic good times to create the buffers necessary to face economic downturns (*Public Finance in EMU, 2007* (2007)).

In the final analysis, when rules start to bite why should ministers punish themselves? Also, the EU is a multipurpose institution. Fiscal policy is just one out of many policies carried out within the same EU governance framework. In such a setup, horse-trading across policy areas is a typical feature of the political process. The situation is different in independent single-purpose institutions like the ECB where political trade-offs across areas of policymaking is excluded by design.

On top of the inherent tendency of policymakers to pursue specific interests in an opportunistic manner, positions are typically not aligned in the Council where in most cases decisions are taken by a qualified majority. Therefore, even if at a given moment there is a majority of countries in favour of upholding the provisions of EU economic governance, they may not represent the necessary majority of votes in the Council; large countries can form a blocking minority: four countries representing 35 per cent of the EU population. During the post-2007 crises, the relative power of large versus small countries was replaced or complemented by the divide between creditors and debtors. The divide became particularly apparent at the intergovernmental level in the Eurogroup, especially in relation to financial assistance programmes, where decisions are taken by unanimity.

Admittedly, the Council makes decisions on the basis of recommendations or proposals put forward by the Commission, which is expected to be the 'guardian of the Treaty'. However, the ultimate responsibility for making Member States observe the provisions of economic governance lies with the Council. This principle was underscored and confirmed by the ruling of the European Court of justice in 2004. The Commission had requested a ruling, in November 2003, after Germany and France chose not to accept the Commission recommendation under the SGP, which would have taken the two countries a step further towards a fine.

More recently, when Spain and Portugal failed to comply with the EU fiscal rules in spring 2015, the Commission took a less confrontational approach. It first postponed recommendations and proposals for the Council and finally decided to forego the sanctions foreseen by the SGP (by setting them to zero). The Commission has been equally cautious with the excessive imbalance procedure. Since inception, it has never recommended a corrective action plan to Member States with excessive imbalances.

The Commission's position can be explained by growing concerns of democratic legitimacy. Against the backdrop of a weak and fragile economic recovery in most euro-area countries, the rationale of fiscal consolidation has been increasingly questioned by the Council, the European Parliament and more generally by growing anti-European, anti-euro sentiments in almost all Member States. In the absence of more political integration which would allow EU legislators to amend (or possibly confirm or even strengthen) the economic surveillance framework, the Commission preferred to avert a clash with the Council which may have further weakened its own position and the governance framework as a whole.

This episode underscores a more fundamental problem inherent in the EMU: the imbalance between economic and financial integration on the one hand and political integration on the other. While an increasing number of economic policy tasks have been moved to the EU level, political integration has been lagging. Complete economic and monetary unions, such as for instance the United States, are endowed with an array of centralised institutions that cover all key macroeconomic functions such as stabilising economic cycles, safeguarding financial stability and offering crisis management support to fend off a systemic meltdown. Most importantly, in complete unions the central government has, within the agreed division of labour across levels of government, the power to enforce decisions. This is not the case in the EMU. Individual nation States still play a central role because of the dominance of the Council in implementing policies. As a result, euro-area governance falls between existing institutional boundaries.

IV. Current Challenges and Future Avenues

The post-2007 crises exposed serious gaps in the Maastricht architecture. Some of the gaps were known since inception (no fiscal and political integration alongside a single currency and a single market), others emerged as painful lessons from the crisis (the crucial and potentially disruptive role of financial systems). Pushing ahead with monetary integration was a deliberate political compromise accepted by the fathers of the euro, built on the assumption that soon 'the horses would be put in front of the cart'.

In response to crises the EU has made great strides towards redressing the governance gaps. At the same time, progress remains limited and resistance hard when it comes to further fiscal and political union; the book of collected articles, *How to Fix Europe's monetary union: views of leading economists* (2016) presents a comprehensive discussion of issues and possible solutions. The hope that monetary union would pave the way for further political and fiscal integration turned out to be wishful thinking. The willingness of participating Member States to devolve core elements of their sovereignty has been overestimated.

In spite of important progress, the current snapshot of the macroeconomy of the euro area still shows important disparities and tensions across countries. Following the usual and stereotypical simplification (for illustrative purposes only), there is a group of core countries exhibiting a sound macroeconomic performance, whereas another group of mostly peripheral countries struggles with persisting high unemployment, shaky public finances and other symptoms of macroeconomic weakness.

Against this backdrop the key question is whether the current EMU framework is sufficiently resilient to endure a conceivably still long period of adjustment in the periphery, with persisting high levels of unemployment, until wages and prices have fallen enough to restore competitiveness, or whether policy interventions from the centre are necessary to facilitate the adjustment process or soften its economic and social impact on the ground.

While it is difficult to determine the exact point of resistance of the EMU construction, there is a growing sense that we are approaching the limits of the current framework. The macroeconomic policy options offered by the current framework have been largely exhausted, and more and more people in key euro-area Member States are increasingly frustrated about how the EU, including the euro, is working or, from their perspective, not working. The rapid advance of nationalist political movements in many EU Member States testifies to this growing frustration. Moreover, the remaining non-participating Member States are less and less inclined to adopt the single currency as it is perceived as a source of instability rather than stability and prosperity.

What significantly complicates matters at the moment and limits the in-built forces of economic adjustment is the persistently low rate of inflation coupled with monetary policy rates at the zero lower bound. In such a context, the required downward adjustment of wages and prices in peripheral countries is much more difficult to achieve. In theory, one could of course envisage a policy aimed at generating higher (above target) inflation in core and surplus countries coupled with wage and price moderation in the periphery, but the feasibility of such a policy is limited for various reasons. First, monetary policy is already stretched. The ECB, like most other central banks in advanced economies, has exhausted its conventional arsenal and the effectiveness of unconventional measures in stimulating output and inflation is still to be determined. Secondly, higher inflation, especially above target, is difficult to reconcile with the statute of the ECB and with preferences in some euro-area countries.

The current framework also limits options to soften the impact of economic adjustment via fiscal policy. The aggregation of national fiscal policies does not necessarily amount to an appropriate fiscal stance for the currency area as a whole. Fiscal space has either been exhausted due to past policy mistakes prior to the crisis, and now sustainability concerns kick in, or is not being used fully where available (European Central Bank (2016), European Commission (2016)). The central level cannot step in because: (a) the current fiscal framework can only prescribe fiscal consolidation but not expansions; (b) there is no centralised fiscal capacity which would allow the EU to directly offer support to aggregate demand in the euro area.

Overall, the current system remains vulnerable to future shocks as the room for macroeconomic policy manoeuvre has been exhausted and structural reforms have been implemented very reluctantly at the national level. Any new disruption could put serious strain on an already exposed framework.

In June 2015, the presidents of the European Council, the European Commission, the European Parliament, the Eurogroup and the ECB outlined an ambitious plan to complete the EMU dubbed the five presidents' report (5PR, European Commission, *Completing Europe's Economic and Monetary Union, report of Jean-Claude Juncker in close collaboration with Donald Tusk, Jeroen Dijsselbloem, Mario Draghi and Martin Schulz*). Over the medium to long run the report includes two main proposals. It strikes a balance between the need to strengthen the structural reform momentum, especially in countries where competitiveness is weak, with the need to make macroeconomic policymaking for the currency area as a whole more effective. What ultimately links the two proposals is the insight that structural reforms will not be implemented unless there are the right incentives. In any monetary and economic union the only instrument the central level holds to ultimately persuade subordinated levels of government to carry out certain economic policies is a central budgetary capacity.

Concretely, the 5PR envisages the establishment of a centralised macroeconomic stabilisation mechanism, where access would be made conditional on compliance with binding economic convergence standards. Such an exchange aims at balancing the need for risk reduction (or responsibility) with the need for risk sharing (or solidarity) across Member States. In parallel, the 5PR also envisages more political integration. This is of crucial importance for two reasons. First, euro-area economic governance has reached a level of considerable complexity where important elements are located outside the Community framework. Secondly, and probably more importantly, the devolution of additional economic policy tasks to the EU level needs the appropriate democratic legitimacy and accountability at the central level. In fact, one of the main limitations of the Maastricht plan was to push ahead with economic and monetary integration, hoping that political integration would follow. *À la longue* the EMU will only succeed if it overcomes the tension between democratic legitimacy and the historical prerogatives of nation States with a view to reap and effectively govern the benefits of economic integration and stability.

Bibliography

Alesina, A and Perotti, R, *The political economy of budget deficits*, NBER [National bureau of economic research] working paper No. 4637 (Cambridge (Mass), 1994) (also online).

Baldwin, R and Giavazzi, F (eds), *How to fix Europe's monetary union: views of leading economists* (London, 2016) (also online).

Bernanke, BS, *The great moderation: remarks by governor Ben S. Bernanke at the meetings of the Eastern economic association* (Washington (DC), 2004) (also online).

Blanchard, REO, Dell'Ariccia, G and Mauro, P (eds), *Rethinking macroeconomic policy*, International Monetary Fund staff position note No. 3 (Washington (DC), 2010) (also online).

Brunila, A, Buti, M and Franco, D (eds), *The stability and growth pact: the architecture of fiscal policy in EMU* (London-New York, 2001).

Buti, M and Sapir, A (eds), *Economic policy in EMU: a study by the European Commission services* (Oxford, 1998).

Buti, M, Deroose Servaas, S and Gaspar, V et al (eds), *The euro: the first decade* (Cambridge-New York, 2010).

Committee for the study of economic and monetary union, *Report on economic and monetary union in the European Community*, s l (Luxembourg, 1989) (also online).

European Central Bank, 'The euro area fiscal stance' (2016) 4 *ECB economic bulletin* 68–87 (also online).

European Commission, *Towards a positive fiscal stance for the euro area. Communication from the Commission to the European Parliament, the Council, the European economic and social committee and the Committee of the regions*, COM(2016) 727 final (Bruxelles, 2016) (also online).

Fleming, M, 'Domestic financial policies under fixed and floating exchange rates' (1962) 9(3) *International monetary fund staff papers* 369–80.

Goodhart, CH and Schoenmaker, D, *Institutional separation between supervisory and monetary agencies*, LSE [London school of economics] financial markets group, special paper No. 52 (London, 1993) (also online).

Mundell, R, 'A Theory of optimum currency areas' (1961) 51(4) *American economic review* 657–65 (also online).

Mundell, R, 'Capital mobility and stabilisation policies under fixed and flexible exchange rates' (1963) 29(4) *Canadian journal of economics and political science* 475–85 (also online).

Obstfeld, M, 'Europe's gamble' (1997) 2 *Brookings papers on economic activity* 241–317 (also online).

Padoa-Schioppa, T, *The road to monetary union in Europe: the emperor, the kings, and the genies* (Oxford, 1992).

'Public finances in EMU, 2007' (2007) 3 *European economy*, monographic issue (also online).

Schoenmaker, D, *Governance of international banking: the financial trilemma* (Oxford, 2013).

Taylor, JB, 'Reassessing discretionary fiscal policy' (2000) 14(3) *Journal of economic perspectives* 21–36 (also online).

Uhlig, H, 'One money, but many fiscal policies in Europe: what are the consequences?' in M Buti (ed), *Monetary and fiscal policies in EMU, interactions and coordination* (Cambridge, 2003) 29–64 (also online).

We are grateful to Niels Thygesen for his precious commentaries, specifically on the history and the economic reasoning behind the European single currency. We would like also to extend our thanks to Luis Fau Sebastian for his commentaries on the part regarding monetary policy. Eric McCoy and Gerda Symens provided essential support during the research stage.

17

The European Central Bank

LUCREZIA REICHLIN

I. Description of the Institution

The European Central Bank (ECB) was established on 1 June 1998, replacing the European Monetary Institute. On that date, 11 of the 19 countries that currently belong to the ECB were members of the Union (Austria, Belgium, Finland, France, Germany, Ireland, Italy, Luxembourg, the Netherlands, Portugal and Spain).

After a brief transition phase, the euro was introduced on 1 January 1999, and the ECB took over all the monetary policy and foreign exchange administration duties that were previously carried out by the central banks of the eurozone countries. The exchange rates of the member countries' national currencies against the euro were also irrevocably established on the same date.

In 2002 the national currencies were definitively taken out of circulation and replaced by the single currency, the euro. Today the euro is the currency of 19 countries (Austria, Belgium, Cyprus, Estonia, Finland, France, Germany, Greece, Ireland, Italy, Latvia, Lithuania, Luxembourg, Malta, the Netherlands, Portugal, Slovakia, Slovenia and Spain). The ECB and the central banks of all the Member States of the Union comprise the European System of Central Banks (Eurosystem).

On 4 November 2014 the ECB took on the additional responsibility of supervising all banks in the Member States participating in the single supervisory mechanism (directly in the case of leading banks and indirectly via the national supervisory authorities for other banks). The Single Supervisory Mechanism (SSM) for banking supervision in Europe comprises the ECB and the national supervisory authorities of the eurozone.

The ECB is a public agency governed by European law with its own legal personality, and exercises its powers and manages its finances independently. Its capital is held by the national central banks of the Member States in shares reflecting the GDP of each country belonging to the monetary union.

Despite being independent, the ECB's actions are monitored by the European Parliament and the ECB president reports on monetary policy to Parliament every quarter. The ECB also reports to Parliament on the various forms of banking supervision introduced by the SSM. In addition, the European Council appoints the executive board of the ECB after consulting the European Parliament and the governing council.

II. Monetary Policy

A. Objectives and Strategy

The primary objective of the ECB's monetary policy is to maintain price stability, which it defines as keeping inflation (harmonised index of consumer prices annual rate) below, but close to 2 per cent over the medium term. This definition of its mandate is based on the idea that price stability is the best way to guarantee employment and economic growth in the long term since, over that horizon, these depend on supply factors, and monetary policy cannot affect their performance. Neo-Keynesian models imply that, under certain conditions, by guaranteeing price stability in the medium term, the central bank can also achieve the objective of full employment (Woodford (2003)). However, in the short term, it is good practice to tolerate temporary deviations of inflation away from its target because these are the consequence of monetary policies aiming to stabilise cyclical fluctuations in the real economy that are necessary when external shocks take the economy to below the full use of its resources. This conceptual framework has inspired the monetary policy of the majority of the world's central banks since the 1990s, even if it has been interpreted in different ways and applied at different discretionary levels.

Some central banks have adopted the strategy of inflation targeting, which is a monetary policy regime in which the central bank has an explicit target inflation rate for the medium term that it is bound to meet because the government has established it by law; in this regime the central bank is independent from the government but is responsible, and as such accountable, for achieving the target. As in the case of the central banks that have adopted this strategy, the target is expressed as a quantifiable objective, which is in turn motivated by a need for transparency. Transparency is defined as the ability to monitor the central bank's performance, a necessary factor for justifying the independence it enjoys. Unlike the pure form of inflation targeting, the ECB leaves a non-quantified margin of ambiguity 'of below 2 per cent'. Furthermore the objective is not symmetrical, which suggests greater tolerance for inflation below 2 per cent than higher than 2 per cent. Both the ambiguity and the asymmetry have been the subject of criticism, the former for not providing a sufficiently clear guide for the markets, and the latter because it introduces a deflationary bias in monetary policy.

The ECB has a two-pillar strategy. The first pillar is based on economic analysis that focuses on the factors that determine short to medium-term price fluctuations and on the financial conditions of the economy. The analysis in this pillar is based on the assessment of various economic indicators by means of forecasting models and qualitative studies. The second pillar focuses on a longer-term horizon and is based on monetary aggregates, in particular M3 (which comprises working capital and overnight deposits, M1; deposits with an agreed maturity of up to and including two years or redeemable at a period of notice of up to and including three months, M2–M1; money market fund shares/units, repurchase agreement transactions and debt securities with a maturity of up to two years, M3–M2), to assess the inflation risks in that horizon and validate the comparative results of the economic analysis and the projections. The ECB uses a benchmark value for M3 growth based on an estimate of the historical relationship between the demand for money and prices (for a description of monetary analysis and its practical use in the precrisis years, see Lenza, Pill, Reichlin (2010)). Analysis of the two pillars then makes it possible to establish the quantity of monetary stimulus appropriate to the target.

This strategy is the result of the combination of two traditions: that of the Bundesbank (the German central bank), which was based exclusively on the currency growth target in order to guarantee price stability, and that of inflation targeting.

B. Instruments

The ECB's monetary policy, like that of the majority of central banks, mainly uses the short-term interest rate.

The key interest rate is that on the main refinancing operations (MROs), which are temporary financing operations with a maturity of one week carried out by national central banks by means of auctions. These 'open market operations' involve the buying (or selling) of securities, which create (or absorb) the monetary base. In general they are repurchase agreements, hence temporary, based on spot sale/purchase contracts with an agreement to buy/sell the securities back later or on collateralised loans. In normal times the monetary base offer is mainly provided by means of MROs. These operations are not to be confused with definitive operations (OMTs, Outright Monetary Transactions), which involve the purchase of government bonds on the secondary market, normally used by the Federal Reserve and the central bank, but only recently by the ECB.

Other rates significant for monetary policy are the rate on the deposit facility, which banks use to make overnight deposits (from the afternoon to the morning of the next day) with the central bank and the rate on the marginal lending facility, which the central bank uses to offer overnight credit to retail banks. These are rates on operations that take place at the initiative of the counterparties that need them for daily liquidity management. The loans are collateralised. The difference between the refinancing rate and the deposit facility rate gives what is known as a corridor, containing the fluctuations in the interbank interest rate. The ECB also requires a compulsory reserve, that is, a percentage of deposits to be held on average over a given month with the central bank (for a detailed description of the monetary policy instruments see the Bank of Italy or ECB websites).

Since the 2008 crisis, the ECB has introduced new monetary policy measures (non-standard measures) to tackle the extraordinary nature of the economic and financial situation (for a short description of these policies, see below).

III. A Stateless Currency

The euro operates through a single monetary policy formulated by the governing council of the ECB, although it is implemented by the national central banks of the Member States (European System of central banks). Fiscal policy on the other hand is decided and implemented by the 19 separate national governments that have adopted the euro as their common currency.

The supranational character of the single monetary policy in a context in which political legitimacy and budget sovereignty are still on a national level is at the core of the bitter controversies over the ECB's action since the crisis of 2008.

To comprehend the unique and ambitious nature of this experiment it is worth bearing in mind a few basic concepts.

IV. The Central Banks

The role of the central banks has evolved over time. The central bank was established as the bank of banks with a role that we could define as their 'strongbox'. Since then it has evolved to become a 'lender of last resort' to financial institutions experiencing liquidity crises, but, at least until recently, has remained a private institution. Today the central banks are almost all governed by public law, although their shareholders, in some jurisdictions, remain formally private. Today the main responsibility of the central bank is monetary policy and, in many cases, banking supervision.

In informal terms, it could be said that today central banks are hybrid institutions: banks, but also part of the State in the provision of banking supervision and in setting monetary policy. Furthermore, in modern democracies, central banks are accountable to Parliament and their profits go to the State.

The central banks have a specific privilege: they can meet their financial obligations to the public and retail banks by creating additional money at practically no cost. For this reason their debt (their balance-sheet liabilities) cannot really be considered debt. In a system like the current one, in which currency does not need to respect convertibility with a tangible good (fiat money) and in which the exchange rate is flexible, the central system can create unlimited liquidity.

This privilege, together with the fact that the central banks are effectively the property of the government, shows how closely linked monetary and budget policy are. The central bank's budget has a unique role in the consolidated public sector budget because the money it creates can in principle be used to finance public spending. In fact, before the principle of the independence of the central bank became established as a rule of good governance, countries used it to finance their current expenditure. When the gold standard was in place, and exceptional costs – for example to fund wars – required the creation of a currency that was incompatible with maintaining the fixed gold parity, it was common to temporarily renounce convertibility with the inevitable cost of inflation and, in some cases, of hyperinflation. In today's fiat money system there is no gold convertibility constraint. In addition, the central bank can operate with negative net assets, and is therefore not subject to normal budget constraints. In fact, should it make losses due to the sale of assets at a lower cost than their balance-sheet entry value, the central bank can still carry on its business and, for example, purchase assets by creating money or granting loans to banks to create reserves. However, monetary base creation could put price stability at risk and undermine the credibility of the issuing institution. It is precisely to avoid such a situation that in recent decades the majority of central banks have, in accordance with the Treasury, set themselves a specific price stability target that they are legally bound to meet. We could say that in a fiat money system, this constraint exists to regulate monetary policy in a similar way to that of the gold standard.

In light of the above, the ECB's statutory objective to maintain the medium-term inflation rate at just below 2 per cent and its independence should be interpreted as a way of ensuring the stability of the eurozone currency, and of protecting the institution and its monetary policy choices from refinancing requests from specific Member States. In general, giving in to such pressures creates moral hazards but, in the context of monetary union, it is particularly controversial because it also means taking budget risks. In fact, should the Union break up, the losses would be borne by everyone and would therefore constitute a transfer of resources between countries without taxpayers sanctioning them within the framework of a political process. Whereas in the event that the Union remains intact and the ECB incurs losses due to the sale of government bonds issued by countries at risk of default, it would be forced to issue reserves in order to perform its monetary policy tasks, with the risk of causing inflation.

However, during a financial crisis, the concept of independence between the central bank and the Treasury, while theoretically clear-cut, is not generally sufficient to guide the action of the central bank, because the need to maintain financial stability and to provide liquidity may come in conflict with the need for price stability. When tension is created between the different objectives and when those of financial stability predominate over those of monetary policy, central banks take risks. To avoid putting taxpayers' money at risk it is important to put in place an institutional architecture involving a clear separation of the duties of central banks, governments and the private sector. As we will see in our short reconstruction of the recent crisis, this was lacking in the eurozone and led to the ECB being excessively involved in managing the crisis.

V. The ECB and the Treaty

From an economic point of view the purpose of monetary union was to avoid the monetary and exchange rate instability that had weighed on Europe for decades and in particular since the end of the Bretton Woods system. The various attempts by the European countries to guarantee exchange rate stability by means of agreements involving semifixed rates had produced an asymmetrical situation in which the most stable country, Germany, acted as the leader in monetary policy and anyone that could not comply – either due to different preferences on stabilisation policy or to an objective economic weakness – became vulnerable to speculative attacks. The monetary union was conceived as a solution to this problem. If on the one hand a country that became a member of the Union lost the exchange rate as a stabilisation instrument, on the other, by taking part in the joint decisions on the single monetary policy, they could express their opinion in a Council in which Germany was only one of the countries sitting around the table. In this way, it was hoped, the asymmetry of the previous system would come to an end.

The creation of the euro, however, was and continues to be an ambitious and unique experiment, because it involves a shared currency being used by a group of countries that have retained sovereignty over their political and fiscal systems and their own economic responsibilities. This is why the single currency would not have been possible if it had not been seen right from the start as part of a more ambitious project of political integration. Despite this, in the Treaty of Maastricht of 1992, with a view to monetary union, the relationship between the two aspects – the economic and the political – was still vague, also in order to avoid creating obstacles to the project.

Obviously renouncing monetary sovereignty was regarded with suspicion, and the architecture created by the Treaty of Maastricht, which constitutes the legal basis for monetary union, was an attempt to establish rules that would reassure the various parties and protect the ECB from government interference in a situation in which the single currency was being introduced without a common budget authority.

The Treaty of Maastricht tackles the problem in two ways. First, it establishes economic convergence criteria to comply with as a condition for being allowed to join the 'club': budget discipline and relatively standardised inflation and interest rates. Secondly, it establishes that, once they have become members of the 'club', countries must respect certain rules that force them to maintain budget discipline. A union based on rules and not on a discretionary policy was also seen as a way of avoiding political negotiations (like those that had taken place during the discussions about parity alignment in the European exchange rate mechanism), which had proven to be a source of financial instability in the 1970s, 1980s and 1990s.

The Treaty also affirms the principle of subsidiarity, according to which decisions are only taken at a federal level when they are not effective if taken at a national level. In this sense the motivation underlying the fiscal rules was to ensure that monetary policy did not create distortions. For example, they avoided the possibility of an 'almost fiscal' monetary policy on the part of the ECB: in other words, a policy in which the financing requirements of non-solvent countries or banks predominated over those of maintaining price stability in the eurozone. However, the credibility of these rules proved to be limited right from the start, and they were in fact revised in 2003–04 with the introduction of the Stability Pact. The crisis then showed that the rules, even in their revised form, were not sufficient to guarantee fiscal discipline and, in certain circumstances, could even be counterproductive. We will go back to this issue at the end of the essay.

The essential elements of the Treaty as far as the ECB is concerned are: (a) the principle of independence, not only in an institutional but also in a financial sense (the latter limits the likelihood that the ECB can develop negative capital); (b) a mandate defined in terms of a single priority objective in which the maintenance of price stability in the eurozone has a central role; and (c) prohibition on the financing of governments by monetary means.

The first principle had been the subject of bitter debate in the run-up to monetary union also because, at the time, the independence of central banks was not yet a shared principle in western democracies. François Mitterrand, for example, was reluctant to accept the principle of a sovereign central bank without a Europe-wide political power (for a historical reconstruction of the debate that led to the establishment of the ECB, see Marsh 2009; James 2012). The same applies to the second principle, as at the time inflation targeting had not yet become a dominant paradigm. In the end, the ECB adopted a hybrid model, which has elements of inflation targeting in as much as it sets a numerical inflation target, but remains tied to the Bundesbank tradition in as much as, in the second pillar, it follows a target for the currency's growth rate. As far as the third principle is concerned, the Treaty sets a legal restriction on the ECB bailing out States. This is the no bail-out principle and was the natural addendum to the idea that the Union should not become a vehicle for fiscal sharing, that is, for redistributive budget policies between countries. We shall see then how, in a situation in which restructuring the sovereign debt of a Member State – Greece – proved to be impossible without consequences for the stability of the euro, this principle became one of the most critical factors during the crisis.

Moreover, the ECB was established without authority over banking supervision which, until a short time ago, was the task of the national central banks. The division of tasks in the European Union (EU) was originally as follows: the national authorities were responsible for supervision, the ECB for monetary policy and the EU for financial regulation. The ECB in any case acquired a key role in safeguarding financial stability, as it is responsible for the payments systems and provides emergency liquidity for the system as a whole (through market operations). Emergency liquidity for individual institutions (ELA, Emergency

Liquidity Assistance) on the other hand remains the task of the national central banks even if subject to the prior approval of the ECB (given the potential fiscal risk in the provision of liquidity during a banking crisis, the responsibility for ELA is assigned to the national banks which implement it at their own risk; the risk of ELA operations, unlike that of monetary policy operations, is not shared between countries).

This division of tasks between national authorities and the ECB, justified by the reluctance to share risk in the event of difficulties for the individual institutions located in a single country, has been the subject of criticism from the outset.

In particular, criticism has centred on the fact that the eurozone was created without a federal authority for resolving cross-border banking crises. For example, in the pre-crisis years, Charles Goodhart (2003) and Xavier Freixas (2003) wrote on this subject, predicting that in cross-border crisis situations the national authorities would fail to respond sufficiently because they would not be able to take into account the systemic effects of such crises. On the other hand, the lack of a federal resolution fund is explained by the political difficulty of setting one up in the absence of a common budget authority.

VI. History and its Lessons

A. The Quiet Times: 1999–2007

The first 10 years of the euro can be considered a success from the point of view of respecting the mandate. The 1999 changeover took place smoothly. In some countries there were one-off price rises, but the inflation rate remained under control throughout the eurozone, fluctuating around the 2 per cent mark, with medium-term forecasts firmly anchored to that level. Furthermore, the differences between inflation rates in the various countries fell to an all-time low, as did the long-term interest rate differences. This latter figure shows the high level of credibility of the ECB in that it implies that the inflation risk premium fell to zero.

From the point of view of the real economy, average GDP growth in that period was 1.5 per cent, compared with 2.4 per cent in the previous two decades. However, this reflects the average international trend, as shown by the quantitative analysis carried out by Domenico Giannone, Michele Lenza and Lucrezia Reichlin (2010).

The decade was therefore one of financial stability, although the fragility caused by a major expansion in cross-border credit, weak local bank governance and the affirmation of a liquidity provision model, operated by banks and based on the interbank market should have sounded alarm bells for the European supervisory authorities. However, at the time the ECB did not have direct supervisory responsibilities over this function.

B. From the Crisis to Quantitative Easing in 2015

During the crisis, the specific peculiarities of European economic governance, with a federal central bank and national budget and banking supervisory authorities, revealed its weak points.

The ECB found itself to be the only institution with the necessary autonomy to take rapid and independent decisions affecting the euro economy as a whole – important for factoring in the 'externalities' resulting from one country's fragility vis-à-vis the rest of the Union. Furthermore, in its capacity as central bank, the ECB was also the only institution to have access to resources free of national policies and budget constraints.

Its action was decisive in maintaining the integrity of the eurozone, but also led to tensions, because it had to take action in areas that should have been the responsibility of institutions with fiscal authority, able to support banks and insolvent countries.

To gain a better understanding of the problem, we will provide a brief critical outline of the ECB's policies during the crisis, divided by subject: liquidity crisis in the financial sector, sovereign debt crisis and deflationary risks.

C. The Liquidity Crises: 2007–09 and 2011–12

The first symptoms of the liquidity crisis in the banking sector emerged in the eurozone in August 2007, with tensions on the money markets. The spreads between guaranteed and non-guaranteed rates shot up and interbank transactions fell. In this context, which could be defined as one of a generalised counterparty risk, the demand for liquidity from the central bank by the banks, both fragile and healthy, increased significantly (see Lenza, Pill, Reichlin (2010)). With the collapse of Lehman Brothers in the US in 2008, the nature of the crisis changed. A number of banks failed, and the economy entered the worst recession since the 1930s. The interbank market effectively collapsed. This was the first financial crisis in the history of the ECB, and therefore the first test of the robustness of its operating system and, more generally, its economic governance of the euro.

The response to this liquidity crisis can be considered a success. The ECB acted aggressively and swiftly, thanks to an operating model that was fit to deal with this kind of crisis.

As Tommaso Padoa-Schioppa had predicted (2004), the ECB's operating model was well-prepared to act as a 'lender of last resort' in cases of a widespread liquidity crisis, because it had both an open market transaction system well-equipped to deal with systemic crises, and an instrument for providing emergency liquidity to individual institutions (the ELA). The ECB had a head start also over the leading central banks, including the Federal Reserve (Fed) in the States. It had a larger budget (in part because it remunerates the bank reserves, a policy only adopted by the Fed after the crisis) and therefore greater capacity to absorb liquidity shocks. In addition, it started from a broader definition of eligible collateral in its operations with banks and accepted a broader category of institutions as counterparties in its operations (Pill, Reichlin (2016)).

This enabled the ECB to adopt a systemic approach to the crisis right from the start, rather than having recourse to specific rescues. The bank's action at this stage respected the classic Bagehot's rule, according to which the central bank must act as a lender of last resort when counterparty risk blocks the entire system and therefore has an effect on both fragile and robust banks. According to Walter Bagehot (1873), this policy must meet three conditions: (1) lending must only be to solvent banks against good collateral; (2) loans must be made at high rates so the beneficiary banks cannot use them to finance current operations; and (3) the central bank must make it clear beforehand that it is ready to loan unlimited liquidity to banks that meet the solvency conditions against adequate collateral (for a discussion of the pros and cons of this vision, see, eg, Freixas, Giannini, Hoggarth et al (2000)).

At the start of 2009 the ECB introduced fixed-rate operations and full-allotment (in order to meet demand) – the so-called LTRO (Long Term Refinancing Operations) – in its operations with banks, thus determining the amount of liquidity to provide to the system endogenously and guaranteeing certainty both of the price and the amount. In addition, it extended the definition of eligible collateral to guarantee such operations and extended the timeframe. These measures undoubtedly helped to stabilise the banking sector at a time of great stress, and were further strengthened in May of the same year when the term of the loans was extended to one year. The liquidity injected into the system was immense and helped to keep down the EONIA (Euro OverNight Index Average) rate, which fell below the MRO (Main Refinancing Operations) rate to a level similar to the rate on deposits. At the same time, the ECB announced the purchase of covered bonds (low-risk, high-liquidity) for a total of 60 billion euro in order to try and support that market and hence facilitate lending terms for banks.

All of these operations led to a 60 per cent increase in the budget of the Eurosystem. Although the ECB did not purchase government securities on the secondary market like the Fed and the Bank of England, it acted aggressively and swiftly and thus stabilised the financial system. The particular nature of these exceptional policies, which distinguishes them from those of the United States and the United Kingdom, was motivated by the fact that the financial system in the eurozone is dominated by the banks and not by the market, and therefore this was the most effective way to act in the circumstances.

As Huw Pill and Reichlin have observed (in press), the action of the ECB at this stage should be interpreted as aimed at keeping the financial system and its infrastructure working by acting as an intermediary for transactions for which the market had stopped acting as an intermediary, thus acting as a central counterparty of last resort. These policies need to be seen as complementary to the traditional policies of setting the MRO interest rate. Quantitative works by Lenza, Pill and Reichlin (2010) and by Giannone, Lenza, Pill et al (2012) have shown their efficacy from the macroeconomic point of view and in supporting lending.

However, this monetary policy action needs to be analysed as part of a broader body of policies of response to the crisis. Given the solvency problem of many banks, the national budget (fiscal) authorities had to mobilise themselves to carry out rescues. These were the years of the crisis of Fortis in Benelux, Hypo Real Estate Bank in Germany and various others. In Ireland, the country with the worst banking crisis in the eurozone, the government spent 64 billion euro on bank rescues between 2008 and 2010. At the same time, the public resources mobilised to rescue the banks amounted to around 5 per cent of eurozone GDP. However, unlike in the United States, no single approach to recapitalising the banks was put in place, and each country followed its own route also with regard to its public expenditure capacity (known as fiscal space). The outcome was that in many countries the capacity and/or the incentives for prompt recapitalisation were lacking.

In this situation, while effective in stabilising the financial system, the action of the ECB, in particular with LTROs, allowed banks that should have recapitalised to stay alive because they could obtain liquidity against low-quality collateral.

This problem became clear with the second liquidity crisis in 2011. The eurozone had not yet emerged from the sovereign crisis that began with Greece in 2010, then spread to Ireland and Portugal, and was starting to threaten Spain and Italy. In addition, in the third quarter, the eurozone entered its second recession.

We should take a minute to look at the difference between what happened in 2007–09 and in 2011. In late 2011, when Mario Draghi took over from Jean-Claude Trichet as president of the ECB, there was the risk of a new banking crisis.

Without the tools for a comprehensive approach to recapitalisation, the ECB found itself the only institution in the eurozone able to act across the Union and with the power, if not to resolve the situation, at least to avoid the worst, enabling governments and the European institutions to take the time to put together other solutions. Against this background, Draghi announced a series of long-term liquidity operations in December 2011 and February 2012 (fixed-rate full allotment three-year refinancing operations).

As for the LTROs adopted by Trichet in 2009, by means of these operations the ECB became a centralised counterparty in the interbank market, but now in the longer term and therefore with more relevance for financing the banks and not just for managing liquidity. LTROs were also crucial in supporting the public sector at a time of great tensions on the sovereign debt market. In fact, with these measures, the banks were able to borrow funds from the ECB at a much lower rate and reinvest them in government bonds of peripheral countries which yielded much higher rates. In this way the banks not only made profits, but supported the very market that foreign investors had fled from.

In this situation the ECB acted as an intermediary for cross-border capital flows in an intra-eurozone market that, given the correlation between bank risk and country risk, was once again segmented by country. This phenomenon, known as the diabolic loop (see Brunnermeier, Langfield, Pagano et al (2016)), consists of the fact that a country that has difficulties refinancing its debt exercises pressure on its banks to purchase national government bonds, while a bank in crisis exercises potential pressure on the public finances of its country if it is at risk of failure. The purchasing of their own country's sovereign bonds by banks, made possible by TLTROs (Targeted Longer-Term Refinancing Operations, that is, loans to banks over a timeframe of up to four years at favourable terms on condition that the beneficiary institutions use the funds to provide credit to the real economy, introduced in June 2014 and again in March 2016), reinforced this correlation between bank risk and sovereign risk, which in turn created heterogeneity between the bank rates to customers, reducing the efficacy of Frankfurt's monetary policy.

The ECB's role in intermediating cross-border flows that were no longer guaranteed by the private market was reflected at the time in the Target2 system (the leading European platform for processing large-value payments), which showed the credit and debit positions of the individual national central banks towards others in the Eurosystem. The following example explains how the mechanism works: when a German investor does not renew their purchase of a Spanish term security, the Spanish bank in question requests a three-year loan from the ECB and uses the funds to repay the German investor. The German bank thus accumulates liquidity which it deposits as reserves with the Bundesbank. The result is that the Bundesbank accumulates a credit in Target2 and the Spanish central bank runs up a debt.

In this phase the ECB clearly acted to support those areas of the eurozone financial sector that would have had to be recapitalised and not, as in the first phase, to support a liquidity crisis involving the whole system. This avoided a banking crisis in 2012, but the underlying problems were not tackled at the root. It is interesting to compare the delayed action on recapitalising the banks with what happened in the United States where, since 2008, the government's TARP (Troubled Asset Relief Program) undertook to purchase the banks' toxic securities, thus facilitating the recovery of lending. In the eurozone it was not until the Asset quality review in 2013 and the formation of the Banking Union that there was an in-depth review of the banks' positions. The euro still does not have a recapitalisation fund or an asset management company operating on a federal level today. In this period, precisely because, despite the liquidity facilitations, the banks were in fact paralysed by a problem of capital, there was a far larger fall in the growth of new loans to businesses and households than during the 2008 crisis (Reichlin (2014)).

The short history provided here shows how monetary policy and liquidity support by a central bank must always be accompanied by other instruments for attacking solvency problems. The latter need resources of a fiscal nature, because they require public funds and therefore taxation powers, and for this reason are not appropriate to a central bank. If the ECB demonstrated at the time that it had the appropriate tools to tackle the liquidity crisis, it also became clear that governance of the single currency needed other instruments in order to be effective. Since in any country solvency and liquidity are not clearly distinct from one another beforehand, every central bank is subject to pressures to exceed its mandate at times of crisis. In the eurozone, given the separation between monetary and political jurisdiction, this causes political tensions between countries that undermine the legitimacy of the institution and are detrimental to the swiftness with which it can act.

D. The Sovereign Debt Crisis: 2010–14

Between the end of 2009 and the beginning of 2010 it became clear that Greece was about to enter a sovereign debt crisis on top of a situation of fragility in its banking system. In spring 2010 the country was no longer able to refinance itself on the market. The eurozone found itself fighting off a sovereign crisis in one of its Member States, and thus testing the robustness of the Treaty system and, in particular, of the no bail-out clause.

The ECB faced a dilemma. On the one hand, allowing Greece to default would have led the country to financial collapse, because its banks held a significant amount of government securities, many of which had been used as collateral in refinancing operations. Default would probably have resulted in the country leaving the euro, as well as having an effect on the German and French creditor banks, and infecting other fragile countries like Ireland, whose banking sector was close to collapse, and Portugal, with its growing foreign debt. On the other hand, the ECB was bound by the no bail-out principle. The crisis revealed the fact that the Treaty led to the impossible 'trinity' of no exit (from the euro), no bail-out and no restructuring, as Citibank economist Willem Buiter put it.

Given the dilemma, the ECB turned to national governments so that they were the ones providing the necessary fiscal support. In April a series of bilateral loans were agreed which ultimately took the form of an institutional framework with the creation of the EFSF (European Financial Stability Facility) and then the ESM (European Stability Mechanism). These vehicles operated within the framework of an adjustment programme monitored by the troika comprising the ECB, the European Union and the International Monetary Fund, the latter having joined as a co-financier of the programme.

However, these initiatives were not sufficient to restore market confidence, in part because the private holders of Greek debt were concerned that in the event of default their debt would be considered junior compared with the official sector. In fact, in 2010, the tension between the risk of the restructuring operation and the no bail-out principle was initially resolved by defining the official sector creditors, including the ECB, holders of senior debt compared with those in the private sector.

At this stage the ECB adopted a pragmatic policy and launched the SMP (Securities Market Programme), a programme to purchase public securities from Greece and other peripheral countries on the secondary market. This avoided Greece defaulting, giving Europe the time to implement the troika's programme, which was extended to Ireland (November 2010) and to Portugal (April 2011). Since, at least on paper, these countries had not failed and were taking part in an adjustment programme, the ECB could purchase their sovereign bonds without violating the veto of the Treaty on the monetary financing of Member States. In addition, given the rules on the valuation of government securities in banking budgets – with all Euro-denominated sovereign bonds treated alike – the purchase price was much higher than the market value and the SMP therefore became a vehicle for indirectly supporting refinancing of the debt.

The SMP was accompanied by other measures, including easing of the conditions on the quality of the collateral for ECB loans to banks, which aimed to encourage the banks to purchase government bonds issued by peripheral countries (for use as collateral in refinancing operations with the ECB), and thus to indirectly support refinancing of the public debt.

Once again the steps taken were far from decisive, but they served to give governments the time to find an agreement on the actions that needed to be taken. These delays, certainly not caused by the ECB, turned out to be extremely costly for the countries involved, in particular for Greece.

At Deauville in October 2010, German chancellor Angela Merkel and French president Nicolas Sarkozy decided to accept the principle of PSI (Private Sector Involvement), according to which financial support for countries in crisis had to be subordinated to restructuring the debt, involving losses for private creditors. The meeting at Deauville was a moment of truth in which the unsustainability of the debt of certain countries was recognised, and the principle that debt does not always need to be fully repaid was accepted (Moody (2014)). However, the announcement caused tensions on the sovereign markets of the countries most at risk, Portugal and Ireland, as well as a very hostile political reaction, in particular from the ECB (see, eg, Bini Smaghi (2011)). There is no doubt that an uncoordinated announcement and the lack of a framework for ordered debt restructuring with set rules led to uncertainty that was very costly, but the alternative of denying the reality about Greece's ability to repay its debts by taking time and gradually transferring the debt from private sector budgets to the budgets of the official sector was equally unacceptable. An initial restructuring of the Greek debt involving the private sector took place in 2012, but there is still no debt restructuring framework within the eurozone and the Greek problem has not been solved (on this point, see Kreplin, Panizza, Zettelmeyer (2017)).

The uncertainty gradually led to the contagion of Italy and Spain between 2011 and 2012, and a jump in the spreads between rates in these countries and Germany. It is reasonable to assume that the reason was not the panic brought about by the Deauville agreement, which initially only had an effect on rates in Portugal and Ireland, but the concern that, in the event of the restructuring of larger countries, such as Italy and Spain, EFSF/ESM resources would not be sufficient to act as a backstop.

In this situation what the economists call self-fulfilling turbulence came about, which could have led to multiple equilibria. If the market is concerned that cash-flow problems can lead to difficulties for a country to renew its debt once it has reached full term, leading to default, rates surge because they reflect a premium for this credit risk. The result is a rise in refinancing costs which makes the risk of default even more pressing, causing a vicious cycle that ultimately turns a liquidity risk into a solvency risk, and pushes the economy towards a 'bad equilibrium'. In such a situation, an institution that can act as a lender of last resort can calm the initial concern by providing the liquidity needed to resolve cash-flow problems, thus reducing the risk premium and producing a good equilibrium.

In the monetary union, a country's debt in euro is as if it were in a foreign currency, and therefore subject to sudden desertion by investors, as happens in emerging countries that typically have debt in a foreign currency. This type of crisis is similar to those that the European countries experienced in the fixed exchange rate systems in the 1990s, and that manifested themselves in attacks on currencies. In such circumstances it is not possible to make a distinction between liquidity and solvency, and the central bank has to act as a lender of last resort (De Grauwe (2012)). Unless there is the certainty of a lender of last resort, at a certain point the liquidity crisis becomes an insolvency crisis, and without a bail-out or debt restructuring it can become impossible for a country to remain in the eurozone. In this area, with different fiscal jurisdictions concerned about the potential distributive effects in the event of default, as well as the perverse incentive for budget discipline that this policy would create, the ECB hesitated to act decisively and tried to introduce partial measures that failed to reassure the market.

In August 2011, the SMP was extended to Italy and Spain. But the programme failed. The main reason was the lack of a solid mandate for that policy which, in fact, the ECB itself described as a limited and temporary programme rather than an actual backstop (which would have reassured the markets). Here it is worth mentioning that the president of the Bundesbank Axel Weber resigned in April 2011 in opposition to the ECB's action.

The ECB also made its intervention conditional on reform policies and exercised bilateral pressures on the governments in that sense, something that led it to take on an almost political role in the case of Italy (in August 2011, the ECB sent a letter to Italian prime minister Silvio Berlusconi signed by president Trichet and the future president Draghi in which it indicated the anti-speculation measures that Italy should adopt as a matter of urgency, expressing the need for a commitment to a sustainable budget and to structural reforms: liberalisations and reform of the labour market, of pensions and of the public administration). In addition, its status as a senior creditor continued to rattle the markets.

The tensions therefore continued. In summer 2012 the ECB reached a turning-point that can be considered a middle ground between two extremes: that of a strict interpretation of the principle prohibiting the monetary financing of a country and that à la De Grauwe, which suggested treating the crisis as a liquidity problem and therefore to act as an unconditional backstop. The solution was the introduction of a new instrument, OMTs (Outright Monetary Transactions), by means of which the ECB committed to directly purchase short-term government bonds on condition that the country entered a programme under the aegis of the ESM. Behind this policy can be seen recognition of the principle that a bad equilibrium can emerge as the result of a self-fulfilling vicious circle. However, at the same time, there was recognition of the moral hazard that unlimited intervention would have created. Draghi's announcement in July on the commitment to do anything to save the euro and then that of the OMT programme caused a drastic reduction in the risk premium and placated the financial instability (see Altavilla, Giannone, Lenza (2016), for a quantitative study on the effect of OMTs). Note that OMTs acted by way of creating a pure expectation, as neither Italy nor Spain ever joined the programme.

The comparison between the efficacy of the SMP and the OMT programme is instructive. While the former was not credible, as it was announced as a temporary and limited intervention within a mechanism in which private creditors were considered 'subordinate' and in the context of a crisis in which countries under stress had no fiscal backstop, OMTs were immediately seen as credible in a changed institutional context in which a conditional support intervention was combined with a fiscal support commitment. This credibility is also linked to other steps to reform governance of the euro, such as the proposal to create a banking union in June 2012, and reflects a process of political maturation and the start of a new compromise between the countries of the Union.

E. The Risks of Deflation and Quantitative Easing

Quantitative easing (QE) involves the direct purchase of private and public securities and is a policy implemented during crises by the leading central banks. The ECB only introduced it at the end of 2014 for private securities and in March 2015 for public securities. Unlike the policies setting short-term MRO interest rates, typical of what are considered normal times, and those in response to the crisis during the 2009–14 phase, which were essentially based on fixed rate collateralised loans to the banks (LTROs and TLTROs), QE involves the direct purchase of bonds on the market and is therefore similar to the SMP implemented by the ECB in 2010. Unlike that programme, which as we have seen had been presented as a temporary emergency measure, QE involves a purchasing programme with precise quantitative objectives for a preannounced period.

While the motivation for extraordinary policies such as LTROs or TLTROs was to be equipped with additional instruments complementary to setting interest rates in a situation in which, regardless of interest rate levels, the banks were unable to collect liquidity on the market, QE aimed to exploit additional channels for monetary policy, and can therefore be considered a replacement for the traditional instrument of short-term interest rates (see Pill, Reichlin, in press).

QE is mainly indicated in situations in which short-term interest rates have reached the 'zero lower bound' or in any case a lower limit under which further interest rate cuts would lead to distortions in the financial markets, making traditional interest rate-based monetary policy ineffective.

QE acts on the economy by generating a rebalancing of the portfolio. When central banks buy medium or long-term public securities and reduce the rate on reserves in excess of the mandatory quota, they reduce the rate on the less risky bonds, such as Treasury securities ('safe assets') and thus increase the incentive for private investors to rebalance their portfolios in favour of securities that are more risky, either due to being either more long-term or due to a higher credit risk. *Ceteris paribus*, this exerts upwards pressure on the prices of the more risky investments and encourages the expansion of credit, thus supporting both prices and the real economy. This policy supports credit by acting on the spreads, because it reduces long-term rates when short-term rates have reached an effective downwards limit, and thus flattens the interest rate curve.

There is no doubt that QE came to the eurozone late, when inflation had already fallen to rates dangerously close to zero, also due to a restrictive monetary policy that had seen the ECB raise rates in both April and July 2011, in the midst of the second eurozone recession since the great crisis of 2008 (on this point, see, eg, Orphanides (2016)).

Between 2013 and 2014 the problem was no longer one of a liquidity crisis of the banks in general, but of a too weak recovery, accompanied by risks of deflation and undercapitalisation in some areas of the banking system. The delay is down to a conflict of orientations within the Council and opposition on the part of many countries, in particular Germany, to a rush to purchase potentially high-risk sovereign securities, which would involve credit risk for the ECB and potential redistribution costs in the event that such a risk materialised.

QE finally found the support of a vast majority of the Council when it became clear that the inflation target which the ECB is required to meet under the Treaty was still not being met and the Union was risking entering a period of deflation like Japan in the 1990s.

The ECB's QE programme has been designed in such a way to reduce sharing of the risk: purchases are made in proportion to the country's GDP and not its debt and only a part of the credit risk weighs on the common budget (note in any case that risk sharing does not apply to liabilities, and in fact the accumulation of reserves corresponding to the sale of bonds by the banks to the ECB is in euro; the latter can therefore be redeemed anywhere in the eurozone). Moreover, the purchase of bonds at rates below the rates on bank deposits with the ECB (currently –0.4) is prohibited.

After more than two years of this policy, it is generally considered that macroeconomic goals have been reached both as regards the support for inflation and for economic activity (Andrade, Breckenfelder, De Fiore et al (2016)), but the debate currently centres on the duration of the programme, given the risks that some believe it poses to financial stability, its dampening effect on the banks' profitability, and the moral hazard that is potentially introduced by the purchase of securities of heavily indebted countries. The ECB announced that it would last at least until the end of 2017, but the programme could last longer as could the policy of low interest rates and negative rates on deposits with the central bank. The decision will depend on the dynamics of the inflation rate in the eurozone, which is in turn linked to the degree of consolidation of economic recovery.

F. The Risks that Remain

Eighteen years after the introduction of the euro and after a devastating economic and financial crisis, despite various errors and constraints, the ECB has shown that it has been capable of saving the euro, maintaining price stability and guaranteeing financial stability. This result was obtained through the construction of complementary instruments to monetary policy in the strict sense and the extension of its responsibilities.

As we have argued, the ECB has had to act in a context in which there was no other authority for managing the crisis at a federal level, without an instrument for coordinating monetary and fiscal policy and without a single banking supervisory body. All of this in a situation in which the countries were clearly divided into creditors and debtors and a financial market that, due to the crisis, had become fragmented at a national level.

The costs of this incompleteness originating from the Treaty of Maastricht have been extremely high in terms of employment and growth, and this has fed radical criticisms of the euro and a debate on the benefits of returning to national currencies. It is certainly difficult to carry out a counterfactual analysis to see what would have happened if the eurozone countries had been able to take advantage of the devaluation of their currencies. However, the past teaches us that in highly integrated economies, competitive devaluations do not deliver long-lasting benefits and this in turn suggests that monetary union, if carried out by the institutions needed to guarantee its financial stability and adequate support to demand when subject to stress, remains a difficult but necessary project in order to strengthen the economy of the eurozone.

The history of the crisis demonstrates that the economic architecture of the euro is still incomplete, and further progress requires greater sharing of the risk between Member States, something that is made difficult by the absence of institutions with the political democracy that would legitimise them.

In this situation the ECB remains a sort of 'institution of last resort' (Pill, Reichlin (2016)), under pressure to carry out the 'mission impossible' of safeguarding the integrity of the single currency in the absence of adequate instruments at federal level to deal with fiscal issues (both disciplinary and those concerning the coordination of monetary and fiscal policy) or financial stability, including a framework for debt restructuring (for a discussion of this issue and possible reforms, see Corsetti, Feld, Koijen et al (2016)).

The future of the ECB and of the euro depends on the ability of the Union countries to reform the Treaty and to move towards economic and political integration of the Union, restoring balance to the responsibilities for economic policy among the various authorities.

Bibliography and Websites

Altavilla, C, Giannone, D and Lenza, M, 'The financial and macroeconomic effects of the OMT announcements' (2016) 12(3) *International journal of Central Banking* 29–57.

Andrade, P, Breckenfelder, J and De Fiore, F et al, *The ECB's asset purchase programme: an early assessment*, European Central Bank, working paper No. 1956 (September 2016) https://www.ecb.europa.eu/pub/pdf/scpwps/ecbwp1956.en.pdf.

Bagehot, W, *Lombard Street. A description of the money market* (London, 1873).

Bini Smaghi, L, The European debt crisis, Atlantik-Brücke, Meeting of Regional Group Frankfurt/Hesse (2011) https://www.bis.org/review/r111026c.pdf.

Brunnermeier, M, Langfield, S and Pagano, M et al, *ESBies: safety in the tranches*, Working Paper Series (2016) 21.

Corsetti, GC, Feld, L and Koijen, R et al, *Reinforcing the eurozone and protecting an open society* (2016) http://www.lucreziareichlin.eu/Content/_Documents/Reinforcing%20the%20Eurozone%20-%20MEZ%202%20-%20April%202016.pdf.

Curdia, V and Woodford, M, 'The central bank balance sheet as an instrument of monetary policy' (2011) 58(1) *Journal of monetary economics* 54–79.

De Grauwe, P, The governance of a fragile eurozone (2012) 45(3) *Australian economic review* 255–68.

Freixas, X, Giannini, C and Hoggarth, G et al, 'Lender of last resort: what have we learned since Bagehot?' (2000) 18(1) *Journal of financial services research* 63–84.

Fisher, B, Lenza, M and Pill, H et al, 'Money and monetary policy: the ECB experience 1999–2006' in A Beyer and L Reichlin (eds), *The role of money: money and monetary policy in the twenty-first century. Proceedings of the 4th ECB central banking conference* (Frankfurt 2007) 102–75 https://www.ecb.europa.eu/events/pdf/conferences/cbc4/ReichlinPillLenzaFisher.pdf.

Freixas, X, 'The role of the lender of last resort in EMU' in JJM Kremers, D Schoenmaker and PJ Wierts (eds), *Financial supervision in Europe* (Cheltenham, 2003).

Giannone, D, Lenza, M and Reichlin, L, 'Business cycles in the euro area' in A Alesina and F Giavazzi (eds) *Europe and the euro* (Chicago-London, 2010).

Giannone, D, Lenza, M and Pill, H et al, 'The ECB and the interbank market' (2012) 122(564) *The economic journal* 467–86.

Goodhart, C, 'The political economy of financial harmonization in Europe' in JJM Kremers, D Schoenmaker and PJ Wierts (eds), *Financial supervision in Europe* (Cheltenham, 2003).

James, H, *Making the European monetary union* (Cambridge (Mass)-London, 2012).

Kreplin, E, Panizza, U and Zettelmeyer, J, *Does Greece need more official debt relief? If so, how much?*, Peterson institute for international economics, working paper 17–6 (April 2017) https://piie.com/publications/working-papers/does-greece-need-more-official-debt-relief-if-so-how-much.

Lenza, M, Pill, H and Reichlin, L, 'Monetary policy in exceptional times' (2010) 25(62) *Economic policy* 295–339.

Marsh, D, *The euro* (New Haven-London, 2009).

Moody, A, 'The ghost of Deauville' *Vox* (2014) https://voxeu.org/article/ghost-deauville.

Orphanides, A, *The Fed-ECB policy divergence*, Shadow open market committee Meeting, Princeton Club, New York City (29 April 2016) http://shadowfed.org/wp-content/uploads/2016/04/OrphanidesSOMC-April2016.pdf.

Padoa-Schioppa, T, *Regulating finance: balancing freedom and risk* (Oxford, 2004).

Pill, H and Reichlin, L, 'Exceptional policies for exceptional times. The ECB's response to the rolling crises of the euro area' in H Badinger and V Nitsch (eds), *Routledge Handbook of the economics of European integration* (London-New York, 2016) 351–75.

Pill, H and Reichlin, L, 'Non-standard monetary policy and financial stability: developing an appropriate macrofinancial policy mix' in *Preparing for the next financial crisis: policies, tools and models* (Cambridge in press).

Reichlin, L, 'Monetary policy and banks in the euro area. The tale of two crises' (2014) 39 part B *Journal of macroeconomics* 387–400.

Reichlin, L and Vallée, S, 'Resolving Europe's banking crisis in Italy' in *Project Syndicate* (October 2016) https://www.project-syndicate.org/commentary/europe-italy-flawed-banking-union-by-lucrezia-reichlin-and-shahin-vallee-2016-10?barrier=accesspaylog.

Reichlin, L, 'Populism and the future of central banking' in *Fatal attraction – The year ahead, Project Syndicate* (January 2017) https://www.project-syndicate.org/onpoint/populism-and-the-future-of-central-banking-by-lucrezia-reichlin-2017-01?barrier=accesspaylog.

Woodford, M, *Interest and prices* (Princeton-Oxford, 2003).

All web pages are understood as having last been visited on 04 June 2018.

18

Fiscal Rules in the Economic and Monetary Union

JUSTINE FELIU AND GUNTRAM B WOLFF

Fiscal policies are at the core public policies. In the euro area, 98 per cent of government spending and almost 100 per cent of revenues are at the country-level. Fiscal policies encompass the allocation and the distribution of government revenue, the taxation system, the management of the budget and its deficit and the government debt. Fiscal policies therefore play a major role in national sovereign decision making, including notably decisions on social policies. Fiscal policies also play a significant role in the economic stabilisation of a country's business cycle. Member States of the European Union (EU) generally share the objectives of enhancing macroeconomic stability. In the case of Member States that are part of the euro area (EA), fiscal policies play an even more important role.

In a monetary union, Member States no longer have the power to implement country-specific monetary and exchange rate policies. Standard macroeconomic models like the Mundell-Fleming model predict that in fixed exchange rate systems, the impact of fiscal policy decisions on the macroeconomy becomes larger than in flexible exchange rate systems.

In a monetary union, national fiscal policies can also have numerous spill-over effects on other member countries.

One aspect concerns the consequences of unsustainable fiscal policies. Outside of a monetary union, a country that has run unsustainable fiscal policies can resort to its own central bank to prevent a nominal default. The consequence of a fiscal crisis solved with monetary means would typically be a weaker exchange rate and higher inflation. The government would therefore not nominally default but use the inflation tax to take care of its fiscal problems. In a monetary union, providing access to the central bank for a national fiscal authority would mean that a national fiscal problem would be solved with a supranational inflation tax. The cost of the fiscal policy would thus be socialised in the monetary union through higher inflation or at least jointly issued currency.

A second aspect concerns the impact of fiscal policies on inflation. In a recession, inflation is typically falling as demand is lower than supply. The fall of inflation expectations triggers a response of monetary policy but that monetary policy response affects the entire union. A recession in one major country of the monetary union therefore triggers monetary policy effects for the entire union. Since national fiscal policies are a part of domestic demand, national fiscal policies indirectly also affect the union's monetary policy.

Conversely, when monetary policy is constrained by the zero lower bound, that is, a situation in which it cannot lower the interest rate further and is therefore becoming less effective, fiscal policies become even more important. In particular, standard macroeconomic theory would suggest that fiscal policy needs to be more active in steering the macroeconomy and preventing a fall in inflation when monetary policy is in a liquidity trap or highly constrained. If fiscal spending and revenues are mostly at the national level, it will be the sum of the national fiscal policies that matter for the union as a whole.

Finally, fiscal policies also have an impact on the relative price and wage developments across countries and this becomes more relevant in a monetary union as the nominal exchange rate instrument is absent. There are various channels for this impact. One is often labelled 'fiscal devaluation' in the literature. It is a shift in taxes away from production factors towards consumption, for example a reduction in labour taxes and an increase in VAT taxes. Such a shift would make exporting easier as the cost of production could be lowered while the VAT tax is not applied to exports. It would directly affect the real exchange rate between members of the monetary union, while outside of it, its effects would be at least partially offset by a nominal exchange rate movement. Another channel concerns the macroeconomic channel of fiscal policy. A relatively contractionary policy in one Member State would lower its relative price and wage levels and thereby its real exchange rate vis-à-vis the other members of the monetary union.

Fiscal policies in a monetary union therefore interact strongly with fiscal and economic policies in other countries as well as with the common monetary policy. Every monetary union therefore has to make decisions on how to manage the relations between its fiscal and monetary policies. In this overview article, we will first present the fiscal framework of the Maastricht Treaty (1992). We will then discuss the changes to the fiscal rules and to the stability and growth Pact (SGP (1997)) over time. Finally, we will discuss the practice of implementation of the fiscal rules, before making a few suggestions for the future development of fiscal policies.

I. The Maastricht Setup

The European Union has decided to let the interaction of national fiscal policies and the common monetary policy be governed by a framework that is set out in the European treaties and that is often labelled the 'Maastricht consensus'. The framework was laid down in the Maastricht Treaty and is detailed in chapter 1 of the Treaty on the Functioning of the European Union (TFEU) on economic policy. It can be characterised as a framework based on rules. One of its major aims is to limit national discretions in that framework and is based on three major pillars:

(a) The first pillar is the so-called no monetary financing rule in article 123 and article 124. The articles are meant to limit the financing of public institutions, that is, governments, by central banks. The aim is to prevent access to the printing press of national governments or preventing the first spill-over explained above, namely the risk that unsustainable fiscal policy is socialised through an inflation tax on the entire euro area. The purpose is therefore to prevent excessive inflation as a result of unsustainable national fiscal policies.

(b) The second pillar is the so-called 'no bail out' clause in article 125 TFEU, which states that the Union or a Member State within the EU cannot pay for the debt of any of the Member States. As written in the article, it 'shall not be liable for or assume the commitments of' any public institution of 'any Member State, without prejudice to mutual financial guarantees for the joint execution of a specific project'.
(c) Finally, the third pillar refers to the set of fiscal rules set out in article 126 TFEU and the secondary legislation based on articles 121 and 126. They are the founding principles of the fiscal and budgetary surveillance in the EU and in the SGP. The first paragraph of article 126 is clear: 'Member States shall avoid excessive government deficits'.

The articles set thresholds for the government deficit – which shall not lie above the reference value of 3 per cent of the gross domestic product – and for the gross government debt – which shall not lie above the reference value of 60 per cent of the gross domestic product.

The SGP sets the operational side of the multilateral fiscal and budgetary surveillance. It defines the preventive and the corrective arms as well as the objectives that each Member State has to meet with respect to its specific fiscal and budgetary situation. As part of the 'preventive arm', the Member State needs to submit to the Commission a stability Programme, for EA countries, or a convergence Programme, for non-EA countries, in April of each year as well as a draft budget Plan (EA members only) in October. These must be in line with the Medium-Term Budgetary Objectives (MTOs) of the country concerned that are set in the SGP (following the reform in 2005). The 'corrective arm' sets the operational rules under the excessive deficit Procedure (EDP) and the sanctions that might be imposed on the country concerned. When a Member State is part of the 'corrective arm' of the SGP, it means that it has to meet additional targets to reduce its government excessive deficit. The main rationale of the SGP is thus to ensure sound budgetary policies on a permanent basis.

The articles as well as the accompanying regulations also establish the governance of the fiscal surveillance. The legal basis underlying the economic governance of the European Union are described by article 3 of the Treaty on European Union (TEU), articles 2–5, 119–144 and 282–284 TFEU. Moreover, article 126 and protocol No. 12 annexed to the Treaty describe the process that has to be followed to monitor governments' deficits. The European Commission is in charge of assessing the fiscal situation and making a recommendation to the Council. The Ecofin (*Economic and Financial Affairs Council*, made up of the economics and finance ministers from all Member States within the European Council) is in charge of taking the decision whether a Member State is in a situation of excessive deficit or not based on the recommendation of the European Commission. If the Council decides that a Member State is in a situation of excessive deficit, the latter enters the EDP that gives guidance on reducing the deficit. In case the Council considers the progress as not sufficient enough, it might start imposing sanctions on the country concerned.

A. Changes to the SGP Over Time

In 2005, the SGP was amended for the first time under the pressure of France and Germany. The 2005 modifications concerned the two arms and the economic governance. One of the major changes was related to the calculation of the MTOs. MTOs are part of the preventive arm and are used as a benchmark for each country to give information on the budgetary situation. Each country has to compute its MTO as part of the stability (or convergence) Programme due in April of each year, as mentioned above. Prior to the 2005 SGP, the MTOs for structural budget balances were calculated according to a 'one-rule-fits-all' method. The 2005 framework allowed the MTOs to be country-specific and to take into account crucial economic differences across Member States, such as the risks associated to demographic changes. As explained in Biraschi, Cacciotti, Iacovoni et al (2010):

> MTO differentiation, in turn, had to consider the countries' government debt and implicit liabilities – especially those associated with rising age-related expenditure –, potential growth, and a safety margin minimizing chances of having budget deficits breaching the Maastricht 3 percent reference value (p 7).

MTOs rely on values according to the economic and budgetary position and sustainability risks of the Member States, based on current debt to GDP ratio and the concerned country's potential output growth. If a country's gross debt is higher than the reference value of 60 per cent of GDP, its MTO has to be strictly higher than the reference value of –0.5 per cent of GDP. Otherwise, it has to be higher than the reference value of –1 per cent of GDP. The structural budget balance (excluding effect of cycle and one-off measures) has to be higher than the MTO. In case of a lower structural budget balance, it has to increase by 0.5 per cent of GDP per year.

Over the last eight years, the European Union faced major economic challenges. The 2007–08 financial crises followed by the sovereign debt crisis in 2011 triggered some Member States' bailouts. The EU had to cope with an unexpected series of shocks that dramatically affected the Member States and led to an unstable economic environment. Financial stability became a source of worries and an issue to be solved at the EU-level. It is in this environment that the EU changed its fiscal governance substantially.

B. The 2011 Six-Pack

The Six-pack is a fiscal law package containing five regulations and one directive. The main objectives of this new series of amendments were to strengthen the procedure to avoid excessive deficits and to address the issue of macroeconomic imbalance, which refers to macroeconomic imbalances such as large current account deficits or surpluses, real estate bubble and others. The Six-pack ultimately aims to reinforce the fiscal and budgetary discipline among the EA Member States by threatening to impose prompt sanctions and introducing a 'reverse qualified majority' voting procedure (with the latter, the burden to find a qualified majority, so as a political decision can be reached, is reversed; that is, the Commission's proposal shall be automatically adopted unless a qualified majority of States that are against it arise within the Council).

Concerning the public debt criterion, the amendment defines the reference value for the debt-to-GDP ratio as 60 per cent of GDP and states that if a country exceeds that value, it will be put under EDP (even if its deficit does not exceed the 3 per cent reference value). Another change made was to provide more guidance for the Member States under the preventive arm of the SGP: the amendment determines a new expenditure benchmark to help assess progress towards the MTOs. Note that, from 13 December 2013 onwards, a Member State can be asked to provide a new version of its draft budget Plan in case of non-compliance with the rules set under the preventive arm.

Finally, the 2011 Six-pack builds up a new surveillance framework called the macroeconomic imbalance Procedure (MIP). It aims at monitoring more closely the macroeconomic and financial stability and imbalances in Member States. According to the European Commission, the main goals of the MIP are to identify, prevent and address the emergence of potentially harmful macroeconomic imbalances. It was created as a result of the financial crisis and the increasing need for more macroeconomic surveillance – especially in the EA in which countries are highly interdependent. Like the excessive deficit Procedure, the MIP is based on a series of reference values – called the MIP scoreboard – that aim at ranking and organising by category (five stages) the Member States according to their macroeconomic and financial situation (ie, the degree of their macroeconomic imbalances). The MIP scoreboard is organised in two categories of indicators: the external imbalances and competitiveness (current account balance, net international investment position, real effective exchange rate, export market shares, unit labour cost) and internal imbalances (consolidated private sector debt, private sector credit flow, change in deflated house prices, public sector debt, unemployment rate, change in total financial sector liabilities). Following an in-depth analysis, each country receives recommendations based on its MIP scoreboard and the stage it has been put under. The Six-pack in principle even foresees a sanction in case of Member States' non-compliance.

C. The 2013 Two-pack and the Fiscal Compact

The Two-pack consists of two new regulations that aim at strengthening the fiscal and budgetary discipline within the EA. It aims mainly at reinforcing the discipline among those EA countries that experienced – or are currently experiencing – financial stability issues. It concerns Member States that are under the EDP, the MIP and a financial assistance programme.

The European Fiscal compact – officially the Treaty on stability, coordination and governance in the Economic and Monetary Union – comprises a 'balanced budget rule', debt brake rule, the automatic correction mechanism, the economic partnership programme, the debt issuance coordination, the commitment always to support EDP recommendations and to embed the balance budget rule and the automatic correction mechanism into domestic law. It also foresees that the debt to GDP ratio needs to be reduced by 1/20 of the difference between the current level and 60 per cent of GDP per year. Finally it foresees the creation of the Euro summit at the level of heads of States and governments to discuss euro-area matters.

All of these reforms were intended to cope with the financial instability and the economic uncertainty prevailing in the European Union. The SGP and its extensions ended up being a very 'sophisticated' set of numerical rules that requires strong fiscal surveillance at the EU-level. They have become so sophisticated that many senior officials have admitted that they do not fully understand them.

D. The European Stability Mechanism and the Outright Monetary Transaction

In the course of the various bail-outs, the euro-area members eventually created a European Stability Mechanism (ESM), which provides financial assistance to EA Member States under strict conditionality. ESM financial assistance loans have been granted to a number of EA Member States (Pisani-Ferry, Sapir, Wolff (2013)). Despite the creation of these instruments, however, sovereign yields in the euro area diverged substantially. The argument made by Paul De Grauwe, that this divergence in yields reflects bad equilibria or self-fulfilling runs on countries, has been widely accepted. Yields only started to narrow when the European Central Bank (ECB) put in place its 'whatever it takes' programme, the OMT (*Outright Monetary Transaction*), a programme announced by the president of the ECB, Mario Draghi, on 6 September 2012, under which the ECB makes transactions in secondary sovereign bond markets within the Eurozone. Under the OMT programme, the ECB can buy sovereign bonds of a specific country as long as there is a valid ESM programme in place.

In fact, the euro area has therefore created a significant bail-out capacity. It has done so in a way that it intends to use it only to address problems of liquidity, which can be solved with the right set of national reforms. For cases of debt insolvencies, the ESM and OMT cannot be activated. This distinction is fundamental in theory but it is actually difficult to put in place in practice. The reason is that debt sustainability analysis is not an exact science. Moreover, those ultimately deciding on whether debt is solvent are not neutral players. It is this blurry line that is at the heart of the problem of whether or not the current EA institutional setup needs major or only minor reforms.

Next, we will analyse how the stability and growth Pact is currently performing in the EU.

II. In Practice

We presented the SGP as it is intended to be implemented in the EU. However, implementation de facto looks different from its original conception.

Table 1 shows the actual figures of general government deficit and gross debt in percentage of GDP in all countries of the EU during 2000–15. We use the two reference values to assess country-specific compliance with the headline numbers, namely 3 per cent for the deficit and 60 per cent for the gross debt. Figures 1 and 2 display respectively the general government deficit in percentage of GDP and the general government debt in percentage of GDP in the EU Member States over 2000–15. They show two data points (2000 and the latest available, 2015) and the increase to a peak – in other words the highest value reached for each country over the same period (highest value in the sense of the thresholds: for the deficit it is the lowest, meaning the largest deficit reached by the country, and for the gross debt it is the highest, meaning the largest level of gross debt reached by the country).

Table 1 General government debt and deficit as % of GDP per country

Country	GG variable	2000	2001	2002	2003	2004	2005	2006	2007	2008	2009	2010	2011	2012	2013	2014	2015
Austria	deficit	−2,1	−0,7	−1,4	−1,8	−4,9	−2,6	−2,6	−1,4	−1,5	−5,4	−4,5	−2,6	−2,2	−1,4	−2,7	−1
	debt	65,9	66,5	66,5	65,7	65,1	68,6	67,3	65,1	68,8	80,1	82,8	82,6	82	81,3	84,4	85,5
Belgium	deficit	−0,1	0,2	0	−1,8	−0,2	−2,6	0,2	0,1	−1,1	−5,4	−4	−4,1	−4,2	−3	−3,1	−2,5
	debt	108,8	107,6	104,7	101,1	96,5	94,6	91	87	92,5	99,5	99,7	102,3	104,1	105,4	106,5	105,8
Bulgaria	deficit	−0,5	1,1	−1,2	−0,4	1,8	1	1,8	1,1	1,6	−4,1	−3,1	−2	−0,3	−0,4	−5,5	−1,7
	debt	71,2	65	51,4	43,7	36	26,8	21	16,3	13	13,7	15,3	15,2	16,7	17	27	26
Croatia	deficit	–	–	−3,5	−4,7	−5,2	−3,9	−3,4	−2,4	−2,8	−6	−6,2	−7,8	−5,3	−5,3	−5,4	−3,3
	debt			36,6	38,1	40,4	41,3	38,9	37,7	39,6	49	58,3	65,2	70,7	82,2	86,6	86,7
Cyprus	deficit	−2,2	−2,1	−4,1	−5,9	−3,7	−2,2	−1	3,2	0,9	−5,4	−4,7	−5,7	−5,8	−4,9	−8,8	−1,1
	debt	54,9	56,5	59,7	63,1	64,1	62,8	58,7	53,5	44,7	53,4	55,8	65,2	79,3	102,2	107,1	107,5
Czech Republic	deficit	−3,5	−5,3	−6,3	−6,4	−2,7	−3,1	−2,3	−0,7	−2,1	−5,5	−4,4	−2,7	−3,9	−1,2	−1,9	−0,6
	debt	17	22,8	25,9	28,1	28,5	28	27,9	27,8	28,7	34,1	38,2	39,8	44,5	44,9	42,2	40,3
Denmark	deficit	1,9	1,1	0	−0,1	2,1	5	5	5	3,2	−2,8	−2,7	−2,1	−3,5	−1,1	1,5	−1,7
	debt	52,4	48,5	49,1	46,2	44,2	37,4	31,5	27,3	33,4	40,4	42,9	46,4	45,2	44,7	44,8	40,4
Estonia	deficit	−0,1	0,2	0,4	1,8	2,4	1,1	2,9	2,7	−2,7	−2,2	0,2	1,2	−0,3	−0,2	0,7	0,1
	debt	5,1	4,8	5,7	5,6	5,1	4,5	4,4	3,7	4,5	7	6,6	6,1	9,7	10,2	10,7	10,1
Finland	deficit	6,9	5	4,1	2,4	2,2	2,6	3,9	5,1	4,2	−2,5	−2,6	−1	−2,2	−2,6	−3,2	−2,8
	debt	42,5	41	40,2	42,8	42,7	40	38,2	34	32,7	41,7	47,1	48,5	53,9	56,5	60,2	63,6
France	deficit	−1,3	−1,4	−3,1	−3,9	−3,5	−3,2	−2,3	−2,5	−3,2	−7,2	−6,8	−5,1	−4,8	−4	−4	−3,5
	debt	58,6	58,1	60	64,1	65,7	67,1	64,4	64,3	68	78,9	81,6	85,2	89,5	92,3	95,3	96,2

(continued)

Table 1 *(Continued)*

Country	GG variable	2000	2001	2002	2003	2004	2005	2006	2007	2008	2009	2010	2011	2012	2013	2014	2015
Germany	deficit	0,9	−3,1	−3,9	−4,2	−3,7	−3,4	−1,7	0,2	−0,2	−3,2	−4,2	−1	0	−0,2	0,3	0,7
	debt	58,9	57,7	59,4	63,1	64,8	67	66,5	63,7	65,1	72,6	81	78,7	79,9	77,5	74,9	71,2
Greece	deficit	−4,1	−5,5	−6	−7,8	−8,8	−6,2	−5,9	−6,7	−10,2	−15,1	−11,2	−10,3	−8,8	−13,2	−3,6	−7,5
	debt	104,9	107,1	104,9	101,5	102,9	107,4	103,6	103,1	109,4	126,7	146,2	172,1	159,6	177,4	179,7	177,4
Hungary	deficit	−3	−4,1	−8,8	−7,1	−6,3	−7,8	−9,3	−5,1	−3,6	−4,6	−4,5	−5,5	−2,3	−2,6	−2,1	−1,6
	debt	55,1	51,7	55	57,6	58,5	60,5	64,6	65,6	71,6	77,8	80,5	80,7	78,2	76,6	75,7	74,7
Ireland	deficit	4,9	1	−0,3	0,4	1,3	1,6	2,8	0,3	−7	−13,8	−32,1	−12,6	−8	−5,7	−3,7	−1,9
	debt	36,1	33,2	30,6	29,9	28,2	26,1	23,6	23,9	42,4	61,7	86,3	109,6	119,5	119,5	105,2	78,6
Italy	deficit	−1,3	−3,4	−3,1	−3,4	−3,6	−4,2	−3,6	−1,5	−2,7	−5,3	−4,2	−3,7	−2,9	−2,7	−3	−2,6
	debt	105,1	104,7	101,9	100,5	100,1	101,9	102,6	99,8	102,4	112,5	115,4	116,5	123,3	129	131,9	132,3
Latvia	deficit	−2,7	−2	−2,2	−1,6	−1	−0,4	−0,6	−0,7	−4,1	−9,1	−8,5	−3,4	−0,8	−0,9	−1,6	−1,3
	debt	12,1	13,9	13,1	13,9	14,3	11,7	9,9	8,4	18,7	36,6	47,4	42,8	41,3	39	40,7	36,3
Lithuania	deficit	−3,2	−3,5	−1,9	−1,3	−1,4	−0,3	−0,3	−0,8	−3,1	−9,1	−6,9	−8,9	−3,1	−2,6	−0,7	−0,2
	debt	23,5	22,9	22,1	20,4	18,7	17,6	17,2	15,9	14,6	28	36,2	37,2	39,8	38,7	40,5	42,7
Luxembourg	deficit	5,9	6	2,5	0,2	−1,3	0,1	2	4,2	3,4	−0,7	−0,7	0,5	0,3	1	1,5	1,6
	debt	6,5	7	6,9	6,9	7,3	7,5	7,9	7,8	15,1	16	19,9	18,8	21,8	23,5	22,7	22,1
Malta	deficit	−5,5	−6,1	−5,4	−9,1	−4,4	−2,7	−2,6	−2,3	−4,2	−3,3	−3,2	−2,5	−3,6	−2,6	−2,1	−1,4
	debt	60,9	65,5	63,2	69,1	72	70,1	64,6	62,4	62,7	67,8	67,6	70	67,6	68,4	67	64
Netherlands	deficit	1,9	−0,3	−2,1	−3	−1,7	−0,3	0,2	0,2	0,2	−5,4	−5	−4,3	−3,9	−2,4	−2,3	−1,9
	debt	51,8	49,2	48,5	49,7	49,9	49,3	44,8	42,7	54,8	56,9	59,3	61,6	66,4	67,7	67,9	65,1
Poland	deficit	−3	−4,8	−4,8	−6,1	−5	−4	−3,6	−1,9	−3,6	−7,3	−7,3	−4,8	−3,7	−4,1	−3,4	−2,6

Country	GG variable	2000	2001	2002	2003	2004	2005	2006	2007	2008	2009	2010	2011	2012	2013	2014	2015
	debt	36,5	37,3	41,8	46,6	45	46,4	46,9	44,2	46,3	49,4	53,1	54,1	53,7	55,7	50,2	51,1
Portugal	deficit	–3,2	–4,8	–3,3	–4,4	–6,2	–6,2	–4,3	–3	–3,8	–9,8	–11,2	–7,4	–5,7	–4,8	–7,2	–4,4
	debt	50,3	53,4	56,2	58,7	62	67,4	69,2	68,4	71,7	83,6	96,2	111,4	126,2	129	130,6	129
Romania	deficit	–4,6	–3,4	–1,9	–1,4	–1,1	–0,8	–2,1	–2,8	–5,5	–9,5	–6,9	–5,4	–3,7	–2,1	–0,8	–0,8
	debt	22,4	25,7	24,8	21,3	18,6	15,7	12,3	12,7	13,2	23,2	29,9	34,2	37,3	37,8	39,4	37,9
Slovakia	deficit	–12	–6,4	–8,1	–2,7	–2,3	–2,9	–3,6	–1,9	–2,4	–7,8	–7,5	–4,3	–4,3	–2,7	–2,7	–2,7
	debt	49,6	48,3	42,9	41,6	40,6	34,1	31	30,1	28,5	36,3	41,2	43,7	52,2	54,7	53,6	52,5
Slovenia	deficit	–3,6	–3,9	–2,4	–2,6	–2	–1,3	–1,2	–0,1	–1,4	–5,9	–5,6	–6,7	–4,1	–15	–5	–2,7
	debt	25,9	26,1	27,3	26,7	26,8	26,3	26	22,8	21,8	34,6	38,4	46,6	53,9	71	80,9	83,1
Spain	deficit	–1	–0,5	–0,4	–0,4	0	1,2	2,2	2	–4,4	–11	–9,4	–9,6	–10,5	–7	–6	–5,1
	debt	58	54,2	51,3	47,6	45,3	42,3	38,9	35,5	39,4	52,7	60,1	69,5	85,7	95,4	100,4	99,8
Sweden	deficit	3,2	1,4	–1,5	–1,3	0,3	1,8	2,2	3,3	1,9	–0,7	–0,1	–0,2	–1	–1,4	–1,6	0,2
	debt	50,7	52,1	50,2	49,7	48,7	48,9	43,7	39	37,5	41	38,3	37,5	37,8	40,4	45,2	43,9
United Kingdom	deficit	1,1	0,4	–2	–3,2	–3,4	–3,3	–2,7	–2,9	–4,9	–10,2	–9,6	–7,6	–8,3	–5,7	–5,7	–4,3
	debt	37,3	34,6	34,7	35,9	38,8	40,1	41	42	50,2	64,5	76	81,6	85,1	86,2	88,1	89,1

Source: Eurostat.

Figure 1 General government deficit in percentage of GDP: general government deficit/surplus is defined in the Maastricht Treaty as general government net lending (+)/net borrowing (−) according to the European system of accounts. The general government sector comprises central government, State government, local government, and social security funds

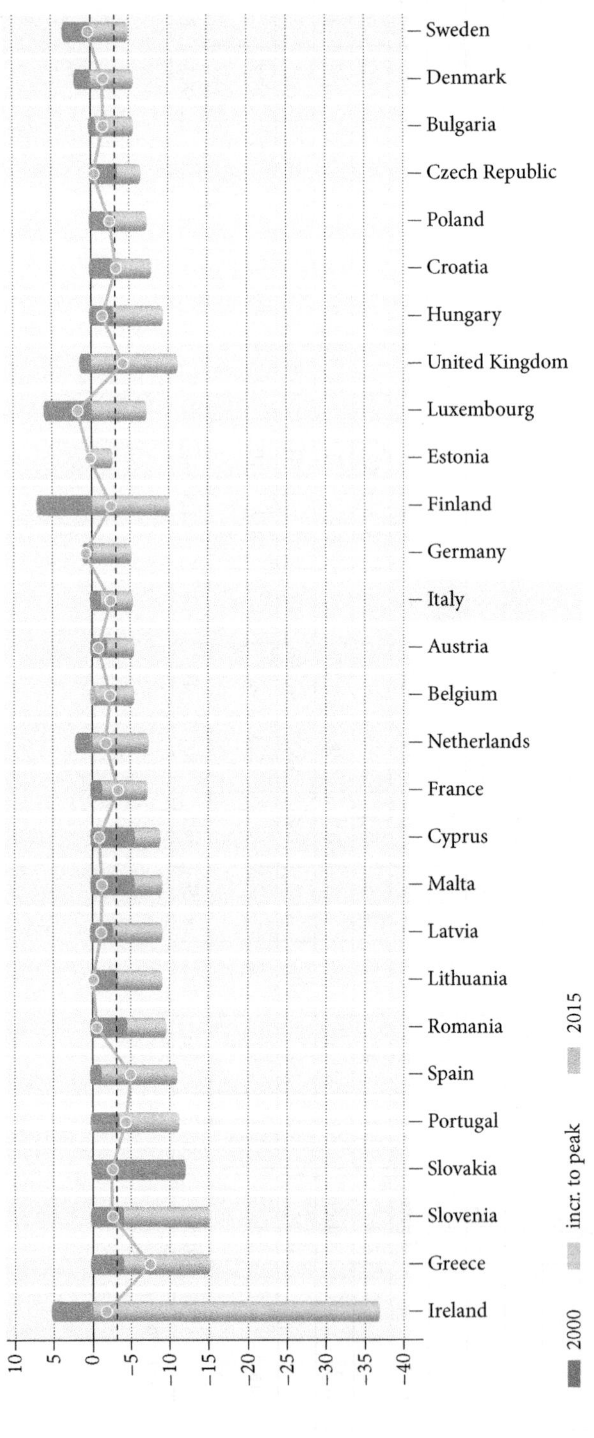

Source: Eurostat.

When we look at figure 1 and the development of the general government deficit/surplus in percent of GDP per Member State, we see that fiscal deficits were corrected after some countries reached really high deficits during the financial crisis and the sovereign debt crisis (Ireland, Greece). The latest data points (values for 2015) are much more encouraging in terms of complying with the fiscal headline numbers. The dashed horizontal line represents the 3 per cent threshold and we note that most of the EU countries are now complying with this threshold.

Only few Member States remain still above that threshold, meaning that their deficit is still too high according to the SGP and the fiscal rules in the EU. The countries that are concerned are: Greece, Portugal, Spain, France, Croatia and the UK, before its withdrawal from the EU (table 2).

Table 2 Overview of ongoing excessive deficit procedure

Country	**Date of the Commission report**	**Council decision on existence of exessive deficit**	**Current deadline for correction**
	(Art. 104.3/126.3)	(Art. 104.6/126.6)	
Croatia	15 November 2013	21 January 2014	2016
Portugal	7 October 2009	2 December 2009	2016
France	18 February 2009	27 April 2009	2017
Greece	18 February 2009	27 April 2009	2017[1]
Spain	18 February 2009	27 April 2009	2018
Un. Kingdom	11 June 2008	8 July 2008	Financial year 2016–17

[1] See the Council decision published on 20 August 2015 for Greece that states that the general government budget deficit will fall below 3% of GDP in 2017. The EC website indicates 2016.

Looking at the development of general government gross debt (figure 2) in the EU, the story is different. Overall, almost all the EU countries reached their maximum level of gross debt in 2015. For those with a current lower value, the progresses seem not to be that significant and encouraging except for Bulgaria or Ireland. General government debt seems to pose a serious problem in the EU, especially for EA countries. This story is in line with the events that occurred over the last years.

Table 3 summarises the situation over the time period 2000–15. As already mentioned above, the classification is only based on general government deficit and general government gross debt. Our goal is to provide an overview of the fiscal and budgetary situation through which the EU Member States have been over the last 15 years. Overall, the striking fact is that the situation seems to have gotten worse over time. The current framework seems not to allow countries to cope with periods of recession. As mentioned in the first part of the chapter, a proper budgetary and fiscal framework should allow the Member States to minimise budgetary troubles during periods of recession and maximise benefits during periods of growth/prosperity (cyclicality of fiscal rules). Moreover, it is clear that some countries have had difficulties going out of the crisis and improving their financial situation (Greece, Spain, and Portugal). While few countries managed to get out of the fiscal 'red zone' (Ireland and Italy for example), other countries have been struggling to improve their situation (Greece).

Figure 2 General government debt in percentage of Gross Domestic Product (GDP): for the purpose of the Excessive Deficit Procedure (EDP) in the Economic and monetary union, as well as for the growth and stability Pact, the current protocol 12, annexed to the 2012 consolidated version of the Treaty on the functioning of the European Union, defines government debt "as total gross debt at nominal value outstanding at the end of the year and consolidated between and within the sectors of general government". The stock of government debt in the EDP is equal to the sum of liabilities, at the end of year, of all units classified within the general government sector (S.13) in the following categories: AF.2 (currency and deposits) + AF.3 (debt securities) + AF.4 (loans). Basic data are expressed in national currency, converted into euro using end-year exchange rates for the euro provided by the European Central Bank (ECB). The Macroeconomic Imbalance Procedure (MIP) headline indicator is calculated as: (Gross Government Debt/GDP)×100. The indicative threshold is 60% of GDP. The data are expressed in millions of units of national currency and in percentage of GDP

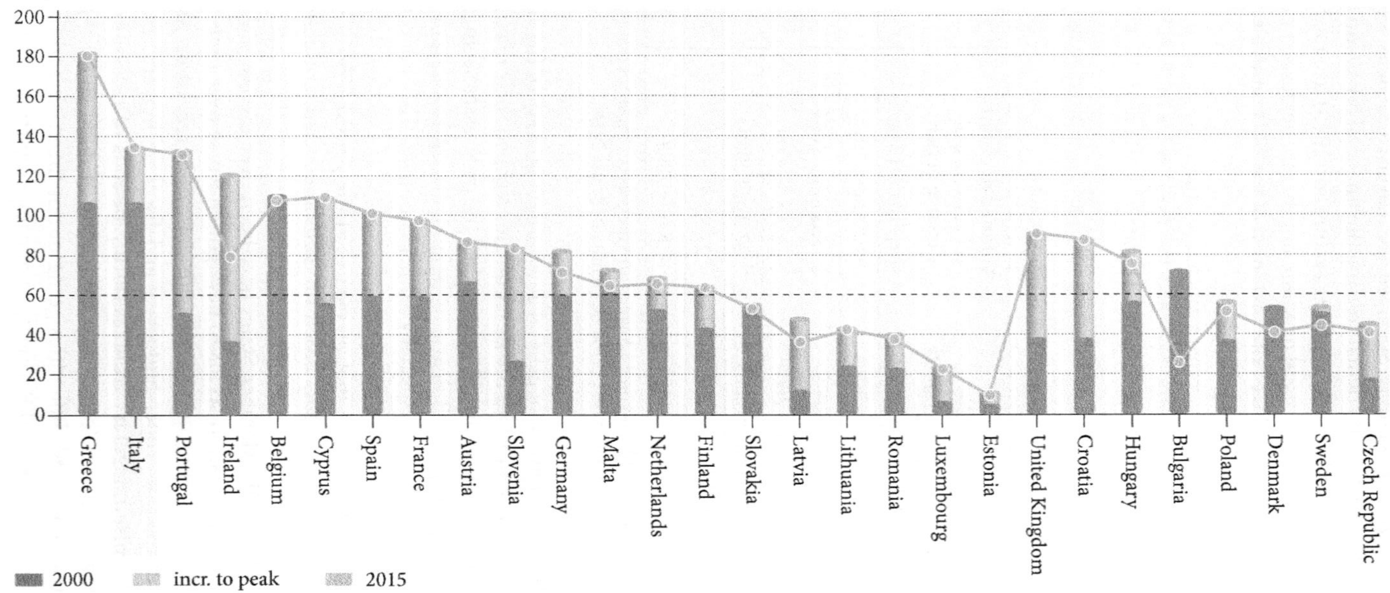

Table 3 Framework summary 2000–2015

Country	2000	2001	2002	2003	2004	2005	2006	2007	2008	2009	2010	2011	2012	2013	2014	2015
Austria																
Belgium																
Bulgaria																
Croatia	–	–														
Cyprus																
Czech Republic																
Denmark																
Estonia																
Finland																
France																
Germany																
Greece																
Hungary																
Ireland																
Italy																
Latvia																
Lithuania																
Luxembourg																
Malta																
Netherlands																

(continued)

Table 3 ***(Continued)***

Country	2000	2001	2002	2003	2004	2005	2006	2007	2008	2009	2010	2011	2012	2013	2014	2015
Poland																
Portugal																
Romania																
Slovakia																
Slovenia																
Spain																
Sweeden																
United Kingdom																

Data used correspond to data in table 1.

Legend: High risk (above 3% deficit and 60% debt)

Medium risk (above 3% deficit or 60% debt)

Low risk (below 3% deficit or 60% debt)

Source: Eurosat.

A. Assessment of the Actual Number of Countries Under EDP

Table 2 shows the currently ongoing EDP along with the associated current deadline for correction. In 2016 there were six countries under an EDP: Croatia, Portugal, France, Greece, Spain and the United Kingdom. Four countries out of the six have been asked to correct their excessive deficit by the end of 2017, namely Greece, France, Croatia and Portugal. Spain will need to correct its deficit by the end of 2018, while the United Kingdom's deadline was the financial year 2016–17. All of the EA countries experienced an EDP over the last 20 years except Estonia. Therefore, the closed EDPs include procedures for: Austria, Belgium, Cyprus, Germany, Italy, Ireland, Finland, Latvia, Lithuania, Luxembourg, Malta, the Netherlands, Slovenia and Slovakia. Among the countries that are currently under the EDP, four countries out of the six have already experienced such a procedure: France (2003–07, 2008), Greece (2004–07), Portugal (2005–08) and the United Kingdom (2004, 2005–07).

In 2011, the European Semester was created in order to 'improve economic policy coordination and ensure the implementation of the EU's economic rules' (Darvas, Leandro (2015) 4). It aims at giving policy recommendations for the eurozone as an entity and for each EU Member State. We start from the European Semester to investigate the reality behind the SGP and the fiscal rules.

One of the latest analyses of the European Semester was carried out by Zsolt Darvas and Alvaro Leandro (2015) in their paper called: *The limitations of policy coordination in the euro area under the European Semester*. The authors created a European Semester reform implementation index that aims at measuring the percentage of reforms fully implemented – or that the government at least started to implement (indicators based on the European Commission's assessment).

Overall, the actual implementation of recommendations in the EU over 2012–14 is low and became worse. Regarding the SGP, it increased in 2013 but then it decreased sharply from more than 50 per cent to 29 per cent. Note that a score higher than 50 per cent means that at least some progress has been achieved on all recommendations, while a score of 29 per cent means that there was very little progress and limited implementation. Darvas and Leandro note that the downward trend is common to all Member States in the EU; however, it is stronger in non-EA countries.

The authors focus also specifically on the SGP and come to sobering conclusions: 'Given that the SGP has strong legal enforcement tools, one would expect a high implementation rate for recommendations related to the SGP' (p 6). Over the time period 2012–14, the rate of implementation for SGP tended to be higher than the rate for the MIP and for other recommendations but '[t]he average SGP implementation rate in 2012–14 was 44 per cent, which is not particularly high and suggests that the European Semester is not particularly effective in enforcing the EU's fiscal rules' (p 7).

The European Semester has also attempted to develop a vision on a euro-area wide fiscal stance but the recommendations are basically empty rhetoric according to Darvas and Leandro. In particular, the authors criticise that the optimal aggregate fiscal stance is not defined. They highlight that the recommendations talk about an aggregate fiscal stance that should be in line with sustainability risks and cyclical conditions, but that they do not clarify what the aggregate stance is in the first place. In conclusion, without a top-down approach to determine national fiscal stances that correspond with the optimal aggregate, it is accidental if the sum of country-specific fiscal stances corresponds with the optimal aggregate fiscal stance.

Overall, what the data and the analysis by Darvas and Leandro tell us is that the current European framework is clearly underperforming and that EU Member States are struggling to improve their budgetary and fiscal situation (table 4).

Table 4 Fiscal sustainability assessment by member state

Country	Overall short-term risk category	Debt sustainability analysis – overall risk assessment	SI indicator – overall risk assessment	Overall medium-term risk category	Overall long-term risk category
Austria					
Belgium					
Bulgaria					
Croatia					
Czech Republic					
Denmark					
Estonia					
Finland					
France					
Germany					
Hungary					
Ireland					
Italy					
Latvia					
Lithuania					
Luxembourg					
Malta					
Netherlands					
Poland					
Portugal					
Romania					
Slovakia					
Slovenia					
Spain					
Sweeden					
United Kingdom					

Legend: High risk (above 3% deficit and 60% debt)
Medium risk (above 3% deficit or 60% debt)
Low risk (below 3% deficit or 60% debt)

Source: European Commission, Fiscal sustainability report (January 2016).

Before moving to the third section and to the possible reforms of the current framework, we will try to list what reasons could actually lie behind the failure of the SGP.

B. The Structural Budget Balance Rule

The structural budget balance is a key indicator of the fiscal situation in a country and is used intensively in the European framework. However, the structural budget balance is an unobserved variable and is estimated with great imprecision. Its objective is to quantify the budget balance without taking into account the impact of temporary effects such as the cyclical effects (tax revenues and unemployment benefits) and the one-off expenditures (banks' bailouts, for instance). According to the OECD definition, the structural budget balance also represents what government revenues and expenditures would be if the output were at its potential level.

The main issue with the structural budget balance is its estimation. It is not clear how to properly estimate that unobserved variable. The EU has agreed on an approach based on an estimate of potential output. However, it is well documented that there have been huge revisions in these estimates after only one year.

In March 2016, finance Ministers of the EU Member States expressed their worries about the estimation of the potential output, like a group of economists before. In a blog post called *Mind the gap (and its revision)!*, Darvas argued that the major source of uncertainty in the estimation of the structural budget balance comes from the estimation of the output gap (namely, the difference between actual and potential GDP).

He also mentioned in a 2013 blog post (*Mind the gap! And the way structural budget balances are calculated*) that the EC's methodology to estimate potential output (D'Auria, Denis, Havik et al (2010)) is based on 'problematic' assumptions about capital, labour and total factor productivity (potential output is estimated using a production function).

The EU's recommendations on national fiscal policy are therefore based on an assessment of national fiscal policies relative to a variable measured with high margins of error. For example, a recommendation may be given to tighten public expenditure by 0.5 per cent of GDP to meet EU objectives. Only one year later, the revisions of the estimates could indicate that the recommendation was totally wrong and that instead a recommendation of a loosening of 0.5 per cent should have been given. These wrong estimates therefore have serious implications for fiscal policy and undermine the credibility of the EU fiscal governance framework.

To summarise, the three major impediments to the calculation of structural budget balances are: the estimation of the potential output, the quantification of its impact on the budget balance, and finally the measurement of the impact of one-off measures on the budget balance. As a result, the credibility of the EU's fiscal framework suffers and Member States often rightly question whether a certain recommendation is sensible.

C. The Lack of Clarity of the Current Framework

The EU's fiscal framework has become extraordinarily complex. The running joke in Brussels is that only one or two people in the European Commission actually understand the rules. Together, the Six-pack and the Two-pack encompass 70 pages of text.

Such complexity can result in a lack of transparency. In fact, for national parliamentarians who are supposed to approve budgets that are in line with EU rules, let alone citizens, it has become close to impossible to understand why a certain budgetary recommendation has been given. At the level of the European Commission, the complexity provides room for interpretation and flexibility. But the way this flexibility is exercised is not clear from the outside.

A priori, the complexity was a result of good intentions. It is generally accepted that mechanically sticking to the simple numerical thresholds of 3 per cent makes little economic sense. The intention was therefore to create 'intelligent' fiscal rules. In particular, policymakers tried to create a framework which would allow automatic stabilisers to operate freely and not be constrained by the 3 per cent threshold. The framework also permits discretionary fiscal spending should the business cycle situation allow for it.

However, at the same time, the new framework was trying to continue to be based on rules and not on economic, let alone political judgement. The result was a very complicated set of rules that aims to achieve this intelligent setup. However, as argued above, the complexity has become so great that the initial purpose is defeated and transparency and clarity of decision is missing.

III. Reform Proposals in the Current Framework

The call for a simplified version of the fiscal European system is becoming more and more vital according to a growing group of economists. According to what Jeffrey Franks stated during a seminar on predictability and transparency of the SGP in Brussels in March 2016, the reforms have already blurred the distinction between the preventive and corrective arms. He presented possible reforms in order to make the current system simpler: 'go back to the two-pillar model: fiscal anchor and operational targets; single fiscal anchor: public debt to GDP; single operational target: an expenditure growth rule, and possibly in combination with an explicit debt correction mechanism'. Overall, there is a 'need to improve economic governance, not just fiscal governance, as private and public imbalances are linked'.

One of the recent proposals for reform was written by Claeys, Darvas and Leandro (2016) in a paper called *A proposal to revive the European fiscal framework*. Their main idea is that fiscal surveillance should not rely on the structural budget balance rule due to the non-reliable estimates of potential output. It should instead rely on an expenditure rule (figure 3).

Since the structural balance rule has been the major and unique rule so far, the SGP and the Fiscal Compact would need to be revised to drop the 3 per cent deficit threshold and to avoid using the structural balance targets as operational targets. One would thereby scrap the complex web of flexibility options, but instead create an expenditure rule with a debt feedback mechanism.

The authors argue that the advantages of expenditure rule over structural budget balance rule are multiple: it is simpler, more transparent, easier to monitor and to explain to public and politicians, it is under the direct control of the government (therefore increases the ownership of the rule), it promotes debt sustainability and countercyclical fiscal policy in periods of growth and recession.

Figure 3 Actual expenditure growth (blue) and real-time expenditure limit estimate (green) based on the expenditure rule proposed by Claeys, Darvas and Leandro (2016)

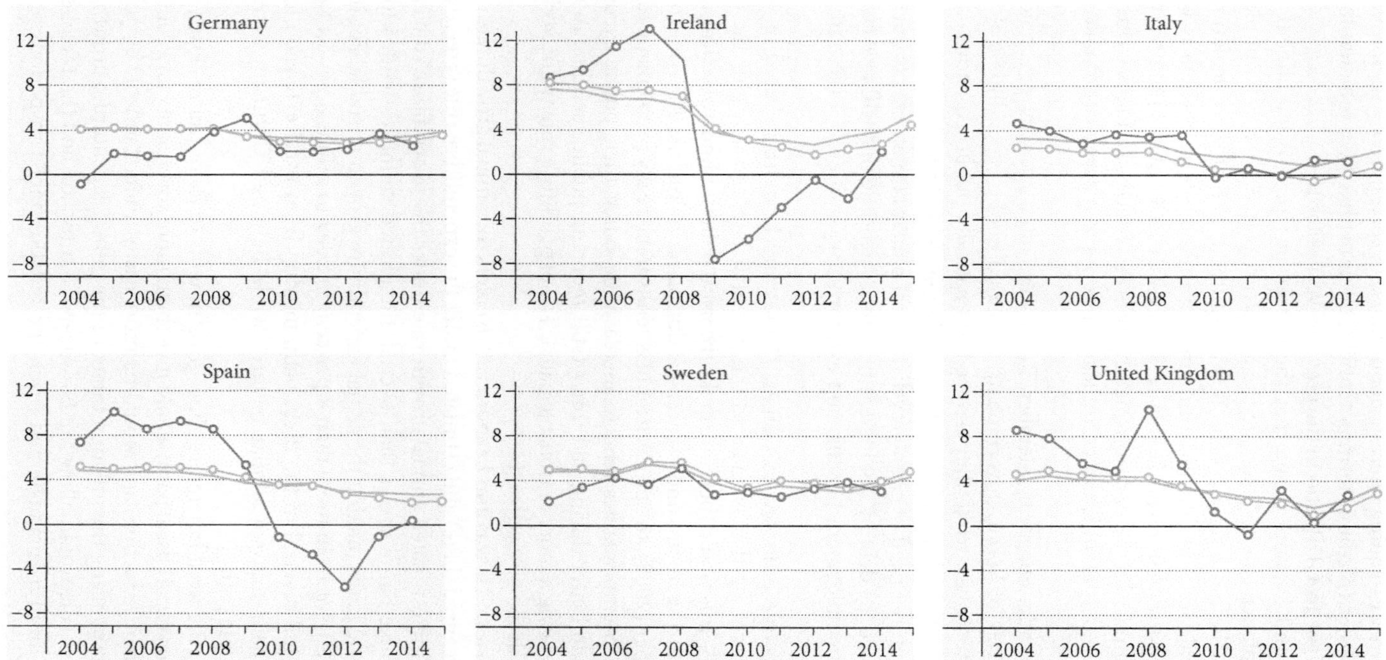

Source: Claeys, Darvas and Leandro 2016.

The formal expression of the proposed expenditure rule is as follows: (growth rate of nominal public expenditures, excluding interest, labour market expenditures + smoothing public investment over years) < (medium-term potential GDP growth + ECB inflation target, 2% in the EA, –0,02 × debt-to-GDP ratio in the previous year –60%).

Claeys, Darvas and Leandro argue that the European Commission should not rely on the structural balance rule to calculate the adjustments that have to be implemented by Member States. The main reason behind this argument is that the calculation of the structural budget balance relies on the estimation of the output gap, which is wrong in real time due to measurement error. Therefore, it creates a series of estimation errors that have a significant impact on the decision-making process. Since the rule is written in the Treaty, it could be used as an index or an indicator but not as a basement to take political decisions.

Over the last decade, European Member States were often running procyclical fiscal policy. During periods of boom, governments increased public expenditures along with the increase of tax revenues, while they reduced dramatically public expenditures during periods of recession, increasing stress and risk of larger debt. There is a wide consensus among economists on the need of countercyclical fiscal policies (make efforts during periods of boom to reduce the debt by not increasing public spending that will give more fiscal space to increase unemployment benefits and extraordinary – one-off – measures during bad times).

The expenditure rule proposed by Claeys, Darvas and Leandro is based on a public expenditure growth ceiling that is equal to the potential GDP growth plus the inflation target set by the ECB. This would therefore make the fiscal policies almost acyclical, allowing for debt reduction during booms and fiscal space during recessions. As Alessandro Turrini concludes in his paper (2008), the procyclical bias tends to be really problematic especially during good times. Member States tend to increase too much their public expenditure, while they tend to do better during bad times (still reducing public spending more than they should but following a more reasonable path). The expenditure rule framework would significantly diminish the procyclical bias.

Figure 3 from Claeys, Darvas and Leandro (2016) plots the annual growth rate of public expenditures both realised (blue) and estimated under the expenditure rule (green) for a set of Member States. The estimated annual growth rate under the expenditure rule is overall more stable. The above figure shows that, overall, the plotted countries tended to implement procyclical fiscal paths making the actual expenditure growth unstable. For instance, Ireland's growth rate went from more than 8 per cent in 2009 to minus 8 per cent in 2010, which represents a full reversal in the fiscal path, moving from fiscal extension to strong fiscal narrowing. Spain shows a similar pattern, while Italy and Germany were overall following a more stable path.

An expenditure rule would therefore allow governments to follow more closely a countercyclical (almost acyclical) fiscal path, would give them more sovereignty and control over fiscal policies and debt reduction, and would be more easily understandable by politicians and citizens. Finally, by using the inflation target in the public expenditure growth ceiling, implementing such a rule would allow the European Commission and the Member States to help the ECB to fulfil its mandate and reach the inflation target in periods of growth and recession.

Claeys, Darvas and Leandro also propose a new framework for the surveillance of the rule. The idea is to have National Fiscal Councils that would monitor the implementation of the rule from drafting the budget to executing and validating the potential growth estimates used in the rule and a European Fiscal Council with a proper mandate and ECB-style governance. The Council would be granted with proper appointment procedure, proper bilateral accountability to the European Parliament, would exercise necessary discretion and could suspend rule for the whole union or particular countries and decide acceptable one-off measures to smooth investment.

The idea behind an expenditure rule and the implementation of national and European fiscal councils is to gradually move away from the use of sanctions to force Member States to reduce their debt and deficit. Fiscal recommendations need to be credible. Moreover, a country should not – and will not in the end – follow the rules because of sanctions, but because it agrees that the rule is the best guidance for fiscal policies to be sustainable.

Overall, it would obviously require an appropriate transition period to implement the whole procedure, but their proposal gives good prospects in practice.

In their paper called *Playing the rules: reforming fiscal governance in Europe* (2015), Luc Eyraud and Tao Wu discuss the issues raised by the steadily increasing public debt in the eurozone. In line with our observations in the second part of our chapter, they show that the EMU is having issues in implementing sound and countercyclical adjustments:

> An important lesson of this exercise is that countries should build sufficient fiscal buffers in good times to accommodate cyclical and exogenous shocks in bad times. [...] most of the deterioration in public finances during the crisis was *not* due to discretionary fiscal stimulus. It was the effect of automatic stabilizers (as revenues fell and expenditures rose in the recession) and exogenous factors (like the bailout of the banking sector or the interest bill). In essence, countries did not enter the crisis with strong enough fiscal positions to withstand such large shocks (Eyraud, Wu (2015) 9).

Even if implemented reforms had an overall positive impact, they failed at reversing the deteriorating trend that public finances are currently following. Along with mentioning design-related issues already stated by Claeys, Darvas and Leandro, such as the growing complexity of the fiscal framework, the reliance on misleading estimates of structural budget balance and the inability to reconcile the two major purposes of the SGP, the authors note that the lack of coordination between the European Commission and the national councils, the poor compliance among Member States and the incomplete separation of powers also participate to the global inefficiency of the European fiscal framework.

Their reform proposal is based on the simplification of the current framework along with the creation of space for more flexibility to deal with shocks. Like monetary policies, a sound fiscal framework should rely on a final objective, which is referred to as 'fiscal anchor', and a medium-term operational target. However, Eyraud and Wu show that the current fiscal rules rely on too many operational targets that are not easy to monitor and too complex. However, defining the fiscal effort variable that will serve as the operational target is not an easy task. It could be a structural balance rule, an expenditure rule or a nominal balance rule. In the literature, a consensus seems to arise. For instance, Xavier Debrun, Natan Epstein and Steven Symansky (2008) proved that implementing an expenditure growth rule along with a debt feedback mechanism allows us to foster convergence to the debt objective and to have more flexibility. It has also been showed that the expenditure growth rule works better when it is put in place with a corrective mechanism (Petrova (2012)). In his paper called *Evaluating fiscal policy: a rule of thumb* (2014), Nicolas Carnot argues that:

> a rule targeting the evolution of primary expenditure relative to trend output growth (adjusted for discretionary revenue measures) can strike a good balance between the objectives of long-term sustainability and short-term macroeconomic stabilization.

Moreover, Eyraud and Wu believe that a structural balance target in level should remain in the fiscal framework, but it should be used as an indicator rather than as an additional target.

Another part of Eyraud and Wu's proposal consists of improving the global governance of the framework. First, they show that formalising the cooperation between national fiscal councils and the European Commission through institutional structures that differ from their degree of integration would help to improve monitoring of the rules. For instance, Fatas, von Hagen, Hallett et al (2003) also argue for the creation of an EU-wide council. Secondly, they argue that reinforcing correction mechanisms by allowing the European Commission to impose sanctions more easily and by enlarging the set of sanctions and increasing Member States' compliance through a more credible no bail-out clause (greater market discipline) or central controls would make the enforcement process stronger.

To summarise, scholars have reached a consensus that the current framework is complex but there is no consensus on whether it should be abandoned altogether or reformed and if the latter, how. In the fourth part, we will introduce proposals that go beyond the reform of the current framework and offer a different approach to fiscal governance altogether.

IV. Moving Beyond the SGP

There is a growing recognition that changes to the EU's fiscal rules can perhaps solve some problems of the fiscal framework but not the fundamental dilemma that fiscal policy in the current monetary union faces. This dilemma is that ultimate sovereign control of fiscal policy is national while the implications of fiscal policy extend well beyond borders and affect the monetary union as a whole. This interdependency is most pronounced when it concerns the possibility of unsustainable fiscal policies. But it is also relevant as it concerns the macroeconomic management of the monetary union.

The debate basically revolves around two polar options. On the one hand, there is the vision to create a European Treasury that would become the institution that would issue most debt of the euro area and be backed by a strong governance framework that would guarantee access to a future stream of tax resources. On the other hand, there is a vision to return to a framework in which national sovereignty and national responsibility are fully reinstated. To achieve this option, a credible no bail-out clause is the fundamental cornerstone that needs to be achieved.

Both options face significant problems. The first option essentially requires a step change in European integration with the creation of a true European sovereign that can raise taxes and limit excessively irresponsible behaviour of national sovereigns if it endangers the

Figure 4 Fiscal Stance in the Euro area over 2000–16

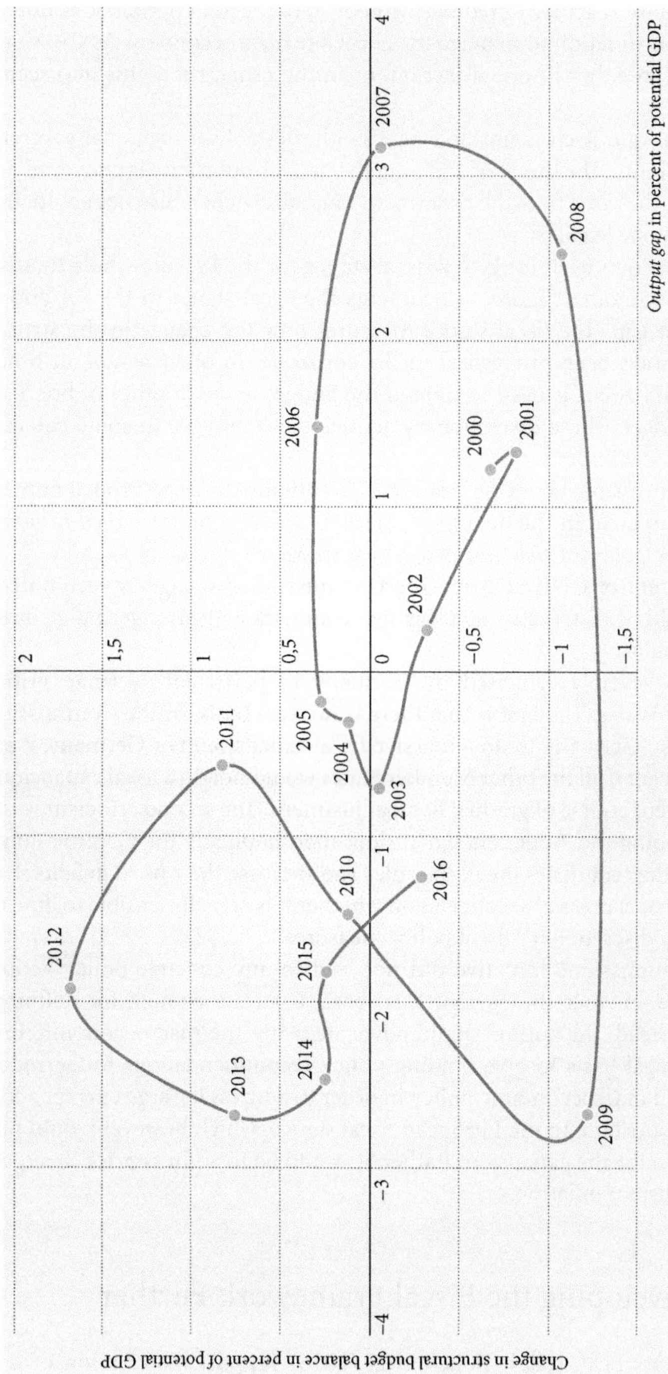

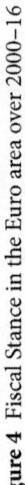

Source: IMF, *World Economic Outlook*, October 2016.

ability of the centre to collect taxes. The second option requires a framework that ensures that the no bail-out clause is actually credible. Moreover, the second option does not allow for any fiscal policy coordination to manage the eurozone macroeconomy. As EA Member States do not want to go either in one direction, or in the other, the status quo seems to prevail.

However, the status quo itself is unstable as it neither establishes national sovereignty nor true joint responsibility. The threat of applying the no bail-out clause is perceived as not being credible while at the same time the promise to mutualise debt is also not acceptable as it lacks a political, let alone legal, basis.

Moreover, the status quo itself leads to a fiscal stance for the EA as a whole that is not supportive of the EA economy. Figure 4 documents the fiscal stance in the EA and how it relates to the output gap. The fiscal stance measures how the change in the structural balance has almost always been procyclical in the eurozone. In other words, in times of recessions, discretionary room is used to tighten the budget while in times of booms it is used to loosen the budget. These discretionary actions offset, at least to some extent, the workings of automatic stabilisers.

The European Commission has recently launched an attempt to set an explicit numerical fiscal target for the euro area. In the document *Recommendation for a Council recommendation on the economic policy of the euro area*, it asked Member States to achieve a fiscal expansion of 0.5 per cent of GDP in 2017. The Commission also vaguely recommended that the stimulus should be distributed in a way that countries with stronger public finance would do a larger stimulus.

The initiative was severely criticised by Germany in particular. German criticism centred on three main issues. The first is that there is no legal basis for the Commission to ask a Member State like Germany to do a massive fiscal expansion. For Germany, it could amount to up to 2 per cent if all the other Member States would not do a fiscal expansion but rather stick to the current course of gradual fiscal adjustment. The second criticism was that if Germany was not doing the 2 per cent expansion, then implicitly the Commission was recommending that other countries break the rules and increase their fiscal deficits. Lastly, the German government expressed scepticism on whether it is actually feasible to 'fine tune' the business cycle with discretionary fiscal policy measures.

The European Commission's initiative did not lead to any concrete policy action. It is indeed questionable whether the current legal basis is strong enough for defining an EA fiscal stimulus. Instead, the author would advocate using the macroeconomic imbalance procedure as a legal basis to give binding policy recommendations to Germany to adjust its structural and macroeconomic policy in order to address its large current account surplus. That would contribute to the European fiscal stance, which however would not be the primary motivation for the expansion. Rather, it would be to address price divergences among States and to sustain inflation.

V. Developing the Fiscal Framework Further

Giamcarlo Corsetti, Lars Feld, Ralph Koijen et al (2016) support the creation of a debt restructuring mechanism that would help the implementation of a credible no bail-out clause in the EA. As the European Union is facing new challenges and is going through its worst time until now, they claim for a need of institutional changes that can be implemented in the short-term, without more political integration, in order to restore growth. The current debt restructuring framework in the EA relies too heavily on rules to enforce discipline, while it should rely more on market mechanism. Since redistributing debt legacy over time is crucial for the wellbeing of the macroeconomy and the financial stability, they propose a steady-state fiscal framework that would deal with that issue without requiring any debt mutualisation or joint debt guarantee.

Their proposal is based on a debt restructuring regime that would complement the ESM. As mentioned in the first part, the ESM is the entity that provides lending to countries during crisis. As part of their framework, the ESM would (and should already) lend only to countries that are defined as solvent (able to pay back the amount of money borrowed on time), while the debt restructuring regime would help solve the issue of excessive debt in insolvent countries. This would require an amendment of the ESM's existing conditions in order to: first give the right incentives to the private lenders ex ante and secondly to prevent ex-post problems implied by minority creditors (procrastination and hold-out problem for instance). The amendment would consist of the implementation of two thresholds (public debt less than 90 per cent of GDP and gross financial needs less than 20 per cent of GDP) and the creation of a clause that would 'extend immunity from judicial process to sovereigns that negotiated a debt restructuring with a (super-)majority of creditors in the context of an ESM programme' (Corsetti, Feld, Koijen et al (2016)).

Along with the new fiscal framework, they propose a new financial and regulatory framework that would deal with the issue of the home bias in banks' sovereign portfolio. Note that both are crucial and needed, and cannot be implemented separately. The main purpose of such a framework is the current necessity to break the bank-sovereign loop. Eurozone banks hold huge amounts of debt securities and especially sovereign from their own origin country. This might have serious consequences in a monetary union since countries cannot use a national currency to adjust for the value of their debt and that countries are heavily dependent on other members' economic situation (shocks spread faster). In order to break the loop, they first propose to assign aggregated average risk weight for each country on sovereigns in order to reduce the home bias. Second, they propose to introduce 'a registration scheme for the private sector' within the ECB in order to create specific kind of collateralised debt obligations that are backed by sovereign debt.

Obviously, the implementation of this new fiscal, financial and regulatory framework would require a period of transition in order to decrease significantly the current level of debt-to-GDP ratios. It could be managed thanks to 'a coordinated one-off solution to remove the debt overhang problem' (Corsetti, Feld, Koijen et al (2016)) in return for stable institutions. This one-off solution would consist of both the creation of a stability fund that would act as a debt buyback and the use of a swap of sovereigns.

Maria Demertzis and Guntram B Wolff start from the observation that it is fundamental to achieve a credible no bail-out clause in order to reduce the reliance of the European policy system on a set of fiscal rules that are dysfunctional (Demertzis, Wolff (2016)). The central question is how the credibility of the no bail-out clause can be established. The central point they are making is that for the no bail-out clause to be credible, more fiscal integration is actually necessary. In fact, at a minimum, the EA would need to be able to decouple the financial system from the fates of national governments.

As long as a sovereign debt restructuring in one Member State can affect the financial stability of the core of the EA financial system, the no bail-out clause is not credible. The authors therefore argue that the next step the EA needs to make is to finish the banking union with full deposit insurance and a fiscal backstop to the resolution fund. To really delink banks from sovereigns, the EA should impose large exposure rules on sovereign debt. As the introduction of such a rule could create a funding squeeze on some sovereigns, it would be advisable to agree ex ante on a buyer of last resort to manage the effects of the introduction of such rules. The authors also underline the importance of the EA and the EU to demonstrate the value added that the union creates. That also means that sufficient resources should be available in the EA to fund EU-wide public goods. A further dimension to strengthen national responsibility and enhance the no bail-out clause would be a minimal joint resource for social needs.

In true federations like the United States, States are credibly subject to a no bail-out clause also because central government functions are exercised by the federal government. Moreover, the fiscal stance of the United States is taken care of by the central government. The eurozone could gradually move in this direction with some more centralised resources for area-wide investments. It could also consider the creation of an EA unemployment reinsurance to prevent excessively procyclical tightening in case of severe recessions that reduce access to borrowing for individual Member States. Together, these steps would allow not only to strengthen national liability but also to gradually discontinue a complicated system of fiscal rules.

One central question that such a nucleus monetary cum fiscal union would leave unanswered is the question of the fiscal stance for the EA as a whole.

Stable monetary unions go hand in hand with fiscal unions that ensure the central functioning of government even in case of default. Demertzis and Wolff therefore propose a long-term process in that direction for the euro area that is divided in the three steps described above. The question is what are the necessary economic and political conditions to:

(a) complete banking union;
(b) create European funds for investment;
(c) increasingly shift other government functions to the centre.

For the first step, they argue that it is imperative to tackle the still significant debt overhang and non-performing loan issue in a number of Member States. The authors argue that for the second step it is crucial to create a common and credible system of checks and balances at the European level, while for the third step, it is actually important that the Member States of the EA have seen a much greater convergence of their economic development levels. The more disparate economic levels of income and susceptibility to shocks are, the more difficult it is to enter into a fiscal union in which explicit risk sharing becomes more important.

Overall, the authors conclude that increasing fiscal capacity is desirable for the economic stability of the eurozone and would improve economic performance while at the same time decentralising fiscal governance and making sovereign debt restructuring possible. But advancing this agenda is politically difficult and raises serious questions about cohesiveness and how much economic convergence is needed.

VI. Conclusions

To summarise, the European Union has created one of the most elaborate fiscal frameworks. The framework developed from one based on simple rules to one that increasingly became more 'intelligent' in order to cater for different contingencies of the economy and prevent procyclical policies. However, compliances with the framework have become weaker and its complexity raises doubts about its legitimacy and transparency. Finally, fiscal outcomes, including concerns about the area-wide fiscal stance, are imperfect and not contributing to growth in the EA. Simultaneously, suspicions about other countries' fiscal policies have increased everywhere and many fear that they have to 'foot the bill' for others. We have proposed a direction of reforms addressing all these concerns by simultaneously increasing the credibility of the no bail-out clause while creating more European fiscal mechanism to achieve better results.

Bibliography

Biraschi, P, Cacciotti, M and Iacovoni, D et al, 'The new medium-term budgetary objectives and the problem of fiscal sustainability after the crisis' (2010) 8 *MEF Working papers* http://www.dt.tesoro.it/export/sites/sitodt/modules/documenti_it/analisi_progammazione/working_papers/WP_8_.pdf.

Carnot, N, 'Evaluating fiscal policy. A rule of thumb' (2014) 526 *Economic papers* http://ec.europa.eu/economy_finance/publications/economic_paper/2014/pdf/ecp526_en.pdf.

Claeys, G, Darvas, Z and Leandro, A, 'A proposal to revive the European fiscal framework' (2016) 7 *Bruegel policy contribution* http://bruegel.org/2016/03/a-proposal-to-revive-the-european-fiscal-framework/.

Corsetti, G, Feld, L and Koijen, R et al, 'Reinforcing the eurozone and protecting an open society' in *Monitoring the Eurozone 2* (CEPR Press, 27 May 2016) https://voxeu.org/article/reinforcing-eurozone-and-protecting-open-society.

D'Auria, F, Denis, C and Havik, K et al, 'The production function methodology for calculating potential growth rates and output gaps' (2010) 420 *Economic papers* http://ec.europa.eu/economy_finance/publications/economic_paper/2010/pdf/ecp420_en.pdf.

Darvas, Z, *Mind the gap (and its revision)!* (20 May 2015) http://bruegel.org/2015/05/mind-the-gap-and-its-revision/.

Darvas, Z and Leandro, A, 'The limitations of policy coordination in the euro area under the European Semester' (2015) 19 *Bruegel policy contribution* http://bruegel.org/2015/11/the-limitations-of-policy-coordination-in-the-euro-area-under-the-european-semester/.

De Grauwe, P, 'The governance of a fragile eurozone' (2011) 346 *Ceps working document* https://www.ceps.eu/system/files/book/2011/05/WD%20346%20De%20Grauwe%20on%20Eurozone%20Governance.pdf.

Debrun, X, Epstein, N and Symansky, S, 'A new fiscal rule: should Israel go Swiss?' (2008) 87 *IMF Working papers* https://papers.ssrn.com/sol3/papers.cfm?abstract_id=1119427.

Demertzis, M and Wolff, GB 'What are the prerequisites for a euro-area fiscal capacity' (2016) 14 *Bruegel policy contribution* http://bruegel.org/2016/09/what-are-the-prerequisites-for-a-euro-area-fiscal-capacity/.
European commission, *Recommendation for a Council recommendation on the economic policy of the euro area* (2016) https://ec.europa.eu/info/sites/info/files/2017-european-semester-recommendation-euro-area_en_0.pdf.
Eyraud, L and Wu, T, 'Playing by the rules: reforming fiscal governance in Europe' (2015) 15/67 IMF Working papers https://www.imf.org/external/pubs/ft/wp/2015/wp1567.pdf.
Hughes Hallett, A, *Stability and growth in Europe: towards a better pact* (London, 2003) http://citeseerx.ist.psu.edu/viewdoc/download?doi=10.1.1.121.7405&rep=rep1&type=pdf.
Petrova, I, 'Iceland's policy objectives under a new fiscal rule' (2012) 12/90 *IMF Country report* https://www.imf.org/external/pubs/ft/scr/2012/cr1290.pdf.
Pisani-Ferry, J, Sapir, A and Wolff, GB, *EU-IMF assistance to euro-area countries: an early assessment* (Bruxelles, 2013) http://bruegel.org/2013/06/eu-imf-assistance-to-euro-area-countries-an-early-assessment/.
Turrini, A, 'Fiscal policy and the cycle in the euro area: the role of government revenue and expenditure' (2008) 323 *Economic papers* http://ec.europa.eu/economy_finance/publications/pages/publication12600_en.pdf.
Zoppè, A, *Fact sheets on the European Union – Economic governance* (2017) 3–6, http://www.europarl.europa.eu/atyourservice/en/displayFtu.html?ftuId=FTU_4.1.4.html.
All web pages are understood as having last been visited on 31 May 2018.

19

The Social Dimension of the European Market: Between Tradition and Challenges

VERA ZAMAGNI

I. The Social Roots of the European Economy

The modern market economy emerged with an intrinsic social dimension in the free cities of the Middle Ages (especially in the Italian Middle Ages), where the productive class – merchants, specialised craftsmen associated in the various guilds, and professionals (jurists, notaries, architects, land surveyors, accountants) – was called upon, both to expand its own affairs 'to make the city rich', and also to directly finance public property – public palaces, churches, convents, walls, fountains, monuments, gardens, squares – and to create and to manage the works that supported those individuals excluded from productive work, temporarily or permanently, or those struggling to make a living – hospitals, pawn banks, Mounts of marriage, conservatories, congregations, confraternities (*Povertà e innovazioni istituzionali in Italia* (2000)). This encouraged a triadic structure of society, with production assigned to the market, regulation to the State, and social works to non-profit organisations created by the citizens themselves. This structure did not entail a rigid division of labour and the citizens tried their hand at various roles (merchants, governors, administrators of non-profit institutions) simultaneously or one after another, so as to realise what was recognised by all as the *common good* of the city: this did not consist only in material wealth, but in decorum, in quality of living, in the promotion of culture, of the arts and of religion, and in the participation of all in the responsibilities that the flowering of the city entailed.

Even after the great upheavals brought about by the birth of capitalism on one hand and the birth of nations on the other, European social life mould continued to structure itself according to the same triadic form previously created, though with an ever more rigid division of labour: *production* fell to the hands of the capitalists, whose responsibility was concentrated ever more exclusively on enterprise; *regulation* was taken up by the public professionalised bureaucracy; and welfare was left in the hands of the civil society (with its charities, the friendly societies, savings and loan banks and similar institutions of a non-profit character). The slogan adopted by the French Revolution in the second half of the eighteenth century still clearly reflected this triadic society: *liberté, égalité, fraternité.* Freedom was guaranteed by a market with little outside interference (*laissez faire* and *laissez passer* were the recommendations of the eighteenth-century Enlightenment, that had to struggle to establish themselves); the State was supposed to police the equality of the citizens before the law; and fraternity was delegated to civil society, in the meantime assuming a more general value, transforming into *solidarity* (Zoll (2000)).

It was with the spread of capitalism in the nineteenth century that a radical change in the structures of European societies commenced: these in fact devolved many welfare tasks to the State, which then became a welfare State. This change happened for a number of reasons.

In the first place the utilitarian development of the economic culture of the Anglo-Saxon countries increased the necessity of support for the working classes. Until the eighteenth century, economic thinkers had taken care to insert their elaborations within a multidimensional vision of economic action, in which policy, philosophy, religion and morality found a place (*Il contributo italiano alla storia del pensiero. Economia* (2012), *passim*). Adam Smith himself (1723–90) remained weded to this approach, having developed, side by side with his thesis of the 'invisible hand' of the market, several considerations about the role of the State and that of civil society, based on moral principles, benevolence and empathy.

The Anglo-Saxon world subsequently embraced an economic theory in which the market and its logic of pure exchange of equivalents, aimed at the maximisation of individual utility, crowded out any other component of economic activity, sketching a *homo oeconomicus* ready to accept any social configuration produced by the market (even extreme inequalities), so as to make the aims of profit for the capital holders prevail. Civil society seemed then no longer to suffice to provide a sufficient safety net against the multiple risks inherent in human life and to 'compensate' for the social damages caused by a productive sector which was preoccupied solely with maximising profits; it was therefore deemed indispensable to have recourse to the State's coercive power, which was capable of imposing decisions at a collective level to satisfy the welfare needs of the multitudes.

In second place, the strong social protest carried forward by the trade unions pushed governments to pass laws favourable to the working class, in order to avoid serious conflicts. Representative parties for the working classes emerged that, when they had ascended to power, utilised the State to answer the calls for social protection. In the end, the guarantee of general coverage for social services could be offered more easily by the public administrations, which by their nature address themselves to the generality of the citizens, rather than through the promotion of charities or the initiative of socially motivated entrepreneurs. These are the principal motives that are at the base of the State solution to the problem of guaranteeing a general welfare, a solution that became widespread in Europe between the end of the nineteenth century and today.

The two basic models of *welfare state* which have arisen in Europe are the German *social market economy* and the Swedish *universal welfare*. The first model established itself in the second post-war period, on an operative framework which had already been put into place by Otto von Bismarck (1815–98) in the 1880s; this framework provided for risk coverage for injuries, sickness and old age for all German employees, through contributions paid by employers (and a smaller participation in financing by the State and by the workers themselves). The very positive results of Bismarckian legislation in terms of economic development, together with a tradition of thought which differed from that of the Anglo-Saxons, brought about a movement in the 1930s known as the Freiburg School, from which Konrad Adenauer (1876–1967) and Ludwig Erhard (1897–1977) took their inspiration in their post-war policies. These policies have taken on the designation of *social market economy* (*60 years of social economy* (2010)). Although the governments that adopted this Bismarckian legislation were centrist, when social democracy came to power no change of course occurred, but rather the reinforcement of this legislation through the development of the *Mitbestimmung*, namely the inclusion of worker representatives in company supervisory boards: an approach that became the second pillar of the German social market economy, and one not imitated in any other European country.

Swedish universal welfare on the other hand had a different origin in the period between the two wars, although it was itself preceded by prior practices. It was the social democratic party SAP (*Sveriges Socialdemokratiska Arbetareparti*), which came to power in Sweden in 1932, to develop a model of social policy influenced especially by the Stockholm School (Gunnar Myrdal and others). The most original aspect of the Swedish model is constituted by its postulation of a reverse causality between economic development and welfare. While in general it is held that development must come first, and then welfare, according to the Swedish model it is social reforms that create the conditions for economic transformation. This is equivalent to saying that social citizenship precedes economic citizenship, because it is the promotion of quality and talents in individual citizens which ensures economic progress. Toward this end, the State has to strive to administer universal welfare, financed by a strongly progressive taxation (and not from the contributions of employers, as in the German model). When discussing universal welfare, we are not referring only to an insurance system for the four big risks (injuries, maladies, retirement and unemployment) but to a number of other provisions: from housing to support for working mothers, from education to work retraining. One can therefore speak in this case of a genuine social state.

It is not just welfare which characterises the social dimension of the European market. The so-called *social economy* should also be added, which includes those forms of enterprise that do not answer exclusively to the objectives of capitalistic profit, such as cooperatives, friendly societies, social enterprises and non-profits, which also arose in the nineteenth century (or even before) and flourish still today. Finally, the European Union (EU) did not just adopt and promote these two social dimensions of national character, offering them a certain coordination and sometimes a contribution to their financing, but it has also introduced a third social dimension which is completely original: that of solidarity between nations, with certain schemes of resource redistribution from the wealthier areas to the less advanced ones.

II. The Welfare State in the Trial of Globalisation

After World War II, all the countries of western Europe introduced a welfare State following the two models outlined above, or a hybrid of them, while the 'liberal' model of American mould is not present in Europe, though some insist on speaking about this model as 'Anglo-Saxon', thereby including Great Britain in it; yet Great Britain rather employs a version of the universalistic model of northern Europe, albeit one which has been somewhat mitigated especially in recent years (Esping-Andersen (1990)). The political scientist Maurizio Ferrera advanced, at the end of the last century (Ranci, Pavolini (2015)), the idea of the existence of a fourth model, that of the Mediterranean countries, which was based on the greater role sustained by the family in the production of welfare services.

Figure 1 Level and efficiency of social spending in 2012

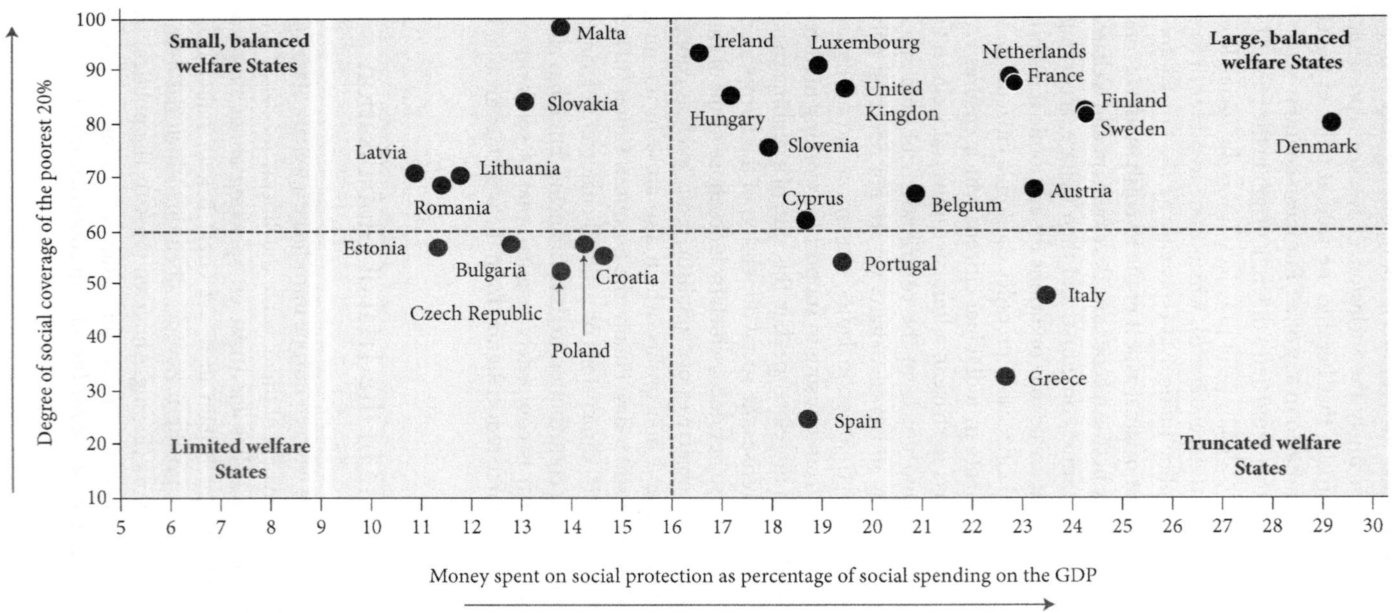

Source: World Bank Group, *EU regular economic report, fall 2015: sustaining recovery, improving living standards*, Washington 2015. The vertical axis shows coverage of the poorest 20% of the population, while the horizontal axis shows the percentage of social spending on GDP.

More recently, the entire modelisation of welfare States was revised on the basis of two indicators: the level of social protection, measured by social spending as percentage of GDP, and the degree of coverage for the poorest categories of the population, measured in terms of the percentage of coverage for the poorest 20 per cent. With this approach, four models of welfare seem to emerge, as can be seen in figure 1, in reference to 2012: these models coincide with the four spaces produced in the chart by the intersection of two lines: the vertical line positioned on the percentage of social spending equal to 16 per cent of the GDP, and the horizontal line positioned at 60 per cent of coverage for the poorest segment of population. Let us review the characteristics of the four spaces.

(1) The States with an elevated and balanced welfare (denominated large, balanced welfare States) are in the upper right quadrant. This includes the States of northern-continental Europe, as well as Hungary, Slovenia and Cyprus. Germany is absent because there were no data during the publication of the report, but surely it is positioned in this quadrant.
(2) The States with a large welfare, but one which is focused on the middle classes (with truncated distribution) are in the lower right quadrant. Only the Mediterranean countries are located here, as their welfare is not sufficiently capable of helping the poorest classes. The existence of a Mediterranean category is therefore confirmed, but it is here identified with multiple indicators with respect to Ferrera's approach.
(3) The States with small but balanced welfare are in the upper left quadrant. Some States of eastern Europe along with Malta are located here; these States have adopted the approach prevalent in northern-continental Europe, but do not yet have the resources for greater spending.
(4) The States with limited welfare are in the lower left quadrant. There are only a few States of eastern Europe. This clearly highlights a temporary situation, given that the countries positioned here all cluster near the demarcation line of coverage of the 20 per cent poorest at 60 per cent.

With these indicators, in reality only two welfare models are emphasised: the northern-continental, which is a hybrid of the two historic welfare State models illustrated in the preceding section, and the Mediterranean one, which is distinct from the others for its low level of family-oriented, housing-oriented and labour market-oriented measures, and its high level of retirement spending, thus prioritising a backward-looking welfare approach. The poorest countries in the EU, in reality, are separated on account of their level of social protection, but not for their disbursement methods as compared to the northern-continental model.

The generalisation of the welfare State, together with a strongly progressive fiscal legislation, had the result of greatly increasing public spending for social protection (table 1), but the elevated growth rates of the European countries and the diffusion of the second industrial revolution supported the burden. The American-style argument that an 'excessive' welfare State has prevented productivity growth in Europe, and in the last analysis also the competitiveness of the European economy, is not supported by the history of the years of the 'economic miracles'. The European countries grew in the presence of rising spending levels for welfare, without this either endangering the public spending balance or introducing perverse incentives to not work.

Table 1 Incidence of social protection spending on the GDP of EU Countries

	1997	2007	2014
European Union (15 Countries)	26	26	30
European Union (28 Countries)		25	29
Austria	–	27	30
Belgium	26	26	30
Bulgaria	–	13	18
Croatia	–	19	22
Cyprus	–	16	23
Czech Republic	–	18	20
Denmark	30	29	33
Estonia	–	12	15
Finland	28	24	32
France	30	30	34
Germany	28	27	29
Greece	20	21	26
Hungary	–	22	20
Ireland	16	17	21
Italy	24	26	30
Latvia	–	11	14
Lihtuania	–	14	15
Luxembourg	20	20	23
Malta	–	18	19
Netherlands	27	26	31
Poland	–	18	19
Portugal	19	23	27
Romania	–	13	15
Slovakia	–	16	18
Slovenia	–	21	24
Spain	20	20	25
Sweden	31	27	30
United Kingdom	24	25	27

Source: Eurostat.

Naturally, all this involved a strong lowering of inequalities (see figure 2) and a general improving of the standard of living (Pestieau (2006)). The welfare State seemed to be so constructive a dimension of the European Union that 1989 saw the adoption of the Charter of Fundamental Rights, which included 12 rights, among which were freedom of movement of workers and citizens within the Union (the first right was already recognised at the time of the establishment of the common market in 1957; the second was granted by the

Schengen Agreement of 1985), social protection, free labour negotiation, participation in the decision-making of enterprises (economic democracy), healthy working environments, equal pay, and vocational training. This charter, after a great deal of debate with the Great Britain, was inserted into the Amsterdam Treaty of 1997 (Geyer (2000)) and subsequently carried over to the Lisbon Treaty of 2007 (in force since 2009, articles 151–164).

However, beginning in the 1980s, the economic and social context changed radically. Not only did the growth rates of the European economies begin to contract, but the costs of welfare were increased exponentially. There are multiple reasons for this. First and foremost, demography: with the collapse of the birth rate and the ageing of the population, welfare has to bear a spending burden which is very elevated compared to revenue (produced by the active population). Secondly, with the introduction of high-cost drugs and ever more advanced diagnostic machines, the performance costs have increased. The declining occupation rate has also contributed to increasing costs. This decline is the result on the one hand of globalisation, which has shifted the most labour-intensive activities toward developing countries, and on the other hand, more recently, of the severe economic world crisis which began in 2008.

Figure 2 Percentage of total GDP held by the highest decile of population, 1910–2010

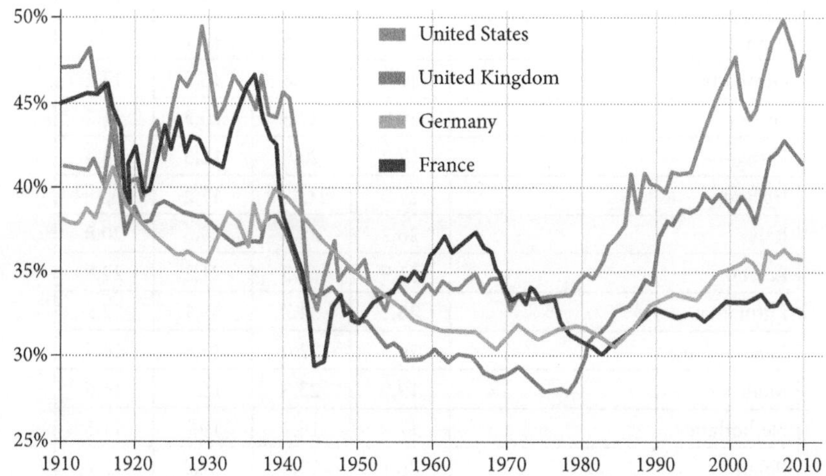

Source: T. Piketty, E Saez, *Top incomes and the great recession. Recent evolutions and policy implications*, «IMF Economic Review», 2013, 61, 3, p. 463, https://eml.berkeley.edu/~saez/piketty-saezIMF13topincomes.pdf.

Once again the third industrial revolution and financialisation have created the conditions for a phenomenal increase in inequalities (more so in the Anglo-Saxon countries than in those of continental Europe) beginning in the 1980s (observe again figure 2), also because many countries, riding the wave of a diffuse neoliberalism, reduced the level of progressivity of taxation (World Bank Group (2016)). Welfare spending has still tended to increase somewhat (table 1), but it is ever more difficult to counter the pressures toward inequality, as is visible in table 2. In that table the levels of relative inequality (the definition for this can be found below the table) are compared before and after the social transfers. It can be seen that the average values of the 28 countries increased between 2007 and 2015 in inequalities before the transfers (0.6 per cent) but still more in those after the transfers (1.1 per cent).

Table 2 Percentage of the population at risk of poverty before and after social transfers[1]

	before transfers		after transfers	
	2007	**2015**	**2007**	**2015**
European Union (28 Countries)	–	24,1	–	17,7
European Union (27 Countries)	23,5	24,1	16,6	17,7
Eurozone (18 Countries)	22,7	23,7	16,1	17,7
Austria	17,0	19,2	12,0	14,3
Belgium	19,5	20,1	15,2	15,6
Bulgaria	28,9	31,3	22,0	23,8
Croatia	–	24,8	–	20,6
Cyprus	22,8	29,3	15,5	17,2
Czech Republic	15,0	15,1	9,6	11,0
Denmark	15,0	17,3	11,7	11,9
Estonia	28,4	31,3	19,4	23,3
Finland	19,1	17,8	13,0	12,6
France	18,5	21,6	13,1	13,9
Germany	21,3	22,8	15,2	17,4
Greece	29,0	27,5	20,3	21,2
Hungary	17,2	20,9	12,3	14,4
Ireland	27,0	24,4[2]	17,2	16,1[2]
Italy	26,2	25,6	19,5	20,8
Latvia	31,9	31,5	21,2	24,8
Lithuania	28,1	34,7	19,1	22,5
Luxembourg	20,3	22,0	13,5	15,7
Malta	19,9	23,5	15,1	16,6
Netherlands	17,9	18,2	10,2	11,5
Poland	26,1	23,8	17,3	17,2
Portugal	32,9	27,8	18,1	20,1
Romania	33,9	31,0	24,6	25,7
Slovakia	14,8	13,9	10,6	12,4
Slovenia	14,9	17,0	11,5	15,6
Spain	26,7	28,6	19,7	21,8
Sweden	13,8	18,1	10,5	15,9
United Kingdom	26,6	26,3	18,6	17,2

[1] The percentage of population with a disposable income per capita inferior to 60% of the average.
[2] The datum refers to 2014.

Source: Eurostat.

The reaction to this new status quo arose sporadically. At the level of the individual European countries, there was a race to carry out reforms on retirement schemes, so as to better take into account the greater longevity of the population, by increasing the retirement age on the one hand, and contributions over the course of the working life on the other. Another sphere which saw many national reforms was that of the 'flexibilisation' of the labour market. Given the speed with which jobs change today, the 'permanent position' can no longer exist and therefore it is necessary to increase geographical and cross-sectorial worker mobility, accompanying it with public support of professional training. This is a phenomenon known as workfare, namely public assistance aimed at reinstating workers in new jobs through workers' agencies and professional courses. Denmark's case is famous, as this country has rendered dismissal totally flexible, followed by the social service taking responsibility for the unemployed worker, not only by supporting their income, but by tending to their reintegration to the workforce, among other things through professional courses financed by the European Union. This approach is also designated 'flexicurity', because it combines flexibility and social security.

The EU paid more attention to the question of the structural unemployment which seemed to afflict it. In 2000 the recommendations for a reform package of the labour market based on the flexibilisation of contracts become insistent, and in fact there were many countries that adopted these reforms. I will recall here the Biagi reform implemented in Italy by the Berlusconi government in 2003 and the contemporary Hartz reform implemented in Germany by the Schröder government. This last was a great success, also because it not only reformed the labour market, but increased the ease of starting new enterprises. With the 2008 crisis and the cyclical increase of unemployment, the EU launched a series of measures to render the European labour market more transparent, through websites in various languages offering jobs, and the support of national workers' agencies.

Other important changes that are happening in European welfare are the increasing supply of social protection services by social enterprises, rather than by public bureaucracy, and the so-called second-level welfare, namely the provision of services additional to the public ones (which are increasingly pared back to their essentials), furnished directly by enterprises via corporate negotiation, and generally with lower taxes. These are both welcome innovations. In fact, the bureaucratic provision of the welfare State had strongly demotivated citizens from being directly responsible for welfare, as had been normal before the advent of the welfare State. This demotivation was reflected in many ways. Tax evasion might be considered one of these, as it is based on the idea of shifting the burden of welfare State financing onto the collective, with an evident underestimation of composition effects (if only a few individuals avoid taxes, they receive benefits without paying; but if many avoid paying taxes, the services can no longer be provided). A second example of deresponsibilisation is that of resource waste, both by citizens and bureaucracy. A third manifestation of deresponsibilisation is the lack of social innovation in the provision of services. By outsourcing welfare services to cooperatives, foundations, associations, and non-profit enterprises, costs have been streamlined by eliminating a great deal of waste; but above all, a process of social innovation was launched that had been non-existent before (for more on this, see *The ramifications of the 'social economy'*).

So far as second-level welfare goes, even this is a very positive novelty, because it encourages enterprises to abandon an exclusive focus on the profit maximisation, thus helping to fill the CSR (*Corporate Social Responsibility*) with more substantial and appropriate contents. Attention to the well-being of their workers, sensitivity to work conditions in enterprises and to not polluting the territory surrounding the company, solidarity toward other territories and countries in collaboration with NGOs, are all much more engaging and positive social objectives than the occasional contribution to the local theatre or art exhibition, and are changing the ways of doing business.

Despite these important changes to the European welfare State, its capacity to counter the strong pressures toward the increased inequalities that issue from the economy as it is currently manifested remains inadequate. The inequalities do nothing but increase, although less in Europe than in the United States. If, therefore, globalisation and financialisation are giving the European welfare State a difficult time of it, there are no signs of a return in Europe toward a society with less welfare – not even as a consequence of the severe crisis which began in 2008. If anything, it is rather true that the alternative welfare model, the non-universal American model, has shown some convergence with the European one, at least up to the Obama presidency. The procedures for provision and the sources of financing are changing, not only so as to render costs sustainable, but also to return to responsibilising citizens and enterprises; however, welfare fundamentally retains its place, even if it is more realistic today to speak of a welfare society than a welfare State, given the greater role that civil society has taken.

The last serious challenge to European welfare at present, and not only to European welfare, comes from the Biblical exodus of populations from militarily and politically destabilised countries, especially in the Southern Mediterranean and sub-Saharan Africa. Already in 2003 with the Dublin regulation, a common regulation was introduced in the EU for the acceptance of asylum-seekers, who at that time were not so many. Starting from 2011, the Syrian and the Libyan crises overwhelmed this regulation as well as the successive measures (the introduction of Frontex in 2006 and the agreements with various countries of origin). This provoked grave tensions between European countries, complicated as well by various political stances, which at present are far from finding resolution. In reality, it is necessary to have the courage to totally rethink the issues of immigration and of relations with developing countries.

III. The Ramifications of the 'Social Economy'

The social dimension of the European Union does not consist only in the welfare State, but also in the creation of economic-productive activities with aims differing from the capitalistic. There are in fact enterprises that do not take as their main end the maximisation of shareholder profits, but instead seek to produce goods and services for the community in question. These are enterprises incorporated in the form of cooperatives, of social enterprises or non-profit enterprises (foundations, associations), that together form the so-called social economy, also designated the third sector (above all in the Anglo-Saxon world; see figure 3).

Figure 3 The social economy

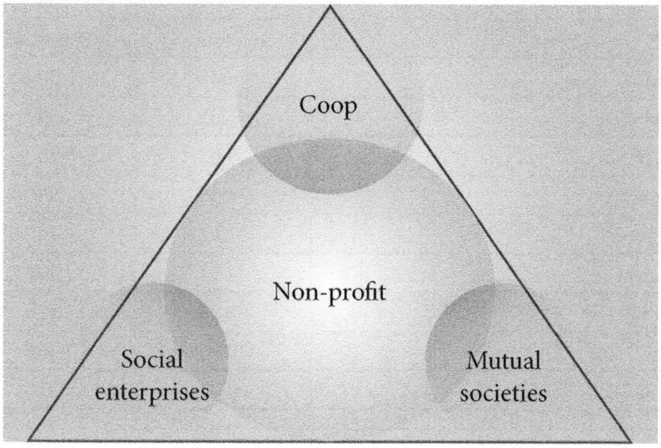

Source: Cooperatives, mutual societies, and social enterprises generally have a juridical form of their own, which in some cases can be categorised as non-profit. The genuine non-profit sector includes associations and foundations.

The size of this social economy within the European Union is considerable. In 2010, over 14 million employees were counted, 5 million of which were in cooperatives and mutual societies, with more than 230 million partners, and 9 million in non-profits enterprises with about 250 million associates. The incidence in total employment in the EU is 6.5 per cent, with the highest points in Sweden (11.1 per cent), Belgium and the Netherlands (10.3 per cent), Italy (9.7 per cent), and France (9 per cent). Added to remunerated employees are volunteers, who support above all non-profit enterprises, the number of which in 2011 was estimated at over 100 million people, equal to a European average of about 25 per cent of the adult population, with spikes in the Netherlands (57 per cent), Denmark (43 per cent), Finland (39 per cent), and Austria (37 per cent). The data per country can be seen in table 3.

Table 3 Paid employment in the social economy as % of total employment and volunteer work as % of adult population (2009–2011)

	%	%
	occupati	**volontari**
Austria	5,70	37
Belgium	10,30	26
Bulgaria	3,97	12
Cyprus	1,32	23
Czech Republic	3,28	23
Denmark	7,22	43

(continued)

Table 3 ***(Continued)***

	%	%
	occupati	**volontari**
Estonia	6.63	30
Finland	7.65	39
France	9.02	24
Germany	6.35	34
Greece	2.67	14
Hungary	4.71	22
Ireland	5.34	32
Italy	9.74	26
Latvia	0.05	22
Lithuania	0.67	24
Luxembourg	7.30	35
Malta	1.02	16
Netherlands	10.23	57
Poland	3.71	9
Portugal	5.04	12
Romania	1.77	14
Slovakia	1.94	29
Slovenia	0.73	34
Spain	6.74	15
Sweden	11.16	21
United Kingdom	5.64	23
Total European Union of 27 Countries	6.53	25

Source: CIRIEC, *The social economy in the European Union*, 2013, https://www.eesc.europa.eu/resources/docs/executive-summary-of-study-of-the-social-economy-in-the-european-union-it.pdf.

The cooperative enterprise (S Zamagni, V Zamagni (2008)) was born in the nineteenth century, after certain anticipations in the late eighteenth century, and already in 1830 there was talk in France of *social economy*, the economy that proposed the aims of peace and social justice. It privileges the sectors of agricultural activities, finance (banks and mutual insurances), retail trade, housing and other services, above all personal services. The diffusion of the social cooperatives in the last 30 years as well as associations/foundations of communities for the supply of welfare services is one of the most striking novelties of the social economy (Borzaga, Ianes (2006)), and contributes to raising the quality of welfare services and to reducing their costs.

Non-profit enterprises have an even more ancient origin in Europe, dating back, as already stated in the first paragraph, to citizen donations in the medieval city-States, aimed toward the constitution of hospitals, pawn banks, conservatories, orphanages and libraries. These have always been genuine enterprises, managed according to the dictates of the accounting system, which guaranteed continuity and sustainability over time, as well as transparency in the use of funds by the city magnates, or by civil and religious congregations. Later, the legal framework of these enterprises was repeatedly remodelled, by adding various public contributions to the basis of donated capital, concluding with the total nationalisation of some of these enterprises (as has been the destiny of many hospitals).

However, the propensity of the citizens to create non-profit businesses with donated capital did not disappear, and other enterprises were created, above all in the form of foundations or associations. The foundations have increasingly taken on an individual character, with people endowed with estates who create one in their own names, or with enterprises that endow themselves with an enterprise foundation; associations meanwhile have generally preserved a more communitarian character. These are concerned with disparate activities, which go from the promotion of culture and research in particular fields (often medical) to the care of babies, the elderly, the disabled, the drug-addicted, the homeless; from the launching of developmental projects in poor areas, even in foreign countries, to measures for dealing with emergencies of every kind, and still others yet (*Libro bianco sul terzo settore* (2011)).

At the EU level, the recognition of the social economy's importance began in 1989, with the patronage of the first European Conference on social economy (held in Paris), which led to the institution of a unity of social economy within the DG XXIII (Directorate general for enterprises policy, distributive trades, tourism and social economy of the European Commission). Other conferences followed, leading to the 1997 recognition of the role of social economy enterprises in local development and in the creation of new jobs, and to the launch of the pilot project *Third system and employment*, meant to explore and promote the potential of the social economy in the area of employment. One of the big problems to resolve was that of the statistic survey of the social enterprises which were lost within national accounts. A lot of work has been done in this direction, beginning with the very definition of the different kinds of social economy enterprises, which have been divided into market enterprises (namely enterprises that produce goods and services intended for sale at economically significant prices) and non-market enterprises (non-profit enterprises that produce family-oriented goods and services which are not destined for sale). At present, market enterprises above all are clearly identified by means of so-called satellite accounts, while the detection of associations and foundations still presents not a few uncertainties, above all of a definitional kind.

From the legislative point of view, the most concrete measure has been that of the European cooperative society's statute, which is proving to be a positive example for the legislation of many countries, but is not used much directly, because the cooperatives prefer to use national legislation.

One should also recall the European Parliament's resolution of 19 February 2009 on the social economy, as well as that of 2 July 2013 on the contribution of the cooperatives for overcoming the crisis. In 2011 (25 October), the Commission formulated a communication entitled *Social business initiative. Creating a favourable climate for social enterprises, key stakeholders in the social economy and innovation*, in which an action plan is presented, aimed at implementing the objective declared in the title, even entering into many practical details. In the same year, a white paper on social innovation was published (Murray, Caulier Grice, Mulgan (2011)) and the measures of foundations and banks were multiplied to finance it, among other things with the so-called social impact bonds, the instrument by which the public sector collects private financing.

More recently, in another communication on *Europe's next leaders: the start-up and the scale-up initiative* of 22 November 2016, paragraph 3.5 of the document is dedicated to the issue of social innovation of small and medium enterprises. It reads:

> Globally, there is increasing interest in social innovation as a way to sustainable growth, e.g. fair trade, distance learning, mobile money transfer, integrating migrants, and zero-carbon housing. Social start-ups therefore have high potential for innovation and positive impact in economy and society at large. Their business model – combining economic efficiency with societal-centred objectives – has proven very resilient (pp 9–10, http://eur-lex.europa.eu/legal-content/EN/TXT/PDF/?uri=CELEX:52016DC0733&from=EN).

This is certainly the most substantial recognition of the role played by the European social economy, but there are still no works that measure the effective aid provided from the EU to the social economy, beyond declarations of intents. It can be observed that this is a most partial recognition, one that does not lead to a pluralistic revision of the enterprise's definition, which remains for the EU exclusively capitalistic. More generally, however, the economic crisis, growing inequalities, and the citizens' impatience toward enterprises and economic policies that enrich the already wealthy are pushing toward a revision of the prevalent theory on the maximisation of shareholder profit by capitalistic enterprises, in favour of a conception referring to 'corporate social responsibility', which has already been popular for decades and reinforced in many forms. Among the first to advocate this revision surely ranks the American economist Michael Porter, with his shared value proposal (Porter, Kramer (1999)), that is an economic activity that offers, together with profits, tangible social benefits. Social budgets formerly generically formulated are becoming more ambitious, transforming into sustainable reports, which involve the achievement of objectives for environmental improvement and social promotion of all the stakeholders in the enterprises and the territories, through explicit ethical codes (in this connection, I will bring to attention the *UN guiding principles on business and human rights*, also called the Ruggie principles from the name of their 2011 drafter: these contain the rules for preventing and dealing with the risks of economic activities having a negative impact on human rights) and the implementation of especially dedicated work projects.

The last frontier in this regard is that of the so-called Benefit corporations, or B Corps, enterprises that are based on an explicit declaration that the aim of an enterprise is not only to create shareholder profits, but also to take direct responsibility towards the community and the world, through precise commitments declared in a company statute and certified by ad hoc agencies. As of 2017 there exist around 2000 certified B Corps in Europe, active in 130 different sectors, and the number is growing exponentially. This is how they present themselves on their site:

> Collectively, B Corps lead a growing global movement of *people using business as a force for good*™. Through the power of their collective voice, one day all companies will compete to be *best for the world*™, and society will enjoy a more shared and durable prosperity for all (https://www.bcorporation.net/what-are-b-corps/why-b-corps-matter).

IV. The Solidarity Measures in the European Union

Title XVIII of the EU Treaty is dedicated to economic, social and territorial cohesion. In its initial article (174), it states:

> In order to promote its overall harmonious development, the Union shall develop and pursue its actions leading to the strengthening of its economic, social and territorial cohesion.
>
> In particular, the Union shall aim at reducing disparities between the levels of development of the various regions and the backwardness of the least favoured regions.
>
> Among the regions concerned, particular attention shall be paid to rural areas, areas affected by industrial transition, and regions which suffer from severe and permanent natural or demographic handicaps such as the northernmost regions with very low population density and island, cross-border and mountain regions.

In question are those policies, originally defined as regional, now often called structural, which began in the 1970s and little by little became ever more important, until absorbing today 40 per cent of the European budget; they have even incorporated the social fund, which principally supports training courses with the view both to alleviation of unemployment, and to migrant integration. Beyond the Regional Fund and the Social Fund, the European Investment Bank (EIB) and the Cohesion Fund are also committed to these kinds of policies, which today appear to be the real heart of EU policies. Basically, those regions with a per capita level of income under 75 per cent of the European average can present a development project which the EU will cofinance. Between 1989 and 2013, the EU financed tens of thousands of projects with about 800 billion euro. These projects include more than 1,200 km of roads and 1,500 of rail for the creation of a trans-European transport network (TEN-T), which is better integrated than the existing one, in addition to urban networks for water provision and supply. For example, the EU has invested 400 million in the Naples metro.

In 2002 the Solidarity Fund was also created, to deal with possible natural catastrophes that might befall the Member States. In the case of the 2012 earthquake in Emilia Romagna, for example, the Fund provided 670 million euro. It might finally be noted that still other characteristic EU measures go in the direction of helping the weakest components of the economy, as in the case of the CAP (*Common Agricultural Policy*), which, while not proposing explicit objectives for territorial redistribution of resources, actually helped a sector – the agricultural sector – which produces average levels of revenue inferior to half that of other sectors. This is a historic policy of the EU, already having commenced in the early 1960s, that contributed to keeping European agriculture alive and with it the food and beverage industry, albeit with high costs for consumers. The restructuring measures in the 1970s and 1980s for sectors in difficulty should also be recalled: principally metallurgy, shipbuilding, and artificial fibres. Recently, these and other measures were brought into better synergy with EU measures through structural policies, so as to more easily achieve the objectives of Horizon 2020, the strategy for sustainable and cooperative growth proposed by the European Commission in 2010. Or again, 'macroregional' strategies have been launched, which connect neighbouring regions that belong to different nations.

Another sector where the 'mutualisation' of measures would be crucial today is that of the migrant crisis, for which, at present, only an EU contribution has been granted for those centres that have to host the migrants awaiting a visa, or for the maintenance of these migrants outside of the EU, as happened with the contribution of three billion euro granted to Turkey. The financial sector is another crucial area in which certain concrete steps have been made in 'mutualisation'. The creation of the ESM (*European Stability Mechanism*) in 2012 will permit future banking rescue measures coordinated on a European level, while the Banking Union, begun in 2014, should help to avoid excessively risky behaviour on the part of the so called 'systemically important' banks (banks of large size which are present in more than one country) through the sharing of rules. Again, quantitative easing, namely the buying of bonds to release liquidity with the aim of stimulating economic growth, started by the European Central Bank in 2015, aims at giving aid to all EU economies with expansionary monetary policies. In 2017, however, we are still far from a mutualisation of the European public debt and a common insurance on deposits.

V. Conclusion

One might really conclude that the European Union is the area of the world where solidarity is most actively and creatively exercised, and where the creation of social capital (Field (2003)) is still held in high regard, albeit in a context which is ever more unfavourable for a still strong liberalism and nationalistic-populistic closures. Indeed, one finds in Europe not only a generalised welfare, which is in many of its members among the highest in the world, but also a robust and lively third sector, both on the quantitative plane, and for the capacity to 'social innovation' that it demonstrates. Millions of EU citizens are committed to working in enterprises that take social impact as their exclusive or complementary objective; millions of EU citizens are shareholders of these enterprises and/or help them, by volunteering their time. But there is also another cooperative dimension that is unique to the EU: namely, the transfer of resources from the richest parts to the poorest ones, with the explicit aim of promoting social cohesion within the EU. This dimension is the most characteristic, because it does not exist in other nations of the world; it is solidarity between countries, and not only within each country, and it should help in the construction of a true European citizenship. The so-called populist movements and parties that predict a return to nationalistic closure underestimate the fact that, in the era of globalisation, solidarity too must be global, or must accept the destiny of being marginalised.

The triadic structure of European society, which has always distinguished it from other societies, therefore persists, by virtue of the presence of a strong civil society which has never surrendered itself, neither to the statism that characterised part of the twentieth century, nor to the more recent liberalism, but which has rather continued to create new forms and new spheres of cooperative measures directed through the third sector, reappropriating the provision of many welfare services that had been withdrawn from the public bureaucracy, and ensuring that the EU acquires a strong cooperative dimension. This triadic approach alone can ensure the capacity to face the many grave challenges facing the EU today.

Bibliography

Borzaga, C and Ianes, A, *L'economia della solidarieta. Storia e prospettive della cooperazione sociale* (Roma, 2006).

Esping-Andersen, G, *The three worlds of welfare capitalism* (Cambridge, 1990).

Field, J, *Social capital* (New York-London, 2003).

Geyer, R, *Exploring European social policy* (Oxford, 2000).

Glossner, C and Gregosz, D (eds), *60 years of social market economy: formation, development and perspectives of a peacemaking formula* (Berlin, 2010) http://www.kas.de/wf/doc/kas_20040-544-2-30.pdf?100630164654.

Il contributo italiano alla storia del pensiero. Economia (Istituto della Enciclopedia Italiana, Roma, 2012).

Murray, R, Caulier Grice, J and Mulgan, G, *Il libro bianco sulla innovazione sociale*, eds A Giordano and A Arvidsson (2011) http://www.societing.org/wp-content/uploads/Open-Book.pdf.

Pestieau, P, *The welfare State in the European Union. Economic and social perspectives* (Oxford, 2006).

Porter, ME and Kramer, MR, 'Philanthropy's new agenda: creating value' (Nov–Dec 1999) 77(6) Harvard business review 121–30, https://hbr.org/1999/11/philanthropys-new-agenda-creating-value.

Ranci, C and Pavolini, E *Le politiche di welfare* (Bologna, 2015).

World Bank Group, *Taking on inequality* (2016).

Zamagni, V (ed), *Povertà e innovazioni istituzionali in Italia dal Medioevo ad oggi* (Bologna, 2000).

Zamagni, S and Zamagni, V, *La cooperazione* (Bologna, 2008).

Zamagni, S (ed) *Libro bianco sul terzo settore* (Bologna, 2011).

Zoll, R, *Was ist Solidarität heute?* (Frankfurt, 2000).

All web pages are understood as having last been visited on 13 June 2018.

Bibliography

20

The European Regional Development Policies

GIANFRANCO VIESTI

I. The Birth of European Development Policies

Regional development and cohesion policies (for simplicity's sake: RDPs) did not emerge with the launch of the European Economic Community (EEC) in 1957. Indeed, in the Treaty of Rome (or Treaty establishing the European Economic Community), they did not play a central role. In its preamble, emphasis is given to the necessity for the Member States to 'strengthen the unity of their economies and to ensure their harmonious development by reducing the differences existing between the various regions and the backwardness of the less favoured regions' (http://eur-lex.europa.eu/legal-content/EN/TXT/?uri=uriserv:OJ.C_.2016.202.01.0001.01.ENG&toc=OJ:C:2016:202:FULL, 7 June 2018). However, as provided for by the Treaty, direct activity at the Community level materialised only in the limited measures of the European Social Fund (ESF) and the European Investment Bank (EIB), which plays a role of some importance, in particular by financing infrastructure in southern Italy. The prevision of an explicit derogation for regional State aid, in the framework of the antitrust laws, proved important for subsequent developments.

Regional policies are in the hands of the Member States for a great many reasons: because, at the Community level, there is great faith in the overall developmental effects of the common market, even in the most backward areas; because, so far as the foundering countries go (Belgium, France, Germany, Italy, Luxembourg, the Netherlands), deep regional disparities are present only within Italy; as national authorities – in particular Italian ones – want to have direct control over RDPs, so as to be able to define the structure and the beneficiaries of the subsidies for private investment, and the composition and allocation of public investments.

The first steps toward a regional development policy were made almost accidentally only in the early part of the Seventies (Manzella (2011)). With the accession of the United Kingdom (1973), the European Regional Development Fund (ERDF) emerged, one of the instruments with which the British were compensated – in the sphere of the Community budget – for their limited payments through the Common Agricultural Policy (CAP; Tsoukalis (1998)). Yet, the role of the ERDF was modest, limited to cofinancing specific definite projects which were managed by the national authorities. Already in that period, however, the authoritative Thompson report of 1973 brought to light the fact that, 15 years after the launch of the common market, regional disparities persisted, and that, without a more decisive action of development policy, these could slow the processes of European integration and reduce its success (Manzella (2011)).

As always in the history of the Community, enlargements make for fundamental stages in the redefinition of policies. The accession Greece (1981) and then of Spain and Portugal (1986) was an occasion to bring to life the Integrated Mediterranean Programmes (IMP), which aimed at avoiding negative effects for the Mediterranean regions of the old Member States (France and Italy and then Greece). These programmes were not particularly important for their quantitative size, but they introduced certain initial elements of that process of programming which would subsequently characterise the RDPs. It was no longer a question simply of Community payments in view of programmes chosen and managed by the Member States. The idea began to appear that these measures should be inserted into long-standing programmes, and entrusted to a cooperative partnership between the national authorities and the regional authorities, with primary management responsibility going to the latter. The principle of national cofinancing of programmes was introduced, and the importance of the processes of policy evaluation was emphasised.

II. The Delors Package

After these first experiments, the regional development policies emerged, and assumed a fundamental importance, only in the second half of the 1980s (*Policy-making in the European Union* (1996)). The Community was a decisive step in its history. With the Single European Act (1986) there was not only a strong renewal of the process of integration, after the so-called Europessimism of the preceding years, but a Europe was drafted which went well beyond the level of a customs union, one based on the four freedoms (movement of goods, people, services, and capital) and on the faith in economic freedom and in the mechanisms of competition as the motors of long-term prosperity. This Europe was the daughter of the great revaluation of Keynesian policies and of welfare in the previous decades, a Europe which was much more confident in the virtue of the market. But at the same time it was a Europe which conserved the conviction that public policies should play a fundamental role of rebalancing in the processes of development and wealth distribution, all of which is personified in the figure of Jacques Delors.

The extremely authoritative Padoa-Schioppa report, published in April 1987, underlined how a greater and deeper Community integration, entrusted principally to the action of the markets, ran the risk of aggravating regional differences, emphasising the spatial polarisation of development. This report arrived at the finding that the common market has not brought a homogeneous development of Community territory. In these analyses the influence of theories from the 1950s and 1960s of uneven development was still strong (these theories would come once again to attention with the development of the so-called new economic geography): regional convergence was neither a guaranteed nor a natural phenomenon, but strong public policies were indispensable for promoting it. The title of the report itself, *Efficiency, stability, and equity*, underlined how the objective of internal equity in Europe had to accompany the objectives of efficiency connected to the single market and the stability of currency.

It is for these reasons that the Single European Act added title V (*Economic and social cohesion*) to the Treaty of Rome, with the provision of a comprehensive reform and of strengthening of the instruments for regional development, namely structural funds (ERDF and ESF). The regional policies of the European Union did not emerge therefore from little compensatory or redistributive ends, but they represent one of the fundamental pillars on which the great revival of European integration is based.

It was in this framework that, together with the reform of the Community budget and the first steps toward redefining the CAP, an initial doubling of the resources earmarked for regional development policies was established with the Delors package of 1987–88, and, with the legislation introduced by the Commission in 1988, its fundamental principles were clarified, which would remain almost unchanged in the successive decades (Viesti, Prota (2004)). The policy followed a principle of territorial concentration and earmarked the better part of its resources to Objective 1 areas, that is to underdeveloped regions. It made two fundamental choices: that of identifying the beneficiaries on the regional rather than national level (followed by an important process of statistical harmonisation with the creation of the so-called NUTS system: in French, *Nomenclature des unités territoriales statistiques*; or *Nomenclature of Territorial Units for Statistics*), and that of defining 75 per cent of the average Community GDP per capita in terms of purchasing power as the eligibility threshold for Objective 1 (an arbitrary measure, but one which, as many compromises at the European level, would withstand the passage of time). Territorial concentration provided also for an Objective 2, resulting from the widespread worries regarding the processes of deindustrialisation which had affected the more developed areas and regions of Europe beginning in the 1970s. There were also other, less relevant objectives which were not defined in a geographical sense, aimed at the issues of employment (Objective 3 on the fight against long-term unemployment and Objective 4 on the promotion of youthful employment) and of agricultural development (Objective 5a on the adjustment of agricultural structures and Objective 5b on the development of rural areas). From these last, a very slow and complex process of interpenetration between RDPs and the CAP would bring, in very recent times, the emergence of the so-called second pillar in the sphere of Community agricultural policies, aimed at rural development.

Beyond their fundamental geographical focus, these policies followed various principles: that of programming, through the definition of development strategies which integrate various instruments and have definite deadlines for their realisation in a multi-year horizon; that of the partnership, both vertical and between regions, States and Community authorities, on the one hand, and horizontal, public-private, on the other; that of cofinancing, by which national or regional resources must compulsorily accompany Community resources; and that of additionality, for which these last must be additional with respect to a predefined level of national measures (a condition which is in reality exceedingly difficult to verify). These were principles which would profoundly influence the action of the national and regional authorities, also in the planning and the realisation of other policies of a territorial nature (Viesti (2001)).

III. The Policies in Action

With the first Delors package, 63 million euro were allocated for the period 1989–93: the RDPs passed therefore from a weight of 18 per cent (1987) to 29 per cent (1993) of the total Community budget. In this initial period, 43 per cent of the European population fell within the two 'objective regions': in particular, Greece, Ireland, Portugal, the better part of Spain, southern Italy, Northern Ireland and Corsica were in Objective 1, for which 70 per cent of the total resources were earmarked (about 44 billion). The principal beneficiary country of the RDPs was Spain (13 billion), followed by Italy (11) and Portugal (8.5).

Just a few years later and the Treaty of Maastricht arrived. Economic and social cohesion remained one of the pillars on which integration was based, and on which policies of regional development were strengthened. It was in fact a widespread conviction that monetary integration might further bring about the processes of geographical polarisation in Europe: the creation of a monetary area would further reduce the obstacles to trade and, with the definitive renunciation of the exchange rate as an instrument of economic policy, the weakest Member States in particular would no longer be able to sustain the competitiveness of the price of their own productions in intra-Community and international exchange. Thus, as compared to the situation then existing from 1979 on with the EMS (*European Monetary System*), the possibility of effecting agreed-upon realignments of currency values in the face of the differentials of inflation was lacking. As would soon be seen with the crisis of the EMS, and as emerged dramatically in the commercial imbalances of the new century (Viesti (2015)), these worries were well founded. Therefore with Maastricht, structural funds assumed a yet more important role: they became the principal, if not the unique, Community instrument aimed at guaranteeing that the processes of economic growth would benefit all the territories (and thus all the citizens) of the Union.

In a controversial decision, in 1994 the Cohesion Fund was created, allocated to infrastructural measures for environment and transport in Member States with a per capita income in terms of purchasing power inferior to 90 per cent of the Community average. This decision was controversial because, in contrast to what had recently before been agreed upon, it fixed the eligibility threshold at the level of nations and not of regions, and also because even in this case the threshold value was arbitrary and excluded Italy (as well as reunified Germany) from these measures, notwithstanding the presence in this country of vast regions of regional underdevelopment. The Fund represents a compensation granted to certain beneficiary countries (in the first place Spain) for accession to the project of the single currency. This last circumstance should not elicit any moralistic evaluations: it is to be expected, in the history of the Community, that the attitudes and also the decisions of the single countries should have been influenced by the concrete compensations which they were able to obtain. The process of defining Community policies has always been complex and the great Community objectives have been known to intersect with the specific interests of the Member States.

Parallel to this, however, with the so-called Delors II package, the action of the structural funds was further reinforced: 167 billion euro were allocated for the period 1994–99, and in the last year they came to represent 36 per cent of the total Community budget. The population they covered rose to 50 per cent of the total, in a framework whose objectives and regulations were not subject to substantial alterations. The principal beneficiary country was still Spain; Germany, following reunification, was now alongside Italy. These were followed by Portugal, Greece, France and the United Kingdom. Meanwhile in 1995 the Union enlarged to Austria, Sweden and Finland, countries with high revenue which contribute to the Community budget. For the two Scandinavian countries a small ad hoc measure was designated: Objective 6 of the structural funds, which regarded those countries' peripheral regions with low population density.

With the 1994–99 programming, the so-called Community initiatives were launched. These were innovative programmes, promoted directly by the European Commission, on issues of particular interest. The most important of these were *Interreg*, to stimulate projects of interregional and international cooperation in more Member States; *Leader*, for rural areas; *Employment* and *Adapt*, on issues relating to the market and jobs; SME (*Small and Medium-sized Enterprises*); *Urban* for urban restoration, and *Rechar*, *Resider*, *Retex* and *Konvar* in cases of sectoral reconversion. The idea, which would be reinforced over time, was that these were experimental actions to be brought later into ordinary programming (through the so-called mainstreaming process), to disseminate good practices and to encourage the creation of stable networks of collaboration (networking).

IV. Toward the Great Enlargement

In 1997, in parallel with the signing of the Treaty of Amsterdam, the Commission published the document *Agenda 2000* (Manzella (2011)). This document reconfirmed the centrality of RDPs, on the basis of progress toward the construction of the single market and monetary unification: it also reiterated that these changes might exacerbate regional unbalances, particularly in light of the poor mobility of labour within the Union. All of this became yet more important, keeping in mind the predicted great EU enlargement toward the East which, with the inclusion of countries and regions with levels of revenue much lower than that of the old Member States, would bring an amplification and an exacerbation of regional problems. *Agenda 2000* proposed earmarking altogether 286 billion euro to RDPs (47 billion of which for the possible admission of countries which were then candidates) and setting a ceiling on the allocations of these resources for each country, equal to 4 per cent of their GDP, to avoid financial flows which might be too heavy, and the risk that these resources – in Community jargon – might not be 'absorbed'. The Commission proposed a reduction of the six objectives to three – Objective 1 (which included also 6) for the least developed regions, 2 (which included also 5b) for the areas in reconversion, and Objective 3 on the labour market; the Commission also proposed a drastic diminution of the population covered by these measures, introducing a modality of decreasing support (phasing out) for the regions targeted by the previous policies, which were to be excluded. Finally, important procedural changes could be seen, and also a greater decentralisation toward regions and State Members: these last elaborated Community support frameworks to locate the Community RDPs in the sphere of the more general processes of development of their own territories, and to render these RDPs as consistent as possible with their own national policies. A deadline was defined for the effective disbursement of funds, once these have been programmed (the so-called N+2 rule), as well as a 'performance reserve', with resources distributed mid-term to incentivise good management of these measures.

The European Council of Berlin of 24–25 March 1999 approved these Commission proposals, but in the framework of a substantially smaller amount of financing. This was a decision with a very important political meaning, above all in light of the then imminent enlargement of the Union, planned for 2004. The era of broad consensus on RDPs ended, and for the first time the resources were to be reduced during the period of programming: from 32 billion euro for the year 2000 to 29 for 2006.

In the period 2000–06, therefore, Objective 1 had at its disposal 150 billion: it covered Greece, large areas of Spain and Portugal, six regions of southern Italy, the eastern *Länder* of Germany, and small parts of other countries. Objective 2, which operated on territories of limited dimension in almost all the Member States, was given 24 billion, and Objective 3, almost 27. To these were added the Cohesion Fund for Spain, Portugal, Greece and Ireland (almost 20 billion) and 11 billion for Community initiatives, which were reduced to four (*Interreg*, *Leader*, *Equal* and *Urban*). The geographical concentration was greatly augmented, especially in Objective 2 regions: the EU population involved fell from 50 per cent to 41 per cent of the total. The 'aid maps' emerged from the conflict of objectives between the RDPs and the competition policies (at first to sustain investments with incentives, then to obstruct State aid); these 'aid maps' fixed intensity ceilings on the subsidies given to businesses, depending on their typology, of the aids and of the regions involved. Among the old Member States, the principal beneficiary of the RDPs was still far and away Spain, followed by Italy and Germany.

In 2004 came the great enlargement to ten new Member States (Cyprus, Estonia, Latvia, Lithuania, Malta, Poland, Czech Republic, Slovakia, Slovenia and Hungary). With their accession the regional disparities within the Union grew geographically, and became considerably more intense. The new Member States were all countries with a low per capita income (97.7 per cent of their population was in Objective 1 or 2 regions): they therefore contributed to a modest degree to the EU budget and at the same time were strong beneficiaries of RDPs, as well as the CAP. 24.5 billion euro were earmarked to them for the three-year period of 2004–06. It should also be noted that their accession, by reducing the average Community revenue, lowered the value of the eligibility threshold for Objective 1 (75 per cent), bringing about – by a simple statistical effect – the exclusion from it of certain regions in the old State Members.

This was a change of great importance. The resources for accession, which the European Council of Berlin of 1999 had reduced, now had to be subdivided between the old and the new Member States. The contribution of the weakest areas of the European Union of 15 (Belgium, France, Germany, Italy, Luxembourg, the Netherlands, Denmark, Ireland, the United Kingdom, Greece, Portugal, Spain, Austria, Finland, Sweden) to enlargement was therefore substantial, in terms of the relinquishment of resources which would have been earmarked for them. At the same time the resources of the RDPs represent about three-quarters of the disbursements of the Community budget toward the new State Members and play a fundamental role in accompanying the restructuring processes of those economies, by assuming an extremely significant burden with respect to the total of their public policies. The fall of communism and the accession to the EU of those countries brought about profound changes in those countries; the strong decline of their easternmost regions (former beneficiaries of the Soviet Union's relative proximity) and the growth of their capitals as well as the areas along their western borders, exacerbated their internal disparities, rendering the role of regional policies yet more important.

V. Controversies in the New Century

After Berlin, in the first years of the new century, the positions of certain countries that aimed at a redimensioning and a profound revision of the RDPs were reinforced. Proposals appeared, contained both in the documents of certain Member States (the United Kingdom, the Netherlands) and in independent reports (such as the Sapir report) to limit the RDPs to Eastern Europe alone, excluding the weak regions of the European Union of 15: in these cases the regional policies were supposed to be 'renationalised' (Viesti, Prota (2004)). This intersected with the desire of the net contributing States (that is, those for which there was a negative net balance, which is to say a negative difference between their contributions to the EU budget and the Community expenditure within their territory) to limit their own payments: to reduce the size of the Union budget and/or to limit the expenditures for the RDPs. This was the position expressed by the influential Group of six (France, Germany, the United Kingdom, the Netherlands, Sweden and Austria).

This was a near-sighted desire. It was based on the idea that the advantage of Union membership is measurable through net balance, but it forgot that precisely for the largest and most advanced countries benefits are determined, to a much more substantial degree, through the possibilities for that expansion of their enterprises which is consented by the single market (and by the single currency), as well as through the development of eligible zones of RDPs, from which arose a strong demand for importations, satisfied to a large extent by the strongest countries.

This climate rendered the discussion of 2007–13 particularly long and complex (Viesti (2006)). The budget negotiation was resolved both by restricting the size of the budget and by introducing new compensations for the net-contributing States: apart from the United Kingdom, these included for the first time also Germany, the Netherlands, Sweden and Austria, for a total of about 60 billion in a total budget of 864. Thanks to opposition on the part of the Commission, the European Parliament, and those Member States that benefitted from the RDPs, the proposals for renationalisation of the policies were rejected. But the appropriations for the RDPs were not increased with respect to their past levels, despite having to accommodate both the old and the new Member States (to which Romania and Bulgaria were added in 2007 and then Croatia in 2013). Compared to a Commission proposal to earmark 339 billion for the expenditure heading 1b (*Cohesion for growth and occupation*), the compromise at which the European Council of December 2005 arrived established the provisions for RDPs at 308 billion euro.

As in the past, these resources were earmarked in substantial measure (177 billion) to the 70 regions with a per capita income inferior to 75 per cent of the Community average, now included in a Convergence Objective. A special appropriation (12.5 billion) was also projected, in the same objective, for phasing out the 16 regions of the old Member States that exceeded that threshold for purely statistical reasons. In total, 140 million Europeans lived in a 'convergence area', 31 per cent of the total of the European Union of 25. To these, between 2007 and 2013, more than 30 million Romanians, Bulgarians, and Croatians would be added.

All the other European regions (155) were included in a new Regional Competitiveness and Employment Objective, for which 39 billion euro were allocated: among these regions were 13 that exceeded the threshold of 75 per cent, independently of the statistical effect (phasing in), and which received ad hoc resources. Thus the practice of zoning which had characterised Objective 2 was definitively surpassed.

The Cohesion Fund had a budget of almost 62 billion. There was also a small (8 billion) new European territorial cooperation objective, which brought the projects first financed by *Interreg* within the structural funds: this included all those regions situated along internal land borders, and along certain external and maritime land borders. The brunt of the policies for cooperating with the world outside the Union, with candidate countries as much as with the others, was instead entrusted to two new funds, external to the RDPs and to heading 1b – respectively IPA (*Instrument for Pre-Accession Assistance*), allocated to those candidate countries which were to enter the EU, and ENPI (*European Neighbourhood and Partnership Instrument*), allocated to nearby countries – whose rationale however in many respects follows that of the structural funds. Especially in the candidate countries, the EU 'exports' one of its best practices, believing this to be useful for favouring the process of transformation, especially in the Balkan economies, in view of their accession. It should be noted that the same thing occurred in extra-European Countries: the RDPs strongly influenced the strategies of regional development in Latin America, Russia, and China.

The decision to go beyond the old logic of 'zones' in Objective 2 had a very important political significance: RDPs, though with a very different intensity depending on the levels of development, covered the entire Union territory. They constituted a policy for development which concerns all Europeans. The Member States were called on to describe 'national policy frameworks' for their entire territory, and to indicate their own strategy of territorial development, to which the RDPs contribute as much as national policies. They must moreover present an annual 'strategic report' and insert a section on regional problems in their 'national reform programmes'.

Therefore RDPs were no longer merely policies to facilitate the growth and convergence of weak regions, but they are rather development policies for the entire Union. This is connected to the circumstance that in the European Union of 15 there is the obligation of using the majority (60 per cent in the 'convergence area', 75 per cent in the 'competitiveness area') of structural funds for objectives consistent with the Lisbon strategy. As has been observed, the strategy defined in 2000 in the extraordinary European Council of Lisbon was aimed at making Europe into the economy based on the most competitive and dynamic knowledge in the world, by 2010. It ended in total failure, given that it provided neither obligations for the Member States in reaching certain objectives (in radical contrast to the logic and the operation of the Stability and Growth Pact, SGP, of 1997), nor allocations of Community-wide resources: and indeed, this strategy was entrusted only to the good will of the Member States and to the so-called method of open coordination. The decisions relative to the RDPs for 2007–13 make structural funds into the principal Community instrument to promote their implementation. About 200 billion euro were invested, taking into account all EU regions, on the objectives of Lisbon, of which about 50 billion were invested in research: the RDPs became the principal policies for innovation and competitiveness in the Union, although on an incomparably smaller scale than was required.

A fundamental aspect of the 2007–13 RDPs was the strong reduction of aid in the European Union of 15. More than half of the 308 billion were allocated to the new Member States, in which the Cohesion Fund was also active. Thus in those countries the impact of the RDPs was reinforced: they contributed to a substantial infrastructural modernisation and to the birth of new economic activities. Only 150 billion were earmarked for the old Member States, with a significant reduction in aid intensity with respect to the preceding period: this circumstance would reveal itself to be of great importance from the start of the 2008 crisis on. To this was added the fact that, thanks to the lack of progress in fiscal harmonisation, the new Member States could implement very favourable policies of corporate taxation: combined with much lower labour costs and, in many cases, with exchange-rate flexibility, these policies exercised a strong effect through the international investment flows inside and outside the European Union, with a substantial 'localised competition' relative to all the Mediterranean regions. With the 2007–13 period the principal beneficiary of the RDPs was Poland (60 billion), followed by Spain, with 31; Italy and Germany received between 22 and 25 billion, but Hungary and the Czech Republic as well; Portugal, Greece, and Romania received less.

Naturally, in light of the varying sizes of these countries, the impact of the RPS on them is very different. In the 2011–13 period, structural funds and the relative national cofinancing covered more than 70 per cent of the public investments in Hungary, Bulgaria, Slovakia and Latvia; between 50 per cent and 70 per cent in Poland and the Czech Republic and in the other two Baltic States, as well as in Portugal. The share was around 10 per cent for Spain and some percentage points fewer for Italy and Germany: by now, the predominant effect of the RDPs was in the new Member States.

VI. European Cohesion Policies in the First Years of the Third Millennium

The construction of the European cohesion policy for 2014–20 was influenced by the publication in 2009 of an authoritative report edited by an independent Italian expert, Fabrizio Barca (Manzella (2011)). The Barca report underlined the enduring importance of the RDPs – place-based policies – both to reduce the underutilisation of the growth potential of all regions, thus augmenting the efficiency of the European economy, as well as to advance social inclusion, for reasons of equity. To this end, the report reiterates the importance of developing integrated intervention programmes built on the basis of the special characteristics of the various regions. To improve its effectiveness, a further concentration of resources is suggested, as well as a strong results orientation (through the choice of useful indicators for the objectives to be reached).

These suggestions were partially put into action. The policy for 2014–20 in many respects mimics that of the previous period, but it also presents several innovations. 351,8 billion euro are available for these seven years, which correspond to little less than a third of the total budget of the EU. Regional allocation varies with respect to the long tradition preceding. There is still the category of less developed regions, which correspond as ever to those with a per capita income in terms of purchasing power inferior to 75 per cent of the Community average, and in which 27 per cent of the population lives: the greater part (181 billion) of the resources is earmarked to these. A category of 'transition' regions (per capita income between 75 per cent and 90 per cent), which receive 38 billion, was created. Finally, there are the most developed regions, above 90 per cent (57 billion). The creation of the intermediate category was the result of the necessity to win the consent of Spain and Germany for the new season of policies. As once large beneficiaries, these two countries would have obtained much less from the RDPs: indeed, as a consequence of their significant development before the great crisis of 2008, almost all their regions (apart from the Spanish Extremadura) had surpassed the threshold of 75 per cent. France, the United Kingdom, and Greece also benefited from the introduction of the new category.

The Cohesion Fund (63 billion), earmarked now only for the new Member States, Portugal and Greece, as well as funding for the territorial cooperation policies (10 billion) both remain. The so-called youth employment initiative was also launched, with a limited budget allocation.

The geography of the beneficiaries shifts ever farther toward the East: the new Member States absorb about 55 per cent of the total resources. Poland alone obtains 77 billion, which is to say more than a fifth of the grand total, but the resources earmarked for the Czech Republic, Hungary, and Romania (more than 20 billion) are also significant, and so forth with the others. The significance of these figures, as has already been recalled, is naturally much greater if they are expressed as a percentage of GDP or per inhabitant. Among the old Member States the biggest beneficiary is Italy, with about 35 billion, followed by Spain, with a little less than 30; the expenditure diminishes significantly in Germany, while it remains substantial in Portugal and Greece.

The 2014–20 policies are organised on 11 thematic objectives, which cover as always extremely large and diversified spheres. Their connection with the initiatives, now included in the Europe 2020 project, for competitiveness and innovation in the European Union has been confirmed. There is an obligation, greater for the more developed regions but significant also for the others, to concentrate at least 50 per cent of ERDF resources on four objectives connected to Europe 2020: research and innovation; information and communication technologies; competitiveness of small and medium-sized enterprises; energy efficiency and renewable energies. The emphasis on the instruments of financial engineering is on the other hand more questionable and, in particular, the emphasis on the connection between the RDPs and the so-called Juncker plan (2014), which provides for the creation of a European fund for strategic investments, aimed at boosting economic growth: there is a push to use structural funds as security instruments to mobilise investments of private capital, through strong leverage. If it is desirable to try to utilise public funds to stimulate private investments, it is evidently necessary that a clear distinction be preserved, both political and operative, between investments which are able to produce remuneration of invested capital, and public investments in the proper sense, which intervene by definition in spheres with no private profitability, but with collective benefit.

A significant emphasis was put, also through the suggestions of the Barca report, on a simplification of regulations, on incentive mechanisms for the quality and the rapidity of expenditure (there is now a performance reserve equal to 6 per cent of the total), and on *ex ante* measures to improve the administrative structures and the framework of national policies connected to structural funds. If these 'conditionalities' for a better use of funds appear to be necessary, the introduction of 'macroeconomic conditionality' raises major doubts. This macroeconomic conditionality comes to subordinate the disbursement of funds in compliance with the prescriptions that each country receives in the sphere of macroeconomic policy coordination and, therefore, also in the implementation of austerity measures connected to Stability Pact infringement proceedings, or to the intervention of the so-called bailout fund.

VII. A View and an Evaluation of the Whole

Comprehensively, four great changes can be identified in RDPs. The first is in their financial dimension: initially they increased (rising from about 0.15 per cent of the Community

GDP in the second half of the 1980s to about 0.3 per cent at the end of the 1990s) and then they remained stable. Their comprehensive burden, therefore, is limited with respect to the whole of the European economy, even if it is much more substantial in the lower-income Member States. The second is in the geography of the beneficiaries: among the old Member States, Germany (after reunification) at first stood side by side the traditional Mediterranean recipients, before diversification in development trajectories brought about a reduction of these policies in Germany and in Spain. All new Member States are included in the policies from the moment of their adhesion: their internal development, with a strong escalation of regional disparities, ensures that certain of their regions (and in particular their capitals) enter into the group of relatively more developed zones, while the rest of the territory is much farther behind. The third is in organisational structuring: the European Social Fund and the European Regional Development Fund were conserved as large containers, but the Cohesion Fund has come to join them. The Community initiatives were launched, and then subsequently integrated to a large extent in ordinary programming. Allocation was distributed first in a multiplicity of geographical and functional objectives, which were then reduced principally to geographical objectives, with the inclusion of the entire European population. The last great change is in the very aims of the policy (Manzella (2011)): an initial compensative aim was substituted by a much greater emphasis on the competitiveness of all the regions and, in particular, on the push for innovation of those policies connected to the objectives of Europe 2020.

Over time, an exceedingly vast literature has been formed, aimed at evaluating the overall experience of the RDPs and, in particular, at quantifying their contribution to Europe's development (Viesti, Prota (2004)). A group of greatly interesting studies, aimed at measuring the impact of RDPs on specific regional conditions, demonstrate convincingly that the impact of these policies has been significant in bringing about changes and improvements in the conditions of regional contexts and in the circumstances that might favour a greater economic development and a more extensive social inclusion. For example, on the Community scale, in 2007–13 RDPs contributed to the creation of about one million new jobs (with respect to a net balance equal to three million), to the support of 250,000 small and medium-sized enterprises, to the realisation or to the renovation of 5,000 kilometres of rail and 30,000 of road, to making broadband connections available to 8.2 million Europeans, and connections to new or improved sources of potable water supplies for 5.9 million inhabitants. More generally, the fundamental contribution of the RDPs is evident in the realisation of large transport networks in the Iberian peninsula and, more recently, in the East, especially in Poland, or the development of airports in southern Italy: these very important structural measures are prerequisite for greater economic development. Such studies are important also because they enable one to compare specific impacts within varied regions, to measure various performances and thus to identify the specific conditions that augment the utility and the effectiveness of the RDPs, thereby progressively increasing their effects.

The very wide spectrum of spheres in which the RDPs are involved should naturally be borne in mind. If on the one hand this is fitting, consistent with a multidimensional vision of development, on the other hand it fragments available resources through a multiplicity of objectives, consenting specific advances to a proportionate degree.

Other studies aim at determining the impact of RDPs on regional growth. These do not present unambiguous results: accompanying those studies which show positive effects are others that remain more sceptical. These are not simple evaluations, given that they must take into account a number of large questions. The comprehensive dimension of these policies, which should by definition be additional with respect to a predefined level of national expenditure, should indeed be borne in mind. But there is a large body of evidence that this occurs only in part and to very different degrees in the national experiences. There is a lesser additionality in those places where only parts of the national territory are classified in the category of less developed regions: as in the Italian case, in which the lack of additionality of RDPs in southern Italy is obvious. If there is a lacking or partial additionality, the impact of the RDPs on the GDP is by definition very limited or even null.

RDPs also principally finance investments: if their impact on the conditions of demand is directly connected to expenditure, their impact on supply conditions – which is much more important and more capable of structurally influencing economic trends over long periods – is much more diffused over time, and subject to the implementation of other development policy measures which do not always come to pass: the realisation of new rail infrastructure (financed or cofinanced by the RDPs) has an impact on supply conditions only when a significant transport service is developed on it, the implementation of which is subject to other conditions and other policies.

The income convergence of a region with respect to the Community average (which is the indicator used in most studies) is moreover the result of two very distinct components: the rate of change relative to the region with respect to the national average, and the rate of change relative to the national average with respect to the Community average. Success relative to a region depends largely on overall trends and on the convergence processes of the national economy of which it is a part. In the contemporary international framework, as is highlighted by the analyses, among others, of the OECD (*Organisation for Economic Cooperation and Development*) of 2016, there have been signs for some time of a widening of regional disparities within many countries. At the same time, significant signs of convergence processes among national economies have also emerged (and at the very least, among some of those that lag most behind together with the vanguard). Many Eastern European regions which showed a significant income convergence in the last decade with respect to the EU average have in reality suffered a widening of internal distances with respect to the strongest areas of their economies (especially their capitals), but they have simultaneously benefited from processes of national convergence.

Finally, the great international crisis has considerably influenced regional dynamics and the effectiveness of RDPs. This crisis has affected European economies and regions selectively, shaking up positions and trends and creating very different dynamics between the eastern and the southern countries of the Union. During the years of the crisis, RDPs were fundamental in countering the very dangerous tendency toward a reduction of public investments in the entire EU, by guaranteeing a minimum level of these, especially in the weakest regions and in those Member States which were grappling with the greatest budgetary difficulties and the most intense applications of austerity policies.

The future of the RDPs after 2020 is already the subject of discussion and it appears shrouded in great uncertainties. It appears that there are strong pressures toward their reduction, even their substantial reduction, or else for their strong thematic or geographical limitation. These pressures originate in net-contributor Member States that, as had already occurred in the debates previous to the last cycle of programming, follow a strictly national interest, trying to limit the expenditure of the Union and thus their own contribution. They also originate in those countries, especially in the countries of Northern Europe, which are favourable to subordinating every European policy to the doctrinaire prescriptions of austerity and of the so-called structural reforms, as well as in a vast ideological alignment on principle against any public intervention in the economy.

On the other hand, within the contemporary European framework RDPs appear to be more useful than ever. Economic theory and decades of economic history show that the phenomena of convergences and regional development are neither spontaneous nor guaranteed. RDPs have to counter strong trends toward polarisation. But there is much more yet: they represent the first European politics, with common rules and objectives for development in all the areas of the continent, capable of favouring economic growth and at the same time of countering social exclusion phenomena, which represent the ideal breeding ground for revanchism, political sovereignism, and anti-Europeanism.

Bibliography

Manzella, GP, *Una politica influente. Vicende, dinamiche e prospettive dell'intervento regionale europeo* (Bologna, 2011).

OECD, *OECD Regions at a glance* (Paris, 2016) http://www.keepeek.com/Digital-Asset-Management/oecd/governance/oecd-regions-at-a-glance-2016_reg_glance-2016-en#page1.

Padoa-Schioppa, T, *Efficienza, stabilità ed equità: una strategia per l'evoluzione del sistema economico della Comunità europea* (Bologna, 1987).

Tsoukalis, L, *La nuova economia europea* (Bologna, 1998).

Viesti, G, 'La politica di sviluppo territoriale fra Europa e Regioni' (2001) 5 *Europa Europe* 39–47.

Viesti, G and Prota, F, *Le nuove politiche regionale dell'Unione Europea* (Bologna, 2004, 2007).

Viesti, G, 'Il difficile policy-making europeo: la discussione sulla politica regionale e sul bilancio dell'Unione (2001–05)' (2006) 1 *Studi sull'integrazione europea* 45–59.

Viesti, G, 'Why Europe is in a trap' (2015) 1 *Stato e mercato* 53–84, http://profgviesti.it/wp-content/uploads/2013/04/2015viestieuropeinatrap.pdf.

Wallace, H and Wallace, W (eds), *Policy-making in the European Union* (Oxford, 1996).

All web pages are understood as having last been visited on 7 June 2018.

PART V

The EU and the World: Competition Within the EU Market and External Relations (With Non-Member Countries)

21

Rules to Guarantee Free Competition

ENZO MOAVERO-MILANESI

I. The Raison D'être of EU Rules to Guarantee Free Competition

Since its very beginning, the process of European integration has been marked by the explicit political choice of fully guaranting freedom of competition to market players. In the early 1950s, it was not an obvious decision – both because of the pull exerted by the alternative scheme of planned economy, which was then applied in an Eastern Europe dominated by the Soviet Union, as well as because of the considerable influence that the governments of Western European countries were used to exercise in economic affairs via the widespread presence of State-owned enterprises, often operating in privileged regimes or as legal monopolies.

The European Union (EU or the Union) rules to protect and guarantee free competition therefore reveal the essence of the founding objective of the complex process of integration among the Member States: to merge the various national markets into one common European internal market, open to the ambition of whoever wants to operate an economic activity, in competition with others. Moreover, in order for that market to be equal and advantageous for the entire society, it is not left to itself but regulated by *ad hoc* norms, which prevent any possible disruption on the market and safeguard an effective freedom of choice for everyone at all market levels.

These prescriptions are of immediate and basic interest for all of us, who interact daily with the market. Any enterprise (be it a multinational or a PMI), craftsman, professional, inventor, artist or anyone else undertaking an economic activity knows very well what competition is. From time to time, competition can be loved or feared, faced or tamed, or avoided. The consumer, who benefits from goods or services offered on the market, also takes advantage from a real competition among sellers or suppliers: broader assortment (selection); range of prices and discounts; customer assistance; innovation and improvement in technology, quality, beauty, style; advertising appeals.

EU competition rules are key for the different Member States, for their governments, and administrations. The observance of those rules – whose enforcement is delegated, in particular, to the Commission and the Court of Justice (to which all the judgments quoted in this text are attributable) – requires a strict discipline often affecting national public policies. For this reason, the bodies in charge of implementing such rules have relevant enforcement powers, and the adopted decisions have a significant and concrete impact often highlighted in the newspapers.

II. The Competition

The concept of *competition* involves the presence of several entities in the market, each of which aiming at its own success and beating the others. Therefore, a resourceful rivalry underpins competition among market players. Freedom of competition offers everyone the opportunity to make choices and to take risks. It allows market operators within the same range of activities (or in those activities that are contiguous) to face each other in order to achieve the best possible result or, at least, their own objectives.

This dynamic process complies with our general interest in having a healthy and evolving economy. The continuous rivalry of those producing and offering goods and services on the market leads them towards a series of actions aimed at obtaining the desired trust from the clients. In the first place, the outcome could be an advantage in terms of business efficiency, since a company consolidates, grows, and creates jobs only by improving the use of resources and services and by innovating. On the other hand, the inability to compete could get the business into difficulty and bankruptcy. Secondly, the consumer as well as the intermediate or final user of goods and services benefits from the competitive dynamics, since they can obtain what they need, taking advantage of a varied and convenient offer available on the market. In this way, the satisfaction of the consumer and the efficiency of the businesses have a positive impact on the whole social context.

Competition is therefore the driving force behind a free market: it encourages its vitality; it redistributes the wealth among economic players, while rewarding the best; it stimulates labour; it benefits consumers. In many respects it appears to be a valid justice factor. For these reasons, the two elements of business efficiency and consumer benefit are usually identified as public interest objectives to be pursued while guaranteeing free competition with appropriate rules. Accordingly, safeguarding free competition does not constitute a purpose in itself, an ideological stand-alone objective, but rather a tool to achieve an overall benefit.

Regardless of the unquestionably positive aspects of a competitive environment, it would not be wise to identify the ideal structure for each market by default. On the contrary, it is very important to ensure full freedom to the market itself, enabling it to adjust spontaneously. It is natural that in an open environment the number of competitors varies depending on economic circumstances. It is also possible that a business becomes dominant or monopolist; at the same time, the other way around, if a business allows its product to degrade or pushes up the price too much, it is likely that new competitors with lower prices and better offers will appear in a free market. As a result, public authorities should always abstain from interfering with the physiological reality of a market, while at the same time they should keep a close watch and redress any distortions therein. This is a sensitive matter that lawmakers have to regulate with suitable norms in order to avoid excessive interventions by public authorities. Norms will protect the smooth functioning of competition as well as the diverse freedoms related to it.

The magnitude, the versatility of the rules guaranteeing competition, and the impact of the bodies responsible to ensure compliance depend on the level of the above-mentioned mechanism and on its interpretation in specific cases. However, the very nature of the matter, the interdisciplinary analysis that it requires, and the importance of the implementing decisions highlight its specific character. It is not without reason that within the EU we talk about *competition policy* with regards to the activity of public authorities responsible for upholding free competition. We are talking about a powerful regulatory tool, which enables getting to the heart of operational strategies of market players, challenging and annulling public measures (in some cases even laws) as well as interfering with the freedom of the market itself.

III. EU Rules Protecting Free Competition

The 'definition of competition rules necessary to the functioning of the internal market' is stated among the exclusive competencies of the Union in article 3 of the Treaty on the functioning of the European Union (TFEU). The basic provisions can be found in other articles from the same treaty and are grouped into two sections.

The first section includes 'rules applicable to undertakings', banning them from certain conducts: any form of agreement that could affect the conditions of competition as well as the wrongful exploitation of a dominant position on the market (articles 101–105: the base of the EU antitrust law, the matrix of which can be found in the American *Sherman Act* of 1890, the forerunner of antitrust laws). Moreover, article 106 concerns 'public undertakings', those benefiting from 'special or exclusive rights' and 'undertakings entrusted with the operation of services of general economic interest'. The second section relates to any form of 'aid granted by States' to market players (articles 107–109).

All these rules are designed to complete the toolbox to protect a free and open internal market of the Union. On the one hand, that is to avoid that market players distort its full competition on the market; on the other hand, to prevent measures by national public authorities that are likely to distort the equality of opportunities among European competitors.

Overall, the approach is pragmatic. There is no intention to protect an abstract model of perfect competition, but a market environment where competition will arise in an efficient manner (so-called workable competition).

Regulations of secondary legislation complement the complex discipline. The most important are the regulations issued by the Council, especially those providing for supervisory procedures and a systematic control of concentrations between enterprises. There are also numerous acts issued by the European Commission, in its authority as guarantor of competition: regulations setting out specific exceptions; directives under article 106 of the TFEU; interpretative documents (so-called *communications*), not mandatory, but essential to evaluate possible illegal situations. Lastly, due to the relevance of case law within the Union, rulings of the Court of Justice, as well as the decision-making practice of the Commission, are always to be considered.

IV. The Concept of Undertaking

EU rules protecting free competition do not define the key concept of undertaking. According to established case law, it is necessary to choose a broader interpretation including each autonomous entity of whatever legal form, actively participating in the economic life, pursuing a specific purpose, via the offer of goods and/or services on a given market.

The great variety of cases includes: public authorities, even when devoid of independent legal status from the public administration (see the judgment of 16.6.1987, case 118/85) or when they carry out tasks of a non-economic nature (see the judgment of 12.12.2000, T-128/98); self-employed individuals (see the judgments of 19.2.2002, C-309/99, lawyers; and 12.9.2002, joined cases 180-184/98, doctors); sports associations and athletes, especially in contexts linked to sponsoring or the organisation of race events (see the judgment of 1.7.2008, C-49/07); artists (see the judgment of 8.6.1971, case 78/70); entities carrying out economic activities even as non-profit organizations (see the judgment of 16.9.1995, C-244/94). Vice versa, it is not considered as an undertaking an entity whose activity has purely social aims, without a real economic underpinning (see the judgment of 11.7.2006, C-205/03, *National Health Service*).

EU Law has also identified the important doctrine of the *single economic entity and parental liability*. When assessing the infringement of rules protecting competition and the punitive consequences, all the companies, even though formally recognised as having their own individuality and legal status but belonging to the same group, where the parent company (holding) is controlling the others, are considered as a single economic unit. A mere relationship of dependency is not considered as sufficient, but an organic relation of effective control is needed, so that the controlled entity is not able to decide independently its own market behaviour (see the judgment of 14.7.1972, case 48/69, and of 31.10.1974, case 15/74). An extension of this doctrine led to establishing an economic unity between two independent companies, which were sufficiently bound by a supply relationship to an extent that any risk to their activity could be eliminated (see the judgment of 11.9.2008, C-279/06).

V. Prohibition of Agreements and Collusions Between Competitors

Article 101 of the TFEU prohibits certain acts put in place by a plurality (at least two) of undertakings: *agreements, concerted practices*, and/or *decisions by associations of undertakings*. The aim of the following list is to cover any type of agreement between competitors affecting the principles of a competitive market: written contracts; verbal deals; collusions, even implicit (see the judgment of 11.1.1990, C-277/87); concerted forms of coordination to reduce uncertainties inherent in a normal competitive environment (see the judgment of 14.7.1972, case 48/69, and of 21.1.2016, C-74/14); recommendations or indications of a business organisation to its members. The arrangement corresponds to what is stated by Section 1 of the Sherman Act, which declares as illegal similar behaviours 'in restraint of trade or commerce' in the United States.

In order to apply the prohibition, two conditions of enforceability shall be fulfilled. The first requires that the acts mentioned earlier 'could' cause *damage to trade among Member States* of the Union: namely, it could affect, even if just potentially, trade. The other condition relates to the *restriction of competition*: the acts must have the purpose (namely the objective) or the impact of obstructing, reducing, or distorting competition within the EU internal market.

Consequently, even if the companies in question are not European, article 101 can be violated if there are implications within the Union territory (this is the so called extra-territoriality principle in the application of competition rules). On the other hand, the breach is disregarded if the impact of the anticompetitive behaviour, real or possible, is of minor importance and not significant (a specific Commission statement clarifies the terms of such situations, defined as *de minimis*). It should be noted that the first condition serves also to define the sphere of competence of EU legislation compared with those of the different Member States: generally, if competition is altered but European trade is not, action is taken under the applicable national laws.

The prohibition under article 101 is not absolute as *non-applicability* (often called *exemption*) can be identified in the case of four interconnected preconditions: (i) a (substantial) improvement in the production or distribution of the products, that is a technical or economic progress, (ii) which would partly be to the benefit of consumers, (iii) though without imposing non-essential restrictions on competition, and (iv) without entirely eliminating competition within a substantial part of the market in question. This involves an important exception, which acknowledges the achievements of some agreements among competitors, which, whilst altering the conditions of competition, can offer objective and proportionate benefits, as set out in article 101.

Interestingly, the character of these benefits can impose an evaluation that goes beyond the mere perspective of free competition, requesting also a diverse logic related to the business activity itself. As a competition authority, the Commission has been given the power to pursue also initiatives driven by industrial policy concerns, by using the exemption under article 101. This option conflicts with the American practice of separating industrial policy from antitrust protection (the borderline case in Europe has been the so-called crisis cartels, which have been authorised in order to allow companies to overcome overcapacity). In this respect, clear evidence can also be found in the Commission regulations (known as *block exemptions regulations*, see below), which exempt certain agreements from the prohibition, while setting out, for this purpose, specific guidelines for the activity of the companies (examples: research, technology transfer, specialisation).

There are many agreements likely to restrict competition. They are split into: *bilateral* and *multilateral* (the latter, called *cartels*, are pernicious, often secret and difficult to detect); *horizontal* (between undertakings operating at the same level of the production and distribution process) and *vertical* (between undertakings operating at different levels, such as wholesale and retail). Their classification depends also on the collusive purpose, for example: (a) to fix the prices of goods and services (including discounts) as well as other terms of sale or purchase, by preventing the consumer choosing according to a comparison of convenience; (b) to limit the produced and marketed outputs in order to reduce the offers and increase the prices; (c) to share the target markets and/or the supply by geographical areas in which there will be no competition (it should be noted that case studies show that in the Union the agreements not to compete in certain territories often follow the borders of the Member States, thus recreating by agreement obstacles that replace the public borders banned by EU internal market rules; (d) to specialise its own productions by avoiding competition over the full range of products; (e) to discriminate, in cooperation with other competitors, against certain buyers or suppliers, to make things difficult for them (in such cases we are talking about a *collective boycott*).

When comparing the mechanism of article 101 with the related American antitrust rule in the *Sherman Act*, there is an immediate basic difference. In the EU system, the rule sets out typical examples of infringement, as well as the reasons to lift the ban. By contrast, in the US system it has been the case law to identify the types of infringement; complementary interpretative doctrines such as *per se violations* or *rule of reason* serve to recognise respectively cases where the infringement is obvious and associated with the act, and cases which, on the contrary, are not to be penalised because the restriction of competition appears to be 'reasonable', due to the benefits that it brings.

VI. Abuse of a Dominant Position on the Market

Article 102 of the TFEU prohibits 'any *abuse* [...] *of a dominant position* within the internal market' of the Union or in a substantial part of it. Illegal conduct can be carried out by one or more players, depending on whether that position is held by only one undertaking or collectively by various undertakings. For the latter situation to occur (commonly in markets with few competitors), there is no need for arrangements, as it is sufficient an economic environment leading the undertakings to a uniform and conscious policy towards the other competitors.

The ban affects the abuse or incorrect exercise of the position of supremacy in the market, not the 'dominant position' as such. Therefore, compared to Section 2 of the Sherman Act, which is in some ways the counterpart, EU regulation covers a more limited scope. The Sherman Act in American antitrust law outlaws any act aiming to 'monopolize, or attempt to monopolize, or combine or conspire with any other [...] to monopolize any part of the trade or commerce' in a market (see also the Robinson-Patman Act of 1936 and some cases of the Clayton Act of 1914).

There are two conditions for the applicability of article 102: the first condition reiterates (see above on article 101 of the TFEU) the need for an *effect on trade between the Member States in the Union*; the second condition requires the existence of a '*dominant position*' in the market.

In order to determine whether there is such a position, the target market must be identified. In jargon we are talking about the *relevant market*, which relates both to the geographical space and the goods offered therein: it is a territory, where competitors can act on a common level playing field (eg, with similar transport costs) and the goods in question are in competition since they are interchangeable in the eyes of consumers. Article 102 specifies that the framework to be taken into account has to comply with the EU internal market or with a 'substantial part' of it, a concept that has been interpreted in the case law very flexibly, even as far as only one State in the Union.

Once the relevant market has been identified, it is necessary to measure the balance of power between the companies operating in that market. Compared to a monopoly, a *dominant position* does not exclude the possibility of a certain competition and enables the dominant companies to decide their own conduct in the market regardless of competitors, suppliers, buyers and consumers. Thanks to its economic power, the dominant player has thus the possibility to evade free competition (see judgment of 13.2.1979, case 85/76). To check if the situation persists, the market share index, while crucial, is not sufficient in itself as the following must be considered: the number of competitors and their comparative importance; the structure of the enterprises themselves (eg, if they are integrated vertically); and the existence of any barriers to entry the market for new competitors.

Article 102, precisely because it has to do with abuse, results in an inescapable total ban. This does not mean that the dominant enterprise cannot pursue its own interests and defend its position, but that needs to be done via the normal use of its market power. Therefore, it is good for the enterprise to act with caution since some of its behaviours, which would be permissible in a competitive market, may prove to be abnormal. For example, if the company significantly reduces its prices (which is usually desirable), it could be objected that it aims at undermining weaker competitors that are unable to sustain the reduction in profit margins (an abuse called *predatory pricing*). In the same way, if the dominant company decides not to sell its products to a customer that is unable to find alternative supplies, this can be construed as an abuse of *refusal to supply* by the dominant company, if the product concerned is essential for the customer to conduct its business.

Other patterns of abuse are: (a) to practice excessive or unfair prices, at the expense of customers and consumers; (b) to offer dissimilar conditions for equivalent services without an objective justification; (c) to offer loyalty discounts to erode the customer base of minor competitors; (d) to make the conclusion of contracts subject to acceptance of additional obligations, which by their nature or according to commercial use are not really needed (we are talking about *tying clauses*; see judgment of 17.9.2007, case T-201/04); and (e) to strengthen the dominant position already held in the market (see judgment of 21.2.1973, case 6/72, and see below: *The control of concentration between undertakings*).

VII. Procedures for Investigating Anticompetitive Agreements and Abuses of a Dominant Position

The application of articles 101 and 102 of the TFEU is governed by Council regulation no. 1/2003; other requirements can be found in a series of regulations issued by the Commission. The complex procedural system involves several bodies: the Commission, as EU authority protecting free competition; the various antitrust authorities of the EU Member States; national courts; the General Court of the European Union and the European Court of Justice. The present system is characterised by significant decentralisation; in the previous framework (in force from 1962 until 2004) the Commission was more directly involved and was specifically the only competent authority to grant the exemption provided for in article 101.

Therefore, EU norms serve as a basis for a plurality of instances. Although it is possible to address directly a judge of the Member State where the anticompetitive conduct has been committed (due to the *direct applicability* of articles 101 and 102), usually before asking a court of law, this goes through an administrative proceeding in front of the Commission or of the antitrust authorities of the various Member States. This makes it essential to have close cooperation among these authorities, ensured by the Commission itself. To this end, there is continuous contact within the appropriate network (the so-called *European Competition Network*) in order to: inform each other; ensure consistent interpretative guidelines;

guarantee that, if the Commission starts a procedure, the national authorities cannot conduct it anymore, with respect to the same concrete issue.

The Commission can start an investigation relating to a potential infringement of articles 101 and 102 on its own initiative or following a complaint, which is usually submitted by competitors or customers claiming to be affected. In this context, extensive powers are conferred upon the Commission: requests for very detailed information; checks and inspections at the business premises, with the power to seize documents and interrogate people; enquiries in certain economic sectors.

On the basis of its findings, in case of unlawful conduct the Commission sends a *statement of objections* to the enterprises involved and by doing so the Commission initiates formal proceedings. In accordance with the principle of respect for the rights of the defence, the enterprises can access the case file (specific measures protect the confidentiality contained therein) and have a structured meeting with the case team (*hearing*). The procedure is terminated by a decision of the Commission: a binding and enforceable act, against which it is possible to lodge a complaint with the General Court; its ruling can be appealed to the European Court of Justice.

Among the final procedural decisions that the Commission is empowered to adopt, the following should be mentioned: (a) *establishment of the infringement*, which can be followed by an order to cease the unlawful conduct (in particular article 101 is explicit about the declaration of retrospective invalidity of the acts performed as part of a prohibited agreement), as well as by administrative fines, *penalties* (up to 10 per cent of the turnover of the companies involved) and periodic *penalty payments* for every day of delay in implementing the decision itself; moreover, those who have suffered damage from the anticompetitive act can ask for compensation before a competent national court (directive no. 2014/104 has harmonised private antitrust actions in the Union); (b) *statement of non-applicability*, which can depend on the absence of motives to intervene under articles 101 and 102 or on the recognition of conditions for the exemption rule under article 101; (c) *adoption of temporary precautionary measures* on grounds of urgency and in cases where the infringement is likely to happen after the investigation; (d) *rejection of a complaint*, if it is unfounded or ineligible.

In order to reduce litigation, the Commission can issue regulations indicating precise conditions to apply the exemption under article 101 to certain categories of agreements. These are the so-called exemption regulations for categories of agreements. These are very important as they allow enterprises to preliminarily assess the compatibility of their agreement with EU rules. Actually, in similar cases there is no individual assessment. Nevertheless, if in a specific case the Commission observes that an agreement disciplined by these regulations causes excessive restriction of competition, it can withdraw the exemption.

The described procedural system in force in the Union outlines various differences compared to the American one. In the United States the observance of antitrust laws is ensured both by the Antitrust Division of the Department of Justice (DOJ) as well as by the Federal Trade Commission (FTC). Both are entitled to bring a case directly before a judge. The cases prepared by the DOJ can also be of criminal nature and lead to a jail sentence for those convicted of serious anti-competition acts. The FTC intervenes especially for the protection of consumers and can facilitate voluntary and settlement solutions. It is not uncommon for the US Supreme Court itself to settle the outstanding matters and novelties, given the more legal nature of the procedures and the tough sanctions imposed.

VIII. The Control of Concentrations Between Undertakings

In 1989, the Council (regulation no. 4064/89; amended by no. 139/2004) completed the Union's antitrust law by setting up an EU system for assessing the impact that concentrations between undertakings can have on free competition. It concerns operations in which: (a) independent undertakings merge; and (b) one or more undertakings take over (gain the possibility to exercise decisive influence on the activities of) other undertakings or parts of their businesses, even by creating a joint subsidiary (joint-venture), provided that this will be able to exercise all the functions of an independent undertaking.

The Commission verifies the Community dimension of concentrations (as defined by the regulation, based upon the turnover of the undertakings, within precise thresholds, and providing that less than two-thirds of their turnover is achieved within one same Member State). The other mergers are, however, being reviewed by national competent antitrust authorities according to national regulations.

The EU procedure provides for an obligation to give *notification* of a concentration to the Commission and suspends the transaction in order to systematically assess its potential negative implications for the competition. For this purpose, the Commission has significant powers equal to those normally used for investigations relating to articles 101 and 102 of the TFEU (see above). Tight deadlines are set for the procedure (a maximum of 90 days following notification) in order to provide quick certainty to companies with regard to operations, which are, by their very nature, structural, often complex and expensive. After the expiry of the time limit set for the control, unless there is a formal decision, the concentration is deemed to be authorised.

The Commission can take a decision stating: (a) the *compatibility* of the concentration, if it does not prevent or 'significantly impede effective competition' in the EU market or in a substantial part of it; (b) the *incompatibility* of the concentration, if the just mentioned restrictive effects occur and this happens specifically when a dominant position is created and strengthened (see above); in that case, the transaction cannot be finalised; (c) on *procedural aspects*, eg, to obtain remedies; and (d) *punitive*, imposing fines and periodic penalty payments (see above), if the standstill obligation of the transaction is not being complied with or if the concentration, despite having been declared incompatible, is pursued (in which event the unbundling of the companies or of its branches merged illegally is also demanded).

Once again, the European antitrust system presents similarities and differences, if compared to the US system, where mergers between companies are regulated by the Clayton Act of 1914 (see also the Celler-Kefauver Act of 1950), which provides for monitoring activities in order to prevent companies from acting to 'substantially […] lessen competition, or […] create a monopoly'. Even the existing American law (see 15 US Code § 18a and the Hart-Scott-Rodino Act of 1976) provides for a notification procedure for the prior examination of the impact of the operations, carried out by the FTC and the Antitrust Division of the DOJ.

IX. Public Aid to Undertakings

In a free market system, there is frequently public (stat, local or other) intervention aimed at encouraging and supporting enterprises, promoting their development or softening the impact of their financial difficulties (or even bankruptcy). Concrete objectives can vary, but the goal is always corrective: as the idea behind it is that the market and competition are not sufficient to guarantee fair results, in line with the general interest.

Therefore, in the name of such interest, public money collected via taxes is spent; thus, with the contribution of all the taxpayers, initiatives benefiting only some of them are financed. If this results in a boost of economic growth or other benefit (eg, a cleaner environment), society in general will benefit in the end. However, if this does not happen, the State will be saddled with a net liability and its ability to bear it may depend on political commitment, the health of public finances, and ultimately the willingness of taxpayers (who should make themselves heard as concerned voters).

This trend poses further questions in a context, such as the one in the EU, where equality among competitors must be ensured in the EU internal market, irrespective of the Member State of which they are nationals. Indeed, competition needs to be fostered among undertakings and not among the various Member States seeking to facilitate operators in their respective territories. And that is why articles 107–109 of the TFEU declare as incompatible the 'aid granted by States' to undertakings.

This concept of 'aid', focused on the negative impact that it has on competition, is quite broad and includes any kind of advantage, in any form: for example, subsidies; reductions or deferrals, not in use, for the payments of levies or charges; funding that is more advantageous than what is available on the market; guarantees to try to get low-interest loans from banks; coverage of losses in the company budget; special export insurances; bailouts from bankruptcy; supply of goods or supply contracts under better conditions compared with the current market.

In order for article 107 to be violated, four conditions have to be met. The first is the public source of the financial *resources* on which the aid is based. The aid could be from the State, from local authorities or from any body or company of a public nature; this may also include private sector resources, granted under the auspices of public authorities (however, if the management is entirely private, completely independent, article 107 is not applied). The second condition requires that the aid must favour 'certain undertakings or the production of certain goods'. On the one hand, there must be a wrongful use, non-compliant with what would have normally happened on the market; on the other hand, the benefit should go to specific competitors or to certain areas of business activities and not to other sectors (it is the *selectivity* of the aid measure, that distinguishes it from *public measures of general nature*, applicable to all, such as a comprehensive reduction of income tax). The third and the fourth conditions reaffirm that the aid has to affect trade between the Member States of the Union and threatens to distort free competition; hence, there is no infringement if the overall scope of the beneficiary is limited to one single Member State or if the aid is mild (known as *de minimis* and quantified by a specific statement of the Commission).

The ban on public aid is not absolute as the EU system recognises that, in certain circumstances, this is justified. Thereby article 107 specifies two groups of exemptions. The first includes the aids: (a) 'having a social character, granted to individual consumers', meaning not to undertakings (eg, the contribution towards the scrapping of old cars); (b) aimed at repairing the damage caused by natural disasters or exceptional events; (c) for regions in Germany affected by the partition following World War II. The second group is related to aids aimed: (a) at European regions with a low standard of living or high unemployment (eg, concessions for enterprises operating in southern Italy); (b) at other regions or at certain areas of activity (this is the case of some urban areas or some industrial sectors); (c) 'to promote the execution of an important project of common European interest' (eg, the launch of the Airbus); (d) at rectifying 'serious disturbance in the economy of a Member State' (such as bailouts of banks that failed because of the global economic crisis in 2007); and (e) atpromoting culture and protecting cultural heritage. In addition, the Council may adopt a decision establishing other exemptions but this has never happened.

X. Procedures to Review Public Aid

Article 108 of the TFEU and Council regulation no. 1589/2015 govern the control of State aids to companies. The authority entrusted with the controlling task is the Commission, and its decisions (as always) can be contested before the two instances of the European Court of Justice. Provision is also made for a kind of extraordinary appeal to the Council, which can authorize, unanimously and in exceptional circumstances, a single case of aid.

Each Member State has the obligation to *notify* the Commission about legislative and non-legislative projects aimed at creating or amending aid measures, so that the Commission can examine them, in joined consultation with the Member State itself. If, on the basis of its analysis, the Commission considers that there are no problems, it will adopt a decision *not to raise objections*. In the opposite case, it will open a formal investigation procedure, where it has the power to request any necessary information from the Member State concerned and from all the entities involved (such as other States or undertakings). The Commission has 18 months to reach its conclusion, after which the notifying Member State is able to ask the Commission to take a decision 'on the basis of information available to it'.

The final decision of the Commission can either declare the aid *compatible* or *incompatible*; namely it can *condition its compatibility* on compliance requirements (eg, to restrict the scope of the aid). During the procedure, the entry into force of the aid measure is always suspended and only upon the Commission's approval the Member State is authorised to implement it, when appropriate, under the specified conditions.

Nowadays, it may happen, and it was even more likely in the past, that a Member State does not consider its own measure as a State aid under article 107, thus failing to notify it. It may also happen that a notified aid is granted before the Commission gives the green light, or that an aid, conditionally authorised, is put in place without respecting the conditions set out. In all these cases we talk about *illegal aids*, and the Commission can carry out all the assessments and take the appropriate decisions; it is to be noted, however, that a failure to notify the aid constitutes an infringement of European law and does not allow the use of the exemptions illustrated above. Illegal aids affect the conditions of free competition, which must be always restored. For this reason, when declaring an aid *incompatible*, the Commission usually order its immediate termination and its *recovery*.

The recovery of unlawful and incompatible aids, aimed at restoring the status quo, has significant consequences: the Member State concerned shall issue a binding act obliging the aid beneficiaries to give back what they have received. The act can be appealed before the competent national judges, but in its case law the Court of Justice has given a narrow interpretation of the notion of *absolute impossibility of recovery* (eg, the refund is due even if: the company would go bankrupt by repaying the aid, see judgment 24.2.1987, case 310/85;

or public order gets disturbed by strike threats, see judgment 9.7.2015, C-63/14; or the company had erroneously trusted the lending national authorities about the compatibility of the aid, see judgment 20.9.1990, case 5/89). This very strict stance by the Court of Justice proves once more the central role of competition rules in the EU system.

The Commission can predetermine by specific legislation the conditions for claiming the exemptions laid down in article 107 (ie, with no duty to notify): these are the *block exemption regulations* for State aids (see above, the similar instrument used for article 101 of the TFEU). These provisions provide the public authorities of Member States with important guidance on how to steer funding in favour of investments complying with the general European interest (for example, regional aid to less-favoured areas; to small and medium enterprises; for innovation and research; for environmental protection; for energy saving; for the training of workers; for the restructuring of undertakings in difficulty).

XI. The Points of Article 106 of the TFEU

Article 106 gives unique outlines to the Union's rules guaranteeing competition. These rules can be explained in the light of the traditions and characteristics of the economic and social European model, which are markedly different from the American model. All the three sections of the provision are of great interest and importance.

The first section reiterates that such rules apply also to *public undertakings* (ie, owned by the State or other public bodies) and to undertakings benefiting from special or exclusive rights assigned by Member States (eg, public or private operators of legal monopolies). Given the obvious interest of national public authorities with regard to such situations, which are quite frequent in Europe, the rule aims at establishing a complete equality between public and private operators. The provision may appear redundant as the concept of 'undertaking' provided for in EU competition rules (see above) is in no way limited to private companies. However, the remarkable casuistry recorded in the application of article 106 proves its importance.

The second section refers to undertakings entrusted with the operation of *services of general economic interest* or having the character of a *revenue-producing monopoly*, and introduces a specific exception to EU competition rules, which do not apply where they prevent those undertakings from fulfilling the 'particular tasks assigned to them'. The aim pursued is to balance two key elements of the European socioeconomic environment: the freedom of competition and the availability of suitable public services. The choice – that is political, rather than legal or economic – is clear. For the sake of services of general economic interest, free competition knows some exemptions (see article 14 of the TFEU; protocol no. 26, annexed to the TFEU; article 36 of the EU Charter of Fundamental Rights). A classic example is given by the *compensation for public service obligation*: whenever the operation of a public service involves costs that are not covered by revenues, companies running such service must be compensated by public entities in order not to compromise the operation of the service itself and the compensation escapes the State aid ban (for the precise conditions, see judgment 24.7.2003, C-280/00).

The third section of article 106 is of an instrumental nature and confers on the Commission the only fully legislative power that the Commission has under EU law, besides its usual power to adopt decisions: issuing directives to regulate the situations mentioned in article 106 of the TFEU (see judgment 12.2.1992, joint cases 48/90 and 66/90). The Commission has made a significant use of it: (a) it provided for the financial relations between Member States and state-controlled companies to be made totally transparent, in order to detect possible public aids within the framework of these relations; (b) it set an evaluation benchmark of the investments and the performance of a public company, in order to systematically compare its decisions with those that would be made by a hypothetical *private investor* in the same market situation (if the conduct of the public company differs from the relevant benchmark, then there is solid evidence that the actions of the public company or of its public shareholders breach the principle of equal treatment of competitors, probably with forms of State aid); (c) it opened up numerous sectoral markets to competition by abolishing the exclusive rights conferred on certain undertakings by Member States to prevent all the other companies from operating in their national markets (these are the so-called directives for liberalisations).

XII. Concluding Remarks

Throughout the integration process, a few provisions within the EU legal order have led to an effective implementation of the rules guaranteeing competition. Their wide reach as well as the strong specific prerogatives assigned to supervisory bodies, have made those rules a versatile mainstay of the whole European framework.

Moreover, in some Member States – and Italy is definitely among them – these free market regulations have led to deep changes in the business culture and in the attitude of public authorities, thus affecting companies' behaviours and the entire balance of the market. From a more general point of view, they have also offered EU citizens the possibility of feeling more involved in economic life and finding a better legal protection of their rights.

In the recurrent debate about the overall set-up of the EU system, in which elements of economic liberalism and mutual solidarity should coexist virtuously, competition rules are often recalled in a negative sense as an example of excessive liberalism. However, as we have seen from the above, provisions on competition correspond to that European rationale, by complementing prohibitions with appropriate exemptions. It is probably for this reason that the wording of the relevant articles has remained virtually unaltered since the Treaty of Rome in 1957 (also considering the regulation on concentrations between undertakings adopted in 2004), despite the frequent debates and the changing political and economic landscape.

Bibliography

Amato, G, *Antitrust and the bounds of power* (Oxford, 1997).
Bacon, K, *European Union law of State aid* (Oxford, 2017).
Bork, RH, *The antitrust paradox* (New York, 1978).
Cook, J and Kerse, C, *EC Merger control* (London, 2009).
Cremona, M, *Market integration and public services in the European Union* (Oxford, 2011).

Dony, M, Renard, F and Smits, C, *Contrôle des aides d'État* (Bruxelles, 2007).
Hancher, L, Ottervanger, T and Slot, PJ, *EU State aid* (London, 2016).
Immenga, U and Mestmäcker, EJ, *Wettbewerbsrecht*, 2 vols (München, 2016).
Jones, CA, *Private enforcement of antitrust law in the UE, UK and USA* (Oxford, 1999).
Kerse, CS and Khan, N, *EU Antitrust procedure* (London, 2012).
Libertini, M, *Diritto della concorrenza dell'Unione Europea* (Milano, 2014).
Moavero-Milanesi, E, *Diritto della concorrenza dell'Unione Europea* (Napoli, 2004).
Rose, V and Bailey, D (eds), *Bellamy & Child, European Union law of competition* (Oxford, 2018).
Rossi, G, *Il conflitto epidemico* (Milano, 2003).
Säcker, FJ and Montag, F (eds), *European State aid law* (München, 2016).
Whish, R and Bailey, D, *Competition law* (Oxford, 2018).
Wils, WPJ, *The optimal enforcement of EC antitrust law* (The Hague, 2002).

22

The Common Commercial Policy: Efficiency and Legitimacy

PASCAL LAMY

The common commercial policy (CCP), or the EU trade policy, is widely recognised as a success story of European integration. Its progressive construction has taken some time and has had to overcome many hurdles. After 60 years it has become a good example of how to build and use collective economic weight to serve both the EU's interests and values in global trade. But if we look into the future, the CCP, as in other areas, is likely to face a number of challenges which will severely test the EU's capacity to keep balancing efficiency with legitimacy.

I. Legitimacy and Efficiency: Building a Common Commercial Policy

Good policy is like good music: it needs a good score, a good instrument and a good conductor. The CCP of today is the result of 60 years of effort to construct, step by step, a score but also an instrument capable of promoting and defending EU's global interests, which are primarily but not exclusively economic. This process has been complex, sometimes cumbersome and conflictual, but overall successful.

It is a history of steady convergence of attitudes towards trade opening, of adaptation to the changing patterns of the world economy as it itself evolves, of tackling evolving obstacles to trade, and to achieve all this, a series of successive improvements resulting in a sophisticated 'score' and 'instrument', all leading to impressive results.

The philosophy underlying the CCP is a crucial part of the EU's foundations and has not changed since 1957. It is governed by the principle of openness. Articles 110 of the Treaty of Rome (1957) and 188 B of the Treaty of Lisbon (2007) are virtually identical, except for 'investment' and 'other barriers' which were not mentioned initially. Like all good foundation texts, it is short:

> By establishing a customs union in accordance with Articles 23 to 27, the Union shall contribute, in the common interest, to the harmonious development of world trade, the progressive abolition of restrictions on international trade and on foreign direct investment, and the lowering of customs and other barriers (http://eur-lex.europa.eu/legal-content/EN/TXT/HTML/?uri=OJ:C:2007:306:FULL&from=EN).

This pro-trade, pro-openness basic stance in the Treaty of Rome was not a given. It resulted from a compromise between Germany and Benelux on the one side, and France and Italy on the other, but in which the views of the first group favouring free trade prevailed over the more protectionist traditions of the other.

The divergences between these postures slowly decreased, while resurfacing from time to time on different topics and with an increasing number of protagonists as the EU enlarged. This has resulted in a high degree of trade openness, with some significant protection of agriculture (see below).

Beyond this 'open' ideological trade policy stance, the CCP has also been increasingly associated with other non-trade related international policies or external actions of the EU. This evolution has culminated in placing the CCP under the umbrella of article 21.2 of the Maastricht Treaty (Treaty on European Union, TEU), signed in 1992 and subsequently amended by the Treaty of Lisbon, according to which:

> The Union shall define and pursue common policies and actions, and shall work for a high degree of cooperation in the fields of international relations, in order to:
>
> (a) safeguard its values, fundamental interests, security, independence and integrity;
> (b) consolidate and support democracy, the rule of law, human rights and the principles of international law;
> (c) preserve peace, prevent conflicts and strengthen international security, in accordance with the purposes and principles of the United Nations Charter, with the principles of the Helsinki Final Act and with the aims of the Charter of Paris, including those relating to external borders;
> (d) foster the sustainable economic, social and environmental development of developing countries, with the primary aim of eradicating poverty;
> (e) encourage integration of all countries in the global economy also through increasing abolition of restrictions to international trade;
> (f) help develop international measures to preserve and improve the quality of the environment and the sustainable management of global natural resources, in order to ensure sustainable development;
> (g) assist populations, countries and regions confronting natural or man-made disasters;
> (h) promote an international system based on stronger multilateral cooperation and good global governance (http://eur-lex.europa.eu/legalcontent/IT/TXT/?uri=celex%3A12012M%2FTXT).

Based on this, the scope of the CCP has expanded over time, as the relative importance of obstacles to trade has morphed in line with the transformations in the domestic and in the international economy.

The original focus on custom duties (the Common external tariff, CET or CXT) has been enlarged in order to cope with other areas where opening markets is also about 'levelling the playing field': subsidies, services, public procurement, intellectual property, non-tariff measures and, more recently, foreign direct investment. The spectrum of measures at stake has logically followed the process of deepening the EU's own economic integration, from a customs union (1968) to a free trade area, and then to an internal market with the Maastricht Treaty (1992).

The economic logic of this movement towards 'uniformity' – with its roots in article 113 of the Treaty of Rome ('The common commercial policy shall be based on uniform principles, particularly in regard to changes in tariff rates, the conclusion of tariff and trade agreements, the achievement of uniformity in measures of liberalisation', https://eur-lex.europa.eu/legal-content/EN/TXT/HTML/?uri=CELEX:12002E133&from=IT) – has had to be translated into new institutional and legal arrangements as the competences of the Union have to be explicitly delegated to the 'federal' level. This evolution took place gradually and, as in other areas, was driven along by a mix of sometimes painfully negotiated treaty changes and the emerging case law of the European Court of Justice (ECJ), from opinion 1/75, recognising 'exclusive competence' to the European Community, to opinion 1/94, limiting this competence and, recently to opinion 2/15. The main issue around which discussions took (and still take) place is how far trade policy competences should go to the Union as opposed to remaining a prerogative of the Member States. A variant of this theme deals with the situation whether trade agreements involving issues of different degrees of EU competence should be treated as 'mixed' or 'exclusive' with important consequences for how the Member States consent to the trade agreement in question. The present articulation stemming from the Treaty of Lisbon and the ECJ opinion 2/15 combines a high degree of federalism ('exclusivity', hence majority), with some remaining national caveats ('mixity', hence unanimity).

Overall, the legal and institutional arrangements governing decision making normally follow the 'community method' model, according to which the European Commission acts upon a mandate from and under the supervision of the two Houses, the Council of Ministers and the European Parliament, by which trade regimes must be approved under their respective majority rules, thus ensuring both efficiency and legitimacy. Under this system, the Commission is entrusted with the exclusive right to propose policy initiatives, and with the authority to negotiate on behalf of the EU. To put it simply, the EU acts not only with one voice, but with one mouth, which makes a lot of difference in an international negotiation, as every Trade commissioner, including myself, can testify.

This simple and 'classical' architecture, which was completed in the Treaty of Lisbon, when the European Parliament was granted the same rights – including the regulation governing the trade defence regime, but with the exception of trade defence measures, such as the determination of duties – as the Council of ministers to oversee and decide on proposals under the CCP made by the Commission (thus establishing the principle of 'co-decision', now called ordinary legislative procedure), ensures legitimacy, as a majority is needed on both sides of the federal construction (both from the States in the Council, and citizens via the Parliament). It is worth noting that even in this case, there are still a number of 'esoteric' elements as a result of residual national competences in some limited areas, which necessitate unanimity in decision making: these are elements resulting from specific sectoral sensitivities, in areas like transport, public services (education, health), cultural diversity, and investment protection.

This sophisticated institutional machinery is now the framework within which international trade policy is conducted via a variety of instruments: agreements governing trade (and now also investment) regimes with EU's trade partners with different degrees of openness and of disciplines, plus the usual tool box of trade defence measures to redress 'unfair' trade practices (ie, anti-dumping or anti-subsidy duties and safeguards).

The various trade regimes progressively established by the EU with third countries can be best seen in juxtaposition, in the form of a pyramid, according to the model used by Paola Conconi (2009), which superposes various degrees of openness of the EU market (see figure 1 below).

Figure 1

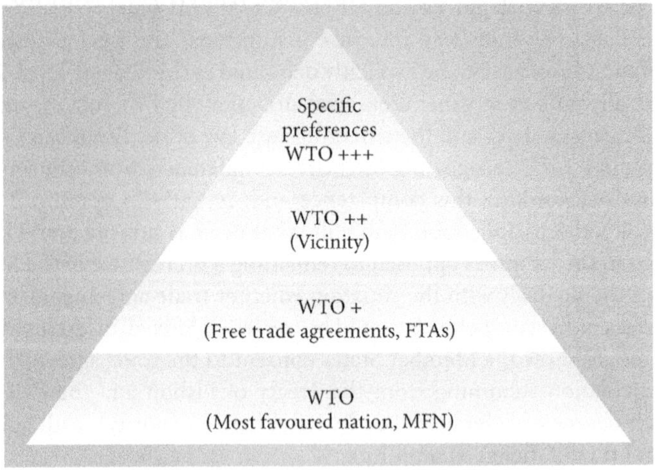

In this model, the three layers starting from the bottom correspond to negotiated arrangements based on reciprocity (with some asymmetry in favour of developing countries according to principles enunciated first by the GATT – *General Agreement on tariffs and trade* – established in 1947 and then, since 1995, by the World Trade Organization, WTO), while the upper layer applies to some developing countries, notably with the *Everything but arms* (EBA) duty-free quota-free regime in favour of least developed countries., by which the least developed countries can export all their products duty free except for one or two limited exceptions, such as armaments.

The first layer, starting from the bottom, represents the multilateral, lowest common denominator, negotiated within the WTO; the second one represents the so-called Free trade agreements (FTAs) with 'normal' trade partners, while the third one the Association Agreements establishing the highest reciprocal available degree of openness, usually between the EU and its neighbours.

This relatively complex geometry governs what is today recognised as a major success of EU integration: the largest market in the world, a high level of openness except for agricultural trade (the EU average tariff protection amounts to 5.5 per cent, as opposed to the 3.5 per cent of the US, the 5 per cent of Japan and the 10 per cent of China, but it increases to 15 per cent when it comes to the agricultural industry), a medium/long term pattern of moderate external surplus, 80 countries having the EU as their most important trade partner, with 50 countries having the EU as their second most important trade partner. More importantly, the EU has done better than comparable countries in the 'great rebalancing' of world trade during recent decades: since 2000 its share in the world exports has shrunk by 10 per cent – much less than both the US and Japan (around 40 per cent).

On a day to day basis, these results are also due to the universally acknowledged quality and expertise of the roughly 600 staff of the Directorate-general for Trade, who assist the Trade commissioner in the negotiation and administration of the EU's trade regime with the rest of the world, including the settlement of trade disputes, where the EU's track record is usually rated at the top of the league table.

To sum up this short history of the progressive construction of the EU's CCP as it stands today, it is a story of succeeding in balancing efficiency and legitimacy: efficiency stemming from the creation of a collective market power, that is, the aggregation of the EU domestic markets, and the institutional capacity to leverage its economic weight on the international trade scene; legitimacy in the democratisation of the decision making system, as the 'lower' chamber representing citizens has gained equal status as the 'higher' chamber representing Member States.

II. The Future of the CCP

Looking ahead, the question is whether a similar synergy between efficiency and legitimacy will be maintained in the future. The answer to this question will be shaped by a number of developments of which we have been seeing the first signs in recent years and which are likely to challenge both the efficiency of the CCP and its legitimacy, as well as the interaction between them.

The efficiency of the CCP will be challenged by both developments in world trade patterns and by Brexit. Its legitimacy will be challenged by higher political sensitivities, hence a risk of less support from public opinion than in the past.

Changing world trade patterns stem from a mixture of long-term factors (mainly related to the ongoing expansion of global value chains and to the changing nature of obstacles to trade) and probable short-term protectionist pressures coming primarily from the US.

The expansion of global value chains, the 'unbundling' of production processes of goods and services – an expression coined by Richard Baldwin (2014) – are likely to continue, although at a slower pace than in recent decades. Investment tends to be driven by a stronger international division of labour, resulting in efficiency gains, but we can expect to see lower returns in the future. The risks entailed by the fragility of some logistical chains are growing. As a consequence, the average import content of exports (ie, the share of imported inputs in the overall exports of a country), which grew rapidly from 15 per cent in the 1990s to above 25 per cent in the 2000s, will probably plateau at around 30 per cent and remain so for some time. This explains why the ratio between the increase of the volume of trade flows and economic growth, having reached 3:1 at the time of this rapid expansion in value chains, is forecast to stabilise at around 1.5:1 in the next decade. That said, a less volatile – and perhaps more relevant – measurement of the relationship between trade and growth can be seen if trade is measured in value added, that is, when the import content of exports is deducted from the volume of exports.

This evolution, if confirmed, will shift attention from obstacles to trade resulting from measures aimed at protecting the producer from foreign competition, to measures aimed at protecting consumers from various risks related to health, safety, the environment or other value-based collective preferences.

In a world of global value chains, protecting producers by increasing the cost of imports is likely to rapidly damage the competitiveness of exports, thereby limiting the appeal of tariff protection. But increasing social demands for 'precaution' will keep pushing standards, norms, certification systems or traceability requirements upwards as has already been happening for some time in the EU and the US trade relationship, driven by higher levels of 'precaution' in either side of the Atlantic, depending on sectors.

Given the aggressively negative trade stance of his platform, the largely unexpected election of Donald Trump in the US in 2016 has recently increased the risk of protectionism which had not materialised, contrary to most expectations, after the 2008 crisis. Even if at the time of writing various protectionists moves initiated in Washington have not degenerated into full blown trade wards with China, or even with Europe, what does seem likely is an acceleration of US disengagement from multilateral institutions such as the WTO, a feature which was already visible during the Obama administration (2009–16).

How these developments will impact the efficiency of the CCP will depend on geoeconomics and to some extent on geopolitical choices vis-à-vis the two major trade partners of the EU, that is, the US and China.

Reducing differences between the EU and US in levels of 'precaution' (a transatlantic priority recognised when the *Transatlantic trade and investment partnership* (TTIP) was launched in 2013) would make a lot of sense. Relaunching this process with the US would serve to open trade in numerous areas. However, finding a compromise in the reciprocal reduction of 'classical' obstacles to trade, such as tariffs or public procurement limitations, might prove even more difficult than with the previous administration.

If the US was to turn anti WTO by, for instance, attacking its dispute settlement system head on, or even threatening to pull out of the WTO, the EU's 'natural' preference for multilateralism would lead it to look at China as an ally to build a coalition against such an American offensive. China, on the other hand, being the primary target of US anti-trade rhetoric obviously would tend to look to the EU for support. This could lead to a closer Sino-EU trade and investment relationship which has been advocated by some on both sides for some times. However, this would imply overcoming serious obstacles to major economic reforms in China, starting with removal of the privileges *de facto* granted to its numerous and powerful State owned enterprises. It would also not be easy for the EU and China to re-energise the negotiations within WTO on a number of issues, such as disciplines on agricultural or industrial subsidies, reduction of tariff ceilings in emerging countries or trade opening in services, which have been pending since the Doha development round came to a halt in 2008. And finally, it would also necessitate better unity in the EU when China tries to 'divide and rule' Member States, a tactic the US have tried, usually unsuccessfully, for some time.

It is in the area of investment that the EU and China are more likely in time to establish a more stable, better regulated and bilateral relationship based on actual reciprocity. This principle is far easier to achieve within investment regimes than in regimes based on trade, specifically in presence of huge differences in terms of economic and social development, which is the case between EU and China.

Even if the US and China remain the EU's main trade partners in the times to come, both geoeconomics and geopolitics should elevate Africa in the priorities of the CCP, in order to create a more active trade and investment relationship that would benefit both sides, based on EU agreements with subcontinental regional groupings which have emerged from Africa's efforts to trade integration. In this sense a more resourced and better focused 'aid for trade' EU programme would be a logical priority for the post Cotonou agreement between EU and Africa, which aims at reducing and eliminating poverty through development support and expires in 2020.

III. The Risks for the CCP

What this broad landscape shows is that the choices for the EU's trade policy are not, as is too often stated, between a multilateral or a bilateral agenda. Both of these approaches have been combined by major trading powers since the 1950s and most of the times have been combined to good effect. The real strategic choice is more about which obstacles to trade to address and with which negotiating partners.

Whatever trade agenda is followed, its efficiency in this more complex environment will be affected by the weakening of the EU's relative strength for three reasons which are there to stay. First, because of Brexit, which will result in a loss of 15 per cent of trade weight for the EU and, possibly, in the UK adopting an unfriendly competitive trade policy. Secondly, because during the next decade, the EU will be more dependent than in the past on foreign markets as world growth is forecast at around 3.5 per cent per year, whereas EU growth should average around 1.5 per cent per year. This means that roughly 90 per cent of world growth will take place outside Europe, hence a higher need for the CCP to open foreign markets resulting in turn in a weaker negotiating position. This evolution is in addition to the inevitable relative shrinking of EU's economic weight on the world stage, from around 25 per cent in the 2000s to around 15 per cent in the 2030s.

Addressing these new challenges will necessitate more European integration. It requires EU institutions to develop more political energy at a time when it is generally less available and at a time when the legitimacy of the CCP is being questioned from various sides.

Higher political sensitivities have surfaced in recent times with a surge of antiglobalisation political attitudes in the western world, leading to (or perhaps flowing from) an increase in public support for more protectionist, isolationist, nativist or even xenophobic postures. Although not shared by the majority of public opinion, if the polls are to be trusted, these attitudes have captured part of the political agenda in Europe and in the US: while trade opening may be globally successful and generally leading to higher growth, jobs and welfare, the local balance between 'winners' and 'losers' may significantly differ. Of course, there is nothing really new here, as it has been clear since David Ricardo (1772–1823) and Joseph Schumpeter (1883–1950) theorised on the effects of opening exchange through both comparative advantage and creative destruction.

Trade opening works to create efficiencies through a process which is often socially painful as economic and social systems have to reallocate production factors, including labour and skills, as well as relocate production facilities, a process understandably more painful for the weak than for the strong. This more negative political mood is easily explained by the speed and force of globalisation in recent decades, in which trade expansion has not been followed by improvements in social protection. It is worth recalling that the initial purpose of social security during the industrial revolution and after was to cushion citizens from these painful disruptions: on the contrary, the 2008 crisis has led to a shrinking of social safety nets in most western countries.

Another major change in the political economy characterised by the opening of trade stems from the aforementioned shift of attention from 'protection' to 'precaution'. Dealing with reducing protection for producers followed a well-established pattern in which producers resist while consumers benefit. Harmonising precaution turns this pattern upside down as producers push in order to obtain economies of scale through a more levelled regulatory playing field, while consumers are inclined to fear that opening trade will result in a reduction of precautionary protection standards (precaution dumping). Such fears, which unfortunately have not been well anticipated, explain why the TTIP bumped, on the European side, into serious political obstacles starting with German public opinion.

As a result of these developments, the legitimacy of the CCP will keep being questioned for both social and broader societal reasons, creating a basis for a potentially much larger 'antitrade' constituency than the traditional battle between vested interests, which the 'authorising' political system of the CCP has learnt to cope with. This will necessitate EU responses in both the social and the societal domains.

Improvement of social safety nets able to cope with social hardship provoked by the need to adjust to change has been prescribed for some time by international economic organisations such as the WTO, the World Bank, the IMF (International Monetary Fund) or the OECD (Organisation for Economic Cooperation and Development). The reaction, however, whether at EU or at national level have been remarkably slow as shown by the disappointing experience of the European globalisation adjustment Fund, which was created in 2006 with a disproportionately small annual financial donation of 150 million euros at that time. The same goes for the modest result of the older and larger US Trade adjustment assistance programme. The EU and its Member States will have to move to a much more ambitious approach comprising considerably superior financial resources, as well as a tighter coordination of industrial, innovation, training and regional programmes, thus strengthening the 'social market economy' pillar of the CCP which is much too weak at the moment.

Social standards such as labour rights, social security, minimum wages are also an area of controversy in Europe: whereas some believe they go hand in hand with high productivity, others fear they create an incentive for 'social dumping' from less developed countries with lower levels of social protection. This should lead the EU to keep pushing at multilateral level for better articulation of trade disciplines in the WTO with labour standards in the ILO (International Labour Organization).

As part of the precaution related agenda, in line with what are clearly Europe's collective preferences, specific attention should be given to the contribution of the CCP to the limitation of carbon dioxide (CO_2) emissions. Numerous studies have shown that the 'green protectionism' advocated by the European Parliament, that is, restrictive interventions regarding CO_2 emission by non-EU metal producers aiming at maintaining the competitiveness of some industrial sectors within the Union, particularly exposed to dumping policies, is not an effective measure. If the EU is to be consistent with the medium and long term commitments it took at the COP 21 in Paris in 2015, a proper, preferably non border-based tariffication of CO_2 emissions is going to be necessary.

In the area of new 'societal' concerns, responses will have to fill what is perceived, wrongly but frequently, as a 'democratic deficit' in the conduct of the CCP.

First steps in this direction have been taken by the Jean-Claude Juncker Commission, in office since 1 November 2014, by increasing the transparency of negotiations, a reform which became indispensable as the proportion of precaution-related issues increases in the agenda of the CCP. Whereas tariff negotiations operate under a 'trade-off' principle, which justifies a level of secrecy for obvious tactical reasons, this does not apply to regulatory convergence which does not operate on a 'give and take' basis and necessitates a higher degree of public scrutiny. In the same vein, the growing intervention of the European Parliament as a result of its new codecision powers (see above) contributes to a wider, both more expert and more political debate, and to significant changes to draft agreements tabled by the Commission. This happened in the case of Peru and Columbia (on human rights), the Republic of Korea (on automotive safeguards), and Canada (on investment disputes). Moreover, the European Parliament used its legislative prerogatives to reject the Anti-counterfeiting trade agreement (ACTA), a multilateral agreement strengthening intellectual property to fight counterfeiting which most civil society organisations believed would have infringed excessively on privacy and civil liberties. These episodes show that the institutional changes are progressively being brought to bear for the very purpose they were conceived. Looking longer term, and considering the example of the US Congress, it remains to be seen whether winning parliamentary and public support for the CCP can happen without allowing special interests to capture the trade policy agenda through intense lobbying.

These ongoing changes will likely not suffice to address the legitimacy challenge of the CCP, and the EU and its Member States will have to revert to the 'mixity' issue which still pitches together various antagonistic positions stemming from different interpretations of the institutional arrangements governing the CCP. Part of the argument was adjudicated recently by the EU Court of Justice, who was asked by the Commission to clarify whether some provisions of the FTA with Singapore pertain to 'exclusive' or 'shared' competences and, if so, have to be ratified by national parliaments in addition to the usual Council/Parliament approval process. Another recent episode concerning the EU-Canada free trade agreement (CETA, *Comprehensive Economic and Trade Agreement*) has shown how far 'mixed competences' involving national ratifications can go: in October 2016, the Parliament of the Belgian region of Wallonia, which according to this country's constitutional statute has to consent in order for Belgium to agree to an international trade treaty, only gave its consent after a heated political debate.

A solution to this conundrum seems to have been endorsed by the Council of ministers in May 2018 hopefully leading to a much clearer devolution of competences: 'trade only agreements' for the Union (oversight and ratification by Council of ministers and European Parliament only), association and investment agreements remaining 'mixed', that is, with ratification both at EU and national level (see Foreign Affairs Council, *Conclusions* (2018)).

Lessons from the recent TTIP or CETA experiences should also be drawn by bringing more clarity to the issues at stake, that is, by distinguishing clearly in the future between four types of agreements: 'trade only', regulatory convergence agreements, investment agreements and 'association' agreements. Even so, such a simplification will require EU institutions, whether the Commission, the Parliament, or the Council, to make the legitimacy case more forcefully than they have so far: they need to point out that EU competences are exercised according to an EU democratic process as prescribed by its arrangements from the moment Member States have accepted to 'federalise' part of their common policies. There can be no going back on this fundamental principle.

As trade globalisation continues both to widen and deepen, accepting this course for the CCP would address both the efficiency and the legitimacy challenge: in particular, it would ensure that, as it has been the case so far, after a lengthy process of building the CCP, efficiency cannot limit legitimacy or the other way around. This is a crucial precondition for the EU to keep exercising its trade strength to the benefit of EU citizens in the future.

Bibliography

Baldwin, R, *Multilateralising 21st century regionalism*, Global Forum on trade (OECD, 11–12 February 2014) https://www.oecd.org/tad/events/OECD-gft-2014-multilateralising-21st-century-regionalism-baldwin-paper.pdf.

Bungenberg, M and Herrmann, C, (eds), *European yearbook of international economic law. Special issue: The common commercial policy of the EU after Lisbon* (Berlin, 2013).

Bureau, D, Schubert, K and Fontaigné, L, 'Commerce et climat: pour une réconciliation' (January 2017) *Note du Conseil d'analyse économique* http://www.cae-eco.fr/IMG/pdf/cae-note037v2.pdf.

Conconi, P, *The EU common commercial policy and global/regional trade regulation* (ULB, 2009) http://conconi.ulb.be/EUtrade.pdf.

Constantinescu, C, Mattoo, A and Ruta, M, 'The global trade slowdown: cyclical or structural?' (January 2015) *World Bank Group. Policy Research Working Paper* 7158 http://documents.worldbank.org/curated/en/991561468127799318/pdf/WPS7158-REPLACEMENT-The-Global-Trade-Slowdown-Cyclical-or-Structural.pdf.

Ederington, J and Michele, R, 'Non-tariff measures and the world trading system' (May 2016) *World bank group. Policy research working paper* 7661 http://documents.worldbank.org/curated/en/882991467989523068/pdf/WPS7661.pdf.

Fabry, E, 'Trump trade: more bark than bite?' (21 April 2017) 193 *Notre Europe Policy Paper* http://www.institutdelors.eu/media/trumptradeandeurope-elvirefabry-april17.pdf?pdf=ok.

Foreign Affairs Council, *Conclusions on the negotiation and conclusion of EU trade agreements*, 8622/18 (22 May 2018) http://data.consilium.europa.eu/doc/document/ST-8622-2018-INIT/en/pdf.

Gstöhl, S, 'The European Union's trade policy' (2013) 11 Ritsumeikan International Affairs 1–22, http://www.ritsumei.ac.jp/acd/re/k-rsc/ras/english/publications/ria_en/11_01.pdf.

IMF, The World Bank, WTO, *Making trade an engine of growth for all. The case for trade and for policies to facilitate adjustment* (March 2017) https://www.wto.org/english/news_e/news17_e/wto_imf_report_07042017.pdf.

Jean, S, 'L'Union européenne, naïve dans sa politique commerciale?' (15 April 2017) *La Tribune* http://www.latribune.fr/opinions/tribunes/l-union-europeenne-naive-dans-sa-politique-commerciale-687408.html.

Kleimann, D, 'Taking stock: EU common commercial policy in the Lisbon era' (April 2011) 345 *CEPS Working Document* https://www.ceps.eu/system/files/book/2011/04/WD%20345%20Kleimann%20on%20EU%20CCP.pdf.

Lamy, P, *The future of trade: the challenges of convergence. Report of the panel on defining the future of trade* (24 April 2013) https://www.wto.org/english/thewto_e/dg_e/dft_panel_e/future_of_trade_report_e.pdf.

Lamy, P, *The Geneva Consensus* (New York, 2013).

Lamy, P, *Looking ahead: the new world of trade*, Jan Tumlir Lecture, ECIPE Conference, (March 2015) http://www.ecipe.org/app/uploads/2015/02/PLamy-Speech-09.03.15.pdf.

Lamy, P, *Où va le monde?* (Paris, 2017).

OECD, WTO, UNCTAD, *Implications of global value chains for trade, investment, development and jobs* (6 August 2013) http://unctad.org/en/PublicationsLibrary/unctad_oecd_wto_2013d1_en.pdf.

Pelkmanns, J and François, J, *Tomorrow's silk road. Assessing an EU-China Free trade agreement* (Brussels, 2016) https://www.ceps.eu/system/files/EUCHINA_FTA_Final.pdf.

Woolcock, S, 'The Treaty of Lisbon and the European Union as an actor in international trade' (2010) 1 *ECIPE Working Paper* http://www.ecipe.org/app/uploads/2014/12/the-treaty-of-lisbon-and-the-european-union-as-an-actor-in-international-trade.pdf.

Woolcock, S, 'European Union trade policy' (April 2011) *LSE Research Online* http://eprints.lse.ac.uk/33488/1/European_Union_Trade_Policy_(LSERO).pdf.

All web pages are understood as having last been visited on 18 April 2018.

PART VI

Political Challenges and Disputes Within the European Union

23

Resisting European Integration: The Variegated Forms of Anti-EU Protest

YVES MÉNY AND GIORGIO MOCAVINI

For a long period of time, up until the 1950s, Europeanism was an ideology, a political inclination unable to transform itself into a concrete political and institutional project. United Europe long remained a dream cultivated exclusively by a few cosmopolitan writers and artists, as well as by a handful of policymakers of various nationalities who had been traumatised by the disaster of World War I. After World War II, a few groups and some individuals began to propose a model of political organisation alternative to the traditional national State. However, to the extent that these visions remained the patrimony of a minority of intellectuals, the idea of a supranational European unity did not attract strong opposition.

Things began to take a rather different turn when, in May of 1950, the French minister of Foreign Affairs, Robert Schumann (1886–1963), became the promoter of an apparently modest proposal, assuming the form of a brief declaration. He suggested bringing the French and German production of coal and steel under the control of a technocratic authority, two industries which had always been considered the symbol and the fundamental cogs of the war machine. It is not necessary to revisit this history, which has already been amply studied and analysed. It should be recalled, however, that the declaration did not exclude the other nations of Europe, but allowed them to take part in the French-German coalition. Belgium, Italy, Luxembourg, and Netherlands immediately made themselves available to pool their respective productions, and unified themselves with France and West Germany. The reaction of the United Kingdom, on the contrary, was completely different. This could be considered almost as a foreshadowing of the complex relation that would be established between Great Britain and the European institutions over the following 60 years. Lord Attlee (1883–1967), the British prime minister of that period, declared that the United Kingdom would not give up its sovereignty to submit to the directives of a supranational authority.

Thus the field was prepared for a debate which has carried on now for half a century between the promoters of an ever more integrated Europe, and those who remain hostile and diffident toward any form of supranational government or authority whatsoever. While the terms of the debate have changed over the years, and have often been redefined by institutional events or by political decisions, the fundamental bases of the confrontation were laid in that period. From 1950 to the Brexit referendum of June 2016, the values that oppose each other in the public debate have not changed so very much. The dimensions and the variety of the debate, however, are different. While this debate was originally circumscribed and reserved to a confined élite, today it extends to the entire population of the European Union: a transformation that already in itself contributes to undermining the conviction that there exists no 'European public sphere'. Paradoxically, anti-European sentiments have created the very conditions for which the pro-Europeanists fought: they have, that is to say, empowered an intellectual and political debate which has expanded beyond national borders. In any case, this debate at the European level must not be overestimated. The meaning, the interpretation and the manipulation of anti-European sentiments have been deeply influenced by strictly national themes, stories, and symbols. As Oliver Daddow (2006) rightly emphasises, 'national contexts remain all-important for understanding and explaining the phenomenon because [anti-Europeanism] is a word that does not pass untrammelled across national borders' (p 327). Those studies that have highlighted the different orientations of Euroscepticism between countries and regions of the European Union have also arrived at similar conclusions (Lubbers, Scheepers (2010)).

With the passing of time, the forms of rejection and of hostility toward the European institutional architecture have considerably amplified and diversified. If the central theme of the debate was initially of an almost philosophical nature (concerning the concepts of nation and of State and the nature of the European project), it has progressively transformed, being linked as it is to the process of constructing institutional architecture, and enlarging and reinforcing the powers and the responsibilities of the EU. For 25 years, the emergence throughout the whole of Europe of populist parties, and the parallel decline of the traditional governing parties, have further influenced the forms, the instruments and the contents of the political debate. The first consideration that can be drawn from the observation of these changes in time and space, given that the opposition to Europe has assumed different guises from one State to the next, and also within the individual States themselves, concerns the extreme variety and ductility of anti-European protests and sentiments. It affects almost every party and contributes to blurring the entire distinction between left and right, since these can unify their forces on occasion of referenda on European issues, using similar arguments which are differentiated only by slight tinctures of the left or the right (Halikiopoulou, Vasilopoulou, Nanou (2012)). That should come as no surprise, because there exists no real definition explaining what Europe is or what it is supposed to be. To reduce every criticism of the project of European integration to a manifestation of Euroscepticism would be too simplistic. One should rather consider the spectrum of positions that go from outright rejection of to enthusiastic adhesion to the European project, and emphasise how indefinite these classifications are: some groups, for example the parties of the extreme left, were opposed to the European Constitution not so much for the idea of a common constitution in itself, as for the level of social protection offered by the Constitutional Treaty, which they do not consider satisfactory.

The semantics of this question have played a leading role in spinning the debate around key words and concepts. The better part of these were elaborated in those Member States with rooted national or nationalist traditions, especially Great Britain and France. These words and concepts have easily embedded themselves in the minds of the people, as they were invented and diffused mostly by mass media. The French have spotlighted the term *eurocrate*, by way of a critique of the technocratic nature of the governing élite. The principal contribution, however, was offered by the British, thanks to the flexibility and the creativity specific to the English language, and to the capacity of the Anglo-Saxon press to elaborate evocative expressions which are capable of conquering public opinion: Euroscepticism, Eurocritics, PIGS (to refer to Portugal, Italy, Greece, Spain), Brexit, Grexit, Club Med countries and so on. Even certain less emphatic and more analytical concepts, such as 'democratic deficit' (coined in 1979 by a university professor favourable to European integration, David Marquand) have been reinterpreted and reused as anti-European instruments. An analogous deviation occurred when the critical analyses formulated by pro-European groups reinforced the argumentation for rejecting Europe. For example, the radical parties of the left or the movements of the extreme right miss no chance to base their own arguments on the critiques of the institutional European architecture advanced by global experts. Such is the case of the economist Joseph Stiglitz (2016), whose analyses are often exploited by populist parties as they explain the reasons why, in his opinion, the common currency will come to threaten the future of Europe.

The difficulty of ascertaining the manifold meanings of the notion of 'anti-Europeanism' was best grasped by the political scientist Peter Mair in the course of an important conference of 2006. While the conference was focused on determining the significance of 'political opposition' to the EU by comparing the ways in which this opposition is included and applied in national systems, Mair brought to light the fundamental difference which characterises the EU:

> [W]hile we now enjoy the right to participate in EU decisions by casting a vote, whether for our putative national representatives who go to the various Councils, or for our European representatives who go to the European Parliament in Strasbourg; and while we also enjoy the right to be represented in Europe – by all accounts, and despite its manifest shortcomings, the European Parliament is a representative body; we emphatically lack the right to organize opposition within the system. We lack the capacity to do so, and, above all, we lack an arena in which to do it. Once we cannot organize opposition *in* the EU, we are then almost forced to organize opposition *to* the EU. To be critical of the policies promulgated by Brussels is therefore to be critical of the polity; to object to the process is therefore to object to the product ((2007) 7).

This is a fundamental point: the moment that one is no longer permitted to oppose the politics of the EU through institutional channels, the only remaining alternative is that of opposing the generator of that politics, that is, the EU in and of itself. This explains the difficulty in defining anti-Europeanism in a precise manner, given that it has been displaced from its original positions (the cessation of sovereignty) to the rejection of specific policies, by appealing almost to the very same principles. The recent case of Brexit is a good illustration of this displacement: the politics of immigration have encountered a firm opposition in that country. The conservative government attempted to mitigate the problem by proposing a referendum: the popular vote did not concern any specific political issue, but concerned rather the decision to remain in or to leave the EU.

Disagreement on the nature of the European project and on its institutions does not implicate being anti-European. On the contrary, it is natural enough that, by way of the ambiguity and the doubts on the *raison d'être* and the final purpose of the EU project, disagreements will appear throughout its entire development. A more general approach has been proposed by Paul Taggart (1998), who defines Euroscepticism as 'contingent or qualified opposition, as well as incorporating outright and unqualified opposition to the process of European integration' (p 366). Moreover, Taggart and Aleks Szczerbiak (2002) have further distinguished between 'strong' and 'weak' Euroscepticism, trying to disentangle simple disagreements from complete rejection. Even this apparently simple and clear distinction is in reality often nuanced, given the evolution of the various positions (which become more radical in time) and the interpretations offered by scholars, by the media and by political groups (Streeck (2014) 20).

The difficulty (and the awkwardness) in proposing a clear definition of the various nuances of resistance to the process of Europeanisation are well illustrated by the considerations of Cécile Leconte in her broad study of this matter. This scholar distinguishes between the hard Eurosceptics, which is to say the anti-Europeanists who oppose European integration on principle, and the Eurosceptics, understood as Eurosceptics:

> who accept the reality of EU membership, while expressing hostility or deep reluctance towards the 'basic political arrangements' [...] underlying the EU political system, which they do not consider as fully legitimate, such as: the pooling of sovereignty; the delegation of state powers to supranational institutions; the primacy of EU law over national norms (including constitutions); and the underlying telos of an 'ever closer union'.

And she adds also that 'what Eurosceptic discourses often have in common is a non-acceptance of the *sui generis* character of the EU as a union "of states and citizens" (which distinguishes the EU from interstate organisations)' (Leconte (2010) 8). Although this effort of clarification is useful, the taxonomy proposed is not entirely convincing, due to the fact that the various components of both groups tend to mingle in the debate into a magmatic protest. For example, it was precisely the hostility for the aspiration toward 'a closer union' that contributed to triggering the withdrawal of the United Kingdom from the EU. Or again, the original demand of certain extremist groups or parties, to bring their countries to withdraw from the Union, was on various occasions supplanted by a different request, namely, withdrawal from the euro. The distinction between 'strong' and 'weak' anti-Europeanism is useful only if the two parts are considered as elements on a continuum, and not as two separate poles.

Other distinctions have been put forward. For example, Petr Kopecký and Cas Mudde (2002) distinguish between Euroenthusiasts, Europragmatists, Eurosceptics, and Eurorejects. Sofia Vasilopoulou (2011) suggests three categories: Euroscepticism which is rejecting, conditional, and compromising. Many other variants have been presented, without being however able to grasp the wide variety of the Eurosceptical movements in time and in space.

In reality these typologies are neither accurate nor very useful, given that the same critical attitude expressed by the dissatisfied pro-Europeans can be shared by the most radical anti-Europeans; or, as happens in many governing parties, all the most contradictory attitudes, ranging from full support to total rejection, can be expressed within one and the same organisation. For this reason, we prefer in what follows to embark upon an alternative course, and to differentiate the variegated forms of opposition along the three core elements of any political system: the polity, the politics and the policies. In other words, opposition to the EU as a nascent political community, opposition through the political instruments of democracy (groups, interests, parties), and opposition to the incremental, but inexorable increase of European policies. For each of these three levels, the targets chosen by the critics of the EU will be the most advanced forms of integration, as these critics perceive them.

I. The Rejection of a European Polity

This peculiar dimension of anti-Europeanism is the most important, and it is the one that carries the longest history on its back. In fact it made its first appearance already in the period of the Schuman proposal, which was aimed at the coal- and steel-producing nations of Western Europe. The other countries were not taken into consideration because many of them rotated in the Soviet orbit or were governed by dictators. This historical fact allows us to understand why the United Kingdom appears to be the country most averse to any given attempt at continental integration. Neither the labour party nor the conservatives were ready to accept the supervision of a supranational authority. The United Kingdom was legitimately considering itself, with good right, as the victor of the war against the Nazi and Fascist regimes, and still the master of the largest empire in the world. For this reason it had no intention of adhering to a supranational authority.

Analogous assertions could be formulated with respect to the French, even if France had been substantially defeated in its own confrontation with Germany, and its empire was beginning to crumble. Its principal difference with Great Britain, however, consisted in the presence of a new party, born after the liberation of the country, which constituted an indispensable element in the formation of any French government, whether it were to be of centre-left or centre-right. Indeed, the Christian Democrats (MRP, *Mouvement Républicain Populaire*), were not only indispensable members of any governing coalition, but they could count on strong homologous parties in most of other partner countries, potential members of the new community, as for instance in Benelux, Italy, and Western Germany. If the opposition to European integration was almost unanimous in Great Britain, it was decidedly marginal in these other countries, while France found itself in the middle. Europe as a project was strongly sustained by the MRP and the moderate left, while a fierce resistance was brought against it by the two extremes of the political spectrum, which is to say the two political forces that emerged strongest from the resistance to the German invasion: the Gaullist party on the one hand, and the communist party on the other. However, while the first began to unravel when De Gaulle decided to withdraw from politics, the second, strongly rooted in the working class and in certain regional strongholds, decided to align itself with the Soviet position, hostile both to the Marshall plan and to the attempts to aggregate the European forces under the protection of the American umbrella.

Despite this opportunistic coinciding of views on the Schuman Declaration, these groups were unable to prevent the launch of this major initiative in 1950 and 1951. They managed however to redeem themselves a few years later, by sabotaging another French initiative, the European Defence Community (EDC). The committed pro-Europeans were as enthusiastic as the American administration to launch this new ambitious project in a period during which the Korea War (1950–53) necessitated American military disengagement in Europe. Since Russian military power still constituted a danger for Western Europe, the Europeanisation of defence in the NATO sphere was considered an ideal solution, one that would allow Germany to rearm and to contribute to a potential war effort. In many respects the recipe was identical to that of the European coal and steel Community (ECSC): an attempt to control a powerful Germany through its integration in a supra-national framework. However, on this occasion, the operation did not end positively, because France, demoralised by the First Indochina War (1946–54), refused to take part in the initiative that it itself had advocated. A 'negative' majority, composed of the left wing of the non-communist left, of the entire communist party and of what remained of the ex-Gaullist party, passed a motion on 30 August 1954 in Parliament, deciding not to proceed with the parliamentary debate. For the Gaullists to vote against that project meant showing that they still counted for something in the French political scene.

Notwithstanding this defeat, the pro-Europeans resumed the debate and were able to negotiate, with the same partners (Great Britain was still refusing the European invitation), what would pass into history as the founding treaty of the European Economic Community (EEC). It is hardly necessary to remind that the return to power of de Gaulle in 1958 was greeted with fear and anxiety by the promoters of this new initiative. Many were wondering if de Gaulle would follow a course of hostility against Europe, as his political group had previously expressed after the war. Fortunately, de Gaulle, a nationalist soldier, was principally motivated by the will to bring his country back to its supposed past glory, and he understood that, at the midway point of the twentieth century, power was intimately connected to economy. He even perceived that necessary changes and appropriate reform could issue from the liberation of new forces and the diminution of the importance of the blocs of conservative interests. He was certainly not a pro-European, but he became an advocate of the EEC for reasons of expediency and of national interest, by forcefully requesting the full implementation of the common agricultural policy, by far the most integrated of all EEC policies.

However, this could not represent a rally to the supranational ideals promoted by the federalists and the Christian Democrats. In that time, the concept of 'red lines', limits beyond which it was not possible to go, an idea subsequently formulated by Tony Blair, was not yet in the air, but de Gaulle was already acting according to that idea, as much in his public speeches as in the particular aspects of his political action. He attempted (in the end successfully) to promote a different kind of vision of Europe: that of a wider Europe, 'from Brest to Vladivostok', which anticipated the Thatcher-inspired motto 'wider is wiser'; a *Europe des patries*, institutionalised through the Fouchet plans of 1959–61 (openly rejected by the others partners); the exclusion of Great Britain, which was thought to be too tied to the United States; a preference for intergovernmental agreements and a rejection of the sovereign pretences formulated by the first European Commission, the Hallstein Commission of 1958–62. These divergent approaches culminated in 1965, when de Gaulle flatly refused the demands of the Commission to bind the financing of the common agricultural policy to the creation of autonomous resources, as part of a budget to be put at the disposal of the same Commission.

The battle ended with the so-called Luxembourg compromise of 30 January 1966, an agreement which clearly confirmed the existence of two alternative visions for Europe: one of a federal mould, supported by the founding fathers, the other of intergovernmental scope, sponsored more or less openly by many governments on the basis of their respective nationalist interests or their own political inclinations. This situation was effectively summarised by the title of a French essay: Europe resembled 'a single bed for two dreams' (Fontaine (1981)). This case demonstrates the difficulty in classifying the Gaullist approach: it certainly was not anti-European, but it posed nonetheless the basis for what later would be defined Euroscepticism. At the same time, for example, an active group of policymakers, jurists and university professors (from Michel Debré to Maurice Duverger), fought against the insidious expansion of the jurisdiction of the Court of Justice through its radical interpretation of the cases that it handled. The language used in the 1960s in France was not so different from what would be used by the 'exiters' and the British UKIP (*UK Independence Party*) 50 years later in their total disapproval of the work of the supranational courts of Luxembourg and of Strasbourg.

Actually, the role played by the Court of Justice has turned out to be decisive in the process of European integration, and it is therefore natural that today it should be the target of the Eurosceptic movements. The Court's decisions, in fact, have progressively allowed Community law to supplement national legal systems, modifying them and integrating them. Performing an almost nomophylactic function with respect to the law derived from the treaties, the Court set about guaranteeing the uniform interpretation of the Community law, allowing its homogeneous application to the various Member States' legal systems. It was the Court, for example, to affirm the principle of autonomy for the Community law relative to that of the Member States, and to recognise the direct efficacy of Community rules in the internal systems of the Member States (judgment of 05.02.1963, *NV Algemene Transport-en Expeditie Onderneming van Gend & Loos v Netherlands Inland Revenue Administration*, case 26/62). This direct application, moreover, was to be understood in the sense that the Community rules were supposed to carry out their effects uniformly in all the Member States (judgment of 09.03.1978, *Amministrazione delle finanze dello Stato v Simmenthal SpA*, case 106/77). And it was always the Court of Justice to enshrine the primacy of the Community law over national law, in any case of conflict, of contradiction or incompatibility between the rules of the two systems (judgment of 15.07.1964, *Flaminio Costa v ENEL*, case 6/64). In any case, the resistance of national judges to the jurisprudence of the Court was not lacking. For a long time, the Italian Constitutional Court continued to refuse to fully recognise the superiority of the Community rules over national ones. Only with the ruling of 8 June 1984, No. 170, did the Constitutional Court recognise the primacy of Community law and the inapplicability, on the part of the judge of the public administration, of national rules which counter the Community law (the supervision of constitutionality was however maintained, in the hypothesis in which Community law violated the fundamental principle of the constitutional order and the inviolable rights of the person).

Similar resistance to the *primauté* of European law was advanced by the federal German Constitutional Court (*Bundesverfassungsgericht*). With the first *Solange* ruling of 29 May 1974, which was followed by *Solange II* on 22 October 1986 and the ruling of 12 October 1993, on the ratification of the Maastricht Treaty, the *Bundesverfassungsgericht* accepted the primacy of Community law, albeit defending the fundamental principles of the German system. Even as regards the mechanisms of references for a preliminary ruling from the Court of Justice, national judges have displayed an attitude of fear if not hostility. The Italian State Council and the French *Conseil d'État* have long avoided asking preliminary rulings from the Court, declaring themselves capable of autonomously solving the interpretative questions brought before them. In particular, the *Conseil d'État* abused the theory of *acte clair*, which permits judges, as a last resort, to avoid the reference for a preliminary ruling when there is no doubt as to the interpretation of the European norm (one recalls the ruling of 19 June 1964, *Société des pétroles Shell-Berre et al*). Only with the *Nicolò* ruling of 20 October 1989 did the French administrative judge, conforming to the guidelines of the *Conseil constitutionnel* and to the *Cour de cassation*, change the guideline. To continue a moment on the subject of the dialogue between the courts, the openness shown by the Italian Constitutional Court is still very recent, while the German *Bundesverfassungsgericht*, urged ever more by citizens and organisations, keeps tight control over EU decisions, ranging from treaties to the decisions and the politics of the EU.

In this context, one cannot fail to report the reference for a preliminary ruling from the Court of Justice, which was made by this latter tribunal in relation to the European programme of Outright Monetary Transactions (OMT). In a ruling of 14 January 2014, the federal German Constitutional Tribunal recognised that the European programme OMT, which was announced by the European Central Bank (ECB) and was relative to the purchase of government bonds of the Member States in secondary markets, might represent a violation of Bank powers for two reasons: the programme did not fall within the ECB's responsibilities on monetary policy, and risked violating article 123 of the TFEU (Treaty on the Functioning of the European Union), which forbids the Bank to purchase the debt securities of Member States. The Tribunal, however, posed for the first time a reference for a preliminary ruling from the EU Court of Justice, which, with the decision of 16 June 2015, held the action of the Bank to be compatible with the governing of monetary policy, as this had been defined by the European treaties. The European Court ruling was followed by the definitive ruling of 21 June 2016, with which the German tribunal welcomed the point of view of the Court of Justice.

The resistance to the integration of European rules, in any case, has not been expressed only by judges, but also by national governments, especially in the policies relating to fundamental rights. The government of Great Britain and Poland, for example, faced with the indirect recall of the Nice Charter (or Charter of the Fundamental Rights of the European Union, 2000) in the Treaty of Lisbon (2007), used the instrument of the opt-out ('withdrawal' from accepting a Union rule), with the aim of precluding the possibility that the provisions of the Charter might be invoked as binding in British and Polish courts. The issue of fundamental rights, incidentally, has caused friction between the European institutions and the Hungarian government, both on the occasion of the constitutional reform proposed by prime minister Viktor Orbán (rejected by the Hungarian Parliament in November 2016), and in relation to the emergency management of migration flows. The tensions internal to the European system certainly derive from the uncertain nature of the EU, which stands equidistant from the model of federation and that of confederation: on the one hand, the EU resembles a federal and State system, which implies a transfer of sovereignty from the Member States' institutions to European ones; on the other hand, the Member States jealously guard many essential prerogatives and are fighting not to cede them to common institutions.

II. European Politics: An Empty Space for the Eurosceptics

Following the failure of the European Constitutional project, due to the rejection of the 2005 referenda in the Netherlands and France, Tommaso Padoa-Schioppa (1940–2010), in his capacity as chairman of the French think tank *Notre Europe*, published a series of papers with the aim of contributing to a better understanding of the European political situation. According to his own words:

> The debate revolves around the word 'politicisation', just as others revolve around words like 'democracy', 'identity', bureaucracy', 'demos', 'social'. The fact that the key words of the political

> vocabulary are gradually poured into the EU mould is in itself significant (Padoa-Schioppa, in *Politics*, 2006, under 'Forward').

In the same publication, two opposite visions about the role and place of politics in the EU were proposed by Simon Hix and by Stefano Bartolini. Hix claimed that '[f]or too long the EU has been isolated from real political battles', and he went so far as to exclaim: 'Finally some politics in the EU!'. He held, also, that a greater politicisation was indispensable for the transformation of EU policies and processes, and concluded by expressing his hope in the introduction of an effective left/right opposition in the entirety of the Union (parties, Parliament, Council, etc), stating that:

> The risk of more politics in the EU is low, yet the costs of not allowing more politics in the EU is potentially high, as citizens will increasingly turn against what they see as a form of bureaucratic 'despotism' (Hix, in *Politics* (2006) 26).

Bartolini, on the contrary, advanced a radical critique of the idea of a further politicisation inside the institutional system, a critique that it is useful to recall here (with the benefit of retrospective analysis), because it has great clarifying value. Indeed, he emphasises six crucial issues:

1. we have no certainty that politicisation will spare constitutive issues;
2. there are legitimate doubts that Euro-parties will manage to offer a coherent and significant left-right alignment and competition;
3. it is difficult that different political mandates for reform can be developed and kept within the narrow policy boundaries of the treaties;
4. it is questionable that such mandates will help foster alliances and coordinate policy positions across EU institutions to overcomes institutional gridlocks;
5. there remain doubts that political mandate of this kind will link the emerging pattern of EU politics to citizens' interest and preferences;
6. and the risk remains that all this may generate frustration (Bartolini, in *Politics*, 2006, p. 46).

The scholar did not call into question the benefits that politicisation might have brought to the project of European integration, but stressed that the suitable conditions were lacking, and that the risks were too high: 'Politicisation is risky because if it fails it is unlikely to leave things as they were. *Failure will strain the integration process to the point of jeopardising its progress*» (p 47, emphasis ours). Unfortunately, Bartolini's dark prediction has come true, and the politicisation of the project of European integration has opened a Pandora's Box that nobody seems able to close again. The principal effect of growing politicisation has been the explosion of all those forces that have passed from critique to total rejection of the EU, and that have managed to impose their ideological schemes on the public debate. In the course of a few years' time, the permissive consensus has failed, and has been replaced by various forms of 'Eurocriticism', which goes from tepid opposition to the total repudiation of the project of European integration.

There is a dilemma and an appraisal that both Hix and Bartolini share completely. Both are of the opinion that the institutional evolution of the EU presents serious risks and that solutions must be found with the aim of avoiding graver dangers. The situation of the EU (as analysed at the time of the redaction of those contributions) is not sustainable in the long term. While for Hix politicisation is the answer, Bartolini does not elaborate alternative solutions, but maintains that the élites and the policymakers should avoid pressing beyond the limited scope of the founding treaties, given that they cannot overcome the contradiction between their capacity for problem solving (the sharing of resources and responsibilities at a supranational level) and the 'nurturing of their sources of rulership' (in other word their legitimacy), which is rooted exclusively in institutions and in national political processes. In fact there is nothing resembling real European parties, but only national parties whose connections to the European level are very weak.

This tension was already identified and examined in the 1970s, although the situation in that period was quite different. The enlargement to Great Britain and to the nations of Northern Europe (1973 and 1995) represented an important change, but did not constitute an inflection point like the entrance of the nations of Eastern Europe of 2004. In addition, the diagnosis of the weakness and of the failures of the EEC was not as dramatic as is the present diagnosis of the EU. There was a genuine conviction and also an authentic trust in the capacity to correct the system and to deliver appropriate remedies. The most evocative expression of this 'constructive critique' was proposed by the academic and labour activist David Marquand in his famous contribution (1979) on the so-called democratic deficit of the Community of the time. Seen from a British perspective, which constantly highlights the political and symbolic role of the national Parliament, it was inconceivable that the most important political decisions could be taken without the involvement of an assembly elected on a universal basis. This was considered a precondition of legitimacy and of accountability. This criticism was in line with the principles of representative democracy and nobody could seriously call that into question in the European democracies that formed the EEC. At the same time, various remedies to the general problem of legitimacy were available, since the juridical toolkit of the parliamentary regimes seemed capable of offering adequate solutions. The election of the European Parliament through universal suffrage (1979) would have constituted a decisive step in the passage from a discredited assembly to a fully fledged European Parliament capable of guaranteeing legitimacy to European politics and of rendering the political decision-makers responsible from a democratic perspective. The destiny of an evocative expression like *democratic deficit* perfectly illustrates how much ideas and concepts can travel from one political camp to another, be manipulated and transformed, or be utilised for purposes extraneous to the intentions of their creator.

Marquand was an authentic pro-European, a reformist eager to improve an institutional framework which was not quite satisfactory. His analysis has been forgotten by most people, with the exception of that famous expression *democratic deficit*, which became in time the slogan of all the Eurosceptical political entities within the various countries of the EU. While the pro-Europeans availed themselves of his analyses to reclaim a more integrated Europe, a more democratic Europe, and one with greater legitimacy, that slogan has been utilised with *polemical function* against the possible realisation of a supranational Europe. In the same way, although that analysis has been employed by scholars or by dissatisfied pro-Europeans, the same considerations were adopted by a large spectrum of hostile groups or parties, which were determined to throw out the baby with the bathwater. Europe was seen by the radical left as a Trojan horse of American power, of corporations and, later, of globalisation. Mirroring this, the opposition of the extreme right – from the Austrian FPÖ (*Freiheitliche Partei Österreichs)* to the French Front national of Jean Marie Le Pen (today led by his daughter Marine), or movements like the Italian Lega and UKIP – bolstered itself with accusations against the destruction of the national States and the invasion of illegal immigrants.

The sensible divergences and disagreements between all these movements certainly have not vanished, but, apart from their evident hostility toward the EU, they share a core of common fundamental values. Very often the content of these values might stand in contrast with their political implications (Taggart, Szczerbiak (2002)). For example, the centrality of national sovereignty is shared by the extreme poles of right and left. However, while the extreme right (Vasilopoulou (2009 and 2011)) brings the idea that the foreigners must be expelled from the national territory and deprived of every right (school education, healthcare, measures of social assistance), the radical left dissociates itself totally from these arguments, and is open to migrants and refugees.

The diffusion of anti-Europeanism is due to the constitution of 'populist' parties, which have appropriated most of the critical arguments against the EU, without worrying too much about safeguarding their ideological consistency. Basing themselves essentially on protest, the various populist movements that have blossomed throughout Europe were able to propose platforms based for the most part on the dichotomy people/élites, and on the strong critique of representative democracy and technocracy, not bothering to equip themselves with a solid and consistent politico-ideological corpus. For such movements, the EU represents the ideal personification of the élites' ills, and the favourite scapegoat of electorates deluded by the policies of the governing parties.

The rapid diffusion of this phenomenon, unknown in Europe until the 1990s, can be explained by a series of ideological and political factors. In the first place, the collapse of the Soviet Union triggered a rather dramatic dealignment of the political forces in all the nations where the communist parties were able to attract a good number of electors. It also freed the parties of centre-right from the constraints of discipline imposed by the fear that the communist forces might attain power, should their coalition fragment. The sudden disappearance of the communist menace also allowed the 'sins' of the governing coalitions (such as endemic corruption) to be denounced with more vigour by the media, and prosecuted by the judiciary without the risk of putting the entire institutional system in jeopardy. In many countries the first victims of this moral purge were the governing parties, usually the Christian Democrats and the social-democrats; that is, the same parties that had strongly and consistently supported the process of European integration.

Many European statesmen, beginning with François Mitterrand (1916–96) and Helmut Kohl (1930–2017), immediately realised the potential risks of this epochal change, and thought it urgent to make a greater effort both to extend the benefits ensured by the EU to the ex-communist nations of Eastern Europe, and to consolidate integration through new instruments, such as the provision of a monetary union. 'Widening and deepening' was the order of the day, and the Treaty of Maastricht (1992) constituted the natural and inevitable political and juridical consequence of this new vision of Europe. It constituted also the watershed event between the permissive consensus of the past and a new era characterised by hard opposition to the integration process. In 1992, the referendum for the ratification of the Maastricht Treaty in Denmark failed, while the one in Ireland passed, as well as, by a fraction, the one in France, where the two principal parties of the right and the left were divided, each with internal minorities (led by Laurent Fabius among the socialists and François Fillon among the Gaullists) which were decidedly contrary to a closer integration and a further transfer of sovereignty. The following 15 years were characterised by a pressing discontent, increasing divisions between the Member States and a desperate effort to consolidate the still fragile and baroque institutional system of the Union through the constitutionalisation of the treaties. The failure of this last project was resounding, and the double referendum rejection in the Netherlands and France (2005) translated into the death sentence of the Constitutional Treaty. Its resurrection in the framework of the Treaty of Lisbon recalled the old method of 'integration by stealth' and illustrated even further the inability to make a clear and open choice in favour of a federal or semi-federal system, the unique political solution which could legitimate such a significant transfer of powers and responsibilities. In the course of the following years, those of the financial and monetary crisis, the contradictions of this approach have been aggravated due to the necessity of increasing the 'federal' powers in the banking, monetary and fiscal sectors, in the midst of a mounting hostility vis-à-vis the European institutions and the Commission, scapegoat *par excellence.*

Other events, internal and international (11 September 2001 and, starting in 2003, the Iraq war), have contributed to increasing the divisions in a significant manner. Euroscepticism was no longer the minority expression of a small cluster of nations like Denmark or haggard radical parties or protest movements. From that time, such a sentiment began to increase even in the parties and in the governing coalitions. This was true almost everywhere, obviously in Great Britain, the so-called mother of all reluctances, but also in founding States, like France, which have always had a non-unanimous approach to the issue, or the Netherlands, where the original integrationist spirit has faded, or, even worse, Italy, a champion of European integration. In this latter country, the coalition led by Silvio Berlusconi was constituted to a large extent by political allies who were critical, not to say hostile, of the EU, which has contributed to transforming, slowly but inexorably, a mass of convinced pro-Europeans into cohorts of anti-Europeans or Eurosceptics. Subsequent crises (the Greek drama and the migration flows), combined with the idea that Europe was subdued to the twin diktat of the German government and of the ECB, have helped yet further to entrench the anti-European sentiments expressed by the protest movements which have blossomed (Della Porta, Parks (2016)) in the course of these periods of difficulties (ten years of prolonged economic stagnation) and which fuelled themselves with the populist victories in other countries (Brexit, Donald Trump).

The unstoppable tide of populist movements cannot be explained only by virtue of the succession of dramatic events on the national and international levels. It is also the by-product of the blindness and the incapacity of the political élites that lead the national and international institutions. Their first error was to refuse to explain to the population the necessary consequences of their actions, postponing to some later period the indispensable clarification of their choices. The expression 'integration by stealth' was often used to describe the attitude of those national policymakers that supposedly deceived their electorate by undertaking actions without assuming the responsibility for them. This is true, but it is only a part of the problem. Because of the many compromises that every collective involves, the policymakers have deceived themselves, ignoring the long-term consequences of their actions: for example, they did not seriously consider the consequences of doubling the number of Member States, or of bringing together nations with extremely different democratic traditions and economical performances; those most favourable to integration refuse to see the contradictions in all this, supporting at the same time, for example, federalism and the enlargement to Turkey (a replica of what had happened in the Seventies with Great Britain); those favourable to international commerce refused to consider the simple fact that the change of the rules would redistribute in a non-uniform way benefits and costs between territories and populations; those favourable to the realisation of monetary union rejected the necessary conditions for rendering it fully successful, such as the institution of a lender of last resort or of a redistributive federal budget. They have ignored the weight of history, and the time necessary for consolidating democracy beyond elections, and were taken by surprise by Euroscepticism and by the illiberal movements that exploded in Central and Eastern Europe (Kopecky, Mudde (2002)).

In other words, the governing élites have forgotten that to take a political decision implies facing its consequences. They have behaved as if the fact that decisions were taken on high levels by 'invisible' hands could release them from paying the collective costs. In other instances, different political actors have pressed too far (as in the case of the economic Union, whose institutional framework is too heavy, intrusive, and complex) or not far enough (the European institutional construction has neither roof nor foundation, that is, it has neither constitution nor grassroots legitimacy). Since the parties and the national coalitions were incapable of providing the indispensable ideological framework for the interpretation of a programme of such a magnitude, they have left the field to critical and simplistic visions which have been exploited by the new political actors (Della Porta, Parks (2016)). In times of crisis and uncertainty, it is indeed simpler to mobilise *against* failed or tough policies and *against* those responsible for them.

Great events, mistaken policies, crises of political parties and protest are the natural ingredients for the emergence of populist movements. But these explanations are not yet sufficient. Usually, the rules of the political arena established by the dominant forces, namely the governing parties, are defined in such a manner as to not permit the entrance of unwelcome guests. To insert oneself among the political élites requires an extraordinary pressure from the base and a minimum core of instruments on which the new arrivals can rely. Some of these instruments were already existent (for instance the mandatory referenda in Ireland), others were introduced when the divided parties were unable to decide without direct consultation (as in Denmark and in the United Kingdom), others again were imposed by the EU itself, as happened in the case of the elections of the European Parliament.

As regards the European parliamentary elections, the electoral rules have introduced two important novelties: the system of proportional representation in countries that traditionally use a majority system, and the necessity, in every country, to draw very few electoral colleges, given the small number of candidates to select per nation. In addition to these mechanisms, another element has played an important role: from the outset, these elections have not stoked a large electoral participation and have been considered as second-order elections. In other words, national issues have gained the upper hand over European questions, and protest has exercised a superior attractive force to that of the support of European policies.

Ultimately it can be affirmed that everything has contributed to weakening the grip of the traditional parties, given that they themselves are divided on the major European issues; there was a larger supply of candidates from small or new parties who have exploited the opportunities offered by the European electoral rules, from generous financing to the possibility of making a break through more easily than at local or national elections. The most evident case is represented by UKIP in Great Britain, which is incapable of breaking through the national elections because of the guillotine of the electoral system's 'first past the post' (namely, the simple majority system), but which was a big winner on the occasion of the European elections or the Brexit referendum. Once this Pandora's box opened, it was impossible to close it again: in the Netherlands, in Denmark, Italy, France, Austria and Finland, populist movements constitute now a stable presence in the national political scene. And most of the eastern Member States are ruled by populist parties or coalitions.

Populist parties vary widely in their style, political programmes and leadership. However they present common characteristics that clearly explain the reasons why they were and are the principal vectors of the anti-European discourse. The first and universal characteristic of populism is the emphasis on the notion of *people*, which, in every democratic context, is the only source of legitimacy and sovereignty. From this point of view, populists differ from the extreme right, even if many aspects of their ideology or of their political repertoire might be drawn from it. They consider themselves not only democratic movements, but also the only true democratic ones: indeed, in their opinion the traditional parties led by narrow ruling classes have betrayed the interests of the people for their exclusive benefit. Therein lies the principal aspect of populism: the rejection of the governing élites and mistrust of the traditional mechanisms of representation. On the one hand, the 'good folk', on the other the corrupt, treacherous, incompetent managerial classes, both national and supranational. These belong to the economical world (banks and corporations), to that of the experts (judges, central banks, independent authorities) or to the political one (parties, parliaments). Nobody is safe from condemnation and from general ostracism (Mény, Surel (2000)): the EU institutions (already accused of being *apatrides* by de Gaulle in 1965) are therefore an ideal target for the populists.

Moreover, everybody is part of the *people*, beginning with the man of the street, but with the relevant exception of whoever is not native to the community. The prime and natural victim becomes therefore the foreigner and, in particular, the immigrant. It is however interesting to note that this fairly clear distinction is then mitigated by a series of considerations that introduce further differentiations: in Great Britain there is a greater opposition to European workers (who 'steal' jobs) than to Indian and Pakistani shop owners. In France, European immigrants do not represent a serious problem (with the exception of the Rom), while there exists a latent hostility toward African immigrants. What is most interesting is not the consistency of these positions, but rather the dichotomous vision between the true and authentic people, however it is identified, and the excluded ones (in the case of Lega Nord, for example, the initial scapegoats were others Italian citizens, the internal immigrants, which is to say the 'southerners', 'terroni' – hicks or rubes).

To insist so much on a notion of the *people* that excludes any components which are considered impure is inevitably reminiscent of the ethnic definition of the nation, even when it is more an 'imagined community', to use the terms of Benedict Anderson, than a homogeneous community from the ethnic, cultural and linguistic points of view. One might observe a return to this nationalistic tradition in countries like Poland or Hungary, which have not been overwhelmed by the effects of colonisation, or by the economic immigration flow. However, even in the United Kingdom, which is now a multicultural country in many ways, the retrieval of interest in the national community has found fertile soil, as the Brexit referendum has demonstrated. The rhetoric of 'national' values, of religion, tradition and of the culture of the country, all reinforced the populist parties' front. For them, only the nation, its sovereignty, its interest and its values matter. In consequence, a 'democracy of peoples' is for the populists not only a dream, but also a contradiction in terms: democracy cannot live beyond the national State, and the decisions assumed by technocratic authorities, like the

Commission, the European Central Bank or the Court of Justice, or by authorities devoid of any real legitimacy, such as the European Parliament, result invariably in conflict with the interests of the nation and its people. These basic principles unite all populist movements, which might then differ in their more particular aspects.

Taking into account the crucial importance of these values and the fact that the EU seems to be the perfect incarnation of everything that the populists hate, it comes as no surprise that the fight against Brussels is central to their programmes. If the traditional parties are often embarrassed to address European issues, on account of the divisive impact that these produce on electors, political activists and elected representatives, and take refuge in vague declarations of principle, in opportunistic positions (whose tenor varies depending on whether they are in the government or in the opposition) or in convoluted proposals, the populist movements exploit such internal divisions to the utmost in order to attract sympathisers from any political alignment. In other words, European questions acquire a different importance in the party system. While these questions are often secondary for the governing parties, they assume a fundamental importance for the populists, given the rhetorical emphasis that they put on terms like 'people', 'élites', 'nation', 'foreigner', 'immigration'. In this connection, a classic example is offered once again by Brexit: the referendum was launched in the attempt to overcome the internal divisions within the conservative party. Labour, whose electoral base was favourable enough to withdrawal from the EU, adopted a low profile to avoid further haemorrhaging of electors and militants. UKIP on the contrary did not have to confront such dilemmas: it was born with only one objective, 'exit', and it was much simpler to celebrate the value of independence than to underline the visible and less visible benefits arising from remaining in the EU.

Furthermore, the governing parties in their programmes have to address on a whole range of questions related to achieved results and future expectations. They carefully balanced their proposals, with the purpose of addressing a great variety of groups with different social and economic interests and with contrasting ideological preferences. Populist movements do not usually have analogous problems, especially in their ascending phase. They do not have to worry about governing, but only about conquering a little bit of space in a political scene which is already filled. If then by any chance they reach power (normally within a coalition), they usually make their voices heard on a single argument (such as immigration, hostility toward the EU or the euro) or else they are obliged to swallow the bitter pill of the exercise of power, namely compromise and adjustment to a hard reality. This has been seen in Finland, in Austria and even in Italy (where for example the fight against immigration was translated into a mass legalisation of irregular migrants thanks to the Bossi-Fini law. It remains to be seen what kind of compromises the new Conte Government will have to accept beyond the so-called *Contratto di governo* of May 2018).

The anti-European position of many populist parties can be interpreted in a myriad of ways (Sitter (2002)). In the first place, it must be taken into account that the politicisation of the European issues along the left/right division, as suggested by Hix, did not occur. However, at the same time, the fears manifested by Bartolini have materialised, given that that politicisation has put the process of an 'ever closer union' in serious jeopardy. His prediction has almost been fulfilled. In any case, the question remains the following: is politicisation avoidable? It is thought that a successful strategy for avoiding negative politicisation might come only by way of integration by stealth and by a sharp reduction of EU responsibilities. However, neither of these conditions can be reached today.

An alternative to this discouraging analysis might be to consider the populist moment as a short-term, but necessary, phase of transition: the party system inherited from the post-war period and connected to the democratisation of the majority of European nations seems to have exhausted its potentiality, and the capacity to structure national politics in a process of Europeanisation, globalisation and technological revolution. The increasing inability of these parties to aggregate public opinion around convincing visions of the world, to formulate credible policies, and to draw up a political platform has led to alternatives which are yet incomplete, unfocused and confused. The conflicts of the past which have contributed to the birth and the development of the party system (Caramani (2016)) are progressively disappearing. A more optimistic vision might emphasise that the anti-European positions of the populist parties foreshadow the tendency toward a greater alignment in many countries of the EU, on the one hand of groups of pro-European, open and liberal parties, and on the other, of a hotchpotch composed of 'antifederal' parties, hostile to the interference of the EU and to centralisation: a renovated, European version of the division between the federalists and the anti-Federalists which is still widespread in the American political system.

III. The Growing Rejection of European Policies

Fritz Scharpf has made an interesting distinction between 'negative integration' and 'positive integration' (1999), emphasising that while the first has been carried out in an effective and systematic way by removing tariff and regulatory barriers, the second has been much more difficult to develop, given the heterogeneity of the views and of the interests of the Member States, and the characteristics of the European decision-making process. The requirements of unanimity and, later on, that of a qualified majority, have therefore represented a serious obstacle for the implementation of ambitious initiatives. In reality, these divisions were present already from the origins of the project of integration: while Germany and, to a certain extent, the countries of the Benelux desired the institution of an economic community with the objective of liberalising the economy and establishing a common market, the French government, conscious of the fact that the French economy would not be competitive enough, insisted that the Treaty in question provide also certain measures of a social character. Due to the tenacious German opposition to this, France had to content itself with a reference to the equality of retribution between men and women, given parity of occupation, and of the commitment to realise a common agricultural policy. This status quo remained unchanged until the Single European Act, proposed and negotiated by Jacques Delors in 1986. The compromise between Thatcherite inclinations and social-democratic aspirations materialised in the provision of structural funds, allocated, in the view of an interventionist combination of economic, social, and territorial policies, for the support of the most depressed areas.

Since then many things have changed. Not only was there an incremental, but constant, growth of the EU policies in the 1980s (through the use of a 'implicit powers' strategy in the fields, for instance, of education or environment), but the Treaty of Schengen (1985), of Maastricht (1992), of Amsterdam (1997) and, subsequently, the Charter of Fundamental Rights of 2000, have also lain the foundations and created the legal basis for important political initiatives. Parallel to this, the consequences of the economic crisis and of commercial liberalisations have made themselves felt in broad strata of the population and/or in certain specific areas. If national governments were long considered responsible for political choices and failures, that outlook has radically changed in the course of the last 20 or 25 years. The European Union (personified in the 'Commission' or in 'Brussels') has become the privileged target of many protests, as well as the scapegoat for the many forms of reluctance of the public opinion.

Public mobilisation against the EU has taken on different contours from country to country, by virtue of the attitudes of the media (de Vreese (2007); *The media and neo-populism* (2003)) and of the national governments. On the other hand, the anti-European movements have not been the only ones to advance critiques against European integration. The original source of such critiques can in fact be found in the governments themselves. These last, while on the one hand being unable to call into question their belonging to the 'club' in which their respective countries had decided to take part, on the other hand have been able to easily criticise the type of *union* that was realised, given the uncertainties regarding the nature and the destination of the path that they had been embarked upon.

The ontological ambiguity of European institutional architecture has often been its strong point, given that it has consented the concealment or the deferment of difficult choices to better times. New members have also adopted diplomatic strategies which are hypocritical enough: in the face of the difficult conditions for entry, the hope for many of these countries consisted in being able to renegotiate the requisites for membership in the EU. Such was the case of France at the time of the crisis of 1965, or the United Kingdom when it requested a reduction of the budget (according to the famous formula of 'I want my money back'), or the United Kingdom once again when it drew red lines with Tony Blair even before the negotiations on the Constitutional Treaty. Naturally, there has always been a form of reciprocal influence between public opinion, media and governments. These last reflect the sensibility of their electorates, but they can decide whether to guide or to be guided in their important political choices. The governments of the Member States have been ever more incapable of explaining and justifying their European choices, and, whenever they have found themselves in some difficulty, they have succeeded in doing nothing other than shifting the blame onto the shoulders of the 'Eurocrats' of Brussels, attempting to hide the fact that they had taken part in those same decisions, or maintaining that they had been put into a minority in the Council. The most striking case was probably that of the United Kingdom, characterised by a vivid contrast between public discourse on the one hand (often enough critical and negative), and practice (the rate of implementation of European decisions in the UK is one of the best among the Member States). The reluctance of many British governments in the face of greater integration was legitimate because it reflected a different vision relative to the unification of the continent. But the official position was further exasperated by the popular press (the so-called gutter press), which has always shown chauvinistic and nationalistic attitudes and has coined hysterical and provocative slogans against the European Union. This press has contributed to reinforcing sentiments against the European Union in Great Britain, systematically caricaturing, through simplistic catchwords, the EU decisions. Charles Grant (2008) head of the pro-Europe *Centre for European Reform* has identified four causes of British Euroscepticism: geography, history, economy, and the fact 'that Britain has a uniquely powerful and eurosceptic popular press' (p 3). Other countries have travelled the road inaugurated by the British government. Even governments that were initially supporters of the EU reveal themselves as being ever more strongly critical of and worried about European policies: Matteo Renzi has often taken a tone unheard in Italy since the creation of the European Union – probably as an attempt to counterweight the tide of the populist movements in the peninsula – the conservative governments of Hungary and Poland have not limited themselves to expressing their dissent, but have also adopted rules which are little compatible with the spirit and the letter of the treaties. Things do not go equally badly in all the Member States, but many governments have the tendency to throw discredit on the EU when they find themselves in difficulty and, on the whole, the press gives great prominence to critical and hostile positions regarding the European Union.

The opposition of some parties and of many populist movements derives in part from their 'fundamentals', which is to say, from their hostility toward the EU itself or toward certain policies which are considered damaging to national interests. However, in many cases, opportunism and cynicism are visible here. In this connection, the populist movements can hardly claim a monopoly, since even the governing parties are expert in such exercises. But the populist movements, not having experience at governing, and nourishing scarce hope of winning the elections, at least at first, set no limits to the exercise of a rhetoric of protest based on a single (contradictory) sequence of events (Semetko, Van Der Brug, Valkenburg (2003)). For example, the French Front national originally presented itself as a fairly neoliberal force in the economy; but then it realised that its electors were composed especially of the 'losers' of certain economic and technological transformations. Today the Front national defends a totally statist, protectionist, protective programme, and one which stands in contrast with the EU treaties and which arrives at the logical conclusion that the choice to exit from the EU should be submitted to the French electors through a special referendum. Yet more exceptional is the inversion of the Italian *Movimento cinque stelle*, which has decided to abandon the group it had already constituted with UKIP in the European Parliament, to request admission into the most pro-European and federalist group, that of the liberals (Alliance of liberals and democrats for Europe) which, in the end, preferred to reject the accession agreement which the group's leader himself, Guy Verhofstadt, sought.

As previously explained, a decisive turning point occurred at the beginning of the 1990s, with the collapse of the Soviet Union. It was believed that the Maastricht Treaty would have consented the management of the new European political setup, while insuring that Germany remained strongly anchored to the EU and 'under control', notwithstanding the new horizons opened up by unification. Although she was not then in power (since she was forced to tender her resignation in November 1990), Margaret Thatcher (1925–2013) had provided the Eurosceptics the entire lexical armoury necessary to contest the reinforcement of the European integration. The famous Bruges speech (September 1988) put Euroscepticism in the foreground and offered the various movements of opposition to the EU the grammar and the vocabulary that they needed to unite. Thatcher claimed that the Community was not an end in itself, or an institutional process determined by some 'abstract intellectual concept', but simply an instrument for 'effective action'. On 25 January 2013, the *Times*, on the basis of various surveys, wrote that, were a referendum for the membership in the EU to be held, the majority of those entitled to vote would opt for Brexit. In that context, it can hardly be surprising that the policies foreseen by Maastricht have provided the pretext for strong critiques against the EU: the euro, Schengen, migrations, fundamental rights, regulations, and the supranational governance soon became the favourite target of whomever wanted to strike out at the EU.

An unexpected, but unsurprising, opposition to EU politics was recently established with respect to the European commercial policy. It was unexpected because the media and public opinion generally do not concern themselves with technical and little-debated issues, like the negotiations on or the ratifications of commercial agreements. According to the treaties, the Commission has the monopoly on eventual negotiations on behalf of the entire Union. In fact, only a monopoly of this kind can guarantee the necessary unity and coherence in the commercial relations between the EU and the rest of the world. In consequence, the treaties confer extensive powers in this matter to the Commission, in charge of concluding agreements on behalf of the richest and most developed entities in the world. During the last half century, such exclusive responsibility never triggered any relevant opposition, with the exception of a few official critical declarations by the French government or the moderate dissatisfaction of small economic groups (like farmers or the environmental movements). However, so far these oppositions have not been so intense as to block the conclusion of these agreements or to impede the Commission from qualifying certain 'mixed agreements' that require approval from national authorities as commercial treaties, falling precisely under its exclusive competence. Public opinion however has radically changed, principally for the following reasons. In the first place, the long-term effects of the treaties have been particularly painful, since national productions have been overwhelmed by the importation of manufactured goods from countries with low labour costs. While at first the almost complete extinction of the textile or shoe-making industry took place without much outcry, it subsequently coupled with the economic and financial crisis. The trade unions and the left-wing parties have denounced with ever more decision the impact of globalisation and of Europeanisation, and have clamoured for the end of commercial liberalisation. Moreover, the negotiations between the EU and the USA or Canada have been conducted as usual in secret, but have alarmed many interest groups, as well as the Eurosceptics of the left and of the right. The negotiations with the United States about the TTIP (*Transatlantic Trade and Investment Partnership*) have entered into a standstill and the French socialist government, under pressure from its most left-wing contingent, even requested that they be entirely suspended. In reality, this has revealed itself as a simple and hypocritical coup de grace, given that everyone knew that it would have been impossible to arrive at an agreement before the conclusion of Barack Obama's term in office. At the same time, the ratification of the agreement between the EU and Canada, the CETA (*Comprehensive Economic and Trade Agreement*), was frozen for a while, on account of the veto brought, in October 2016, by the region of Wallonia, which, according to the Belgian Constitution, must approve every international treaty which falls, even only in part, within its own sphere of jurisdiction. The movement was sustained by the pro-European (if critically pro-European) president of the region, Paul Magnette, but popular support originated above all in those movements of the left which are critical of the EU, and in particular the trade unions.

Hostility toward migrants is probably what most unites the opposition to the European Union, notwithstanding the fact that the European institutions have only limited powers in this area. The EU is considered responsible for the situation for two principal reasons: The first is that European integration is based on four freedoms, among which is movement within the Union. Although initially this freedom was limited by border checks and the myriad obstacles of a practical and bureaucratic order (transfer of currency, residency permits, healthcare and pension systems), the circulation of persons has been facilitated and favoured by the signature of the Agreement (1985) and the Convention (1990) of

Schengen, as well as by its successive extensions. Originally, its implementation was favourably perceived. To move freely facilitated the life of cross-border workers, of businessmen, of tourists and students, while the migratory flow tended to follow the directing legacies of the various countries' colonial heritage. Resentment began to grow when the migrations augmented, and in many respects changed. In the first place, the number of asylum-seekers has grown in an exponential way, owing to the insecurity and the wars in many parts of the world, and particularly in the Mediterranean basin. Secondly, the demographic balance between rich old Europe on the one hand, and a continent that displays the fastest population growth in the world (Africa) on the other, has driven millions of economic migrants to face any danger in order to look for a better life elsewhere. Thirdly, the noteworthy differences in income and well-being between the Member States after the 2004 enlargement have upended the underlying sense of the freedom of movement granted to European citizens.

If the movement of EU citizens from one State to another was contained up until 2004, over the past ten years, on the contrary, it has become a mass phenomenon. We are dealing with a rather spontaneous and natural movement in accord with the realisation of the goals of the treaties, which is to say the progressive realisation of a single market. However this has certainly been facilitated by the 'services directive' or the 'Bolkenstein directive' (directive 2006/123/EC) which proposed to grant to immigrant workers from another Member State salaries identical to those recognised in the State of migration (while the social costs were paid at the rate of the nation of origin). These rules have been rendered more protective, by correcting the line traced by the sketch of the directive, so as to avoid social dumping. The rhetoric of the 'Polish plumber' played a crucial role in the French debate and contributed to the rejection of the Constitutional Treaty in the referendum of 2005. These norms were full of good intentions, but their promoters did not realise that, by protecting the pay of national workers from plummeting, they were in fact offering salaries eight or ten times higher than those of the countries of origin, thus rendering these jobs extremely appealing.

This was not the first time that a large-scale immigration had taken place in the most developed European nations: millions of Italians, Portuguese, Maghreb citizens, Turks, Latin-Americans, and Asians relocated within Europe. The true problem is that the most recent immigrations have occurred in a period of financial and security crises. Growing unemployment, moreover, has brought about cut-throat competition in unskilled labour, triggering a genuine 'war among the poor'. The theme of migration was far and away the most debated in the course of the campaign on Brexit, to such a point that the British prime minister Theresa May, in office since July 2016, felt obliged to prefer the so-called hard Brexit, which would allow her to close the borders. The labour party is divided and uncertain on the question, on account of the fact that its electorate was attracted by the propaganda of UKIP. The paradox is that, after the enlargement of 2004, the United Kingdom was the country that, despite its refusal to adhere to the Schengen Treaty, had, more than anyone else facilitated the free circulation of European citizens from central, southern and eastern Europe into its territories.

Hostility to immigration assumes different forms according to the peculiar characteristics of each nation: in Scandinavia the populist parties have accused the migrants of abusing the social protection system, and in Sweden and Denmark in particular, these parties have contributed to the defeat of the social-democrats and to the adoption of more stringent rules on immigration (Bering (2000)). This manifestation of 'welfare chauvinism' was observed even in the United Kingdom, and the restriction of social benefits to new immigrants was part of a package of measures negotiated by David Cameron, prime minister at the time of the referendum of 2016, to weaken the supporters of Brexit. In other States, the opposition of anti-European movements was shared by the main parties (albeit with very different tones), given that the larger question was the difficulty or the incapacity to manage the irregular immigrant fluxes. This was the case in Greece and in Germany, where the Christian socialists of the CSU (*Christlich-Soziale Union*) have manifested fears and advanced objections analogous to the arguments of the party of the right, the AFD(*Alternative für Deutschland*). In Italy, the migration issue has been decisive in the victory of the two populist movements, Lega and cinque stelle. In the Central and Eastern European countries, opposition on the part of the governments to the Commission's plan for redistributing refugee quotas has been more of a cultural, regulatory character, and is marked by a sort of old-fashioned 'nativism'. In fact the numbers proposed were rather modest: for example, 1294 migrants were to be relocated in Hungary. But the offer was still very contentious for a nation that has already received around 2000 asylum requests in 2012 and more than 180.000 in 2015 (of which only 146 were accepted). Tradition, history, culture, religion, and ethnicity constituted a powerful mix that allowed the extreme right to extend its influence beyond its natural limits. In any case, the referendum organised by Orbán to give strength and legitimacy to his own opposition to the quotas for relocation missed its target in October 2016 (despite a favourable vote of 98 per cent), since the quorum for participation (50 per cent) was not reached, with only 30 per cent of the electorate having voted.

There is however a baseline common to all these different contexts: the ruling governments have everywhere attempted to render the policies regarding migrants more onerous, under the influence of parties or movements which are hostile to a possible open-border policy, of which the European Community is thought to be the instigator. Thus, walls were built in Hungary, border checkpoints were reinstated, provision was made for the repatriation of irregular migrants or their accommodation in reception centres, simultaneously limiting the granting of asylum rights or economic and social benefits. Denmark, since 2016, has gone so far as to provide for the confiscation of the money and of the goods of migrants over a certain minimum level.

Monetary union was another policy that was strongly contested by the Europhobes (and not only by them). This is the hottest and most debated theme in Europe, together with that of immigration. From the start, scepticism has made inroads here in the United Kingdom, which availed itself of an 'opt-out', and also in Denmark, where in 2000, 53 per cent of the voters refused monetary integration by referendum. In addition, a great confusion reigns among critics and experts in no area as much as that of monetary policy, and above all among economists and populist movements hostile to the euro. Some economists are against the establishment of the monetary union under the EU. Others (such as two Nobel prize winners, Robert Mundell and Stiglitz) support the single European currency on the level of theory and principle, but indicate its political and economic defects, and see concrete risks for its failure on account of the imperfection of the overall institutional architecture. In particular, many critical economists point their finger at those political choices adopted by Maastricht which were taken without adequate examination of their radical implications in the institutional and political field. In this connection one recalls the insufficient accountability of the European Central Bank to its restricted mandate (limited to controlling inflation), or to the ban on operating in certain cases as a lender of last resort, the ban on bailouts (namely, the rescue of institutions, like banks or insurance agencies, that are in a state of insolvency), the failure to adopt Eurobonds, and the absence of a real federal budget capable of alleviating the unbalanced effects of the monetary policy on the single countries.

The main arguments of the populist movements are twofold, and their attention is concentrated on one or the other depending on the specific interests of these same parties. The first is relative to national independence and sovereignty. Since the crisis has produced different consequences among the States that are part of the monetary union, there has been much debate regarding the impossibility of using devaluation to recuperate competitiveness, a technique that can normally be used when the currency is under the control of the State. The second was elaborated in countries that, despite having drawn the greatest benefits from the monetary union, now fear that they will have to pay the bill in case of a collapse of a euro-member. This is the case, for example, of the Netherlands and Germany. In the latter, various arguments merge together, such as the nostalgia for the supremacy of the Deutschmark and the contemptuous critique against the countries of the so-called Club Med, which are accused of jeopardising monetary stability and throwing their problems on the shoulders of virtuous nations. In Germany the problem seems therefore to be framed in a *moral* dimension. We should also add that, in many cases, the withdrawal from the Eurozone might be seen as a surrogate for withdrawal from the European Union. It is indeed easier to demand the withdrawal from the euro (which is not yet totally accepted, especially by the oldest segments of the population), whose short life has been stormy enough, rather than to clamour for a complete secession from the EU, the effects of which would surely be more traumatic.

The link between experts and populists is tightened thanks to the manipulation of the arguments of the former on behalf of the latter. The classic case is that of Stiglitz (2016), who has bitterly criticised the monetary union as it is today, hoping however for a reform of the system. The anti-euro movements did not miss the opportunity to exploit his critiques and to underline that experts of clear international fame were on their side.

The rejection of European policies on the part of certain anti-European groups is an interesting indicator of changes in course, and helps us to better illustrate many rarely debated issues.

The first question is the concrete formation of a kind of 'Eurosphere' on a selected number of issues. It is no longer possible to maintain that these debates are exclusively national. Certainly, the traditions, the specific characteristics of each country (Lubbers, Scheepers (2010)) and linguistic barriers do not permit a constant and reciprocal exchange of different points of view. Nevertheless, one can observe the simultaneity, the use and/or manipulation, the passage of arguments from one State to another, as well as transnational conferences and agreements. The experts of social movements have measured, for example, the growth of transnational mobilisation and the transversal dimension of populism on certain themes (Halikiopoulou, Vasilopoulou, Nanou (2012)). As Thomas Risse has observed, 'contestation is a crucial pre-condition for the emergence of a European public sphere rather than an indicator for its absence' ((2003) 5).

The second consideration regards the progressive formation of a new alignment which opposes pro-European/globalist/liberal groups to anti-European/nationalistic/illiberal groups (Leconte (2008)). Certainly, one cannot claim that the left/right cleavage has been eclipsed, but its value as an instrument of organisation and interpretation of politics is not as useful and precise as it was in the past. This new opposition, which recalls that between the federalists and the anti-federalists in the USA, is still in formation, and many subtleties and nuances might blur tis ideal-type. Nevertheless, if this trend were confirmed, it would have positive effects for the development of a new system of European parties aligned along this deep division. As Daniele Caramani (2016) has clearly pointed out:

> The impact of common expressions of voice is increased compared to separate claims directed to several national systems and conveyed through different legislative chambers. Accountability, rather than working through 30 separate electorates, operates through integrated fronts across national boundaries (p 286).

The third observation concerns the capacity of anti-European parties and movements to contribute to policy making. There is not a single Eurosceptic party which has been able to attain power and to impose its agenda. Nevertheless, certain conservative parties, which are very near to the new populist parties, have implemented part of the agenda of the anti-Europeans, for example in Hungary and in Poland. In other countries, the influence of the Eurosceptics has been more indirect, but still decisive, as in Austria and in the United Kingdom, where UKIP contributed in a decisive way to the most dramatic decision of the last 50 years. The anti-European movements have also been crucial in certain sectors of public policies, such as immigration or the policies of welfare in Denmark or in Finland. In the Netherlands, Geert Wilders, leader of the nationalist and populist party PVV (*Partij Voor de Vrijheid*, Party for freedom), convened a referendum on the agreement between the EU and Ukraine and, in April 2016, won the referendum contest, notwithstanding a very low turnout and the merely advisory nature of the vote. Populist movements (both on the left and on the right) played a crucial role in the referenda campaigns of 2005 in France and in the Netherlands. In 2018, for the first time ever, Italy, one of the EU founding countries will be governed by an unexpected alliance of two populist countries often labelled as Eurosceptics (with quite a lot of nuances between them). More generally, even in countries where populist movements (such as the Front national) have been ostracised by the most important parties, they have succeeded in dictating the political agenda on many political and economic issues, such as social benefits, freedom of movement, immigration, and safety, not to speak of the euro and the united Europe. Many parties have been forced to take a position with respect to the proposals of the populists and have not developed their own autonomous visions. At the European level, policy agenda has practically been 'frozen', given that certain questions are treated as taboo (beginning with the exclusion of any new treaty whatsoever, as we have had opportunity to observe in the pre-Brexit negotiations with Cameron). The initiatives of the Commission has been pared to the bone, because many European governments have misgivings about any potentially explosive reform, as for instance international agreements, the harmonisation of taxation, and so forth.

The fundamental problem today consists in the capacity of the EU to overcome this difficult phase in an extremely uncertain and unpredictable world. There is no reason to nourish many hopes regarding further forward steps in the process of European integration in the years to come. On the contrary, one might express justified fears relating to a whole sequence of unexpected events, from Brexit to the election of Trump as the president of the United States. It cannot be ruled out that the worst is yet to come; but this notwithstanding, if the European Union learns how to translate the motto of the city of

Paris, *Fluctuat nec mergitur* ('Tossed by the waves but never sunk'), into reality, its utility and its necessity will become more evident than ever. History is long, and the worst does not always arise from an inevitable fatality.

Bibliography

Bering, H, 'Denmark, the euro and fear of the foreign' (2000) 104 *Policy review* 63–74.

Caramani, D, *The Europeanization of politics. The formation of a European electorate and party system in historical perspective* (New York-Cambridge, 2016).

Daddow, OJ, 'Euroscepticism and the culture of the discipline of history' (2006) 32 *Review of international studies* 309–28.

de Vreese, CH, 'A spiral of Euroscepticism: The media's fault?' (2007) 42 *Acta politica* 271–86.

Della Porta, D and Parks, L, 'Social movements, the European crisis and EU political opportunities' (2016) *Comparative European politics* 1–18.

Fontaine, A, *Un seul lit pour deux rêves. Histoire de la détente. 1962–1981* (Paris, 1981).

Halikiopoulou, D, Vasilopoulou, S and Nanou, K, 'The paradox of nationalism: the common denominator of radical left and radical right Euroscepticism' (2012) 51(4) *European Journal of political research* 504–29.

Kopecký, P and Mudde, C, 'The two sides of Euroscepticism. Party positions on European integration in East Central Europe' (2002) 3(3) European Union politics 297–396.

Leconte, C, 'Opposing integration on matters of social and normative preferences: a new dimension of political contestation in the EU' (2008) 46(5) *Journal of common market studies* 1071–91.

Leconte, C, *Understanding Euroscepticism* (London, 2010).

Lubbers, M and Scheepers, P, 'Divergent trends of Euroscepticism in countries and regions of the European Union' (2010) 49 *European Journal of political research* 787–817.

Mair, P, 'Political opposition and the European Union' (2007) 42(1) *Government and opposition* 1–17.

Marquand, D, *Parliament for Europe* (London, 1979).

Mazzoleni, G, Stewart, J and Horsfield, B (eds), *The media and neo-populism. A contemporary comparative analysis* (Westport, 2003).

Mény, Y and Surel, Y, *Par le peuple, pour le peuple* (Paris, 2000) (Eng transl *Democracies and the populist challenge* (London, 2002)).

Scharpf, F, *Governing in Europe: effective and democratic?* (Oxford, 1999).

Semetko, HA, Van Der Brug, W and Valkenburg, P, 'The influence of political events on attitudes towards European Union' (2003) 33(4) British Journal of political science 621–34.

Stiglitz, J, *The euro: how a common currency threatens the future of Europe* (London, 2016).

Streeck, W, *Buying time: the delayed crisis of democratic capitalism* (London, 2014) (orig *Gekaufte Zeit: die vertagte Krise des demokratischen Kapitalismus* (Berlin, 2013)).

Taggart, P, 'A touchstone of dissent: Euroscepticism in contemporary Western European party system' (1998) 33 *European Journal of Political Research* 363–88.

Vasilopoulou, S, 'Varieties of Euroscepticism: The case of the European extreme right' (2009) 5(1) *Journal of contemporary European research* 3–23, www.jcer.net/index.php/jcer/article/download/106/131.

Vasilopoulou, S, 'European integration and the radical right: three patterns of opposition' (2011) 46(2) *Government and opposition* 223–44.

Websites

Grant, C, 'Why is Britain eurosceptic?' (2008) *Centre for European reform essays* https://www.cer.eu/sites/default/files/publications/attachments/pdf/2011/essay_eurosceptic_19dec08-1345.pdf.

'Politics: the right or the wrong sort of medicine for the EU?' (2006) 19 *Notre Europe. Policy paper* (in partic. T Padoa-Schioppa, 'Foreword'); S Hix, 'Why the EU needs (left-right) politics? Policy reform and accountability are impossible without it', 1–28; S Bartolini, 'Should the Union be 'politicised'? Prospects and risks' 29–47) http://personal.lse.ac.uk/hix/Working_Papers/NotreEurope_Hix%20_Bartolini.pdf.

Risse, T, *An emerging European public sphere? Theoretical clarifications and empirical indicators* (2003) http://userpage.fu-berlin.de/~atasp/texte/030322_europe_public.pdf.

Sitter, N, 'Opposing Europe: Euro-scepticism, opposition and party competition' (2002) 56 *SEI working paper* https://www.sussex.ac.uk/webteam/gateway/file.php?name=epern-working-paper-9.pdf&site=266.

Taggart, P and Szczerbiak, A, 'The party politics of Euroscepticism in EU Member and candidate States' (2002) 51 *SEI working paper* https://www.sussex.ac.uk/webteam/gateway/file.php?name=sei-working-paper-no-51.pdf&site=266.

All web pages are understood as having last been visited on 12 June 2018.

24

The Union Facing Fractures, Centrifugal Thrusts and New Applications for Accession

SYLVIE GOULARD

'We are leaving the European Union, but we are not leaving Europe'; so spoke the British prime minister Theresa May on 17 January 2017, in a press release on Brexit; and she added: '[We do not seek] anything that leaves us half-in, half-out. [...] We do not seek to hold on to bits of membership as we leave'.

By delineating the framework of the next negotiations between the European Union (EU) and the United Kingdom in this way, May brought an end to two fundamental strategies of Great Britain over the last 50 years: participating in the single market, and at the same time curbing the construction of a supranational political entity. Supposing that the negotiations have a positive outcome (which should not be taken for granted, given the complexity of the treaties and their impact on the prosperity of the country) the British prime minister has confronted the Europeans with their responsibilities: will they carry to fulfilment the political union which they claimed they wanted to build? What will they conserve of a European Union which they in part have moulded? The British people have disavowed their own ideal objectives, since the greater market, a Europe enlarged to continental dimensions and even certain aspects of an open society were all consigned to the flames of the referendum bonfire.

For the Brexiteers, Europe has failed in its mission: it has eroded the sovereignty of its members without succeeding in sufficiently conciliating their interests, and it has not proved able to manage the migration flows.

This is a rather short-sighted analysis. It is not so much 'Brussels' that has whittled away at the sovereignty of the States, as the inescapable reality of a world in which nations are ever more interdependent. May has always declared the need 'to take back control of our own affairs': these are nice words, but they will not suffice to free one from the so-called yoke of the European institutions (starting from the Court of Justice, guarantor of a State of supranational law) to be strong and happy in the world of Donald Trump, Vladimir Putin and Recep Tayyip Ergoğan. May continues to make professions of multilateralism – as she did in the course of the 46th edition of the World Economic Forum (Davos, Switzerland, January 2017) – and in the meantime abandons the EU. A reckless position: the City is in danger of paying dearly for its exit from the single market. And perhaps the EU will be better off, without the continuous attacks on supranationality, the budget, and the idea itself of a European Parliament.

What is the present state of the EU, which in 20 years has more than doubled the number of its Member States? It is necessary to make an objective assessment of the errors committed. Objective, yes, but rigorous, in contrast to that which was made during the British referendum campaign.

It is an undeniable fact that the EU is in crisis. It is subject to centrifugal forces without precedent and it is run through with division, both internal and external. There are those who, in making a critical assessment of it, impute the present difficulties of the Union to a badly managed enlargement dynamic. But one cannot forget that the EU remains nonetheless an audacious political project, a democratic construction without precedents, one of the great economic powers of the world. Rather than complaining, would it not be more sensible to get once more to work, and to draw lessons from the past so as to prepare better for the future?

It is more urgent than ever to make a critical assessment of the last twenty-five years and to redefine a positive project, oriented toward the future and capable of speaking to the young.

I. The EU Subject to Tensions Without Precedents

A. Internal Points of Fragility

It is evident that the EU is in crisis. It is run through in particular with unprecedented internal divisions, as: the prospect of the United Kingdom's departure (Brexit); the chronic fragility of the eurozone; the weakness of the relations between France and Germany; the rise of nationalism; the day-to-day scepticism. Such tensions compromise the continuity of the European project and loom like a dark atmosphere over the entirety of Europe.

The prospect of the United Kingdom's departure (Brexit) – 23 June 2016, the British citizens decided, via referendum, with 51.9 per cent of the vote, to leave the EU. For the first time, a Member State chooses to leave the Union, or at least (in the present state of things, in January 2017) intends to resort to article 50 of the Treaty on European Union (TEU). Brexit signals the end of a process of uninterrupted enlargement which in the course of a few decades has changed the nature of the EU, bringing the number of the Member states from 6 to 28.

In reality the founding fathers had not provided for the possibility of withdrawing from the EU. To the contrary, the entire architecture of the Union was conceived to create the strongest possible bonds: a 'de facto solidarity', to cite the expression used by Robert Schuman in his declaration of 9 May 1950. It is precisely for this reason that separation today is so complex.

Even if the voluntary character of the European construction has always been beyond question, no withdrawal procedure for the Member States was originally provided for. It was introduced belatedly in the European legal framework, with the Treaty of Lisbon (which came into force in 2009).

The provisions of article 50 of the TEU delineate the procedure in broad strokes, without furnishing many details. For want of precedents and definite rules, no responsible politician is able to establish a calendar for negotiations or to specify the modalities of their implementation. On 29 March 2017, the British government launched the procedure described in article 50. According to Michel Barnier, the lead negotiator for the European Union, the agreement which will bring an end to the present relations must imperatively be concluded by October 2018, so that it might be ratified before the European elections of 27 States in the spring of 2019. It will then be necessary to restructure the relations between the EU and the United Kingdom, which will become a third country. Ivan Rogers, permanent British representative to Brussels, resigned on 3 January 2017, after having declared that the negotiations for a new commercial agreement could last more than 10 years.

The withdrawal of the United Kingdom could provoke very substantial changes for the European institutions, the 27 Member States, and the British people. In particular, numerous enterprises will have to plan a new long-term strategy, while millions of households will have to gain a more precise idea of their own rights and their own opportunities. What will become of the enactment of the right to free movement of goods, people, services and capital between the continental Europe and the United Kingdom? In this situation of uncertainty, disquiet grows.

At the centre of the negotiations, precisely as it was at the centre of the referendum campaign of 2016, will be the free movement of persons and workers. UKIP (United Kingdom Independence Party) has leveraged on the 'identitarian' anxieties connected to the arrival in the British labour market, beginning from 2004, of the workforce coming from central and eastern Europe.

And yet it was precisely Tony Blair (British prime minister from 1997 to 2007) who encouraged this arrival, explicitly refusing the possibility of a transition period in expectation that the standards of living might equalise. In that period, those governments of western Europe that decided to take such a precaution attracted the criticism of the British government. Beyond the migratory question, the impact of Brexit on workers, students, and British pensioners residing in southern Europe is not negligible.

On the other hand, the departure of Great Britain from the EU threatens to call into question the unity of the Kingdom itself. In the referendum of 23 June, Scotland voted 62 per cent in favour of continued EU membership, and it has the intention of maintaining close relations with the Union. On 20 December 2016, in a speech read before the Scottish Parliament in Edinburgh, Scottish prime minister Nicola Sturgeon presented a strategy in three phases in the Brexit framework, and requested that the United Kingdom stay in the single European market. If this should be impossible, she will request that Scotland stay, whilst remaining an integral part of the United Kingdom. If not even this is possible, 'Scottish independence [from the United Kingdom] is not off the table', and she clarified that this last possibility is her 'preferred option'. Spain has already announced its own veto to the admission into the EU of any dissident Spanish region.

Analogously, the consequences of Brexit on the relations between Ireland and the United Kingdom provoke a series of worries: indeed, even Ulster voted for continued EU membership. The reintroduction of border controls between the two countries threatens to reawaken old dormant grievances, if it not indeed to generate new violence. The peace process (the so-called Good Friday Agreement of 1993) rested effectively on the EU and on the juridical authority of the European Council (the European Convention for the protection of human rights and fundamental freedoms).

These reflections on the British reality offer a gloomy portrait of the state of the Union and of the weakening of the countries that compose it. The United Kingdom has always had a complicated relationship with the European construction, formed of repugnance and calculation more than accession. It is nonetheless true that in recent times Great Britain seems to have lost all of its most characteristic traits: pragmatism, consciousness of its own interests, and an exceptional national cohesion. That its highest functionaries openly write as much does nothing but reveal the depth of the moral crisis the country is going through.

Even if various Balkan countries, such as Turkey, remain official candidates for accession, the uncertainty of the present situation gives no grounds to predict a new wave of entries into the EU.

The chronic instability of the eurozone – The economic and monetary union instituted by the Treaty of Maastricht (in effect since 1993) should have brought prosperity and improved the living and working conditions of the Europeans, given the political rapprochement. Notwithstanding a promising start, such hopes were unfortunately widely dashed. It is useless to deny it.

The first years were happy, not to say euphoric, but beginning in 2008 dire turbulence afflicted the eurozone. On the one hand, the eurozone suffered the backlash of the financial crisis originating in the United States in the summer of 2007, which worsened in September 2008. On the other hand, the macroeconomic management of the eurozone has not proved entirely satisfying.

On account of the bad management of its public finances, Greece was the first to be stricken. Ireland followed, victim of a real-estate bubble which forced its government to take extensive and onerous measures to come to the aid of the banks. All these actions were adopted in a state of urgency, not to say improvised.

Drastic budget cuts, carried by the wave of alarmism, contributed to nourishing an undoubted political radicalisation. Tensions appeared between the various peoples and the various Member States (consider the violent protest on occasion of the visit of German chancellor Angela Merkel to Athens, on 9 October 2012: the protestors held her responsible for the austerity measures inflicted on the Greek populace).

A North-South fracture was then drawn between certain particularly unbending States, near to Germany (such as the Netherlands and Finland), and certain Southern States that were in financial difficulty. So as not to alienate confidence in the markets or incentivise deviant behaviours, the former requested a rigorous application of the treaties and of the Stability and Growth Pact (a mechanism devised by the countries of the eurozone to coordinate national budgetary policies and to avoid the appearance of excessive public deficits). The latter, on the contrary, asked for a bit of oxygen, pointing out that political stability is well worth a little bending of the rules.

In 2015, after the election of Alexis Tsipras as prime minister of Greece, the possibility was even raised of the withdrawal of that State from the eurozone. But the French president François Hollande and the German chancellor, together with their colleagues in the European Council, dismissed the possibility.

The current situation of the eurozone is very different from that of 2009–10, at the start of the Greek crisis: the institution of a European Stability Mechanism (ESM) calmed the markets. The measures adopted by the European Central Bank (ECB) in the framework of its mandate – measures which were defined 'unconventional' by certain specialists – contributed to avoiding the worst. Thanks to considerable efforts, the situation of some Member States (Ireland, Portugal, and, although to a lesser extent, Spain) has been redressed. Under the guidance of Mario Monti, called in emergency to head a technical government, Italy too did its part. But the crisis of the euro revealed the absence of a lasting consensus among the States that share the single currency.

In Germany, public opinion seems no longer to perceive the enormous benefits that the country derived from the single market and from the now largely depreciated common currency, and concentrates its attention on the low level of interest rates for savers, imputed to the lenient policy of the ECB.

Italy too gives some cause for concern. The banks of the peninsula, too numerous and too often undercapitalised, suffering from the downturn which has been weighting on the country now for years, find tens of billions in nonperforming loans on their hands. The public debt in 2016 reached 132.6 per cent of the gross domestic product (GDP; Eurostat (April, 2017) http://ec.europa.eu/eurostat/statistics-explained/index.php/Government_finance_statistics). Already starting in the early 2000s, the Italian growth rate has always been beneath the eurozone average. At times the tone of the debate has become hotly anti-European and anti-euro, and this in a country which from its very origins had professed an unwavering adherence to the European project.

True, the European citizens remain connected to the euro – according to the latest 'Eurobarometer' (*Eurobarometro* 87, May 2017), 73 per cent of the residents in the eurozone thought that the single currency was an advantage for their country, 58 per cent in Italy.

The weakness of the relations between France and Germany – On 16 November 2016, Barack Obama took his leave of the Old Continent from Berlin. It was the sixth time that the United States president had visited Germany. The choice is significant: even though the German leadership is restrained by a modest military commitment and by the legacy of its history, the country is by now indisputably the first European power.

The figures tell us everything: in 2016, Germany recorded a record budgetary surplus of 19.2 billion euro (FT, 'Germania, nel 2016 PIL a +1.9%' (12 January 2017) *Il Fatto Quotidiano*; the article cites the data published by the Federal Statistical Office, the Destatis), while France remains burdened by a public debt equal to 96 per cent of the GDP (INSEE, *Institut National de la Statistique et des Études Économiques*, cited in A Feertchak, 'Le gouvernement rate son objectif de déficit public pour 2016' (24 March 2017) *Le Figaro*). The French State finances its own operating expenditures and a by now moribund social security system on credit, on the back of the future generations. From the point of view of Brussels, France enjoys preferential treatment: by no particular merit of its own, but rather, to some extent, through a phenomenon of usury. 'Because France is France', according to a curious declaration by the president of the European Commission, Jean-Claude Juncker (speech to the 99th Salon des maires de France, Paris, 31 May 2016).

The relations between France and Germany clearly suffer from the French weakness, which unbalances them.

In the third 2016 trimester (July-September), the unemployment rate stood at 9.7 per cent for metropolitan France and at 10 per cent for the whole of the country (INSEE, November 2016; https://www.insee.fr/fr/statistiques/2491592). In the same period, Germany recorded a rate of 5.7 per cent (Bundesagentur für Arbeit, November 2016, https://statistik.arbeitsagentur.de/Navigation/Statistik/Statistik-nach-Themen/Arbeitslose-und-gemeldetes-Stellenangebot/Arbeisloseund-gemeldetes-Stellenangebot-Nav.html). Moreover, in the course of November 2016 the French trade balance recorded a deficit of 4.4 billion euro (Ministère de l'Èconomie et des Finances, November 2016, http://www.douane.gouv.fr/articles/a11899-consulter-les-statistiques-du-commerce-exterieur-de-la-france) and the German trade balance a surplus of 22.6 billion (Destatis, November 2016, https://www.destatis.de/DE/PresseService/Presse/Pressemitteilungen/2017/01/PD17_006_51.html).

Not only this: while the influence of chancellor Merkel is decisive, the governing French élites of every orientation renounced advocating a structured European vision. Furthermore, this is one of the reasons for the rise of Emmanuel Macron, elected president of the French Republic in May 2017, who, on the contrary, upheld a clearly pro-European commitment.

At this point, it is difficult to evaluate the effect of this change. It might prove decisive for the European Union. Nor have single and important actions failed to join to this: for example, the work of the chancellor and of the French president to find a peaceful solution in Ukraine, or the management of the European sovereign-debt crisis, in June 2012 and in January 2015. However, a vision of the whole is lacking. And yet, without a shared plan, without the certainty of a 'common destiny' planned over the long-term, the contingent divergences and the incomprehension tied to cultural differences are quick to re-emerge. The heterogeneity of the enlarged Europe, the number of its Member States, the external threats, the internal scepticisms, all demand much more energy than ordinary management would require. The lack of decisive action for Europe in part explains the rise of aggressive nationalism, whose ruinous consequences can be observed in the United Kingdom.

The rise of nationalism – Almost everywhere in Europe, nationalist protest parties, sometimes openly xenophobic, have seen their consensus grow. The electoral results are clear. In France, the Front national reached the second round of the presidential elections with 21.3 per cent of the votes and, in the run-off, Marine Le Pen – although roundly defeated by Macron – was nonetheless allotted 33.9 per cent of the votes. In Germany, the growth of Alternative für Deutschland appeared as a phenomenon without precedents since the end of World War II. No matter how much more picturesque it might be, the nationalism of Beppe Grillo is not for this reason less deplorable.

Economic and social difficulties, migration flows and global upheavals contribute to creating a fertile ground for these movements. Some citizens, troubled by a difficult economic or political situation, or simply by the prospect of a social declassification or identitarian aggression, let themselves be seduced by a deceptive or wrong-headed propaganda. On the grounds that they must listen to the grievances of the people, moderate politicians abandon their positions, or even jump on the nationalistic wagon (in Austria, for example, apropos of a preference for the original workers of the country; not to speak of the Hungarian Viktor Orbán, an erstwhile liberal).

While it is perfectly legitimate to pose questions about the evolution of our societies, there are some who use this as a formidable springboard. The fear of foreigners, whose presence is by now tangible everywhere, or Islamic radicalisation are issues that 'loosen the tongue'. And there is no lack of scapegoats: from Muslims to finance, and the technocrats with them.

A recent editorial in the weekly *The Economist* coined a label for this phenomenon: post-truth politics (*Post-truth politics: art of the lie*, 10 September 2016). The term designates the new tendency of certain politicians to manipulate the public opinion by exploiting the electors' mistrust of the 'experts'. At the same time, it is true that the failure of the traditional parties, which have been unable to give adequate response to the financial crisis or to the inequalities provoked by globalisation, does nothing but encourage such a reading of reality. The speeches of these politicians presently have the aim of reinforcing the prejudices of the populace and relegating facts, figures, and truth itself to a subordinate position. The electoral campaign of the new American president, Donald Trump, is a manifest example of this.

The nationalist parties appeal to the 'gut'. They often advance the idea of recuperating national sovereignty (without bothering to learn if this might perhaps still exist) or else rediscovering a lost position of dominance (the *grandeur de la France* of general Charles de Gaulle, or the British Commonwealth of nations). National myths are overestimated and largely valorised at the expense of a more objective reading of History. By combining nostalgia and a turning inward on themselves, they colour their speeches with Europhobia, accusing the EU of all those evils, of which the citizens are well aware. An example: 23 October 2016, the nationalist Orbán, prime minister of Hungary, in a speech delivered in Budapest on occasion of the 40th anniversary of the anti-Soviet revolt, declared, alluding to the European policy on refugees, that his country must resist the 'Sovietisation' of Europe desired by Brussels (in reference to the refugee quotas allocated among the Member States, approved by the EU in September 2015; see below). He forgets that Hungary was not invaded, but acceded to the Union spontaneously.

Daily scepticism – Even setting aside the fervent nationalists, pro-European sentiment is significantly losing steam. According to a recent study of the American Pew Research Center of June 2016, which took into consideration the inhabitants of 10 EU countries (Great Britain, Italy, France, Germany, Spain, Poland, the Netherlands, Hungary, Sweden, Greece; B Stokes, *Euroskepticism beyond Brexit*, 7 June 2016; http://www.pewglobal.org/files/2016/06/Pew-Research-Center-Brexit-Report-FINAL-June-7-2016.pdf), only 51 per cent had a positive opinion of the Union, as against 61 per cent of the year before. A large portion (42 per cent) held that the Member States should regain certain prerogatives, 27 per cent wished to conserve the present equilibrium, and only 19 per cent would support an expansion of Community policies.

The percentage of EU-favourable opinions declined markedly on occasion of the crises of the eurozone (from 2010) and of the influx of refugees (2015). The most perceptible decline was recorded in France: while 10 years ago the favourable opinion was at a little more than 60 per cent, today it stands at less than 40 per cent. The most Eurosceptical are the Greeks, followed by the French and the Britons. It is however worth noting that the youths under the age of 35 are for the most part favourable to the EU (except in Greece). Unfortunately, their vote in the UK did not suffice to safeguard their future.

Presently, Euroscepticism is gaining ground in Italy more quickly than in any other country. On occasion of the referendum of last 4 December, the Italians rejected, by a vote of 59.1 per cent, the constitutional reforms proposed by the Renzi government, which led the prime minister to resign. The *Movimento 5 Stelle*, which is nationalist and anti-euro, as well as being the principal Eurosceptic formation in Italy, took credit for the victory, immediately demanding early elections. If it should come to power, the Movement has promised to organise a referendum on withdrawal from the euro.

According to a study carried out by the German foundation Bertelsmann, immediately after Brexit a slight increase of sympathy for the EU was recorded: 'between March 2016 and August 2016 the support for being a member of the Union grew by five per cent, and is now at 62% across Europe' (*Brexit has raised support for the European Union* (21 November 2016) 1; https://www.bertelsmann-stiftung.de/fileadmin/files/user_upload/EZ_flashlight_europe_02_2016_EN.pdf).

These internal tensions put the Community project hard to the test, precisely at the moment in which Europe is shaken also by external pressures.

B. External Pressures

The refugee crisis – For years the various Italian governments, and then Pope Francis in Lampedusa in July 2013, condemned the indifference toward the drama that is unfolding on the migratory routes between Africa and Sicily. They received almost no response at all from the EU until Germany was hit in its turn with a massive arrival of refugees.

In 2015, more than a million people fled toward the EU on account of conflicts devastating their countries or in search of better living conditions. In 2016 the flows were significantly alleviated, reaching a little under 363.000 individuals: this contraction seems predominately due to the agreement on migrants signed by the EU with Turkey, which produced a reduction in the arrivals along the eastern Mediterranean route. On the other hand, the arrivals along the central Mediterranean route have risen by almost a fifth, with Italy as the natural point of arrival. This route was the most travelled in the first months of 2017: indeed, according to the statistics of the UNHCR (*United Nations High Commissioner for Refugees*), from 1 January to 31 May, 60,305 migrants disembarked in Italy, as compared with the 7,274 to reach Greece. These massive arrivals of migrants put the countries which they cross into particular difficulty, especially Turkey, Greece, and Libya, which often are not able to put adequate emergency measures into effect.

To arrive in Europe, the migrants are ready to undertake an exceedingly difficult voyage, by way of land or sea. Upon their arrival they are deprived of everything, and they must receive assistance: basic humanitarian aid, potable water, medical care, lodging, legal assistance and so forth. There are numerous children and minors among them, who have need of further forms of protection.

In the face of the Member States' difficulties in managing the migratory flows, on 13 May 2015 the European Commission adopted a European Agenda on migration, which proposes a global approach to improving the management of all aspects of these migrations. The EU has also on several occasions earmarked funds for emergency relief projects for the most affected States: for example, in April 2016, the European Commission announced (in the framework of a new instrument of humanitarian aid designated Euro ECHO) that it had allocated 83 million euro, intended for the 50.000 refugees and migrants received in some 30 sites in Greece.

This issue has provoked strong tensions among the Member States. In September 2015, to give Greece and Italy (the principal ports of entry to Europe) some respite, the Member

States agreed to relocate 160.000 individuals who manifestly had need of international protection to other EU countries, over the course of two years. This measure was approved by a qualified majority of the Interior ministers of the Member States. As of today, however, the established quotas are rather far from having been reached (as of March 2017, only 14,438 individuals, equal to 9 per cent of the objective, have been relocated).

In 2016, in France, protection status (refugees and beneficiaries of subsidiary protection) was granted 26.351 times by the *Office français de protection des réfugiés et apatrides* (OFPRA) and by the *Cour nationale du droit d'asile*. In the same year, the OFPRA recorded 85,244 requests. The commitment accepted with the other Member States was to accept 30,000 by 2017.

On the other hand, four countries of eastern Europe (Romania, the Czech Republic, Slovakia and Hungary) continue to oppose the very principle of 'burden-sharing'. Hungary and Slovakia, condemning what they call 'a diktat' of the EU, decided to appeal the decision before the European Court of Justice, but they lost. On 2 October 2016, a referendum in Hungary rejected, by 98.3 per cent of the vote, the binding decision for relocation of the candidates for right of asylum among the Member States (but the vote was invalidated on account of insufficient turnout, 39.9 per cent). The text of the proposal was, in any case, partisan ('Do you want to allow the European Union to mandate the resettlement of non-Hungarian citizens to Hungary without the approval of the National Assembly?') and it must be said that the misinformation of prime minister Orbán is shocking.

Moreover, following the terrorist attacks on Paris, Nice, and Berlin, many European leaders changed their positions. The priority shifted onto the security of the citizens and the protection of the maritime borders in the Mediterranean. 'If there is no effective border control, no mechanism of distribution [within the EU] can be implemented', declared president Hollande on 16 September 2016, at the European Summit in Bratislava. During that same summit, chancellor Merkel acknowledged the failure of the quota system established by the Union, which she herself had supported.

The instability of nearby countries – In the 1990s, 13 States applied for accession to the EU: Cyprus, Malta, 10 countries of central and eastern Europe (Bulgaria, Estonia, Hungary, Latvia, Lithuania, Poland, the Czech Republic, Romania, Slovakia and Slovenia) and Turkey. In 2004 10 of these became members (Cyprus, Malta, Estonia, Hungary, Latvia, Lithuania, Poland, the Czech Republic, Slovakia, Slovenia), followed in 2007 by Romania and Bulgaria. In 2013, Croatia became the 28th State of the EU.

The consequence of the enlargements contributed to stabilising the periphery of the Union. And yet the instability has grown for some time.

The 'Arab spring' and its consequences shook numerous political systems, causing them to pass from stable authoritarian regimes to more or less open but fragile ones. Islamic fundamentalist movements in some cases took power, or create a climate of destabilisation through terrorist acts. The chaotic situation in Syria, Libya and Iraq exacerbates the instability and creates a strong migratory pressure on the Union, above all through Greece and Italy.

Also, since the fall of the Soviet bloc, the bilateral relations between Russia and Ukraine are tense, above all on account of Crimea and the Sea of Azov. The 'orange revolution' of 2004, the struggles over gas and the Russian invasion of Crimea in 2014 (with the consequent dispute on the division of international waters in the adjacent Sea of Azov), demonstrate the strong tensions between the two countries. Russia's violations of international law and of the commitments taken with the European Council have led the EU to react with various sanctions.

The relationship between the EU and Turkey is also particularly complex. In 1995, an initial customs union agreement was signed, and on 12 December 1999, in Helsinki, Turkey's candidacy was officially received. But the negotiations remain difficult. The arrival to power in 2003 of the Justice and Development Party (AKP, *Adalet ve Kalkınma Partisi*), an Islamic party founded by Recep Tayyip Erdoğan, raised at first certain hopes, on the basis of which it was decided to open negotiations for accession. On 3 October 2005, a 'negotiating framework' was agreed upon between the EU and Turkey, specifying that 'these negotiations are an open-ended process, the outcome of which cannot be guaranteed beforehand' and that they depend on the absorption capacity of the EU as much as on the capacity of Turkey to assume its obligations; should it not be able to do so, Turkey must be 'fully anchored in the European structures through the strongest possible bond'. But the evolution of the party and of the regime today inspires a more lively disquiet, given the extent to which arbitrariness rules today in that country.

Far from gradually approaching the EU, Turkey, after an initial positive phase, has sunk again into an authoritarianism which is incompatible with European values. The uncertainties were aggravated after the Turkish State declared a state of emergency, following a failed attempt at a coup d'état on 15 July 2016. In the face of the disproportionate measures it adopted, on 24 December 2016 the European Parliament officially requested the freezing of the accession process (*European Parliament resolution of 24 November 2016 on EU-Turkey relations*, 2016/2993[RSP]). This is also presently the position of Angela Merkel.

These external pressures bring to light the difficulty that the Member States have in sharing a common position. The Eastern European Member States are less sensitive to the problems of the Mediterranean. The commercial relations of certain Member States with Russia discourage them from applying sanctions, while the countries bordering on Russia live in fear of their neighbour. The repressive measures of Turkey irritate some Member States, but others are more interested in the global strategy coordinated with Ankara on 18 March 2016 to reduce migration toward Europe (the plan, as illustrated in a joint EU-Turkey 'declaration', has the aim of offering Syrian refugees safe and legal access to the EU, and reducing illegal migration; http://www.consilium.europa.eu/en/press/press-releases/2016/03/18/eu-turkey-statement/).

Some commentators explain these tensions and the difficulties of the EU in forming a bloc with reference to the various enlargements that have taken place, which have brought together extremely heterogeneous Member States.

II. The Question of Enlargement Reopened

A. Enlargement Justified by History

The founding fathers firmly rejected the artificial division of Yalta between western and Soviet spheres of influence. Established during a series of conferences that were held between 4 and 11 February 1945, on the banks of the Black Sea, between the leaders of the Allies, Joseph Stalin, Winston Churchill and Franklin D Roosevelt, it arbitrarily split the European continent into two blocs. Ideological division and decades of 'separate life' widened the division.

With the fall of the Berlin Wall and the subsequent emancipation movement, the central and eastern European countries regained their liberty, but they had to build a new future for themselves. In an exceedingly short period of time the question of their entry into the European Economic Community (EEC) was raised. At the start of the 1990s, the French president François Mitterrand proposed the idea of a 'confederation'. In the end, on account of the fluid character of his proposal, the vision of a full and integral accession was established.

In Germany, the will to pacify and normalise the relations with neighbours near and far, all victims of the Nazi catastrophe, became an absolute priority. From the moment of unification, under the urging of chancellor Helmut Kohl and of the Foreign minister Hans-Dietrich Genscher, the country concluded a series of bilateral treaties which pressed the countries of eastern Europe toward accession to the EU. France followed the same approach, although less programmatically.

With the end of the Cold War, Vienna literally recovered its *Hinterland*, that is, the old area of influence of its Habsburg Empire. Northern Italy, too, was reintegrated into that *Mitteleuropa* of which it had once been a part.

In one of his recent articles ('La terza alba della Mitteleuropa. Dopo gli inverni, una nuova sfida' (9 April 2013) *Corriere della Sera* https://www.micciacorta.it/2013/04/la-terza-alba-della-mitteleuropa/:

> a politico-economic space dominated by the Austro-Germans and the Hungarians. When one says *Mitteleuropa*, rather than using the merely geographical expression central Europe, one indicates a multilingual and multicultural mosaic crossed by common elements which underlie national differences. [...] Today more than ever there is need of that Mitteleuropean civilisation, so sensitive to hardship, so diffident in the face of all totalising political and philosophical systems which command the world to march like an army and which claim to triumphally interpret and guide the march of History itself.

Certainly, the wounds suffered and decades of reciprocal ignorance have complicated the process of accession. Most likely the 'western' Europeans did not exert themselves enough in explaining the aims of the Community project, such as the consequences of accession in terms of sovereignty and the relations with the United States (where the 'diaspora' of central and eastern Europe is particularly strong).

Apart from these difficulties, Europe was able in a rather short period of time – a result which would have been inconceivable only a few years before – to reunite the European States, which for the entire Cold War had been adversaries and which had even verged on nuclear war (see the 2015 German television miniseries *Deutschland 83*, set in the epoch of the Euromissile crisis). In Germany, Gerhard Schröder, having arrived at the federal chancellery in October 1998, continued Kohl's work, also evoking German responsibility in the face of the countries of central and eastern Europe (see his speech to the German Parliament of 10 November 1998; http://dip21.bundestag.de/dip21/btp/14/14003.pdf).

In the end, the enlargement of the EU permitted the exportation of its democratic values and its market economy into all the Member States. Articles 49 and 6 of the TEU effectively define the conditions which the countries must meet if they would like to accede to the EU.

Reference is made to the 'criteria of eligibility approved by the European Council', adopted in Copenhagen in 1993 and reinforced in 1995 and in 2006:

(a) respect for human rights, for the fundamental freedoms and for the rights of minorities;
(b) a functioning market economy capable of sustaining competition;
(c) the acceptance of the EU *acquis*, that is, the accumulated laws and obligations which unite the States as Members of the Union;
(d) inserted *in extremis* in 2006, the 'Union's capacity to absorb new members, while maintaining the momentum of European integration'.

It is indisputable that accession to the EU is a determining factor for modernisation and democratisation, that it has had good results in central and eastern Europe, after having sustained, during the 1980s, the march of the southern countries (Spain, Greece and Portugal) toward democracy.

On 6 December 2002, in Brussels, Romano Prodi (president of the European Commission) enumerated the advantages which had pushed the ten new Member States toward accession, thus: 'stability, prosperity, solidarity, democracy and freedom' (p 2). More recently, the former Kosovan Minister of European Integration, Vlora Çitaku, declared that 'for us, to enter the European Union is synonymous with peace and stability' (television interview for touteleurope.eu, Paris, 25 November 2013; https://www.touteleurope.eu/actualite/vlora-citaku-pour-nous-rentrer-dans-l-ue-est-synonyme-de-paix-et-de-stabilite.html).

B. The Enlargement and Development of the EU

There were also strategic reasons which justified the enlargement: a broader and more populous EU would have a greater weight in the world, both in the economic sphere and in the diplomatic one. Unfortunately, this last objective, lacking an adequate deepening action, was never reached. And yet in the 1990s and in the first years of 2000 the idea was kept well in mind, as is indicated by the positions of the European commissioner for trade, Pascal Lamy (2002), or the European strategy with regard to security approved in December 2003 (replaced by the global strategy of the EU on 28 June 2016).

Economic interests also represented an important component of enlargement. On the one hand, the founding States opened their single market and their free movement space to the new Member States; on the other hand, they benefited in their turn from the opening of new markets. The French president Jacques Chirac and chancellor Kohl separately visited Warsaw and the other central European capitals to promote acceleration of the timescales for accession. On 12 September 1996, Chirac addressed the two Chambers of the Polish Parliament (the Sejm and the Senat) to express his support for a rapid integration of the county in the EU, and at the same time to exhort the French enterprises to 'have a yet greater spirit of conquest'. The hosting president, Aleksander Kwaśniewski, strongly reinforced the message, affirming that 'between France and Poland, we have to pass from Chopin to Michelin' (P Haski, 'Chirac invite la Pologne dans l'UE. À Varsovie, il a souhaité que l'intégration ait lieu dès l'an 2000' (1 September 1996) *Libération*).

C. A Policy of Enlargement Justified by Geopolitical Motivations

Since the aforementioned Copenhagen 'criteria of eligibility' of 1993 are founded on the values of peace and democracy, admission into the EU consolidates and facilitates the *process of internal pacification* of those new Member States which in the previous years had seen disorder or armed conflict. On the other hand, a refusal might provoke in the rejected candidate a distancing from those values, if not even an outright radicalisation.

In the third millennium, various 'neighbour' States to the EU have seen popular revolutions that demanded greater democracy and transparency in their political system, and expressed their hope in a rapprochement with the EU. In November 2003, in Georgia, the 'revolution of roses' brought Mikhail Saakašvili to power, consenting him to then promote a policy of pro-European reforms. In December 2004, the 'orange revolution' in Ukraine brought the pro-European Victor Juščenko to the presidency of the Republic. According to a study of the European Parliament on the politics of the areas near the Union, 'it seems, therefore, that EU enlargement can act as a catalyst for reform in the eastern neighbourhood, but only sometimes, since some undemocratic regimes are able to shore up their power and stifle the opposition' (Perchoc (2015) 11).

These popular movements found themselves before the opposition of Russia, which views with diffidence a western influence in which it considers its own zone of influence (that is, the ex-Soviet bloc). On 25 April 2005, in its sixth annual message to Parliament, Russian president Vladimir Putin defined the collapse of the USSR as 'the greatest geopolitical catastrophe of the 20th century'. Then from words he passed over to deeds.

The war in Donbass, which broke out in Ukraine in April 2014, is an example of this. Putin denounced the will to dominion on the part of the United States. 'This is an attempt to freeze the present global order with the existence of a single leader [the United States], which established itself in the course of the decades after the fall of the Soviet Union', he declared the day after his meeting with president Hollande and chancellor Merkel on the project of a peace plan for Ukraine ('Poutine dément vouloir faire la guerre mais s'en prend aux Etats-Unis' (7 February 2015) *La Tribune*).

Thus, while the opposition between the blocs gathered around the great powers (the United States, Russia, China) is still topical, the enlargement of the EU was perceived as a way of limiting the Russian influence on the countries of the East. Consider the accusations levelled against the United States for having employed certain NGOs (Non-Governmental Organisations) to finance pro-European political groups in Ukraine. Or consider what happened in November-December 2013: on 28–29 November in Vilnius, Latvia, on the occasion of the third Eastern Partnership Summit (the programme of association of the EU with certain countries of the ex-Soviet Union), the Ukrainian prime minister Victor Janukovič refused to sign the planned association agreement between his country and the Union; in compensation, on 17 December the Ukrainian government obtained 15 billion dollars' worth of aid from Russia. These occurrences unleashed a period of fierce popular protests in Ukraine which culminated one year later in the aforementioned 'orange revolution'.

Thus there can be no doubt: the policy of EU enlargement was justified. And yet it has generated great difficulties.

D. Growth of Opposition to the EU

In England, the free movement of citizens of central and eastern European origin has without doubt favoured the rejection of the EU. And yet it was precisely the various British governments that desired it so strongly. According to a statistic published by the market research firm YouGov, the determining factor for the Brexiteers in their choice of vote was the desire that Great Britain might act in an independent way (45 per cent), followed by the aspiration for a better management of immigration (35 per cent) and by economic questions (8 per cent; YouGov, *Time survey results*, 22 June 2016; https://d25d2506sfb94s.cloudfront.net/cumulus_uploads/document/atmwrgevvj/TimesResults_160622_EVEOFPOLL.pdf).

In the other Member States, the opposition to the EU has similar motivations, stemming from various consequences of expansion.

Competition in the labour force originating in central and eastern Europe – It is necessary in the first place to make a distinction between free movement of permanent workers and the so-called posting of workers. One speaks of posting when an employer temporarily sends one of their dependents to work in another country. To avoid the effect of social dumping, the European directive which regulates posting (96/71/EC, 16 December 1996; http://www.secola.org/db/3_60/en-96-71-ec.pdf) stipulates that the salary of the country of arrival should be applied. However, to protect employees and to guarantee them a contributory continuity, the tax burdens remain those of the country of origin. It has happened that unscrupulous employers have profited from fraudulent posting of workers, and the suspicions surrounding this practice are exacerbated by these frauds.

The enlargements of 2004 and 2007 substantially expanded the EU: its Member States passed from 15 to 27, its surface augmented by more than 25 per cent and its population by more than 20 per cent; however, its wealth grew only by 5 per cent.

After the accession, the economic development of the 'new' Member States accelerated, thanks to the financial support of the EU (through structural funds), but also thanks to access to its internal market. They therefore obtained a net gain.

These countries grew also thanks to the wealth produced by their citizens in the 'old' Member States, which was then sent back to their homeland. The 'old' Member States could count on a low-cost workforce. Even if these individuals worked hard in thankless jobs (butchers, fruit and vegetable harvesters, personal services, etc), a sense of frustration spread in the local populations, which were convinced that they were suffering from unfair competition, above all in the field of transport and construction. In France, during the referendum campaign of 2005 on the ratification of the project of the EU Constitution, the opponents of the treaty leveraged on the myth of the so-called Polish plumber; and yet less than 3 per cent of Europeans live in another Member State. These anxieties are more a bugbear worked up by the Eurosceptics than an economic reality.

For some years the European Commission has been working to safeguard the equilibrium between fair competition in terms of wage and social costs and free movement of workers. On 8 March 2016, the Commission proposed a revision of the rules on posting of workers in the area of the EU, so as to adapt them to present needs. Soon this revision will be submitted to the scrutiny of the European Parliament.

Sense of 'uncontrolled liberalisation' – The European bloc oscillates between contrary positions also on the question of trade openness.

In a report presented on 8 May 2010 by Mario Monti (*Una nuova strategia per il mercato unicoal servizio dell'economia e della società europea. Rapporto al Presidente della Commissione europea,* José Manuel Barroso) four groups of countries are distinguished on the basis of their different expectations for the common market (https://www.ecc-netitalia.it/files/Una%20nuova%20strategia%20per%20il%20Mercato%20Unico_Mario%20Monti%20-%20Maggio%202010.pdf, *I timori degli Stati membri* (29–32)):

- The continental countries with social market economies, particularly critical of the competition and more generally of the regulations relative to the single market, on account of the greater attention they give to social problems.
- The Anglo-Saxon countries that, at least until Brexit, have favoured the opening of the market and an energetic policy of competition. They respond to worries of a social order by concentrating on the growth of the market. The Anglo-Saxon countries played a decisive role in the integration of the single market and in the policy of European competition.
- The new Member States, which on account of their political and economic history would like to recuperate the time they have lost in decades of ineffectual economy management, and are fervent supporters of the market and of competition. Moreover, as they are the latest arrivals, and are often of small dimensions, they care greatly about the strict application of the rules of the single market and of competition, which guarantee them an equal treatment with respect to the old Member States. Their enthusiasm represented a new boost to the single market during a period in which the financial crisis attenuated, at least for the moment, the force of conviction in the Anglo-Saxon countries in their defence of the market.
- The Nordic Countries, which have successfully harmonised the opening of the market and social protection, basing this last above all on security nets for individual workers.

Keeping these different categories in mind, Monti's new strategy to combat the erosion of confidence in the single market proposes a 'proactive' and global approach, also integrating policies that are not generally thought to be connected to the single market (competition policies, industrial policies, energy and transport policies, digital policies, social and environmental policies). The initiatives proposed aim at making a consensus emerge, which might reinforce the single market. Unfortunately, the report was applied only in part.

The EU must however continually attempt to reconcile the interest of the States with their differing experiences and traumas, so as to pursue the construction of the European edifice by reconciling contradictory expectations. Certainly, greater attention should be paid to the psychological and cultural aspects of the question. But geopolitical pitfalls and the common economic and environmental challenges are as many reasons to persevere.

E. Difficulty in Functioning Owing to Numbers

Obviously, it is more difficult for 28 States to come to a decision than six, above all when unanimity is required (as in the case of fiscal matters). The same difficulty is encountered in the field of harmonising the respective national regulations.

Moreover, it is natural that there should be difficulties in comprehension between 28 Member States with very heterogeneous histories, cultures, political regimes and interests. It might be arduous to find a common position, for example, on the issues of foreign policy or with respect to the economic and migratory crises. Many citizens hold that so heterogeneous a Europe is unmanageable.

The effects of these numbers and their heterogeneity are experienced also within the Community institutions. The new framework of the European Commission, with one 'representative' per State, has profoundly modified its nature. This Commission, an institution which is supposed to be independent from the States, incarnates the general interest of the Union, pursuant to article 17(1) TEU. It originally counted nine members, six originating from the major countries (Germany, France and Italy) and three from Benelux. Until 1 May 2004, a certain equilibrium was maintained, with 10 commissioners from five 'major' States and 10 from 10 'minor' ones: all national sensibilities had the opportunity to express themselves, and at the same time the States with numerous populations felt themselves to be adequately represented. With the arrival of the new Members, the Union undertook a kind of 'nationalisation' of the commissioners: the Treaty of Nice which came into force in 2003) permitted the enlargement of the Commission to 10 new members, with a commissioner for every State. This is a wretched solution, because it compromises the independence of the commissioners (who could now be confused with national 'representatives') and provokes a dispersion of the Commission's tasks, which is detrimental to its good functioning.

Inadequate budget – The EU budget did not expand at the same rate as enlargement. Today it is particularly reduced, as it comes to not even 1 per cent of the GDP of the Member States. Originally, the Community was able to finance itself thanks to the profits generated by its market and by the taxes on products imported from outside of the zone. But little by little, as the customs duties were lowered, the quantity of its own resources (that is, of a specifically European origin) was drastically reduced. So much so that today the Union depends on the contributions of the single States, agreed upon during very tense negotiations, which little take into account the general interest. Not only: given the fact that a good part of the credits are still absorbed by the common agricultural policy (CAP) and by the structural funds, the resources allocated to future issues, such as control of external borders, innovation and digitisation, tend to be insufficient.

Relationship between the 'major' and 'minor' States – Following its progressive enlargement, the EU is today composed of States which one might call 'major' and 'minor' States, on the basis of the breadth of their population, territory, and economy. There has been a shift from a (more than legitimate) over-representation of the minor Members to a demand for equality among the States, which is much less commendable. The most evident example is the presence of a 'nationalised' Commission, the result of demands for equality on the part of the minor States (see above); and today certain German *Länder* are much wealthier and more populated than many Member States. This has provoked a certain nervousness in the major States, even though the double majority vote (of States and of population) adopted by the Treaty of Lisbon (articles 16, TEU and 238, TFEU, Treaty on the Functioning of the European Union) represents significant progress.

F. A Short-Sighted Management

Enlargement without deepening – Contrary to what was hoped by the founding fathers, the enlargement of the EU was not accompanied by an adequate deepening. And yet the arrival of numerous new States and their heterogeneity would have justified a revision of the architecture of a Community originally conceived for only six States.

In 1997, after the signing of the Treaty of Amsterdam – which left certain fundamental institutional questions open – three of the founder States – France, Belgium and Italy – publicly declared that the 'the Treaty of Amsterdam does not meet the need, reaffirmed at the Madrid European Council, for substantial progress towards reinforcing the institutions'. Still in the same declaration, one reads: 'such reinforcement is an indispensable condition for the conclusion of the first accession negotiations' (Agence Europe, 15 and 16 September 1997; https://europa.eu/european-union/sites/europaeu/files/docs/body/treaty_of_amsterdam_en.pdf). Institutional reform was presented as an indispensable condition of the expansion of the EU.

In December 2000, on the occasion of the Nice European Council, the question was once more on the agenda. But the Fifteen (the number of the EU States at that time), for want of political courage on the part of the French president, limited themselves to a minimal institutional reform: consecration of the right to veto, a hypertrophic Commission (the major States renounced their second commissioners, conceding that all future Member States should have a commissioner) and reinforced national claims.

It was on this basis, as fragile as it is dubious, that the enlargement of 1 May 2004 took place. Also in Nice, perhaps on account of their bad conscience, the governments committed to pursuing the negotiations for institutional reform ('Declaration No. 23 on the future of the Union' *Official Journal of the European Communities*, C 80/85, 10 March 2001). Thus a Convention was instituted, charged with the drafting of a European Constitution. The result was a plan for a constitutional treaty, approved in an abridged version in the European Council of 17–18 June 2004, but rejected by France and by the Netherlands through the May–June 2015 referendum, and thus never adopted.

The 2009 Treaty of Lisbon, approved after years of vacillation, did not modify the institutional triangle. Though far indeed from the objectives of the constitutional treaty, it nonetheless has the merit of introducing a certain degree of simplification (abolition of the 'pillars' of Maastricht, clarification of the distribution of powers) and a greater degree of democracy (the Charter of fundamental rights becomes legally binding, the right of petition is recognised to the citizens, the prerogatives of the national parliaments are reinforced). The Treaty also defines the fields of action of the Union more clearly: recognition of the legal status of the EU, extension of the legislative powers of the Parliament, adoption of the double majority principle, lengthening of the term of the president of the European Council to two years, entrusting the election of the president of the Commission to the European Parliament (through a majority of the Members that compose it), institution of the post for High Representative of the Union for Foreign affairs and Security policy, reinforcement of the Eurogroup (a coordination forum which gathers the Finance ministers of the eurozone), introduction of new methods of cooperation in matters of defence, justice and international affairs.

With a view to a true deepening of the European project, the Treaty of Lisbon represents an important, but nonetheless insufficient, step forward. Moreover, some of the measures adopted reflect still certain mistrust toward the EU and the Commission. In fear of raising suspicions of federalism, it rejected the adoption of a clearer terminology and the simplification of legal instruments, including all the symbols connected to federalism. It is distressing that certain countries accepted these on an individual level (Treaty of Lisbon, annex, 'Final act of the intergovernmental conference' *Official Journal of the European Union*, C 306/02 267; https://eur-lex.europa.eu/legal-content/EN/TXT/PDF/?uri=OJ:C:2007:306:FULL&from=EN).

The indispensable participation of the national Parliaments constitutes a form of control (through the 'yellow' and 'red cards') rather than a harmonious collaboration between several decisional levels involved in the same project (article 5(3), all. 2, TEU, and article 12b, TEU and protocol No. 2 'On the application of the principles of subsidiarity and proportionality').

Despite everything, the EU continued to enlarge with the accession of Croatia on 1 July 2013. But today, facing the various crises, the process seems to have suffered a setback. The dynamic has slowed.

Incomplete accession criteria – The already cited criteria of Copenhagen of 1993, and in particular the fourth (the 'Union's capacity to absorb new members, while maintaining the momentum of European integration'), have neglected the essential. Cold and technical, they neglect the human aspects; they make no reference to a common project capable of mobilising the Europeans and giving them a sense of belonging. The governments are concentrating on what one might call the *hardware*: democracy and human rights, economy and market, capacity to sustain competition, assimilation to the EU *acquis*. However they have requested nothing in terms of *software*: among the necessary accession criteria there is no mention of the capacity to reconcile with one's own neighbours and to call one's own history into question, nor the acceptance of the supranational character of the Union.

The EU should have established more ambitious and more complete criteria. According to certain commentators, the enlargement process was a way of 'making Europe' by conserving the illusion that nothing would have to be ceded in the way of sovereignty. 'Making Europe without unmaking France', as the French prime minister put it on 28 May 2001, in a speech given in Paris (*L'avenir de l'Europe élargie*).

Not only: the collaboration with the new Member States has never sufficiently involved the societies of the founding countries. And yet the differences in culture, ideology and mentality require a labour of reciprocal rapprochement, above all through the learning of their respective languages and town-twinning arrangements. And this is still more important when we are dealing with distant countries and countries which had been divided by the iron curtain.

In one of his writings, the great Czech writer Milan Kundera (1983) describes central Europe as a culture or a destiny of incredible richness. A crucible of little nations mistreated by History, it is distinguished by a personal vision of the world, diffident in the face of totalitarian powers and profoundly tied to Europe. 'It's the disabused view of history that is the source of their culture, of their wisdom, of their 'nonserious spirit' that mocks grandeur and glory'.

This painful history, this culture rich with great writers, composers and painters, deserves to be known by the Europeans of the West. One might have hoped for more from the cultural and human dialogue around the EU, if for no other reason than to improve the European project together.

Lack of open political debate – Enlargement was never the object of an open political debate. The debate over the purpose of the EU was eluded.

The citizens, moreover, were almost always kept out of the enlargement process. It was treated as a diplomatic affair conducted by the executive power, and not as a democratic choice, so much so that the approval on part of national parliaments was provided for only in the final phase.

In contrast to what had been done in 1973 for the United Kingdom, Denmark, and Ireland, recourse to a referendum was not allowed in the latest enlargements – both for the ratification of the accession treaty of Austria, Sweden, and Finland in 1995, and for the admission of the 'Ten' in May 2004. The referendum was certainly not the only road that could be taken. Indeed, the EU is composed of representative democracies. But the national Parliaments must be the true centres of the debate and assume their responsibilities.

The European Parliament exercises partial control, since it can furnish an 'assent' expressed through the absolute majority of its members (article 49(1), TEU). But this assent is adopted only toward the end of the negotiations with the candidate country, after the signature of the treaty of accession. Though it draws up interim reports, the Parliament does not have the same supervisory power during the previous stages (presentation of candidacy, recognition of candidate status, opening and conduct of negotiations). In particular, the decision to open negotiations, the most important of all, is not sufficiently debated; once it has been taken at the highest level, that of the European Council, it is difficult to back away.

On the other hand, politicians of various orientations, who brought the Union from six to 28 members, almost never presented themselves before the people to explain their reasons or to give an account for them. They did not seek to objectively present the advantages and the disadvantages of the new accessions. Being little convinced themselves, they were almost not at all convincing.

This exclusion of the public opinion contributed to weakening the legitimacy of the EU enlargement, of the European edifice as a whole and more generally of democracy.

The politicians have led us to believe in the possibility of a perpetual enlargement, nourishing the hope or the frustration of the populations. As Giuliano Amato (2004) said, 'when the Americans want to exercise a strong influence on another country, they usually invade it. When we want to exercise an influence on another country, we usually propose accession to the Union' (p 15).

The EU was not the victim so much of enlargement – which should be considered a positive fact, for all the reasons mentioned above – as of the way in which this was managed, and the lack of awareness of what was at stake. Today the gravity of the situation urges a reformation of the European policies and of the European institutions themselves.

III. Lessons for the Future of the European Union

Too often the pro-Europeans regard the anti-European or even simply the Eurosceptic parties with condescension. This is an error. Many defects of the Union are evident; many errors have been committed and require immediate correction. The populist propaganda feeds in part off of the faint-heartedness of all those who ought to defend the European project. A radical change presupposes, on the one hand, the remediation of specific deficiencies so as to restart the EU and, on the other hand, to get back to work, even in small numbers, encouraging a model for a multi-speed Europe.

A. Restarting the European Union

It is important that the EU draws a lesson from the crises that it has undergone and that it is undergoing now. It must above all remedy its defects in the field of democracy, improve the implementation of its decisions, and propose a more mature European project.

Insufficient democratic legitimacy – It is a widespread opinion today that the EU suffers from a *democratic deficit.*

But analysts and detractors often forget that the crisis of democracy is considerably wider.

The phenomenon involves the other western democracies as well, above all the United States. The election of Donald Trump demonstrates the breadth of the crisis of confidence, which is artfully ridden by unscrupulous politicians.

So far as the EU goes, the problem arises above all in the interweaving of various levels of public action, on the part of the States and the Union.

Considering the ever more important role played by the European Council, which assembles the Members' heads of State and government, the core of the problem has been clearly identified by the great German philosopher Jürgen Habermas (2011): the EU suffers from having become a system of 'executive federalism' ((2012) 52).

The problem is not so much, as one often hears, the non-elected Commission – which all things told is well enough controlled by the European Parliament and can even have a motion of censure brought against it – but the anomalous primacy of the Council. The principal executive body, the European Council, is not elected as such, holds its sittings behind closed doors and gives no account of the whole process to the citizens. Every national parliament checks its respective government – at least in parliamentary democracy – but in their totality they are not accountable. Since opacity reigns, the national leaders commandeer the European debate, with sometimes grave consequences, as the crisis of the euro and the negotiations with the United Kingdom of February 2016 have demonstrated (see S Goulard, *Goodbye Europe* (2016) 35).

If choices are not made openly, errors cannot be punished. As in 2010, in Deauville, when the French president Nicolas Sarkozy and chancellor Merkel took the decision to obtain redress in a brutal manner from the private creditors of Greece. The decision, which was never the object of debate, precipitated the crisis. In the same way, no lesson was drawn from the collective error of judgement on the appalling agreement stipulated on 18–19 February 2016 between the European Council and the United Kingdom, which reinforced the special status of the latter within the EU. In democracy, this is unacceptable.

A Europe without a voice – On the other hand, the absence, or worse yet, the misrepresentation of Europe in the press and in public speeches is detrimental.

In the better part of the Member States, the national media, which are a fundamental element of democracy, rarely speak of the Union in a favourable way, or else they demonstrate indifference. This silence reinforces the prejudices regarding a technocratic, expensive, useless, even dangerous EU. The citizens are not informed and have no points of reference when they vote for a referendum or elect their members of the European Parliament (MEPs).

The principal French television channel, TF1, has never deemed it useful to have a permanent correspondent in Brussels. Various newspapers flaunt Eurosceptic positions, such as the *Sun*, the *Telegraph*, or the *Daily Mail* in Great Britain.

The appearance of European media – bearers of a pan-European point of view, and one not connected to a specific Member State – might perhaps evolve the public opinion, but for now their distribution is limited to a restricted public. This is the case for the American newspaper *Politico*, addressed essentially to an audience of specialists.

Scarred by the experience of the war, strongly inspired by an ideal, the founding fathers undertook to explain their vision to the general public with enthusiasm and humility. Thus, Jean Monnet (1888–1979) dedicated great energy to the dissemination of his ideas through an action committee (*Comité d'action pour les États-Unis d'Europe* (1955)), including the representatives of labour unions and parties (and he would have liked to include also workers). Today, the political leaders have more contacts with employers than with labour unions, and the representatives of the workers themselves no longer have, at least in France, the influence they once did. One does not address oneself to the segments of the population which feel excluded (the unemployed, the precarious workers, etc).

Moreover, the present-day political debate tends to *concentrate on national interests* in the short term. The populist formations embrace an egoistic logic, the vanity of which is encapsulated by the Trump slogan, 'America first'. The British prime minister May holds indefensible positions. In this context of all-out simplifications, promotion of the European compromise becomes very difficult.

Despite its representative offices, located in the capitals and in the principal European cities, the Commission remains an institution unknown to the citizens, who also generally know nothing about the European role of their national ministers and the prerogatives of their MEPs. The parties often send personages to Brussels who are shallow and little inclined to commitment. And yet, the EU will not be heard if it does not have solid points of reference at the national level. Moreover, many legitimate questions remain unanswered, the fears are not alleviated, and the lies multiply with ease. The 'media coverage' of the European Parliament in France is particularly weak (37 per cent); the average European value is higher (60 per cent; Eurobarometer (October 2016)).

The 'European demos': requirement or consequence of a European democracy? – The non-existence of an already-constituted European people (*demos*) is an argument frequently utilised to demonstrate that the Union can never be democratic. Naturally, David Cameron ceded to this oversimplification in his Bloomberg speech of 23 January 2013, which cleared the way for Brexit.

Apart from being horribly static, this vision of the world ignores the historical truth. In ancient Athens, the *demos* was not anterior to the development of democracy. On the contrary, historians maintain that the *demos* of the city emerged only in the sixth century, at the behest of Cleisthenes, thanks to his exercise of new prerogatives. According to the scholar of Greek history, the Frenchman Claude Mossé (1971):

> Cleisthenes did not create Athenian democracy, but rather the conditions which would permit the birth of that democracy. He made all citizens equal before the law, a law that from then on would be the expression of the will of the entire demos (p 25).

The *demos*, therefore, is not a preliminary condition for the existence of a democracy, but a consequence of the conditions of equality between citizens (for a more detailed treatment, see S Goulard, M Monti, *La democrazia in Europa: guardare lontano* (2012) 71 et seq). Democracy transformed the family or tribal bonds into a new sense of belonging. In the same way, in nineteenth century Italy and Germany, there did not exist a homogeneous people at the moment of unification: union within the national crucible gradually gave life to the two nation-States. As compared to Jacobin France, the concept of belonging to Italy and Germany is much more varied, and this is a richness rather than a weakness.

It falls therefore to the policy makers but also to the whole of civil society to create, amplify, or implement the conditions necessary for consolidating the European people. There already exist certain instruments, such as the Erasmus exchange programme, cultural town-twinning arrangements between cities, and numerous European associations. But more can be done. And the joint operation of political power will do the rest.

The rapid development of new technologies, such as the Internet or Twitter, contributes to the dissemination of ideas beyond national borders. Notwithstanding possible degeneration (see C Cadwalladr, 'Google, democracy and the truth about Internet search' (4 December 2016) *The Guardian*), such instruments represent opportunities that the European Union ought to seize.

The need to better implement decisions – When it is a question of implementing the commitments made in Brussels, or furnishing financial means for a fruitful collaboration, everything becomes complicated.

In the first place, the rules are violated continuously. Such is the case with the Stability Pact, much reviled by the national political exponents; and some have gone so far as to publicly boast of their own nonchalant attitude. In a passage from a book interview (which was commented on less in France than elsewhere), Hollande explains that to violate the 3 per cent deficit rule is 'the prerogative of the major countries'; and he adds: 'something that many no longer [*sic*] accept' (F Lhomme and G Davet, *Un président ne devrait pas dire ça ...: les secrets d'un quinquennat* (2016)). And yet the EU is a community of law founded on equality. Reciprocal trust is indispensable to share a single currency.

There sometimes exist fundamental divergences on the means to employ so as to reach determinate objectives. Competition, for example, is considered by many countries of the EU as the best means for distributing resources and opening the markets to new participants. In France on the other hand it is demonised by a large portion of the political class and by the public opinion, notwithstanding the excellent work of the *Autorité pour la concurrence*.

Some pretend not to know that certain contentious issues have already been resolved, such as the independence of the ECB and the scope of its responsibilities (limited to the battle against inflation), which are even choices that were made already with Maastricht in 1992. The same thing holds for the German press, when it attacks the excessively lenient policy of the ECB in the name of German savers: the ECB does not act for the good of one country alone, even the most important, but of 19.

In this moment, the national leaders tend to avoid their responsibilities. They stubbornly resist every European project which would force them to take on risks in their internal politics. Thus, the Italian ex-prime minister Renzi accused the EU of hampering the reconstruction of Italy after the earthquake of 2016. And yet, it is thanks to the objective level reached by the Italian public debt (as well as, unfortunately, a certain corruption in the public markets of certain regions) that the country is not sufficiently equipped with buildings compliant with earthquake standards.

This comportment represents an important change with respect to the past: let us recall Mitterrand, who in 1983, during the Euromissile crisis, gave his support to Kohl, against the opinion of the entire European left. Or let us recall Kohl himself, who promoted a project for single currency, notwithstanding strong resistance from his own party.

The lack of commitment on the part of national leaders clears the way for every kind of unrest. The critiques turned against the EU are sometimes legitimate, but sometimes baseless, or even bereft of any relation to reality. One fears the lobbies which operate in Brussels, and does not see those which interfere with one's own national parliament. One denounces a commercial agreement with Canada, an allied country respectful of the rights of man, as 'unclear', and one is not alarmed by the multiple military cooperation agreements or arms supply made with Saudi Arabia or certain African countries.

Finally, the States have almost completely given up on certain objectives: what remains of the 'Europe as a global power' or the 'social Europe', so often promised in France at the end of the twentieth century? Who has done something, internally, in the face of hostile public opinion and lobbies (foremost among them those of the national diplomats), to see to it that such objectives might be realised?

In an interview with a French newspaper, Monti (2015), ex-European commissioner and Italian ex-prime minister, explained the matter thus:

> We have passed from a historical phase in which Europe was perceived as a grand investment for the future, which justified some sacrifice in terms of national interests, to a new phase in which the Union represents simply a commodity. National leaders no longer go to Brussels to add value to the European edifice, but to dismantle it piece by piece.

Paul-Henri Spaak expressed the matter of the European Community in this way: 'Those who measure their commitment to Europe by the approval they receive for having defended some particular interest, without worrying about the general interest and the future, are not equal to the historical mission which has been entrusted them' (interview with the Brussels newspaper *Le Soir*, 15 November 1969).

B. Realising a True European Project

To realise a true European project, it is necessary to act in the first place on the level of defence and external border control. The national governments reproach the Union for not having an effective European policy for defence and immigration. These critiques, which are repeated in the media, are largely shared by the public opinion. Often one hears the question: 'And Europe? What is Europe doing?'.

This is an evident example of denying reality, because the EU has neither the jurisdiction nor the means to act in areas of this kind. In 2001, Prodi proposed the creation of a European coast guard. In 2013, the European Parliament proposed augmenting the finances for Frontex, the European border and coast guard agency. These initiatives received a categorical rejection on the part of the Member States, which were worried about preserving their own national sovereignty. Rather than anticipating the needs created at the external borders of the EU by the disappearance of the borders between the Member States, they denied these needs altogether.

So far as the budget goes, the decision-making process is in the hands of the States alone. Indeed, with customs duties lowered, the budget of the EU is based ever less (as mentioned above) on properly European resources, and depends therefore to a large extent on national contributions. Now, in a climate dominated by the general dissemination of the slogan (once British) 'I want my money back', both the common interest and the imperative to solidarity wind up being denied. How can the concept of solidarity gain influence when everyone wants to recover all the money they have spent? Or when countries like Poland and Hungary recover 69 and 19 billion euro of European funds respectively during the period covered by the multiannual finance perspective, without feeling themselves tied to the common values?

Moreover, this situation brings it about that in the budget debate the European Parliament has been relegated to a marginal position. And yet, over the course of history, parliamentary democracy has been built through consensus in fiscal matters. Not to speak of the fact that the search for the general interest comes about through the concession of adequate funds, the determination of which must be discussed collectively.

The attitude of the States tends to create a worrying situation. However loath they are to augment their own contribution, the States simultaneously want to conserve the subsidies they have obtained: for example, the common agricultural policy in France, or the structural funds in the southern, central, and eastern European countries. This obstructs the transition toward a more far-sighted spending. The multiannual financial perspective voted in 2013 might have been fine in the last century, but it does not take into consideration new issues like internal security, research and innovation, and information technology.

Finally, although some progress is being made in the issue of fiscal convergence, there remain too many incomplete projects: the projects of social uniformity, the European judiciary, and European diplomacy have been obstructed (the last notwithstanding the efforts of Federica Mogherini, High Representative of the European Union for Foreign affairs and Security policy, and vice president of the Commission). The method of compromises devoid of a general vision, in which every national government haggles over every least concession, has rendered the EU ineffectual and unpopular.

It is not a question of asking 'more Europe' for every last thing, but rather of providing the means necessary for acting when Europe decides it wants to do so.

Recently (December 2016), an inter-institutional group guided by Monti published an excellent report, *Future financing of the EU. Final report and recommendations of the High level group on own resources* (http://ec.europa.eu/budget/mff/hlgor/library/reports-communication/hlgor-report_20170104.pdf), which denounces negligence and aberrations in the EU budget, requesting the institution of a simplified, transparent, and more democratic process of financing through own resources. The 10 analysts gathered around Monti (all members of the Council, of the Commission, or of the European Parliament) propose bold initiatives, such as the creation of a European tax (on electricity and fuel for cars) or the collection of funds through a European policy of border control or of the digital market. They hold that Brexit might represent a good opportunity to reform the budget without enduring pressures from Great Britain. The objective of such proposals is not so much to augment the EU budget as to choose appropriate sources for it, above all through the collection of own resources (article 311, TFEU). A reform of the kind would moreover permit a better distribution of the budgetary burden amidst the various Member States.

C. Sustain the Model of a 'Multi-Speed' Europe?

The possibility of a differentiation has long existed. Not all the countries of the European Community participated in the first European monetary system, the EMS, created in 1979. The Treaty of Maastricht of 1992 established conditions for entrance into the economic and monetary Union, and some countries had to carry out certain reforms before being able to reach the eurozone; others, such as the United Kingdom and Denmark, negotiated permanent derogations.

The Schengen area (a zone formed by the European States which have abolished the controls on persons at their common borders), which includes today only 22 of the Members of the EU, was originally constituted independently from the Community construction. More recently, the Treaty of Lisbon made recourse to 'enhanced cooperation' easier (introduced with the Treaty of Amsterdam, 1997): when it is not possible to secure unanimity of the 28 countries, as was the case for the European patent, a group of at least nine countries can decide to go ahead on a common project, leaving the others free to join them at a later moment.

The existence of a eurozone of 19 States in the sphere of a Union of 28 is perhaps the most evident example of an internal differentiation. Europe has need of a new political framework, with its own executive under the control of a Parliament, if we want to overcome the problems of transparency in inter-governmental management. Today, the Eurogroup does not answer to the European Parliament, and not even the European Court of Justice has any control over it. Many have hoped for a deepening of the process of integration: Jean-Claude Trichet, Mario Draghi, Herman Van Rompuy, the Commission, the European Parliament, and so forth.

According to some, it is necessary to restart the European project with a more limited kernel of Member States, for example the six founder States. The idea has been advanced on numerous occasions to construct such a project with a 'little Europe', or else thanks to an 'avant-garde' sustained by a new generation of courageous and ambitious pioneers.

This idea should not be dismissed, above all in a geopolitical context in which Trump openly mentions, and not without a certain relish, a disintegration of the EU. However, the question of the choice of the participants remains open: a 'limited' option might create unnecessary fractures within the continent.

A smaller number would probably favour a certain homogeneity, but it threatens to deprive the Union of the possibility of having sufficient weight, in the eyes of the world, on the level of its dimensions (population, economy, territory). The advantage of conserving a large market and the risk of a return to rival alliances on the European continent invite us to confront these questions with no taboos, but with discernment. For example, the (recent but significant) entry of the Baltic countries in the Eurozone notwithstanding the Greek crisis, necessitates a certain loyalty with regard to these partners.

In any case the joint exercise of sovereignty remains difficult, even for a limited group. For all those who are nostalgic for the period of collaboration 'of Six' (1951–73), in particular the French, it is worth recalling the failure of the European Defence Community (EDC) in 1954 and the political paralysis due to the 'empty chair crisis' (from 30 June 1965 to 30 January 1966, France – under the de Gualle government – boycotted the sittings of the Council of ministers of the Economic European Community). Even in Six things were not easy.

Rendered apprehensive by their historical experience, some recently acceded countries do not want to be considered 'second tier' Members. This was the mood which provoked their rejection of the European Confederation proposed in 1990 by Mitterrand.

An analogous controversy derived in 1994 from the 'central European core' elaborated in Germany by Karl Lamers (Christian-democratic spokesperson for questions of foreign policy) and by Wolfgang Schaüble (president of the CDU/CSU parliamentary group at the Bundestag and ex-minister of the Interior). In a document entitled *Reflections on European policy*, the two proposed a political union composed of few Member States, around a central French-German nucleus. The pretext of Italy's absence (that the creators of the project did not want so much to exclude it as to spur it to play a part) permitted the French authorities to refuse the proposal, which they held to be too 'federalist'. A fine missed opportunity.

In the present context two new elements should be considered. First of all, Brexit (supposing that it is carried through) changes the terms of the question: as of now, all the EU countries, except for Denmark (whose currency is however already tied to the euro), have implicitly made the commitment to enter into the eurozone for the long run. This is a return to the logic which inspired the Treaty of Maastricht, the logic of the single currency. It should not be forgotten, for example, that in the 1990s, prime minister Tony Blair promised once again to submit the adoption of the euro in the United Kingdom to a referendum vote. Moreover, article 3(4) of the TEU reads: 'The Union shall establish an economic and monetary union whose currency is the euro', while protocol No. 14 on the Eurogroup recognises 'the need to lay down special provisions for enhanced dialogue between the Member States whose currency is the euro, pending the euro becoming the currency of all Member States of the Union'. Not only: in a resolution of the European Parliament of 12 December 2013 (2012/2078[INI]) we read that 'if this supposedly transitory situation is to last, an appropriate accountability mechanism for the current euro area and the Member States committed to joining must be considered within Parliament'.

Although it rejected the single currency, the United Kingdom was granted an extraordinary statute which authorised it to participate in all the decisions regarding the eurozone, and to oppose any future revision of the treaties, including the provisions regarding the eurozone. From this point of view, Brexit represents a welcome simplification.

This does not mean that everything will be easier. The difficult question of the necessary connection, in the long term, between the monetary policy and defence policy remains open. The Treaty does not explicitly state it – and various States of the eurozone would prefer to remain neutral on this matter – but it is indisputable that these two aspects constitute the core of political sovereignty and should go hand in hand.

Among the non-delegable duties of the State are generally included the adoption of laws and the penalisation of those who violate them, through the monopoly on legitimate violence (police) and the judiciary. Toward countries abroad, on the other hand, the faculty of negotiating international rules and the management of the armed forces are enumerated. The exercise of these functions requires the ability to draw on own resources, furnished by the national collective through the instrument of taxation.

It is therefore difficult to separate monetary policy from defence policy. Europe cannot pretend to reinforce the sovereignty of its Member States without tackling the problems inherent in foreign and security policy. But the Member States have always shown themselves rather fearful and reticent about these issues, and certainly the present crisis, with the decline in mutual trust that derives from it, does not improve matters.

The new geopolitical context connected to the election of Trump and to the prospect of a rapprochement with the authoritarian regimes of Russia and Turkey will perhaps bring the positions of the Europeans up to date. But it cannot be said that they are ready, and time is pressing.

IV. Conclusions

If one thinks of what the Europeans have done, starting from the fall of the Berlin Wall, the balance appears in chiaroscuro.

Enlargement was a fundamental and necessary objective, for which the EU has no need to feel ashamed. Even if these passed in silence, there have been positive effects that should not be underestimated: in particular, the reprieve in the potential conflicts between minorities in central Europe, the 'containment' of Russia (consider the destiny of Ukraine), the democratisation and stabilisation of the new Member States.

The problems emerged early on, more than anything in the management of the enlargement on the part of the 'old' Member States: the refusal to launch serious institutional reforms has clipped the wings of the Community bodies, not to speak of the flippancy with which the implications of enlargement on the level of national identity have been confronted. The near-sightedness of Blair regarding the consequences of free movement of persons is perhaps the gravest example of this.

In the new accession countries, some individuals have quickly come to the conclusion that the entire process was spoilt and that they were only the victims of it. The souverainist politics of Orbán in Hungary and of the Law and Justice Party (*Prawo i sprawiedliwość*) in Poland represent a defeat, and not just for the EU, even if the civil society continues to courageously resist.

The errors and inadequacies are indisputable:

- Enlargement was considered, wrongly, as an objective in itself. To construct an *affectio societatis* it was necessary to know what the common objectives were. Instead, some used the policy of enlargement as a simple instrument of foreign policy (through the 'carrot' of accession).
- The EU has not undergone a serious process of deepening. This is today the result of a series of mediocre treaties (the Treaty of Amsterdam in 1997, the Treaty of Nice in 2000, the failed constitutional treaty which then became the Treaty of Lisbon). The aforementioned fourth Copenhagen criterion, namely the EU's 'capacity to absorb', has been neglected. If it had seriously been taken into consideration in due course, the Union would never have launched the Turkish adventure. The absence of real political will and team spirit have undermined the ambitious European project of the founding fathers.

- The citizens are excluded from the process of building the European edifice, thus nourishing the sensation of a Union which is distant and foreign, above all in the West (France, United Kingdom) and in the South (Italy) of the continent.

In the same period of time, the EU has had to face also the rise of a globalisation which was less cooperative than what one might have hoped, and a financial crisis which it did not have adequate instruments to react to.

Any European revival must pass through a critical examination of the last 25 years. But such exercise in introspection is senseless if it does not take into consideration the developments of 2016: the internal shock represented by Brexit and the external upheaval caused by the election of Trump. A cycle has closed which opened with the end of the Cold War, and perhaps even a longer and more important cycle, that which commenced at the end of World War II, if the change of direction undertaken by the new president of the United States is confirmed. We are living in a more uncertain universe, marked by new geopolitical, climactic, economic anxieties. In this context, the unity of the Europeans, however unattainable it might sometimes seem, conserves all of its pertinence and greatness. In the face of the egoism and the parochialism of the souverainists the commitment to unite people beyond borders is not an ambition of which we should be ashamed.

Bibliography

Amato, G, 'Comment mettre l'Union Europeenne en situation de bien fonctionner en s'elargissant?, and De l'accessibilité des documents européens et de la transparence des activités institutionnelles', in Europartenaires, Friedrich Ebert Stiftung, *Le projet de la gauche pour l'Europe elargie. Compte rendudu séminaire du 28 janvier*, ENA (Paris 200) 5–8; http://library.fes.de/pdf-files/bueros/paris/50146.pdf.

Habermas, J, *Zur Verfassung Europas: ein Essay* (Berlin, 2011) (English trans *The crisis of the European Union: a response* (Cambridge, 2012)).

Kundera, M, 'Un Occident kidnappé, ou La tragédie de l'Europe centrale' (1983) 5(7) Débat 3–23 (English trans in *New York Review of Books* (1984) 31(007) 33–38, https://is.muni.cz/el/1423/jaro2016/MEB404/um/Kundera_1984.pdf).

Lamy, P, *L'Union Européenne et les Etats-Unis face à la globalisation: un enjeu pour le monde*, speech given on occasion of the 2002 Cycle of the Conférences Glaverbel, Louvain-la-Neuve (28 October 2002) http://europa.eu/rapid/press-release_SPEECH-02-527_en.htm.

Monti, M, 'L'Europe est devenue un simple bien de consommation', interview with I Marchais (22 December 2015) *L'Opinion* https://www.sylviegoulard.eu/lopinion-interview-de-mario-monti-par-isabelle-marchais/

Mossé, C, *Histoire d'une démocratie: Athènes. Des origines à la conquête macédonienne* (Paris, 1971) 25 et seq.

Perchoc, P, *The European neighbourhood policy*, Research service of the European Parliament, PE 569.048, Luxembourg 2015; http://www.europarl.europa.eu/RegData/etudes/IDAN/2015/569048/EPRS_IDA%282015%29569048_EN.pdf).

Prodi, R, *L'Europe élargie: une politique de proximité comme clé de la stabilité*, 'Peace, security and stability – International dialogue and the role of the EU'", sixth ECSA-World conference. Jean Monnet Project, 5 and 6 December (Brussels, 2002); http://europa.eu/rapid/press-release_SPEECH-02-619_fr.pdf.

All web pages are understood as having last been visited on 18 June 2018.

The author thanks Sylvain Maréchal and Marie Alix Dadillon for their help in drafting this article.

Author's note: This text was written before being able to evaluate the outcome of the elections in the Netherlands and in France (held in March and April–May 2017, respectively). With the choice of the electors of these two Member States of the European Union, in a few months, what seemed to be a Eurosceptic wave subsided. The support for Europe is growing in many countries. Emmanuel Macron was elected president by the French citizens, after having maintained, during his electoral campaign, a very clear pro-European attitude; in particular, he promised to make the necessary reforms toward the end of once more giving France economic growth and strong credibility in foreign policy. At the centre of his vision are to be found extremely strong French-German relations and a revival of the democratic ambition of the Union and of the so-called eurozone. In consequence, we can expect that, on the one hand, he will not hesitate to stand up to the governments of Poland and Hungary should they negate the fundamental EU values or the conditions of fair competition; and, on the other hand, with regard to Brexit, he is ready to defend a rigorous and demanding conception of the single market and of European interests.

25

The Democratic Deficit

GIANFRANCO PASQUINO

It is said by some that there is a democratic deficit in the European Union (EU) – where, no one knows. Despite this, or perhaps precisely because of it, the critique of lack of democracy, or rather say of the democratic insufficiencies in the institutions, in the procedures, in the services and in the comprehensive functioning of the EU, is as wide-spread and persistent as it is, most likely, founded on shaky grounds, uncertain data, and badly formulated interpretations.

It seems that the term was used for the first time at the 1977 Congress of Berlin, by the supranational political movement *Jeunesse européenne fédéraliste*, which complained of a sense of alienation and a lack of confidence in the ability of the (European) political system to face the difficulties of the youths. The request to create institutions capable of resolving, on a European scale, problems that escaped the control of the Nation-States was pressed, somewhat contradictorily, in the direction of giving greater power to the lower levels, nearer to the people, and introducing democracy in local communities and in the workplace. Drawing it in part from this source, it was then the English Labourist David Marquand, in 1979, who was to launch the expression 'democratic deficit', considering it 'structural' (but by then, all the European institutions had been widely 'democratised') without, however, proceeding to clarify and deepen what he meant.

The best analytical, and perhaps essential, point of departure consists, on the one hand, in giving the most correct and most precise definition possible to the two terms, *deficit* and *democratic*; and on the other hand, thus equipped, in seeking out its possible and effective location. In which institutions, precisely? In the entire institutional circuit? Only once this indispensable terminological, conceptual, and 'spacial' work has been completed, will it become possible to deepen the discourse, to arrive, first of all, at a convincing assessment of the existence and the scope of the democratic deficit, and then, at the debated propositions for possible remedies and solutions.

I. Deficit

Deficit means, obviously, *lack*. Deficit indicates a disparity between expectations and realisations, between promise and performance, between constitutive tasks and the degree of success with which they have been carried out. It is possible to maintain that, over the course of time, ever more complex tasks have been attributed to the EU and, more precisely, to its institutions; that the promises have multiplied; that the expectations, as often occurs in a multiplicity of contexts, on account of the successes attained, have mounted. In consequence, deficit understood as disparity might be enlarged despite, or perhaps because of, what the EU has succeeded in doing for its Member States and for its citizens, thus contributing to the growth of their expectations. These last might regard the goods, of any given kind, that the citizens believe the EU should produce and distribute and which they expect from the EU; or else, they might refer to the EU institutions' mode of functioning, to their transparency and to the responsibility of the officeholders; or else, finally, to the role that the citizens intend to have and to perform and to their concrete participation in the government of the Union. From time to time, those who analyse not only the formation and the functioning of the EU, but also the relations between the citizens of the Union and its institutions, might make additions to and clarifications of the substantial meaning, only in some small mutable part, of the term 'deficit'. To the degree to which one refers precisely to a deficit defined as being *democratic*, it becomes, however, essential to clarify from the start what the word *democratic* might mean.

II. Democratic

Democratic is, above all, that which conforms to the exercise of power (*kratos*) of the people (demos). We know that all constitutions establish that the power, the sovereignty of the people (and I cite article 1 of the Constitution), 'is exercised by the people in the forms and within the limits of the Constitution'. In the case of the EU, in the absence of a proper Constitution, it is the Treaties, most recently that of Lisbon, which, read in sequence, delineate a more than significant list of the principles of constitutional value, to which, therefore, it is imperative to make reference for everything regarding institutions and citizens, tasks, powers, responsibilities, and, naturally, connections to the principles and values of democracy. However indispensable it might be, the connection between the power of the people and electoral procedures is naturally not sufficient to constitute and exhaust the content of the adjective *democratic*. Surely, the absence of electoral procedures for the formation of representative and governing institutions reflects the non-existence of democracy, but if, on the one hand, elections are only an element, albeit an absolutely essential and indispensable element for any political system which desires to remain democratic, on the other hand, democracy also requires, and is founded on, the recognition and the exercise, the protection and the promotion, of a wide and articulated battery of civil, political, and social rights.

However, the adjective *democratic* cannot be referred exclusively to the rules and to the modalities for the formation of institutions, but must regard their functioning with specific reference to two procedures: the first relative to representation (of the citizens), the second to *accountability*, which is to say, responsibilisation (of officeholders). Therefore, whoever desires to analyse the possible existence of a democratic deficit of or in the EU must know how to direct their gaze beyond electoral procedures, to encompass the functioning and the performance of the institutions, and the possibility that the officeholders in those institutions are competent to, that they desire to, that they are able to render account of their actions to their electors (and, perhaps, in a wider sense, to the public opinion).

All political systems can be evaluated individually, once specific criteria have been established with which to proceed in evaluation, by identifying the best indicators (for example, freedom, equality, participation, production, satisfaction) and making the necessary calculations. However, in order to know more, it is always necessary to proceed to opportune comparisons; both the citizens, even the least informed, and the most refined analysts, regularly resort to this method, more or less consciously. Having clarified the definitions of the terms *deficit* and *democratic* and having established this proviso of methodological caution concerning comparison, be it implicit or explicit, it is now possible to confront the overall problem, that is, whether there exists a democratic deficit in the EU, where, if it exists, it might be located and how extensive it might be, and what remedies are imaginable and practicable. I will proceed first to analyse the mode of formation and operation of each institution: the Parliament, the Council, the Commission (not the Central Bank and the Court of Justice, since these institutions are not held to requisites of democraticalness even in national political systems); I will then evaluate their performance. I will conclude with a comprehensive glance over all the elements of the political system of the Union, to understand in the most complete way possible, on the basis of what motivations the European citizens have come to consider the EU democratically deficit.

III. Electoral Deficit? The Parliament

Inevitably when one speaks of democratic deficit, one's focus races, before all, to the elections. Even if it is not always true that wherever there are elections there is democracy, it is absolutely true that there exists no democracy without free and fair electoral procedures which produce political consequences on the formation, the functioning, and the evaluation of the institutions put in place by the respective elections. Accordingly, in the search for a possible deficit in the European institutions, it is more than appropriate, it is truly imperative to proceed from the procedures through which the three most important institutions are put in place.

To begin with, inasmuch as it is elected by the citizens of the Member States of the Union, the European Parliament should not suffer from democratic deficit, as long as we limit the assessment of this deficit to electoral democracy. In truth, there are not a few scholars who underline how the electoral procedures in the broadest sense which lead to the formation of the European Parliament might be exceptionable, even from the point of view of electoral democracy itself. First, as has been acutely observed by Karlheinz Reif and Hermann Schmitt (1980), starting from the first election on the part of the citizens of the 1979 European Parliament (up till then the European parliamentarians were nominated by their colleagues, or rather, by the parties of national parliamentarians to which they belonged), the European elections are elections of a second order and degree. In the eyes of the leaders of the party, of the candidates themselves and of the citizens, they are considered to be of a clearly inferior importance with respect to national elections. Analysing the indispensable constitutive elements of a democratic election, the first element which reveals problems pertaining to democracy in the wide sense, is the decline, over the course of time, in voter turnout. Particularly worrying is the percentage of the participants in the most recent elections (May 2014), in which overall less than half of those with the right to vote participated, that is, 42.44 per cent (in Italy, a country of traditionally high participation, 57.22 per cent). The data relative to the Netherlands, one of the founding countries of the Union, are alarming – 37.32 per cent – and, above all, those of Slovakia, a Member State since 2004 – 13.05 per cent, the lowest participation absolutely.

To vote or not to vote are responses that the citizen electors give to the offers of policies, of candidates, of comprehensive vision that, a little bit in all national elections, the parties are forced to propose and to promise. These are therefore worrying signs: on the one hand, the decline in the capacity, if not even in the will, to mobilise their electorates through the national parties; on the other hand, the exceedingly limited interest for the European elections blatantly manifested by the principal political actors, with all the variations in the different cases, including also the evident inadequacies of the transnational parties and of the European parliamentary groups. Decline and disinterest of the parties oblige one to shift one's attention first onto the candidates, then onto the elected representatives, and, finally, onto those who seek re-election. Though it lacks the necessary comparable national statistical information, the available research (see, above all, *Routledge handbook of European elections* (2016)) concurs in signalling that there are but exceedingly rare cases in which the European electoral campaigns are conducted effectively in the name of explicitly and specifically European issues. On the contrary, the European electoral campaigns are often almost essentially a pallid continuation of the national ones. A significant paradox follows from this: it is the anti-European parties themselves, often classified en bloc as *populists* – a polemical label that does not correspond to reality, is misleading and often even counterproductive – who conduct campaigns strongly centred on the extent to which the Commission and the Parliament act in a dissatisfying way or, more often, against the 'national interests'. So far as the candidates go, while it is true that over the course of time the phenomenon of the election to the European Parliament of men (and, more rarely women) who have come to the end or almost to the end of their national politico-parliamentary careers has become rarer, it is also true that for many a seat in the European Parliament is often rather the springboard into a political career which these individuals subsequently prefer to continue on the national level.

Both these paths, in the form of a golden finale or else a promising beginning to a national political career, have important effects both on representation and on accountability. The elected representatives in the European Parliament, in an overwhelming majority, are aware that they represent parties whose members include many more citizens than have elected them, and, above all, they know they must account for their actions to those who have the power to re-nominate them, which is to say, to the leaders of the respective parties. Therefore, notwithstanding the existence of parliamentary Eurogroups composed of parliamentarians of akin European parties, it is not surprising that in the votes on specific national interests the needs of the national parties, duly communicated to their Members of European Parliament (MEPs), should be held in consideration almost as much as their kindred Europe policies, if not more. This, however, is the opinion of the

European citizens (see below). Yet more debatable than the ways the nominations to the European Parliament are pre-selected, is the process of reselection of the candidates, which has exceedingly little to do with their presences and their performance, but in the better part of the cases depends on the position occupied by the MEPs in the power-structure of the party to which they belong. All of this goes, obviously, to the almost total detriment of accountability. The candidates seeking renomination and re-election will obtain it more easily if they have been receptive to the needs and the preferences of their party leaders. It is known that a similar phenomenon occurs also in the case of candidacies in national elections, but in that of the European Parliament its negative impact on accountability is greater, in particular as regards the very functioning of the Parliament. Indeed, MEPs released from responsibility toward their electors would/will vote following indications, influences, and pressures of other actors, often of interested groups. Very briefly, a deficiency in democraticalness is to be found in the European Parliament already beginning from the electoral procedures that stand at the basis of its formation, and which, at least in part, affect its functioning.

Figure 1 Overall vision and opinions of the Europeans on the European Parliament (in percentages)

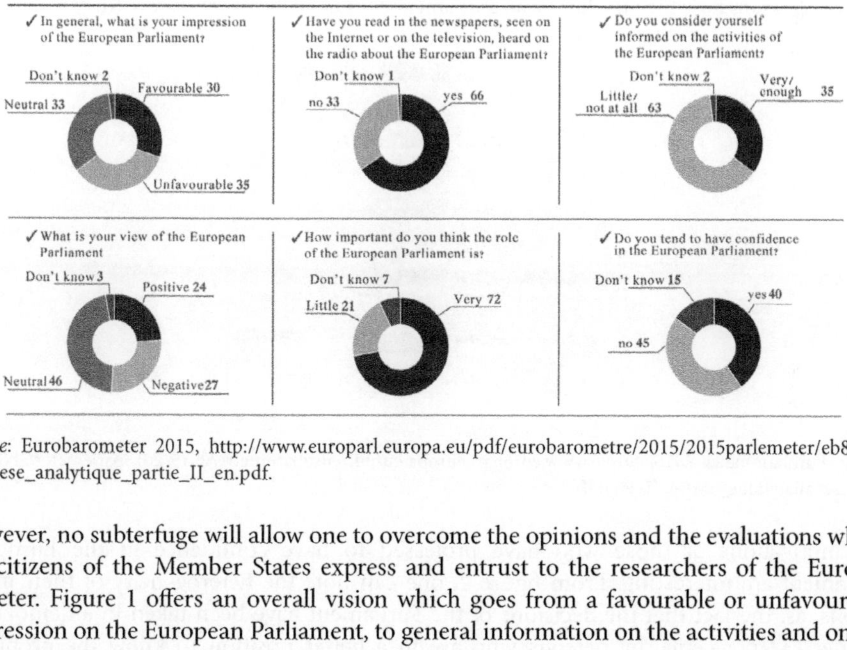

Source: Eurobarometer 2015, http://www.europarl.europa.eu/pdf/eurobarometre/2015/2015parlemeter/eb84_1_synthese_analytique_partie_II_en.pdf.

However, no subterfuge will allow one to overcome the opinions and the evaluations which the citizens of the Member States express and entrust to the researchers of the Eurobarometer. Figure 1 offers an overall vision which goes from a favourable or unfavourable impression on the European Parliament, to general information on the activities and on the role it plays, up to the level of confidence in it. It is not a very positive picture, still less if it is compared to the corresponding national Parliaments.

As for that, more or less two thirds of the European citizens interviewed had heard something about the European Parliament, not even one third of them derive a favourable impression and only about one fourth have a positive impression. However, no less than 72 per cent hold that the role of the European Parliament is very relevant; but only 40 per cent have confidence in the institution, as against 45 per cent who have none at all.

Figure 2 Reasons for which the European Parliament deserves confidence (in percentages)

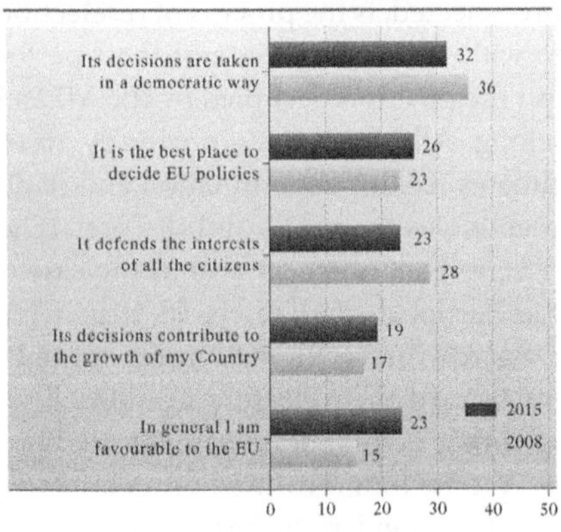

Source: Eurobarometer 2015, http://www.europarl.europa.eu/pdf/eurobarometre/2015/2015parlemeter/eb84_1_synthese_analytique_partie_II_en.pdf.

Figure 3 Reasons for which the European Parliament does not deserve confidence (in percentages)

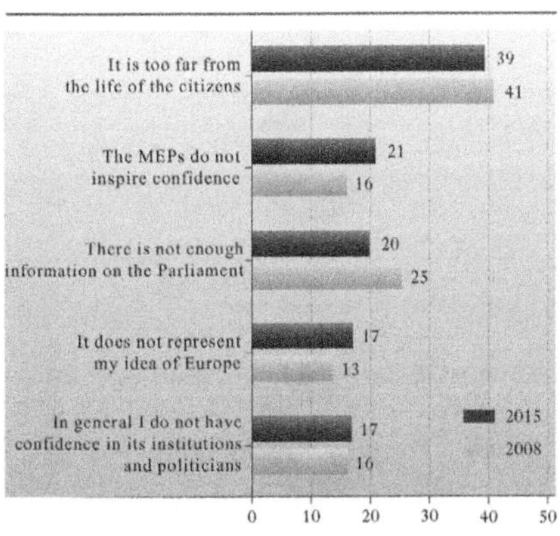

Source: Eurobarometer 2015, http://www.europarl.europa.eu/pdf/eurobarometre/2015/2015parlemeter/eb84_1_synthese_analytique_partie_II_en.pdf.

The motivations of those who have professed to have confidence in the European Parliament are interesting. From figure 2, one can note the heterogeneity of their motivations, as: the fact that the decisions of the Parliament have been taken in a democratic manner (32 per cent), by persons who are in a better position to know the problems (26 per cent), because the Parliament defends the interests of European citizens (23 per cent) and because its decisions contribute to the economic growth the interviewee's country (19 per cent). The trend of these percentages in 2015 with respect to 2008 is not unambiguous. It signals, in part, a worsening, while the percentage of those favourable to the EU in its totality is clearly on the rise.

Those who show lack of confidence in the Parliament adduce motivations which, as can be seen in figure 3, have to do predominantly with aspects connected to democracy. They feel that the European Parliament is distant (39 per cent), they do not trust certain

MEPs (21 per cent), they think that the European Parliament does not represent their idea of Europe (17 per cent) and they do not have confidence in its institutions and politicians (17 per cent).

The lack of confidence in the European Parliament is not accompanied by a devaluation of its political or institutional role. On the contrary, 72 per cent of the Europeans as opposed to 21 per cent (roughly the percentage obtained in the elections of 2014 by the parties which were, in the broad sense, anti-European and populist) think that the European Parliament has a very important role in the functioning of the EU (see figure 1 above). Indeed, in a very important statistic, 44 per cent hold that it ought to have a more important role in the near future, 25 per cent the same as now, 21 per cent less important. All these percentages, as can be seen in figure 4, have fluctuated moderately in the last decade, beginning from October–November 2007.

Figure 4 Result of the survey of European citizens on how important the role of the European Parliament should be in the future with respect to today (in percentages)

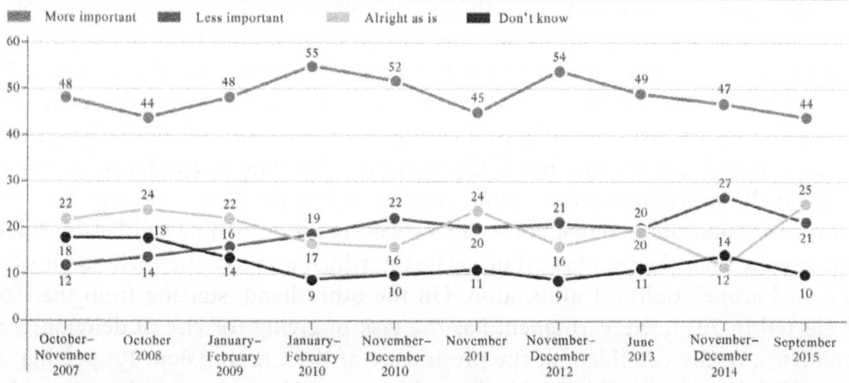

Source: Eurobarometer 2015, http://www.europarl.europa.eu/pdf/eurobarometre/2015/2015parlemeter/eb84_1_synthese_analytique_partie_II_en.pdf.

As for the functioning of the EU, 38 per cent of the European citizens hold that its decisions are adopted on the basis of the political affinities of the MEPs, as against 32 per cent, according to whom national interests count for more; 20 per cent, meanwhile, attribute equal weight to both motivations. With a view to the perception of democratic deficit deriving from the European Parliament's mode of functioning, these percentages do not contain a clear and unambiguous message for opposing academic or political positions. For the intergovernmentalists, that is, those who hold that Europe works better if its interest and its path are defined by representatives of the Member States, the fact that almost a third of the European citizens affirm that the MEPs express national interests might be comforting. For the federalists, who desire a politically unified Europe, that 38 per cent who believe that the MEPs act on the basis of political affinities might be encouraging. Perhaps, however, the European Parliament would function better if it succeeded effectively and efficaciously, as 20 per cent of the interviewees believe, in combining national interests with European ones, not letting the national interest be monopolised by representatives who are, in the broad sense, populist.

The overall picture which emerges is that the Parliament still has a long way to go if it wishes to affirm itself as an institution worthy of the confidence of the Europeans and capable of convincing them of its utility and of its efficacy. The data of the survey indicate that there exists a concrete disparity between the democratic procedures with which the Parliament is elected and through which it functions, and the perception of the European citizens that, however, would like to attribute it a more important role than it presently has. In that disparity, like it or not, justified or not, is located a part, in my opinion not a particularly important part, of the Parliament's democratic deficit. It matters little if the respective national Parliaments (but this is surely not the case, for example, of Westminster, the Parliament of Great Britain) are susceptible to criticism not dissimilar to that directed against the European Parliament. The problem of its image, of its role, of its democraticalness remains, not grave, but open.

It cannot help but seem paradoxical that the positive evaluation of the European Parliament's role and of its importance in the institutional system is diminished, if only a little, in the eyes of the European citizens, and is accompanied by a decline in electoral participation precisely at the moment its powers have significantly augmented. Not only does the Parliament possess the most important power of all Parliaments in parliamentary, presidential and semi-presidential democracies, which is to say, that of voting down the budget (of the Union), but it intervenes also in a decisive way in the formation of the European Commission, which, in a certain sense (see below), is the 'government' of the EU. Indeed, on the one hand, the European Parliament conducts *confirmation hearings* on all the commissioners nominated by each of the Member States, toward the end of ascertaining their competencies, investigating their possible conflicts of interest, and measuring their degree of pro-Europeanism, which is to say, their will to pursue the process of Europe's political unification. On the other hand, starting from the Parliament elected in 2014, the Parliament has the task of giving (or else of denying) a vote of confidence to the candidate of the presidency of the Commission. Respecting what has been laid down in the Treaty of Lisbon, this man or this woman is the person designated before the election of the Parliament by the leaders of the parties represented in Parliament. The candidate of the parliamentary group which has obtained the most seats merits, save in conspicuous exceptions, to be nominated by the Council of the heads of government and enters into office after a formal vote delivered by the Parliament. This procedure was rigorously adopted in 2014 such that the candidate of the European People's Party, the Luxembourg ex-prime minister, but also ex-MEP, Jean-Claude Juncker, became President of the Commission. There is nothing here which contrasts with the normal procedures of formation of parliamentary governments, or in which one might perceive any democratic deficit whatever with respect to those kinds of governments. If anything, one should note the involvement, from the outset, of the electors, and, during the process, of the heads of government of the Member States, up till the completion of the procedure entrusted to the MEPs, elected representatives of the citizens of the Member States.

In light of the elements analysed, it is possible to hold that the European Parliament should not be charged with any electoral deficit at all. At the same time, however, at least from the point of view of the voting citizens – a point of view which it is imperative to consider with the greatest respect – while 50 per cent of them consider it 'the institution that best represents them' (16 per cent say that this is the Commission; only 9 per cent choose the Council, while 23 per cent state that they do not know), the Parliament suffers from a deficiency of representation, confidence, and functioning.

IV. Electoral Deficit? The Council

The Council of the heads of government plays a role which is at once clear and ambiguous. The Member States are directly represented in it through the presence of their heads of State, which is to say, of the men and women who have won the elections in their respective countries, and who will remain there as long as they continue to enjoy the support of their respective majorities. Their political legitimacy is full and undeniable. They cannot be accused of any democratic deficit, neither from the electoral point of view, nor from that of the representation of their citizens, nor finally form the point of view of accountability. Indeed, as is common democratic practice, all of them return periodically before their electorate, so as to reconquer the necessary consensus to remain as their State's head of government. If not one of the components of the Council suffers from any electoral deficit, it is difficult to understand why the Council in its entirety should do so. Perhaps, however, the situation is more complicated than the simple existence of an albeit functional circuit of politico-electoral accountability, and concerns instead the internal dynamic of the Council.

We do not know enough of what occurs in the Council meetings, save through the indiscretions which certain heads of government entrust to the mass media, favouring, naturally, their preferences and their interpretations, and that which all those heads of government convey through bland official communiqués, in which one can rarely glimpse, for good or ill, the different opinions and arguments, the points of true disagreement and the types of compromises which are reached. That which occurs in the Council is not entirely definable as *arcana imperii*, but, certainly, this form of confidentiality permits the public opinion to wonder if the heads of state sometimes might arrive at unspeakable bargains to protect or advantage their national interests, rather than promoting genuinely European ones.

Although the barriers are many and high against the production of accurate analyses on how the various heads of government relate to the Union, and how they take it into account in their internal policies, some hypotheses seem corroborated by the facts. The first hypothesis is that not one of the heads of State has acquired his/her office and the necessary votes, nor conducted his/her electoral campaign under the banner of European problems, proposals and priorities. The second hypothesis is that, whenever these problems emerged in the electoral campaign and, afterwards, in many controversial political decisions, they were actually introduced by certain opponents (too often united in the category of populism) as their contingent or permanent rallying cry. The third hypothesis is that by now most all the heads of government have elaborated a double strategy of damage control, whenever the issues tied to Europe succeed in entering into the national politics. On the one hand, while it is compulsory that the directives, regulations, and policies that issue from the EU be implemented, the strategy of the involved heads of government is that of the *alibi*: 'We should have liked to do otherwise, but Europe imposes this on us with the threat of sanctions. We must submit'. This alibi contains also, to some extent, the possibility of curbing internal opponents, who, however, being 'souverainists', will appeal to the necessity of recovering the national sovereignty. On the other hand, when the heads of State implement inadequate policies, which do not work and which produce harmful effects, they very often attempt to shift the blame for whatever has gone awry onto the EU. This is the strategy founded on the identification of the *scapegoat*.

The two strategies can be used conjointly. They can deceive everyone once. They can deceive many several times. They cannot, however, deceive everyone every time. Nevertheless, on the one hand, they cultivate scepticism in the citizens regarding the capacity of the EU to succeed in providing a solution to a problem, and to the suspicions that it has become, rather, the origin of those problems. On the other hand, they stoke in the citizens themselves negative sentiments regarding the Union, its institutions, above all the Commission, and those politicians, technocrats, and bureaucrats who occupy important offices: offices of responsibility, of command, thus contributing to a dangerous overall delegitimisation.

Having observed this, in the case of the Council of the heads of the government, where would the democratic deficit really be located? I believe that, at least in a first, but good, approximation, it is possible to suppose that the deficit makes its appearance in the stances of the heads of state regarding their implicit refusal to address two very 'democratic' issues with the citizens. The first concerns the respect of the commitments made to the Union and to the other Member States, which deserve to be clarified and explained to the electors, also in their implications, but above all in their costs and benefits. The second concerns the implementation of the public European policies, decided according to pre-established procedures through votes that are as protective of the national interest as possible. Since the discussion has been up to now centred on the possible existence of a democratic-electoral deficit, it is important to highlight that the decision-making procedures of the Council are translated into votes of various kinds: the much criticised unanimity, qualified majorities and weighted majorities. Without going into particulars, but underlining that the procedures for voting have a primary objective – namely not to crush the little States – and an objective which follows from this, and is almost equally important to not consign the power of veto to any head of government – there exist two general circumstances. First circumstance: when the Council votes on a proposal of the Commission, approval comes through 55 per cent of the Member States that represent at least 65 per cent of the population. Second circumstance: when the Council acts on its initiative or on the proposal of a Member State, of the Central Bank or of the High Representative for Foreign Policy, the qualified majority rises to 72 per cent of the Member States which represent 65 per cent of the population.

There exist a series of issues for which the unanimity of the heads of government is required: membership to the Union; the concession of new rights to the European citizens; the harmonisation of national laws on indirect taxation; the financing of the Union; certain provisions in the judiciary sector and in internal affairs, among which is operational police cooperation; the harmonisation of national legislation in sectors of social security and social protection; and foreign policy and security. Finally, the Council must reach unanimity to reject a proposal of the Commission, when the latter has not reached an agreement on the amendments proposed by the Council. It should be underlined that possible abstentions do not prevent the decision from being taken.

In a certain sense, unanimity is the least democratic procedure, since it confers to only a single head of government the power of veto. It is true that, sometimes, perhaps often, unanimity is attained thanks to the acquiescence of one or more (but very few) heads of government who refrain from formal and public opposition, since they know that they will be in some way compensated in other places, on the occasion of other votes on other subjects which they consider to be of greater importance. It is equally true, however, that sometimes, precisely to attain unanimity and to avoid the 'blackmail' of some head of government, by applying the rule of 'anticipated reactions', a watered-down decision, already in the making, is brought before the Council. However, on the whole, to affirm that the Council of the heads of government suffers a democratic deficit in its functioning appears on the one hand excessive, and on the other misleading. It is excessive because all the heads of government who compose the Council are the expression of democratic procedures. It is misleading because it prevents one from grasping the true *punctum dolens*, which is to say that too many heads of government suffer, if anything, from a deficit of pro-Europeanism and, what is worse yet, they think (and they might be right) that they would lose the national elections were they to increase, in the most various and original forms and ways, according to their respective countries, their commitment toward a closer union.

Thus there emerges, not so much a democratic deficit, as a genuine paradox. If the heads of government of the Member States decided to increase their pro-European commitment, it is not at all a given that they should reduce the democratic deficit of the Council; but they would open a gap between themselves and their national electorates so far as the representation of precisely national interests and preferences goes. That gap could be spanned by a long-lasting measure of pro-European political pedagogy, but, in the short run, the risk of an electoral defeat would probably become for many heads of government extremely high. Unfortunately, there is not as of now any specific research which corroborates the thesis of risk for any country/head of government who has staked his/her office by emphasising his/her pro-European commitment. Therefore, it is possible to affirm that the Council of the heads of government of the Member States presents/manifests a very limited democratic deficit, almost non-existent as concerns its composition and its functioning. The deficit is, however, visible if one analyses how those heads of government obtain their national office, which is the necessary condition whereby they become and remain members of that consensus.

Not even the exercise of power collectively conferred to the Council suffers from a democratic deficit, but only from certain impediments owing predominantly to voting procedures. One might rather say that in the Council there exists a dose/quantity of negative power, both in its entirety and for each of its components – namely the power of blocking decisions – which is generally superior to its quantity of positive power – namely, that of directly producing decisions or ensuring that other institutions, the Parliament and the Commission, proceed according to the indications and the preferences of the Council and its components. At this point, the democratic deficit would end up drowning in the sometimes churning, but rarely stormy, waters of the inter-institutional circuit. This shift, almost a transference, occurs rarely in such a way that the decisional deficit of the Council appears very visibly.

V. Electoral Deficit? The Commission

Whoever holds that the essential element for defining a democracy is constituted by elections, and that those institutions to which legitimacy is conferred by a popular vote alone are democratic, must consequently attribute the greatest degree of democratic deficit to the Commission. In principle, the Commission is democratically deficit on all levels: for its formation, for its operation, for its ways of exercising the power it has been conferred, perhaps also for the procedures with which it might be made to answer for its accountability, or its lack thereof. Naturally, the actual situation is rather more complex. It would be well to take one's bearings by a cutting definition of the Commission from the mid-1970s, given by General Charles de Gaulle, who was at the time President of the French Fifth Republic: he called it an institution composed of *technocrates apatrides et irresponsables*. Given that, naturally, a supranational institution prefiguring a federal Europe could not in any way be acceptable and desirable to de Gaulle, champion of a Europe of confederate nations, his definition contained many elements which are absolutely worthy of notice and analysis.

In the first place, the critique of technocrats was curious, coming from a President of the Republic who had received support and esteem from persons surely definable as *technocrates* in the movement that sent him up, and that had already nominated in his governments, and would continue to nominate, the cream of the crop of technocrats, not last among them Georges Pompidou (President of the Republic in his turn from 1969 to 1974). Using the term *technocrats*, it is much more likely that de Gaulle wished to place emphasis on the fact that the commissioners were not elected like politicians, but nominated on the basis of their more or less specialist competencies. It is certainly true that the commissioners are not elected but nominated. However, their level of 'politicalness' has grown enormously over the course of time. Practically all the commissioners of the two or three most recent Commissions (2005, 2010, 2015), at the moment of their nomination, could boast of having fulfilled prestigious governmental offices, in some cases up to having been the heads of their national governments. Today, the criticism derogatorily directed at the commissioners of their being 'technocrats' and 'bureaucrats' (like the famous *grand commis* of the French Republic) not only reveals an all too prevalent ignorance regarding the European institutions and the personalities that fulfilled their offices, but it is of clearly populist mould and, therefore, not attributable to the intentions and evaluations of de Gaulle.

In the second place, *apatrides*, which is to say 'without country', was, in the language of de Gaulle, probably the gravest of offences, absolutely disqualifying. But on the contrary, for whomever wishes to become and accepts being a European commissioner, it is an essential quality. Indeed, statutorily, all the commissioners commit to and have the responsibility of stripping themselves of their national affiliations. They must think and act in the exclusive interest of the Union, pursuing purely supranational objectives. In a certain sense, with a little rhetoric, one might say that the commissioners' country is Europe.

The Gaullist crescendo of cutting criticism against the commissioners was completed and concluded with the adjective *irresponsables*. On the one hand, we can and we must appreciate the conception of politics that de Gaulle expresses and summarises, based on responsibility, recalling the words of Max Weber that it is precisely the ethics of responsibility which distinguishes the best of the politicians. On the other hand, we must observe that, technically, de Gaulle grasps a very relevant point which must be analysed in depth. I will define it *the irresponsibilisation of the European commissioners*. Surely, the commissioners cannot and must not be politically responsible before the fellow citizens of their State for what they decide and do; but they are not responsible even before the European citizens.

They have not been elected, neither by their fellow citizens nor by the European citizens; they will be evaluated by none of these; they will have to address themselves to none of these to request a second term on the basis of what they have done, not done, or done badly. Electorally and, in a slightly more problematic manner, politically, the commissioners are unequivocally irresponsible. With regard to the commissioners, the democratic circuit 'election-action-re-election' does not ever come into being. Statutorily, that circuit can in no way contemplate responsibility and responsibilisation. And yet, we have apprehended something of great importance from the interviews, the writings, the memories of not a few commissioners (eg, Walter Hallstein, Ralf Dahrendorf, Antonio Giolitti, Roy Jenkins, Altiero Spinelli, Jacques Delors). At various times and in various ways, with different tones and emphases, all of them proudly proclaimed – here, as a homage, I will paraphrase the first lines of de Gaulle's autobiography – that they were constantly forced to operate in a responsible way in the face of a 'certain idea of Europe' (Bardi, Pasquino (1994)), that which shaped their pro-European commitment. It remains beyond doubt, however, that even that idea of Europe is unable to elide the democratic electoral deficit at the fount of the Commission's formation and of the nomination of its components.

It is the Council of the heads of governments of the Member States which nominates the commissioners and, as we have seen previously, the president of the Commission as well, taking into consideration the results of the election of the European Parliament. However, no commissioner has a direct electoral legitimacy; yet they do have an indirect legitimacy, since the head of the government of the Member State that nominates them has a clear and, often, authoritative electoral legitimacy. It is interesting to add that the nomination of a commissioner by a head of government of the Member State intersects with something more than a simple opinion expressed by the other heads of government. It is a nomination which is debated even with the president of the Commission, who, usually, confers his endorsement; but we do not know how many times his/her dissent can be expressed in a formal way, or how many times he/she might suggest and obtain a search for alternative personalities. Finally, it is a nomination that must be ratified after the confirmation hearings conducted in the special Parliamentary Commissions of the European Parliament, but it can also be voted down or else it can be withdrawn before a formal open vote.

So far as responsibility goes, it is certain that the individual commissioners can fall under a vote of censure delivered by the European Parliament and motivated by the visible incompetence of the commissioner, by his/her inadequacy, and by a variety of improper actions (eg, appointing, to the role of counsellor, his/her dentist, as the French commissioner Edith Cresson did, the first woman to arrive in the office of prime minister nominated by president François Mitterrand). When it became clear that the other commissioners too were being lapped by waves of corruption of various kinds, the president of the Commission, the Luxembourg Jacques Santer, imposed the resignation of the entire Commission (15 March 1999) in an action which, as the then Italian commissioner Emma Bonino complained, was excessive and punitive even against those who were not touched by that scandal. On the one hand, it is true that the Commission acts as a collegial organisation and, therefore, must collegially assume its responsibilities; but, on the other hand, the drastic gesture of Santer is only partially justifiable, even bearing in mind that around half the Commission ought to have been dismissed and rapidly substituted, and that, in any case, the term of that Commission would have concluded within the year.

The most significant consequence of those resignations en bloc, was the unexpected necessity of nominating a new President, in the person of Romano Prodi, and a totally new Commission.

Given that the functioning of the Commission is collegial, although with the assignment of delegations in specific materials and areas, the personality of the President of the Commission makes a great difference, sometimes going so far as to constitute a phenomenon already underway in certain national political systems: the presidentialisation of the Commission. The minimal essential definition of presidentialisation is 'centring of powers in the hands of a leader and their exercise outside of specific control'. This phenomenon does not necessarily always implicate, nor even at all, a slide toward forms of authoritarianism, but it certainly involves certain functional and democratic risks. Some authors add that presidentialisation is favoured and characterised also by expansion in number and resources of the bureaucratic bodies, thanks to which the 'presidentialising' leader grows and extends his/her political power. It is the Commission itself which offers the best examples of the awareness, amply supported by the best research, that presidentialisation is neither an inevitable phenomenon nor an unstoppable and irreversible one. The personalisation/presidentialisation of the Commission of Delors (1985–94) was clear and committed; that of Santer (1995–99) non-existent; that of Romano Prodi (1999–2004) extremely weak and unsought for; and that of Manuel Barroso (2005–14) sought for, but never acquired.

Finally, it is even possible to maintain that the Commission has absolute need of a very authoritative leadership, centred on visible qualities, which are personal and capable and ready to move toward an effective presidentialisation. This is not the dynamic established by Juncker (2014), which, however, could strengthen itself with a certain procedure of electoral legitimation obtained through the vote of the European People's Party, which had indicated him as its candidate. To a(n un)certain degree, the recurring proposal of the Commission President's direct popular election by the European citizens (so far insufficiently supported by the Member States' heads of government) has garnered the favour of some authoritative pro-Europeans like Delors, previously the President of the Commission, and of Joschka Fischer, Foreign Minister of Germany (1998–2005). According to the Eurobarometer of September 2013, no fewer than 70 per cent of the Europeans approve, only 13 per cent are contrary, and 13 per cent do not know. Direct election is intended and envisaged, on the one hand, to strengthen the role of the President in the Commission in the face of the Council and of the single heads of government, and on the other, to increase, thanks to the electoral process, the democratic legitimacy and power of whomever would be elected. Obviously, the personal and political characteristics of the elected person will do the rest, if relevant.

It would be, however, illusory to think that the democratic deficit of the Commission might be completely resolved by a direct popular election of its President. Let it be noted, however, that the arrangements which led to the designation of Juncker are already considered significant progress by 63 per cent of the Europeans, and negative by 18 per cent (while those who do not know correspond to 19 per cent: Eurobarometer 2015). According to 31 per cent of the European citizens, the direct election of the President of the Commission, by itself or else united to the team of commissioners, would serve to confer greater legitimacy to decisions; for 30 per cent it would reinforce democracy; for 26 per cent it would both increase the feeling of being citizens and strengthen the ties between the Union and the citizens themselves. Finally, it is very probable that the direct popular election of the president of the Commission would lead to an important step forward on the tortuous road of political representation and accountability, thanks also to a hard-fought electoral campaign which would disseminate information and proposals, and which would involve many tens of millions of European citizens, attributing real power to them, putting the candidates in touch with the electors, their problems, their demands. The change in playing field, from the asphyxiated Brussels with all its rites to the European territory with all its turbulences, would create, from many points of view, unpredictable challenges and opportunities. By changing the players, the conditions would be established to change the game – metaphors aside, to change, for the better, not only the operation of the Commission, but of the entire EU.

The Commission is a collegial institution whose operation is characterised by two elements: maximal openness and the search for standardised solutions. Within it, its working method pursues essentially the maximum degree of agreement possible between all its components, even if, sometimes, some commissioner or other demands *carte blanche* in the sector of his competence. The Commission recognises clearly that if it wants to oppose those sometimes genuine interferences and pressures of the Council of the heads of government, it can do this effectively only if it is able to maintain a unified front, in its intents and in its actions/reactions. The same unity is necessary whenever the Commission must confront the Parliament, even if the Commission and the Parliament learned long ago that the efficacy of both depends on achieving points of equilibrium and agreement on the greatest number of subjects possible. The most problematic sphere of action of the Commission concerns its relations with that which, at the moment, I will define in an extremely vague manner as the *external*. The questions here are many: how open is the Commission to external contributions, in the form of information, materials, advice, pressures? Does all of this signal the opportunity for the exercise of influence, operated also by the European citizens, or else only by organised groups, by the lobbies? How much does this opening complicate the decision-making procedures and, potentially, distort them? The point of departure of every analysis in this subject cannot help but be constituted by the needs and the preferences of the European citizens.

VI. The Voice of the Citizens

In the issue of democratic deficit, any decision relative to the access of groups and persons to the decision-making processes in the Commission, but also, evidently, in the European Parliament, cannot help but have two foundations: the open society and pluralism. The open society, read in Popperian key (with reference to the famous 1945 book of Karl Popper, *The open society and its enemies*), not only cannot, by definition, in any way restrict the access of any group, but it actually derives benefits from the information, the proposals, the priorities, the problems that, thanks to its 'openness,' enjoy the greatest possible circulation within it. As for pluralism, its existence is ever and everywhere the best guarantee of democraticalness in a political system. However much the EU is a political system constantly *in fieri*, probably *in progress*, it is inevitably and positively characterised by the existence of an irrepressible pluralism. Having sung the well merited elegy of the open society and pluralism, it is well to underline that among the harshest criticisms to the functioning of the Commission, is to be found the conviction that it is not pluralism which dominates its decision-making process, but rather a kind of confusion, not always and necessarily creative, from which it is difficult to disentangle oneself. All of this, along with the criticisms aimed at lobbies, some of which are inevitably powerful (interest groups originating from all the Member States, but also any non-European corporation, large or small, which operates in the space of the Union), leads almost to the impossibility of ascertaining responsibility for the decisions that are made and, above all, for deferrals and the decisions that are not made. In the framework of the reflection on democratic deficit, the lack of accountability, wherever 'comitology' is affirmed (which is to say the unlimited entrustment of the execution of decisions to very diverse committees composed of an elevated number of representatives of the Member States), occupies an absolutely prominent place. Who can be held and assessed responsible for decisions made (and not made) with the tumultuous participation of a multiplicity of agents?

Perhaps because they were aware both of the excesses of comitology and of the complications relative to it (in terms of a congestion of proposals, length of discussions, the necessity of negotiations and compromises, all phenomena which occur in opacity), the Member States' heads of government have sought a rebalancing. Without, unfortunately, thinning the committees and the exponents of the organisations, two important procedures of citizen participation in the formation of European decisions were inserted into the Treaty of Lisbon: legislative initiative and petition. Legislative initiative allows a million citizens of the EU, belonging to at least seven Member States, to appeal to the Commission to propose legislative acts in questions of Union competence. The Petition, in the form of a complaint or a request, can be presented to the European Parliament, individually or in association with others, on all the subjects which come within the European Union's field of activities and which directly affect that citizen or that group of citizens. However, the commendable periodic investigations of the Eurobarometer reveal that in 2015 (see figure 5) only 39 per cent of the Europeans hold that their voices have a weight in the EU (27 per cent of the Italians) as compared to 63 per cent (38 per cent of the Italians) who hold that their voices have weight in their respective country. It is interesting to underline that, in order, 96 per cent of the Swedes, 94 per cent of the Danes, and 85 per cent of the Finns say that their voices count in their country. Swedes (65 per cent), Danes (62 per cent) and, a little surprisingly, Croatians (58 per cent, but the surprise extends also to the statistic, 80 per cent, relative to their declaration of influence in national affairs) lead the classification of those who think that their voices count in the EU. There is a significant discrepancy, however, of around 30 per cent on average, between their perception of influence in their country and in the EU. In the light of Brexit, it is useful to report also the data relative to Great Britain: 62 per cent held that their voices counted in their country and 33 per cent in the EU.

As for the procedure through which they might make their voices heard, 57 per cent (38 per cent of the Italians) hold that one should vote in the elections of the European Parliament (but let it be remembered that in 2014 only 42.44 per cent of the European electors effectively went to the ballot box), that one can make one's voice heard by exercising the right of initiative (20 per cent, percentage which rises to 30 per cent among the Italians, a referendary people), by writing to one's MEP (17 per cent) and to the institutions (14 per cent), by participating in debate on the Internet and on the social media (12 per cent).

Figure 5 Results of the survey on the importance that the citizens believe they have in their own country and in the EU (in percentages)

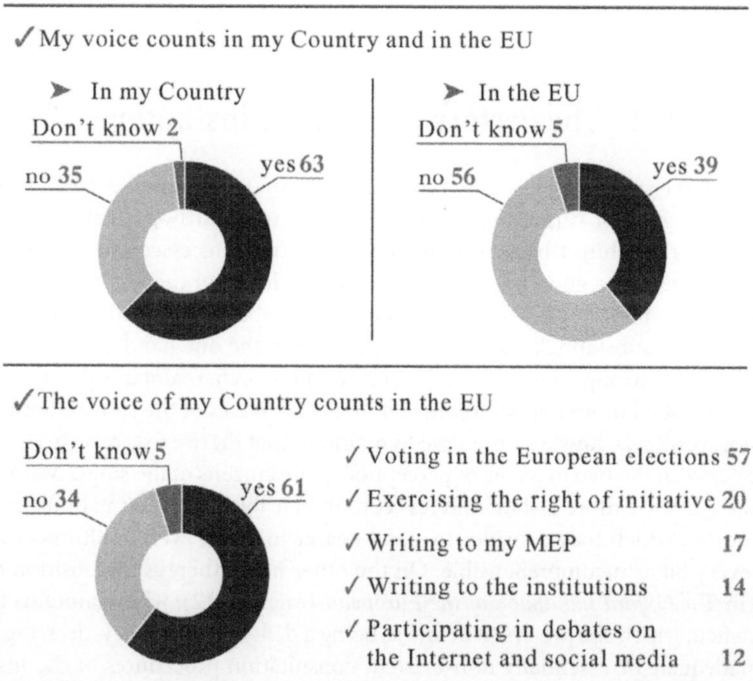

Source: Eurobarometre 2015, http://www.europarl.europa.eu/pdf/eurobarometre/2015/2015parlemeter/eb84_1_synthese_analytique_partie_II_en.pdf.

It is permissible to doubt the efficacy of these procedures, but it would be wrong to hold that the Commission and the Parliament are not places in which the Popperian open society effectively manifests itself. In short, from the side of input, which is to say of questions, the democratic deficit seems to be substantially non-existent, or else, in any case, it is very contained, and, if anything, depends on the citizens rather than on the institutions. It should be added, remaining in the terminology of systemic analysis, that sometimes the scholars and the commentators underestimate, if not even neglect, another procedure with which the Commission more than the Parliament seeks to respond to the problems of the European citizens and of the Union institutions, by identifying the questions to answer, the problems to resolve. The great political scientist David Easton (1965) defined *withinput* as those political impulses which originate in the authorities and from within the institutions without being elicited by questions originating from outside, in the form of input. These 'internal immissions' can sometimes compensate for the insufficiencies of input which originate in the European citizens, who, for a multiplicity of reasons – among which, perhaps dominant, is a deficiency in knowledge of the tasks and functioning of the EU – do not make their needs felt. It is not comforting that the percentage of Europeans to declare themselves very interested in the policies of the Union (43 per cent) is clearly inferior to that (56 per cent) of those who are little or not interested. A glimmer of optimism can be found in the fact that 42 per cent of the Europeans declare that in 2025 they will be more involved in these policies (30 per cent hold that they will be then as they are today; 20 per cent less involved; 8 per cent do not know), but, certainly, they are still too few, and, perhaps, also a little too far in the future.

VII. The Performance of the Institutions

Systemic analysis suggests that the transformation of inputs into outputs – of social questions of the greatest variety into more or less adequate answers which are, precisely, systemic – occurs within a black box whose procedures are essentially inscrutable. We might hypothesise that a good part of the democratic deficit of the EU is located precisely within this box, and not, therefore, in the sphere of any specific institution. In this connection, there are two substantially opposing positions. On the one hand, Andrew Moravcsik (2002), a scholar of strong convictions based on solid research, maintains that the European black box is not at all more impenetrable than the black boxes of the single Member States. Against Moravcsik it is, however, possible to maintain that there exists a far from negligible difference between the two in terms of perceptions. The citizens of the single Member States perceive the EU to be more distant and less comprehensible than their national authorities and institutions, which they consider to stand nearer to them, even if, ultimately, they are probably every bit as incomprehensible. On the other hand, there is the position of Vivien Schmidt (in *The Oxford handbook of the European Union*, 2012), who maintains the existence of a deficit, which she prefers to define as being a deficit of *legitimacy*, deriving from the limited, inadequate or essentially non-existent consultation procedures of the institutions with the European citizens, and of intermediation through their organisations of concern. More precisely, the deficit regards what happens in the black box, which is to say, what connects, according to procedures which are not easily known, the inputs to the outputs, and which Schmidt defines in an innovative way as *throughput*.

If an acceptable synonym of input is *immission* and of output *emission*, it appears to be plausible to supply the synonym 'transmission' for *throughput*, that which passes through, which travels within the black box of decision-making procedures. Here one might find adequate placement also for that criticism of a predominantly, but not exclusively, English mould: namely, the criticism of the excess of bureaucracy and regulation (red tape). The repeated enlargements, but above all the massive one of 2004, to States whose political and administrative culture was not homogeneous to that of the States that were already Members, and to bureaucracies which were certainly not recruited on the basis of merit and capacity, have inevitably contributed both to the obscurity of the procedures of transmission/transit of input, and to the inexplicability of the appearance of withinputs, 'intraimmissions', not to speak of the many actors who are sheltered by that obscurity and that inexplicability from the necessity of assuming their responsibilities.

The risk of an analysis conducted in the shadow of the difficulty, if not the impenetrability, of the decision-making processes in the institutional sphere, consists in thinking that the possible democratic deficit depends essentially on a shortage of information at the disposal of the European citizens. Obviously, such a risk is much more substantial so far as the Council and the Commission go, since the European Parliament is certainly more transparent and, to the extent that I have already indicated, relatively more responsibilised/responsibilisable in what it does, does not do, and does badly. It might be, on the other hand, the European citizens themselves who do not have enough interest in and adequate information on the activities of the three principal European institutions. It might equally be that the great 'intermediaries', which is to say the mass-media operators and, to a considerably lesser degree, the representatives of interest groups, are neither prepared enough nor sufficiently equipped to perform a task which is complex, inasmuch as the entire political system of the Union functions in an inevitably complicated manner. In point of fact, the democratic deficit, to the degree to which it exists and does not derive merely from more or less significant electoral legitimation, belongs to no specific institution, but to the circuit of and the relations between the institutions and, secondarily, to the ways in which associations and the citizens interact with the institutional system of the EU. Finally, insofar as it exists, the democratic deficit cannot be found within and attributed to a single institution or a specific procedure alone.

The democratic deficit is a systemic defect. Then it is to the system that one must look, more precisely to the institutional model (as Karry Siedentop (2001) has done in a general way, though, in my view, unconvincingly). In a systemic key, it is necessary to know how to propose and formulate solutions. Very briefly: more functionalism, which is to say to extend as far as possible the integration between activities and sectors; more intergovernmentalism, which is to say, to ask the Member States to move toward the greatest number of shared decisions; more federalism, which is to say to proceed to the political unification of the people of the EU. Each of these modes would give a different, but, according to one's visions and preferences, acceptable, solution to the present democratic deficit.

Too many scholars have dedicated themselves, without obtaining the necessary consensus from other scholars or from the public European opinion, to the research of complicated formulae that have no roots in the thought and the institutional practice of Western democracies. We know, however, that federalism is a State model which goes hand in hand both with presidential Republics (as in the United States and Brazil) and with models of parliamentary government (as those from Great Britain to Germany and from Australia to Canada). We also know that the EU can evolve in both directions, and that there exist proposals for both alternatives. We know, finally, that it is not at all true, as is said and repeated by various parties, that if the EU were to apply for accession to the EU, it would be rejected because it does not satisfy its own canons of democraticalness. On the contrary, the EU as such is certainly a 'liberal-constitutional' political system as regards the rights enjoyed by its citizens (who are protected and promoted in a tireless and irreproachable manner by the European Court of Justice) and as regards the limits it places on political power: its checks and balances, through the freedom of media and through political, social, religious, economic, cultural pluralism. I would go so far as to maintain that, in a hypothetical classification of rights, of functioning, of responsibilisation, the EU as a political system would occupy an intermediate position among the 28 (27 once the withdrawal of Great Britain has been finalised) Member States.

Only once it has been fully recognised that the EU belongs among the open societies and the constitutional-democratic political regimes, is it correct and appropriate to reflect on the possible existence of a democratic deficit. It is then conceivable that the democratic deficit appears in the EU precisely because it is neither a parliamentary model of government nor a presidential model of government. In brief, the EU is not a presidential model because it is not the voting citizens who grant executive power directly to a president whom they have elected. Nor is it a parliamentary model either, since there are no parties in Parliament who give life to a majority coalition, which in turn would appoint and sustain the head of the government. The EU approaches the parliamentary model, but two conditions are lacking to construct that model and to keep it alive and vital: that the Parliament be granted the power to give and to withdraw confidence to that coalition and to its head, potentially so as to install another; and that the European citizens be put into a condition such that they might evaluate the performance of the outgoing coalition and the promises of the challenging coalition. Naturally, in this kind of analysis one must give full legitimacy to the objection that at least some of the parliamentary governments of the Union's Member States themselves betray specific democratic deficits in considerable quantities. Without proceeding through an exhaustive classification – the cases are well known and much debated – I limit myself to the most obvious: Austria, with whom the countries of the EU for some time suspended bilateral relations following the participation in its government of the extreme right leader Jörg Haider; Hungary, which has been 'reprimanded' various times and even now is reprehensible on account of the policies adopted by its President Viktor Orbán; Slovakia, for the attitude of total obstruction to migration policies on the part of its prime minister Robert Fico; and, with its genuine sleights of hand in its public finances, Greece.

In brief, the democratic deficit of the EU is to be found almost entirely in the inadequacy of the accountability procedures of the European rulers (the Council and the Commission), which inadequacy eludes the (little) voting citizens, on account of the very structuring of those mechanisms and those procedures. Since especially in parliamentary democracies (to a much greater degree than in presidential Republics), a key role – not only for what concerns the full responsibilisation of the rulers, but the preliminary formation of the executive itself – is played by the political parties, it is precisely to the parties that one must turn one's attention, to understand how to confront the problem of democratic deficit at the European level. Some scepticism is in order, because the political parties themselves suffer from an almost permanent democratic deficit, and in all the European democracies straddling the twentieth and the twenty-first centuries, these parties have seen their prestige decline to the lowest levels ever. Since up till now, no one has found a way of revitalising the prestige of the national parties and making it grow, scepticism on operations of this kind on the European level is absolutely justified. However, if the elections for the European Parliament were to take place, not State by State, but on an effectively European scale, and if the Commission and its President were elected by the European citizens, this would probably create the conditions for relaunching those parties which are capable of becoming European, and for consistently reducing democratic deficit from the electoral point of view. One should not expect any breakthrough proposals on the initiative of the Member States' heads of the government, since they are concerned with the issues which their electors consider to be salient, unemployment and immigration. The conclusion of the term of the 2019 European Parliament and Commission will not reveal any novelties in the subject of institutional reforms. In one way or another, all the agents, European and national, institutional and political, will continue to 'chase their tales' in everything they claim they cannot do, or would not know how to do.

Figure 6 Degree of satisfaction in the functioning of democracy in the EU (in percentages)

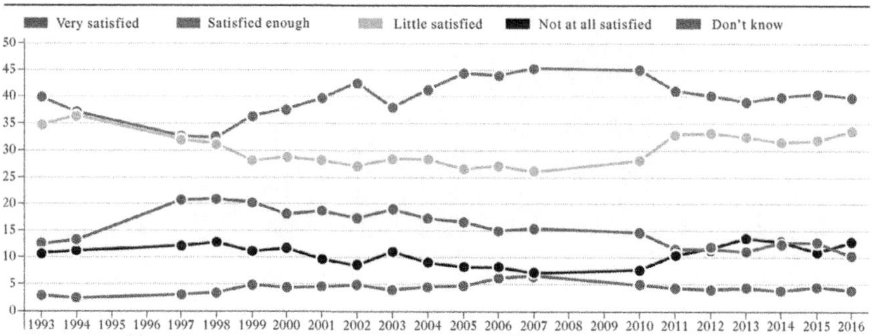

Source: European Commission 2016, http://ec.europa.eu/commfrontoffice/publicopinion/index.cfm/Chart/getChart/chartType/lineChart//themeKy/2/groupKy/228/countries/EU/savFiles/54,129,179,555,6,194,554,661,137,143,184,191,201,521,632,702,8,698,805,41,3,7,49,186,190,192,195,196,187,646,838/periodStart/031993/periodEnd/112016.

VIII. Finally: The Functioning of Democracy

Some of the European citizens have a sense of how the Union's democracy works, even if rarely with reference to appropriate studies and research, targeted journalistic reportage, and, least of all, by direct experience, for example, through contacts with those who they might define 'their' MEPs, or else with the Eurobureaucrats. In many Member States, the citizens stand, with few exceptions, almost as far from their national politics as from the European politics. What counts, however, and what is never to be underestimated, is that the sense of the European citizens on European politics and democracy reflects that which circulates in their environment, that which is variously recounted by the media and by the politicians, that which blows in the wind. And the wind for some time has not blown in a positive direction. Figure 6 shows a slight growth in the absolute dissatisfaction of the European citizens with regard to the functioning of EU democracy, and a slight decline, above all as compared to its peak between 2005 and 2010, in moderate satisfaction. Evidently, the economic difficulties have had an inevitable impact, and their continuation threatens to carry dissatisfaction very far into the future.

In figure 7, on the other hand, one can follow the different levels of satisfaction of the European citizens for the functioning of democracy in their States. We can underline in every way that the democratic deficit, if it is evaluated coolly and with adequate parameters, is certainly inferior to what is commonly thought, and that, at bottom, many of the 'democratic' difficulties on the European level are detectable also in the single Member States; but the verdict of the Europeans – that which, in the final analysis, truly counts – is clear and distinct, unequivocal. The functioning of Union democracy does not satisfy half of them.

Figure 7 Degree of satisfaction in the functioning of democracy in the Member States (in percentages)

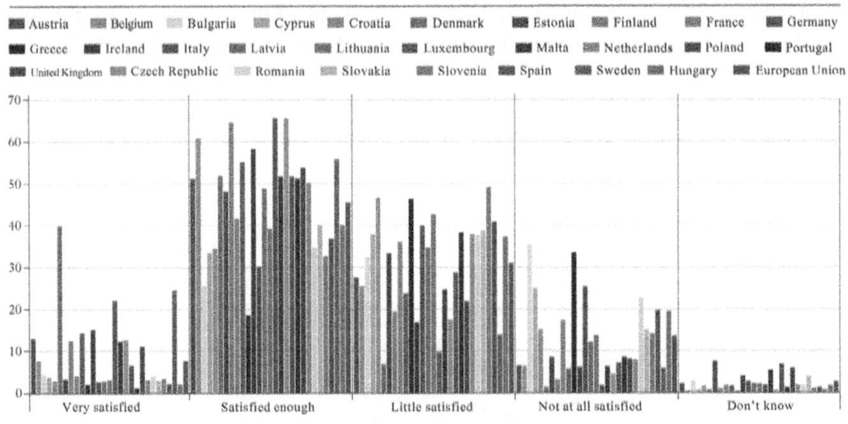

Source: European Commission 2016, http://ec.europa.eu/commfrontoffice/publicopinion/index.cfm/Chart/getChart/chartType/barChart//themeKy/45/groupKy/226/countries/EU/savFiles/54,78,83,129,138,179,555,6,59,76,77,194,554,10000,66,70,72,86,88,112,661,68,81,85,96,119,137,143,184,201,521,632,702,8,61,63,74,75,698,805,41,71,80,93,107,3,7,49,186,190,195,196,60,62,65,73,79,103,118,187,646,660,838/periodStart/091973/periodEnd/112016.

To answer the question of what must and can be done to obtain improvements is a task which lies beyond the scope of this essay. It would be too easy (even if this is surely, at least in part, the correct response) to affirm with passionate emphatic rhetoric that it is up to politics to change Europe (but who changes politics?). Politics does not consist only in furnishing goods, services, capital, work. It consists also in the production of immaterial goods, of symbols, of identity, of a sense of belonging. Therefore, if politics wants to face the problem of the democratic deficit in the EU, to limit it and reduce its dimensions – in the full consciousness that no democracy anywhere will ever succeed in spanning the disparity between expectations and realisations, and that, indeed, this ever mobile disparity is the very essence of real and ideal democracy – politics must be (re-)interpreted as an activity which is carried out as much by the representatives and the rulers, as by the citizens. If there is a 'demo-cratic' deficit, which is to say, etymologically, a deficit in the power of the people, let it be also the people to take action, to make good that deficit.

Bibliography

Bardi, L and Pasquino, G, *Euroministri. Il governo dell'Europa* (Milano, 1994).

Bassanini, F and Tiberi, G (eds), *Le nuove istituzioni europee. Commento al Trattato di Lisbona* (Bologna, 2010).

Easton, D, *A systems analysis of political life* (New York, 1965).

Ferín, M and Kriesi, H (eds), *How Europeans view and evaluate democracy* (Oxford, 2016).

Hix, S and Høyland, B, *The political system of the European Union* (Basingstoke, 2011).

Jones, E, Menon, A and Weatherill, S (eds), *The Oxford handbook of the European Union* (Oxford, 2012) (in partic VA Schmidt, *Democracy and legitimacy in the European Union* 661–75).

Marquand, D, *Parliament for Europe* (London, 1979).

Moravcsik, A, 'In defence of the 'democratic deficit': reassessing legitimacy in the European Union' (2002) 4 *Journal of common market studies* 603–24.

Norris, P, *Democratic deficit* (Cambridge, 2011).

Pasquino, G, *L'Europa in trenta lezioni* (Milano, 2017).

Pasquinucci, D and Verzichelli, L (eds), *Contro l'Europa? I diversi scetticismi verso l'integrazione europea* (Bologna, 2016).

Piattoni, S, *The European Union. Democratic principles and institutional architectures in times of crisis* (Oxford, 2015).

Reif, K and Schmitt, H, 'Nine second-order national elections. A conceptual framework for the analysis of European elections results' (1980) 8(1) *European journal of political research* 3–44.

Santaniello, R, *Capire l'Unione Europa* (Bologna, 2016).

Schmitter, PC, *How to democratize the European Union ... and why bother?* (Lanham, 2000).

Siedentop, L, *Democracy in Europe* (New York, 2001).

Vai, L, Tortola, PD and Pirozzi, N (eds), *Governing Europe. How to make the UE more efficient and democratic* (Bruxelles-Bern-Berlin-Frankfurt a. M.-New York-Oxford-Wien, 2017).

Viola, DM (ed) *Routledge handbook of European elections* (London-New York, 2016).

26

Towards a New Constitutional Debate?

RENAUD DEHOUSSE

Sixty years after the signature of the Treaties of Rome (1957), the European Union (EU) is called to come to terms with a series of structural weakness which have been present since its origin. The events that have affected Europe since 2007, *annus horribilis* of international finance marked by the subprime mortgage crisis in the United States, have brought to light different structural weaknesses of that monetary and economic union which some had considered the basis for the future political union. Moreover, the crisis hotspots have multiplied in the countries bordering Europe: this, in addition to being a great threat to security, has meant that European countries have been affected by a wave of immigration unequalled since 1945, to which they have been unable to provide a common answer.

Ten years of recession seem to have fractured the relations between the EU and its citizens, who now look with diffidence, if not open hostility, on everything that comes from distant Brussels. Great Britain, already traditionally reluctant about the idea of integrating with a broader whole, has voted in favour of leaving the Union. This multiplication of difficulties makes an overall examination of the ambitions of the Union, along with the reforms necessary to accomplish them, feel ever more urgent. The withdrawal of the United Kingdom almost mechanically invites a reflection on the future of the EU.

Some people, faithful to the earlier federalist ideals, invoke a qualitative leap toward more intense forms of integration among the countries that intend to remain, or at least among some of these; and hence the resumption of a debate brutally interrupted by the French and Dutch referenda, which in 2005 signalled the failure of the draft European Constitution. But the present political climate – with tensions among the national governments and institutions, between peoples and governments – makes every discussion difficult.

Where might these opposing pressures lead? Is there space for a new constituent phase that would allow the confrontation of such structural challenges? In attempting to identify a possible response to such questions, this essay will retrace certain critical phases of European integration, seeking to emphasise some of the structural mechanisms which have had an impact on the tortuous journey of the European project.

From the initial phases of the Community experience, there have been questions not only on the final objective – that is, the structural form that integrated Europe would have had – but also on the best way to achieve it. The failure of various attempts undertaken toward a federal turnaround or a constitutionalisation invites us to reflect on the very nature of the exercise and on the difficulties that it might entail. On the other hand, the progressive development of bonds based on compromises – apparently more modest – perhaps suggests an alternative road.

After having examined this long-term tendency, we will dwell on the contradictions which have emerged in the course of recent years: on the one hand, the ever greater resistance of the governments to the development of power in Brussels and the consolidation of an open opposition to Europe in the vast majority of Member States; on the other hand the reinforcement of the economic powers of the EU in response to the many doubts on the viability of the euro in the years following the financial shock of 2007–08. Integration has traditionally been a process guided from above, by the governing elites, rather than a request originating from below. Ultimately, its path has been yet more singular, with forward steps reluctantly conceded by the elites – rather than being actively desired and promoted. Hence the question that we will face in conclusion: is this a good basis for attempting to strengthen the political ties between the European States?

I. Europe and the Constitutional Idea

In contrast to other composite political systems, for example federal States, the EU is not the fruit of a dramatic and sudden revolution, nor is it founded on a pre-existent doctrine.

The long period which opens in the aftermath of World War II seems characterised by an uncertain succession of advances and failures. The defenders of the federal revolution, the advocates of a more gradual approach, and the supporters of a more traditional Europe have regularly collided. However, compromise after compromise, this evolution has given birth to a form of international governance without precedents. In this process, the idea of a constitution has been present from the initial phases, although on the political plane it achieved only ephemeral successes. Contrary to expectations, the most significant innovations, those to which we owe the so-called constitutionalism without constitution characteristic of the European project in its present stage, are the fruit of the activity of the European Courts.

A. The Defeats of the Constitutional Idea

From the start, the possibility of taking the constitutional route to attain political unification has been at the centre of the debates on European integration.

At the Hague congress, organised on the initiative of the European movements in May 1948, a great many maintained the necessity of convoking a consistent Assembly to define the foundational laws at the basis of the cooperation between the Member States. The American model was a source of constant inspiration for the federalist movements, who insistently demanded that Europe too should have a 'Philadelphia Convention', inspired on the model of the convention in which the Constitution of the United States (1787) was drafted. However, in the months that followed, the confrontation between the governments maintaining this federal vision and those that looked to Europe's future according to more traditional canons would prove that the times were not yet ripe. Finally, in May 1949, 10 governments agreed to sign the treaty that instituted the Council of Europe. However, the consensus undergirding the launch of what was, at the time, defined as a greater Europe, was anything but broad, thus condemning the project to stagnation.

The Schuman Declaration of 9 May 1950, with which France proposed a 'coal and steel pool', signalled a change in strategy. 'Europe', the text reads, 'will not be made all at once, or according to a single plan. It will be built through concrete achievements which first create a de facto solidarity' (https://www.robert-schuman.eu/en/doc/questions-d-europe/qe-204-en.pdf). Following the ideology herein expressed, the States most favourable to European integration adopted a functionalist approach: they intended to proceed, step by step, towards an ambitious political construction, multiplying the cooperation projects. In reality, federalism and functionalism conflicted only on the tactical plane, while their long-term objectives were similar.

Immediately after the signing of the Treaty of Paris (18 April 1951), the dynamic of integration seemed indeed to accelerate. In an international context marked by the escalation of the Cold War, the six Member States of the ECSC (*European Coal and Steel Community*) considered, again through France's initiative, extending their cooperation to the military sector. Toward that end, a treaty instituting a European Defence Community (EDC) was negotiated. Since the European army provided for in this draft would have been placed under the control of a political authority, the governments of the six Countries convoked a constitutional assembly (in reality, this was an enlarged ECSC Assembly, cautiously designated 'ad hoc Assembly' in the official texts) to define the institutional framework in which the various forms of cooperation between the European States might be inserted.

In March 1953, the Assembly adopted a project of Constitution for a European political Community, clearly inspired by federalist principles (Griffith (2000)). This constitutional phase was brief; only one year later, the French National Assembly rejected the EDC after a public debate of some particular intensity, and the political community foundered with it. The failure of the EDC rekindled the interest for the functionalist approach.

The 'relaunch' triggered by the Messina conference in 1955 led, with the Treaty of Rome (1957), to the creation of the European Economic Community (EEC) and the European Atomic Energy Community (EAEC or Euratom). In the subsequent quarter century, numerous adjustments were made in this framework or in the margins of the treaties. The constitutional route seemed by then barricaded. Although the draft Treaty establishing the European Union, adopted in 1984 by the first elected European Parliament on the initiative of a fervent supporter of federalism, Altiero Spinelli (1907–86), was inspired by the federal model, it prudently avoided any explicit reference to a Constitution. This did not preserve it from failure. The four great constitutional reforms that followed, up until the 2001 Treaty of Nice, all presented themselves as modifications to existing treaties. Among these, the principal ones, like the Single European Act (1986) and the Treaty of Maastricht (1992), were of a functionalist mould. The first appeared as the institutional corollary to the project of the 'single market' launched by the Delors Commission (1985–95). The second, on the other hand, passed into history (not without difficulty) as the text that established the creation of the single currency.

The chaotic path of the European construction seems, therefore, to refer to two key ideas. The federalist idea has always been a point of reference and, for some, an objective. But, it is the functional approach to which we owe the principal advances. The history of Europe can be interpreted as a succession of great projects, from the 'coal and steel pool' to the single currency, passing through the common market or the single market. The history of the constitutional path is every bit as linear: all the attempts made to create a constitutional basis have proven unsuccessful. From this perspective, the rejection of the draft

Treaty establishing a Constitution for Europe should be located in an extraordinary historical continuity. Later on, I will have occasion to return to the causes underlying so clear a tendency. For the moment, it is sufficient to note that the predominance of the functionalist path is in great part due to the role of the governments in the process of the treaties' reform. Since any modification requires their unanimous agreement, every transfer of power to the European level must be the object of negotiations between the Member States. And, in a Union of States with different traditions, whose immediate interests do not always coincide, it will be easier to reach an agreement on projects with – relatively – circumscribed limits, whose benefits can be evaluated more or less precisely, without lingering on an abstract vision of the just and the good.

B. A Constitutionalism without Constitution

If the classical constitutional option, that through which the representatives of a society determine the way in which they would like to be governed, has up to now proven to be beyond grasp, the institutional construction of Europe in the most recent decades has nonetheless been characterised by facets that are not dissimilar to the concept of constitutionalism.

For the pioneers of the European cause, and in the aftermath of two global conflicts that brought Europe to its knees, carrying with them devastation and barbarities, it was clear that it was necessary to overcome the system inherited from the 1648 Peace of Westphalia, a system based on the principle of an unlimited sovereignty of the States, which relate to one another on the basis of force. The idea of a new European order in which the States are subject to a set of regulatory principles seemed therefore the single alternative to the 'state of nature' in which the State systems had coexisted up until then.

It was natural that this effort of reorganisation should deal above all with human rights, before Jean Monnet (1888–1979) and Robert Schuman (1886–1963) discovered, with the idea of 'de facto solidarity', the means of introducing a logic of collaboration. The necessity of measures to safeguard the States from the atrocities that marked World War II found broad consensus. The preamble of the European Convention for the protection of human rights and fundamental freedoms (ECHR), signed in Rome on 4 November 1950, references 'a common heritage of political traditions, ideals, freedom and the rule of law' (https://www.coe.int/en/web/conventions/full-list/-/conventions/rms/0900001680063765). Behind a discourse strongly characterised by references to natural right, there clearly emerges the political will to subject the action of the States to the control of what would subsequently be called, the international community. It is precisely because this 'common heritage' had not prevented the atrocities of the two world wars, that it was deemed necessary to confer to these higher principles the force of rules of law, from which no government would have been able to withdraw. For many supporters of a European declaration of the rights of man, the binding character of the convention was essential. It was necessary to go beyond merely declarative principles which had led to the signing of the Universal Declaration of human rights, adopted by the United Nations General Assembly in December 1948, binding the States to a network of international commitments which could be invoked, with recourse to sanctions against them in case of violations of the principles of democracy and of fundamental rights.

The internationalisation of the protection of fundamental rights adopted thus the same function as their recognition at the constitutional level: in both cases, the essential principles were elevated to superior status, so that they might be protected from the errors of occasional majorities. 'International constitutionalism' does nothing but extend the constitutionalism that we already know on the national level. Naturally, one no longer makes reference here solely to the relations between governments and those who are subject to their authority, but also to relations between States. In both cases, moreover, the objective is the same: to combat absolutism and arbitrariness, subjugating the rulers' actions to law.

While the 'constitutionalising' ambition of the ECHR is apparent, the same cannot be said for the treaties which established the various European communities in the 1950s (the 1950 Treaty of Paris on ECSC, the 1957 Treaties of Rome on the European Economic Community and on atomic energy). The latter created a revolutionary institutional architecture, hinging on the idea of transfer of sovereignty to supranational institutions. However, according to the functionalist approach, the treaties appeared at first sight as a catalogue of provisions of an essentially technical character. This did not prevent a German school of thought, *Ordoliberalismus*, from discerning in them a recognition of the market economy, elevated to a metajuridical principle and called upon to structure numerous interpretations of the treaty and of the Community jurisprudence, and thus, indirectly, the behaviour of the Member States. Although this vision of Community 'economic constitution' was challenged, its existence is evidence of a tendency to see European integration with constitutional lenses, a vision which has been raised often in debates on economic integration.

The Luxembourg Court of Justice has done a great deal to promote a constitutionalisation of the treaties. Without dwelling here on an evolution that all legal manuals retrace in a deeper manner, it might be useful to review certain key elements of this process. As early as 1962, the Court has given an extremely extensive interpretation of the prohibitions on discrimination contained in the Treaty establishing the European Economic Community (EEC), in which it has discerned a source of rights that complainants might invoke before national courts, even when the formulation of these provisions clearly suggested that they were principally directed at the Member States (judgment of 05.02.1963, *NV Algemene Transport- en Expeditie Onderneming van Gend & Loos v Netherlands Inland Revenue Administration*, case 26/62). Elevating the Treaty to a catalogue of individual rights has simultaneously opened the doors for individuals to an arsenal of arguments to which they might appeal, whenever they believe that the national authorities have violated their rights. Subsequently, overstepping the silence of the treaties on the question, the Court would soon affirm that in case of conflict with national provisions – even with constitutional law – the Community rules should always prevail (judgment of 15.07.1964, *Costa v ENEL*, case 6/64). Finally, responding to the concerns expressed by some national judges who feared that the primacy of Community law might lead to calling the constitutional provisions relative to the protection of fundamental rights into question, the Court of Justice progressively admitted the need to check the conformity first of the Community decisions, and then of the national decisions which refer to them, against the 'fundamental rights recognized and protected by the constitutions of those States', and against the 'international treaties for the protection of human rights on which the Member States have collaborated or of which they are signatories' (judgment of 14.05.1974, *J Nold, Kohlen- und Baustoffgroßhandlung v Commission of the European Communities*, case 4/73). The language was perhaps a touch sibylline, but it referred clearly to the ECHR.

Decision after decision, the Community judges have thus lain the groundwork for a normative edifice that is imposed on the Member States. Toward that end, they have adopted methods of interpretation very similar to those of national courts. Rather than remaining attached to the real or supposed intention of the contracting parties – an obligatory point of reference in the interpretation of international agreements – they have been broadly inspired by the final objectives of integration, laid down in general terms in the preamble of the Treaty of Rome.

If in this connection it has been possible to speak of 'constitutionisation' of the treaties (Stein (1981) 1–27), this is because it seemed clear that, proclaiming the primacy of Community law over national rules, this process tended toward an implicit transfer of sovereignty, thus laying the groundwork for that conflict which would shake Europe at the moment of the ratification of the Treaty of Maastricht (1992) and, subsequently, on occasion of the debates on the draft of the Constitutional Treaty in the early 2000s. The national judges were not fooled, and often they accepted with reluctance the primacy of Community law. This attitude was particularly widespread in the constitutional courts: often, even while recognising the principle and its effects – the necessity to apply a national rule which violates the Community law – in reality they based their decision on the fact that supremacy corresponds to a will of the Member States, which have acquiesced to entrusting Europe with the management of certain tasks, while the Court of Justice saw the specific character of integration rather as the source of supremacy. The difference might seem subtle but it is not without importance. Indeed, if we accept the thesis of the constitutional courts, we must also accept the fact that the States could take back that what they have ceded. This idea of primacy claimed by the European Union, and freely conceded by the national legal systems, confers a peculiar authority to the European institutional systems, greater than that of classic international law, but less stable than that which might derive from a State Constitution (Weiler (2002) 151–76). On this point, the 2003 draft of an institutional treaty, to which we will return, by officially proclaiming the primacy of Community law, expressly rendered compulsory what before had been only freely accepted.

C. Constitutionalisation and Judicialisation

To proclaim a set of constitutional rules was not sufficient; it was necessary also to ensure that they would be respected. The subjection of the States to law had, as a corollary, the creation of international courts, charged with monitoring the application of superior principles defined in the basic texts. The novelty in the procedure was even more significant, considering that the States had long shown opposition to every form of 'judicialisation' of international relations, insofar as this last might have violated their autonomy. However, the wind of constitutionalism that was blowing on post-war Europe pushed toward the search of counterweights capable of opposing totalitarianism. In light of the weakness shown by the European parliamentarian regimes in the face of the rise of Nazism and fascism, it was natural to turn to specialised institutions. The reasoning was similar to that which inspired the creation of constitutional courts on a national level: in both cases, the recourse to a specialised jurisdiction court seemed indispensable to guarantee the efficacy of the fundamental rules that had just been solemnly recognised.

However, it would be excessive to define such a development as a triumphal march from darkness into light. On the contrary, when one retraces the steps of the debate that accompanied the birth of the ECHR, what strikes one the most are the many objections, inspired by a classic vision of international law, raised against what appeared as a threat for omnipotent States. The jurisdictional system instituted by the Convention multiplied safeguard measures, seeking a synthesis between judicial and diplomatic action. The decision to create a Court of Justice aroused fewer concerns at the time of the creation of the ECSC, but it is also true that this new judicial institution was designed to check the high authority of the ECSC, rather than to check the States. As the ECSC had been attributed important managerial powers, it seemed natural to provide for the possibility of jurisdictional control of its decisions. The Treaty of Paris therefore provided for an arsenal of means of redress inspired by the French administrative law. In the same vein, the Member States of the European Community accepted the Court's authority, whose competence was obligatory. The treaties also confer an essential prosecution role, in case of violations of Community law, to an autonomous institution, namely the European Commission. This centralised enforcement model contrasts with the principle of free choice, on the part of the States, of the mechanisms for controversy resolution, which remains the rule in international law.

Irrespective of its importance, the creation of international courts was not sufficient to guarantee the respect of law, insofar as in many cases, a government would prefer to turn a blind eye, in the name of the superior interests of the nation, rather than get involved in the 'internal affairs' of its partners. The constitutional logic at the basis of European integration required another step: to give to the holders of the new rights the possibility of acting in court to protect them.

The qualitative leap was important: it allowed the entry onto the international scene – traditionally reserved to the States – to individuals they did not control. There is thus no reason to wonder at the strong opposition with which these innovations were met. These reservations might have led to a limited recognition of the possibility of individual recourse to the European Courts. But the Court of Justice itself decided to open the doors of the courtroom to individuals. While the Treaty of Rome reserved the task of initiating the procedures aimed at ensuring the enforcement of Community law to the Commission, the Court acquiesced to assess the behaviour of the States in the framework of the preliminary proceedings, provided for in article 267 of the Treaty on the Functioning of the European Union (TFEU) of 2008. After having recognised that the Community law confers to individuals 'rights which become part of their legal heritage', it agreed to take up the (often unequivocal) questions that were addressed to it by the national courts, as regards the compatibility of the national regulations with Community law (judgment of 05.02.1963, *NV Algemene Transport- en Expeditie Onderneming van Gend & Loos v Netherlands Inland Revenue Administration*, case 26/62). This decision, which was supposed to encourage private individuals to appeal to national courts whenever they believed a national decision had ignored the rights guaranteed by Community law, has had an extremely important impact on the evolution of Community litigation. Today, it is fundamentally through the channel of the reference for a preliminary ruling – and therefore, indirectly, on private initiative – that the behaviour of the Member States is subject to the Court's judgment. The success of this form of constitutional control on the actions of the Member States has never been called into question. This explains the number of references for a preliminary ruling that, at present, represent an essential part of the rulings issued by the Court of Justice every year. Some of the main rulings of the Court were issued following individual proceedings: the alliance between the Court and private individuals has thus modified the course of the European integration on several occasions.

However, this genuine revolution, that raises the individual to the level of an actor of the integration process, has its limits. The proceedings in the Strasbourg and Luxembourg courts remain a road full of long and onerous obstacles, inaccessible to the marginalised who do not have specialised counsel or economic resources at their disposal. At the EU level, the individual remedies against the institutions' decisions remain limited, even if they have been occasionally extended by the Court in the name of the rule of law. Constitutional justice has clear limits: it was designed to protect individual rights and the democratic debate; not to supplant the latter.

D. Transnational Constitutionalism: Innovation or Transitional Synthesis?

Thus, while the 'ordinary' constitutional path had apparently been barricaded, Europe after World War II brought to life an original alternative. This form of 'transnational constitutionalism' is a by-product of the liberal climate which inspired the development of constitutional guarantees at the national level in the nineteenth century. In recognising the limits of State sovereignty and the necessity of a jurisdictional control on the governments' actions, Europe has gone beyond the initial stage in which relations between States are mainly power relationships, and has progressively entered into a world of regulation. The change is not limited to interstate relations, since even the discretionary powers of the national administrations have been subjected to European rules. In the emerging European society, what happens within the national borders is no longer the exclusive domain of the States.

Nevertheless, this form of integration has been accompanied by relatively limited transnational socialisation. Europeans continue to define themselves primarily in relation to their countries. In the best of cases, European identity is considered at most a secondary element: hindered in particular by the absence of a common political language and culture, the European political debate remains limited and transnational movements relatively weak. Despite the references to European citizenship inserted into the Treaty of Maastricht, the common people still struggle to make their voices heard: a limited elite makes the decisions. The growing resistance that emerged from the 1990s has demonstrated that public opinion was no longer satisfied with this situation.

One could say that, just like the bourgeois society of the nineteenth century, which had combatted the arbitrariness of the monarchs while ignoring the rights of the women and of the poor, European society now must complete its constitutional revolution through a democratic revolution. This would require a leap in quality: a Europe based no longer on the defence of subjective rights, but on the possibility of the citizens to influence decisions that are taken at a European level. Seen in this light, the recognition of fundamental rights in a treaty cannot suffice: what good does it serve to proclaim loudly new rights, which in the best of cases, will be effectively invoked only by a narrow minority of persons?

After having invented a constitutionalism without Constitution, Europe must thus come to terms anew with a problem without precedents: how to succeed in giving greater weight to the citizens, without dramatically undermining the role of the State – with which these citizens themselves identify always and before every other.

Is there a need for a genuine constitution? A great many have responded positively to this question, maintaining both the utility of a symbolic affirmation of the creation of a new political system and the necessity to bring order to the jungle of texts that today regulate the life of the European Union. However, none of these arguments resolves the question. Neither the simplification nor the democratisation of the European architecture require the shift to a constitutional regime. The present treaties have been modified many times to reinforce the rights of the European Parliament and they could be modified anew if, for example, there were the desire to reinforce the links between the European elections and the appointment of a European Commission. Furthermore, in most of the old European countries national identity is so strong that the legitimacy which Europe would obtain through a Constitution appears uncertain, as suggested by former constitutional judge Dieter Grimm 'without the people, there is no constitution' (Grimm, in *Une constitution pour l'Europe?* (2002) 69–78).

If the European construction clearly represents a political innovation, as we have already said, why seek at all costs to cast it into the traditional mould of the constitutions (Weiler, in *Une constitution pour l'Europe?* (2002) 151–76)? The final objective of the process is not that of progressively bringing about the creation of a centralised super-State but, on the contrary, to regulate the peaceful and harmonious coexistence of old nations, which are often attached to their traditions, and to invent rules to handle matters of joint interest in line with the expectations of the people. This notwithstanding, the idea of a European constitution has aroused a new interest at the beginning of this century.

II. The Lessons of the Constitutional Treaty's Failure

Interest in the constitutional idea was rekindled at the start of the twenty-first century, thanks to the debate on what was soon to be defined as a constitutional treaty. In a speech delivered in Berlin in May 2000, in the wake of the 50th anniversary of the Schuman Declaration, the then German Foreign minister Joschka Fischer endorsed the critique of functionalism, firmly rejecting what he defined as the 'inductive communitarization as per the "Monnet method"':

> This gradual process of integration, with no blueprint for the final state, was conceived in the 1950s for the economic integration of a small group of countries. Successful as it was in that scenario, this approach has proved to be of only limited use for the political integration and democratization of Europe. […] Even today a crisis of the Monnet method can no longer be overlooked, a crisis that cannot be solved according to the method's own logic. (http://ec.europa.eu/dorie/fileDownload.do?docId=192161&cardId=192161)

At the same time, Fischer invited his listeners to reflect on what the political architecture of the Union would be once the process of integration had been completed. His analysis, largely endorsed at the time, was decisive for the subsequent change in direction. Already in 1999, during the German presidency, the European Council had entrusted the drafting of a Charter of Fundamental Rights of the Union to an assembly composed of representatives of the national governments and Parliaments, and of members of the European

Parliament, so as to render visible that which – as Fischer would say later – had before been invisible, which is to say Europe's interest in the fundamental freedoms. After the partial failure of the Nice European Council in December 2000, when the Member States were effectively unable to come to an agreement on the principles that should have governed the functioning of the Union after its enlargement, the Laeken European Council (2001) assumed the responsibility for diagnosing the crisis of the 'Monnet method'. The formula of the convention was therefore the same as was used to launch the reflection on the 'goals of Europe' so desired by the German minister. Thus, a draft European Constitution was prepared and solemnly signed in Rome in October of 2004. However, after being rejected in the referenda of France and the Netherlands in 2005, it never came into force. This failure deserves further analysis, because it is rich in lessons, both regarding the reasoning beneath the institutional change, and the way in which these lessons themselves might be interpreted by public opinion.

A. A Fictitious Constitution

The extremely diplomatic language of the draft's first articles, which make reference to the heads of State on whose behalf the agreement had been sealed, left no doubt regarding the intentions of its authors: in their minds, this was a fully-fledged international treaty, even if it would have had to institute a Constitution for Europe. The last part of the text made systematic reference to a treaty that would have entered into force only after the ratification on part of all the 'high contracting parties', in accordance with the respective constitutional rules (articles 4–447). Yet more significant was the fact that, as all previous European agreements, it could be modified only subject to the approval of each Member State. This provision clearly aimed to protect the States from potential modifications beyond their control. Some will speak in this connection of legal cavils, which however did not prejudice the effective bearing of the text. Yet the difference is essential; while a Constitution establishes the manner in which a population intends to be governed, in the so-called European Constitution the States – or better said, the governments – remained the masters. It was they who decided the final content of the draft at the Intergovernmental Conference, and they clearly intended to maintain control over its future evolution. In contrast, the 'We the people' of the American Constitution clearly established, at least in principle, the advent of a new political body: the people of the United States, distinct from the 13 colonies. Moreover, in line with what had been provided for in Philadelphia in 1787, this Constitution came into force immediately after its ratification on the part of nine States. The decisive ratification, that of New Hampshire, occurred while a fierce debate was still underway in New York and in Virginia, a State in which a fifth of the Union's inhabitants lived at the time. The famous *Federalist papers* were written to convince the members of the Assembly of the New York Convention to ratify the new charter. Nothing like this for the European Constitution, whose dismissal was dictated by the negative outcome of referenda in two founding countries.

Surely, in many respects, this treaty resembled a Constitution. In the material sense, it established the conditions for the attribution and exercise of power at the European level. Formally, it was a single text which laid claim to a higher legal value than any other rule (articles 1–6, concerning the primacy of Union law). However, the change was marginal since, as stated above, these two aspects were already present, albeit in different form, in the previous constitutional order.

To speak of Constitution in a system which had hitherto been ruled by treaties suggests a break with the past. However, this constitutional treaty itself bore witness to the firm will to keep the preestablished order intact, especially as concerned with the equilibrium between the European institutions and the States. Many of the novelties introduced by the constitutional treaty were nothing more than preexisting elements reintroduced in a new guise. Indeed, the genesis of the constitutional treaty seems to have been dominated by the respective fears of the States regarding a weakening of their influence within the European political system. The nature of these fears varied from country to country. The large States (with the single exception of Germany) shared the will to limit the influence of supranational institutions; the smaller States, on the other hand, were worried about possible concentration of power in the hands of the larger countries. These worries were the watermark of the institutional structure defined by the Constitution. Somewhat paradoxically, the interpretation of this text is easier if one focuses on what it sought to avoid. Clearly, it did not aim to foster the emergence of a strong power directly founded on the will of the European citizens. Thus, the European Council seemed to benefit the most from the changes introduced by the Convention: its political leadership was reaffirmed and its power of political orientation was expanded to cover the entirety of external relations of the Union. At the request of the large States, it was decided that its efficacy should be improved through the institution of a permanent presidency. In other words, in a context dominated by fears regarding the consequences of enlargement, the individual and short-term concerns of the governments prevailed over the common interest, in defining a model for a sustainable government for the new Europe. Hence the importance attributed to defence mechanisms: maintenance of unanimity for Great Britain, voting rights for the Poles and the Spanish, the possibility of protecting their own culture for the French. Drawing a parallel with the American Constitution, we might say that while in Philadelphia the supporters of a stronger central power prevailed, in this case the 'antifederalists', the defenders of States rights, won the day. This continuity is easily explained: already from the start, it was clear that the debates within the Convention would be followed by a classical intergovernmental conference. The members of the Convention could not therefore ignore the preferences of the national governments without running the risk of being censured. In many respects, therefore, this text was in line with the history of successive treaties of the European construction, which was entirely made through progressive modifications: the references to a constitutional big bang were merely rhetorical.

B. A Reform Lacking Clear Objectives

If the analysis just made is correct, and if the draft treaty was much less revolutionary than its name led one to believe, how then to interpret the difficulties experienced by supporters of the Constitutional Treaty in presenting the concrete advantages of the project?

Many of the previous treaties, as we have said, were associated with important and easily explained projects: the single market for the Single European Act, the single currency for Maastricht. On the other hand, although the convention was conceived as an opportunity to do away with the mistakes of the past, in truth it was the daughter of the very Treaty of

Nice, which it was supposed to modify. Just as the latter had done, it concentrated above all on institutional reforms: the dominant view at that time, defended with great emphasis by Joschka Fischer, held that the functional method of Monnet had been overcome, along with integration by 'small steps' and '*de facto* solidarity'. But nobody was able to explain what great ambitions the Constitution pursued. The enlargement of the EU, which was its starting point, was treated as a technical problem, while in reality it raised a fundamental political question, namely: what are the ambitions of an enlarged Europe?

The debate awakened national sensitivities, transforming the negotiation into a zero-sum game and making it more difficult to come to an agreement. The artificial division between 'large' and 'small' States, almost non-existent in previous years, became a central problem: this explains the quite turbulent end of the process that gave birth to the draft Constitution, with an agreement reached laboriously, only then to be foundered by the results of the referenda. At the same time it became more difficult to 'sell' the public opinion on a text whose principal ambitions were of an institutional nature. In the absence of clear explanations, the draft became a source of widespread concerns, which were amply used by opponents in the 2005 referendum campaigns (relocation, fiscal dumping, levelling downward on social protection etc).

This episode is a lesson that must be taken into account. For the vast majority of people, institutional questions are secondary. With its many nations and diverse cultures, Europe cannot hope to generate the same sense of belonging that might be experienced by a community founded on ethnic or linguistic bonds. The popular adhesion to a particular form of institutional architecture remains a rare phenomenon, with the single exception being a country like the United States, where there seems to be a large consensus on the superiority of national institutions.

Ultimately, it would seem that Europe's legitimation depends to a large extent on its capacity of demonstrating its utility in everyday life, which brings us back to functionalism. Although this method is associated with the idea of agreements between elites, it offers the enormous advantage of providing simple answers to a fundamental question: what is the purpose of this construction? The Coal and Steel Community served the cause of peace and freedom; the common market intended to reinforce the economic prosperity of western Europe, precisely through the Single European Act in the 1980s. The clear functional objectives permitted the citizens to make sense of the European construction, providing at the same time simple parameters to assess its efficacy. In other words: the European Union is judged above all on the basis of the policies that it pursues and on the results that it attains. Certainly, the same consideration could be made about States, within which disenchantment against the *res publica* has greatly increased over the last years. But on the European level, the phenomenon is rendered still more evident by the almost complete absence of other forms of legitimation. Unlike the nation States, Europe has failed to create an 'imagined community' (Anderson (1983)): its legitimation depends firstly on its capacity to obtain positives results (Scharpf (2000)). As a result, institutional change in itself can hardly be a source of legitimacy.

From this perspective, the failure of the attempt at constitutionalisation of the European treaties at the dawn of the twenty-first century only confirms the lessons of more than 60 years of integration. Europe seems able to evolve only when its members are able to agree on how to achieve precise objectives; abstract speeches on good governance at the EU level were never able to mobilise sufficient consensus.

III. The Response of the EU to the Crisis

As has been observed, the strong economic and financial crisis which struck Europe beginning in 2008 has led to a tightening of European control on macroeconomic politics. Analyses of the decisions taken in this period tend to highlight the central role that the national governments – Germany first and foremost – have assumed during that period, but perhaps not enough consideration was given to the fact that, parallel to this, the supranational institutions saw their role strengthened in numerous sectors.

From the outbreak of the crisis, the European Central Bank (ECB) assumed a very enterprising attitude, broadening the range of tools at its disposal, in particular through the adoption of outright monetary transactions (OMT) in 2012 which enabled it to reassure the financial markets as to its determination to defend the euro, and the programme of quantitative easing (QE) launched in 2015. In this way, the ECB effectively assumed *de facto* the functions of lender of last resort, which everyone thought had been denied to it by the Treaty of Maastricht (Buiter, Rahbari (2012)), and it likewise began to play a primary role in European macroeconomic policies. Although these changes were introduced without the formal agreement of the Member States, the governments did not object to them.

Germany, which had systematically rejected everything which resembled a mutualisation of the national debt, decided not to comment on the initiatives of the ECB, even though, in both cases, everyone knew that the German member within the Bank's Governing Council was opposed to them. Likewise, contrary to widespread expectations, the powers of the Commission in the field of macroeconomic governance were significantly strengthened by a series of reforms adopted in 2011–2012. The crisis seems to have brought a consolidation of the power of supranational institutions.

We thus find ourselves standing before a paradox: why have the national governments, which declared themselves categorically contrary to new transfers of power at the European level, wound up conceding, willingly or unwillingly, substantial transfers of authority to institutions over which they can exercise no direct control? The paradox becomes yet more apparent if one considers the strong decline in support in favour of the European Union and of the idea of European integration which was observed in the same period.

A. The Reform of Macroeconomic Governance

The Economic and Monetary Union (EMU), part of the Treaty of Maastricht, was based on a clear distinction between the principles underpinning monetary policy – centralised and entrusted to a very powerful institution, namely the ECB – and the economic policies – decentralised but subject to coordination procedures regulated by rules (cf Dyson, Featherstone (1999)). One of the problems immediately identified in the literature was the 'unbalanced' character of the enforcement mechanism: indeed, the national authorities were obliged to apply the rules to themselves, which incentivised collusion and haggling. Unsurprisingly, in the first years of the implementation of the Stability and Growth Pact (SGP) underwritten in 1997, the Council routinely sweetened the recommendations of the Commission. The shortcomings of the system came to light in 2003, when the Economic and financial affairs Council (Ecofin) failed to obtain the qualified majority necessary to adopt the recommendations of the Commission, which proposed to sanction France and

Germany in the field of the excessive deficit procedure, although it was supported by a majority of countries. In 2005, following the discovery of repeated irregularities in Greece's public finances, the national governments reaffirmed their aversion to the conferral of additional powers to the Commission by rejecting a draft regulation aimed at strengthening the control capacities of the statistical Office of the European Union (Eurostat) on national accounts.

The European response to the crisis of the euro was slow and fragmentary, but it nonetheless contributed to a substantial consolidation of the European economic governance. A first part of the reform provided for the establishment of support mechanisms to assist countries at risk of default, culminating in the creation of the 2012 European Stability Mechanism (ESM). However, the 'creditor' countries imposed a significant consolidation of the oversight system in exchange for their solidarity, in order to prevent the reemergence of similar problems. In little more than a year came the adoption of two important legislative packets (the Six pack and the Two pack) and a new treaty, the Fiscal Compact, strongly promoted by chancellor Angela Merkel. This is not the place to make a systematic analysis of these reforms, but it is important to note that these reforms have significantly consolidated economic policy coordination, reinforcing the Commission's control over of the State Members' fiscal policy in a variety of ways (Keppenne (2014)). The scope of the Commission's powers was also extended to encompass the whole of macroeconomic policy.

The 'European Semester' was instituted, which multiplied the interactions between the national authorities and the Commission *before* the presentation of draft budgets. To guarantee the efficacy of the new normative system, there was a general shift from 'measures without binding consequences toward a binding framework' (Keppenne (2014) 211) to avoid the repetition of episodes like that of 2003. If the Commission finds that the rules of the Stability and Growth Pact have been violated, its 'recommendations' become binding, unless the Council overrules it within 10 days through a qualified majority decision. This system of 'reverse qualified majority', introduced by the Six pack and consolidated by the Fiscal Compact, makes it difficult to reverse the choices of the Commission – thus rendering the implementation process less 'partisan'. To quote the former European Council president Herman Van Rompuy: 'We were not fooled: we knew that the Commission's position would never be overruled' (cited in Dehousse (2016) 624). Finally, the German government and its allies also attempted to impose an extension of the supervisory powers of the European Court of Justice in matters of economic policy. Given the British opposition to any treaty modification, they had to settle for a parallel mechanism with regard to violations, in order to monitor the implementation of the Fiscal Compact (Keppenne (2014)).

However, the idea of a greater automaticity in the implementation of European rules has encountered strong resistance on the part of certain States, France in particular. The compromise established by the Six pack was rather ambiguous: the recommendations were maintained and could thus be modified by a qualified majority, but, to reject them, a reverse qualified majority was necessary. After months of great uncertainty in the financial markets, the question was finally resolved with the Fiscal Compact, which established the commitment of the contracting parties to systematically endorse the proposals and the recommendations of the Commission, the exception being cases where a qualified majority opposes the proposed decision (article 7).

In a certain sense, things were easier as regards banking union, as a juridical basis was immediately available: article 127(6) TFEU authorised the transfer of powers in the field of the prudential supervision of the ECB credit institutions. This simplified the implementation of decisions taken by the EU leaders – a consideration which should not be underestimated, given the dramatic character of the crisis. Therefore, in the spring of 2012 when the president of the ECB Mario Draghi began to apply pressure towards making the European Central Bank become the anchor of what was called a 'banking union', no alternative proposals were put forward. Once the decision was taken, it took only a few months to agree on the project of a Single Supervisory Mechanism (SSM). The Commission granted this question expedited treatment, and its proposals were then clarified by ECB experts during the summer. A roadmap was brought to the table in September of 2012 and approved by the European leaders in the following month. The ECB is now the single institution to decide whether to concede or revoke a banking licence in the eurozone. It had to hire about a thousand functionaries for its supervisory tasks and, at the moment, it occupies about a fifth of the entire personnel responsible for banking supervision in the area.

This episode, together with the reinforcement of the Commission's powers of oversight as regards macroeconomic policy, illustrates the singular character of the events that followed in the wake of the Euro crisis. In both cases, notwithstanding the sovereignly concerns of the Member States, and a political climate which was ever more hostile toward the EU, the supranational institutions have seen their power significantly reinforced in areas of strategic importance.

B. European Control as the Lesser Evil

The transfer of larger powers to supranational institutions did not occur from one day to the next, as if it were caused by a sort of big bang. On the contrary, it is the result of a series of decisions taken during countless dramatic meetings, in which a great rift between the eurozone States clearly emerged, determined by their respective financial situations; on the one hand, northern European countries with sound public finances and on the other, southern European countries with varying solvency problems. The power shift was so gradual that the first analyses of the crisis tended to underline the absence of a strong transfer of competences to the EU or to the eurozone level, concentrating instead on the cumulative nature of the successive reforms that essentially preserved the philosophy behind the Maastricht project and the SCP. For example, using the models of institutional change put forward by Streeck and Thelen (in *Beyond continuity* (2005)), some scholars have described the attribution of new powers of surveillance to the ECB as a case of *stratification*, in which new institutional elements come to integrate existing ones, and the reform of the economic governance framework as a *redirection* of existing instruments through the definition of new criteria (Salines, Glöckler, Truchlewski (2012)). This gradualism was in great part due to the absence of a broad consensus on the nature of the reforms to be pursued, or, in the first place, on the need itself for reforms. The negotiations often took place following the same scheme, with Germany and its closest allies, initially reticent at the idea of a greater solidarity, obliged in the end to accept it, in order to avert the risks for the Euro due to the instability of the financial markets, but imposing, in exchange, stronger EU control mechanisms. The fragmentary character of the reform process could even explain why, despite the growing attention addressed to European affairs in national policies, as post-functionalist scholars have observed (Hooghe, Marks (2009)), the opposition to greater integration did not prevent a significant transfer of authority to the European level. Not only have various tactics been employed to avoid risky debates, but the absence of a great 'leap forward', the sense of urgency and the technical complexity of the proposed reforms, have combined in the last analysis to justify ad hoc solutions. As regards the motivation of key actors, it has been suggested that the final result owes a great deal to the appearance of a new endogenous preference among national governments, 'the common interest to save the euro and the eurozone' (Schimmelfennig (2014) 329). All of this finds an echo in the words of key actors of the period. According to Van Rompuy, for example, 'with the passing of time the governments have come to understand that the problem was systemic and that it could have exploded the entire monetary union' (interview with Van Rompuy (April 2015) cit. in Dehousse (2016)). The ex-president of the Italian Council Enrico Letta was even more direct: 'Germany has found itself constrained to accept the banking union because the alternative was the end of euro' (interview with Letta (21 January 2016) cit. in Dehousse (2016)). In other words, the existential threat over the common currency has softened the long-standing opposition to the reinforcement of the EU's regulatory powers.

This, however, leaves us with a question related to the choice of political instruments. Having reluctantly accepted the reinforcement of EU powers in areas where they would have clearly preferred, since the beginning, to preserve the widest discretionary powers possible, why have the governments decided to confer power on supranational institutions, over which they exercise (in principle) limited control, notwithstanding the intergovernmental spirit of the moment? This choice can be explained through a simple concept: lack of confidence. The years of crisis have seen an increase in polarisation, with the Member States of the eurozone divided into two blocs. According to the interpretation of the so-called creditor countries, the crisis was principally due to the lax budgetary policies pursued by southern European countries. The crisis revealed a series of deviant behaviours – the worst of which were in Greece, which had forged its public accounts – and this inevitably came to erode mutual trust. A survey published by the Pew Research Center at the moment of greatest intensity in the crisis showed the deep lack of confidence of the citizens amongst the various EU countries. The majority of Germans believed that the Italians were the most corrupt, and the Greeks the laziest, of the European peoples, and it seems that the situation was no better with respect to relations between the governments. It is no wonder, then, that the countries that were asked to contribute to various solidarity mechanisms should show so little enthusiasm. For that entire period, the German leaders and their allies opposed the fiscal transfers and expressed their desire to avoid any kind of moral hazard. In their opinion, shared responsibility mechanisms would have created perverse incentives for States that were already too self-indulgent in the field of fiscal policy or banking regulation. Even in countries like France, there was a widespread conviction that the public authorities of some southern European countries should be controlled more closely. For its part, Finland demanded a collateral from Greece as a condition for its contributing to the 2011 rescue package. Economic studies have shown that lack of confidence generally translates into requests for greater regulation, even in societies where there is limited support for the State (Aghion, Algan, Cahuc et al (2010)). If applied to the EU, this model helps us to explain why, in the absence of any possibility of an orderly exit, the lack of confidence between the countries of northern Europe and those of southern Europe has led to a compromise on the basis of which a more rigorous European discipline has been imposed, in exchange for the commitment to financial solidarity among eurozone countries.

The lack of confidence was so strong that creditor countries insisted on a depoliticisation of the enforcement mechanisms. And, as former president Van Rompuy underlined, 'in the EU there exists only one way to depolicitise a process: to "communitarise" it' (cit. in Dehousse (2016) 627).

As for macroeconomic policy, the Commission has proven to be the most natural choice for a function of oversight which, in many respects, reflects its role as guardian of treaties according to the 'Community method'. In the same way, in the banking sector, the institution of a strong European regulator was a prerequisite to the mutualisation of the guarantees offered to banks. In both cases, the delegation of authority to supranational institutions was perhaps no one's favourite choice, but, in a situation characterised by radical divergences between national preferences, it represented a second-best situation, acceptable to everyone. To the 'hawks', it offered guarantees against risks of incorrect applications on the part of lax and unreliable governments; while to the 'doves', whose contractual power was weaker, the submission to control by an independent institution appeared less menacing than submission to foreign administrations. To put it more simply: for the Greek government it was preferable to be controlled by faceless institutions (which then could be criticised for their bureaucratic character) than by the dreaded German Finance minister Wolfgang Schaüble.

IV. Politicisation and Institutional Reforms

The common wisdom is that EU policymaking is characterised by the absence of politicisation. European policies are generally considered the fruit of interactions between the national and European bureaucracies and stakeholders of various kinds. The European elections are seen as 'second-order elections', carried out on the basis of the model established on occasion of the first direct elections of the members of the European Parliament in 1979; the candidates are selected by national parties and national issues dominate both in the electoral campaign and at the ballot-box (Reif, Schmitt (1980)). Equally emphasised are the lack of a strong European party system and the almost complete absence of 'political parties at the European level' – to take up the words of the Treaty on the Functioning of the European Union – in the national scene. In the vast literature on the all-encompassing concept of Europeanisation, attention has focused on the influence of Europe on national policies rather than on that of political systems. In 2000, the political scientist Peter Mair (1951–2011) identified a disparity between the effective responsibilities of the European Union and its Member States on the one hand, and the issues at the centre of electoral competition at each of these levels on the other. According to him, issues such as the direction and the scope of the integration process continued to occupy a central place at the time of the European elections, even if the European Parliament, notwithstanding its repeated requests, exercised only a limited influence on such questions. In contrast, conflicts over national policy issues still dominate national elections, although those issues are ever more conditioned by decisions taken at the European level. In consequence, the choices of the electorate had a limited impact on the important decisions taken at both levels.

Since this diagnosis was made, however, things have changed in many respects. Developments at the European level tend to matter more in national elections. This evolution affects both the behaviour of the parties and that of voters. As far as the former go, expert surveys and manifesto data have revealed the greater importance attributed to European issues by political parties across the whole Union (Steenberger, Scott (2004)). Since these issues may be divisive, party leaders often seek to avoid the debate, so as to preserve party cohesiveness (Ladrech (2012)). In some cases, however, disagreements become so strong as to lead to the emergence of new political parties (*Front de gauche* in France after the 2005 referendum, or else the *Independent Greeks* (ANEL) in response to the 2011 memorandum imposed on Greece by the EU). As far as electoral behaviour is concerned, a number of scholars have suggested we might be shifting to a new era, as contestation over European issues has appeared at the national level, notably after the economic and financial crisis of 2008.

On account of the key role of European decisions in successive rescue packages and in the development of a policy of fiscal austerity, the domestic salience of EU membership has significantly increased, in particular in those countries worst affected by the crisis. The elections of 2012 and 2015 in Greece were widely considered, by the parties and by the electorate, to be a referendum on the permanence of the country in the eurozone. European issues played a central role also in the Italian political elections of 2013, albeit not in such drastically binary terms. According to the outgoing president of the Council Mario Monti, national policies and those of the EU were so closely intertwined that their respective agendas had to be considered together: Italy needed the support of the Union, but for this it needed to become a reliable partner, by stabilising among other things its public finances. In contrast, the electoral programme of Silvio Berlusconi's party, the *Popolo della libertà*, openly attacked austerity and Europe, just as opposition parties did (*Lega nord* and the *Movimento cinque stelle*). Parties' attitude towards Europe thus became a basic element of their strategic choices. This makes it easier to understand why, after its victory in the 2015 Greek elections, the leftist party Syriza decided to form an alliance with the right-wing ANEL: although divided on many sociocultural questions, both found themselves in agreement on one of the most contentious issues of the time, that is, the necessity of renegotiating the memorandum of understanding imposed by the EU.

Thus, an important characteristic of elections in times of crisis emerges: when European issues play a central role in the electoral campaign, there is a notable growth in opposition of both parties and candidates to EU policies. This is nothing new as regards populist parties; in almost all European countries, anti-establishment movements, both on the extreme left and on the extreme right, have regularly used EU issue in order to garner electoral consensus (Kriesi (2007)). However, one of the most surprising aspects of the process of Europeanisation, which we have witnessed in recent times, has been the appearance of a negative rhetoric amongst the leaders of government parties traditionally well disposed toward the EU. Nicolas Sarkozy in France or Matteo Renzi in Italy have clearly sought to leverage on hostile feelings toward Brussels, in order to obtain greater support. Even former European commissioner Mario Monti warned against the dangers of 'creditocracy', a system in which all decisions are dictated by countries with solid public finances, regardless of the situation of their partners (Goulard, Monti (2012)). In times of crisis, one gains more votes by criticising the EU than by supporting it. In general, this new rhetoric has contributed to fanning the flames of Euroscepticism in the public opinion.

Therefore, EU politics seem to have abandoned that classical model which dominated its first decades of existence. That model was characterised by a double separation: between policies and politics on the one hand, and between the national level and that of the EU on the other. On both levels, the distance between the poles has decreased. Macroeconomic policy issues, largely determined at the EU level, have become so important as to occupy a central place in national political debates. The same thing holds for other political issues. In consequence, to fully understand the attention reserved to European questions, it is no longer possible to consider the 'EU issue' as an element limited to the debate over greater or lesser integration, as used to be the case in the past. It is necessary to take into consideration a much wider range of EU-related issues, covering topics such as unemployment, macroeconomic politics, immigration or welfare reform. Political parties, including the mainstream ones, traditionally loath to adventure onto uncertain European ground, have been obliged to adapt themselves to this evolution. In the same way, the attitudes towards EU-related issues have played an important role, directly or indirectly, in the recent electoral contests. The two trends seem to be mutually reinforcing. Parties are obviously very sensitive to what they know about the potential voters' feelings, while the growing Euroscepticism in the contemporary political discourse has contributed to the reflux of pro-European attitudes among the general public. While the phenomenon was evident enough in most of the debtor countries, the same causes seem to have led to similar effects in other countries. True, neither Germany nor Finland have experienced the tightening of European control that has caused such strong reactions in Greece, nevertheless, they have seen the development of anti-European forces such as True Finns or *Alternativ für Deutschland*. Clearly, all these elements owe a great deal to the dramatic character of the economic and financial crisis which Europe has been experiencing since 2008; however, it is improbable that they will disappear with the end of the crisis. The emergence of European issues in national debates preceded the outbreak of the crisis and, since it constituted a reaction to structural factors – namely, the strengthening of control exercised by the EU institutions in certain sectors – it can be supposed that the phenomenon will persist also in the future.

The current process of 'negative Europeanisation' is ambivalent. One the one hand, it does not necessarily indicate a total rejection of Europe and it might even contribute to the intensification of the debates on European issues, as has long been hoped by the federalists; on the other hand, it clearly complicates the decision-making process at the level of the Union by polarising the national positions. For this reason, Liesbet Hooghe and Gary Marks (2009) maintain that the growing attention given to EU matters at the domestic level, after decades of relative indifference, could make it more difficult to carry on business as usual at the EU level, with the high reliance on experts and on decisions by consensus that characterise EU policymaking. If this is true, the future of Europe is likely to be marked by growing political conflicts.

Could the Europeanisation of national politics in the final analysis encourage the politicisation of EU policymaking? It is interesting to note that with the 2014 European elections we have witnessed the institution of a system of indirect election of the president of the Commission, with candidates presented by the principal political parties. Although this novelty does not seem to have had a strong impact on the electorate (Hobalt, Schmitt, Popa (2015)), the European Council, against the will of many of its members, in the end agreed to yield and to follow the indications of the Parliament in the choice of the president of the Commission. This might encourage the parties to up the ante in the future, thus contributing to the development of political parties on the EU level. So far, apart from Jean-Claude Juncker's success in 2014, it seems that the impact of the system of

Spitzenkandidaten on the political system of the Union has been modest. Contrary to the initial expectations, it has not brought about a clear political realignment of the Union's decision-making process, with clearer political alternatives offered to the electorate. The slight centripetal shift felt at the moment of the choice of the Commission's president does not seem sufficient to counterbalance the strong centrifugal pressures of recent years. If we want to achieve important institutional reforms, these must be the result of great compromises between national governments and, for now, the dominant winds do not seem to be blowing in the right direction.

V. Some Lessons for the Future

As indicated in the introduction, Europe today is facing great structural challenges. Although the crises that followed from 2007 have led to major reforms, economic and monetary union are far from being complete. Essential aspects, necessary to guarantee stability to the banking system, are missing, such as a European mechanism of deposit insurance or a more robust banking resolution fund, which could be adopted on the basis of the present treaty. Above all, Europe is deprived of the instruments that might allow it to develop a true countercyclical policy in case of regression: the plan of investment launched by president Juncker at the beginning of his term has in fact only a limited scope. Moreover, the massive influx of refugees in 2015 has emphasised clear weaknesses in the field of border controls and in the management of migratory flows. The awakening of Russia and the exacerbation of relations with Turkey create instability at the borders. Finally, the United States, which has always supported the project of European integration, seems much more distant under the Trump Presidency. In his time, Barack Obama showed little regard for European affairs, proving much more interested in strengthening ties with Asia. The first steps of the Trump presidency have been characterised by unfavourable, if not openly hostile signs, towards both the European Union and NATO. The protectionist agenda of the present administration cannot help but create problems in relations with Europe.

Given their interdependence, it is difficult to imagine that the European States might effectively respond to these challenges by acting independently. Moreover, the formal request for withdrawal from the European Union presented by the United Kingdom indirectly forces the remaining 27 Members to ask themselves what sense they give to their membership in the European Union. At the same time, it is obvious that the growing diffidence of broad segments of the population with respect to Europe renders agreement more difficult.

In light of what has been said previously on the long-term evolution of European integration, it is hard to imagine that the response to these difficulties might issue from a confrontation between various abstract models of organisation of the European continent. The somewhat surreal debate which was sparked by the celebratory declaration of the 60 years of the Rome Treaties illustrated the limits of this approach. Time and energy have been wasted on theoretical discussions regarding the possibilities of integration at two or more speeds, whereas a multispeed Europe has been a fact since the launch of the European construction. Suffice it to mention that, when the six founding countries decided to institute the ECSC in 1950, there were protests against what seemed even then to be the forging ahead of a small squad of pro-integration States. Other illustrious examples are the Treaty of Schengen on the free movement of persons (1985) or the single currency, which even today regards a limited number of Member countries. Nevertheless the debate that we have witnessed on that occasion has only succeeded in creating principled oppositions between the Member States. As has been said, whenever one has sought to change method and to confront abstract issues such as the geographical limits of Europe or its ultimate institutional framework, we have witnessed resounding failures, as in the case of the draft European Constitution. Institutions are a means for reaching objectives; they must not become an end in and of themselves. The Treaties of Rome show us the sequence we should pursue: first they list the objectives, then the policies and only afterwards the institutions. The same road should be followed: a debate is needed, but it must first deal with the challenges which the European countries are facing, and the responses to these. Only afterwards, on the basis of the preferences which have emerged in this first phase, or perhaps on the basis of a coalition of States which declare themselves ready to accept possible reforms, can one pass to a discussion on the reforms that might be necessary to reach these objectives.

Some will perhaps assert that this reminder inspired by the 'Monnet method' neglects the importance of the legitimacy crisis which Europe must face. This critique should not blind us to the advantage of that approach, which renders European construction more easily comprehensible. The possibility of giving a sense to what has been decided is essential in the eyes of the citizens. The many referenda tied to Europe over the course of the last 20 years have shown that voters find it easier to decide on the basis of its judgement as to the benefits (real or supposed) of European policy, than on the basis of an abstract vision of institutional balance. Sometimes, it will even accept heavy sacrifices if it can be convinced that these are indispensable. Thus, the Irish accepted by referendum the Fiscal Compact, as well as the austerity that it entailed, not certainly on account of their adhesion to an abstract project, but because it seemed to them the only way out of the crisis into which their country had then fallen. The emphasis placed on concrete objectives also offers the advantage of facilitating the choice of performance indicators. How many times have we heard: 'At Maastricht we were told that the euro would make us more prosperous, that it would even protect us from instability. But this has not happened'? In other words, the more public opinion matters, the more functionalism will be necessary, because, as we have seen, the legitimacy of Europe depends above all on its achievement rather than on its being.

Having said this, it seems clear that future reforms will have to address the Union's legitimacy problem: to restore confidence in Europe, it is necessary to give greater weight to the voice of the peoples. The emergence of populist movements in the great majority of European countries shows that the model of the 'government by elites' which has marked the history of European integration is no longer regarded as legitimate. How can one give greater weight to the concerns of the citizens without denying the traditional *modus operandi* of Europe, that is, the patient search of compromises between divergent national interests? This will be without any doubt one of the greatest challenges in the years to come. But it is every bit as clear that a debate which addresses this issue alone will stand little chance of resulting in a positive outcome.

Bibliography

Aghion, P, Algan, Y and Cahuc, P et al, 'Regulation and distrust' (2010) 125(3) *The quarterly journal of economics* 1015–49, https://scholar.harvard.edu/files/shleifer/files/regulation_trust_qje.pdf.

Amato, G, Bribosia, H and de Witte, B (eds), *Genèse et destinée de la Constitution européenne/Genesis and destiny of the European constitution* (Brussels, 2007).

Anderson, B, *Imagined communities. Reflections on the origin and spread of nationalism* (London, 1983).

Buiter, W and Rahbari, E, 'The ECB as lender of last resort for sovereigns in the euro area' (2012) 50(2) *Journal of common market studies* 6–35.

Dehousse, R (ed), *Une constitution pour l'Europe?* (Paris, 2002), (esp R Dehousse, *Un nouveau constitutionnalisme?* 19–38; D Grimm, *Le moment est-il venu d'élaborer une constitution européenne?* 69–78; JHH Weiler, *Fédéralisme et constitutionnalisme: le sonderweg de l'Europe* 151–76).

Dehousse, R, 'Why has EU macroeconomic governance become more supranational?' (2016) 38(5) *Journal of European integration* 617–31.

Dyson, K and Featherstone, K, *The road to Maastricht: negotiating economic and monetary union* (Oxford, 1999).

Goulard, S and Monti, M, *La democrazia in Europa. Guardare lontano* (Milano, 2012).

Griffith, RT, *Europe's first Constitution* (London, 2000).

Hobolt, S, Schmitt, H and Popa, SA, 'Does personalization increase turnout? Spitzenkandidaten in the 2014 European Parliament elections' (2015) 16(3) *European Union politics* 347–68.

Hooghe, L and Marks, G, 'A postfunctionalist theory of European integration: from permissive consensus to constraining dissensus' (2009) 39(1) *British journal of political science* 1–23.

Keppenne, J-P, 'Institutional report', in U Neegaard, C Jacqueson and J Hartig Danielsen (eds), *The economic and monetary Union: constitutional and institutional aspects of the economic governance within the EU*, XXVI FIDE Congress, 1, (Copenhagen, 2014) 179–257, http://fide2014.eu/pdf/FINAL-Topic-1-on-the-EMU.pdf.

Kriesi, H, 'The role of European integration in national election campaigns' (2007) 8(1) *European Union politics* 83–108.

Ladrech, R, 'Party change and europeanization: elements of an integrated approach' (2012) 35(3) *West European politic* 544–88.

Mair, P in KH Goetz and S Hix (eds), *The limited impact of Europe on national party systems, in Europeanised politics? European integration and national political systems* (Portland (Oregon), 2000) 27–51.

Reif, K and Schmitt, H, 'Nine second-order national elections – A conceptual framework for the analysis of European election results' (1980) 8(1) *European journal of political research* 3–44.

Salines, M, Glöckler, G and Truchlewski, Z, 'Existential crisis, incremental response: the eurozone's dual institutional evolution 2007–2011' (2012) 19(5) *Journal of European public policy* 665–81.

Scharpf, F, *Gouverner l'Europe* (Paris, 2000).

Schimmelfennig, F, 'European integration in the euro crisis: the limits of postfunctionalism' (2014) 36(3) *Journal of European integration* 321–37.

Steenbergen, MR and Scott, DJ in G Marks and MR Steenbergen (eds), *Contesting Europe? The salience of European integration as a party issue*, in *European integration and political conflict* (Cambridge, 2004) 165–92.

Stein, E, 'Lawyers, judges, and the making of a transnational constitution' (1981) 75(1) *American journal of international law* 1–27.

Streeck, W and Thelen, K (eds), *Beyond continuity. Institutional change in advanced political economie* (Oxford, 2005).

All web pages are understood as having last been visited on 26 June 2018.

PART VII

Conclusion

27

The States' Upcoming Choice: Move Ahead All Together, Some Members Only or Alone?

JOSEPH HH WEILER AND JOHANN JUSTUS VASEL

All together, some members only or alone? This is the choice that Member States must address. Surely it all depends on the direction we choose to move ahead.

But if moving all together is not obvious, moving ahead, too, is not without its problems. Euro speak has always had a messianic fervour to it: 'An ever closer Union' are the iconic words of the Treaties. But if it is to be *ever closer* it must always be moving, closer and closer (even when it gets hot and sticky) to some illusive promised land of integration, with that facile and well-worn example of the bicycle which falls if its stops moving. But why should the question of all together or only some be tied to that problematic *Drang nach Elisium*? What about the option of staying (partnership-wise) all together, but also staying (destination-wise) exactly where we are, content with what we have created and, perhaps, not risking it with ever new ventures and expanding frontiers, geographical, political or functional.

To complexify even further, one has to add the manner in which we move that destination: The manner in which Europe is governed – in what areas does a State retain its veto, to give but one example or how adept will the Union be in respecting the democratic traditions of the Member States to give another – will also determine whether a Member State wants to move all together, only with some, or maybe even exit – as its only option if it feels an unacceptable loss of voice.

In this chapter we will try to untangle some of these complexities exploring in depth the 'alone-exit' option. It is critical in our view to address two 'alone' narratives which are current in Europe: the obvious one which is exit from the European Union (EU) – à la Brexit. But no less important is the interconnected narrative of exit from a Member State à la Catalonia, Scotland and others. They are interconnected in two ways: first, it is the prospect of finding a safe haven within the EU which emboldens the call for secession from within Member States. Secondly, and even more importantly, there is a common mindset to these two narratives of aloneness which requires exploration. Both are a problem and a challenge to Europe, the second even more than the first.

We will then turn to the 'all together' and the 'some members only' options. Our thesis here is simple enough: this is a false dichotomy. At least since the 1970s, Europe has been practicing in myriad ways, big and small, a combination of 'all together' and 'some members only'. It is but another manifestation of 'united in diversity'. There is no going back on this combined model. Our preferred term for such is *differentiated integration*. It is part of Europe's very ontology. It is a complex matrix with differentiation occurring along axes of time, space and subject matter. But central to our analysis is the differentiation between 'in Treaty' differentiated integration – through the mechanism of enhanced cooperation, and 'ex Treaty' differentiated integration – through ad hoc arrangements, international treaties and some mechanisms which straddle both in and ex. We will highlight two features of this empirical matrix. First, a paradox whereby the 'in Treaty' enhanced cooperation though functional has been marginal, whereas the 'ex Treaty' model has captured the centre stage in importance – think about the Fiscal Compact – even if of dubious legality. Secondly, the status quo even if functional and pragmatic is messy and contentious and often leaves a bitter taste of a two-class Europe rather than a two-speed Europe.

I. The 'Alone' Option

One can forgive the authors of the hopelessly drafted article 50 TEU (Treaty on European Union). It was obviously, like nuclear weapons, never meant to be used. And yet Brexit suddenly made this option a reality. Unlike some, we do not entertain great fear of contagion and even if one or two Member States were to follow the UK example, we do not think such an (unlikely) eventuality would be quite as disastrous as is often presented. Such Member States would clearly stand in the way of any meaningful reform of the European construct and, thus, better out than in.

It is not our intention in this chapter to examine the viability and pros and cons of the 'alone' option from the perspective of an exiting Member State, let alone advocate it.

The main importance of Brexit in our view is that it points to deep seated and widespread phenomena across the Union of which the UK decision was but an extreme manifestation. The enthusiasm for a hard Brexit and the closing of European ranks in adopting a tough negotiating stance towards the UK – mainly as an internal elite strategy of scaring off any other 'exiters' – comes with three heavy price tags.

The first is that part and parcel of this strategy is to underscore 'British exceptionalism' ('We should have listened to de Gaulle'; 'the British were never true Europeans' etc etc *ad nauseam* and *ad tedium*) and in this way shut our eyes to the deep seated problems which are pan-European. The second price tag is that by forcing a hard 'alone' option on the UK, the Union is shutting itself to some options which may serve it well in its future. The third and final is that even in the short term this strategy is probably counterproductive in maximising the chances of the outcome which would serve best both parties.

A. The Two Narratives of the 'Alone' Option

There are currently in Europe two trends sweeping across and within the Member States which, at first glance, appear contradictory.

The first trend is an internal yearning for 'alone': the turn to secessionism *within* Member States, the two most visible, but certainly not unique, instances being Catalonia and Scotland. Interestingly in the internal discourse of secessionism, European integration is considered favourably and the European Union is viewed as the safe haven within which the newly independent State would be firmly anchored. Take away that safe haven and the appetite for secession would considerably diminish.

The second trend is the normalisation and mainstreaming of Euroscepticism in various forms. From a sideline show usually associated with the lunatic fringes of established politics, Euroscepticism now enjoys considerable support, is an official part of the platform of established parties and has made considerable electoral gains. On some counts at least seven out of the remaining 27 governments of the Member States could be counted as Eurosceptic to one degree or another.

In fact, though the surface language of the two trends seems to be contradictory (internal secessionism Europhilic, external secession an extreme manifestation of Euroscepticism), the deep structure of both discourses draws from the same well: the (re)turn to (national) identity as a potent mobilising and coalescing factor in social and political life. Note that the (re)turn is to national identity what ruptures the usual assumption that Member State identity equals national identity. This turn to identity is almost in all places associated with dissatisfaction with the functioning of democracy either within the State or within the Union, and in some well-known instances is associated with an attraction of what is not euphemistically called illiberal democracy. Whether an illiberal regime is consistent with a modern understanding of democracy may or may not be just a question of definition, but the sanctifying power of the word democracy represents in this respect a certification of guarantee for the States.

What complicates the picture even further is the oft intermingling of these two issues with the problems associated with the mass immigration/refugee and the growing xenophobia associated with such. One notes, for example, that in the UK debate, which had been largely shielded from the mass of immigration from the Middle East disasters, internal EU free movement was conflated with migrations and exploited as such.

We want to give two contrasting normative readings to the phenomenon underlying the two trends – secessionism and Euroscepticism: one antipathetic and the other sympathetic. We do this purposefully because we think neither trend can be dismissed by painting it with a simple black and white brush.

The demand for secession from the Union – with Brexit being an extreme manifestation of Euroscepticism – or from within a State is often couched in moral terms. The moral argument is typically understood in its negative manifestation: that it would be immoral (and illegal) to deny such independence to distinct nations such as the Scots or the Catalans. At its most powerful, the moral argument is linked to some form of democratic claim. At its starkest this could be expressed by the proposition that majoritarian democracy is predicated on the majority and minority being part of the same *demos*, and that, by contrast, the absence of independence in effect enshrines the rule of one *demos* over another or some *demoi* over another. This would be true as regards both types of secession discourses. It is the precise point at which the vocabulary of sovereignty and identity meets the vocabulary of democracy.

One difference lies in the legal dimension: no one calls into question the legal right of the UK to secede from the Union, whereas the legal right of, say, Catalonia to secede from Spain is hotly disputed. But other elements of this type of argument seem to be of the same cloth.

The alleged legal difference as regards the right to secession between the two narratives is of little concern to us in this chapter. Though we take the view that under international law neither Catalonia nor Scotland enjoy a right to secede, we do not give much moral weight to the international legal position as a valid proxy for a real moral argument.

The international legal position was articulated most cogently in the 1960s declaration on friendly relations and it is clear to us that it was impacted by quite a cynical political position by States which had won independence in the post-World War II decolonisation process and were eager not to give legal space to a partition of their newly won independent territories.

Indeed, for this reason we applaud the political maturity of both the UK and Canada, which allowed a referendum on exit of Scotland and Quebec respectively, whilst holding to the position that neither one nor the other enjoyed a legal right to secede. It is an open and vexed question whether in those cases (and in the case of Catalonia) such a referendum should include the citizens of the entire union or of the subunit alone. It is understandable why in Spain, a much younger modern democracy, there is far greater reluctance to allow Catalonia alone to decide on the break-up of the Kingdom.

Beyond legality, at a deeper level the nexus between the two secession discourses is that they represent, reflect and reinforce a general trend in Europe which has two characteristics.

The first is a turn away from one of the fundamental moral drivers of the post-World War II European circumstance: a turn to politics which view with abhorrence some of the ills of nationalism and seek policies (and a polity) which transcend such and place the individual in his or her full humanity at the centre.

The second, even more worrying and particularly manifest in certain strands of the Eurosceptic discourse, is a fatigue with post-World War II humdrum and greyness of democracy itself, which is concerned with the day-to-day business of economic management and individual and collective welfare and safety.

Mark Mazower, in his brilliant and original history and historiography of twentieth century Europe (*Dark continent: Europe's 20th century* (1998)), insightfully describes a cyclical pattern of the rise and demise of democracy and messianic narratives in twentieth century Europe. The Europe of monarchs and emperors which entered World War I was often rooted in a political messianic narrative in various States (in Germany, Italy, Russia and even Britain and France). It then oscillated after the war towards new democratic orders, which then oscillated back into new forms of political messianism, in fascism and communism. As the tale is usually told, after World War II Western Europe was said to oscillate back to democracy shorn of messianic dreams as expressed in our Member States old and new. The fear is that we are now at the moment of cyclical turn yet again. It is noticeable how frequently Eurosceptic discourse not only reemploys national and even nationalist images, but how notions of 'destiny', 'masters of our own fate', 'taking back control', and some form of promise of a better 'kingdom to come' creep into this imagery, the staples of messianic politics replacing democratic processes.

The ground is fertile for such imagery when our inevitably imperfect democracies fail to deliver the goods, as has been the perception for close to a decade now in both economic and security terms or when it fails to distribute its sweets in an equitable manner which has been the case for even longer.

Fatigue sets in and the scene is set for yet another European turn to narratives such as those which appeared in the interwar period. The writing is clearly on the wall in bold graffiti in Hungary, Poland, the Netherlands, Denmark, Sweden, Germany and Italy, but the ascendance of these temptations is present elsewhere both in East and West.

Some readers might be bristling at the way we have indicated a nexus between some of these ugly manifestations of Euroscepticism, illiberal democracy and reemergence of political messianic imagery with the secession movements in, say, Scotland and Catalonia, the plans of which are to be as independent and democratic States.

It is precisely this allusion to the previous European cycles in the wake of World War I which justifies in our view the claim of such a nexus. So in what way may we regard the drive for an independent Scotland or Catalonia, at least in some way, made of the same cloth as the uglier features of Euroscepticism?

The claims of Catalonia, Scotland and the like eerily revert to that very period, the early twentieth century post-World War I, and to the then prevailing mentality in understanding the building blocks of national democracy. It was a period when self-determination as an operational and legal concept was invented (or rediscovered) and at that period appeared a progressive idea, indeed in some respects was, associated as it were with the breakup of empires and the domination of one people over another. It reemerged, with even greater moral force and legal solidity in the post-World War II era with the process of decolonisation. The post-World War I statutes of minorities were an expression of that form of progressiveness and were motivated by the same impulse of limiting domination.

But the very fact of those special regimes for the protection of minorities was the supposed solution to the notion that a single 'nation State' had to be just that: a single nation State and that encompassing more than one nationality within the nation State was a problem which required a 'progressive' solution – hence the special treaties on minorities which abounded in the breakup of the Ottoman and the Austro-Hungarian Empires.

These arrangements, representing perhaps progress at their time, also embodied a very dark side eventually, let us not hide the ugly facts, feeding and leading to that poisonous logic of national purity and ethnic cleansing. Make no mistake: we are not suggesting for one minute that anyone in Catalonia, or Scotland or elsewhere, is an ethnic cleanser. What we are suggesting is that the 'do it alone' mentality is associated with that kind of mindset.

The secessionist movements represent a turn away from the double shift which occurred in the post-colonial era in the second half of the twentieth century: a more inclusive notion of the nation itself and a more inclusive notion of the State to allow for the possibility of uniting, under single citizenship, more than one nationality. At its simplest this part of our claim is that the secessionist movement is a turning of one's back on these more inclusive and tolerant mindsets and a revival of an earlier, more purist, but normatively less compelling notion of State, nation and national sovereignty. There is some poetic political irony to the possibility that the exit of the UK from the Union will also bring about the breakup of the UK union – everyone happily purer and basking in their national sovereign identity.

Revival and reconstruction of historical narratives of grievance and oppression are fuelling this turn back. Yes, Catalans and Basques suffered serious historical wrongs in the pre-democracy era in Spain (it takes a Braveheart to ascribe the same to modern Scotland).

For thousands of people, maybe the majority, as in the case of Catalans, this is really claiming and living their own distinct cultural and politic identity. But to play, say, the 'Franco card' as a justification for secession is but a fig leaf not only for an outdated sense of the collective self, but for seriously misdirected social and economic egoism, cultural and national hubris and often the naked ambition of local politicians.

It is with this light that one can read the zeal of internal secessionists for the European Union. It is not only, as we argued above, that it provides a safe haven of political and economic comfort, but also supposed moral legitimacy in being 'good Europeans'.

However, in our view it actually runs diametrically contrary to the historical ethos of European integration. The commanding moral authority of the founding fathers of European integration – Robert Schumann (1868–1963), Konrad Adenauer (1876–1967), Alcide De Gasperi (1881–1954) and Jean Monnet himself (1888–1979) – was a result of their rootedness in the Christian ethic of forgiveness coupled with an enlightened political wisdom which understood that it is better to look forward to a future of reconciliation and integration rather than wallow in a past, which, notably, was infinitely worse than the worst excesses of, say, the execrable Franco.

Leaning toward the 'alone option' inevitably has a general spillover effect to all 'foreigners' feeding at its worst atavistic xenophobia. One cannot but notice, in this context, the speed with which the UK in the run up to the Brexit referendum announced that it would not be part of any resettlement of Syrian refugee deal worked out with Turkey, thus bringing back up the old alliance of nationalism with atavism and 'dehumanism'.

Should we celebrate, encourage or morally validate every distinct national, cultural and linguistic minority in Europe willing to hold a referendum about secession and independence? Dig deep enough and far enough in the past and grievances galore could be found. The Corsicans? The Bretons? The Welsh? The German-speaking people of the Alto Adige? The list is endless given the wonderful cultural richness of Europe. We would argue that it is only under conditions of political and cultural veritable repression that a case for regional secession can convincingly be made. Catalan arguments for independence are simply laughable and impossible to take seriously even when taking into account the extensive (even if deeply flawed) Catalan Statute of autonomy. Moreover, such arguments end up cheapening and insulting meritorious – if inconclusive – cases such as, for example, the Chechens.

The very ethos of European integration should, in our view, discourage the Union – as such – from welcoming these movements and encouraging them with the promise of easy accession. In part the argument here is utilitarian too. The Union is struggling today with a decisional structure which is already overloaded with 27 Member States. But more importantly with a socio-political reality which makes it difficult to persuade a Dutch or a Finn or a German that they have a human and economic stake in the welfare of a Greek or a Portuguese or, yes, a Spaniard. Why would there be an interest to welcome into the Union a polity such as an independent Catalonia predicated on such a regressive and outmoded nationalist ethos which apparently cannot stomach the discipline of loyalty and solidarity which one would expect it would owe to its fellow citizens in Spain? Or the UK? Or Italy? Or France, if they were to follow the same principles? To take Catalonia again as an example, the very demand for independence from Spain, an independence from the need to work out political, social, cultural and economic differences within the Spanish polity, independence from the need to work through and transcend history, arguably disqualify morally and politically Catalonia and the likes as future Member States of the European Union.

On this antipathetic reading, Europe should not seem as a Nirvana for that form of irredentist 'Eurotribalism', which contradicts the deep values and needs not only of the Union as a political institution, but of Europe's noble attempt to move away from its sanguinary past. It would be hugely ironic, this time with no poetic tinge, if the prospect of membership in the Union ended up providing an incentive for an ethos of political disintegration. There really is a fundamental difference to the welcoming into the Union of a Spain or a Portugal or a Greece emerging from ugly and repressive dictatorships and a Catalonia or Scotland, which are part of functioning democracies which at this very moment are in need of the deepest expression of internal and external solidarity. In seeking separation the secessionists are betraying the very ideals of solidarity and human integration on which the European construct stands.

B. The Sympathetic Reading of 'Aloneness'

What then would a sympathetic reading of 'aloneness' look like?

First there is the circumstance of Europe itself, and in particular the circumstance of European democracy. Europe bears considerable responsibility for the turn against itself.

This is an interesting time to be reflecting on European democracy, given an overall nadir of the European construct which one cannot remember for many decades. To many the issue of democracy had been definitively solved with the Lisbon Treaty. The surface manifestations of crisis are with us every day on the front pages: the euro crisis and the migration crisis being the most current. Beneath this surface, at the structural level, lurk more profound and long-term signs of enduring challenge and even dysfunction and malaise. Let us refract them through the lens of democratic legitimacy. For Lisbon notwithstanding, there is a persistent, chronic, troubling democracy deficit, which cannot be talked away and which, in our view, feeds and nourishes, not without some justification, the 'alone' instinct.

First, despite the 'no-demos thesis' – a lack of transcendent responsibility for the lot of one's fellow citizens and nationals – seems to have receded in recent discourse, its relevance is suddenly more acute than ever. The difficulties of, say, constructing some form of 'fiscal union' type of solutions for the euro crisis are explainable in no small measure as the result of the lack of demos. Germans, Dutch and Finns are not saying: 'a bailout is the wrong policy'. They are saying, 'why should we, Germans, or Dutch, or Finns, help those lazy Italians or Portuguese or Greeks?'. A very visible manifestation of the no-demos thesis of Europe's democracy crisis.

Secondly, there are failures of democracy which simply make it difficult to speak of governance 'by and of' the people. The historical error was the belief that simply granting extensive powers to the European Parliament – an absolutely necessary step – would be enough to close the deficit. The essence of the problem is the inability of the Union to develop structures and processes which adequately replicate or 'translate' at the Union level even the imperfect habits of governmental control, parliamentary accountability and administrative responsibility that are practiced with different modalities in the various Member States. Make no mistake: it is perfectly understood that the Union is not a State. But it is in the business of governance and has taken over extensive areas previously in the hands of the Member States. In some critical areas, such as the interface of the Union with the international trading system, the competences of the Union are exclusive. In others, they are dominant. Democracy is not about States. Democracy is about the exercise of public power – and the Union exercises a huge amount of public power. We live by the credo that any exercise of public power has to be legitimated democratically and it is exactly here that the legitimacy process fails.

And yet two primordial features of any functioning democracy are missing – the grand principles of accountability and representation.

As regards accountability, even the basic condition of representative democracy, that is, that at election time the citizens 'can throw the scoundrels out' – that is replace the government – does not operate in Europe. The *Spitzenkandidaten* exercise (the candidate that the various political families in the European Parliament propose to the European Commission) was a hugely important step in the right direction but it will take several cycles to transform the political culture.

The form of European governance, governance without government, is and will remain for considerable time – perhaps forever – such that there is no 'government' to throw out. Dismissing the Commission by Parliament (or approving the appointment of the Commission president) is not quite the same, not even remotely so.

Startlingly, but not surprisingly, political accountability of Europe is remarkably weak. There have been some spectacular political failures of European governance. The embarrassing Copenhagen climate fiasco, the weak (at best) realisation of the much touted Lisbon Agenda (also known as Lisbon Strategy or Lisbon Process), or the very story of the defunct Constitution to mention but three. It is hard to point in these instances to any measure of political accountability of someone paying a political price as would be the case in national politics. In fact it is difficult to point to a single instance of accountability for political failure as distinct from personal accountability for misconduct in the annals of European integration. This is not, decidedly not, a story of corruption or malfeasance. Our argument is that this failure is rooted in the very structure of European governance. It is not designed for political accountability. In a similar vein, it is impossible to link in any systematically meaningful way the results of elections to the European Parliament to the performance of the political groups within the preceding parliamentary session, in the way that is part of the mainstay of political accountability within the Member States. Structurally, dissatisfaction with Europe, when it exists, has no channel to affect, at the European level, the agents of European governance. Depressingly, Parliament has reverted to its 'rotation exercise' between the two big centre-left, centre-right blocs, and the European Council has made its dissatisfaction with the *Spitzenkandidaten* exercise quite clear with a determination not to allow a repetition.

Likewise, at the most primitive level of democracy, there is simply no moment in the civic calendar of Europe where the citizen can influence directly the outcome of any policy choice facing the Community and the Union in the way citizens can when choosing between parties which offer sharply distinct programmes at the national level. The political colour of the European Parliament only very weakly gets translated into the legislative and administrative output of the Union.

This political deficit, to use the felicitous phrase of Renaud Dehousse is at the core of the democracy deficit. The Commission, by its self-understanding linked to its very ontology, cannot be 'partisan' in a right-left sense; neither can the Council, by virtue of the haphazard political nature of its composition. Democracy normally must have some meaningful mechanism for expression of voter preference predicated on choice among options, typically informed by stronger or weaker ideological orientation. That is an indispensable component of politics. Democracy without politics is an oxymoron. And yet that is not only Europe, but it is a feature of Europe – the 'non-partisan' nature of the Commission – which is celebrated. The stock phrase found in endless student text books and the like, that the supranational Commission vindicates the European interest, whereas the intergovernmental Council is a clearing house for Member State interest, is at best naïve. Does not the 'European interest' necessarily involve political and ideological choices? At times explicit, but always implicit? Again, the president of the European Commission Jean-Claude Junker has been able only marginally or in a Machiavellian way (we use this term in the best sense of the word) to redress this problem in the selection of his Commission. He could allocate portfolios with imagination but could not choose candidates of Member States based on programmatic commitment.

Thus the two most primordial norms of democracy, the principle of accountability and the principle of representation, are compromised in the very structure and process of the Union.

This structural argument is consistent with the noticeable paradox of the extraordinary decline in voter participation in elections for the European Parliament. In Europe as a whole the rate of participation is below 45 per cent, with several countries, notably in the East, with a rate below 30 per cent. The correct comparison is, of course, with political elections to national Parliaments where the numbers are considerably higher. What is striking about these figures is that the decline coincides with a continuous shift in powers to the European Parliament, which today is a veritable colegislator with the Council. The more powers the European Parliament, supposedly the *vox populi*, has gained, the greater popular indifference to it seems to have developed. The last elections saw the lowest turnout of voters in the history of direct elections and in all likelihood it would have been even lower but for the Eurosceptic mobilisation. It is sobering but not surprising to note the relative absence of the European Parliament as a major player in the current crisis.

The critique of the democracy deficit of the Union has itself been subjected to two types of critique. The first has simply contested the reality of the democracy deficit by essentially claiming that wrong criteria have been applied to the Union. The lines of debate are well known. But we are more interested in the second type of critique, which implicitly is an invocation of result or output legitimacy. Since the Union, not being a State, cannot replicate or adequately translate the habits and practices of State democratic governance, its legitimacy may be found elsewhere.

In analysing the legitimacy (and mobilising force) of the European Union, in particular against the background of its persistent democracy deficit, political and social science has indeed long used the distinction between process legitimacy and outcome legitimacy (also known as input/output, process/result etc). The legitimacy of the Union more generally and the Commission more specifically, even if suffering from deficiencies in the democratic State sense, are said to rest on the results achieved – in the economic, social and, ultimately, political realms. The idea hearkens back to the most classic functionalist and neofunctionalist theories.

We do not want to take issue with the implied normativity of this position – a latter day *panem et circenses* approach to democracy, which at some level at least could be considered quite troubling. It is with its empirical reality that we want to take some issue. We do not think that outcome legitimacy explains all or perhaps even most of the mobilising force of the European construct. But whatever role it plays, it is dependent on the *panem*. Rightly or wrongly, the economic woes of Europe, which are manifest in the euro crisis, are attributed to the European construct. So when there suddenly is no bread, and certainly no cake, we are treated to a different kind of circus whereby the citizens' growing indifference is turning to hostility and the ability of Europe to act as a political mobilising force seems not only spent, but even reversed. Europe is suddenly seen not as an icon of success but as an emblem of austerity, thus in terms of its promise of prosperity, failure. And now, the migration crisis too is scandalously but persistently associated with Europe.

If success breeds legitimacy, failure, even if wrongly allocated, leads to the opposite. The abject failure of Europe and its Member States (with the usual finger-pointing) to deal adequately with the migration/refugee crisis adds oil to the conflagration.

This brings us back to the phenomenon of secessionism, internal and external, which is the extreme manifestation of the seemingly contagious spread of anti-Europeanism in national politics. What was once in the province of fringe parties on the far right and left has inched its way to more central political forces. The 'question of Europe' as a central issue in political discourse was for long regarded as an 'English disease'. There is a growing contagion in Member States in North and South, East and West, where political capital is to be made among non-fringe parties by anti-European advocacy. The spillover effect of this phenomenon is the shift of mainstream parties in this direction as a way of countering the gains at their flanks. If we are surprised by this it is only because we seem to have airbrushed out of our historical consciousness the rejection of the so-called European Constitution, an understandable amnesia since it represented a defeat of the collective political class in Europe by the *vox populi*, albeit not speaking through, but instead giving a slap in the face to the European construct itself. We had earlier stated that internal secessionism trends, such as Scotland and Catalonia, see in the European Union a safe haven. This however does not contradict our argument that the failures of European democracy are a catalyst in undermining democracy itself, which is one of the feeders of secessionism.

In the antipathetic reading of 'secessionism' we described this turn to national identity as a lamentable regression to post-World War I notions of nation, State, nation State and democracy which deserved at least some measure of normative contempt.

Nationalism, however, may also be seen as a response, surely not the only one, rooted deeply in the human condition, namely an existential yearning for life meaning, one expression of which is given (and often abused) by a sense of collective belongingness. It is easy to see the appeal of such meaning in more than one way. The (national) collective transcends the life of any individual – and thus automatically bestows on each and every one who belongs to it both a past and a future. National identity oft breeds distinct forms of creativity – and both elements of the equation, creativity and distinctiveness, are important since they are the ones responding to the yearning for meaning. The distinctiveness can be in all forms of culture from the obvious linguistic distinctiveness and its derivatives in narratives, literature, poetry etc to the kitchen and the wardrobe. But it is the belongingness in and of itself which is the most intriguing. Johann Gottfried von Herder's (1744–1803) 'community of fate' was, notoriously, an idea abused by National Socialism. But read through the eyes of, say, Isaiah Berlin (1909–97), one understands the appeal which the community of fate holds in its sense of mutual responsibility, its demands of a certain measure of selflessness and not least one of the powerful antidotes to an existential sense of individual loneliness which itself is part of the human condition. In the community of fate everyone has some form of a family. One finds manifestations of such in the most interesting of contexts such as fans of football clubs, especially those who hardly (if ever) win.

Since its inception the European Union aspired to an ever closer union among the distinct peoples of Europe to be such a community of fate.

This was a compelling vision which animated at least three generations of European idealists, for whom the ever closer union among the people of Europe, with peace and prosperity an icing on the cake, constituted the beckoning promised land.

It is worth exploring further the mobilising force of this new plan for Europe. At a superficial level, it is its straightforward pragmatic objective of consolidating peace and reconstructing European prosperity. But there is much more within the deep structure of the plan.

Peace, at all times an attractive desideratum, would have had its appeal in purely utilitarian terms. But it is readily apparent that in the historical context in which the Schumann Plan was put forward with the Declaration of 9 May 1950 the notion of peace as an ideal probes a far deeper stratum than the classic Biblical metaphor for peace ('swords into ploughshares', 'sitting under ones' vines and fig trees', 'lambs and Wolves' etc.). The dilemma posed was an acute example of the alleged tension between Grace and Justice which has taxed philosophers and theologians through the ages – from William of Ockham (premodern), to Friedrich Nietzsche (modernist) and the controversial but profound Martin Heidegger (postmodern).

These were, after all, the early 1950s with the horrors of the war still fresh in the mind and, in particular, the memory of the unspeakable savagery of German occupation. It would take many years for the hatred in countries such as the Netherlands, Denmark or France to fully subside. The idea, then in 1950, of a community of equals as providing the structural underpinning for long-term peace among yesterday's enemies, represented more than the wise counsel of experienced statesmen. It was, first, a 'peace of the brave' requiring courage and audacity.

At a deeper level it managed to tap into the two civilisational pillars of Europe: the Enlightenment and the heritage of the French Revolution and the European Christian tradition.

Liberty was already achieved with the defeat of Nazi Germany, and Germans (like their Austrian brethren-in-crime) embraced with zeal the notion that they, too, were liberated from National Socialism. But here was a project, encapsulated in the Schuman Declaration, which added to the transnational level both equality and fraternity. The post-World War I Versailles version of peace was to take yesterday's enemy, diminish him and keep his neck firmly under one's heel, with, of course, disastrous results. After World War II, on the other hand, a vision in which yesteryear's enemy was regarded as an equal took shape: Germany was to be treated as a full and equal partner in the venture and engaged in a fraternal interdependent lock that made the thought of resolving future disputes with a conflict unthinkable. This was, in fact, the project of the Enlightenment taken to the international level as Kant himself had dreamt. To embrace the Schuman Plan was to tap into one of the most powerful idealistic seams in Europe's civilisational mines.

The Schuman plan was also a call for forgiveness, a challenge to overcome an understandable hatred. In that particular historical context the Schumannian notion of peace resonated with, and was evocative of, the distinct teaching, imagery and values of the Christian call for forgiving one's enemies, for Love, for Grace – values so recently consecrated in their wholesale breach. The Schuman plan was in this sense, evocative of both confession and expiation, and redolent with the Christian belief in the power of repentance and renewal and the ultimate goodness of humankind. This evocation is not particularly astonishing given the personal backgrounds of the founding fathers, all seriously committed Catholics.

The mobilising force, especially among elites, the political classes who felt more directly responsible for the calamities of which Europe was just exiting, is not surprising given the remarkable subterranean appeal to the two most potent visions of the idyllic 'Kingdom' – the humanist and religious combined in one project. This also explains how, for the most part, both right and left, conservative and progressive, could embrace the project.

It is the model which explains (in part) why for so long the Union could operate without a veritable commitment to the principles it demanded of its aspiring members – democracy and human rights. Aspirant States had to become members of the European Convention of human rights, but the Union itself did not. They had to prove their democratic credentials, but the Union itself did not – two anomalies which hardly raised eyebrows.

It was a 'Lets-just-do-it' type of programme animated by great idealism (and a goodly measure of good old State interest, as a whole generation of historians such as Alan Milward and Charles Maier among others have demonstrated).

The European double helix has from its inception been Commission and Council: an international (supposedly) a-political transnational administration/executive (the Commission) collaborating not, as we habitually say, with the Member States (Council), but with the governments, the executive branch of the Member States, which for years and years had a forum that escaped in day-to-day matters the scrutiny of any Parliament, European or national. Democracy is simply not part of the original vision of European integration.

This observation is hardly shocking or even radical. Is it altogether fanciful to tell the narrative of Europe as one in which 'doers and believers' (notably the most original of its institutions, the Commission, coupled with an empowered executive branch of the Member States, in the guise of the Council, and COREPER, the Permanent Representatives Committee, that is, the executive branch of Member States with full power), an elitist (if well-paid) vanguard, were the self-appointed leaders from whom grudgingly, over decades, power had to be arrested by the European Parliament? And even the European Parliament has been a strange *vox populi*. For has not it been, for most of its life, a champion of European integration, to the extent that, inevitably, when the Union and European integration inspired fear and caution among citizens (only natural in such a radical transformation of European politics), the European Parliament did not represent the place citizens would go to express those fears and concerns?

This narrative produced a culture of praxis, achievement, and ever-expanding agendas. Given the noble dimensions of European integration one ought to see and acknowledge their virtuous facets.

But that is only part of the story. They also explain some of the story of decline in European legitimacy and mobilising pull which is so obvious in the current circumstance. *Part* of the very phenomenology of political vision is that it always collapses as a mechanism for mobilisation and legitimation. It obviously collapses when the project fails; when the revolution does not come. But interestingly, and more germane to the narrative of European integration, even when successful it sows its seeds of collapse. At one level the collapse is inevitable, part of the very phenomenology of any such project. Reality is always more complicated, challenging, banal and ultimately less satisfying than the dream which preceded it. The result is not only absence of mobilisation and legitimation, but actual rancour.

Europe became a victim of its success in two ways. First, its stupendous achievement in making war unthinkable as a means for resolving differences has been so compelling that to new generations acculturated within this culture of peace, the sense of achievement has disappeared, it is taken for granted – and one should not lament such. Since, as we outlined above, the project progressed with a deep seated structural democratic deficit, its legitimation was increasingly based on results, on outputs. The point we are making is not the obvious one that as results falter, the legitimacy that comes with them falters too. It is the deeper point that result discourse displaced the original ideal discourse: the sense of mutual responsibility, the sense of polity and community. In 'selling' European citizenship the vocabulary was always one of rights, never duties; one of benefits, never sacrifice or selflessness. The deep tragedy of the European construct has been its failure to engrain itself, implant itself in social and political consciousness as a community of fate.

It is this void of meaning which is now occupied increasingly by the two different but interconnected strands of secessionism including their regressive atavistic appeals.

Europe's tragedy is however also its future potential promise. Since in an increasingly complex world, the economic, security and population challenges are such that they simply cannot be solved by any single State, what these challenges are offering is the potential of revival of that transcendent responsibility, both within its Member States and among them.

We offer this extensive analysis of the 'alone' option as an important cautionary tale as Europe 'moves ahead'. The current thinking is all focused on new projects which will appeal to European citizens and 'prove' to them the importance of the Union. This is important and understandable. But it is also a regression, yet again, to result or output legitimacy – a contingent and precarious long-term strategy. A structural reform, through politicisation, of European governance, the only remedy to the deep seated enduring democracy and political deficits, is critical if not more to Europe's future. If output legitimacy is not matched by input legitimacy, the next crisis is just round the corner.

II. All Together or With Some Member Only?

Our principal thesis in this part of our chapter is that this dichotomy is fictitious. A single set of disciplines for all partners may have existed in the 1960s and early 1970s with a Community of six Member States, the scope of action of which was relatively limited – not even a veritable common market existed then. But starting already with the first enlargement in 1973, that vision was fractured and increasingly so ever since. From inception, Denmark had a carve-out to free movement as regards the purchase of properties on its southern shores by Germans, to give but one example; a careful perusal of the small print – especially in annexes and declarations appended to the evolving Treaties (Single European Act, Maastricht, Amsterdam, Nice, Lisbon) – is a story of carve-outs, opt-ins and opt-outs not to mention fundamental – bold print – developments, such as the Euro and Schengen which give lie to a simplistic notion of 'all together'.

As the legendary judge of the European Court of Justice (ECJ), Pierre Pescatore, explained decades ago, federalism does not necessarily mean a federal State but any form of shared governance. The Union is no exception – it is a form of federalism, surely unique and special but possessing the essential tensions inherent in any federal construct. The late Martin Diamond described the classic position of federalism by the song that Jimmy Durante, the American comedian, belted out in the film *The man who came to dinner* (1942): 'Did you ever have the feeling that you want to go, and the feeling that you want to stay?'. That is the classic problem for which federalism, as a technology, was invented. 'United in diversity' is but another expression of that problem. At one and the same time we want to be united, but we do not want to lose our specificity and separateness. We want to govern ourselves and govern together with our partners. We want to go and we want to stay. Typically, this tension manifests itself in the tension between that which needs to be integrated and that which should be left to the constituent members.

There is, we would argue, no solution to this problem. It is an ontological tension inherent in federal arrangements. All together or some members only is but a manifestation of this ontological tension to which there can neither be a clear normative resolution.

Consider the circumstance of the European Union when it comes to its basic constitutional moments such as Treaty revision. The prevailing constitutional norm is one of unanimity. Treaty revision requires consent of all Member States in accordance with their constitutional provisions. Imagine that all are in agreement as regards some modification, say, a European income tax, except for, say again, Malta or Luxembourg. Should the collective will of virtually all Member States and an overwhelming number of European citizens be thwarted by a miniscule number of citizens in a miniscule Member State? The seductive answer would be that as long as the new discipline (which requires treaty amendment) is not imposed on the opposing Member State, why not allow the 26 to move ahead? Or to put it differently, why allow the one to thwart the will of the overwhelming many? Schengen is an example of the practicability of this theory, as in its own way is the euro. Of course, it would be nicer if border controls were removed among all Member States, but is not a second best solution (at least some) better than an all-or-nothing solution which in this case would mean nothing? But this answer, seductive as it may appear, is not without considerable difficulties. There are various 'salami' type problems. It seems easy enough when we postulate 26 versus Malta. But what if Malta were joined by one or two or three others? Would we, should we, feel so comfortable to 'leave them behind' and just move ahead? And what if it were not Malta, but, say, France or Germany? This is not hypothetical: when Denmark and then Ireland rejected new Treaties they were told to think (and vote) again or else. When France and the Netherlands voted against the Constitutional Treaty, that was its burial place.

We can frame the dilemma in a more abstract way. The European integration project is an invitation to Member States and their national societies to tie their future and destiny. In some areas they are required to accept a majoritarian decision. In other areas, especially as concerns the very framework of integration itself, the deal is that one 'moves ahead' only with the assent of all partners, for good or for bad. This is not just a pragmatic political arrangement: it embeds and embodies the very notion of a common destiny, of moving together. Just as the requirement of a qualified majority means that sometimes, frustratingly, a simple majority will not have its way, but accepts this as part of the discipline of democracy, so is in constitutionalism the principles of unanimity.

And here is yet another way to conceptualise the dilemma. At what point would a variable geometry of integration, different subject matters with different combination of Member States, undermine what is actually meant by integration?

It is, we think, clear that going too far in either of these directions would implode the federal arrangement whatever it may be and that any rigid rule will just call and impose pragmatic exceptions, but when exceptions become rules the result will be the same.

The matter is easier *within* the framework of the Treaties and in this respect the procedure of enhanced cooperation was designed to allow such a variable geometry to operate within predetermined procedures and conditions.

III. The Praxis of Differentiated Integration

Differentiated integration is permitted by more than 50 provisions or protocols of the Treaties.

The European Council meeting of 27 June 2014, in the height of the crisis, stated that 'ever closer union [...] allows for different paths of integration for different countries, allowing those that want to deepen integration to move ahead, while respecting the wish of those who do not want to deepen any further'.

The real and only question facing Europe in its future reinvention is the balance between the two.

The 'some members only' option, or in our preferred term, differentiated integration, may operate on different axes: time (when or multispeed), space (who, including, like Schengen, even extra-Union participation) and subject matter (in which areas). In the diagrams and tables (figures 1 and 2) we present in graphic and tabulated form the myriad practices which characterise the Union in this respect.

The most important formal mechanism for differentiated integration is that of enhanced cooperation, which is to be found in the Treaties and to which we will devote considerable attention. But it should be noted that enhanced cooperation is but one example of differentiated integration and to date has been of relative minor importance in the bigger picture of differentiated integration, as will be evident from the graphics. It has been infrequently used and only on peripheral subject matters. Ever since the 'poly-crisis' affecting Europe, most examples of differentiated integration have been nestled in intergovernmental realm and even in extra-treaty instruments of dubious legality, notable examples being: the Turkey refugee deal, the Fiscal Compact, which circumvented a debilitating potential veto by going outside the treaties, the Weimar Triangle (an agreement between France, Germany and Poland aimed at strengthening political and economic interdependence) and others.

Figure 1 Diagram of differentiated integration

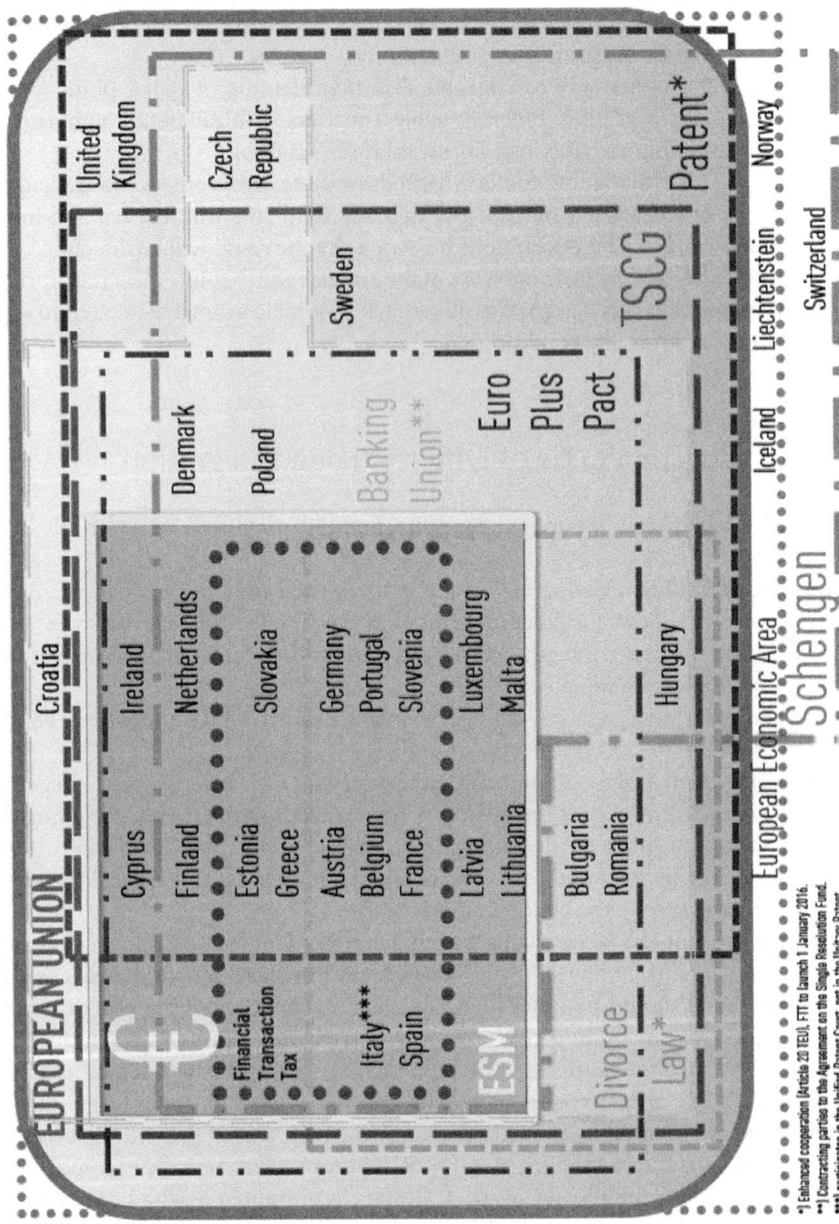

Source: V. Kreilinger, *Differentiated integration in one graphic*, 2015, https://tineurope.files.wordpress.com/2015/04/differentiatedintegration_kreilinger2015.jpg.

Figure 2 Diagram of differentiated integration

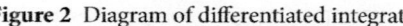

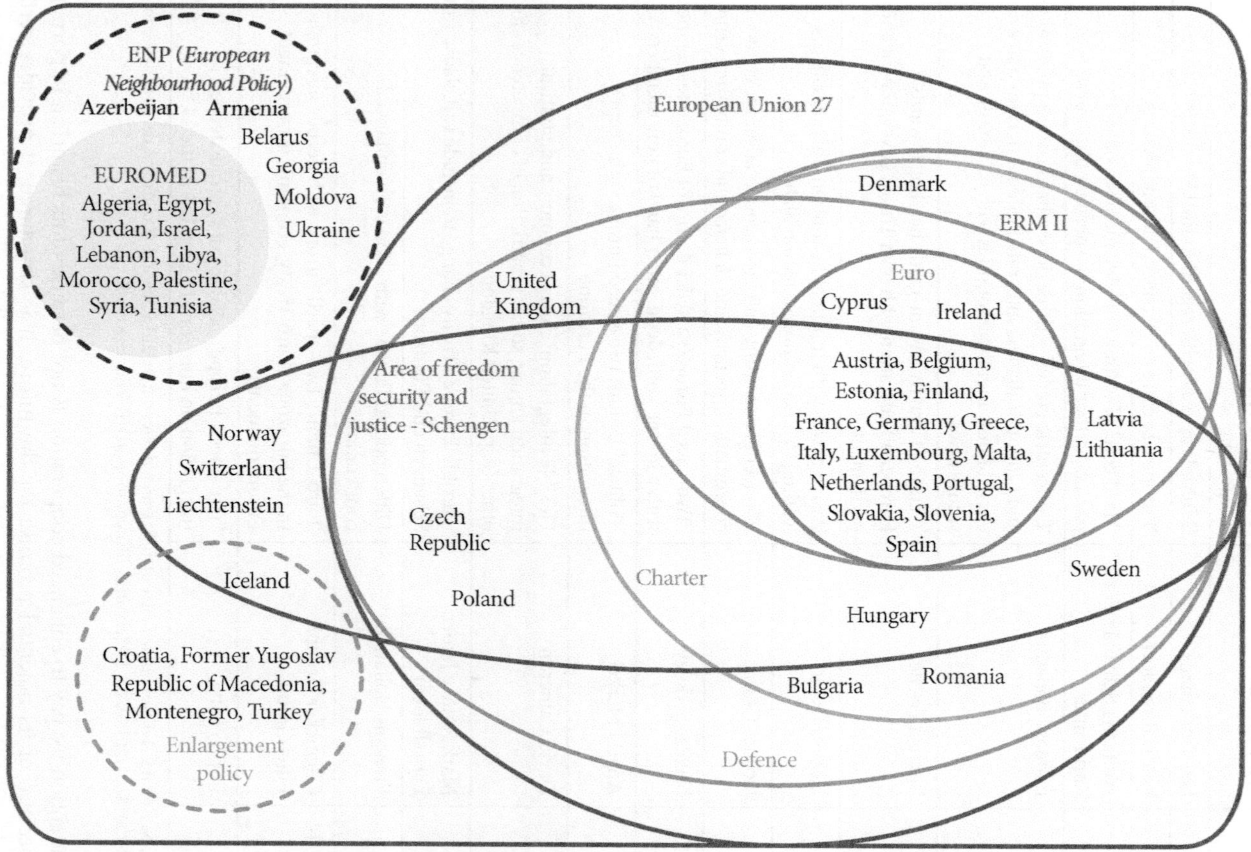

Source: F. Tekin, *Differentiated integration at work. The institutionalisation and implementation of opt-outs from European integration in the area of freedom, security and justice*, 2012, p. 20.

Models of differentiated integration proposed by prominent proponents

Date	Personality	Model of differentiated integration
1973	Willy Brandt	'Functional' rather than constitutional approach to EU integration
1975	Léo Tindemans	'Multiple speeds' with regard to EMU
1979	Ralf Dahrendorf	'Europe à la carte' to pursue common interests
1994	Wolfgang Schäuble e Karl Lamers	'Hard core' of willing and able member states that pursuesfurther integration in specific policy areas
1994	Édouard Balladur	'Concentric circles' – three tiers: a hard core; a politically and economically less integrated middle tier; un outer circle of non-member Counties with economic and security ties
2000	Joschka Fischer	'Centre of gravity': avant-garde heading towards a European Federation with own Treaty, governement and parliament
2000	Jacques Delors	'Avant-garde' with minimal institutional arrangements, leading to a Federation of nation States
2001	Jacques Chirac	'Pioneer group' using enhanced cooperation for economic coordination, security and defence and combatting crime
2011	Nicolas Sarkozy	'Two-speed Europe': a 'federal' core of Eurozone members with a looser 'confederal' outer band of non-members
2012	Angela Merkel	'Political Union': two-speed Europe with deeper integration in the Eurozone
2013	David Cameron	Flexible integration: closer economic and political integration among some, repatriation of competences for other (e.g., United Kingdom)
2013	Mark Rutte e Jeroen Dijsselbloem	'Flexible Europe': Treaty change to include exit clause from Schengen and Eurozone
2013	François Hollande	Differentiated Europe with a focus on enhanced cooperation
2013/14	Glienicker Group/ Eiffel Group	'Euro-Union': Two-speed Europe with deeper integration in the Eurozona (Euro Treaty, economic governement, Europarliament)
2015	Enrico Letta	'Two-speed Europe': need to concentrate deeper integration on Eurozone to keep UK in the EU

Source: N. Koenig, *A differentiated view of differentieted integration*, 2015, www.delorsinstitut.de/2015/wp-content/uploads/2015/ 07/20150723_DifferentiatedIntegration_JDIB_Nicole-Koenig.pdf.

The attention we pay to enhanced cooperation is not because of its historical importance, but because of its potential promise for the future. It is structured, it provides certain procedural guarantees, it limits its subject matter, and it is subject to judicial review by the European judicial system. There is no doubt that in its future outlook, differentiated integration will play an important role. We believe that it is better if it follows predetermined rules and limits rather than follow the ad hoc nature of previous practice.

IV. Enhanced Cooperation: Introduction and Overview

A. Precursors, Origins and Contextualisation

As just noted, enhanced cooperation (*coopération renforcée, verstärkte Zusammenarbeit*) is the only formalised procedure for the 'some members only' option, though it is far from being the most important (in its political and economic consequence). In fact, the underlying concept has an intricate and diverse history. In a very abstract sense Europe's post-war reconciliation and reconstruction had always been marked by a division of periphery and centre, pioneers and followers. Various early forms of enhanced cooperation are deeply inscribed into the process of European integration. A salient example was the Franco-German partnership since the 1963 Élysee Treaty introducing the paradigmatic shift from enmity (*Erbfeindschaft*) to elementary agreement (*entente élémentaire*) and building a nucleus of European integration foreshadowing the later idea of a 'core Europe'.

Other forerunners of enhanced cooperation can at the latest be traced back to the early 1970s and were provoked by the stagnation – if not paralysis – of European integration. It has always been these moments of stagnation which brought to the fore the notion of 'some members only'.

Former German chancellor Willy Brandt (1913–92) in a speech he addressed to the European Movement in Paris in 1974 mentioned the idea of a 'pioneer role' in Community policies. Soon after, the former prime minister of Belgium, Léo Tindemans (1922–2014) stated in the report on the European Union (Tindemans report): 'It is impossible [...] to submit a credible programme of action if it is deemed absolutely necessary that in every single case all stages should be reached by all the States at the same time'. Another prominent model of integration dating back to the early 1970s – though the very antithesis to uniform integration – is the idea of a Europe *à la carte*, as formulated by Ralf Dahrendorf (1929–2009) and later politically promoted by John Major. In 1994, Èdouard Balladur, back then France's prime minister, proposed a 'Europe of concentric circles': an inner core of the single currency, a middle tier of those being Members of the EU but not participating in the single currency, and an outer circle of non-Members with close links to the EU. In the same year Karl Lamers and Wolfgang Schäuble suggested the model of a 'core Europe' (*Kerneuropa*).

The legal concept of enhanced cooperation took a more definite shape in an exchange of correspondence between Helmut Kohl (1930–2017) and Jacques Chirac in December 1995 ahead of the negotiations of the Treaty of Amsterdam. In a letter to the presidency of the EU they expressed the idea that 'where one of the partners faces temporary difficulties in keeping up with the pace of progress in the Union, it would be desirable and feasible to introduce a general clause in the Treaties enabling those Member States which have the will and the capacity to do so to develop closer cooperation among themselves within the single institutional framework of the Union'.

The legal concept of enhanced cooperation as introduced by the Treaty of Amsterdam as well as its current structure can neither be qualified as an implementation of *Kerneuropa*, given that there is no fixed core of States for enhanced cooperation, nor as a tiered temporal or geographical process of integration. Enhanced cooperation *strictu sensu* is also not a Europe *à la carte* since the limits to 'pick and choose' – to stick with this culinary metaphor – are extremely limited. Thus, enhanced cooperation is best captured by the idea of a Europe of concentric circles or a *géométrie variable*.

B. The Early Legal Concept and its Development

While the concept of enhanced cooperation was formally introduced by the Treaty of Amsterdam (1997), the practice of enhanced cooperation by a small group of Member States is not novel within the Union. Already the Single European Act (1987) created the possibility of additional multiannual programmes undertaken by several Member States (see now articles 184, 188(2) TFEU). Article 27 TFEU allows exceptions from the principle of uniformity for certain economies showing differences in development and particularly the regime for an Economic and Monetary Union (article 120, TFEU et seq) is an expression of differentiated integration.

Another form of enhanced cooperation has also previously been practiced with regards to Schengen and social policies. Thus, the project of integration exhibits various types of enhanced cooperation and the *géométrie variable* seems to be more an indisputable element of European integration than a guiding idea for its future architecture. Nevertheless, the concept of enhanced cooperation as established by the Treaty of Amsterdam remains a milestone since it introduced, in its subject matter, for the first time the generalised unlimited and unspecified possibility of differentiated integration. Enhanced cooperation was ushered in view of the eastern enlargement to attenuate the potential threat of stagnation, which allegedly correlates with the increased heterogeneity.

The Treaty of Nice (2001) led to substantial amendments and changes of the regime. Irrespective of the multitude of changes, enhanced cooperation remained subject to strict requirements which ultimately made it unsuitable to resolve the tension between enlargement and deepening of integration. Finally, in reaction to the failure of the Constitutional Treaty, enhanced cooperation experienced a renaissance. The Treaty of Lisbon (2007) adopted the essential features of the regime of Amsterdam and Nice, but also restructured them significantly, streamlined the norms and contrasted the simplification in implementation by an impeded authorisation.

C. The Concept of Enhanced Cooperation – Article 20 of the Treaty on European Union and Articles 326–334 of the Treaty on the Functioning of the European Union

Article 20 of the Treaty on European Union (TEU) functions as a general provision with regards to the regime of enhanced cooperation. This prominent inclusion in the TEU reflects both a political valorisation as well as the understanding that it will serve as the predominant tool of integration in the absence of further treaty changes in the near future. It shall provide the possibility for States aiming at more integration to realise 'an ever closer Union' (article 1(2), TEU) without amending the treaties. Enhanced cooperation is based on a 'mutual give and take': while the enhanced cooperation must be in line with the aims of the union, it allows recourse to the infrastructure of the Union (*Organleihe*), meaning its personnel, resources, institutions and instruments.

The legal regime of enhanced cooperation – Article 20 TEU establishes the general framework of enhanced cooperation and refers to articles 326–334 TFEU, which lay down more detailed conditions and rules of procedure for enhanced cooperation. While article 20(1) TEU outlines and calibrates the idea of enhanced cooperation, article 20(2) TEU deals with its authorisation. Article 20(3)–(4) TEU focus on the conduct, implementation and consequences of enhanced cooperation once the authorising decision is issued.

Authorisation – Enhanced cooperation is based on an agreement between at least nine Member States, which must be authorised by the Council (article 20(2), TEU). The procedure of authorisation is governed by article 329 TFEU. It differs based on whether the area of enhanced cooperation is part of the internal EU policies (article 329(1), TFEU) or concerns the (intergovernmental) field of **C**ommon **F**oreign and **S**ecurity **P**olicy (CFSP, article 329(2), TFEU). While in internal policies, Member States intending to establish enhanced cooperation initiate the procedure by first notifying the Commission, which then may submit a proposal to the Council, the Council is addressed directly in the field of CFSP. Differences also apply with regards to the required majorities and the involvement of other institutions. Authorisation in the field of internal policies requires a qualified majority of the Council (article 16(3), TEU), while authorisation within the realm of CFSP needs unanimity (article 329(2), subpara 2, TFEU). While in matters of internal policies the consent of the European Parliament is needed prior to the Council's decision, this is not a prerequisite in matters of CFSP. It remains within the discretion of the Parliament to give an opinion (see article 329(2), subpara 1, TFEU). This differentiation also has repercussions on judicial review. The Council's decision on authorisation in CFSP matters is not subject to the jurisdiction of the ECJ (article 24(1), subparas 2–6, TEU). In contrast, the refusal of the Commission in matters concerning internal policies can be challenged by an action for nullity (article 263, TFEU).

In addition to the regular procedure, articles 82(3) sub paragraph 2, 83(3) sub paragraph 2, 86(1) sub paragraph 3 TFEU and article 87(3) TFEU provide a special regime for enhanced cooperation regarding judicial cooperation and criminal justice.

General Conditions – Article 20(1) TEU establishes certain prerequisites for enhanced cooperation. First, enhanced cooperation must not fall within the field of exclusive competences of the Union (see article 3, TFEU). Moreover, enhanced cooperation shall not exceed the competency framework of the Union. It follows that enhanced cooperation is limited to the regulatory power of article 2(2)–(4) TFEU, which in turn leads to difficulties in the area of external relations of the EU.

Article 20(1) sub paragraph 2 also ties enhanced cooperation to the fundamental objections of the Union. Thus, enhanced cooperation shall aim to further the objectives of the Union, protect its interests and reinforce its integration process. This obligation secures that the progressing Member States are heading to a direction that is generally in alignment with the other Member States and is not in contradiction with the commonly endorsed programme of integration. Moreover, this restriction allegedly comprises a principle of non-regression. Further limitations are set out in article 326(2) TFEU, which holds that the cooperation must comply with the Treaties as well as acts and measures based thereupon, it must not undermine the internal market (article 26(2), TFEU) or the economic, social and territorial cohesion (article 174, TFEU), and neither impede trade between the Member States nor distort competition (article 101, TFEU et seq).

By reference to article 328(1) TFEU, article 20(1) sub paragraph 2 TEU also underscores the principle of openness of enhanced cooperation to all Member States and thus embosses the guiding aim of unitary integration. Moreover, article 328(1) sub paragraph 2 TFEU obligates the Commission as well as the Member States to ensure and promote participation. The relationship between Member States participating in enhanced cooperation and other Member States shall also be guided by mutual respect and those not participating shall not impede the cooperation (article 327, TFEU).

The overarching, still prevailing principle of unitary integration also finds expression in article 20(2) TEU. First, it establishes an ultima-ratio precept/last-resort test. Enhanced cooperation can only be authorised when the objectives of such cooperation cannot be attained within a reasonable period by the Union as a whole. In the absence of any enumerated criteria within the treaties for assessing such a situation of last resort, the Council is supposed to have a wide discretion. While this wide discretion has been acknowledged by the ECJ, enhanced cooperation can nevertheless only be considered if serious attempts to find a resolution have been made and even a minimal consensus under exclusion of contentious issues has not been reached. In line with this, the Commission has justified and substantiated its first proposal for authorising enhanced cooperation with unsurmountable disagreements among the Member States regarding core elements of the objective.

Secondly, article 20(2) TEU requires a minimum participation of nine Member States. This requirement is meant to attenuate the risk of disintegration by a large amount of smaller, inner circles. However, the fixation of this (arbitrary) number (a quorum of one third after Brexit) has been subject to critique. Provided that enhanced cooperation meets all the other requirements, the overarching aim of coherent integration would not be put at risk if a smaller group of Member States would take the lead. Moreover, the number of people represented by the Member States engaging in enhanced cooperation would arguably suffice as a better safeguard against segmentation.

Apart from that, one exception to the minimum requirement of nine Member States is explicitly acknowledged in article 350 TFEU (Benelux-cooperation).

Article 20(3) TEU is a manifestation of the principle of transparency, as it determines that all Member States of the Council can participate in its deliberations. However, only those Member States engaged in the enhanced cooperation shall take part in the vote, which follows the rules laid down in article 330 TFEU. This right to participate in the deliberations serves two needs: first, it allows all Member States to voice their interests and ensures coherence of enhanced cooperation with Union law. Secondly, it provides access to information on the development of enhanced cooperation for those Member States that are not (yet) part of it. This is of particular importance to enable a future participation in enhanced cooperation.

Article 20(4) TEU clarifies the limited scope of enhanced cooperation, whose binding effect extends only to the Member States participating in it. Apart from this territorial limitation, legislation enacted under the auspices of enhanced cooperation shares the same functional characteristics as secondary EU law, for example, direct applicability and supremacy. This status of 'special secondary EU law' causes difficulties with respect to regular secondary law, which illustrate some of the doctrinal problems of enhanced cooperation. Since the Council acting within enhanced cooperation differs from the regular Council of the EU, the *lex-posterior* and the *lex-specialis* rule cannot be applied to resolve conflicts of law. This incongruence of organs is also suggested by the 'lending of organs' according to article 20(1) TEU. To resolve this potential conflict, it has been argued that EU secondary law prevails over secondary law generated by enhanced cooperation.

Furthermore, article 20(4) TEU states that secondary law generated by enhanced cooperation is not regarded as *acquis communautaire*. Thus, there is no obligation for future Member States of the European Union to adopt this law.

Financing and costs – According to article 332 TFEU the administrative costs created by the institutions of the Union while carrying out enhanced cooperation are part of the general budget of the Union. The other costs are borne by the participating Member States, unless the Council – representing all Member States – unanimously decides otherwise.

Accession, exit, cessation – The procedure for joining an enhanced cooperation is laid down in article 331 TFEU. In parallel with the initiation of enhanced cooperation, the procedure differs based on whether the enhanced cooperation falls within the ambit of internal policy (article 331(1), TFEU) or CFSP (article 331(2), TFEU). In case of the former, the applicant informs the Council and the Commission and then the Commission decides upon the application. To be able to join, the Member State needs to fulfil the conditions for participation set out in the authorising decision (article 328(1), TFEU). The Commission is empowered to enact certain transitional provisions and grace periods if necessary. If the Commission ultimately decides that the conditions have not been met, the Member State may refer the matter to the Council, which shall decide upon the request (article 331(1), subpara 2, TFEU). If the enhanced cooperation is a matter of CFSP the applicant also needs to notify his intention to join to the High Representative and the final decision on accession is taken unanimously by the Council.

The participation in enhanced cooperation creates the obligation to adopt all legal acts and decision enacted within the enhanced cooperation ('partial acquis'). Given the clear wording, a partial membership seems to be foreclosed.

The legal regime of enhanced cooperation does not provide a procedure to exit enhanced cooperation. Arguably, this seems to be permitted based on the *actus-contrarius* principle. Moreover, a Member State can be released from enhanced cooperation by an amicable agreement of all Member States. The admissibility of a unilateral, extraordinary termination has to be assessed on the basis of articles 356 and 344 TFEU, as well as of unwritten principles of Union law while public international law (article 54 et seq, Vienna Convention) shall not be applied.

The legal regime of enhanced cooperation also does not provide rules for the cessation of enhanced cooperation. Generally, an agreement on enhanced cooperation seems to be of unlimited duration (see article 356, TFEU). It can either end with the accession of all Member States or if the Council representing the participating Member States repeals the constitutive act.

Justiciability of enhanced cooperation – The competence of the ECJ extends to all activities of the Union (article 19, TEU, article 251, TFEU) except CFSP (article 275, TFEU). In accordance with this, all measures and acts undertaken within enhanced cooperation fall within the jurisdiction of the Court as long as they do not touch upon CFSP. Consequently, resolutions pursuant to article 329(2) TFEU and decision pursuant to article 331(2) TFEU as well as implementing measures in the realm of CFSP pursuant to article 330 TFEU are exempted.

V. The Practice of Enhanced Cooperation

Since its inception the enhanced cooperation mechanism has been used in five instances: the divorce in the Rome III regulation (2010), the unitary patent protection (2011), the financial transaction tax (2013), the property regimes of international couples (2016), and most recently the European public prosecutor's office (2017).

These five applications of enhanced cooperation have proved who doubted that enhanced cooperation would ever be authorised wrong. The increasing frequency of its use indicates its usefulness to continue integration given the difficult circumstances prevailing in Europe. Moreover, criticisms that enhanced cooperation will turn the Union into a fragmented, incoherent project are clearly seen as overstated. While it certainly adds to complexity and opacity of European integration, it can only be qualified as a pinprick to uniformity. In most cases, enhanced cooperation has created a certain 'pull effect' – the number of participating Member States significantly increasing over time. Furthermore, enhanced cooperation has not lead to a 'core Europe' since the joining Member States differ depending on the subject matter in question and cannot be divided into clear categories of 'old' and 'new', North and South or West and East. Notably, only two out of the five enhanced cooperation procedures ended up before Court.

Nevertheless, there is also the already mentioned dark side to enhanced cooperation. The welcomed 'pull effect' correlates with the threat to be overrun, a tyranny of the majority and the *de facto* coercion (by market pressure) to join. Diversity and cultural identity are not taken seriously and lack protection.

In short, it is a perfect manifestation of the inherent tension we outlined above. It is a visible manifestation of the rejection of *E pluribus unum* and the adoption of 'united in diversity'. Ultimately the issue will always be one of frequency and measure. Enhanced cooperation is neither a panacea nor the end of European integration. In the strict sense, the subject matters of enhanced cooperation have been seen to be both peripheral and ephemeral. In fact, it is possible that its most important effect is as deterrent and catalyst for integration, prompted by the fear of some going it alone. No empirical work exists to substantiate this hypothesis but it appears plausible in at least some respect.

VI. Cutting the Gordian Knot of Differentiated Integration

The 'all together' and 'some members only' options are destined to live side by side in any future vision of European integration. Differentiated integration is, as we have argued, embedded in the very ontology of Europe, 'united in diversity'. But the arrangements for practicing it at the moment are messy, legally contentious, and on occasion politically divisive. Differentiated integration has always been *en vogue* in times of crisis since it can be invoked by both sides – Eurosceptics as well as Europhiles. It can be seen as a tool for deepening or as a tool to enhance flexibility giving more respect to national sovereignty and diversity. But it is at the same time associated with deep ambivalence. The Europhiles often regard it as a 'second best', a solution to get around recalcitrant Member States, and the Eurosceptics often regard it with suspicion as a plot to leave them behind and create a two-class Europe.

There is, in our view, one bold measure which could cut this Gordian knot, a single constitutional change with the potential to alter the destiny of Europe and put to rest both the ambivalence and the contentiousness of differentiated integration. The moment has arrived where Europe should accept treaty amendment by (super)majority vote as is the norm in all functioning constitutional orders. The requirements of the composition of the majority are a second-order question. If Europe were to take this step, the problem of differentiated integration would be simplified overnight. There would be but two basic procedures for differentiated integration. Within the treaties it would be enhanced cooperation, which of course could be refined and streamlined. Anything else would require a formal treaty amendment. Those who want to 'move ahead' would have to accept that if the supermajority is not achieved, Europe as a community of destiny and fate will have to wait with any large plans of deepened integration until such a majority is found. That is the nature of constitutional democracy. Those who oppose such change would also have to accept that if a majority (however defined) exists for future development they would have to go along (or exit – a very remote possibility). That, too, is the nature of constitutional democracy, which in our view is the make-or-break condition for an enduring and stable European construct.

Bibliography

Blanke, H-J, 'Art. 20 und Art. 326 ff.', in E Grabitz, M Hilf and M Nettesheim et al (eds), *Das Recht der Europäischen Union: EUV/AEUV* (München, 2016).

Cadet, F and Vascega, M, 'Fewer woods for Robin Hood: financial transaction tax under enhanced cooperation' (2013) 15 *Europäische Zeitschrift für Wirtschaftsrecht* 574–78.

De Witte, B, Ott, A and Vos, E (eds), *Between flexibility and desintegration: the trajectory of differentiation in EU law* (Cheltenham Glos, 2017) (esp D Thym, *Competing models for understanding differentiated integration*; S Peers, *Enhanced cooperation: the Cinderella of differentiated integration*).

Harratsch, A, Koenig, C and Pechstein, M, *Europarecht* (Tübingen, 2016).

Pechstein, M, 'Art. 20' in R Streinz, T Kruis and W Michl (eds), *EUV/AEUV Kommentar* (München, 2012).

Peers, S, 'Divorce, European style: the first authorization of enhanced cooperation' (2010) 6 *European constitutional law review* 339–58.

Streinz, R, 'Die verstärkte Zusammenarbeit: Eine realistische Form abgestufter Integration?' (2013) *Juristische Schulung* 892–95.

Thym, D, *Ungleichzeitigkeit und Europäisches Verfassungsrecht. Die Einbettung der verstärkten Zusammenarbeit, des Schengener Rechts und anderer Formen von Ungleichzeitigkeit in den einheitlichen rechtlichen und institutionellen Rahmen der Europäischen* (Union, Baden-Baden, 2004).

Thym, D, 'Flexible Integration: Garant oder Gefahr für die Einheit und die Legitimation des Unionsrechts?' (2013) 2 *Europarecht/Beiheft* 23–49.

Zeitzmann, S, 'Das Verfahren der verstärkten Zusammenarbeit und dessen erstmalige Anwendung: Ein Ehescheidungs- und Trennungsrecht für Europa' (2011) *Zeitschrift Für Europarechtliche Studien* 87–113.

INDEX

Please note that pager references in **bold** refer to information in tables and those in *italics* refer to information in figures.